D0217263

An Introduction to Family Social Work

FOURTH EDITION

 Brooks/Cole Empowerment Series 24964

Donald Collins
University of Calgary

Catheleen Jordan
The University of Texas at Arlington

Heather Coleman
University of Calgary

Authorship is equal

BROOKS/COLE
CENGAGE Learning·

Australia • Brazil • Japan • Korea • Mexico • Singapore • Spain • United Kingdom • United States

BROOKS/COLE
CENGAGE Learning·

An Introduction to Family Social Work, **Fourth Edition**
Donald Collins, Catheleen Jordan, and Heather Coleman

Publisher: Jon-David Hague

Acquisition Editor: Seth Dobrin

Editorial Assistant: Suzanna Kincaid

Media Editor: Elizabeth Momb

Marketing Program Manager: Tami Strang

Art and Cover Direction, Production Management, and Composition: PreMediaGlobal

Manufacturing Planner: Judy Inouye

Rights Acquisitions Specialist: Don Schlotman

Text Researcher: Bill Smith Group

Cover Image: © Özgür Donmaz/ iStockphoto

For product information and technology assistance, contact us at **Cengage Learning Customer & Sales Support, 1-800-354-9706**

For permission to use material from this text or product, submit all requests online at **www.cengage.com/permissions** Further permissions questions can be e-mailed to **permissionrequest@cengage.com**

Library of Congress Control Number: 2012931449

ISBN-13: 978-1-133-31262-8

ISBN-10: 1-133-31262-4

Brooks/Cole
20 Davis Drive
Belmont, CA 94002-3098
USA

Cengage Learning is a leading provider of customized learning solutions with office locations around the globe, including Singapore, the United Kingdom, Australia, Mexico, Brazil, and Japan. Locate your local office at **www.cengage.com/global**

Cengage Learning products are represented in Canada by Nelson Education, Ltd.

To learn more about Brooks/Cole, visit **www.cengage.com/brookscole**

Purchase any of our products at your local college store or at our preferred online store **www.cengagebrain.com**

Printed in the United States of America
1 2 3 4 5 6 7 16 15 14 13 12

DEDICATION

*To Kaydence: At the ripe old age of eleven months,
your happy spirit (and red hair!) infectiously touches
all who know you. (Catheleen)*

*To our granddaughters Kaydan, now four years old,
and Jasmyn, now 11: You continue to brighten the lives
of all around you. (Heather and Donald)*

To families everywhere, regardless of shape, size, or form.

Contents

Preface

We are pleased to offer the fourth edition of *Family Social Work* to the social work profession. Social work has a proud history of working with families and was the first profession to do so. Many current family textbooks emphasize *family therapy*, a specialized activity that is usually practiced at the graduate social work level. Additionally, many family therapy books are not, for the most part, written by social workers. This is despite the fact that the family has been a focus of social work practice since the beginnings of the profession. Social work pioneers such as Mary Richmond argued for a family focus five decades before the modern family therapy movement; yet social work often has been humble in acknowledging its contributions to families. This book aims to help the profession reclaim its heritage.

At the time of publishing this fourth edition, 473 accredited baccalaureate social work programs in the United States and 35 in Canada educated students to work with families. Additional programs attained candidacy status. As was true at the times of our previous editions, few courses and textbooks specifically target the role that BSWs (Bachelor of Social Work) will play after graduation in assisting families. The number of accredited baccalaureate programs has grown considerably since the first edition (1999) of our book, making the importance of a social work-focused book on families even more imperative. Again, we remain committed to the primary goal of this book—to provide undergraduate social work students with a strong beginning knowledge and the skills to work with families in a variety of settings beyond the traditional office environment.

Many undergraduate social workers are employed in agencies that do not provide office-based family therapy, and few BSW student field placements are offered in traditional family therapy (office-based) settings. Indeed, many beginning social workers work for agencies that provide support, teaching, and concrete services to families with a variety of needs and problems. Settings for family intervention include child welfare, women's shelters, family support, mental health, schools, and correctional facilities, to name a few. Families continue to experience multiple problems, perhaps more so than ever before. The social service community is working hard to ameliorate challenges to families, but some issues need to be tackled from a broader perspective.

The book's approach to beginning social work also is useful in first-year MSW (Master of Social Work) programs. It may be used as the beginning text to provide an overview of initial work with families and children from a generalist perspective. The generalist perspective often is required of master's level students in the first year; an advanced second-year curriculum then builds on the generalist framework.

The global recession, widespread unemployment, political partisan bickering, wrangling and gridlock, violence, substance abuse, wars, discrimination, and oppression of vulnerable members of society continue to undermine and threaten family well-being. Structural poverty lies at the heart of many difficulties. Problems are therefore not exclusively in the domain of relationship dysfunction or disrupted homeostasis, which are the focal points of traditional family therapy approaches. Now perhaps more than any time in our history, families need advocates to fight on their behalf. Eminent economist Albert Hirschman suggested that people respond to the decline of the state by either "exiting" or "voicing." For most, exiting is not an option. The most viable option for family social workers is to "voice," that is, to speak out, advocate, rally, and fight for their families. In this book, we honor our social work heritage by placing families within an ecological niche and by advocating for "voice." We recognize that families require a wide range of services to deal with different types of problems.

This is a challenging time to be a social worker. Social workers of both micro and macro persuasions must work together harder than ever to ensure that the lives of families are not sabotaged by larger social issues. The number and types of issues experienced by families may overwhelm social work students and new graduates. We hope to ease these feelings by equipping students with knowledge and skills to stand by their client families and face these challenges head-on.

New social workers may find it difficult to anticipate what it will be like to see an overburdened family for the first time. They may have basic questions about what they need to know to prepare to see a family for the first, second, and even third time. In addition, they may wonder how to engage families, earn their trust, and encourage meaningful and lasting changes. Social workers need access to practical information and skills to help families deal with a particular issue or set of issues. This book is intended for undergraduate social work students and new social work graduates who are (or will soon be) working with families for the first time. In it, we provide a framework for thinking about "family," as well as practical suggestions to guide family social work practice.

Working with families is both exciting and challenging. Family work requires knowledge and skills beyond those required for working with individuals. It is perhaps a meeting place in which to synthesize the bulk of the social work curriculum— group work, human development, P-I-E, social policy, research, social work values, communication skills, and so on. We cannot rely on theoretical texts that explicate family therapy models, most often at a level of abstraction that removes the family social worker from the practical day-to-day realities that families face. The family therapy focus is an important aspect of social work education, but usually occurs at a graduate level. Moreover, family therapy theory is often too abstract and office-specific to assist students to learn about the basics of family social work. Social work educators are challenged to be comprehensive enough to equip students with sufficient knowledge and skills to work effectively with families and also be specific enough to address concrete situations that students may encounter.

In this book, we continue to attempt to present in a clear, succinct manner the knowledge and practical skills needed to engage in family social work. We want to make family social work alive and stimulating for family social workers. This book can be used in a beginning interview course or a family course as an introductory text on basic family social work theory and practice. It can also be used as a preparatory text before exposing students to the range of theoretical models offered in family therapy texts.

WHAT IS NEW IN THIS FOURTH EDITION?

We would like to thank the reviewers of our third edition, whose feedback helped to bring this fourth edition to fruition. Based on their reviews, we restructured and updated the material in this edition. We continue to hold true to our social work value base of social justice and anti-oppressive practice by entering the debate and advocating for an open-minded approach to the family. Family diversity continues to be infused throughout the book rather than being a single chapter full of checklists of traits based on culture. We believe that making diversity part of the core of the book rather than standing out as something "different" helps normalize diversity throughout the book, making it an integral and natural part of family social work. Cultural diversity, gender issues, and different family forms are infused naturally throughout the book. We struggled with the "languaging" of diversity, particularly given the international usage of the text. Our rhetoric about diversity is designed to move forward current thinking, to dissect and critique the political correctness of our language, and to recognize that diversity is viewed differently across the globe.

We introduce family systems theory early to create a foundation for the theoretical basis of the book, and this theoretical basis infiltrates the entire book. Although we have a chapter devoted to family strengths and resilience, we have also incorporated this strengths-based perspective throughout the book. We acknowledge culture as a repository of strength and resilience for families. The focus on strengths and resilience will help family workers see through a different lens to appreciate the many possibilities that "differentness" can offer the family and the family social worker in times of difficulty. We have worked to keep the balance of theoretical and practical aspects of family social work to assist new family social workers to understand and balance the two and hopefully provide a framework with which to integrate theory and practice.

As mentioned, we are very aware of the importance and power of language. In the words of Ann Hartman, "Words create worlds." In this text, we have become particularly attuned to the language of family therapy versus family social work practice and have tried to remain true to our social work legacy by infusing the language of the latter throughout the book. Languaging is also an issue when speaking about diversity. We were struck by the language surrounding family diversity—ethnicity, culture, family structure, sexual orientation, and so on. We quickly started to recognize that politically correct use of language is bound by the location and time surrounding the use of a particular term. Terms that were considered politically correct a year or so ago have been replaced by new language. And, what is appropriate in one location or one country may be inappropriate in another. The use of "minority" is but one example. This term is not universally appropriate in the United States, whereas in Canada, the common usage is "visible minority." We realize, in fact, that everyone is ethnic! In the process of trying to locate the ideal language that captures diversity without alienating any group, we discovered that the ideal language does not yet exist and that concepts and language describing diversity are truly diverse! Our presentation of the issues surrounding diversity is intended to stimulate further discussion and keep the issue alive. We hope that our approach to discussing diversity and the issues we have raised will produce lively classroom discussion without offending any one particular group.

The book also incorporates the competencies identified in the Educational Policy and Accreditation Standards (EPAS) articulated by the Council on Social Work Education (CSWE). According to CSWE, "Core competencies are measureable practice behaviors that are comprised of knowledge, values and skills" (http://www.cswe.org/File.aspx?id=13780). In this book, we refer to the ten EPAS core competencies and related practice behaviors. These practice behaviors suggested by CSWE for each of the core competencies may be used to operationalize the curriculum. We have linked these core competencies and suggested practice behaviors to the appropriate sections of the book.

This book also includes suggested readings and key terms in each chapter. Exercises have been moved to the appropriate places in the chapters rather than appearing at the end of each chapter. The literature, wording, and case examples, where appropriate, have been updated and better linked to the case examples in this edition. Culturally sensitive language and information is included. EPAS icons are located throughout, and competency notes are new at the end of the chapters. References are updated and we recommend further readings, and key term definitions have been added to the end of each chapter.

The structure of the book orients the reader to the step-by-step process of family social work (FSW). We have reorganized the book in response to our reviewers' suggestions. We have also updated many references and related text. New exercises have been added and placed strategically within the chapters. Chapter 1, which discusses the field of family social work, has been updated with new references. Chapter 2, entitled "What is Family?" includes a look at "family diversity" as well as a discussion of the language of diversity and the cultural dimensions of the many expressions of "family." Chapters 1 and 2 continue to provide students with a philosophical perspective on family social work and a conceptual understanding of different family forms. Chapter 3 offers an understanding of family functioning from a systems perspective. Based on the feedback from reviewers, the flow of the chapters has been revised. Chapter 4 discusses family development and the family life cycle. Again, family diversity, as well as modern-day variations in the family life cycle, is discussed. Family strengths and resilience are discussed in Chapter 5. The discussion has been updated with new references, and factors contributing to resilience—including the strengths of families from diverse backgrounds—have been placed within an ecological framework. The family strengths perspective remains a theme throughout this edition. In Chapter 6 (formerly Chapter 4), we describe the practical aspects of family social work, such as how to prepare for a home visit. Chapter 7 introduces the beginning phase of family social work, including basic interviewing and relationship skills. Chapters 8 and 9 introduce assessment skills and techniques. Chapter 8 focuses on qualitative methods such as genograms and ecomaps, while Chapter 9 discusses the use of quantitative methods including standardized measures. These remain important for the managed care environment in the United States and for evidence-based practice.

Chapter 10 continues with family assessment techniques useful for intervention and also discusses interventions that fit into a family systems framework. Now included in Chapter 10 is "Intervention with Minority Families" following a family systems framework. Chapter 11 follows with the skills necessary for the intervention phase, including techniques that can be used as well as various intervention strategies. We have added a new section on specialized family intervention approaches that includes solution-focused, communication/experiential, structural, and narrative family approaches. Chapters 12 and 13 focus on parent-child and couple intervention skills, respectively. In Chapter 12, we have added information on interventions with children of substance abusers as well as interventions in families with substance abusers. Chapter 13 addresses gender-sensitive practice, which includes a discussion of family violence with a particular focus on marital violence. The final chapter, Chapter 14, provides information and skills related to the termination phase of FSW. We have added to this chapter a method to evaluate student learning of family social work based on relevant Council on Social Work and Canadian Association of Schools of Social Work Accreditation Standards. Finally, Chapter 14 includes a new section entitled "Future Trends." Some future trends discussed include population trends such as baby boomers, increasing disparities between the richest and poorest in society, and populations affected by increasing military endeavors. Professional issues such as recruitment into the profession, changing technologies, and evidence-informed practice are also discussed. We have also updated the PowerPoint presentations for each chapter to accompany the text. Finally, we have provided a Test Bank, Instructor's Manual, and Student Workbook, all of which are new to this edition.

This book is designed to assist students and other new family social workers to understand the dynamics and principles of family social work. It can be used in a family social work course, with each chapter providing the structure for a weekly class. Throughout each chapter, a number of exercises are provided to give students an opportunity to apply the concepts presented in the chapter. Finally, this text can serve as a primer to a family therapy text. We have synthesized major family concepts from different schools of family thought to create a generalist family social work text.

It is within the spirit of the profession that we close with a quote by the late Jack Layton. His vision can be an inspiration for social workers everywhere:

We can be a better ... country of greater equality, justice, and opportunity. We can build a prosperous economy and a society that shares its benefits more fairly. We can look after our seniors. We can offer better futures for our children. We can do our part to save the world's environment. We can restore our good name in the world.... My friends, love is better than anger. Hope is better than fear. Optimism is better than despair. So let us be loving, hopeful, and optimistic. And we'll change the world.

The late Jack Layton (1950-2011)

We would like to point out that while the order of authorship was decided a long time ago, the authors in fact contributed equally to the writing of this book. The authors are continually indebted to the support given us by Seth Dobrin, acquisitions editor for Brooks/Cole, Cengage Learning. It is always a pleasure to work with Seth, who provides a supportive work environment and useful feedback. We appreciate the hard work of the production staff, the reviewers of the draft of the manuscript, as well, including Annie Chavis, Fayetteville State University; Linda Kardos, Georgian Court University; Robert Karolich, Eastern Kentucky University; Scottye Cash, Ohio State University; Shari Miller, University of Georgia; and Tracy A. Marschall, University of Indianapolis. Finally, we continue to be ever grateful to our children and to our families, who have provided us with the experiential learning aspects of family work!

About the Authors

Donald Collins, Ph.D., is a Professor, Faculty of Social Work, University of Calgary, Southern Alberta Region. **Catheleen Jordan, Ph.D.,** is a Cheryl Milkes Moore Professor in Mental Health Research, School of Social Work, The University of Texas at Arlington. **Heather Coleman, Ph.D.,** is a Professor, Faculty of Social Work, University of Calgary, Southern Alberta Region.

Address correspondence to Catheleen Jordan; UTA-SSW; Box 19129; Arlington, Texas 76019-1029 USA.

The Field of Family Social Work

LEARNING OBJECTIVES

- Conceptual: Understand the contribution of social work in the history of working with families. Understand the difference between family social work and family therapy.
- Perceptual: Perceive the uniqueness of family social work.
- Valuational/Attitudinal: Appreciate the role of social workers in the helping professions.
- Behavioral: Learn about different family social work approaches and related skills.

S ocial work students often experience anxiety and doubt when first learning about family social work. They quickly realize that work with families is more complex than work with individuals. Students thus have many questions that must be answered before they see their first family. These questions include:

- What is the purpose of family social work?
- How is family social work different from family therapy?
- What is my role as a family social worker?
- How can I work effectively with families that are different from my own?
- How will I know what factors contribute to the family's difficulties?
- How should I work with an entire family and with all the members in the same room at the same time?
- How will I know what questions to ask family members? What do I say to the family?

- How can I encourage family members to participate if they are resistant, feeling blamed, uncommunicative, or overpowered by another family member?
- What should I do if family members get angry at me or at another family member?
- How should I prioritize a family's problems?
- What do I need to know when making a home visit?
- How can I protect my safety when making home visits in dangerous neighborhoods?
- What do I need to know to help families change? What knowledge will help the family begin to change?
- What skills will I need when there are young children in the interview? What skills do I need when there are older children in the family?
- What can I do to protect individual family members when the rest of the family is blaming or attacking them?
- How do I help families that are paralyzed by a crisis to rise above it and solve their problems?
- What do I need to know about family social work when working with families of diverse ethnic, racial, or sexual orientation backgrounds?
- What skills are needed by the family social worker throughout the different phases of family social work?

In this book, we answer these and other questions about family social work. Our goals are to help you be effective in assisting families and to build a strong foundation for you in family theory and practice. We will provide tools with which to assess families, develop a relationship and rapport with them, learn about fundamental intervention theory, and develop skills to terminate productively with the families that you see.

WHAT IS FAMILY SOCIAL WORK?

We present family social work using a generalist approach for working with at-risk families. It can embrace many different types of programs such as intensive family preservation services, in-home family support, and instruction in parenting skills. It will also serve as a basis for learning more advanced skills. If you are planning on working in child protection, the knowledge and skills obtained will assist you in understanding complex family issues and give you direction in decision making about child safety, family assessment, and what is needed to help families change. This book will also give you a foundation to work in the areas of children's mental health, pediatric social work, or social work in schools. The overarching purpose of this book is to teach you to assess and work with families so they can learn to function more competently in meeting the developmental and emotional needs of *all* their members.

Many of the families that social workers see are burdened with multiple problems. Working with these families can be challenging and intimidating for new and experienced social workers alike. We will prepare you to work with these families. Social workers have been involved with multi-stressed families since the beginning of the profession, and to work with them is unique. At times, families can encounter difficulties when one family member's needs are sacrificed for the needs of other members or when an individual family member suffers as a result of the combined actions of other family members.

Family social work embraces the following objectives:

1. Reinforce family strengths to prepare families for long-term change (or intervention).
2. Create concrete changes in family functioning to sustain effective and satisfying daily routines independent of formal helpers.
3. Provide additional support following family therapy so families will maintain effective family functioning.
4. Build relationships between families and their environmental supports to ensure that basic needs of members are being met (Nichols, 2010).
5. Address the crisis needs of the family in a timely fashion so they can effectively address more long-standing issues.

Family *social work* is not the same as family *therapy*. Family therapy relies on office-based intervention to help families make systemic changes. Family social work can be both home-based and community-based, often unfolding in the same time and space as family life and focusing on daily routines, family interactions, and social environment. Although the family social worker may sometimes interview a family in an office, much of the work is conducted in the family's home. Home-based intervention opens the door to a greater understanding of the family's daily routines, patterns, and functioning. This is particularly useful for families who are plagued by crises and need to resolve their immediate issues before stabilizing in more adaptive ways. The family social worker often concentrates on concrete *needs,* daily *routines, skills,* and *interactions* within client families as targets for change, a focus matching the needs and expectations of many high-risk families (Wood & Geismar, 1986).

A family social worker has many ways to provide on-the-spot and concrete assistance. For example, when a teenager and a parent become embroiled in conflict, the family social worker can work with the dyad to identify the source of the problem and intervene in "teachable moments." A family social worker can help the pair discover what led up to the argument by identifying problematic and repetitive interactions that solidify into ongoing dysfunctional patterns. The family social worker does not view arguments and crises as paralyzing; rather, they are gifts that generate rich opportunities for change at a time when the family is most vulnerable and open to working on issues. The family social worker can assist the parent and teenager to replace problem behavior with healthier and more satisfying interactions. When a young child throws a temper tantrum, the family social worker can teach the parent more effective methods of dealing with the child in the moment. Similarly, a family social worker may be in the home or readily available when a family member threatens suicide, when a parent loses a job, or when a landlord threatens to evict the family onto the street. The family social worker thus shares critical and intimate experiences with the family. Ultimately, the family

dyad – 2 ladies

social worker capitalizes on what is happening in the here-and-now to support, encourage, and direct healthy family dynamics in the physical place and time that problems emerge.

Family social workers within the home or community have an advantage over many office-based interventions. Instead of having the family conjure up a critical family incident verbally in the office, the family social worker has a unique opportunity to understand the dynamics of a situation as it unfolds. Home-based family work gives the opportunity to "show an interest in the things that define [the family's] identity—children, pets, religious artifacts, mementos, awards(Nichols, 2010, p. 233). Family social workers also have the opportunity to teach families new skills in a situation on-the-spot. The home is where problems often arise, making it an opportune place to create and implement solutions. Because family social workers operate primarily within the family home and close neighborhood, they can make an *immediate* difference in the lives of troubled families within their *environment*.

Although family social work addresses a range of individual and family problems in the home, including challenges facing the frail elderly and adults with mental health challenges, the focus of this book is on family social work involving children. We do, however, discuss interventions with couples since we believe a strong marital relationship fosters healthy parental skills (see Chapter 13). We approach family social work from a strengths perspective. The strengths perspective reveals to family social workers how to discover and explore, enhance, and exploit families' strengths and resources in the journey of achieving their goals, realizing their dreams, and shedding the shackles of their own lack of confidence, shortage of skills, and misgivings (Saleebey, 2000). Chapter 5 describes strengths and resilience in greater depth.

Our guiding vision is to promote the well-being of children in their families. We believe that it is a basic human right for children to grow up in healthy, supportive, and growth-promoting families and communities. We also believe that parents have the right to receive support to raise children. Consequently, the foundation of family social work rests on the conviction that children are best assisted when their family functions well. Parenting is one of the most demanding roles in life and requires a rich repertoire of skills, buttressed by a strong social support system. For most people, parenting skills are not instinctual. However, we believe that parents are capable of learning more effective parenting skills. In essence, "The problem with being a parent is that by the time you're experienced, you're unemployed" (Efron & Rowe, 1987). A family social worker can accelerate this learning process for parents so that they can enjoy their children and family life.

Effective family social work utilizes a number of skills throughout the four phases of family work. This book is organized around these four phases: engagement, assessment, intervention, and termination. A number of skills are embedded within each phase. Social work is a value-based profession, and these values guide practice. We refer to these skills as value-based or attitudinal. Attitudinal skills permeate every phase of family work; this is why we have devoted much attention to beliefs and assumptions about families in this chapter. Social work has always valued the importance of relationship; hence relational skills are also imperative and form the basis of the work. Relationship skills are necessary but not sufficient. Other skills, as delineated earlier by Tomm and Wright (1979), include perceptual, conceptual, and executive skills.

Perceptual and conceptual skills refer to what is taking place in the mind of the worker. They form the basis for the actions of the family social worker (Tomm & Wright, 1979, p. 2). Perceptual skills involve what the family social worker observes in family meetings. These observations need to be accurate and pertinent to the work. Conceptual skills entail the meaning that the family social worker attributes to these observations. As such, theory, particularly family systems theory, plays a role in framing the observations that the family social worker makes. When possible, we identify the appropriate skills during the various phases of family social work.

Historically, society has assumed that raising children is intuitive, contributing to the belief that parents should raise children without outside intervention. In other words, society expects every parent to raise children with the least amount of assistance and support from the state or other external agencies. This assumption bolsters the belief that support is necessary only for bad, failing, or incompetent parents, thus contributing to a stigma about receiving help.

EXERCISE 1.1   Parenting Skills

Do you think that parenting is instinctual? Make a list of parenting skills that you think are important. How do parents learn these skills? What skills do you think parents often lack when they are dealing with their children? Make a list of things that impede the acquisition of parenting skills. How can parents develop these skills? Discuss in class.

Ironically, although failing to ensure that parents receive necessary support, society holds high expectations for them. When parents struggle, social institutions have often taken intrusive and punitive paths, contributing to resentment and resistance by the family. For example, child welfare agencies might remove at-risk children from their homes, rather than first trying to equip families with adequate resources in the home to enable them to resolve difficulties and remain intact (Fraser, Pecora, & Haapala, 1991). These comments are not meant to diminish the role of child protective services, which often struggle with high caseloads, limited resources, negative public opinion, excessive paperwork, and complex bureaucracies. Nevertheless, punitive interventions seldom resolve parent or child problems. Social institutions often wait until parents fail, rather than providing timely assistance to them beforehand. Unfortunately, the function of many agencies has been to monitor, correct, or evaluate families only *after* a problem has surfaced. At one extreme, agencies may remove a child from a home without having provided support and aid proactively to *prevent* the child's removal. Rather than "lend a hand," the motto often seems to have been "point a finger."

Family social work can enhance the effectiveness of child protection services. As a professional practice, it is built on the premise that parents, children, and the family as a unit deserve support to avoid the need for later (and often more intrusive and severe) correction. All families need support from peers, neighbors, communities, and agencies at one time or another, and we believe that families have a right to receive services from family agencies that provide a family-centered approach. In keeping with a holistic philosophy, family social work differs from traditional approaches that work with family members individually, fractured from the family unit and isolated from their social context. Family social workers

Seldom — raramente   motto — lema

work under the assumption that what affects one member of a family affects other family members. Therefore, the family unit is the client.

Based on these philosophical underpinnings, a family-centered strengths-based approach in family social work is both necessary and practical. Family social workers may work with families that have faced longstanding problems and had multiple interventions from a variety of helping systems. Because of previous experiences, many vulnerable families frequently have become either treatment-resistant or treatment-sophisticated. Family social workers might become disconcerted when working with families that have spent more hours in intervention than the worker has! Families may be hesitant to discuss family problems with a professional who, in their view, operates from within a distant office environment, disconnected from the family's daily and natural life experiences. Families may have negative opinions of helpers who, in the past, have taken a punitive approach with them.

EXERCISE 1.2 Family-Serving Agencies

As a class, compile a list of family-serving agencies in your communities. Then, complete the following grid:.

Mandate of Agency	Purpose of Intervention	Level of Intrusiveness/Punitiveness
1.		
2.		
3.		
4.		
5.		
6.		
7.		
8.		
9.		
10.		

What are the themes embedded in this list?

EXERCISE 1.3 Individual-Serving Agencies

Building upon Exercise 1.2, make a list of agencies in your community that focus on interventions with individuals. How do these agencies involve families, if at all? How would the individual focus affect families?

EP 2.1.1c

The Field of Family Social Work

Social work's involvement with the family predates modern family therapy approaches that emerged in the 1960s. The long tradition of family social work began with early efforts to alleviate human suffering—efforts that removed social problems from the exclusive domain of individual responsibility and embedded them in a *context* where they were perceived to originate, that is, the broader family and community context. The earliest social workers recognized that the family was central both to human behavior and social organization. Social work's focus on the contexts within which clients live out their lives is one of the profession's outstanding contributions and is a benchmark of the profession, distinguishing it from other helping disciplines. The long-standing focus on context—a perspective that is now increasingly being valued and adopted by other professions—places social workers in a unique and cutting-edge profession. The contextual approach of social work is best identified as the Person-In-Environment (P-I-E), or ecological perspective. This perspective understands an individual not in isolation, but as a social being affecting and being affected by her or his social context (environment). Family social workers recognize the influence of the social context. After all, they are context specialists! The environment consists of dyadic interactions, triads, small groups, large groups, small communities, large communities, country, and even the global community and global environment. The March 2011 earthquake and tsunami in Japan is a stark example of how the global community and environment affects all of us.

The P-I-E perspective has been the hallmark of professional social work since its inception. It is evidenced through beliefs about the family as the crucible of human life and through understanding the influential features of the social environment such as social relationships, culture, and oppression. The social environment plays a central role in the quality of life for social work clients. P-I-E is a particularly useful lens with which to understand and work with "multiproblem" or "multiburdened" families. Also known as the ecological approach, it contributes to services that are relevant and responsive to families' needs. P-I-E emphasizes *doing* in addition to *talking*. Studies support this emphasis. When social workers convey a willingness to help; be with the family; provide support, encouragement, and attentive listening; and offer concrete services, families fare better (Ribner & Knei-Paz, 2002).

Authors such as Pinsof (2002) suggest that marriage and family as foci of science and intervention has existed for only five decades. We disagree. In fact, Mary Richmond, the first family social work pioneer, argued for a family perspective in order to understand human problems over half a century before Pinsof made his observations (see, for example, *Social Diagnosis*, 1917). She transformed the art of helping people beyond religious, moral, and psychoanalytic perspectives into a contextually- and scientifically-based practice, proposing that the family is an essential context in which to understand individual and social problems. Her formulations about the role of family were based on an empirical analysis of case records. Nichols and Schwartz (2007) suggest that the centrality of social workers in the field of family work might have been overlooked because social workers were in the trenches delivering services rather than writing. Moreover, early social workers were mostly women. Beels (2002) describes Richmond as one of the first social systems thinkers, whose thinking took hold much later in family therapy literature. Richmond's vision also propelled social workers to think beyond the family by understanding that families are also situated within broader communities and social systems. As a result of Richmond's work, social workers have long considered the family as the "case" of focus and an important contributor to individual well-being.

We admire Richmond's vision and courage in challenging mainstream perspectives that were commonly accepted in her day—namely, that problems were due to psychodynamic or moral shortcomings. (We do, however, acknowledge her psycho-analytic leanings.) We also admire her tenacity to study social problems through scientific investigation, which was considered rigorous in that day. Richmond's visionary thinking argued for a collaborative posture with families, an open mind, and viewing the family in interaction with the community and larger society in order to arrive at a comprehensive assessment of problems (Beels, 2002). Social work involvement with families has remained steadfast for over a century, often taking different forms. More recently, the "discovery" of child abuse, the war on poverty in the 1970s, and the growing awareness that too many children are being placed in out-of-home care without sufficient attention to families, have renewed and enhanced efforts in working with families. Social workers who followed Richmond, such as Virginia Satir, Carol Anderson, Peggy Papp, Betty Carter, Monica McGoldrick, Michael White, and David Epston, among others, advanced the importance of the family through their own unique way of understanding family functioning. Since Richmond's day, society has become more complex, creating even more complicated problems for families. This makes the P-I-E approach to working with families even more crucial (see Chapters 5 and 8).

In this book, we capitalize on these early professional traditions by extending and integrating Richmond's thinking to include more recent theories of family functioning. We also synthesize the contributions of other disciplines and place them within a social work context. The theory we present involves the social work tradition woven into an eclectic framework for families. The basis of our approach is a family systems foundation, within which we merge various ideas about family (discussed in more detail in Chapters 5 and 8).

EP 2.1.1c

FAMILY SOCIAL WORK AND FAMILY THERAPY

Richmond's friendly visitor movement was the beginning of modern family social work and later evolved into work with multiproblem families (Wood & Geismar, 1986). Today, educated professionals still visit families, offering concrete support and education. Sometimes family social work starts when a family first enters the helping network, and interventions may eventually lead to family therapy. In other situations, families enter into family social work during or after family therapy.

While family therapy does not fall under the domain of a single profession, family social work has existed since the end of the nineteenth century. Family social work differs from family therapy in several ways. The broad focus of family social work emphasizes the complex interrelationships of individuals within the family unit and the multilayered impact of social systems. Family social work focuses on clearly defined, concrete events and interactions that play out in the daily life of a family. Nichols (2010) suggests that the difference between the two is that the home-based approach focuses more on enhancing family resources than on repairing system dysfunction (p. 233). We partly agree with this observation, but not entirely. In fact, family social workers' interventions can "repair systemic dysfunction."

By comparison, family therapy is more formal, usually conducted in an office setting, and typically focused on more abstract patterns and structures of relationships and family functioning. Family social work is primarily focused on first-order change, while family therapy is primarily focused on second-order change (see the discussion in Chapter 3 on how a family operates according to established rules). The family therapist addresses intrafamilial issues, processes, and organization that make up internal family functioning. His or her goal is to restructure roles and relationships, with the assumption that the newly learned roles and relationships will culminate in more effective family functioning and the eventual elimination of presenting problems (Frankel & Frankel, 2006). Family therapists believe that individual problems often develop because of dysfunction within the family unit. For family therapists, the family, as a unit, is the target of intervention, and they seldom focus on individual family members. However, family therapy has fallen short in addressing the deleterious effects of the environment—particularly the effects of poverty, racism, and sexism—on children and their families (Frankel & Frankel, 2006).

By comparison, family social workers have greater latitude to focus on specific problematic issues such as parent-child conflicts or school-related problems that emerge as a subset of family dynamics. Thus, family social workers can flexibly respond to a wide range of family member needs and relationships. Often responses involve concrete problem solving through supporting and teaching skills and competencies to individuals, dyads, or the whole family. Family social workers have the leverage to help the family access concrete services and resources within the community such as job training, substance abuse programs, or programs for special-needs children. Issues that emerge can be dealt with either individually or within the family arena.

Both family therapists and family social workers have roles that are important and distinct, and it is essential that the roles of each be clearly understood to avoid role confusion and working at cross-purposes. Clearly understood roles are particularly crucial when a family therapist and a family social worker are working simultaneously with the same family. In such instances, family therapists and family social workers must work together to provide focused and mutually reinforcing interventions for the family.

EXERCISE 1.4   Family Theorists

Make a list of social workers who have promoted the family over the past century. Provide dates, the name of the theory, and the specific concepts. Determine the unique contributions each has made to family social work. Next, make a list of professionals from other disciplines who have contributed to family theory. Note dates, names of the theories, and the unique concepts. What social work contributions have they used to enhance their theories? Here is an initial list: Mary Richmond, Jane Addams, Bertha Reynolds, Ruth Smalley, Helen Harris Perlman, Virginia Satir, Michael White, Peggy Papp, Carol Anderson, Monica McGoldrick, Betty Carter. Expand on this list. Present the list in class.

EP 2.1.1c

REALITIES OF FAMILY SOCIAL WORK PRACTICE

Family social work differs from the traditional family therapy approach of the 50-minute, once-a-week interview with the family in a therapist's office. Instead, family social workers typically work in the home or community, learning the intricacies of the daily fabric of the family's life and patterns. Intervention with the family often occurs when the need for assistance is most acute and when the family is most receptive to intervention and change. The family may have experienced a recent crisis that is causing distress. In other situations, the family may be experiencing long-standing, chronic issues that require concrete intervention. Assistance may entail working alone or in collaboration with a wide range of other services and agencies.

The varied needs and demands of families might require that the family social worker become directly involved in the home beyond the traditional once-a-week interview. Some family social workers are available to families around the clock during crises. These time demands can be stressful for the family social worker who needs to restructure his or her personal life around a highly demanding caseload. Working in a client's home instead of an office can also challenge a worker's beliefs about both therapy and professional relationships (Snyder & McCollum, 1999). For example, a worker may find the level of intimacy to be different from that of office-based work, as he or she partakes in deeply personal family routines including the eruption of arguments, people dropping by or telephoning, children playing, and the expression of raw emotions in response to distressing events. It is also not unusual for television sets to blare in the background during an interview. At the very least, families have more difficulty maintaining a façade at home than in an office. Nichols (2010) suggests that the worker can ask the family to reduce these distractions——but only after a positive relationship has been created.

The direct and immediate witnessing of family events as they unfold allows family social workers to become engaged with the daily life routines and experiences of families. Family social workers provide support, knowledge, and skills in the here and now and on-the-spot. Because family social workers are acquainted with daily family events and dynamics, families do not have to wait for a weekly appointment to address their issues. Workers therefore become more familiar with home-based clients than they would with office-based clients (Snyder & McCollum, 1999, p. 240). Moreover, when family social workers are not in the home, they might be just a phone call away, enabling them to avail themselves for critical family incidents. Thus, family social work tends to be hands-on, practical, and action-oriented.

A worker can provide emotional and concrete support to an isolated and overwhelmed mother; teach a misunderstood or acting-out 10-year-old to express her or his needs and feelings more appropriately; or help a chaotic family structure mealtimes, homework, and bedtime routines so it can operate more smoothly and experience less stress and conflict as the result of routines that give the family greater structure and predictability. At the agency and community level, a family social worker can advocate for families and help them access other helping systems in the community. One overarching purpose of family social work within the community is to enhance environments for family members while concurrently meeting social expectations and community standards.

During work with the family, the family social worker must be prepared to address concrete issues related to family problem areas. Families, especially those that are poor and overburdened, are most concerned about meeting concrete needs and respond well to an honest and straightforward approach (Wood & Geismar, 1986).

In addition, home-based workers must coordinate their efforts with other service providers (Nichols, 2010).

In response to these issues, some families might see family social work as more informal and less intimidating than family therapy, in part because of the emphasis on developing a worker-family coalition. Conversely, other families might feel vulnerable because of the intense exposure of their family issues to someone from outside the home. Physical, social, and emotional boundary issues may emerge because the relationship might appear to be friendlier and less professional. Family social workers must be aware that relationships might appear more social than professional (Snyder & McCollum, 1999), challenging workers to stay focused on the task and require the family to work, rather than just chitchat. Engagement and relationship skills form the basis of this work to allow a problem-solving, growth-oriented partnership with families to evolve. Workers must also learn to work in a territory where many factors are outside their control and where they may feel less in control of the sessions and the ensuing work.

Although workers have access to extensive information about the family, they need to develop skills to integrate and organize this complex information for a professional intervention. Through joining with the family and participating in daily events for several hours at a time, rich opportunities emerge with which to develop a worker-family partnership. Empathy and understanding are the bedrock of this collaboration. One of the strengths of family social work lies in the fact that family social workers challenge family members to try new or different problem-solving skills and develop alternative daily-living skills that can be obtained both during and after the helping process.

On the other hand, a downside of home- or community-based family work is that it is not as structured as office-based family work, which makes focusing on issues more difficult for the worker. Seeing people in their living rooms also increases the pressures of induction into a family's problematic patterns, necessitating that home-based workers make special efforts to maintain professional boundaries (Nichols, 2010). Relationships contain the seeds of potentially more social interactions, and both the worker and the family might be tempted to make the professional boundaries looser. For example, some workers might be tempted to take the children home for their own family functions, lend money to the family, or take the family with them on their personal vacation. These activities are counterproductive and undermine the work that needs to be accomplished. They might also violate the profession's Code of Ethics.

Essentially, family social workers reconstruct the family system one building block at a time. A key assumption underlying family social work is that if enough problematic interaction patterns can be addressed, the family's future ability to problem solve and thus meet the needs of members will be enhanced. In addition, as the result of a strengths-based approach (see Chapter 5), families are more likely to feel supported instead of criticized. This emphasis builds stronger families and healthier individuals. Increased competence in problem solving improves the immediate environment of the family, equipping children to become more capable parents later in life. Ideally, family social work will have a multigenerational impact.

John, age 44, his wife Mary, 43, and their three children, 14-year-old son Marvin, 13-year-old son Michael, and 11-year-old daughter Sharon, were referred to you by their family doctor because Mary is feeling depressed and overwhelmed primarily because of family issues. These issues include poverty. John works evenings as a pizza delivery person making minimum wage. He has a history of unemployment. Mary works a couple of days a week cleaning houses. Back problems and fatigue prevent her from working more hours. They live in a small, two-bedroom, low-income housing unit.

They regularly attend church, and all three children attend a Christian-based school. Since the school is private, the family's educational expenses are greater than the cost of attending a public school. There is no extra money for recreational activities for the children outside of school. They are doing reasonably well academically, although Marvin is struggling in math. Sharon is overweight and also suffering from acute eczema.

Since the family lives in cramped quarters, there is little privacy in their home. The two boys often fight with each other, as well as excessively tease their sister. Since the father is often at work in the evenings, discipline is left to the mother. None of the children pay much attention to her. They rarely help out with household chores.

The family moved to this state in the past year and has no friends or relatives nearby.

© Cengage Learning 2013

EXERCISE 1.5   Concrete Needs

Break into groups of four or five students. On the basis of Case Example 1.1, make a list of concrete needs required by this family and connect these needs with an agency or resource in your community.

EXERCISE 1.6   Differences between Family Social Work and Family Therapy

Divide the class into two groups. Using Case Example 1.1, list the advantages and disadvantages of family social work and family therapy on the basis of the differences listed there. Debate the advantages and disadvantages as a class. The advantages and disadvantages can be for the family or for the family social worker. In addition to the differences outlined in this section, what other differences do you see?

Family Social Work

Advantages   Disadvantages

Family Therapy

Advantages   Disadvantages

EP 2.1.1c

ASSUMPTIONS OF FAMILY SOCIAL WORK

Assumptions intrinsic to family social work flow out of beliefs and principles (examined in Chapter 2) that form the foundation of family social work. These assumptions include valuing *family-centered* and *home-based* practice, coupled with recognizing the importance of *crisis intervention*. Another foundational emphasis is on the importance of *teaching* families so that they become competent in their problem-solving abilities and in their social functioning and family relationships. Finally, family social work recognizes that families are embedded in a set of nested social systems that generate both risks and opportunities for families (*ecological*). We briefly present these assumptions about family social work in the following sections and in more detail throughout the text.

Home-Based Support for Families

Mary Richmond (1917) advocated for the importance of seeing families in their own homes. Half a century later, Nathan Ackerman (1958) also pointed out the merits of home visits. He suggested that home visits open a window into the emotional climate of the home and allow the worker to see firsthand the psychosocial identity of the family and its specific expressions in a defined environment (p. 129). Ackerman was particularly interested in family mealtime as a useful assessment tool.

In part, due to the field of child protection, interest in home-based family work has reignited over the past quarter-century. Conducting family work in the home provides several advantages. For example, home-based assessments of family functioning might produce more accurate and complete evaluations of families than office-based assessments (Ledbetter, Hancock, & Pelton, 1989). In the home, family social workers receive immediate and direct information about family functioning and develop a more complete picture about the family relationships as members interact within a familiar environment. This is known as "ecological validity" (Masse & McNeil, 2008). Ecological validity allows the worker to witness "real-life behaviors" in that family members often do not exhibit the same behavioral intensity in an office that usually occurs in homes. This allows the worker to individualize the intervention based on a family's living situation.

Most families also appreciate receiving services in the home. For example, in some programs, parents rate highly the importance of therapists coming to the home, highlighting client receptiveness to home-based services (Fraser, Pecora, & Haapala, 1991). This finding was supported in another study; in one program, a parent stated, "I liked the home-based services so my child could be observed in a normal atmosphere" (Coleman & Collins, 1997).

Advantages of family social work in the home extend beyond assessment. Office-based family therapy operates under the assumption that changes made by clients during an office interview can be easily applied (generalized) to settings and situations outside the office in the home and community. Yet, these changes do not consistently or easily transfer from office settings to the home (Masse & McNeil, 2008; Sanders & James, 1983). For example, some studies show that parents who have abused their children have difficulty transferring skills from office to home

(Isaacs, 1982). Other researchers found that mothers and conduct disordered adolescents who had received home-based services reported more improvement than did those who experienced office-based counseling (Foster, Prinz, & O'Leary, 1983). These studies are just two in a cluster of studies suggesting that interventions done in settings where problems spontaneously occur are more effective than office-based interventions. This suggests that transfer of learning from interventions is easier when family work occurs in client homes.

Home-based services also overcome treatment obstacles such as lack of transportation and other reasons for missed appointments. In overcoming such obstacles, home-based intervention offers several unique advantages: (1) services are accessible to a wider range of clients, particularly those who are disadvantaged or disabled, (2) counseling dropouts and appointment no-shows are reduced, (3) *all* family members are more readily engaged, and (4) the home is a natural setting in which interventions take hold (Fraser, Pecora, & Haapala, 1991; Kinney, Haapala, & Booth, 1991). However, caution should be exercised in assuming that *all* family members are more easily engaged through home-based services since some might consider them intrusive and an invasion of privacy.

The home and family are training grounds for children's social adjustment (Patterson, DeBaryshe, & Ramsey, 1989). Providing family social work in the home, with a flexible service schedule, engages reluctant family members more readily in treatment—a pivotal issue for family social workers given that some families might resist intervention. Additionally, entrance into clients' worlds where problems naturally emerge produces opportunities to use teachable moments. Family social workers can respond immediately to client problems.

With the family social worker working in the home, face-to-face contact with all family members becomes easier, which is an important issue when involvement of all family members is critical to success. Involvement of the entire family does not always happen when families are required to travel to agencies for appointments that are often inconvenient. Home-based family social work is also effective with isolated or impoverished families, as well as with families who are ambivalent, resistant to professional intervention, or otherwise suspicious of service. Although home-based family social work increases opportunities to meet with all family members, a family member may still avoid meeting with family workers by not being at home when a social worker visits. In Chapter 6, we discuss practical strategies for involving family members in the helping process.

The issue of portability and transferability of changes is a double-edged sword, since behavioral changes learned at home face similar obstacles when needed in places outside the home, such as school. High placement rates for adolescents with problem behaviors reveal the complexity of generalization to different settings. Delinquent adolescents, in particular, are often influenced by peers and situations outside the family and become buffered from family and social worker influences as they grow older and attain greater independence. Thus, family social workers must also teach families to transfer their learning to settings where family members work and play, including schools and recreational organizations. Additionally, early intervention, when problems are less entrenched, could halt the development of more severe problems later.

Despite the advantages of providing services in the home, home-based intervention also poses some difficulties for which the family social worker can prepare. For example, family social workers can lose some control when intervening in the home (Masse & McNeil, 2008). Loss of control can occur for a number of reasons. For example, family homes are dissimilar, creating an unfamiliar, unpredictable, and uncontrolled environment for the worker (p. 128). Moreover, home visits are threatened by a number of distractions such as television, electronic equipment, telephones, visitors, and toys. Home visits are also challenging because family social workers have fewer available resources; for example, they can bring only a small amount of play activities with them. Finally, traveling to a family home can be more expensive for the agency and individual family social worker because of fuel costs, vehicle depreciation, and travel time.

The best way to address these challenges is to plan ahead and anticipate potential obstacles. This might mean that the family social worker explore the layout of the house, examine resources, and discuss possible distractions with the family before starting out. Making a contract with the family at the outset would also facilitate future work with the family. The contract might include how to handle distractions (such as by not answering the telephone, turning off the television, and informing friends that they are busy for a specified period of time). The contract can be negotiated and signed to maximize social worker control over the direction of meetings.

EXERCISE 1.7   Boundaries in Family Social Work

Knowing the difference between professional and personal boundaries is extremely important for family social work. Get into small groups of four or five students. Construct a list of boundary issues, and try to differentiate between the personal and the professional in the following areas: money, time, sharing space, sharing personal information, sexuality, and relationship issues. Present this list to the class and discuss. In your discussion, try to make reference to how reciprocal these issues are. Refer to the Social Work Code of Ethics for other ideas.

Personal Boundaries   Professional Boundaries

Family-Centered Philosophy

A central belief of family social work is that the family is the context within which treatment originates. Social workers have always been context specialists through their ecological understanding, and family-centered work affirms the importance of understanding people's behavior within its natural context. Therefore, understanding that the family is pivotal to children's well-being provides a clear rationale for the value of family social work. Family social workers assert that every child has the right to grow up in a nurturing and protective environment.

Placing the family in the center of treatment is beneficial. Parents may experience problems with several children or have difficulties with other children once a targeted child receives treatment. A family-based intervention can therefore address wider problems beyond those presented by the target child. By working with the entire family, parents can use what they have learned regarding the target child and not repeat the same mistakes with other children. In this way, family social work can be preventative. Many families value the family-centered philosophy of family social work, as revealed in the following comments from parents: "The worker put the whole family on a contract," and "[The worker] directed attention to the entire family. It was useful to keep the whole family unit perspective and to value the family as a unit" (Coleman & Collins, 1997).

Changes beyond the target child are an important goal of family work. "Sibling generalization," which involves bringing about changes in the behavior of siblings who are not the specific focus of family work, can occur through family social work. Teaching parents about child management techniques is a core skill in family social work. Other siblings will be affected by these changes since, logically, skills learned by parents can be used with all children in the family. Teaching parents to manage child behavior problems more effectively promises to produce changes in the entire family unit, making it less likely that similar problems will reappear. For example, one program found that when mothers decreased punishment for inappropriate child behaviors, fathers stepped into the disciplinary role (Patterson & Fleischman, 1979). Family structure adapts to incorporate new behaviors learned within the family.

Working with the entire family has been useful in working with delinquent youth. Parents can use what they learned in dealing with socially aggressive boys with other children in the family (Arnold, Levine, & Patterson, 1975; Baum & Forehand, 1981; Klein, Alexander, & Parsons, 1977). Family interventions are based on the belief that parents are effective and preferred therapists for their children and that a change in the family system can also affect the behavior of other children in the family. Such programs show a decrease in behavior problems of siblings by more than two-thirds, compared with behavior before treatment. Research also suggests that positive changes can continue for several years after services end (Coleman, 1995). Declines in problematic child behavior beyond target child improvement therefore support the importance of family-based social work.

Crisis Intervention

Because of immediate, on-the-spot intervention, the family social worker provides crisis intervention during stressful family events. This is particularly important when interventions are triggered by the endangerment of a family member, such as suicide threats or abuse. Accordingly, the prompt and on-site presence of the family social worker can reduce the risk to vulnerable family members, at least until healthy family functioning and individual safety have been restored. During a crisis, the worker's intervention with the family focuses on problem solving and decision making, and the goal is to resolve the crisis and help the family develop adaptive coping skills. Through crisis intervention, family social work targets moving family members beyond their collective pain to a point of renewed growth and improved coping. To achieve these results, interventions can target concrete and practical problems experienced by the family.

Crisis intervention is effective in working with families that have a variety of problems, and under some circumstances it can be as effective as traditional long-term therapies (Powers, 1990). The dual aims of crisis intervention include the immediate resolution of urgent problems and adaptation to disruptive life events and the promotion of long-term skill building to reduce failure and maximize the ability to deal with future crises. Ideally, changes made during crisis intervention remain intact long after services end. For example, family crisis intervention has been effective in preventing hospitalization for some children and contributing to shorter psychiatric hospital stays for others (Langsley, Pittman, Machotka, & Flomenhaft, 1968).

Family social workers sometimes believe that more is better in terms of hours devoted to a particular problem. This is not always the case, as some interventions have a threshold effect. For example, spending fewer hours on a problem does not consistently result in less success. What matters is the clarity and focus of assessment and intervention. This means that family social workers must not be overwhelmed by the sum total of a family's difficulties. Instead, they must learn to prioritize existing problems and deal with each of them on the basis of their urgency. Each targeted problem will have a unique intervention. Family social workers not only deal with family crises but also dissect what led up to a particular crisis in addition to the long-term impact of a crisis on family functioning.

"Teachability" of Families

Family social workers often work with family members to increase skills that are integral to family harmony. Parenting and child management techniques are necessary skills that family social workers can help parents develop. These skills may involve a variety of methods, including: (1) reinforcing effective or desired behaviors; (2) helping family members deal with hurt and anger more effectively; (3) teaching parents how to observe and track children's behavior; (4) using time-outs when family conflict or child behaviors become unmanageable or too stressful; (5) practicing positive behaviors by using techniques such as role-playing; (6) focusing on the development of social skills for parents and children; (7) teaching relaxation techniques to help parents cope with stress and learn to self-nurture more effectively; and (8) developing more effective parenting skills and child management techniques.

Studies support the effectiveness of teaching parenting skills to eliminate abuse and change children's behaviors in a positive way (Baum & Forehand, 1981; Foster, Prinz, & O'Leary, 1983; Wolfe, Sandler, & Kaufman, 1981). Abuse and behavior problems are two primary reasons for family social work involvement with families. Also, behavioral training for parents has been effective in teaching self-control techniques (Isaacs, 1982) and changing behaviors of delinquent children (Webster-Stratton & Hammond, 1990).

Parent training to eliminate abuse and child behavior problems is built on observations of family interactions on a moment-by-moment basis. Family social workers can pay close attention to patterns of parent-child interaction and help the family to change these patterns in tangible ways. It is noteworthy that families with abused and conduct-disordered children show similar types of minute-by-minute interactions. Observations of parent-child interaction reveal ongoing interaction patterns within families, particularly repetitive behavior patterns between parent and child. In these patterns, abusive parents and parents of children with behavior problems communicate less frequently than other parents and use more negative and aversive parenting styles, ignoring prosocial child behavior (Patterson, DeBaryshe, & Ramsey, 1989). One component of parent skills training involves changing dysfunctional molecular patterns by teaching parents to respond positively to children's prosocial behavior, first within short time frames and later extending into longer periods (see Chapter 12).

Ecological Approach

Our democracy has become, in large measure, a democracy of the fortunate.
—*John Kenneth Galbraith*

Social workers and other professionals have begun to recognize the importance of understanding behavior within a social context. The ecological approach is born out of biological theories that explain the interdependencies between organisms and their environments (Payne, 2005). The field of family social work, being informed by family systems theory (Chapter 3), found ecological theory acceptable; theorists such as Germain and Gitterman were informed by both ecological and systems perspectives when they created their life model (Germain & Gitterman, 1996).

The ecological approach is especially relevant when working with families who are marginalized or disadvantaged. "Assessing families' connections to work, friends, and their broader community is essential to understanding their problems and to figuring out strategies for intervention" (Carter & McGoldrick, 2005, p. 19). A family's social context promises both risk and opportunity. For example, living in a high-crime area where families do not know one another presents ecological risk. In such neighborhoods, neighbors cannot watch out for one another and offer support during stressful times. By contrast, ecological opportunity is present in a close-knit neighborhood. When neighbors know and support one another, they are more likely to help a family in need. To develop a comprehensive understanding of families, social workers can identify potential sources of ecological risk and opportunity. Also, roles performed by family members within the family may parallel the roles they play outside the family (Geismar & Ayres, 1959).

A common error of social workers is to focus solely on the internal functioning of a family or its social environment, a split that oversimplifies a complex problem (Wood & Geismar, 1986). In fact, some work with families has met with limited success because all of the family's problems are attributed to patterns of family interaction. This leads to the limiting idea that only family interaction needs to be changed. Conversely, effective family social work involves identifying strengths and resources in each family member's social environment, as well as assessing the match between the two. Family social work accounts for factors beyond family boundaries and focuses on multiple dimensions of family functioning that go beyond relationships and communication. For example, parental effectiveness is closely linked with the quality of the social environment in which parents raise their children (Garbarino, 1992).

Families live in relationship with their larger environment. Many times, forces in the family's larger environment challenge its survival. Social barriers sometimes prevent families from reaching their potential. Family social workers work with families in their neighborhoods and communities to expand the material and social supports for families. It is a mistake to see families as single and isolated units; all families are intricately connected with their environment. Every family is embedded within layers of overlapping systems and is affected by each of these layers. Family social environments are complex and dynamic. Recognizing the complexity of the interactions between families and their social contexts offers social workers a new set of conceptual lenses to use as they describe, analyze, and intervene. Family social workers must be comfortable with assessing and interviewing in the social environment of each family member. This assessment balances the strengths and resources of the family with the strengths and resources of the environment, examining mismatches between the two. Family social workers assess family coping and recognize the ways in which the environment impinges on family functioning.

Even healthy families, if living in oppressive, stressful, or unsupportive environments, eventually show symptoms of strain, despite their abilities and strengths. The need for intervention to span home, school, and community and to promote give-and-take between systems is fundamental to the family social work approach. Building bridges between families and appropriate social support systems in the environment is therefore an essential ingredient of family social work. Family social workers using an ecological approach need to focus on "inter-relational transactions between systems" (Ungar, 2002) and see these transactions as reciprocal, each having influence over the other over time through many exchanges. A goal of family social work is to "increase the fit between people and their environments" (Payne, 2005). Germain and Gitterman's life model of social work practice is based on the metaphor of ecology, in which people are seen as interdependent with each other and with their environment (1966). The concept of P-I-E germinated from this thinking.

Many valuable resources are available within the social environment. These resources can include material or monetary supports, as well as social resources. The social environment can be understood by looking at the availability of social support. The need for social support has mistakenly been identified as a source of dependence. An absence of social support might imply independence to some, although it usually reflects vulnerability and isolation. Family privacy and geographic mobility in our society have often amputated families from sources of valuable social support.

Significant people in the family's environment can provide support and feedback to family members and to the family as a whole. When social resources are adequate, crises can be averted (Berry, 1997); on the contrary, when resources such as social support are inadequate, family members are more apt to display emotional distress or physical illness. Carter and McGoldrick (2006) caution that, "It is extremely important that we not 'psychologize' social problems by searching for the roots of every problem in the interior motivations and actions of the individual and/or the family" (p. 20). For example, women with little social support are more likely to experience complications during pregnancy than are women who receive a wider range of support, and women who receive sufficient emotional and physical support during pregnancy are likely to give birth to a healthier baby. Thus, social support benefits not only women but also their unborn children and the family as a whole. Helping a family nurture new support networks will not only optimize competencies but also help the family avoid becoming dependent on the worker. By the time the social worker terminates with a particular family, the family members should have consolidated skills and resources from which to draw upon later.

Considering the environment of the family has direct practice implications for family social workers. Traditionally, family services consisted of interventions restricted to externally predefined needs of children and families. Outside authorities, such as public health, school, or child protection officials, decided what the family was missing and implemented remedial interventions to fix the problem. The interventions were imposed on families, and the expertise of families regarding their own lives was ignored. These interventions frequently resulted in failure because workers did not consider the context within which the problems were occurring.

Working within a comprehensive framework allows a comprehensive response to the needs of all family members. Families receiving services are usually families under stress, and responding to stressors requires resources (Berry, 1997). An effective and collaborative partnership between a social worker and a family addresses the family's concerns when identifying needs, priorities, and options for service. Developing services tailored to the unique situation of each family replaces standardized interventions to which the family must conform. This approach respects the self-responsibility that family members should assume to obtain the services they need. Conversely, dictating a course of action does not respect self-sufficiency, nor does prescribing a standard package of services for all families. *One size does not fit all.*

Although the trend is toward providing more comprehensive services, the family's right to negotiate services and to individualize interventions implies that not all families will desire or require such a broad-based approach. The family social worker and the family negotiate a contract, specifying services to be provided. The social worker should be aware that some families might want help with one specific issue (such as remedial education assistance with a learning-disadvantaged young person) rather than broader interventions. Broader services are not better services if they do not fit the unique needs and expectations of the family. The importance of formulating a mutually acceptable contract with specific goals cannot be overemphasized. The process of negotiating a contract is a key aspect of family social work and will be discussed in more detail in Chapter 7.

There is growing interest in providing early intervention for problems, before concerns become full-blown or unmanageable, instead of intervening only after the situation has become explosive or destructive. Prevention is preferable to picking up pieces later. Helping people learn parenting skills is more effective if done before, rather than after, an adult has abused a child. Interest in prevention is also reflected in the increased attention to early childhood stimulation programs, as opposed to later remedial programs for school-aged children. Early intervention assumes two forms: intervention early in the life cycle and intervention early in the problem cycle. Family social workers conduct both types of intervention.

TABLE 1.1	Example of Assessing Family Roles and Responsibilities in the Social Environment

Social Environment	Roles of Family Members	Responsibilities
Neighborhood	Parents:	
	• Adult	To look out for the safety and well-being of neighborhood children
	• Coach	To coach a baseball team comprised of 9- and 10-year-old children
	• Neighbor	To reach out to neighbors and provide support if necessary
	Children:	
	• Family member	To let parents know who their playmates and friends are and where they are going
	• Team member	To follow the rules and help teammates

© Cengage Learning 2013

Another changing direction in family social work is the emphasis on building family strengths rather than responding solely to deficits and problems. For example, programs for children with special needs are focusing not only on the medical needs of the child but also on helping families include members with social and developmental disabilities in the family's ongoing activities. These principles promote growth and recognize the need to consider the family as part of a larger community of extended resources.

The broad focus of the family social worker does not make decisions easier when she or he must set priorities for services or address conflicting demands within the family. Instead, a wide focus forces the family social worker to consider the needs of all family members, not just the child whose problems may provoke the initiation of services. On the basis of these considerations, the family social worker must identify the needs of family members, decide how to best address specific problems, and locate available internal and external resources. Whenever possible, these considerations should be made in collaboration with the family.

EXERCISE 1.8   Families and the Social Environment

To prepare for work with families, we need to think about how families function within their social environments or communities. Think about your own family and other families you know. List four social environments in which family members live, work, and play. Next, write down the roles and responsibilities of family members that might be associated with each of these social environments. See Table 1.1 for an example to help you get started.

The Family as a Special Group Form

The family is the primary group in which members share close and personal relationships, which are developed through shared activities, that last over a prolonged period of time. "Those who first sought to understand and treat families found a ready parallel in small groups" (Nichols, 2010, p. 8). Emotional ties are intense, whether they are negative or positive. Some believe that the family group is the prototype for all other groups and is the first group that a child knows. The experience in this group will influence that child's experience in every other group throughout life. Every child is born into a family group and grows up in that group, if even for a short time. Unlike many other groups, we do not choose the family group into which we are born. Furthermore, families have a history and future together, unlike many other groups (Nichols, 2010). Therefore, the family exerts tremendous influence over its members in terms of behaviors, beliefs, communication styles, cultural transmission, social skills, and efforts to meet basic human needs. From birth onward, every human being is a member of a primary group.

EXERCISE 1.9   Groups and Families

In small groups, make a list of similarities and differences between groups and families. If you have studied group theory before, pull some of this theory into the list. What are the implications of these similarities for the work that you will do as a family social worker? Present the group's discussion to the rest of the class and compare responses.

As a child grows and develops, the number of groups of which he or she is a member expands. Yet the family remains the first group experience, a group that is organized to meet daily demands for food, clothing, shelter, growth, and development. The family group helps members learn unique attachment styles and teaches children how to relate in other group settings outside the family unit. Clearly, all families are organized in unique ways, with different capabilities and different levels of success in meeting their members' needs.

The family is also a natural group. It forms spontaneously on the basis of life events, interpersonal attraction, or the mutually perceived needs of members (Toseland & Rivas, 1984). Family groups form independently of professional involvement and usually have an extensive history well before the initial family social worker contact. Families incorporate new members only by birth, adoption, commitment, or marriage. Members can leave only by death (Carter & McGoldrick, 2005). Family members are also irreplaceable. Therefore, family groupings have an extensive history, and relationships are well established and are created independently of a professional helper or leader. Therefore, there are both similarities and differences between the natural family group and groups formed around specific professional or recreational objectives and tasks, and similar concepts and tasks apply to the different forms of groups.

Lewin (cited in Nichols, 2010) draws parallels between group and family dynamics first suggesting that group dynamics are a complex blend of individuals and personalities and superordinate properties of the group. Second, the group is more than the sum of its parts. Third, group discussions, and by extension family discussions, are more effective than separate meetings with individuals. Nichols and Schwartz (2007) cite Bion, who noted that patterns of fight/flight, dependency, and pairing are also group patterns applicable to families. The dependency pattern is manifested through the need for a leader (parent) who can nurture and protect. The group also must protect itself (fight/flight), either through fighting or running away. There is a need for pairing (creation of subsystems) by members.

Nichols and Schwartz also draw parallels between Bennis's stages of group development and the family life cycle. Bennis suggested that groups go through predictable stages of development, an observation echoed in the family life cycle. Finally, role theory has been adapted to apply to family work. Early family theorists adapted group concepts to work with families.

EP 2.1.3b

CHAPTER SUMMARY

Social work has a proud history of working with families. Although social workers can do family therapy, family social work is different from family therapy. It is much more concrete, as well as strength-based. Family social work is usually home-based, family-centered, and ecologically focused and believes that families are teachable.

KEY TERMS

Crisis intervention We recognize that families are often in crisis when they start family work and that this immediate crisis needs to be stabilized before longer-term work occurs. Often immediate problems need to be resolved before the longer-term problem-solving skills can be taught and implemented.

Ecological approach The ecological approach encourages the family social worker to consider challenges, strengths, supports, and barriers at multiple levels— including the individual, family, and community, as well as from within a cultural and societal context that affects the experiences of a person facing problems within a family.

Family-centered Our focus is not on individuals but on the family as an interacting system. We value all family members and their input into each other's lives.

Family social work Family social work usually occurs in a family's home and often concentrates on concrete needs, daily routines, skills, family patterns, and functioning. Problem-solving, strength-based, and crisis-intervention approaches are all utilized.

Family therapy Family therapy is office-based and primarily focused on second-order changes—that is, changing thinking patterns that govern rules and thus behaviors, thoughts, and feelings. It effects more abstract change compared to the first-order concrete change of family social work.

Person-in-environment (PIE) Similar to the ecological approach, PIE does not focus on the individual in isolation but looks at the individual in relationship to another significant person (dyad), families (triads), small groups, large groups, local communities, larger communities like state and country, and even the global community and global environment.

Strengths-based approach The strengths-based perspective reveals to family social workers how to discover and explore, enhance, and exploit families' strengths and resources in the journey of achieving their goals, realizing their dreams, and shedding the shackles of their own lack of confidence and misgivings (Saleeby, 2000).

SUGGESTED READING

Richmond, M. (1917, reprinted 1964). *Social diagnosis*. Philadelphia, PA: Russell Sage Foundation. This book is a recommended read, as it is a "classic." The roots of direct social work practice are based on this classic text by Mary Richmond, one of the founding figures of social work. Although influenced by psychoanalytic thought and the medical model, Richmond's work contains the beginnings of the unique contribution of social work that laid the foundation for social work to become a recognized profession.

COMPETENCY NOTES

EP 2.1.1c. Attend to professional roles and boundaries: Family social work is not the same as family therapy; family social work may be home-based or community-based.

EP 2.1.3b. Analyze models of assessment, prevention, intervention, and evaluation: The broad focus of the family social worker does not make decisions easier when she or he must set priorities for services or address conflicting demands within the family. The family social worker must use critical-thinking skills to identify the needs of family members, decide how to best address specific problems, and locate available internal and external resources.

From a psychological perspective, it is hard to imagine the value of defining any major social group that is not physically or emotionally harming itself or others as deviant or undesirable.

—Nathan W. Ackerman Family Institute, Beatrice L. Wood, William M. Pinsof, Mental Research Institute

What Is Family?

CHAPTER 2

LEARNING OBJECTIVES

- Conceptual: Understand different family forms, diversity, and beliefs about families.
- Perceptual: Observe and define different family structures.
- Valuational/Attitudinal: Value diversity as richness.
- Behavioral: Be nonjudgmental and anti-oppressive. Put into practice the family social work principles.

One of the most challenging issues in learning about families originates from the deceptively simple question: What is a family? The complexity in answering this question partially springs from the ever-changing nature of social relationships, making a single, all-inclusive definition difficult to arrive at. Attempts to define *family* encounter challenges similar to defining such emotionally laden and even politically constructed concepts as masculinity, motherhood, or love. Everyone seems to have a personal definition of each, but a single agreed-on definition does not exist. Despite this difficulty, social workers are challenged to understand what they mean by *family* if they are to decide on service eligibility from a particular agency and who is to be included in services. The definition of family membership can help family social workers determine who should be included in a family intervention (Hartman & Laird, 1983). A clear definition of *family* will determine who is eligible to receive such benefits as maternity leave, day care subsidies, public assistance, or health care. It will also help the family social worker make a decision about the particular unit that will be the focus of family social worker services.

EXERCISE 2.1 Personal Biases and Beliefs about Families

On the basis of your own family of origin, create a definition of family. Then join with one other person and incorporate that person's definition into your definition. Your dyad should then join up with another dyad to incorporate that dyad's definition of family. Then join with another group of four to synthesize a new definition. Keep joining groups until you have a class definition of family. Write the class definition down. How has the definition changed throughout the process of integrating others' definitions? Compare this definition with other definitions in this text.

The picture of family that family social workers develop must encompass a range of family structures, roles, and functions. For many new family social workers, their primary experience with family has been in their family of origin. Yet, family social workers must move beyond individual experience because limited and deeply held personal beliefs about what families are will decrease sensitivity to the validity of diverse family structures and functioning. Without critical reflection about what *health* and *dysfunction* mean, biases will creep into the meaning of these terms.

On a political level, the definition of family is debated even more contentiously. The term *family values* is embedded in everyday discourse, and families that fail to adhere to these values are considered undesirable. But few people can, in fact, actually define the term *family values*. In the process of using it to judge, women who work outside the home are criticized, poor families become marginalized, families from other cultures are made to feel defective, and single parents sometimes believe that their family has suffered a critical amputation because it is incomplete. The simplistic argument has even been forwarded that if families were more traditional, social problems would be eradicated. Embedded in this argument is the suggestion that the so-called disintegration of the traditional family has created many social problems for the rest of us. The following quotation illustrates how family values play out in families:

> *What we often take to be family values—the work ethic, honesty, clean living, marital fidelity, and individual responsibility—are in fact social, religious or cultural values. To be sure, these values are transmitted by parents to their children and are familial in that sense. They do not, however, originate within the family. It is the value of close relationships with other family members, and the importance of these bonds relative to other needs...*
> —David Elkind (www.Bartleby.com)

EXERCISE 2.2 Family Values

Make a list of the characteristics embedded in the term family values. Build on this list with the class. How much do you agree or disagree with this list? What will the characteristics in this list mean for your family social work role?

Therefore, rigid adherence to a single and traditional type of family would rob us of considerable diversity and richness. Perhaps we have created more confusion than necessary in our discussion of the definition of family. Yet, as critical thinkers, family social workers need to think beyond personal opinion or the policies of a single agency and ask: What kind of grouping qualifies as a family, as compared to friends or roommates? Where do extended family members fit in? What about common-law relationships? How do gay and lesbian families fit into the definition of family? Similarly, how do communal relationships or polygamous relationships fit into the category of family? How do cross-cultural variations of family structure and form fit into the conceptualization of family? Finally, are alternative family forms the enemy of families?

Defining *family* is not easy! Yet, a working definition of *family* is a crucial preliminary task for family social workers. Beyond the direct practice level, family social workers need to critically consider how policy makers have attempted to control family behaviors and structures on the basis of preferred political and moral agendas (Pinsof, 2002). Policy makers have options to support a variety of family forms. Without a clear definition and conceptualization, social workers would have only personal assumptions, beliefs, and social stereotypes of family to rely on. Family social workers need to think critically about how to define their target client group so they can design and focus appropriate interventions. One of our first tasks in this book, then, is to unearth common biases and beliefs about families. Some of the biases are rooted in history, which has perpetuated the hegemonic interests of the powerful few.

Generally, people think of the traditional family when referring to the nuclear family. Static definitions have been limited to members related by blood (i.e., biological parents and children) or legally sanctioned relationships. Clearly, a monolithic view of family would exclude more people than it includes. The idea of a traditional family conjures up an image of the mother at home, father at work, and 2.2 children. Distress about the current state of the family has been accompanied by the belief that the best way to resolve serious social problems is to return to this traditional form.

In reality, North American family structures have always been diverse, and the traditional nuclear family existed more in fiction than fact. The family with a male breadwinner and female full-time homemaker existed as a dominant family form for only a brief period, most commonly in white, middle-class households (Coontz, 1996). During the 1920s, a small majority of children grew up in a family where the male was the breadwinner and the female was the homemaker. Today, this type of family comprises less than 10 percent of all households. The current idealized traditional nuclear family espoused by conservative politicians existed primarily in the 1950s (Coontz, 1996). Recognizing and accepting family diversity is a necessary attitude underpinning family social work.

Family forms have always been diverse. In colonial and pioneer times, wealthier settlers established independent households by relying upon the services of poor immigrant workers and slaves. African Americans were denied the legal protection of marriage and parenthood and, in response, developed extensive kinship networks (Coontz, 1996). Middle-class white women were able to enjoy domesticity because working-class women liberated them from household tasks. Carter and

McGoldrick (2005) remind us that "the traditional stable multigenerational extended family of yore was supported by sexism, classism, and racism" (p. 3). Perhaps this observation is as true today as it was yesterday!

Throughout history, death, desertion, divorce, separation, single parenthood, and blended families have been woven into the social fabric, challenging beliefs about the erosion of society because of family breakdown. Blended families are not a recent development. High mortality rates of women during childbirth and illness made blended families common. Historically, disease and war claimed lives, leaving some adults single several times over during their lives and making remarriage common. In addition, many poor women and children worked outside the home even before the Industrial Revolution, again challenging the discourse that feminism and women in the workforce are responsible for the breakdown of the family. Whose interests are served by claims that women working outside the home hurt families? What does the research say about this? Given this sketch of family history, we see that the traditional nuclear family primarily existed in middle and upper classes of European lineage, supported by the toils of poor and oppressed workers.

We argue that the absence of a supportive environment contributes to family disintegration. As family social workers, we celebrate family diversity since diversity, rather than being a threat to families, honors all families. For example, legal recognition of gay and lesbian unions reinforces the importance of families. Rather than being deficit-based, diversity provides families with depth, character, and richness. We argue that hostile social environments that are opposed to diversity are largely responsible for family difficulties. Families encounter difficulties for many reasons, not the least of which is a *one-size-fits-all* notion that everyone must conform to the same structure and rules. When social attitudes oppress those who do not fit, difficulties arise. By embracing a broader definition of *family*, family social workers will be prepared to work nonjudgmentally with all types of families. Anti-oppression and respect for diversity are two cornerstones of our maturing profession.

PURPOSES OF FAMILIES

EXERCISE 2.3 Family Purposes

What purposes (benefits) do families serve? List five purposes for its members and five purposes for society.

Families exist both for the well-being of their members and for the well-being of society. Ideally, they offer predictability, structure, and safety as members mature and participate in the community. It is within families that children develop skills that prepare them for life outside the family—first in school and friendships, and later in the workforce, and romantic partners. Through families, members meet basic human needs; when families fail to meet these needs, outside intervention becomes necessary. One of the first tasks for a family social worker is to assess whose needs are and whose needs are not being met in a family. When families do well, society also thrives.

Over 40 years ago, Satir (1967), a well-known family social worker, identified seven functions of families. Many functions are outdated, revealing the metamorphosis of the family in only four decades. Which ones do you believe still exist? The seven functions include:

1. To provide heterosexual experience for mates
2. To contribute to the continuity of the race by producing and nurturing children
3. To cooperate economically by dividing labors between the adults according to sex, convenience, and precedents
4. To maintain a boundary (e.g., incest as taboo) so that tasks can be performed smoothly and stable relationships maintained
5. To transmit culture to the children through teaching communication, expression of emotions, coping with the inanimate environment, and roles
6. To recognize when one of its members reaches adulthood
7. To provide for the eventual care of parents by their children (pp. 26–27).

EXERCISE 2.4   Outdated Family Functions

Discuss in class which of Satir's seven functions listed previously are now outdated.

Families also pass down cultural traditions from one generation to another, including language, beliefs, religion, knowledge, and rituals. However, cultural traditions are in a constant state of flux and evolution. Some people are nostalgic because society is changing so rapidly, while others welcome these changes. Which traditions do you miss, and which do you embrace? The mass media combined with the integration and synthesis of global ideas seem to be hastening cultural and family changes.

Through family teachings, children mature and learn how to survive outside the family. Within the family, children learn how to get along with others. They also learn about gender roles, peer relationships, and responsibility to self and others. Moreover, they develop a work ethic and first realize their potential. Freud once claimed that a healthy person is one who knows how to "play and work," and it is through the family that children develop skills with which to play and work throughout their lifelong journey.

Families also produce workers and consumers, two requirements for a strong economy. A journalist interviewed one of the authors of this textbook about the meaning and implications of the declining birth rate. This author was curious why a declining birth rate was a problem and asked the interviewer to explain. The interviewer responded, " We need babies to fill the empty houses of course." Perhaps the interviewer had it backward: People should not have babies in order to fill houses; rather, houses should be built to accommodate people! The interview was never published, but it was evident that the interviewer's assumption was the importance of a growing consumer population to support the economy. Families produce children who become both workers and consumers. Many industrialized countries are increasing immigration quotas because of a low birth rate that interferes with economic growth. From this discussion, the interdependence between families and the larger society should be clear.

Therefore, blaming social problems on changing families places the cart before the horse. Another angle from which to view social problems is to consider how such problems *contribute* to the breakdown of the family. As proposed by Coontz (1996):

> These inequities are not driven by changes in family forms, contrary to ideologues that persist in confusing correlation with causes; but they certainly exacerbate such changes, and they tend to bring out the worst in all families. The result has been an accumulation of stresses on families, alongside some important expansions of personal options. Working couples with children try to balance three full-time jobs, as employers and schools cling to policies that assume every employee has a "wife" at home to take care of family matters. Divorce and remarriage have allowed many adults and children to escape from toxic family environments, yet our lack of social support networks and failure to forge new values for sustaining intergenerational obligations have let many children fall through the cracks in the process. (p. 47)

Over fifty years ago, Nathan Ackerman (1958) pointed out the poor fit between social needs and individual needs:

> Whatever the term, all are agreed on the trend toward a sense of lostness, aloneness, confusion of personal identity, and a driven search for acceptance through conformity. One effect of this trend toward disorientation is to throw each person back on his (sic) family group for the restoration of a sense of security, belongingness, dignity and worth. The family is called upon to make up to its individual members in affection and closeness for the anxiety and distress which is the result of failure to find a safe place in the wider world. (cited in Satir, 1967)

Both Coontz and Ackerman are critical of the failure of society to support and help families to foster nurturing environments for children and parents. Both agree that difficulties of living in a hostile and alienating social world heap additional burdens on the family to meet members' needs *and* fail to buffer family members from social stress. Perhaps families are doing more for society than society is doing for its members. What do you think?

Despite the fact that throughout history and across the globe the family has assumed diverse forms, all people come from a nuclear family of one form or another. The nuclear family is any kinship group of more than one person residing in the same household and related by marriage, blood, or societal or self-sanction. This definition is so broad that one could easily ask, "What grouping does not qualify as a family?" The definition is broad enough to include all who have been or are currently members of a nuclear family. Indeed, being a member of more than one nuclear family in a lifetime is both possible and likely.

EXERCISE 2.5   History of the Family

Discuss in class:

1. How has the family evolved since the Middle Ages?
2. How have cultures outside of a Eurocentric perspective addressed issues of divorce, separation, and so on?
3. What has been the role of women with regard to families over the past 200 years?

DIVERSE FAMILY STRUCTURES

Regardless of cultural group or socioeconomic status, families include a range of structures. The most common family structures that include children are presented in the following sections. The same family can fit into two or more categories.

> *Children live in a variety of family forms; they develop normally with single parents, with unmarried parents, with multiple caretakers in a communal setting, and with traditional two-parent families. What children require is loving and attentive adults, not a particular family type.*
> —Sandra Scarr (www.Bartleby.com)

Family of Orientation/Family of Origin

Most individuals belong to at least two family groupings over a lifetime. All have belonged to a family of orientation, commonly referred to as the family of origin. This is the family into which a person is born or raised. It is possible for some people to come from two or more families of origin. For example, a child who is adopted during infancy was, at least briefly, part of a family of orientation with the birth mother. To the child, however, the family of origin is more likely to be that of the adoptive parents. One definition of the family of origin is "the living unit in which a person has his or her beginnings physiologically, physically, and emotionally" (Hovestadt, Anderson, Piercy, Cochran, & Fine, 1985, cited in Rovers, DesRoches, Hunter, & Taylor, 2000).

Family of Procreation

A family of procreation consists of a couple, whether through self or state sanction, that has developed a relationship and has children. The couple in a family of procreation may be opposite- or same-sex, and procreation may occur through heterosexual intercourse or through one of the assisted reproductive technologies, such as artificial insemination or surrogate parenthood.

Extended Family

An extended family includes two or more family units. For example, an extended family may consist of a household in which a grandmother or grandfather lives with a married son, daughter-in-law, and grandchildren. Although grandparents are the most common extension, an extended family may also include aunts, uncles, or cousins. For members of some ethnic groups, the extended family plays an especially important role. Grandparenting is discussed in more detail in Chapter 4. In recent years, often due to economic reasons, more families have been extended with children returning home—sometimes with their children as well. According to one study, the likelihood of an adult child returning home has tripled since 1945 (http://www.statcan.gc.ca/pub/11-008-x/2006003/9480-eng.htm). In addition, an elderly parent may move into this home. "According to Census data, the number of parents living with their adult children increased 67% from 2000 to 2007" (http://womensissues.about.com/od/startingover/a/MomMovesStats.htm).

We wonder if the term "extended family" needs to be changed to the "over-extended" family! Indeed, the baby boomer generation (those born from 1945 to 1964) is now referred to as the "sandwich generation" due to being squeezed between their adult children and their elderly parents. For these stressed-out boomers, an eagerly anticipated, quieter, less family-responsible retirement has become an unfulfilled dream.

Blended Family

A blended family, or stepfamily, consists of two people living with at least one child from a previous relationship. The parents may also have biological children together. Half of all children born since 1970 will live in a blended family, as statistics show that 80 percent of divorced men and 75 percent of divorced women under the age of 45 will marry again within three to four years (http://www.trust4u.com/Resources/BlendedFamilies.htm).

Adoptive Family

Adoption involves a legal commitment to raise children who have been born to others. Adoption has become more complicated in recent years, with fewer children available to be adopted. Prospective parents can now adopt through an open process, informally, internationally, and interracially. Families may be formed by more than one way of adopting. Moreover, single parents can now adopt and, in some states, gay and lesbian parents are also free to adopt (Carter, 2005). Adopt Help Law Center reports that 21 states and Washington, DC have court precedents that allow for second-parent adoptions of their partner's child(ren) for same-sex couples; however, since same-sex couples are barred from legal marriage in most states, they are barred from adopting an unrelated child since adoption laws favor married couples as adoptive parents (http://www.adopthelp.com/alternativeadoptions/alternatives2.html).

Foster Family

In a foster family, parents temporarily nurture children born to others. The length of time in which a foster child is in the home can vary from several days to most of his or her childhood. Although most foster families have a formal arrangement with child welfare authorities, other fostering arrangements can be made informally with friends or relatives. In the United States, nearly half a million children are in foster care. Two thirds are African American or mixed race; most are between the ages of 5 and 11; and many have behavioral or emotional problems (Carter, 2005). Carter also notes that for-profit businesses in the field of foster care are emerging.

Single-Parent Family

A single-parent family consists of one parent and one or more children. The parent can be either male or female and can be single as a result of the death of a partner, divorce, separation, desertion, or never having been married. A growing number of single parents are single by choice. Over one-quarter of Caucasian babies and over two-thirds of African American children in the United States are born to unmarried women (Pinsof, 2002). That is equal to nearly half of the children born in Scandinavia. Single parents need the support of family, friends, and community (Carter, 2005) because there is no partner to share the responsibilities.

EXERCISE 2.6   A Single-Parent Family

Describe a single-parent family that you know. How did the single parenthood come about? What is the impact of single parenthood on the family (e.g., economic, social status, family identity, social perception)?

EP 2.1.4c

DEFINING *FAMILY*

Murray Bowen, one of the first great systemic thinkers, views the family as a system. "The family is a number of different kinds of systems. It can accurately be designated as a social system, a cultural system, a games system, a communication system, a biological system…. I think of the family as a combination of emotional and relationship systems" (1971, p. 169). Bowen's definition can easily be used to define other groups as well, such as a classroom group, a basketball team, or a therapy group. (Ideas about how emotions and relationships play out are discussed later in this book.)

Eichler's (1988) definition of *family* provides a foundation on which to build:

> *A family is a social group that may or may not include one or more children (e.g., childless couples), who may or may not have been born in their wedlock (e.g., adopted children, or children by one adult partner of a previous union). The relationship of the adults may or may not have its origin in marriage (e.g., common-law couples); they may or may not occupy the same residence (e.g., commuting couples). The adults may or may not cohabit sexually, and the relationship may or may not involve such socially patterned feelings as love, attraction, piety, and awe. (p. 4)*

Compare Eichler's definition of *family* with this outmoded definition provided by Satir over 45 years ago (1967):

> *When Mary and Joe added the parental role to their individual and marital roles, they then qualified, sociologically speaking, as a family…. [Sociologists]: (1) Generally seem to agree that the nuclear family (made up of parents and children) is found in all societies. (2) They define a family as a group composed of adults of both sexes, two of whom (the mates) live under the same roof and maintain a socially accepted sexual relationship. (3) Families also include children created or adopted by these mates. (p. 26)*

The Vanier Institute of the Family (www.vifamily.ca) defines *family* as:

> *Any combination of two or more persons who are bound together over time by ties of mutual consent, birth and/or adoption or placement and who, together, assume responsibilities for variant combinations of some of the following:*
> * *Physical maintenance and care of group members*
> * *Addition of new members through procreation or adoption*

- *Socialization of children*
- *Social control of members*
- *Production, consumption, distribution of goods and services, and*
- *Affective nurturance–love.*

Finally, Carter and McGoldrick's (2005) definition of *family* offers yet another perspective:

> *Families comprise people who have a shared history and a shared future. They encompass the entire emotional system of at least three, and frequently now four or even five generations held together by blood, legal, and/or historical ties. (p. 1)*

EXERCISE 2.7   Creating Your Own Definition of Family

Review the definitions of family and then create your own personal definition. After creating this definition, share it with another person in the class and explain what it means.

EXERCISE 2.8   Definition of Family

Divide into groups of four. In your small group, compare the different definitions of family provided in this chapter. Do you see any biases? How inclusive is each definition? Are there any definitions so loose and vague that they can apply to any group of people? Are there difficulties with any definition that might pose a challenge to social policies or family-serving agencies?

Cultures differ in how they define *family* and who is included. The definition derived from the dominant culture focuses on the traditional nuclear family, whereas African American families include an extended kinship network, Chinese families focus on ancestors, and Italians embrace several generations of extended kin (McGoldrick, Giordano, & Garcia-Preto, 2005). Some Native American families consider the entire community in their web of family affiliations (Coleman, Unrau, & Manyfingers, 2001). In some families that adhere to traditional cultures, relationships with extended family and kin networks are often based on interdependence, group orientation, and reliance on others. Cultural values and practices about family that someone from another culture may label as strange or unhealthy may also be embedded in what is considered to be *family*. Family activities may diverge markedly from the dominant culture.

For example, some cultures practice arranged marriages, polygamy, communal sharing of resources, and different family life cycle transitions. Other families are structured "traditionally" with a clear line of authority, with males or elders as heads of households. Moreover, various religious groups affirm patriarchal values within the family. Difficulties can emerge when children or females from one culture encounter differences in the dominant culture. These values and beliefs might pose special challenges to workers who utilize theories that are based on the equality of family members. For example, feminist theory challenges power inequities within the family. Take a look at Table 2.1, which depicts the results of a survey completed by Gallagher based on interviews of 2,087 religiously

TABLE 2.1 | Gender and Marriage Ideals among Religiously Committed Christians (percent)

	Evangel.	Fundamntlst.	Mainline	Liberal	Catholic
Empty/unfulfilling marriages should be ended in divorce.	13.3	22.4	29.0	40.9	34.9
Marriage should be an equal partnership.	87.4	82.6	88.3	91.9	92.2
The husband should be the head of the family.	90.4	82.8	70.5	59.0	38.1

© Cengage Learning 2013

committed individuals. This survey did not include interviews with individuals who had no religious affiliation or who ascribed to religions other than Christianity. The table reveals that beliefs about family structure differ depending on religious affiliation.

EXERCISE 2.9 Religion and the Family

Review Table 2.1 and answer the following:

Describe an empty or unfulfilling marriage.

Describe an equal partnership in terms of concrete behaviors.

What does "head of the family" mean in terms of describable behaviors?

Where do you stand with regard to each of the statements?

Discuss your responses in class. Break into small groups and analyze how these responses would affect a family social worker's approach to working with religious families. How would his or her approach be different from working with families for whom religion is less important?

Both a lack of self-awareness and critical thinking might lead family social workers to be less objective about families whose backgrounds are either very different from or very much like their own families. In either case, they might have blind spots or personal "hot buttons", fail to understand parents, or encounter communication and cultural barriers such as language, religious differences, or divergent styles of parenting. Another risk is that social workers may construct inaccurate assessments about family strengths and weaknesses. Thus, family social workers must critically reflect upon personal motivations, biases, and blind spots. Doing so clears the way to enable them to work empathetically with parents from different backgrounds. Cultural sensitivity is discussed in more detail throughout the book.

In conclusion, contemporary family lifestyles and structures are fluid and evolving, necessitating that the family social worker adopt a broad definition of *family*. Judgments and decisions about family structures play an important role in deciding which resources and barriers a family will encounter in getting its needs met. Despite the difficulty of developing a clear and simple definition of *family*, most people can construct an unambiguous description to fit their own particular family, and working definitions of *family* can be established for most situations. The family, in its most basic conceptualization, is what a person in a family says it is. The experienced family reality, instead of reliance on a static, one-dimensional, and rigid definition, is crucial to family social work and opens the mind for the work ahead.

EXERCISE 2.10   Your Family Defined

Develop a definition of family based on your particular family. How has the definition of family changed over the years, and at what times has your family fit into the standard social definitions?

EP 2.1.4c

DIVERSITY AND FAMILIES

> *If history has a lesson for us, it is that no one family form has ever been able to satisfy the human need for love, comfort, and security.*
> —Gillis, 1996, cited in Carter & McGoldrick, 2005, p. 15

> *Marriage as a relationship between two individuals is taken more seriously and comes with higher emotional expectations than ever before. But marriage as an institution exerts less power over people's lives than it once did. It is no longer the main mechanism for regulating sexual behavior, conferring differential economic and political rights, ordering the relations between the sexes, or organizing interpersonal rights and obligations, including reproduction and dependent care.*
> —Coontz, 2006

A historical overview of the family in Western culture confirms the existence of a variety of family structures that diverge from the traditional view of the family as a single, monolithic form. Pinsof (2002) argues that marriages seldom lasted for 15 years, with death as the primary reason for the end of a marriage. It was not until the middle to end of the twenty-first century that divorce overtook death as the primary reason for marital dissolution. Coontz (2006) suggests that the frequency of divorce in modern American society is not entirely unprecedented, although the reasons for divorce in the past were different than in complex, stratified societies. The reasons were different because the reasons for marriage were different. Unlike before, when marriage was based on practical reasons, in the present time, marriage is usually based on the search for personal fulfillment. Coontz also argues that, "it is naïve to think that we can ever again reduce divorce to a minor part of family terrain by tinkering with law and social policy" (p. 14).

The divorce rate has leveled off (and even dropped during the recession) (http://www.coloradoconnection.com/news/story.aspx?id=272784). Looking beyond family structure will help you develop an accurate understanding of unique family experiences and the common needs of family units across society. A childless couple; a couple with two (or ten) biological, adopted, or foster children; a single mother or father with children; and a gay or lesbian couple with children are all examples of different family structures, but are families nonetheless. So are families that embrace extended kin and families from cultures that assume forms that differ from what we consider the traditional family. It is interesting that many definitions define a group as a family only if children are present in the relationship, revealing a subtle bias for children. Do you think two people should be considered a family, even if there are no children present?

Family structure across North America is especially diverse. Families differ in many ways beyond the structures discussed above, including differences in lifestyle, cultural heritage, gender role expressions, sexual orientation, and the decision whether or not to have children, to name a few. Newcomers to North America bring with them unique cultural and religious beliefs and heritages that affect family structure and family functioning. Culture also plays an instrumental role in how families proceed through the family life cycle (Carter & McGoldrick, 2005). (The family life cycle is discussed in more detail in Chapter 4.) Families are also affected by the sociohistorical era in which they live. Gender relations within families vary greatly, and we are still a long way from total gender equality, both inside and outside the family. Nevertheless, gender is a major organizing factor in families because it influences behavior in families and how problems are constructed Ramage, F. (2005).

All families exist within a particular culture and social environment. Many are disadvantaged because of lack of access to social resources and the willingness of social institutions to support them. In many ways, the traditional nuclear family encapsulates a Eurocentric perspective and, in doing so, sets the stage for subtle discrimination that is based on race and gender. As such, individuals and groups that fall outside the mainstream definition of family can encounter discrimination and ineligibility to receive services from a particular agency because the dominant group does not acknowledge or value their unique experiences and practices. This contributes to marginalization and distancing from social resources. At the same time, "different" families are blamed for their own victimization. Typically, those doing the blaming have little compassion for or understanding of powerlessness and discrimination and fail to empathize with the obstacles that others face. Consequently, children in some of these families feel stigmatized and ostracized by the larger community in which their families struggle to get their basic human needs met with dignity.

Family social workers are challenged to develop awareness and sensitivity by understanding differences from both a structural and a cultural point of view. *Awareness* includes the openness and ability to recognize that differences exist and understand how they shape reality in inequitable and unjust ways (Laszloffy & Hardy, 2000). Those who are sensitive to differences are not only aware of issues embedded in these differences, but are also capable of acting on them. They can take their awareness to a political level and challenge institutional racism, rigid gender beliefs, or oppressive family policies and practices. We therefore recommend that every family assessment include an analysis of oppression and the impact of racism on each family.

Garbarino (1992) cautions that children should not be made to feel as though they are growing up in a war zone! In Canada and in the United States, for example, indigenous or native peoples remain an underserved and marginalized group, leading us to reflect on Maslow's hierarchy of needs (Maslow, 1968). The premise of this book is that children and families have a *right* to the necessities of life: food, shelter, clothing, safety at home and in the community, education, health care, and so on. Family social workers understand families by using a wide-angle lens and critically analyze the social influences that affect their ability to thrive and survive. For example, according to Sims (2002), with whom we agree, one of the outcomes of living on a low income is that families cannot afford a healthy diet, creating multiple disadvantages for children: their growing bodies and developing minds perform more poorly in school and play. The playing field for these children is uneven from the outset. Moreover, in families where parents are stressed, parents have greater difficulty engaging in nurturing relationships because their energies are siphoned elsewhere. Two of the authors of this book live in a country where health care is considered a basic human right and is accessible to everyone. They have been quite surprised by the arguments against universal health care in the United States. When children and families do not have their basic needs met, they face an increased risk of experiencing unfavorable outcomes (Sims, 2002).

Family social workers are challenged to recognize, accept, and respect a range of family expressions. For our clients, beliefs about the ideal or "real" family have led some to believe that they grew up in abnormal or dysfunctional families because their families of origin did not conform to the accepted mold. Others, particularly those who hold firm beliefs about what constitutes a "real" family, might be critical of family forms that diverge from their beliefs. This is particularly true for family forms that are not middle-class, white, intact, or based on heterosexual unions. For example, many cultures believe in selfless loyalty to their families, whereas members of mainstream North American culture may consider such loyalty as over-involvement or enmeshment (Nichols & Schwartz, 2007).

In learning about diversity and alternative expressions of family, it is necessary for family social workers to examine their biases and assumptions about what the term *family* means and then deconstruct these beliefs as being a singular "truth." Although geographic mobility is quite common, it is also still common for people to reside in the general vicinity in which they grew up. Local realities and lack of exposure to alternative ways of thinking can prevent family social workers from embracing broader ways of seeing the world. Exposure to new ways of thinking is the first step in understanding the world.

Definitions of family contribute to how we practice, and if a family social worker adheres to limited beliefs about an ideal family type, those who do not resemble the ideal quickly become marginalized (Hartman & Laird, 1983). However, it is important to remember that the notion of what is "normal" is vague and value-laden. Once armed with the awareness and acceptance that many forms of family exist and are indeed widespread, the family social worker can help dismantle barriers and attitudes so that people who were raised in atypical households do not feel dysfunctional or judged. The heart of social work involves establishing relationships with and valuing people from diverse backgrounds and experiences.

EXERCISE 2.11   Cultural Diversity among Families

Become aware of the cultural diversity among families around you. Compare different beliefs about the family, as well as who is included in the family unit. Make a class list of your observations.

EXERCISE 2.12   Addressing Differences

Break into small groups and answer the following questions:

1. How do I define myself culturally from a family perspective?
2. When did I first become aware of race, ethnicity, or color in general? When did I first become aware of different family structures?
3. What messages did I learn about race or ethnicity based on that first experience? What messages did I learn about different family structures based on that first experience?
4. What direct and indirect messages did I receive about race or ethnicity from my family and friends throughout my childhood? Throughout my adulthood? What direct and indirect messages did I receive about different family structures from my family and friends throughout my childhood? Throughout my adulthood?
5. How did the messages I received about race or ethnicity affect how I thought and felt about myself? About others? How did the messages I received about family structure affect how I thought and felt about myself? About others?
6. How did I benefit from my race or ethnicity? How did I benefit as a result of my family structure?
7. How was I at a disadvantage because of my race or ethnicity? How was I disadvantaged because of my family structure?
8. How many friends from a different race or ethnicity do I have? How many friends from a different family structure do I have? (adapted from Laszloffy & Hardy, 2000)

Diversity can teach us much about ourselves, about other people, and about the world. We then need to take a closer look at what we think *normal* means. The term takes on different hues when examined by the twelve dimensions listed below. We will use divorce as the example, but many behaviors can be substituted (e.g., monogamy, incest, having children, etc.).

- *Historical*: Sometimes "normal" is defined according to historical practices. People believe that what has happened before us is what should be considered normal. Therefore, people tend to argue that the family is breaking down due to feminism and women working outside the home. It is assumed that, historically, marriages remained intact. Coontz (2006), a historian of "family," dismantles much of the historical romanticizing about the family. For example, she argues that divorce has always existed, but the reasons for divorce have changed because the reasons for marriage have also changed.
- *Religious/Moral*: "Normal" can also be defined through a religious or moral lens where "family" becomes a moral issue. For example, a common religious saying is, "The man is the head and the woman is the neck;" then the man's natural and God-given place in the family is as head of the household. Or in terms of child rearing, "Spare the rod and spoil the child" is considered a biblical sanction for corporal punishment of children. (Others argue that the rod actually referred to the staff held by a shepherd who used it to guide the sheep, not beat them.)
- *Statistical*: Something is normal, then, when the majority of people do it. For example, if the divorce rate were 10 percent, divorce would be considered

"abnormal." However, if the divorce rate were greater than 50 percent, divorce would be considered normal since the majority of people have experienced this event. The term "minority" frequently refers to a statistical minority, although it has also taken on the meaning of "other" or "different."

- *Cross-cultural*: Another way of defining normal would be dependent upon whether a certain behavior is present in other cultures. This standard has been applied to such behaviors as premarital sex, sexual orientation, monogamy, and so on. If the divorce rate is lower in other countries than in North America, one might conclude that North America, in comparison with other cultures, has an abnormally high rate of divorce.

- *Biological*: Sociobiologists might argue that marriage was "invented" when life spans were much shorter and that, given the longer life spans of people living in North America, long marriages are neither natural nor desirable as humans are not equipped to be with one person for such an extended period of time.

- *Medical*: From a medical perspective, it has been argued that marriage is physically and emotionally harder on women than men. This could be one reason why women initiate divorce more frequently than men.

- *Psychiatric*: This category involves whether there is a psychiatric (a term used very broadly that can include social work, psychology, etc.) opinion about whether a particular behavior (divorce) is "normal." For example, it has been argued that family therapists are inherently biased against divorce (perhaps because it would mean intervention failure).

- *Scientific*: Through science, particularly research, divorce can be normalized through investigation of how common it is, the effects of divorce on individuals, and so on. Science can also investigate any of the other categories in this list.

- *Zoological*: This argument is based on the question of whether animals remain with the same mate for life. The fact is, some do and some do not.

- *Cultural*: Another standard for defining "normal" is the extent to which a particular behavior is condoned in a particular culture.

- *Political*: Legislation made by political institutions influences whether to legalize a particular behavior. For example, laws in North America define marriage as the union of two people. Some jurisdictions allow for these unions to be same-sex unions; other jurisdictions do not. Across North America, polygamy is not legal (although there is currently a court challenge in Canada asserting that this law discriminates based on religious freedom). Divorce, until the latter half of the twentieth century, was difficult to obtain.

- *Personal values*: Personal values involve the subjective values of individuals. Subjective values arise from a combination of family upbringing, cultural values, religious and legislative values, and media influence. While personal values are distinct, it is often these values that people use to judge others.

Each standard examines "normal" from a different angle. Family social workers therefore need to go beyond their "gut reaction" and consider what normal entails from multiple angles. For example, some might define the family in traditional ways (e.g., two parents, father works and mother stays at home, two children, and one dog named Spot). This definition might be both a political and religious one, based on the values of a certain group. It is also a historical artifact. Definitions differ based on the combination and relative weighting of the perspectives listed above. This leads to the question of who has a right to impose the definition of what is normal. Imposition of values and beliefs is a widespread practice that benefits those with social power and control. Subscribing to the dominant view inherently disadvantages and disempowers those who hold other beliefs.

EXERCISE 2.13 Ways of Looking at "Normal" and "Family"

Select a definition of family from either this book or another resource. Using each of the dimensions listed in this chapter, determine how your definition fits with each dimension.

Definition:

How it fits or does not fit with:

Historical

Religious

Statistical

Cross-cultural

Biological

Medical

Psychiatric

Scientific

Zoological

Political

Personal values (With which dimension do your personal values best align?)

FAMILY DIVERSITY NOW AND BEYOND

> *Your basic extended family today includes your ex-husband or -wife, your ex's new mate, your new mate, possibly your new mate's ex and any new mates that your new mate's ex has acquired.*
> —*Delia Ephron (www.Bartleby.com)*

Families are changing globally. Carter and McGoldrick (2005a) point out the changing trends in family structure in the United States:

- More people are remaining single, with approximately 25 percent of all households being single-person households.
- The percentage of single-parent families, both female-headed and male-headed, is rising. Of all families with children, one-fourth consists of single-parent households, and many of these parents are employed outside the home.
- The nuclear family comprised 25 percent of all households in 1996.
- Most unwed mothers live in poverty and have less education than married women.

- Birth rates vary according to the mother's education, race, and ethnicity, with less-educated women having the highest rates. Latino women have the highest birth rates.
- The median age of first marriage was 24.5 for women and 26.7 for men in 1996, a significant increase since 1970.
- The divorce rate stabilized in the mid-1990s at about 46 percent.
- Fewer people are remarrying after a divorce. Half of fathers lose contact with their children within one year after a divorce, and two-fifths of divorced men do not pay child support.
- Remarried families are the most common family structure.
- Most married women work (pp. 13–14).

In addition, fewer than 10 percent of families conform to the traditional nuclear family structure in which the mother stays home and the father works. In 1996, over 60 percent of all children had spent at least part of their childhood in a single-parent household by the age of 18 (Gavin & Bramble, 1996). 2009 Census data indicated that 26 percent of U.S. children under 21 were living in single-parent (mostly mother, 84 percent) homes (http://singleparents.about.com/od/legalissues/p/portrait.htm). Single-parent families face a greater risk of living in poverty. Though 79.5 percent of single mothers and 90 percent of single fathers are employed, 27 percent of mothers and 12.9 percent of fathers in single-parent homes live in poverty (http://singleparents. about.com/od/legalissues/p/portrait.htm). Today, families are smaller, women are having children later in life, and people are marrying later. The average household size is smaller, and more couples are choosing to remain childless. Although nearly 70 percent of divorced individuals eventually remarry, second marriages have a higher risk of divorce. Serial relationships and serial marriages are now commonplace. While some things have changed rapidly, others have changed more slowly. Women still earn less than men. Men still spend less time on child care and household tasks, although this latter trend appears to be easing somewhat.

Cultural diversity is also altering the North American landscape, and the white "majority" is slowly becoming a statistical minority (McGoldrick, Giordano, & Garcia-Preto, 2005). Cultural family values may differ from the dominant culture and at times bear little resemblance to beliefs and assumptions that guide mainstream family work. Sims (2002) considers culture as social capital on which to build strong relationships that form the foundation of community connections. A cultural connection is important, and strong connections to a particular culture can be a potent source of social support that is linked to parenting competence. Conversely, amputating people from cultural connections undermines parenting competence. Socially rich neighborhoods are those places where people are a community resource that gives back to others. Hence, a perspective that goes beyond the family can enrich the work that family social workers do.

To be effective, family social workers must discard ethnocentrism *and* develop sensitivity and competence in working with different cultures. Of utmost importance is learning that the socially dominant values and beliefs about families can be oppressive and inapplicable to families from other cultures. Nichols and

Schwartz (2007) remind us not to assume that just because a family is different it is sick. Unfortunately, in past practices, we have done just that. Valuing diversity also includes acknowledging the impact of sexism, racism, and heterosexism on how we work with families and the theoretical models from which we draw. In this book, we argue that memorizing a list of cultural characteristics is not helpful. There are far too many cultures and differences *within* cultures to suggest that a list is capable of embracing a specific cluster of characteristics and beliefs. Moreover, overemphasizing culture can exaggerate the differences and ignore similarities between the worker and the family (Nichols & Schwartz, 2007).

EXERCISE 2.14   Terminology

Terminology surrounding diversity seems to be at a stalemate. Difficulties surround such terms as minority, majority, white, ethnicity, ethnic, Euro, people of color, and so on. Discuss in class what term(s) would be appropriate and respectful in discussing these issues.

EXERCISE 2.15   Examples of Diversity

Consider the following families that have been assigned to your caseload at your family social work field placement. How is each family like or not like your own family of origin? What beliefs and assumptions about these families will you bring to working with them? What unique challenges, if any, will you face in working with each family?

- The Peat family was referred to you by their children's high school due to their poor attendance and low grades. Connie is 42 years old, Caucasian, and a housewife. Her husband, Jerry, is 43 years old, Native American, and works as a mechanic at a gas station. During your initial interview with Connie and her teenage daughter, Kaylee, Kaylee tells you that many of the family's problems stem from her father's drinking, bad temper, and physical abuse of his wife. Connie says she stays with her husband because of her religious beliefs, which require that wives submit to their husbands.
- The Gunn family was referred to you by the local mental health clinic where Teresa Gunn, receives medication for schizophrenia. Teresa is a single African American female in her twenties who lives with her parents, Jim and Stella. Jim and Stella are concerned because Teresa takes her medication sporadically and disappears for weeks at a time when off her medication. The Gunns have been informed that Teresa has been living on the streets during these periods. They are afraid for her safety.
- Liz Rocheleau, a 23-year-old Caucasian female, and her 4-year-old daughter Jackie were referred to you by Child Protective Services (CPS). Jackie's day care teacher reported the family to CPS when Liz recently divorced Jackie's father and moved herself and her daughter in with her new partner, Katie. The teacher reports that Jackie frequently appears at school hungry, unwashed, and dressed in clothes that she appears to have slept in.
- John Bells and Craig Boyd, a gay couple raising their 7-year-old son, have come to see you. Recently they have had arguments over different parenting approaches and are seeking your help in parenting skills training.

- Rosa Jimenez, a 39-year-old Hispanic female, referred herself and her family to your agency. Rosa is a recently divorced mother of seven children: 16-year-old Alicia, 13-year-old Joe, 11-year-old Maria, 7-year-old twins Carlos and Juan, and 4-year-old Dora. Rosa, her boyfriend Ricky, and the children moved in with Rosa's mother and stepfather last week. Rosa's parents have volunteered to help out with the children, as Rosa's job takes her away from home for many hours each day. Rosa and her common-law partner Ricky have a 1-year-old child, Anna. Ricky also has a 13-year-old daughter, Sydney, from a previous relationship and a 7-year-old daughter, Sadie, from another relationship. They have come to CPS because they found out that Sadie's biological and custodial mother hit her one day, and she went to school with bruises on her face. They would like CPS to investigate and consider granting their family custody of Sadie.

EP 2.1.4c

CULTURAL DIMENSIONS OF FAMILIES

Family social workers must be able to work with clients from diverse ethnic and cultural backgrounds without imposing a particular ethnocentric view on them. Culture exerts an enormous influence on families, providing a sense of identity, meaning, belonging, rituals, and continuity. Culture and ethnicity are related but not interchangeable concepts: **Culture** concerns the common patterns of behavior and experience that emerge when people live together. "Diverse value orientations, life experiences, and worldviews are all implicit in the term multiculturalism" (Jordan & Franklin, 2011, p. 359). Ethnicity includes culture but also speaks to the common ancestry through which people have developed shared values and customs, as well as identity, commitment, and loyalty to an ethnic group (Jordan & Franklin, 2009).

Racism and discrimination usually peak in times of limited resources and when large ethnic groups immigrate together (McGoldrick, Giordano, & Garcia-Petro, 2005). The word "ethnic" and its derivatives have connoted subtle racism and a perpetuation of the "them-versus-us" mentality. Warren Clements (2011) points out the subtleties of discrimination:

> "Consider ethnic origins—or, rather, the origin of "ethnic." The word "ethnic" is derived ultimately from the Greek ethnos, meaning "nation or people." Ethnicity refers to a person's linguistic, cultural, religious, or racial origins. By that measure, all humans are ethnic. However, that's not how it works. "Ethnic is used as a euphemism for people with a different background from whoever is using the word. It's a handy catch-all, short for ethnic minority. Its chief benefit is that it telegraphs in a single word what might otherwise take several to express. Its chief sin is that it can make people who use the word forget that ethnicity—differences in speech, look, national origin, cultural behaviour—covers all of us.

> The term "ethnic" entered English in the Middle Ages with just that sense of "them-versus-us." Although ethnos meant nation, the people who first translated the Old Testament into Greek used the phrase ta ethne (foreign nations) for the Hebrew word goyim, meaning gentiles or people who weren't Jews. From this usage emerged the Greek ethnikos and the Latin ethnicus, which had the sense of "heathen." By the time the term ethnic reached English, it referred to nations that weren't Christian or Jewish. It's a measure of the fluctuations in language that Conservatives now use it to refer to Canadians who are Jewish.

By the mid-1800s, the adjective had largely shaken off its earlier us-and-them sense, having acquired the relatively neutral, anthropological meaning of a group with common cultural, linguistic, racial, or religious aspects. But by the 1960s, the distancing definition had crept back. The Sun in London, England, observed in 1965 that ethnic "has come to mean foreign, or un-American, or plain quaint."

It should be obvious then, that even though we think we are aware of our biases, they leak out through our use of language. We present this caveat, fully acknowledging that "all of us are ethnic."

When a family has a sense of belonging to a particular culture, they have a built-in support network in times of distress. Because intercultural relationships have had a rather checkered history (racism, colonization, genocide, systemic discrimination, oppression), discussing ethnicity and culture has become awkward, and even taboo. At the same time, political correctness and "languaging" about ethnicity is fluid, and what is acceptable one day becomes unacceptable the next. For example, the use of the term "minority," as the passage above suggests, "marginalizes groups whose heritage is not European whereas the term 'Black' eclipses the ancestral roots of people with African heritage" (McGoldrick, Giordano, & Garcia-Preto, 2005, p. 7). We agree with this observation and acknowledge that our language is in a state of flux. We struggled with language in this edition. We also agree that the term "minority" (implying a statistical minority?) marginalizes, but also recognize that the phrase "people of color" (in the United States) or "visible minorities" (in Canada) clusters "other" groups who "have no color" into a single European monolith, while the term "non-dominant group" fails to recognize that the "dominant group" is in fact multicultural. Given these caveats, we do our best to adhere to the language that is currently correct, recognizing that language about culture and ethnicity will be revised when words become politically loaded. We appreciate the dialogue.

It is critical that family social workers be aware of their biases and ethnocentric views so that they can work nonoffensively and sensitively with families of different cultures and ethnicities, as well as capitalize on the strengths that all families possess regardless of cultural heritage. Until recently, the approach to teaching cultural sensitivity and competence has been to compile a "laundry list" of characteristics and traits with which to understand the different cultures that social workers may encounter. We now know that culture is too complex and multi-dimensional to be understood in terms of checklists that reduce it to a static and homogeneous entity; rather, it must be recognized as a dynamic process affecting everything from worldview to communication styles to food preferences to beliefs about family to daily behavior and practices. Checklists convey one-dimensional images; overlook heterogeneity within "single" cultures; and risk presenting stereotypes rather than conveying culture as dynamic, evolving, and fluid.

There are *differences within groups;* no culture is homogeneous. Although we refer to the "dominant" or "mainstream" culture, it is apparent that many cultures and belief systems coexist within it. Differences are both subtle and complex. For example, the terms "Hispanic" and "Latino" describe people from different countries with different cultures and sociopolitical histories who in their countries of origin would have difficulty seeing the similarities (Garcia-Preto, 2005). Both includes peoples from South (mostly) and Central America and the Caribbean (p. 155). The term "Hispanic "refers to the influence of the Spanish culture and language on various groups who have suffered years of colonization, but excludes indigenous cultures (who have been the most severely colonized of all). The term "Latino" is more inclusive but excludes Brazilians, whose heritage is Portuguese. Another example is the seeping use of the adjective "Euro," which is used to describe the 53 nationalities among European Americans (Giordano & McGoldrick, 2005, p. 502)! With regard to American Indians, there are 562 federally recognized tribes in the United States (Sutton & Broken Nose, 2005, p. 45), and it is the individual tribe that determines roles and family obligations (p. 46). The same argument holds true for "Asian American" families, for whom the use of a single term could not possibly embrace the diversity and complexity of what it means to be Asian American (Lee & Mock, 2005, p. 269). As such, the term collectively refers to Americans whose families originated in many different Asian countries; there are at least 32 different primary languages spoken (p. 270) and even more dialects, just to point out a single aspect of uniqueness. All of this leads to the conclusion that, "Shared ethnic heritage hardly produces homogeneity of thought, emotions, or group loyalty" (Giordano & McGoldrick, 2005, p. 503).

The degree to which one adheres to the "dominant" beliefs of a culture denotes the level of belonging one feels to that culture. People who do not primarily identify with the dominant culture differ in their degree of identification. "Acculturation" is a term that captures the process known as the "melting pot" (United States) or the "cultural mosaic" (Canada). Acculturation involves the extent to which one group adopts the values and practices of another group. In everyday vernacular, it typically refers to a statistical "minority" group assuming the attitudes and behaviors of the statistical "majority." In fact, the influence is reciprocal, but perhaps not equally so. Some people may draw strength exclusively from a single culture, whereas others are bicultural or multicultural and can navigate cultures other than their primary one with relative ease. While there might be common threads among "similar" groups of people, classifying them based on terms such as "Asian," "European," "Hispanic/Latino," or "African" is just slightly more refined than calling someone "ethnic."

Instead of learning about culture "horizontally" by listing typical characteristics of a group, which perpetuates stereotypes, we present culture "vertically"; that is, we discuss dimensions common to all cultures. Unique cultural expressions within each dimension are presented about specific cultures, keeping in mind that there is *heterogeneity* within a single cultural group. We argue that viewing culture vertically uncovers the richness of each culture, as well as the commonalities among different cultures. Elsewhere we discussed some distinct dimensions of culture, and we refine and build upon these dimensions here (Coleman, Collins, & Collins, 2005). We see these dimensions as sources of strength and richness upon which families can construct an identity, establish routines and rituals, build valuable social connections, and develop a sense of mutuality with their communities by drawing from the wealth that these traditions offer. Awareness of the historical background of different ethnic groups is important, as is knowledge of the customs and beliefs shared by members of each. Such awareness demands that family social workers tune into the nuances of cultures and avoid labeling what they do not understand as "pathological" just because the beliefs and practices differ from what is familiar. We would like to emphasize, however, that in researching the various cultures, each and every single culture considers "family" central. The expressions of family are unique and are neither inferior nor superior.

Let us now examine the cultural dimensions of family:

1. *Cultural identity:* Culture provides a sense of belonging to at least one particular cultural group. Interestingly, across North America, most people do not derive from a single cultural, ethnic, or racial heritage. Instead, most are "multicultural" due to intermarriage. "Cultural identity has a profound impact on our sense of well-being within our society and on our physical and mental health" (McGoldrick, Giordano, & Garcia-Preto, 2005, p. 1).

   Here are some examples of how cultural identity plays out for various cultures: North American Indians identify themselves as belonging to a particular tribe, band, or clan (Sutton & Broken Nose, 2005, p. 47), and the customs and values of each tribe are critical to individual identity and family dynamics. Each tribe has a distinct worldview, and religious practices, customs, and family structures are each unique. In Brazil, identities are based on who one is, not on what one does (Catao de Korin & de Carvalho Petry, 2005, p. 170). For Cubans, *Familismo* is a cultural attitude that places the interests of the family over the interest of the individual ... *respecto* is a means of reinforcing male authority over women and children (Bernal & Shapiro, 2005, p. 207). Collectivist cultures, such as Lebanese and Syrians, "define their identities based on group membership" (Haboush, 2005, p. 475). Similarly, African Americans also have a communal sense, expressed as "We are, therefore I am," compared with the European ideal, which translates to "I think, therefore I am" (McGoldrick, Giordano & Garcia-Petry, 2005, p. 3; Moore Hines & Boyd-Franklin, 2005, p. 88). For Africans, community comprises the core of their spiritual identity, and their sense of communal identity involves both the living and the dead (Kamya, 2005, p. 108).

2. *Belief systems and worldviews:* Beliefs govern actions, and within the context of culture, beliefs are transmitted in great part through families. A worldview provides a way to understand and function in a larger society. It is important to know about the cultural values of a family in order to understand behavior (McGoldrick, Giordano, & Garcia-Preto, 2005, p. 24). Values might concern definition of family, intergenerational patterns, and life transitions.

   Some cultures, for example, emphasize communal responsibility, whereas "mainstream" North American society ascribes to individualism. Individualism emphasizes independence and self-responsibility. Anglo-Americans (a term that risks collapsing and force-fitting a number of different ethnicities into one term) have a strong future orientation, prize individual achievement, and consider themselves dominant over the natural world (McGill & Pearce, 2005, pp. 524–525). By comparison, the African American culture stresses "collectivity, sharing, affiliation, deference to authority, spirituality, and respect for the elderly" (Kamya, 2005). Similarly, while members of various Native American tribes hold different beliefs, certain common beliefs distinguish them from members of other cultures. One of these is that nature is important and that they are a part of the whole, leading to an appreciation of nature and the maintenance of a balance with all life. As such, all life has a spirit that should be respected, leading to a view of time in terms of natural cycles or seasons. Furthermore, sharing is a traditional Native American practice (Sutton & Broken Nose, 2005, p. 48). Similarly, Hawaiian culture emphasizes the significance of connections to family and communities through love, care, aid, unity, generosity, humility, spirituality and righteousness, and caring for family members over the lifespan (Obana, 2005, pp. 66–67). Systems of support are also embedded in the Cuban community ... [where] religious, social, health, political, and neighborhood organizations are an important part of community life (Bernal & Shapiro, 2005, p. 209). Broadly speaking, the Latino culture is hierarchical, family-oriented, and fatalistic and emphasizes personalism, interdependence, and spiritualism (Kusnir, 2005, p. 259). The Japanese also emphasize interdependence in human relationships, revealed through group behavior. In the United States, Japanese Americans honor affiliation, sensitivity toward the attitudes of others, a tendency for self-abnegation, and avoidance of conflicts (Shibusawa, 2005, p. 342). Finally, halfway across the globe, the socialist ideal that society is more important than the individual pervades Scandinavian life (Erickson, 2005, p. 645), with a firm belief in social welfare and collective responsibility for societal problems (p. 649). Scandinavians hold the egalitarian value that no one is better or worse than anyone else (p. 649), a belief that is embedded in attitudes about marriage and family. The concept also permeates Scandinavian social policies, some of which are the most advanced on earth. (Some people confuse the concepts of socialism and totalitarianism when, in fact, they are very different.)

3. *History of a culture, including history of colonization:* Through a culture's history, people develop an identity and based on the historical factors that contribute to this identity at various points in time. Slavery (Black & Jackson, 2005), genocide (Sutton & Broken Nose, 2005), religious missionaries (Tafoya & Del Vecchio, 2005), war (Lee & Mock, 2005), colonization (Kamya, 2005, p. 102), famine (McGoldrick, 2005b), and political upheaval and oppression have all played a role in the formation of a cultural identity. African Americans were uprooted from their homelands and brought to the West involuntarily and have since experienced long-standing institutional discrimination and racism. American Indians were slaughtered, witnessed the forced removal of their children to residential schools, and were forced to abandon their languages and traditions.

   By making sense of the harshness of their history, peoples can rise above difficulties imposed on them by their oppressors. As we mention in Chapter 5, African American culture contains the seeds of resilience through qualities that have helped them survive a hostile environment. These include: strong kinship bonds, an educational and work-achievement orientation, flexibility in family roles, a commitment to religious values and church participation, and a humanistic orientation.

4. *Communicating meaning and the use of language, including self-expressiveness:* Perhaps the primary source of intercultural misunderstanding occurs because of communication. How we use language reflects how we view

the world. Below we offer a snippet of various cultures' use of language, again keeping in mind the differences within cultures as well as varying degrees of acculturation:

- Cambodians experience confrontation or direct questioning as very rude and threatening (McKenzie-Pollock, 2005, p. 293).
- Indonesians consider it more polite to "talk around" sensitive issues than to discuss them directly; directness is considered impolite (Piercy, Soekandar, Limansubroto, & Davis, 2005, p. 334).
- Japanese culture values nonverbal over verbal communication. They place emphasis on what is not said, partly because they feel that emotions and sentiments cannot necessarily be captured or communicated by words (Shibusawa, 2005, p. 342).
- Koreans are most spontaneous among their peers and social equals, and they are reserved and deferential in the presence of superiors and during official occasions (Kim & Ryu, 2005).
- The communication style of Arabs is hierarchical, creating vertical as opposed to horizontal communication between those in authority and those who are subservient. This relationship ... leads to styles of communication between parents and children in which parents use anger and punishment and children respond by crying, self-censorship, covering up, or deception (Abudabbeh, 2005, p. 427).
- In Lebanese/Syrian families, especially in males, expressions of anger can be strong and even dramatic, inasmuch as aggressiveness is valued. At the same time, displays of affection and expressions of endearment are also common and might quickly follow an angry outburst (Haboush, 2005, p. 480).
- For centuries, the Irish have used words to enrich their dismal reality (McGoldrick, 2005, p. 598). Because the Irish have difficulty in dealing directly with differences and conflict, feelings tend to be submerged (p. 599).
- For Scandinavians, shyness is seen as positive, and shy people are considered to be sensitive, reflective, and nonpushy (Erickson, 2005, p. 646). Moreover, the Scandinavian languages do not have a rich vocabulary of aggressive words (p. 647).
- Native cultures value listening; silence may connote respect (Sutton & Broken Nose, 2005, p. 51), making it important to tune into nonverbal communication. In the Sioux tradition, talking is banned in certain relationships; for example, it is not acceptable for a wife to speak directly to her father-in-law.
- Indirect, implicit, or covert communication is consonant with Mexicans' emphasis on family harmony, "getting along," and not making others uncomfortable (Falicov, 2005, p. 235).
- Among Asian groups, silence may be viewed as a virtue (Lee & Mock, 2005, p. 272). They often speak in an oblique, understated way, with little emotion, implying that a problem is milder than it really is. Negative and even positive emotions ... may be expressed in an indirect way (p. 287).

Different communication styles will no doubt play a role in family social work. Communication styles interact with the history and worldview of a particular culture. For example, African American families might be uncommunicative with family social workers that represent the dominant group, because of distrust. Their attitudes toward whites often depend on their class as well as the particular politics of their home countries (Kamya, 2005, p. 105). Jews like to analyze; the British believe in the utilitarian use of words; Italians use words for drama and convey the emotional intensity of an experience; the Irish are embarrassed when talking about feelings; Norwegians also withhold emotional expressions; and so on.

Generally, workers should avoid using bilingual children as interpreters, especially when the presenting problem involves parent-child issues (Lee & Mock, 2005, p. 287). The worker should understand the family's communication style, which may include indirect communication and avoidance of direct confrontations.

5. *History of migration:* It is important to explore the reasons for, experience of, and history of the family's or the family's ancestors' migration to North America. Reasons for migration to North America vary and might include new opportunities (economic, employment) or to escape intolerable conditions in the homeland (war, famine, political upheaval, or torture). Moreover, many encounter further oppression in their adoptive country.

Diverse migration experiences are discussed in the following examples. Columbians migrate to obtain a better job, escape violence or difficult family situations, or attain an international experience (Rojano & Duncan-Rojano, 2005, p. 195). Currently, the primary reason for Dominicans to leave their country is to search for a better life, compared with those in the 1960s who left because of political reasons (Vazquez, 2005, p. 220). Mexicans, by comparison, move back and forth depending upon the economic circumstances of the United States (Falicov, 2005, p. 230), placing stress on families and fracturing the structures of emotional support, advice, and material aid (p. 232). Many Asian countries suffered from war or political turmoil where families were exposed to loss, separation, changes in health status, torture, or other forms of direct or secondary trauma before immigrating (Lee & Mock, 2005, p. 271).

Migrating families bring with them hopes and expectations, and it is important to ask to what extent they have been met. What were their challenges and struggles? It takes courage to leave a country of origin and move to another country that is thousands of miles away, often with few, if any, family relations, friends, and other natural social supports in the new land. Many have to overcome language barriers, job skill challenges, and discrimination. The resilience of these new immigrants is to be acknowledged in family social work by helping people make sense out of their struggles through the development of awareness and developing the ability to make meaning that inspires a sense of hope (Hernandez, 2002). Making meaning out of hope is also Walsh's (1998) focus. Family social workers can explore what the meaning of migration is for the family (Black & Jackson, 2005, p. 80). Families may need to grieve the loss of their homeland (Kamya, 2005, p. 103). For example, many Central American refugee families have to depart suddenly, with no time for farewells. They fear not returning; often a few members of the family emigrate first (Hernandez, 2005, p. 185). Asian families might experience differences in rates of acculturation of family members (Lee & Mock, 2005, p. 278). Families may experience stress as a result of role reversal stemming from migration. When they live within Asian communities, support systems usually provide a cushion against the stresses of migration. These communities provide a sense of belonging, connectedness, and validation (p. 279). The process of migration disrupts the family life cycle (Chapter 4) by adding an extra stage (Carter & McGoldrick, 2005) and affects each phase of the family life cycle uniquely.

6. *Beliefs about family, family structure, and kinship bonds:* "Family" is expressed uniquely in each culture. For example, in African American families, there is a high ratio of female-headed households, in part due to the high mortality rates of African American males. This structure affects family functioning; families tend toward egalitarian sharing of roles while mothers shoulder the economic, breadwinner burden and assume responsibility for child care. The extended family network is likely to be involved in supporting the family, as is the church family (Moore Hines & Boyd-Franklin, 2005).

In some cultures, boundaries surrounding the family include extended families; cousins are referred to as brother and sister, and children have a primary relationship with their grandparents (Sutton & Broken Nose, 2005, p. 45). Others have no language to describe an in-law. For Brazilians, concepts of loyalty and obligation, or accountability toward the family, influence personal choices (Catao de Korin & Carvalho Petry, 2005, p. 170). Solidarity, empathy, and hospitality are important values ... Brazilians are not usually concerned about having their own space, preferring physical closeness. The Hispanic/Latino American family system is both patriarchal and hierarchical; the father is the head of the household, and parents have authority over children (Garcia-Preto, 2005).

In Native American families, extended family (which may include nonkin namesakes) is important. These groups may or may not live together in one household, but extended family groups are an important means of support. Support may come in the form of role modeling, and it is not uncommon for grandparents to parent their grandchildren (Mooradian, Cross, & Stutzky, 2006). Intermarriage is common between members of different Native American groups and between Native Americans and members of other groups, and divorce and remarriage are acceptable practices.

For African Americans, kinship bonds are traceable to life in Africa, where various tribes shared commonalities that were broader than bloodlines. Later, slaves were prohibited from marrying, with an extensive kinship network being a by-product of this. The kinship network is broader than traditional bloodlines and has been a critical resource for African Americans. New African immigrants place great emphasis on the family, which includes kin relationships that extend beyond ties of blood or marriage to include other individuals—especially members of the tribe or clan (Kamya, 2005, p. 109). Interestingly, immigration to the United States by Africans is restricted through social policy because of the narrow American definition of family (p. 109).

Mexican American families take many forms and can be nuclear, extended, blended, single-parent, never married, divorced, or widowed. Nuclear families often live near extended families, and family collectivism and inclusiveness are central to Mexican American families. Family boundaries include grandparents, uncles, aunts, and cousins. Kinship ties, extending to third and fourth uncles and to cousins, are often close (Falicov, 2005, p. 234). Strong sibling ties are stressed early. *Familismo,* or family interdependence, involves extended family members sharing the nurturing and disciplining of children, financial responsibility, companionship for lonely isolated members, and problem solving (p. 234). Similarly, for Puerto Rican families, "family" is usually an extended system that encompasses those related by blood and marriage, godparents, and even informally adopted children (Garcia-Preto, 2005, p. 245). Marriage for Puerto Ricans is a union of two families. Traditionally, the families are patriarchal (p. 246).

In traditional Asian American families, the family unit, rather than the individual, is preferred (Lee & Mock, 2005, p. 274). The individual is the sum of previous generations, and the behavior of an individual reflects on the individual, the extended family, and ancestors. Obligation, shame, and guilt are traditional mechanisms used to reinforce social expectations and behavior. Asian American families are guided by Confucian philosophy that creates a familial hierarchy requiring loyalty, respect, and obedience, particularly to parents. Children are expected to respect and obey parents, and wives to respect and obey husbands. Because time orientation for Asian American families focuses on the past and present rather than the future, ancestors are central. Asian American parents also play a role in their children's mate selection. A sense of obligation is the backbone for these families; consequently, families feel shame if expectations are not met. Siblings' roles and obligations are based on birth order, and the eldest son is obliged to provide a home for his widowed mother. The eldest son has the highest status among the siblings; the youngest daughter may be obliged to care for her elderly parents (Lee & Mock, 2005).

In the Cambodian culture, familial relationships are stratified, with the husband at the head of the household and the eldest son holding a special position. The unique structure of the traditional Chinese family is related to Confucianism, which emphasizes harmonious interpersonal relationships and interdependence. Family interactions are governed by prescribed roles defined by family hierarchy, obligation, and duties; independent behavior is discouraged (Lee & Mock, 2005b, p. 305). Indonesian families value closeness, loyalty, obligation, and respect. Children must obey their parents and preserve the family's honor, and parents approve their children's choice of a mate. Hierarchy is important: the wife should respect and obey her husband, and children should respect and obey their parents (p. 333).

In Arab families, men have specific duties toward their wives and children, wives are given instruction about how to treat their husbands, and children are instructed to honor their mothers (Abudabbeh, 2005, p. 437). The Arab family is patriarchal, and pyramidically hierarchical with regard to age and sex and extended family (p. 427).

Euro families vary considerably, which is not surprising given the large number of different groups that fall under the "Euro" umbrella. For example, in Dutch families, roles and responsibilities are very clear. The relationship between husband and wife is considered sacred; there is often a strong emotional commitment, buttressed by religious belief, between them

(De Master & Dros Giordano, 2005, p. 543). Family is central to the lives of Franco Americans, similar to their French Canadian ancestors where family rituals center on family gatherings—weddings, baptism, wakes, and Christmas mass (Langelier & Langelier, 2005). Extended family relationships among the Irish are often not close, although families may get together for "duty visits." Family members tend not to rely on one another for support, and when they have a problem, they may see it as an added burden if the family finds out (McGoldrick, 2005, p. 605). In the Italian family, family members must never do anything to hurt or disgrace the family (Giordano, McGoldrick, & Guarino Klages, 2005, p. 620).

7. *Beliefs about children and child rearing:* Every culture has a unique approach to child rearing, part of which involves discipline. Parent-child relationships appear to change when families immigrate, particularly when children acculturate faster than their parents. For example, Puerto Rican children acculturate faster than their parents and are often caught in cultural conflicts (Garcia Preto, 2005).

   In African American families, children are treated in an egalitarian fashion and assigned responsibility according to age. The oldest child may be responsible for looking after younger sisters and brothers (Black & Jackson, 2005). In Native American families, children are integral to the renewal of tribal life and historically have been highly valued. Children are disciplined and taught by extended family members in an egalitarian fashion, often through modeling. Corporal punishment is not used; rather, "observation and participation" are preferred child-rearing techniques. Within an extended family environment, siblings and cousins surround the child, with the older children often caring for and teaching the younger children (Sutton & Broken Nose, 2005).

   Religious beliefs, which are intricately linked with culture, have both a positive and negative effect on parenting. For example, Stewart and Mezzich (2006) point out that negative parenting outcomes are generally associated with conservative religious beliefs that support authoritative parenting philosophies and techniques such as corporal punishment. On the other hand, religiosity has also been helpful in providing assumptions critical to warm parent-child relationships, social support, and closeness.

   Among Jamaicans, spankings are the primary form of punishment and are often accompanied by a scolding or "tongue lashing," neither of which is considered abusive. Rather, spankings are considered a necessary means of teaching children to distinguish right from wrong and to learn respect for elders and other authority figures (Brice-Bake, 2005, p. 122). In the Haitian culture, children are valued and the entire family participates in raising a child (Menos, 2005, p. 133). Nevertheless, Haitian children are raised with the belief that they must be obedient and that physical discipline with a belt or switch is sometimes necessary (p. 133). Puerto Rican parents also consider spankings. At the same time, they may be hesitant to reward good behavior lest children lose feelings of respect. Although fathers are supposed to be the disciplinarian, mothers carry most of the responsibility (Garcia-Preto, 2005, p. 246). Many Dominican parents encounter forced separation from their children for long periods because of undocumented immigration status (Vazquez, 2005, p. 222).

Lifelong parent-child connectedness and respect for parental authority are valued over the husband-wife bond in Mexican families (Falicov, 2005, p. 234). At home, children are expected to speak their minds, challenge, and debate. Parents might encounter difficulty advocating for their children at school because of the language difficulties. Mexican American parents sometimes resort to punishment, shaming, belittling, deception, promises, and threats in response to their children's misbehavior. Often the father disciplines the children and compels them to obey their mother, whereas she tends to defend and protect them (p. 235).

In general, Muslim families emphasize education and studious, well-behaved children (McAdams-Mahmoud, 2005, p. 145); there are also restrictions on dress and eating requirements, posing challenges to parents and children when they interface with mainstream culture. Children are raised to perpetuate the customs and traditions of the family (Abudabbeh, 2005, p. 429). Methods of discipline vary between mild punishment for unacceptable behavior and instilling fear in a child with warnings of what happens to those who do bad things. Children, especially sons, receive unconditional love, and differential treatment of boys is not uncommon (p. 429).

In Asian American families, the traditional role of mother is as nurturer and supporter, while the father's role is that of disciplinarian (Lee & Mock, 2005a, p. 274). Childcare often falls to older siblings when there are many children. Sibling emotional ties are strong for those who escaped and survived war in their homelands. Again, sons are favored (p. 275).

Anglo-Americans raise their children to be self-contained, principled, responsible, independent, self-reliant, self-determining, and perhaps, from the vantage point of other cultures, self-centered individuals (McGill & Pearce, 2005, p. 525). "The muted Anglo American approach may be puzzling to the non-Anglo American therapist" (p. 525). In the German family, infants and young children are raised with structure, limits on spatial exploration, and precise schedules (Winawer & Wetzel, 2005, p. 564). Among the Irish, ridicule, belittling, and shaming play a major role in child discipline (McGoldrick, 2005, p. 605). Jews tend to raise children through reasoning and explanation about expectations. Jewish parents are permissive, overprotective, and concerned about their children's happiness at the expense of their own. Traditionally, the Jewish mother was viewed as her children's primary educator (Rosen & Weltman, 2005, p. 675).

8. *Family life cycle issues and cultural rituals related to life cycle:* Family rituals including rituals associated with cultural membership are important sources of family strength and resilience (discussed in more detail in Chapter 5) and enhance group identity. Some cultural rituals celebrate life-cycle events such as weddings, funerals, and births. For other cultures, different expectations accompany the various phases of the family life cycle, such as when to leave home, whom to involve in child care, and so on. The Irish have considered death the most significant life-cycle transition (McGoldrick, 2005, p. 606), leading to stories about Irish wakes. African families also use elaborate traditions to mark major life transitions (Kamya, 2005, p. 111). Values related to collectivism and respect for authority, large family networks, and Roman

Catholicism influence the definitions, stages, and rituals of the Mexican American family life cycle (Falicov, 2005, p. 237). Their family life cycle includes longer periods of interdependence between mothers and children and a relaxed attitude about children's self-reliance (often mistaken for overprotection); the absence of an independent living situation for most unmarried young adults; the absence of the "empty nest," or a crisis and refocusing on marital issues in middle age; and continuous involvement, a respected position, and the usefulness of parents and grandparents in the family (p. 237). Leaving home occurs primarily through marriage, and the divorce rate is not very high. By comparison, Anglo American families do not struggle to keep children at home or closely involved in family life as do, for example, Jewish or Italian families (McGill & Pearce, 2005, p. 526).

9. *Partnering:* How people find a partner has a lot to do with their cultural background. It is worthwhile to explore not only a person's expectations about whom they hope to partner with but also the extended family's expectations for that person's partnership. While marrying outside a culture is sometimes frowned upon, currently there is much cultural and racial mixing, with more than 50 percent of people marrying outside their ethnic group.

   In Islam, marriage is considered a religious duty entered into via contract as a social necessity (McAdams-Mahmoud, 2005, p. 146). Muslims do not date; mates are selected by recommendation and arrangement; and both parties must consent. Islam considers marriage an important duty (Abudabbeh, 2005, p. 427). Marriage is considered a family affair in which a partner is chosen by a person's family; it is not based on the Western concept of romantic love (p. 428). Practices such as endogamy continue to occur in many Arab families in which marriage within the same lineage (cousins) is preferred (p. 428). While traditional Islamic law allows men to have up to four wives, some Arab countries have outlawed polygyny. Muslim girls cannot marry non-Muslims, but Muslim men can marry women from monotheistic religions.

   Dominicans typically marry early and have children early, mostly through legal and religious marriages although consensual unions are also common. It is still a practice for Dominican men to have more than one partner and more than one household (Vazquez, C. 2005). Because of poverty, many are forced to divorce their Dominican spouse and marry American citizens to obtain residency (p. 219). In traditional Asian families, parents or grandparents arrange marriages to ensure family prosperity and continuance of the husband's family line. However, the primary relationship is more likely to be the parent-child dyad, rather than that of the husband-wife (Lee & Mock, 2005a, p. 274). Anglo Americans tend to experience marriage as a contractual relationship between individuals to meet individual needs (McGill & Pearce, 2005, p. 527).

10. *Gender roles:* In Chapter 13, we explore gender issues. Gender is a central organizing feature of families. Some cultures strictly adhere to traditional gender roles (often patriarchal), which can be difficult for family social workers who are expected to operate from a position of gender equality. We form beliefs about gender roles from parents, culture, historical context, and current social attitudes, which are often propagated by the mass media. Where did a person get her or his gender role beliefs? Is the person making changes to

accommodate these modern times? Gender arrangements permeate family life and intimate relationships within all cultural groups. Gender roles and customs vary greatly across the world, but, interestingly, most cultures are patriarchal.

Gender relations in communities of African origin have been affected by the subjugation of males and females during enslavement and colonization and the imposition of European values on African descendent communities. However, patriarchal values shaped male-female relationships prior to contact (Black & Jackson, 2005; Kamya, 2005). Despite fairly egalitarian values related to gender and work, families of African origin continue to struggle with issues of patriarchal control (Black & Jackson, 2005, p. 82). The high unemployment rate among African American men affects the willingness to marry; women are more easily employed. In Columbia, *machismo* and *mariansismo* separate male-female roles (Rojano & Duncan-Rojano, 2005, p. 195). Immigration for Puerto Ricans can be stressful since women obtain employment more easily, causing marital tension due to reversal of traditional gender roles (Garcia-Preto, 2005, p. 249). Generally, Puerto Rican men don't seek help because doing so threatens their machismo or because they are already feeling oppressed and marginalized and seeking help is further evidence of their failure (p. 253). Indonesian men are expected to marry and be the providers and leaders of their families, and women are expected to defer to their husbands (Piercy, Soekandar, Limansubroto, & Davis, 2005, p. 335). Although Arabic countries, including Lebanon and Syria, are largely patriarchal, women have a certain degree of power within the family because of their role in maintaining family ties (Haboush, 2005, p. 476). In the German family, gender is a central aspect of family organization, as revealed in gender-determined roles (Winawer & Wetzel, 2005, p. 563). Greek culture is patriarchal, and male individualism is celebrated (Killian & Agathangelou, 2005, p. 577). Similarly, in Italian families, the father is the undisputed head of the household, while the mother represents the heart of the home (Giordano, McGoldrick, & Guarino Klages, 2005, p. 621).

11. *Social values, sense of community, and social supports:* Some cultures support rugged individualism, whereas others greatly value community affiliation. For example, Puerto Ricans have flexible boundaries between the family and surrounding community, whereas Italians have clear boundaries within the family and draw rigid lines between outsiders and insiders (McGoldrick, Giordano, & Garcia-Preto, 2005, p. 31). Native Americans display a cooperative spirit, rather than a competitive orientation, when interacting with others. "This concept of collaterality reflects the integrated view of the universe where all people, animals, plants, and objects in nature have their place in creating a harmonious whole" (Sutton & Broken Nose, 2005, p. 44).

12. *Religion and spirituality:* The United States is a highly religious country; Canada is less so. "In America, despite the fact that separation of church and state is one of our most cherished core beliefs and a bedrock of our Constitution, our country has always had a quasi-religious understanding of itself as a model society blessed by God" (Giordano & McGoldrick, 205, p. 512). Religion provides a deep sense of community and a means of coping with stress or powerlessness (p. 512). Ethnicity often has a religious character, and religious

life is influenced by ethnic customs and rituals (p. 513). Religion and spirituality can be integral parts of family life, and we are just beginning to acknowledge the importance of working with a family's religious and spiritual values. When people adhere to a belief system, some beliefs and practices can have a positive buffering effect on difficulties (Thayne, 1998).

We discuss these aspects here (for a more comprehensive discussion of religion and spirituality, see Walsh, 1998). Religion and family life are deeply intertwined. A system of values and "shared beliefs that transcend the limits of a family's experience and knowledge enables family members to better accept the inevitable risks and losses in living and loving fully" (Walsh, 1999, p. 9). Religion helps families construct or enact rituals about such transitions as marriage, birth, and death that mark progression through the family life cycle.

In considering religion or spirituality in family social work, workers struggle with a number of ethical issues. The tricky piece is for workers to not allow their personal religious beliefs to contaminate their work with families (Haug, 1998). Imposing religious beliefs on clients is akin to colonization in much the same way that missionaries sought to colonize native peoples across the globe. The legacy of colonization still haunts us to this day, which might explain the reluctance of helpers to enter the religious world of clients. In addition, for many years, the helping professions viewed religion as either a form of pathology to be treated or something that was best left outside the therapeutic process (Wendel, 2003, p. 165). Religion may also take on a negative connotation for deeply religious family workers who have been taught that theirs is only one true religion or conversely for those who are skeptical about religion believing that religion has sown the seeds of national and international conflict. Others struggle with the tenets of any religion that discriminates or oppresses others, such as women and gays. Respecting families whose religious or spiritual teachings differ from our own is integral to ethical social work practice. Family social workers need to work with the client's belief systems first by avoiding value judgments that are isolated from the client's reality (Thayne, 1998).

Religion and spirituality go hand-in-hand with culture; they are related, but distinct concepts. All cultures have at least one religion attached to it. Religion is seen as extrinsic (being imposed from outside as through religious institutions), whereas spirituality is intrinsic (coming from within). Religious practices can support family cohesion through prescribed family rituals and customs associated with religious events. "If, as many social scientists argue, religion has to do with two major foci of concerns—*personal meaning* and *social belonging*—then most certainly it is around the first of these that religious energies revolve primarily today" (Roof, 1999, cited in Wendel, 2003, p. 172). The concept of *lived religion* tries to understand the space between official religions and the day-to-day experience of people and is considered to be the concrete expression of the personal and sacred dimensions of human life (pp. 173–175). Religion is a subjective and personal experience, although intricately tied to the institutional expressions of religion.

According to Walsh (1998), "suffering invites us into the spiritual domain" (p. 71). Spirituality provides meaning and purpose beyond the individual, the family, and troubles. Suffering can be a spiritual issue and can create meaning for human troubles. Rituals such as prayer and meditation or the support of a spiritual or religious community can provide strength during difficult times. Crises can clarify an individual's moral compass and make relationships more meaningful. Creative changes may arise out of a crisis—a true feature of resilience.

In a number of ways, religion is an institutional manifestation of ethnicity and culture. Even though people are somewhat free to convert to the religion of their choice, they typically follow the religious teaching of their parents and their society. Currently, religion and spirituality contain sources of strength for families. In assessment and intervention, it is therefore important to account for both the religious and spiritual dimensions of a family. While addressing spirituality shows respect for a diversity of beliefs, not imposing religious beliefs on clients might be difficult since one of the tenets of many religions is to convert unbelievers. The purpose is not to determine how religious a particular family is; rather, the purpose is to find out about the family's world and what beliefs, social networks, and rituals guide its passage through the life cycle (Wiggins Frame, 2001). Church, for some, might be considered part of the family's extended family.

Respecting clients' religion and spirituality will help social workers to understand the central role of each in client decisions, thoughts, and feelings about particular issues such as divorce, abortion, gender roles, and child rearing. Research also indicates that religion greatly affects family relationships (Marks, 2004). Religious experience, including beliefs, practices, and the religious community, correlate with higher marital quality, stability, satisfaction, and parental involvement. There is also a connection between certain expressions of religiosity and undesirable outcomes such as prejudice, authoritarianism, abuse, and tolerance for abuse. Intermarriage of two people from different religious backgrounds can also challenge relationships. Nevertheless, shared religious activities can contribute to intimacy and commitment in marriage. Religious practices contribute to the creation of family rituals. "Acknowledging that religion is vital to some families is one issue, but arguing that therapists *should* include and address religion in a substantive way is another" (Marks, 2004, p. 228).

There are multiple examples of various cultures and their associated spiritual/religious beliefs: Aboriginal peoples refer to "all my relations" (Sutton & Broken Nose, 2005, p. 46), the spiritual bond with nature, the family of man, mother nature (p. 46), and harmony with rather than dominance over nature. Similarly, spirituality has historically been an important factor in the lives of Africans. A family's strong spiritual values may influence the meaning it assigns to a crisis and the options for resolutions it considers. The strong spiritual orientation of African Americans has led to highly emotional religious services as a means of dealing with oppression (Moore Hines & Boyd-Franklin, 2005, p. 93). For Haitians, Catholicism and voodoo can coexist. Islam practices segregation of sexes during social and religious occasions (Menos, 2005). While Roman Catholicism provides continuity for a large number of Mexican Americans (Falicov, 2005, p. 232), folk medicine and indigenous spirituality coexist with mainstream religion and medical practices (p. 232). In Asian American families, the religious leader is highly respected

(Lee & Mock, 2005a, p. 280), and family social workers are cautioned to respect the spiritual perspective of the Chinese family.

Frame (2001) recommends developing a spiritual genogram (see Chapter 8 for a general discussion of genograms) with families for whom religion and spirituality play an important role. The genogram will portray a visual history of how spiritual and religious issues across generations shape and affect the client's beliefs and values. When focusing a genogram on religion or spirituality, it is important to look at the family history of denomination, interfaith marriages, baptisms, first communions, events in religious communities, stable and unstable affiliations, religious closeness, divorces, religious messages, and so on. Frame cautions family workers to know their own religious beliefs and attitudes before working on religious beliefs and attitudes with others.

Discussing spirituality and how to work with it can create anxiety in students and seasoned practitioners alike, especially given the great diversity both within and between religions. We urge students to assume a humble and "not-knowing" stance, one that is equally applicable to working with cultural diversity and religious diversity. Griffith (1999) recommends the following stance in working with a family:

- Do not assume that you know what God means to a particular family, even if you are of the same religion.
- Do not assume that you know what a family's language about God means.
- Do not assume that a family must have the same image of God that you do.
- Do not use psychological theory to explain another's belief in God.

13. *Cultural expressions related to dress, food, music, and the arts:* Again, shared cultural expressions related to aesthetic concerns give families a sense of belonging and stability. In recent years, mainstream society has developed a great appreciation for ethnic food. At the same time, clothing may be different and have religious or social significance. Perhaps aesthetic issues, more than any other cultural facet, opens the door to cross-cultural understanding and acceptance (perhaps with the exception of dress). North America is blessed with an abundance of selection in terms of the aesthetic concerns.

14. *Work, education, and social class:* Social class (level of education, income, standing in the community) is important to assess, as higher status usually leads to a higher level of well-being and greater access to a range of resources. In some cases, however, families may be discriminated against by the dominant culture despite their high social standing, while at the same time being rejected by members of their ethnic group because of their high level of acculturation into the mainstream culture. This places them in double jeopardy.

15. Beliefs about social troubles and help-seeking behavior, including the use of indigenous and traditional healing practices: Studies in ethnicity (McGoldrick, Giordano, & Garcia-Petro, 2005) reveal that people differ in:
- Their experience of emotional pain
- What they label as a symptom
- How they communicate about their pain or symptoms
- Their beliefs about the cause of their difficulties
- Their attitudes toward helpers
- The intervention they expect (p. 28).

Despite the lists of characteristics discussed in the subheadings above, family social workers must be careful not to stereotype groups since individual differences exist among people of similar ethnic and cultural backgrounds. Some of these differences may be related to varying levels of acculturation. Still, certain characteristics distinguish ethnic minority cultures from the dominant or majority white middle-class culture in the United States and Canada.

1. *Ethnic minority reality:* Members of many ethnic minority groups experience poverty and discrimination, resulting in underutilization of social services. Poverty and discrimination are risk factors in the macro- and exosystems that permeate a family's everyday life. These risk factors create vulnerability to stress and adversity impinging on the individual and family.

2. *Impact of external system on minority cultures:* Values of various cultural and ethnic groups may conflict with those of the dominant culture on issues such as exerting control versus living in harmony with the environment, orientation to time (past, present, future), "doing versus being" orientation, individual autonomy versus collectivity, and the importance of nuclear versus extended family relationships.

3. *Biculturalism:* The ethnic minority person belongs to two cultures. The level of acculturation into the dominant culture is an important aspect of the assessment of ethnic minority families seeking outside intervention.

4. *Ethnic differences in minority status:* The status of various ethnic minority groups differs. Some groups experience more discrimination than others. For instance, refugees may receive better treatment than the descendants of slaves do. Skin color is another determinant of status; visible minorities often experience more severe societal discrimination.

EP 2.1.4c

BELIEFS ABOUT FAMILIES

As mentioned, a mindset that values diversity and is nonjudgmental about differences is a fundamental ingredient of family social work. Without acceptance and a nonjudgmental attitude toward differences, the family social worker is unlikely to be trusted and accepted by families. Therefore, family work starts with an examination of our fundamental beliefs about families and family life. Beliefs and attitudes guide what we see and what we do in our work with families. In the words of Karl Marx, "It is not the consciousness of men that determines their being, but, on the contrary, their social being that determines their consciousness." In other words, the way we see the world depends upon the economic and social contexts in which we live. Some attitudes are not conducive to family work: these include blaming parents (versus holding them responsible), failing to value and embrace diversity, imposing singular or restrictive views, and erecting barriers that prevent understanding and acceptance of the struggles of family life and its members. Negative attitudes and preconceived notions about families interfere with the partnership that workers must nurture in family work.

Attitudes about families can make or undermine a constructive basis for family work. Family workers can believe that people want to do the best with what they have. Optimistic beliefs that family problems can be successfully addressed and that a family can grow to become a healthy and supportive unit are also helpful. Sensitivity to the realities of family life will help form ethical and humane practice with families and produce a road map for viable worker-family relationships. Accompanying this perspective, the following beliefs guide family social work:

Belief I: Families Want to Be Healthy

People who are committed to an intimate relationship usually intend to stay together. When people have children, their objective is to be competent parents. Unfortunately, marriages terminate and children are raised in less than optimal environments. This does not mean that the family did not want to resolve its difficulties. Rather, it may mean that the family considered its problems to be insurmountable or that it lacked the knowledge, skills, resources, and support to change the situation. To overcome these challenges, early and timely intervention can create potent opportunities for change. Early intervention to promote lasting change is important to help the family deal with difficulties. It also allows problems to be dealt with before they become firmly established and intractable.

Belief II: Families Want to Stay Together and Overcome Their Differences

Most people prefer to remain in a relationship, provided that it meets their needs. They also possess varying degrees of skill and motivation to remain together and resolve their differences if they have hope and believe that their relationship can improve. Most people do not suddenly decide to leave a relationship; instead they attempt to use existing knowledge, skills, and supports to resolve differences and overcome pain. Often when people struggle to change their situation, they end up doing "more of the same thing," despite the fact that more does not mean better. They do not need to learn how to do "more"—they need to learn how to do "different." Nevertheless, many families do not know how to handle their difficulties and require outside assistance to resolve them in constructive and mutually satisfying ways. For some, and this is true of many culturally diverse families, the first step is to turn to friends and family for guidance. When these close supports fail to provide what is needed, the family might turn to family social workers who can provide practical, supportive, concrete assistance without the biases that friends and family members might have. Many children across North America are removed from their homes and placed in foster care when their health and safety are in jeopardy, and most are returned back home when it is believed that the family living conditions have improved. When children are removed from the home and placed into foster care, the family social worker can intervene to help the family prepare for their return home (Lewandowski & Pierce, 2004).

Belief III: Parents Need Understanding and Support for the Challenges Involved in Keeping Relationships Satisfying and Raising Children

Few people receive training or education on how to be effective partners or parents. Many base their relational styles and child-rearing practices on what they learned during their own childhood. Being an intimate partner and raising children requires skills, knowledge, patience, consistency, and unselfishness. People who are struggling with these issues need understanding and support. Often, they are blamed when a marriage fails or when their parenting is inconsistent or ineffective. Observers may be judgmental without appreciating a family's struggle and pain when a relationship deteriorates or when problems become intractable. Defensiveness and anger are created through blame. Family social workers can hold parents responsible without resorting to blame. Moreover, understanding and support can create new opportunities for learning, constructive change, and possible reunification of families.

Belief IV: Parents Can Learn Positive, Effective Ways of Responding to Their Children if They Have Opportunities to Obtain Support, Knowledge, and Skills

All people—and parents in particular—benefit from support from friends, relatives, and community resources. This challenges the popular notion that only those who are independent are healthy and functional. In reality, social support is necessary for adequate social functioning of everyone. Nevertheless, some parents have had little opportunity to learn about effective parenting and receive adequate knowledge. Helping parents acquire the necessary knowledge and skills benefits everyone. This fourth belief underscores the understanding that all people would like to do their best and that they can improve their parenting skills when they learn more effective and positive techniques.

Belief V: Parents' Basic Needs Must Be Met before They Can Respond Effectively and Positively to the Needs of Their Children

Unemployed parents, parents distressed about housing or food, or those who are experiencing other forms of debilitating distress usually have difficulty meeting the needs of others, despite their best intentions. Thus, even when the goal of family social work is to help parents develop more effective ways of enhancing their children's development, attention also must be directed toward helping parents meet their own needs. Remember the airplane metaphor: passengers are advised to put on their own oxygen mask first before helping their children! Working with parents to eliminate stress can free them up to relate to and interact with their children in more positive and productive ways.

Belief VI: Every Family Member Needs Nurturing

People need to feel cared for and connected to other people. Sometimes becoming angry and blaming others is easier than sharing love and connecting with others. Every home should be a haven in which *each and every member* experiences nurturing, love, support, and acceptance. If one family member is getting his or her needs met at the expense of others, then the family is not functioning properly.

Belief VII: Family Members, Regardless of Gender or Age, Deserve Respect from Each Other

Within the context of culture, family social workers need to understand existing power structures in a family rather than assuming that one person is the "head of the household." This means respecting differences in and unique contributions to the marriage, parenting, and family unit. Children have a right to be respected, and gender differences also should be respected. *Equal* opportunities for growth and participation must be guaranteed to *all* family members, regardless of age or gender. At the same time, social workers should understand that roles related to gender and age vary in different cultures. Family social workers must grapple with the difficult task of respecting culture and at the same time valuing equality of family members. At times, the two may be opposing values. In the words of McGoldrick, Giordano, & Garcia-Preto (2005): "Just because a culture espouses certain values or beliefs does not make them sacrosanct. All cultural practices are not ethical. Mistreatment of women or children, or gays or lesbians, through disrespect, as well as physical or sexual abuse, is a human rights issue, no matter in what cultural context it occurs" (p. 31).

Belief VIII: A Child's Emotional and Behavioral Difficulties Should Be Viewed within the Context of the Family and the Larger Social Environment

This belief stems from the overarching definition of a social worker: Social workers are *context specialists!* Thus, in order to understand the behaviors, emotions, and beliefs of children, we need to understand their families. Moreover, to work effectively with children, we must work effectively with their families. Problems experienced by families generally reside neither within the parents nor within the child. Instead, from a family perspective, individual problems are intricately linked to the daily pattern of family interactions and relationships, as well as to the family's interactions with their environment.

Belief IX: All People Need a Family

All children (and indeed most people) need to feel a positive connection with at least one other person who cares for them. This is known as "unconditional positive regard" and combined with acceptance from another person creates the building blocks of healthy development.

Belief X: Most Family Difficulties Do Not Appear Overnight but Have Developed Gradually over the Years

Although a situational crisis is often the catalyst for families to receive help, most problems in families have evolved over a protracted period. Consequently, change is unlikely to occur overnight because the problem is entrenched in the family's patterns. Family social workers need to help families understand the need for long-term work and support during the change process. This belief also speaks to the importance of early intervention.

Belief XI: A Difference Exists between Thoughts and Actions in Parenting

At times, parents may experience overwhelming levels of frustration and even distress when managing children. They may even consider leaving their families. Although some people do leave their families, for most, these are only escape fantasies. The family social worker needs to read between the lines to discern whether a parent is unloving or uncaring. Saying something or thinking something is different from doing it. Nevertheless, family social workers are cautioned to take seriously any threat to individuals in the family or to the family unit. These include but are not limited to threats of suicide, homicide, or abuse, as well as threats that would cause any type of harm to another person. If the threats are serious, then the family social worker needs to deal with them first before addressing more long-standing family issues.

Belief XII: A Difference Exists between Being a Perfect Parent and Being a Good Enough Parent

No parent, not even the best, does the right thing at the right time all the time. Parents yell at their children and sometimes fail to meet their children's needs. These actions or inactions seldom destroy a child. Rather than being a perfect parent (which is unattainable), the goal is to help parents meet *enough*, rather than *all*, of their children's needs. The definition of what is good enough will be modified over time, paralleling the child's evolving developmental needs. For example, ignoring a child for half a day has different consequences if the child is an infant compared with if the child is a teenager. Family social workers must also take into account whether such incidents are long-standing chronic patterns or incidental behaviors. Parents need to work toward consistency in parenting. Instead of placing blame, we need to recognize that parents are not perfect and give them permission to make mistakes while at the same time taking responsibility for them. Children will realize that there is no such thing as a "perfect" parent.

Belief XIII: Families Require Fair and Equal Treatment from Environmental Systems

Many families from various cultures and ethnicities have not been treated justly or respectfully by society and the social institutions designed to meet human needs. Historically, members of different groups have been denied equal access to the same resources, opportunities, and systems of helping that mainstream members have enjoyed. We describe these populations as underserved. Social workers seek to equalize resource imbalances between groups and to promote social justice for all families. Single-parent families or other family types that do not conform to the prescribed norms suffer when resources and support fall short of their needs. The value base of the social work profession requires that social workers take a political stance to advocate for oppressed and underserviced client groups.

EXERCISE 2.16 Beliefs and Problems

List some of your beliefs about families, parents, and family social work that will facilitate your work with families. Then list some of your beliefs that might be problematic.

EP 2.1.4c

GUIDING PRINCIPLES OF FAMILY SOCIAL WORK

The following principles equip social workers to emphasize family strengths and positive choices in family work. They will lay the foundation of family social work and convey a belief in the family's capacity to institute positive change.

Principle I: The Best Place to Help Families Is in Their Home

The home is the natural living environment for the family. Through observing the home patterns of family interactions and behaviors, the family social worker is best able to develop a comprehensive assessment of the family. Interventions based on accurate and more complete knowledge of the families in their social context provide optimal opportunities for intervention success. In this way, families do not have to face the difficult task of translating office-based interventions and transferring the acquired learning to their world; one step in the application process is eliminated. Family issues may require the family social worker to be in the home for many hours a week, focusing on daily issues and interactions. Working out of the home, the family social worker can give immediate feedback and intervention, teaching new ways to interact and solve problems.

Principle II: Family Social Work Empowers Families to Solve Their Own Problems

A primary goal of family social work is to assist family members to become competent as a parent, as a partner, or as a functioning member of society. Imposed solutions suggested by the family social worker (if they are even acted upon) may alleviate current stresses, but usually do not equip the family to deal with future issues. Families change by learning and then practicing new skills. It is critical for the family social worker to be aware that the overarching goal of family social work is to promote family participation in change in a way that increases self-reliance and independence.

Families vary in their ability to function and change while under stress. Some have effective coping and problem-solving skills but require a special boost during a particularly stressful time. Other families require ongoing assistance and support, often from several agencies. All families have a unique set of strengths and weaknesses; no family is completely lacking in abilities or strengths. An accurate assessment of the specific capabilities of families should come before the design of the intervention.

Principle III: Intervention Should Be Individualized and Based on an Assessment of the Social, Psychological, Cultural, Educational, Economic, and Physical Characteristics of the Particular Family

Family social work begins where the particular family is. This principle is true whether it is the social worker's first or twenty-first interview with the family. Family strengths and issues must be assessed in an ongoing way and then evaluated to ensure appropriate and timely intervention. What is effective for one family may not work for another with similar problems.

Interventions based on prescribed formulae do not permit modifications tailored to the special needs of a particular family. One advantage of family social work is its capacity to implement interventions based on the unique qualities of families. A strengths-based approach also helps. In the 1980s, family workers were challenged to become culturally sensitive because characteristics of culturally diverse families such as extended kinship networks had been considered dysfunctional by conventional family practice standards (Nichols & Schwartz, 2007).

Principle IV: Family Social Workers Must Respond First to the Immediate Needs of Families and Then to Their Long-Term Goals

Hungry children need food; children in homeless families require shelter; sick children need medical care. They cannot grow and develop on promises for the future while their parents learn a trade or seek employment. The family social worker must assess a family's immediate needs and ensure that these needs are met first. At the same time, the social worker can help the parents plan for the future to ensure that long-term needs will also be met.

Maslow's hierarchy of needs is a useful road map for assessing the needs of children and families. On the basis of this assessment, plans can be made to build a foundation for meeting these needs, beginning with basic physical needs. Starting with an assessment of basic physical needs, such as the need for food and shelter, can help family social workers develop a plan for intervention. The second level of needs involves safety. Satisfying these needs involves protection from physical harm and living in safe homes and neighborhoods. The third level includes needs related to belonging. Belonging needs are met when one is accepted and valued by a group, the family group being primary. The next tier involves esteem needs, and the final level is the need for self-actualization. The family social worker first ensures that family members' basic physical and safety needs are met and then works with the family on meeting its other needs.

EP 2.1.7b

CHAPTER SUMMARY

Effective family social work is contingent on the application of a set of core beliefs, assumptions, and positive valuing of families and family social work. These beliefs assist the worker to develop competency-based, respectful interventions designed to promote collaborative relationships with the family. They also involve being open-minded to the many expressions of diversity. Through such teamwork, family social workers can help families capitalize on their own particular strengths and attributes.

KEY TERMS

Culture   Culture refers to the culmination of values, beliefs, customs, and norms that people have acquired, usually in the context of their family and community.

Different family forms/structures   Families include various configurations, including family of orientation, family of origin, family of procreation, extended family, over-extended family, blended family, adoptive family, foster family, single parent family.

Ethnicity   Ethnicity relates to a person's identity, commitment, and loyalty to an ethnic group (Jordan & Franklin, 2009).

Family   A family is a social group that may or may not include one or more children (e.g., childless couple), who may or may not have been born in wedlock (e.g., adopted, or children of one partner from a previous union). The relationship of the adults may or may not originate in marriage (e.g., common-law). The adults may or may not cohabit sexually, and the relationship may or may not involve such socially patterned feelings as love, attraction, piety, and awe (Eichler, 1988).

SUGGESTED READINGS

Coontz, S. (1996). The way we weren't: The myth and reality of the "Traditional Family." National Forum, 76(4), 45–48.

Coontz provides searing insight into myths about the current family and dismantles common misconceptions and arguments about how families are deteriorating.

McGoldrick, M., Giordano, J., & Garcia-Preto, N. (Eds.). (2005). *Ethnicity and family therapy*. New York, NY: Guilford.

This is a comprehensive resource on families and ethnicity that should be read by students and family social workers. By highlighting culture as a crucial factor in family functioning, the book is seminal. It challenges cultural blindness and places ethnicity and culture at the forefront. It surpasses other discussions of culture and family therapy, which present cultures as a checklist of characteristics.

COMPETENCY NOTES

EP 2.1.4c. Recognize and communicate their understanding of the importance of difference in shaping life experiences: Cultures differ in how they define family as well as who is included.

EP 2.1.7b. Critique and apply knowledge to understand person and environment: Hungry children need food; children in homeless families require shelter; sick children need medical care. Maslow's hierarchy of needs is a useful road map for assessing the needs of children and families.

Changing a family changes the lives of its members.

— **Nichols and Schwartz, 2007**

Crisis is opportunity on the tail of a dragon.

— **Chinese Proverb**

[handwritten: home visit you a can give a richer picture of what's happening w/ the family]

[handwritten: assessment is an ongoing process. If you fix one person is not going to fix the family system you have to treat to whole family]

CHAPTER CONTENTS	LEARNING OBJECTIVES
What Is a Family System?	• Conceptual: Understand the concept of family systems and its components.
Key Assumptions about Family Systems	
Family Boundaries	• Perceptual: See families as interconnected and interactive units within themselves as well as within the larger ecological environment.
Family Subsystems	
Chapter Summary	• Valuational/Attitudinal: Value the strength of family systems to resolve problems.
Key Terms	
Suggested Readings	• Behavioral: Move from an individual practice focus to a systems interactional focus.
Competency Notes	

Family systems theory is the heart of most existing approaches to family work. It also has a long history in social work. As early as 1917, Mary Richmond advised workers to consider the potential effects of all interventions at every systemic level and to use the reciprocal interaction of the systemic hierarchy for the purpose of working toward change (Bardill & Saunders, 1988). Adapted from biology, family systems theory now provides a foundational assessment and intervention framework with which to understand family functioning. Systems concepts have gained increasing prominence in family social work over the past several decades and have helped social workers understand the dynamics of family functioning and how families relate to various situations within their environment. Systems theory also guides the direction of intervention.

Over four decades ago, Satir (1967) pointed out that, "Numerous studies have shown that the family behaves as if it were a unit" (p. 17). Watzlawick, Beavin, and Jackson (1967) further developed this concept, noting that families are systems "in which *objects* are the components or parts of the system, *attributes* are the properties of the objects, and *relationships* tie the system together" (p. 120).

Three main ideas form the bedrock of systemic family work:

1. Problems occur as the result of ongoing patterns of communication within the family.
2. Crises encountered by the family create both instability and opportunities for change. *Look what's behind the behavior.*
3. Families function according to established rules that must be altered before problems can be effectively and permanently resolved.

At the outset of our discussion about family systems, we urge caution about how the theory falls short of explaining abuse within families. In particular, family systems theory fails to capture abuses of power, such as domestic violence and sexual or physical abuse. In response to this shortcoming, feminists criticize family systems theory for its built-in gender bias, pointing out how it discounts the importance of power within family. (These issues are addressed later in this chapter.) Others have also criticized rigid and uncritical adherence to family systems concepts. For example, early theorists attributed family systems dynamics to the development of schizophrenia and autism, often singling out mothers for their children's difficulties. The term *schizophrenogenic mother* is but one example of the pejorative and blaming concepts put forward by family systems theory, particularly in its early conceptualizations. Moreover, others have criticized systems theory as being too mechanical, through the application of unyielding universal principles such as rules, homeostasis, and circular causality to every family. Nevertheless, we still see much benefit in understanding family systems as both a *metaphor* and a *framework*.

The family is a powerful environment in which individuals grow and develop. Families are extremely complex, and without an organizing framework, it would be easy to become overwhelmed and confused by the information and behaviors that families present. Perhaps the most useful understanding that family systems theory has to offer is that it teaches us that families are organized in specific ways for a reason. It also teaches us that every family functions on the basis of predictable patterns. Nevertheless, we encourage students to use any theory with a critical lens and avoid applying every theoretical concept rigidly or insensitively to every situation or case. *punctuality.*

loss, financial issues, divorce, addiction, a diagnostic

WHAT IS A FAMILY SYSTEM?

According to family systems theory, all families are social systems, and it is this belief that guides understanding and work with families. Because family members are interdependent (rely on one another), behaviors do not exist in a vacuum. As such, family systems theory helps us see how problems spring from family relationships and transactions. In family work, the overall web of patterned relationships within the family becomes the focus. Thus, one of the key beliefs of family systems theory is that problems that arise in families cannot usually be attributed to individual dysfunction or pathology. Rather, understanding family dynamics will help uncover family processes that seem to foster and maintain the presenting problem.

Therefore, problems such as parent-child conflicts, behavior problems, mental health issues, and so on develop and continue within the family context.

When family social workers work with families, they must look beyond individual behaviors and understand the family context, which becomes the catalyst for the creation and maintenance of ongoing communication patterns, rules, family relationships, and, ultimately, problems within the family. Thus, family systems theory provides a conceptual framework for assessing family relationships and for understanding problems within the context of family relationships.

This central organizing belief is perhaps the hardest for families (and sometimes workers) to understand. We have found in our practice that many parents bring their children into counseling to be "fixed." They would like nothing better than to drop off their child at the agency and pick up that child later "all better." This does not work for several reasons. First, as mentioned, problems seldom develop or are maintained in isolation. When people live in close relationship with one another, they constantly affect and are affected by one another. The way people affect one another becomes entrenched in predictable and repetitive *patterns* over time. Because these patterns become habitual, they usually escape conscious awareness of the key players. It is quite natural to act unthinkingly in daily life. It simply would take too much energy to be aware of every single behavior and response on a minute-to-minute basis (and be mindful about every action). Whereas we expect family social workers to be aware of everything that goes on in a family session, we also realize that people often respond habitually in their personal lives. Wouldn't it be nice if everything people did on a daily basis were *intentional*? Carter and McGoldrick (1999) suggest that when predictable interactional flows are altered, "other family members will be jarred out of their own unthinking responses and, in the automatic move toward homeostasis that is inherent in all systems (discussed below), will react by trying to get the disrupter back into place again" (pp. 437–438).

Second, even if problems develop at the individual level, how people *respond* to the behaviors tends to keep the behaviors going. We also realize that when problems occur, doing more of the same thing does not make them better, although it is the tendency of families to do so. Families need help to get out of their entrenched ways of responding and make changes so that solutions to problems become more effective. Unfortunately, many people within a family have a hard time accepting that they are contributing to the problem. They have spent much time and effort being angry or concerned about the problematic family member and may become defensive when the family social worker suggests that they are playing a role in the creation and development of the problem. It is only through a sensitive and thorough exploration of the process that families can understand their contribution.

In keeping with this belief, the family social worker views a family system as a complex set of elements in mutual and constant interaction. When a family worker sees a family as a system, he or she conceptualizes a set of interconnected units. The focus of intervention is on how family members and subsets of family members influence one another, rather than on each individual's behavior in isolation. In other words, the behavior of one family member is intricately connected with the behaviors and reactions of all other family members.

The key to working with families as systems is to understand that family interactions and relationships are *reciprocal, patterned,* and *repetitive.* Relationships are reciprocal in that family members affect one another in a back-and-forth fashion. They are also patterned because over time, responses to one another become solidified and predictable. Finally, behaviors are repetitive because they occur over and over again in much the same way. Through these reciprocal, patterned, and repetitive responses, family relationships and interactions become interwoven to create a complex, but patterned, family quilt. In the process, family social workers develop an understanding of how family life becomes the backdrop for individual behavior, particularly how each member interacts with others in the family in reciprocal, patterned, and repetitive ways. The focus on family interactions means that the family social worker looks first for *what* is happening, rather than *why.*

The late Michael Crichton (1995) wrote the following passage in *The Lost World,* which can serve as a metaphor for understanding the family as a system:

> *It did not take long before the scientists began to notice that complex systems showed certain common behaviors. They started to think of these behaviors as characteristic of all complex systems. They realized that these behaviors could not be explained by analyzing single components of the systems. The time-honored scientific approach of reductionism—taking the watch apart to see how it worked—didn't get you anywhere with complex systems, because the interesting behavior seemed to arise from the spontaneous interaction of the components. The behavior wasn't planned or directed; it just happened. Such behavior was therefore called "self-organizing." (p. 2)*

Crichton's observations highlight the shortcomings of observing one family member in isolation from the others. Like a proverbial watch, the movement of the dial cannot be understood without understanding the various mechanisms in the watch. Similarly, behavior within families is interdependent, and one person cannot be understood by looking at his or her behavior alone and in isolation. In other words, the thoughts, feelings, and actions of each family member influence the thoughts, feelings, and actions of each other member. In addition, families in chaos have great potential for creativity (Suissa, 2005).

EXERCISE 3.1 Understanding Family Systems

Take time to reflect on your family when you were growing up and try to understand your family of origin as a family system. The following will guide your understanding:

List the members of your family system.

Identify family subsystems in your family. How were they divided: by generation, gender, interests, and functions?

Describe the family boundaries using an open-to-closed continuum. Describe family relationships.

Describe the informal and formal roles assumed by each member of your family. Account for role conflicts and role clarity in the family.

What cultural influences affected the family, and how would you describe them?

EXERCISE 3.2   Family Systems

Go to family systems literature, particularly early conceptualizations, and find out how it explains:

Schizophrenia

Wife battering

Incest

Autism

What are the biases you discovered? Share your findings with the class.

EXERCISE 3.3   Individual versus Family Causes

Select a problem that has been described from an individualistic perspective (e.g., child behavior problems, eating disorders, mental health issues). Compare the theories describing individual causes versus family causes of the difficulty. Report back to your class.

KEY ASSUMPTIONS ABOUT FAMILY SYSTEMS

It is important to understand the six central concepts within family systems thinking. Just as one person's behavior cannot be understood by looking at his or her behavior alone, family workers should also be aware that these six central ingredients overlap with each other. These six ingredients include:

EP 2.1.7a

1. A change in one family member affects all of the family members.
2. The family as a whole is more than the sum of its parts.
3. Families try to balance change and stability.
4. Family members' behaviors are best explained by circular causality.
5. A family belongs to a larger social system and encompasses many subsystems.
6. A family operates according to established rules.

A Change in One Family Member Affects All of the Family Members

To understand families as social systems, it is important to recognize that a change in one family member affects every other family member (Bowen, 1971). In other words, what happens to one person in the family alters the entire family. Recognizing this tendency can explain a family's response to a member's attempts at change, as well as the response to the family social worker's attempts to stimulate change. Satir (1967) observed that when early workers tried to change one family member's way of operating, they were actually changing the entire family's way of operating (p. 4). However, focusing on just one person in the family, usually the one with symptoms, places a burden on the one with the presenting problems. If one family member begins to behave differently, other members may resist this new behavior in an effort to keep the family the same. Some authors suggest, for example, that after one family member's symptoms improve, another individual in the family may develop symptoms. They refer to the original person with the symptoms as the "symptom bearer." Further, if this member changes successfully, the family will be unable to revert to previous patterns because of the changes. In other words, change in one part of the system forces change in other parts of the system. "In a family, if any person changes, his or her emotional input and reactions also change, interrupting the predictable flow" (Carter & McGoldrick, 1999, p. 437).

For example, if a parent yells at the children to complete their homework but eventually does the work for them, children may learn to rely on the parent's help every evening. However, if the parent stops doing the children's homework, the children must learn to finish their own homework, either by getting someone else to do it, doing the homework themselves, or suffering the consequences of not doing it at all. We see, then, that the family system adapts in response to one member's altered behavior.

We recall one humorous incident relayed to us by a friend who observed that when she and her husband were driving in the car together, she would always sit in the passenger side of the car. She decided to see what would happen if she took over the driver's side seat. She took the driver's seat and reached her right arm over the back of the passenger's seat as she casually drove down the road. She did not tell him what she was doing. Her husband's response was quite amusing. At first, he rode in the passenger seat without saying a word. Then he asked her what the matter was. A couple of days later, he attempted to reclaim his role as driver. This change was obviously too much for the man, and he worked hard to revert to the original state of homeostasis! Our friend's husband had no choice but to change in response to his wife's new behavior. This example also shows, in a very simplistic way, how when one family member changes behavior, others have no choice but to change theirs.

Although this example is seemingly trivial, it does highlight how challenging even the smallest change can be for a family. It demonstrates that when one person changes a particular behavior, others have to concomitantly change their behavior in response. Finally, it also illustrates the importance of first-order and second-order change (discussed in the section on family rules).

The Family as a Whole Is More than the Sum of Its Parts

Family systems theory, as a general organizing framework, can help family workers understand the family as a social system that is more than the sum of the individual characteristics or behaviors of each family member. Von Bertalanffy, the biologist who first formulated general systems theory, suggested that when the component parts of a system become organized into a pattern, the outcome of that organization is an entity greater than the individual parts. No matter how well we know individuals in the family, we can understand a person's behavior better by observing her or him within the context of interactions with others. Families have a tremendous influence on how people develop their identities, roles, beliefs, and behaviors.

EXERCISE 3.4   More than the Sum of Its Parts?

What are the parts of a family system? Consider, for example, the Hagel family in which there are five children—three boys (John, Peter, and Steve) and two girls (Meagan and Paige)— plus the mother, Jane, and father, Mark. The most obvious answer is that the parts are merely the sum total of John plus Peter plus Steve plus Meagan plus Paige plus Jane plus Mark. A simple answer is that there are seven parts or subsystems in this particular family. Yet, there are many other subsystems (parts) in this family beyond the initial observation. Subsystems might be identified by family role (parent and child), gender (father and sons, mother and daughters), possible triangles (father, mother, and John), and so on.

Examine the family described in this exercise. Map out all the potential subsystems in this family. How do these various subsystems support the belief that the family is more than the sum of its parts?

When the focus of family work is on children, family social workers can best understand them by observing the interactions within the family—how parents and siblings respond to them and how they respond to the responses of others in the family. Through this emphasis, the family social worker develops a deeper appreciation of the patterns of family relationships. Although children are born with unique temperaments, they are also deeply affected by family dynamics. Thus, the child who is noncompliant with parental and family rules is not understood as a "bad" child. The child is acting out because of the patterns of family members' interactions both before and after the noncompliant episode. Getting the family to understand the child's behavior through this lens can be a quite challenging, yet necessary, part of change.

Family assessment entails identifying both a family's strengths and problems. Assessment also involves understanding how the interactions of individual family members detract from or contribute to effective family functioning in general and to the presenting problem in particular. Many kinds of individual problems either originate or are expressed through family interaction. Consequently, both the challenge and goal of family work is to transform dysfunction into mutually supportive and growth-enhancing family relationships. Altered family interaction is both an end in itself and a vehicle with which to understand and address individual difficulties. The overarching goal of family intervention is to improve family functioning by promoting better interpersonal relationships and interactions.

Another way to understand how a system can be more than the sum of its parts is to think of how musical notes are organized in such a way as to make a tune. Separately, the notes mean nothing, but together, the notes are organized to create a melody. The combination of single notes creates a unique melody that has characteristics completely different from the individual notes in isolation or from a different combination of notes. How many possible notes are there? Even with the limited number of notes available, the number of songs is infinite! Therefore, despite how much the family social worker knows about individual family members and different subsets, ultimately, their behavior is best understood through observations of family interaction—the family melody. In conclusion, the interaction of family members creates an entity that is more than the sum of the individual personalities.

Families Try to Balance Change and Stability

To survive and fulfill their functions and also to grow and develop, families need stability, order, and consistency. The struggle to stay the same and retain the status quo is known as *homeostasis*, wherein the family acts to achieve balance in relationships (Satir, 1967; Satir & Baldwin, 1983). Stability and predictability allow family members to anticipate behaviors and events that are energy-efficient. Maintaining homeostasis is a demanding, although on the surface it might appear that the family is stable. However, under the surface the family is paddling like the proverbial duck (calm on the surface but paddling frantically underneath) to keep the system on track. Satir (1967) suggests that members help maintain this balance overtly and covertly (p. 2). Family rules help to keep homeostasis in check by determining which behaviors are acceptable or forbidden. Just as a thermostat in a house keeps the furnace or air conditioner operating to maintain a stable temperature, homeostasis works to keep the family in constant balance. In families, the "thermostat" represents family rules (discussed below) through which families strive to function consistently and predictably. Some believe that families are self-correcting systems, although change typically occurs through feedback.

The concept of homeostasis was first identified by Jackson (Watzlawick, Beavin, & Jackson, 1967), who discovered that families of psychiatric patients deteriorated after the patient improved. He suggested that family behaviors, and hence the psychiatric illness, were "homeostatic mechanisms" functioning to bring the disturbed system back into its delicate balance (p. 134). Ackerman (1958) added to this view by seeing family homeostasis as vital to the family in maintaining effective, coordinated functioning under constantly changing conditions (p. 69).

Families attempt to maintain the status quo to conserve energy and keep conditions the same. At the same time, they encounter continuous pressure to change in response to the external environment and the evolving needs of family members. For example, children in different developmental stages require different things from their parents. Behaviors that were appropriate for a toddler become inappropriate for teenagers. When families have difficulty responding and adapting to developmental demands of children, they are said to be stuck or frozen. In the process, families must also find a balance between conflicting demands for consistency and change.

Family social workers should not assume that stability and health are interchangeable. Stability merely releases family members from constantly needing to respond to unpredictable demands, giving members the energy to function adequately in daily routines. As families progress through the different stages of the family life cycle, tasks differ according to the activities that are demanded to maintain stability and the activities that are conducive to development.

While homeostasis is a necessary state for families, at times, homeostasis can hurt a family. A family crisis, for example, disturbs the homeostasis of a family, but after a time, the family will adjust rules, behaviors, interactions, and patterns as it adapts to the new situation. The arrival of a new child is but one example of a family crisis. New behaviors are demanded of every family member to adjust. Eventually these new patterns become entrenched in the family as the family system adapts and settles down. Imagine a family that did not get used to a new baby.

What would be the consequences? What if a family did not adapt to death, unemployment, or other threatening family event? For some crises, it is impossible not to adapt.

Because of movement through the family life cycle and because individual family members are also experiencing their own developmental stages, it is paradoxical that families must constantly adapt and change to remain stable. Nevertheless, families eventually develop a rhythm that enables both stability and change over the life cycle of the family. Destabilizing crises embedded in each of these stages disrupt family patterns, making life both unpredictable and stressful. Each stage of the family life cycle contains a potentially destabilizing experience. Arguably, one of the most destabilizing experiences in a family is the birth of the first child.

Moreover, after certain crises or change-inducing situations, family functioning becomes reestablished. Yet, many crises are unpredictable or unavoidable. After a crisis, the tendency is for the family to revert to the way they functioned before the crisis. For example, if a parent becomes drug- or alcohol-free, the initial stage of adjustment might be marked by crisis while family members adjust to living with a sober parent (who may also be depressed). However, after this temporary disruption, the family develops new responses and functioning in the form of routines and patterns based on the new set of circumstances. If the parent relapses, the family may slowly revert to previous patterns of functioning. That is, the family returns to its "normal" state.

A family's typical reaction is to deny and resist impending change imposed by a crisis. Homeostasis is an important concept as it relates to the particular problem the family is experiencing since homeostasis built around a problem can remain stable and entrench that problem (Satir, 1967, p. 49). However, it is important to remember that resistance is based on the desire to maintain balance and stability. Resistance to change can be intense, as social workers who have attempted to challenge rigidly maintained behavior can attest. This is one reason why family work can be so taxing. The family worker not only has to deal with individual family member resistance; the worker must also address the resistance of the entire unit and that of the different family subsystems. Changes in family functioning may be difficult to maintain unless intervention creates ways to ensure that the family will incorporate the changes permanently. Because of this, we know that families can experience distress or discomfort with new behaviors even when changes are positive, such as when an alcoholic member stops drinking.

Resistance involves opposing or avoiding something that is painful or unpleasant. Because the need for stability is so strong, resistance to change by families is normal and should be anticipated. People may seek relief from anxiety, guilt, and shame through resistance. They may see the direction of the family work as too unpleasant or painful to change. We have found, for example, that many families resist the initial shift from identifying one person as the problem to framing the presenting problem as a family problem.

In addition, zealous actions of the family social worker might contribute to family resistance. One important skill for addressing resistance is to recognize the right amount of pressure to use to avoid pushing family members too hard, and yet be challenging enough to move the family past its "stuckness." The family social worker can develop skills to enter the family's world unobtrusively and join with them in a mutual endeavor designed to address presenting concerns. The task becomes even more complex when you consider that individual family members might all see the problem in different ways. One view is to consider the individual with the presenting problem as the sole owner of the problem and hold this person responsible for the family distress. Another way to view the problem might be to see a particular subsystem as the problem, such as an overly harsh parent scapegoating a child. Nevertheless, it is a natural (and safe) tendency of family members to view the problem as belonging to someone else.

Countering resistance requires skills to disarm and neutralize behavior while instilling mutual willingness to discuss what is happening in the family work. Even an appropriate intervention may incite resistance because the social worker has asked the family to do something that makes no sense to them, they feel anxious about, or they do not wish to do at a particular point. Resistance can be lessened when the family becomes more comfortable with the social worker, when trust has developed, when individual family members feel validated and supported, and when the family senses empathy, honesty, and genuineness from the worker.

When a specific change is targeted, the family social worker can help the family determine how to arrive at a new point of homeostasis. Talking to the family about change and stability might be the first step. A shift in family homeostasis demands that the family reorganize and devise new patterns of behavior and communication. For example, when a child is placed into foster care, the family will reorganize to deal with this loss. Remaining family members might assume the various roles and functions of the child. For example, if a child is parentified (taking on the adult roles of a parent), another child might assume the role of caretaker for the younger children and even for the parents. In fact, reorganization is necessary since failure to achieve a new balance means that some, if not all, of the family members will not get their needs met, perhaps leading to family chaos, disintegration, or the generation of new problems to replace the old. Once a family reorganizes and settles into a new state of homeostasis organized around the absence of the child (as when a child is placed into foster care), reintegration of the child back into the home might be challenging. If the family does revert to more familiar patterns, the reasons for the child's removal in the first place may not be addressed. The urge to reestablish stability and equilibrium (that is, "normal family functioning") during periods of change is a powerful force that should be considered very carefully by social workers who are trying to create permanent change that will continue after the social worker is no longer seeing the family. This example speaks to the necessity of ongoing work with families whose children have been removed from the home but whose eventual return authorities have determined should be the goal.

The family social worker might assume an educational stance and, together with the family, talk about homeostasis and stability and how they play out in this particular family using an explanation the family can understand. Connecting theory with what you see happening in the family could lead to an "aha" experience. However, it is important not to force families to agree with you if they see the issue from another perspective.

Although it appears that families prefer equilibrium, in fact families are never static. According to Michael Crichton (1995), complex systems seem to strike a balance between the need for order and the imperative for change: "Complex systems tend to locate themselves at a place we call 'the edge of chaos'" (p. 2). The survival of a social system necessitates that it remain on the edge of chaos where there is sufficient vibrancy to keep the system alive but sufficient stability to keep it from falling into chaos. Boredom and chronic crises are equally threatening to a family, in different ways.

Because families are always changing, they may be unbalanced and stable at the same time. When families face pressure to change or adapt through an extended crisis, a new pattern of family functioning emerges, creating an altered state of family balance. This is a very important point for family social workers to keep in mind, as much family work is started because of a family crisis. The hope is that the longer parents adopt a new parenting strategy, the better the chance that they will incorporate this strategy into a habitual parenting style after the social worker leaves. Similarly, it is hoped that new child behavior will continue when family work ends. The threat is that if one side of the equation reverts to old patterns, the entire system will shift to previous levels of functioning that brought the family to seek assistance in the first place.

Part of the discussion with the family involves what they must do to continue the changes they make after family social work ends. Families can think about how they can apply their new learning over time, with different people, and in different situations; this is known as transfer of learning or generalization.

The coexistence of change and stability is one of the most difficult concepts of systems theory to understand in terms of family social work practice. Often, social workers will view families either as stuck or as being in total disequilibrium (i.e., chaotic). Experienced family social workers appreciate the complexity of families, without being overwhelmed by it. They recognize that when families seem stuck or appear to be moving from one crisis to another, they may be maintaining either rigid equilibrium or chaotic change. Thus upsetting a stuck family will be required. The risk is that families will blame the family social worker for this upset, making it precarious for the family social worker-family relationship. We advise not provoking a crisis before the relationship has developed sufficiently; otherwise, the family might terminate prematurely. Conversely, if avoiding important issues, the family work might become stagnant and meaningless. Eventually, the family will need to adopt solutions that include a balance between stability and change.

EXERCISE 3.5 Crises and Stability

Identify three possible unpredictable family crises that might threaten the stability in a family. How would each of these crises affect family stability? What might a family do to try to reestablish stability?

EXERCISE 3.6 Positive Change and Family Stability

Identify one positive change in a family. Speculate on how this change might disrupt family stability. Compare your answers with those of the rest of the class.

Some family theorists suggest that presenting problems (often child-related problems) are primarily an attempt for the family to maintain homeostasis. However, caution should be exercised in seeing the homeostatic mechanism in families solely in this way, since it has been used to rationalize and justify a range of problem behaviors in the family such as sexual abuse and domestic violence. This thinking has served as a rationale for not placing responsibility for the abuse on the perpetrator. It has also led some to suggest that victims of abuse play a role in the initiation of abuse and that the perpetrator might even be a victim (see, for example, Coleman & Collins, 1990; Trepper & Barrett, 1986). Indeed family systems theory is problematic when used to explain sexual abuse and domestic violence and family systems intervention has been banned by several states' laws to regulate batterer intervention programs, for example, those of Massachusetts and Michigan (Murray, 2006).

Family homeostasis has implications for crisis intervention. Family social workers often encounter families that have experienced a destabilizing crisis such as a report of child abuse. Often the crisis brings the family to the attention of official agencies in the family's community, such as child welfare, schools, or the criminal justice system. Being aware of the tendency to fall back to "normal" (maybe even habitual) functioning after a crisis can teach family social workers to capitalize on destabilizing periods by helping a family create second-order, long-lasting changes. The task of family social workers, then, is to challenge the family to move to a new state of balance by reorganizing patterns of interaction and creating new rules to regulate these patterns. In this way, the family will abandon past preferred states of balance in favor of new ones.

EXERCISE 3.7   Family Homeostasis

In reflecting back on your family of origin, try to recall a couple of crisis situations. Describe one situation in which the family reverted to homeostasis. Describe another crisis in which the family did not revert to homeostasis quickly. Contrast the two.

EXERCISE 3.8   Family Adjustments

Break into small groups and make a list of the kinds of adjustments that a family must make to adapt to the sobriety of a family member. Share your list with the class.

EXERCISE 3.9   Crisis Events

Break into groups of four or five students. In your small group, make a list of crisis events that can unbalance a family and discuss how the family might react when it becomes unbalanced. Compare your answers with those of other small groups.

Family Members' Behaviors Are Best Explained by Circular Causality

As mentioned, even the most chaotic families function in predictable and patterned ways. For example, it is usually the same person who feeds the dog every day or does the laundry. Patterns of communication in the family are also predictable. We can accurately guess which child will do homework without coaxing or threats and which child will start to argue when asked to do something by a parent. We can also predict, with some certainty, how a particular parent will respond to a child who is throwing a temper tantrum or refusing to comply with a demand. Many of these patterns fall outside the awareness of those following them. (These patterns are habits that maintain family stability and homeostasis by making daily family routines and interactions predictable.) While patterns are unavoidable and even desirable in families, when they become hurtful or dysfunctional to individuals or to the whole family, they must be altered.

Bateson and Jackson (1974) define the circularity of interactions as:

> *where A is stimulated to do more of this because B has done this same thing; and where B does more of this because A did some of it; and A does more of it because B did some, and so on. This is the sort of symmetry characteristic of keeping up with the Joneses, some armaments races, and so forth. (p. 200)*

Communication patterns in a family are therefore reciprocal and mutually reinforcing. That is, each pattern of communication, in the form of a transactional sequence, cycles back and forth between the two people involved. The responses of one person will influence the responses of the other. Eventually the responses solidify into a fairly predictable and patterned sequence of exchanges between two people. Thus, an early task of the family social worker is to identify the *repetitive patterns* of communication within the family. These patterns are known as circular causality. (See Chapter 10 for assessment of and intervention with circular patterns.) Although most people think in terms of causation, or linear causality whereby one event is believed to directly *cause* another event, circular causality is different. In linear causality, for example, when a parent tells a child to do his or her homework, the child either does the homework as requested or refuses to do the homework. In the first example, the child is said to be obedient. In the second example, the child is described as "bad." The parent is doing what parents do, but whether the child does the homework or not depends solely on the child. Looking at behavior in this way removes behavior from its context and fails to put the parent in the equation. How did the parent make the demand of the child? What can the child expect in terms of a parental response if he or she refuses to do the homework? How does the child make meaning of the parental request? What is the relationship like between the parent and the child? These and other questions can be understood once the sequence of exchanges is taken out of a linear context and placed within the context of circular causality.

Similar to the preceding example, temper tantrums often are considered linear events. Parents report that when they say no to the child's demands, the child protests. This conceptualization of tantrums allows parents to call the child "bad" or "spoiled." Beliefs about linear causality allow other family members to disown or detach from the role they play in the development and continuation of the temper tantrums. Lineal explanations for behavior problems exclude an understanding of relationships, history, and ongoing communication patterns that start, reinforce, or support the problematic behavior. Ultimately, lineal explanations of individual problems attribute problems to personality factors. Blaming personality relieves others of the role they play in the problem and also relieves them of the responsibility to change. Earlier, Watzlawick, Beavin, and Jackson (1967) cautioned against taking a linear perspective, in part because the *punctuation* of the sequence places it in an individual context. "What is typical about the sequence and makes it a problem of punctuation is that the individual concerned conceives of himself only as reacting to, but not as provoking, those attitudes" (p. 99).

Conversely, circular causality places ongoing interaction patterns within a *context* of patterned family relationships. In working with a family, the social worker should look for circular patterns of interaction between family members. Circular causality accounts for how the behaviors are perceived and how members feel about the interaction. It also sets behavior as a response to the behavior of another person. Circular causality challenges the notion that events simply move in one direction, with each event being caused by a single previous event.

Circular causality, then, describes a situation in which event B influences event A, which in turn contributes to event B, and so on. For example, a parent shows interest in the child's homework, and the child then explains the assignment to the parent. This is likely to result in an ongoing circular and reciprocal pattern of interaction. The parent continues to take an interest in and offer support regarding the child's homework; the child feels supported and rewarded and may make an extra effort when doing homework and ask the parent for help, thus reinforcing the pattern. Circular patterns are characteristic of ongoing family relationships. Rather than one event causing another, events become entangled in a series of *causal chains*. The success of circular interactions depends, to a large degree, on the skill and sensitivity with which both parties can understand and respond to one another. In problematic circular interactions, one or both members of the dyad have difficulty understanding and responding to the other person.

Family social workers will often become involved in altering maladaptive circular patterns within the family. Consider another homework example. A parent yells at a child to do her homework. The child interprets the yelling as a message that she is bad and a failure, which causes her to feel anxious and have difficulty concentrating, which ultimately leads to avoidance of homework. The parent, upon observing that the child is not concentrating or doing her homework, interprets the child's behavior as laziness and defiance. In response, the parent scolds the child about her poor attitude and performance, and the circular maladaptive pattern becomes entrenched after a number of repetitions of the cycle.

Several authors (e.g., Caffrey & Erdman, 2000; Kozlowska & Hanney, 2002) also use systems theory and circular causality to examine attachment relationships within the family, particularly relationships involving the parent and child. In part, early attachment styles can determine the nature and quality of future adult relationships. As such, in the parent-child relationship, the behaviors of each member are both a stimulus and a response to the other person. Attachment behaviors develop in circular and behavioral and affective sequences. For example, a crying child typically brings out nurturing or caregiving responses from the parent. A child who continues to cry draws out further responses from the caregiver. Moreover, factors outside the parent-child relationship will also affect the nature of the parent-child attachment loop, such as stress, poverty, or violence in the parental relationship. If parents in the family are unable to provide a secure environment for one another, it is quite possible that the children's needs will not be met. Instead, the parents will be preoccupied with meeting their own needs. Caregivers can respond to child distress in a number of ways, including behaviors that comfort, escalate the distress, or are unpredictable. Parental responses help children structure and organize their behaviors and relationship patterns. In discussing attachment, we remind you that both the expression and interpretation of attachment behaviors are partially determined by culture (Neckoway, Brownlee, Jourdain, & Miller, 2003), and not all cultural groups assign the same meaning to an infant's cry or share the same beliefs about what to do in response. For example, in the Native American culture, the child belongs to the family group, making attachment not just dyadic. Moreover, attachment theory has historically considered the mother as the primary caretaker, thus implicating her in a host of attachment disorders of children.

Over time, patterns of interaction among family members become repetitive and predictable. In conceptualizing circular causality, however, we must be careful to incorporate power into the analysis. Until recently, power was considered too linear to be applied to family interactional patterns. However, whereas a mobile can be a metaphor for a family system, just as certain components of a mobile are heavier than others, different family members exert more influence over others. As feminists have argued, power imbalances must be taken into account in understanding family relationships. "Power is inherent in the system and every family member participates in its distribution, management, and use" (Suissa, 2005, p. 17). Power relations involve who holds the balance of power and in a practical way address the following questions: Who speaks for whom? Who speaks first? Who interrupts whom? Who agrees with whom? Who "takes up the most space"? Who makes decisions for whom? Who seems to hold the ultimate decision-making authority? (p. 17).

Figure 3.1 demonstrates how interaction might unfold in a family in patterned and regular ways. The circular patterns account for thoughts, feelings, and behaviors of two people that become engrained over time. Sometimes the interaction is between parents, and other times the interaction occurs between parent and child. Some interactions are adaptive and positive. For example, when a person is hurting, another person might give support and affection. Positive interactions are healthy for family members and should be encouraged to continue. It is when interactions are negative and hurtful that family social workers should intervene. Pattern E demonstrates a problematic circular exchange between a parent and a child.

Consider the example of a teenager who is acting out. The teen and the parent are in conflict, and there is much anger and resentment between the two. The teen might be coming home late and violating curfew. This occurs on a regular basis. In response, the parent might be thinking that she or he is a poor parent and feeling like a failure. The parent becomes depressed and angry (the two feelings often go together). Affectively (on a feeling level), the parent is feeling inadequate, like a failure, and might even feel rejected, hopeless, and powerless. In response, the parent's behavior is perceived as irritability and anger by the adolescent; the parent yells and has very little tolerance for the teen's behaviors, including the breaking of curfew and anything else the young person does at the home. The parent might also ignore the teen. The teen, in response to the parent's behavior, feels anxious and unwanted because there is little positive interaction between the two. The teen wonders if he was wanted and does not think that he can please the parent. The affective response to these feelings is guilt, anger, and hurt. What does the teen do when he feels guilt,

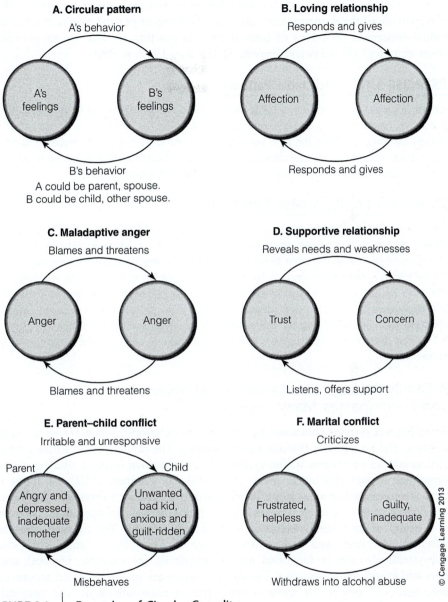

A. Circular pattern

A's behavior

A's feelings   B's feelings

B's behavior

A could be parent, spouse.
B could be child, other spouse.

B. Loving relationship

Responds and gives

Affection   Affection

Responds and gives

C. Maladaptive anger

Blames and threatens

Anger   Anger

Blames and threatens

D. Supportive relationship

Reveals needs and weaknesses

Trust   Concern

Listens, offers support

E. Parent–child conflict

Irritable and unresponsive

Parent   Child

Angry and depressed, inadequate mother   Unwanted bad kid, anxious and guilt-ridden

Misbehaves

F. Marital conflict

Criticizes

Frustrated, helpless   Guilty, inadequate

Withdraws into alcohol abuse

© Cengage Learning 2013

FIGURE 3.1 | Examples of Circular Causality

anger, and hurt? Like many teens, the young person turns to friends who can meet his needs for acceptance and caring. He enjoys the company of friends so much and forgets to watch the time, only to arrive home late and upset his parent. The parent, in response, feels angry and upset, thinks she is a failure as a parent, and feels inadequate, powerless, hopeless, and rejected. When the parent experiences these thoughts and feelings, the response to the teen is to show irritability, yell, or ignore him. The teen views the parent's behavior, and the pattern continues. "What is typical about the sequence and makes it a problem of punctuation is that the individual concerned conceives of himself only as reacting to, but not as provoking these attitudes" (Watzlawick, Beavin, & Jackson, 1967, p. 99)!

EXERCISE 3.10   Predictable Patterns

Identify a predictable pattern in a social relationship you have. The relationship might be in a classroom, board meeting, or work setting. Without telling the other person(s), do something entirely different. Continue the new behavior for several days, noting the reactions of people around you. Report back to the class. How did other people change in response to what you did? How did they attempt to get the patterns back to the original state?

EXERCISE 3.11   Predictable Pattern Change

Select one of your intimate relationships, preferably within a family context. The relationship should be one that has been established long enough for predictable patterns to emerge. Identify one of your predictable behaviors and then do the opposite for one day. Select a behavior that is not threatening to the other person, but be as ridiculous as you want. How did other people in your system respond to your new behavior? What kind of pressure did you experience to revert to your original behavior? How did the others respond when you changed your behavior? Discuss the differences in responses between Exercises 3.10 and 3.11. What difference does closeness and intimacy make in terms of the responses to your behaviors?

A Family Belongs to a Larger Social System and Encompasses Many Subsystems

An important systems characteristic concerns the relationship between systems, subsystems, and larger-scale systems (suprasystems). The family system forms multileveled structures of systems within systems. Each subsystem forms a whole and at the same time is part of a larger whole (Kozlowska & Hanney, 2002). All living systems are composed of subsystems in relationship with other subsystems. Subsystems can consist of two or more relationships with unique ways of operating. The family is a group of individuals within a wider family system. The marital subsystem, parental subsystem, and child subsystem are all examples of family subsystems. Subsystems also can be identified within individuals, for example, physical, cognitive, and emotional subsystems. Family subsystems are often organized around gender, age, and power, to name a few. The marital subsystem (the parents) is considered the "architect of the family" because it is (or should be) the most influential subsystem within the family (Satir, 1967). Therefore, the success of the family is largely dependent on the parental subsystem, whether it consists of a single parent or two parents.

EXERCISE 3.12   Family Subsystems

Identify the family subsystems in your family of origin. Describe the nature of the boundaries between these subsystems as, for example, enmeshed or disengaged.

Larger systems to which families may belong include the extended family, the city, the neighborhood, recreational organizations, the church, and so on. These in turn are part of even larger systems, such as countries or groups of nations. The family social worker will focus on the family, its subsystems, and, to some extent, the larger systems to which the family belongs. We call this the ecological perspective. Cultural blueprints from the wider society have a definite impact on families. For example, in families that are part of a larger patriarchal system, women and children typically have less power than men. As mentioned in Chapter 1, the person-in-environment (P-I-E) perspective is a benchmark of good social work practice.

Environmental support is necessary for family and individual well-being (Garbarino, 1992), particularly informal support from friends and family. Yet formal sources of support dominate the support network of many families, and many have a pattern of negative interactions with the social service system (Kaplan, 1986). Excessive involvement of formal agencies can exacerbate chaotic family functioning. (Ecological assessment is discussed in more detail in Chapter 8.)

On the other hand, a rich and diverse network of social relationships is a sign of maturation and health. For example, young children start out in a relationship with one significant person (often the mother), gradually relating to other children and adults in the family. Eventually, children incorporate other children and adults outside the family circle into their support networks. This occurs through school and exposure to others through family activities. Children, and indeed the entire family, are disadvantaged when their parents have limited support networks.

FAMILY BOUNDARIES

Individuals who consider themselves part of a family do so within the context of family boundaries. A *boundary* is a symbolic line demarcating who is included in the family or subsystem and who is not, and who fits within a particular system or subsystem and who does not. Boundaries should exist between generations, as between the parent-child subsystems, and a boundary around parents allows them to

EP 2.1.7a

have a private life apart from their children. Parents share confidences and intimacy and trust that these issues will remain within that subsystem and not be shared with children and other people. Boundaries therefore keep some information private, whereas other information can pass through easily. Ideally, there should be clear but flexible boundaries between the parental subsystem and the child subsystem. In particular, boundaries around the parental subsystem are extremely important for the functioning of the family as a whole. Boundaries around the parental subsystem that are too porous allow information and behaviors to spill into the child subsystem. For example, failure to create clear boundaries might contribute to problems in the family such as sexual abuse or the "parentification" of a child. Boundaries between subsystems and individuals are also important indicators of family functioning. Boundaries between generations are particularly important in family work. Boundaries between parental and sibling subsystems should be clear and allow for role differentiation based on appropriate development and socially sanctioned functions.

Most theories about healthy families suggest that families should have not only flexible, clear boundaries with the outside world, but also well-established intergenerational boundaries. In other words, the parents should be partners in parenting the children. A dysfunctional intergenerational boundary can exist when one or more children form a coalition or alliance with one parent against the other. This is common in divorcing or otherwise conflicted families. Similarly, families experience intergenerational boundary problems when a parent abandons his or her role and a child assumes the parental role. These children are described as *parentified* because the child assumes an adult role, and the parent assumes the role of a child. This pattern can occur due to a variety of circumstances such as the presence of an alcoholic or physically or mentally ill parent. It is then common for one child to step into a parental role. If a child becomes primarily responsible for household chores, child care, or meeting the emotional needs of family members, intergenerational boundaries are breached. One of the authors worked in an outpatient mental health facility. One time when she was on call, she was approached by a young teenager whose mother was suffering from schizophrenia. His mother was going through a psychotic episode and it was his responsibility to get her hospitalized. He was a very responsible young man who had taken on the adult responsibility of caring for his mentally ill mother.

Healthy boundaries are therefore semipermeable. Healthy families have clear, flexible boundaries that are open and permeable enough to assimilate new thoughts, ideas, and resources when needed, but sufficiently closed that the family maintains a sense of identity and purpose. Flexible boundaries should also allow information and resources to leave the family freely. Boundaries must be firm enough to protect family members from harm outside the family. Ideally, closeness is neither overbearing nor intrusive (in other words, not enmeshed) to family members.

Family rules define who is and who is not included in a particular system or subsystem, as well as how they are included (Minuchin, 1974). Boundaries also help to regulate relationships. The nature of family boundaries varies according to definitions based on culture and lifestyle. In Native American communities, for example, the extended family plays a central role in raising children (Pimento, 1985) and in-laws are considered part of the primary family unit (Sutton & Broken Nose, 1996, 2005). A boundary related to lifestyle could include a family in which both parents have demanding jobs and have hired a live-in nanny or have a grandparent who lives with the family. Live-in nannies are sometimes considered members of an immediate family.

Some families have very definite boundaries, whereas in others the boundary between the family and the outside world is loose and unclear. When boundaries between the family and outside world are loose, children might be exposed to sexual abuse by someone outside the family. Children in loose-knit, disengaged families may be at risk of sexual abuse by perpetrators external to the family because these offenders are able to move in and out of the family freely, and children may lack adequate supervision and be exposed to high-risk adults. Part of a family assessment will involve looking at family boundaries in order to describe who belongs within the family system and who interacts with whom. Services most often target individuals within family boundaries.

In rigid families, boundaries surrounding the family unit are closed, and no information enters or leaves the family. Families with boundaries that are too closed or too open expose members to greater risk than do families with more balanced boundaries. In some families with rigid boundaries, for example, a child may be sexually abused or a woman may be battered, but family boundaries block this information from leaving the family since there are rules that govern the disclosure of information to the outside world. Sexual abuse and domestic violence victims are often isolated from the outside world, and their activities and connections with the outside world are limited—often by the abuser. The perpetrator controls family members and may convey to the victim that disclosure is a betrayal of family loyalty. Friendships, particularly for the victim, are tightly controlled. At the same time, incest is a profound breach of intergenerational and personal boundaries, whereas domestic violence is a violation of interpersonal boundaries. Gender also influences whether the abuse will be intrafamilial or extrafamilial. Male children usually have more independence in Western culture (and probably in most other cultures as well), making it more likely that they will encounter sexual abuse from people outside the family.

When families have rigid or overly closed external boundaries, the involvement of members with the outside world is restricted, creating difficulty in accessing external resources. To the detriment of many families, Western culture values autonomy and devalues interdependence (Garbarino, 1992). "Self-sufficient" families may come close to imploding before being able to ask for and accept external assistance. Garbarino (1992) has noted that a positive orientation toward relationships beyond the family and even beyond the larger kinship group is important to complement or counteract the idiosyncrasies of individual family patterns.

Internal family relationships fall along a continuum of rigidity or diffusion, known as disengagement and enmeshment. When family members are cut off from one another both emotionally and in terms of involvement, they are described as *disengaged,* or not very involved with one another (Kaplan, 1986; Minuchin, 1974). In disengaged families, members share few activities together. Members may be overly independent and autonomous and disconnected from other family members, having little influence on one another. Interpersonal boundaries that are too open and overlapping are known as *enmeshed,* and they weaken individual integrity and prevent family members from acting autonomously. Enmeshed relationships occur when family members are locked into tight relationships with one another, undermining individual autonomy. They may be extremely devoted to the family, sacrificing their autonomy for the family.

Families with rigid boundaries concerning the outside world often have enmeshed relationships within the family, whereas families that experience loose boundaries tend to be more disengaged with one another. Neglect is one sign of disengagement (Kaplan, 1986). Both disengaged and enmeshed family relationships can indicate poor functioning in families. This is particularly problematic as children get older, because adolescents strive to be independent of their families. When looking at boundaries, it is important to factor in culture and gender. For instance, when a male worldview is superimposed on family relationships, female relationships may appear to be enmeshed. Similarly, in some cultures the relationship among family members might be quite close, and it is important not to label the family as enmeshed. North American culture emphasizes individualism and independence, which are often apparent in family relationships.

Consider the following example illustrating a family's problems with boundaries:

Phil and Katie Gunn, a Caucasian couple in their mid-thirties, were referred to you by Family Court Mediation Services. The couple was seeing the court mediator as required during their divorce proceedings for the purpose of establishing child custody, visitation, and support payments for their only child, James, age 3. The mediator noted that James seemed to be having difficulties adjusting to his parents' divorce, showing aggression toward his classmates and his parents. The boy had been expelled from two day care centers for hitting and biting the other children. The parents reported that James's behavior ranged from angry rages to clinging when making transitions between his parents' separate homes.

Mr. Gunn initiated the divorce proceedings against his wife's wishes, though both report marital problems during most of their 10-year marriage. Mr. Gunn reported that the relationship had been tolerable until the birth of their son. Prior to James's arrival, Mr. Gunn described the marriage as "two people going our separate ways." He said he and his wife had little in common, few mutual friends, and different life goals. After James was born, his wife became very attached to the baby, and Mr. Gunn reported having felt excluded by his wife. She wouldn't let him hold or care for the baby unless he insisted. In addition, she breastfed James until he was 2 years old, against her husband's wishes. Mr. Gunn now believes his ex-wife to be angry about the divorce and especially upset that he initiated it. He describes her as "unable to move on with her life" and claims she is using James to "get revenge" on him and is also "trying to turn James against him." He reported that his ex-wife is over-involved with and overprotective of James and that consequently James is a "Mommy's boy, afraid of his own shadow."

Katie Gunn denies her ex-husband's allegations, though she does report that they "could have tried harder" to stay together. She reports that they went to marital counseling for a few months, but that Mr. Gunn felt it was not helping and dropped out. She said that this kind of behavior was typical of her ex-husband; that he withdraws emotionally at any sign of conflict and that he was "unable to establish a truly intimate relationship." She believes that she is now teaching James how to have a close relationship. She is fearful that Mr. Gunn cannot provide an appropriate male role model for her son. In sum, Katie Gunn feels her son's problems stem from her ex-husband's inability to establish an intimate relationship, while Phil Gunn feels James's problems originate from his mother's over-involvement with him.

A Family Operates According to Established Rules

Family rules determine what is allowed and what is forbidden in the family. As mentioned in the discussion of family boundaries, rules also regulate family members' behavior toward one another such as boundary setting and the degree of enmeshment or disengagement. Family rules are unwritten and are established through diverse mechanisms related to gender, age, culturally-linked expectations, personal experience, and so on. Understanding patterns of interaction within a family allows observers to understand implicit (unspoken) family rules. Family rules determine what behaviors are permitted in the family, including patterns of acceptable

EP 2.1.7a

and unacceptable behaviors. For example, all families have a power hierarchy, and rules govern the nature of this hierarchy (Minuchin, 1974). In many families, both mainstream and minority, the adult male possesses the most authority. Some families experience difficulties because children (often adolescents) are seen to have more power than their parents. Families vary both by the nature of the rules they have and by the quantity of rules that govern them. A family with few rules might be chaotic, whereas a family possessing many rules may be static and rigid.

Satir (1971) suggests that in order to function as an open system, the family needs rules to allow it to meet changes head-on. The family will inevitably encounter three kinds of changes:

1. Changes within family members that occur between birth and maturity in the use of perception of authority, independence, sexuality, and productivity
2. Changes between family members such as between a child and parent or husband and wife
3. Changes that are demanded by the social environment such as a new job, school, neighborhood, and so on. (p. 129)

As mentioned in the discussion on homeostasis, family rules act as a family thermostat, keeping the family environment comfortable and stable. Because they regulate behavior, rules can become entrenched but unexamined aspects of family life. Rules also contribute to predictable patterns of behaviors and interactions within the family. It is through this predictability and the establishment of patterns that homeostasis solidifies within the family. For example, family members know who will make supper one night, who will put the children to bed, and how parents will react if a child breaches the family's rules about speaking out of turn. Without at least an implicit (unspoken) understanding of the rules, families would be overcome by chaos, with no one knowing who is supposed to behave in a particular way and how others are to respond.

Families often inherit and adapt rules based on adult members' experiences with their own families while growing up. Conflict might occur throughout the family's life about which rules will come into play in this new family. In addition, when two people get together, they might also blend rules on the basis of their mutual experiences. Roles, for example, become established on the basis of family rules, such as how children will be cared for, who does the laundry, who works outside the home, and how the money is spent. Because rules are value-based, understanding them will tell workers much about what the family believes. Division of family labor evolves over time, and children might assume distinct roles. Gendered rules governing males and females in the family, for example, will tell workers a lot about beliefs concerning men and women. The rules surrounding gender also reveal how family boundaries are operating and how the family is connected to belief systems outside the family unit. Understanding family rules allows workers to see how family members view their relationships with one another.

It is possible to change the rules once they become clear and explicit. A family social worker might say, for example, "It appears that in this family, females are responsible for all the housework." However, family social workers should also be aware that there are *rules about rules* that dictate how members interpret them as well as how they change them. For example, in some families, talking about a parent's substance abuse might not be allowed. A family social worker might ask, "What rules does this family have concerning speaking about the father's drinking?"

EXERCISE 3.13   Unspoken Family Rules

Unspoken rules regulate all families. Identify some rules from the family in which you grew up. Describe how the rules differed according to age and gender of family members. Think of other family rules not related to age or gender. What were these rules? What rules have you brought from your family that are very important to you but that might conflict with the rules that another person might bring into a relationship with you?

Two types of change can occur within a family: *first-order* and *second-order* change (Watzlawick, Beavin, & Jackson, 1967). First- and second-order changes revolve around rules (Watzlawick, Weakland, & Fisch, 1974). First-order change occurs when the behavior of one family member changes, but *rules* governing the family stay the same. In second-order change, the rules are altered. First-order change does not permanently achieve the intended result, and it does not change the core attitudes and values causing the behaviors. Consequently, first-order change is likely to result in families reverting to their "normal" pre-crisis patterns because the change involves merely changing the superficial aspects of behaviors and interactions within a family. It might involve something as simple as parents making a conscious decision to stop yelling at their children and their children, in response, making a conscious decision to comply with their parents' requests (so long as the parents do not yell). First-order change might mean that people do less or more of something. This type of change is less enduring and less meaningful than second-order change.

Second-order change, on the other hand, is likely to generate more enduring family changes. Second-order change involves permanent attitude shifts that result in new behaviors. For example, a family worker might encounter a family in which the father makes the decision about where the family will go on vacation. Having other members make the decision will create first-order change. In this case, the behaviors of family members might change, but the rules about decision making are not examined at all. However, if the family worker initiated discussion in the family about how decisions are made, it would not be surprising to learn that the rule governing decision making is "the male is the boss."

Thus, in second-order change, people develop new ways of understanding their family life. Second-order change has many dimensions to it and involves changing attitudes, behaviors, relationships, and rules about interactions with one another. This type of change essentially involves changing the structure of the family, and, in the process, family functioning also changes. Once the rules governing behaviors and interactions within the family are altered, change is more likely to endure and be meaningful within the family.

FAMILY SUBSYSTEMS

As mentioned, family systems are made up of many different subsystems. Perhaps the simplest family structure is the single-parent family with one child. This family does not consist of subsystems made up of other family systems, but does consist of subsystems based on age, role, and gender. The more components (individuals) included in the family unit, the more subsystems that exist. Every family member is part of a number of different subsystems. The basic subsystems include the parental and sibling subsystems.

Spousal and Parental Subsystems

The emotional health of children in a family is affected by the emotional relationship between the parents.
—*Froma Walsh (1998)*

Early family workers recognized the centrality of parents in family functioning and child behavior (Minuchin, 1974; Satir, 1967; Satir & Baldwin, 1983). The parents perform critical roles that are integral to family functioning. As a couple, they must learn to negotiate their roles and support one another. Many times the roles are complementary.

Given the importance of parents in the formation and functioning of the family, it is important to understand the circumstances under which parents got together. Satir, for example, suggests that when people get together because of low self-esteem, problems ensue. It is important to involve the child in the parental subsystem and at the same time ensure that the child not be included in matters that pertain to the spouses as a couple. Doing so requires a delicate balancing act. Parental subsystems need their own space as individuals and as a couple, without interference from the children (Suissa, 2005). The parental subsystem also needs to set common rules and positions for the functioning of family members (Suissa, 2005).

Triangulation

Triangles are an important family systems concept and thus need to be uncovered by the family social worker in the assessment phase. Triangulation constitutes circular patterns with a third person involved. Triangles can appear when a dyadic relationship is under stress and unstable and a third party, often a child, is drawn into the relationship to stabilize the situation and diffuse the tension. Triangulation usually happens when tension or conflict appears in the relationship between two individuals. All intimate relationships contain the seeds of instability and sometimes require a third party to maintain stability. Triangles are not a preferred family subsystem because they allow the two people the opportunity to avoid dealing with their issues (Carter & McGoldrick, 1999, 2005; McGoldrick, Gerson, & Petry, 2008). They usually appear when something negative is going on in a relationship and are usually harmful to the well-being of the third party. According to Bowen (1978), triangulation occurs when people are insufficiently differentiated and when they are oversensitive to other important people.

The "original triangle" is the mother-father-baby triangle. The formation of this triangle diminishes the emotional intensity of the couple dyad as the parents strive to meet the needs of the newborn. This basic triangle is necessary and can be functional. When a triangle is functional, the parents are able to acknowledge and support the child having a healthy relationship with the other parent. Young babies require intense and selfless caretaking, and this caretaking omits the other parent. The other parent is not threatened by that parent-child relationship. Once children are introduced into the family, it is the parents who play the largest role in the behaviors, values, interactions, and so on. The nature and quality of the parental relationship has an enormous influence on the relationship among subsystems in the family. When the parental relationship encounters difficulty, problems often reverberate throughout the entire family. One of the biggest difficulties in families occurs when one child is pulled or triangulated into the parental relationship. The child is said to be triangulated.

However, at other times, such triangles become dysfunctional and problematic, particularly when the third person is used to allow two people to avoid facing their dyadic issues. In this instance, a triangle develops into a two-against-one scenario in which the third person reduces anxiety and stabilizes the relationship. The third person is hurt in some way through this triangulation. Nichols and Schwartz (2007) suggest that triangulation prevents personal and open one-on-one relationships from developing and evolving. This is then a problematic triangle. Although such triangles might create stability for the family, they also create problems for the unit. In a problematic triangle, trouble emerges when the parents trap a child in the middle of their conflict. "Each parent now sees the child as a potential: (1) Ally against the other mate; (2) Messenger through whom he can communicate with the other mate; and (3) Pacifier of the other mate" (Satir, 1967, p. 37).

One classic triangle occurs when two parents are locked in conflict over an extended time. One child might develop behaviors or symptoms that draw the parents' attention away from their troubled relationship. One example is when the parents argue and the child jumps in and draws attention to herself or himself. As the tension between the parents diminishes, the behaviors of the child become more intense and entrenched, stabilizing the family. The child with the problem behaviors is said to be scapegoated. All of these behaviors happen unconsciously. Yet the pattern must be interrupted since the child is being sacrificed for the marriage through the development of problems. When parents expect the child to choose sides, the child suffers. In one program, for example, workers found that parents redirected their attention toward the distress, anxiety, and attachment needs of their children rather than directing hostility toward one another (Kozwlowska & Hanney, 2002). Thus, unresolved or masked parental conflict can disrupt and even damage parent-child attachments. For example, some research suggests that preoccupied adults are likely to have children with ambivalent attachment (Rothbaum, Rosen, Ujiie, & Uchida, 2002).

Thus, marital conflict has a detrimental effect on children. Perhaps the most important awareness about triangulation is how a negative marital relationship is associated with a poor parent-child relationship. On one hand, the child might become the scapegoat, diverting parental anger onto himself or herself. Alternatively, the child might elicit other feelings such as concern and worry such that one or both parents satisfy their needs for closeness through the children. Some children are so drawn into the relationship that they comfort, defend, or distract parents during conflict. An extreme form of this might be when children develop severe problems to draw their parents' anger away from each other and to focus their parents on themselves. We recall that in one family we saw, the family was very child-centered and the children all slept in a family bed with their parents. Once the children started demanding their own beds (a unique twist for sure), the marriage broke up.

Another common family triangle occurs when two siblings are fighting and one or both tries to draw in a parent. "Katy just hit me," is one example of siblings triangulating parents. Therefore, one task of a family social worker is to understand the presence of triangles, assess how they operate within the family, and make plans to help the family *detriangulate* when problems exist. Sometimes triangles can include previous generations "whereby patterns of relating and functioning are transmitted over generations in a family" (Carter & McGoldrick, 1999, p. 438; Carter & McGoldrick, 2005). McGoldrick, Gerson, and Petry (2008) give a fascinating account of the role of triangles in Freud's life.

Which child is selected to be the third arm of a problematic triangle depends on several factors, most of which are unique to a particular family. It may be based on a special characteristic of the child, such as a disability or a child that reminds one parent of another person. Other possible factors might include birth order, gender of the child, or age. Alternatively, the child might be a stepchild, adopted child, or a child with special needs such as a child with ADHD. It is important to explore all possibilities regarding how this child came to fill this particular role in this particular family.

Family workers can easily be triangulated into the family system. Suissa (2004) urges them to beware of the pitfalls of a social worker entering into an alliance with one family member against another. This alliance may be viewed by another family member as a "hostile coalition" (p. 20). Workers may experience a pull to support either the parental subsystem or the autonomy and well-being of the child. Sometimes, workers side with one member of the family. For example, if in the worker's opinion a parent is too harsh with an adolescent, the worker might develop loyalty to the teen, colluding against the parent. Should this behavior become a pattern, it would not be surprising to see the parent refuse to participate in further family work. To prevent worker blind spots from interfering with family work, family workers should reflect on issues from their own family of origin and anticipate what personal issues might blind them to the real issues in the family. For example, some parents, in discussing their experiences in a family preservation program, reported feeling resentful when social workers allied themselves with some family members at the expense of others. Forming an alliance with a child is perceived as a sabotage of parental authority (Coleman & Collins, 1997). For this reason, worker neutrality is usually recommended, unless of course a family member is at immediate risk.

Workers also can be triangulated into a family when secrets are shared in the absence of one family member (Brendel & Nelson, 1999). This triangulation is very challenging for the worker, who faces an ethical dilemma about what to do with the secret. On one hand, the worker is bound by confidentiality; however, on the other hand, the worker is acutely aware of the impact of the secret on family functioning. Similarly, sharing the information breaks a trust with the person who disclosed. In addition, the worker might be colluding with family dysfunction by keeping the secret. According to the International Association of Marriage and Family Counselors, confidences gained in individual work are not to be shared without permission. At the same time, if these confidences interfere with family work, the worker might have to terminate work with the family (cited in Brendel & Nelson, 1999, p. 113). There are also situations in which it is necessary to divulge the secret, such as in sexual abuse disclosure. It is only fair to tell the informer that you have a professional and legal obligation to report this information.

The Sibling Subsystem: Fellow Travelers

In a big family the first child is kind of like the first pancake. If it's not perfect, that's okay, there are a lot more coming along!
—Antonin Scalia (www.Bartleby.com)

As siblings we were inextricably bound, even though our connections were loose and frayed..... And each time we met, we discovered to our surprise and dismay how quickly the intensity of childhood feelings reappeared.... No matter how old we got or how often we tried to show another face, reality was filtered through yesterday's memories.
—Jane Mersky Leder (www.Bartleby.com)

We believe that the sibling subsystem is the most ignored subsystem in family work and in family theory. Yet sibling relationships are the first context through which children learn to relate with peers. Siblings teach each other about peer relationships and cooperation. Adler (cited in Prochaska & Norcross, 2003) provides an intriguing analysis of the impact of birth order on child and personality development. For most people, the sibling relationship is lifelong because siblings usually outlive parents and the sibling bond is second only to the parent-child bond in importance (McGoldrick, Watson, & Benton, 2005). In fact, the death of a child is a major family life cycle disruption that few families are adequately prepared to handle. Because of the centrality of sibling relationships in a person's life, some suggest having a sibling session without parents to gain an understanding of family issues (McGoldrick, Watson, & Benton, 1999, 2005). The nature of sibling bonds ranges between close and conflictual relationships. Moreover, there may be a combination of siblings, stepsiblings and half-siblings. In looking at sibling relationships, age spacing is probably an important issue and determines the amount of time siblings spend together as children.

Sibling relationships can be close, distant, or conflicted. Some suggest that sibling conflict and abuse is the most common type of conflict within families (Straus, Gelles, & Steinmetz, 1980). Because sibling conflict might be predictive of later anti-social behaviors in adolescents, helping siblings develop interpersonal competence to improve sibling relationships is important (Kramer & Radley, 1997). Doing so will assist children in the development of both peer and sibling relationships.

Early writings about sibling rivalry fail to do justice to the powerful bonds that siblings might experience throughout a lifetime. The nature of the sibling relationship differs on the basis of a number of factors such as age, gender, physical challenges, and sexual orientation, to name a few (McGoldrick, Watson, & Benton, 1999, 2005). For example, children who are close in age share similar family life cycle issues, whereas children in families with a wide spread in children's ages have very divergent experiences. In addition, we hear much about the destinies of older versus younger children in the family. For example, it is suggested that older children are more likely to be leaders, whereas younger children are more pampered and may expect others to do things for them. Moreover, with the declining birth rate, families with only one child are becoming more common; some suggest that children without siblings are more adult-oriented and their challenge is to learn to relate to peers (McGoldrick, Watson, & Benton, 1999).

Although many cultures prefer male children to female children, families with female children derive much benefit (McGoldrick, Watson, & Benton, 1999, 2005). In large families, older female children are likely to assume caretaking responsibility for younger siblings.

When a problematic triangle involving one of the siblings appears in the family, it is important to remember that despite the fact that only one child has a "problem," the problem affects every other family member. In many ways, when there is a dysfunctional parent-parent-child triangle, this triangle receives the most attention from the family worker. At the same time, other children in the family might be ignored. This is a mistake! Other children in the family have unique insights and needs when their family is suffering, and ignoring them is not recommended. It is our experience that when one sibling is in pain, the other children react to that pain. We recall a family in which the father was sexually abusing the oldest sister. The worker met individually with the other children in the family and was very touched by the sensitivity and concerns each of these children expressed about what was happening in their family. Moreover, when the worker asked one child, "What do you worry about?," the child unveiled a litany of worries about his family that kept him awake and crying every night. Until that point, no one had thought to ask him what he was going through. He related worries about his sister, his mother, his other siblings, his father, and the family as a whole, and felt very much alone with his heartaches.

Birth order is also an interesting facet in the personality profiles of children. For example, oldest children are likely to be over-responsible and conscientious, while the oldest daughter is also responsible and cares for others. By comparison, middle children risk being lost in the family and youngest children have a sense of specialness that allows self-indulgence. Disabled children play a unique role in the family by requiring adjustment and caretaking responsibilities of the siblings. Siblings respond to the disabled child and to the parents' distress about the needs of the child (McGoldrick, Watson, & Benton, 2005).

Family System Disruptions

It is rare for a family to pass through its entire cycle without any disruption. Death, divorce, separation, mental illness, chronic illness, and disability are but six examples of how a family's life course might be disrupted. With every disruption, it is important to find out how members of the family coped as well as what happened to the marriage at each critical point.

For example, the birth of a physically or mentally challenged child poses many demands on the family system. Both the nature and severity of the disability determine the impact on the family unit as well as the ability of the family to cope with the challenges. The birth of this child affects both parents and siblings. At the very least, the birth of any child places a family in a state of disequilibrium. However, the extra emotional, physical, and financial demands of a disabled child create additional burdens on the entire family unit, provoking a family crisis as family members scramble to reestablish homeostasis. The arrival of a disabled child into a family is usually unplanned, and parents experience stress and disruption on many levels. Parents may place additional demands on other children in the family to assist with caretaking, although caretaking expectations vary widely from family to family. "Small families tend to experience more pressure when there is a handicapped child because there are fewer siblings to share the responsibility" (McGoldrick, Watson, & Benton, 1999, p. 148). Age and gender influence the expectations placed on other children in the family. Sometimes families must struggle with institutionalizing the disabled child. If the child remains at home, parents must then decide what happens during the "launching" phase. Should the child remain with the parents for life? If this is the case, what happens when the parents die? Alternatively, parents may struggle with placing the disabled child in a group home or institution when the child reaches adulthood or even earlier.

Death is another family disruption that leaves "a hole in the fabric of family life ... and disrupts established patterns of interaction" (Walsh, 1998, p. 187). Walsh suggests that, "the ability to accept loss is at the heart of all skills in healthy family systems" (p. 178). When a family member dies, the system experiences upheaval as members maneuver to adapt to the loss. Some loss is expected, as in the death of an elderly parent or grandparent. Other losses, such as the death of a child or a young spouse, are unexpected and may aggravate and prolong the grieving process (McGoldrick & Walsh, 1999, 2005). When a family member dies, homeostasis is disrupted as others attempt to fill the void left by the departed member. McGoldrick and Walsh suggest paying special attention when the birth of a child or a marriage coincides with a death because it may interfere with parenting or assume a replacement function. Family adaptation is also challenged if the deceased member was the breadwinner or filled an otherwise central instrumental or affective role in the family. When the loss is of a child, the marital relationship becomes particularly vulnerable (1999, p. 141). And women typically outlive men, making widowhood for many a grim reality.

Death through suicide has long-lasting repercussions within the family. Suicide demands that surviving family members develop individual interpretations of the act. At the same time, they must renegotiate ongoing relationships with surviving family members. One important aspect of family reorganization is the need to recognize and respect differences in grief reactions and coping styles among members of the family. These differences might entail a lack of synchronicity in grieving. Interpersonal tension and marital discord may result from grief incongruence between surviving adult partners, and family members may find themselves out of step with one another as they seek to regain personal and family balance. One challenge for adult survivors is to understand why. The search for meaning is one element of children's grief, but not the central agonizing and organizing theme for child survivors. Children also worry about losing the surviving parent and may feel personally responsible for the suicide. Funeral rituals vary according to culture, and family social workers should investigate what they are and what death means to a family (Barlow & Coleman, 2004; Barlow & Coleman, 2003).

Alcohol and other substance abuse problems also cause disruption in a family system. It is a particularly challenging problem to deal with because denial is a major issue (Hudak, Krestan, & Bepko, 1999, 2005). Alcoholism, affecting between 10 and 15 percent of the population, is progressive and usually ends in either abstinence or death (p. 456). It is impacted by gender, race, and amount of reinforcement one receives for drinking, in combination with a host of other sociodemographic factors. Hudak and colleagues provide some insight into the presence of addiction in the family, noting that family boundaries may be too rigid or diffuse. There may also be role reversal in which a child is parentified by stepping in and assuming the role of the disabled caretaker. When alcoholism is advanced, the family may become socially isolated from extended kin and from the community. The authors suggest beginning assessment with the basic question: How much pain has been caused by drinking? (p. 459). This pain can be far-reaching and involve such difficulties as unemployment; illness; marital conflict; domestic violence; depression; sexual, physical, or emotional abuse; and so on. Accessing specialized addiction services can be useful, and it is important to remember that denial can and usually does affect every family member. Despite the pain and family upheaval caused by the substance abuse, it may be difficult for the addicted member to admit to the problem.

We refer you to the "stages of change" model developed by Prochaska and DiClemente as a source for understanding denial on the part of the alcoholic and developing some options about how to handle alcoholics who do not believe they have a problem. This model suggests that when a problem arises (not exclusive to addictions), individuals progress through different phases of admitting and taking action on the problem:

- Precontemplation (I do not have a problem and have no intention to change.)
- Contemplation (I have a problem but have not formulated a plan for change.)
- Preparation (I have a problem and will try to find a solution.)
- Action (I am going to change my behavior, environment, or experiences.)
- Maintenance (I have dealt with my problem and will make changes to ensure that these changes last.)
- Termination (I have successfully dealt with my problem for five years and have no temptation to resume my problematic behaviors.)

Because the family patterns discussed in the previous sections become set and organized around the problem over time, intervention is necessary even after the alcoholic member stops drinking. The family will need to address family dynamics that have solidified around the problematic drinking. Hudak and colleagues warn that early sobriety may be a difficult time for the entire family.

Immigration creates another disruption in family dynamics, particularly when immigration occurs in a stepwise fashion, with one adult immigrating and getting established before sending for the other family members. Immigrant children in particular can feel the impact of family disruption. Immigrant families are in constant flux, as they must constantly reorganize to accommodate the loss and gain of family members. In addition, relationships may be marked by several responses such as grief, guilt, and detachment as the family proceeds through the process.

Multigenerational Transmission of Patterns

Murray Bowen (1978) formulated ideas to capture how families transmit values, beliefs, and behaviors from one generation to another. He was fascinated by the historical context of family patterns as they are passed down from one generation to another. In particular, Bowen was concerned with family patterns over several generations such that children leave home and marry partners with similar levels of differentiation to themselves (Piercy & Sprenkle, 1986).

Genograms (discussed in Chapter 8) have the unique capability of capturing these intergenerational patterns. Bowen (1978) determined that patterns occur over several generations, suggesting that learning in a family over generations plays a role in the development of symptoms. Bowen believed that multigenerational relationship patterns of reciprocal functioning between spouses and child were associated with the same patterns in the nuclear family and that symptoms were reproduced in the areas of physical, emotional, and social functioning. For example, the quality of infants' attachments to their mothers is associated with the dynamics observed in the grandmother-mother relationship (Krechmar & Jacobvitch, 2002).

The core of Bowen's theory is differentiation of self, which affects key family relationships. Differentiated people are able to maintain a psychological separation from others, separate the emotions and the intellect, and have independence of self from others. The more one is differentiated, the easier it is to avoid being drawn into the dysfunctional patterns of other family members. In all families, members develop on a continuum based on differentiating the self, and the degree of differentiation is determined, in part, by the relationship patterns in a particular family. People are attracted to partners who have similar levels of differentiation and these levels of differentiation are reproduced over multiple generations. In North America, high levels of differentiation are preferable to low levels of differentiation.

"The multigenerational transmission concept" is that the roots of the most severe human problems, as well as the highest levels of human adaptation, are generations deep (Bowen, 1978).

CHAPTER SUMMARY

The family systems approach allows the family social worker to assess a family within the context of interactions and relationships. The systems approach complements the developmental approach. The developmental approach considers stages in the family's life cycle. With a systems perspective, relationships at each stage of the family life cycle are the focus of assessment.

EP 2.1.9a

From a systems view, the social worker focuses on the family as a whole, rather than on individual family members. The family is seen as trying to achieve a balance between change and stability. Change that affects one member affects the whole family. Causality is circular rather than linear. The family system includes many subsystems and also is part of larger suprasystems.

KEY TERMS

Circular causality Circular causality relates to patterned and repetitive interactions between a dyad within a family. In circular interactions, individuals both affect and are affected by the other person in the dyad in a mutually influencing way.

Family boundaries   A boundary is a symbolic line demarcating who is included in the family or subsystem and who is not, and who fits within a particular system or subsystem.

Family systems   A system is a unit of interactional components. Systems become patterned based on their interactions. A family system consists of individuals interacting with each other in the family. Family system interactions and relationships are reciprocal, patterned, and repetitive.

Homeostasis   Is a term used to describe the need for a family system to act in ways to achieve balance in relationships. Families need homeostasis for stability, order, and consistency.

Subsystems   The family system forms multileveled structures of systems within systems. Subsystems can consist of two or more relationships with unique ways of operating, for example, the marital subsystem, parental subsystem, and child subsystem.

SUGGESTED READINGS

Minuchin, S. (1974). *Families and family therapy*. Cambridge, MS: Harvard University Press. An early classic text by Minuchin outlining the basic principles related to structural family therapy.

Satir, V. (1983). *Conjoint family therapy* (3rd ed.). Palo Alto, CA: Science and Behavior. Originally published in 1964, this is a seminal book written in bullet form. It contains a wealth of information on communication theory within families, stressing the dynamics behind marriage and communication problems and depicting parents as "architects of the family." The book addresses normal family issues, including mate selection, stresses of family life, communication problems, and solutions within the family.

Von Bertalanffy, L. (1968). *General system theory*. New York: Braziller. This classic book was the catalyst behind the adaptation of social systems theory to family systems theory. This book will help readers understand the genesis of family systems theory and could be used as an initiation to the field of family work.

Watzlawick, P., Beavin, J., & Jackson, D. (1967). *Pragmatics of human communication*. New York, NY: W.W. Norton. This book is a classic analysis of communication. The principles of communication outlined in this book will provide the groundwork for anyone wanting to develop expertise in working with families. The book contains many gems and treasures that are highly applicable to social work practice. For example, one axiom of communication is that "You cannot NOT communicate."

COMPETENCY NOTES

EP 2.1.7a. Utilize conceptual frameworks to guide the processes of assessment, intervention, and evaluation: Assumptions about family work underlie this approach. These include conceptual framework concepts from systems theory, such as circularity and boundaries.

EP 2.1.9a. Continuously discover, appraise, and attend to changing locales, populations, scientific and technological developments, and emerging societal trends to provide relevant services: Contexts of practice include family systems and subsystems. Examples are spousal, parental, and sibling subsystems, as well as multigenerational systems.

Other things may change us, but we start and end with the family.
— Anthony Brandt (www.Bartleby.com)

CHAPTER 4

Family Development and the Life Cycle

CHAPTER CONTENTS

LEARNING OBJECTIVES

- Conceptual: Identify the various developmental family stages.

- Perceptual: Observe the challenges of family developmental tasks.

- Valuational/Attitudinal: Value the strengths of families to meet developmental challenges.

- Behavioral: Ask questions about various family developmental challenges, and use knowledge about family development to intervene effectively with families.

UNDERSTANDING A DEVELOPMENTAL PERSPECTIVE

One assessment task for family social workers is to understand how a family is functioning at particular points in its evolution. In this chapter we build on family systems theory by discussing family development, an important theoretical framework with which to understand the predictable growth and crises of family life. Most people are familiar with stages of child and adult development, but few are aware of family developmental stages. Knowledge about the family life cycle focuses on the developmental tasks facing families and their members and reveals why family stress appears at critical points of development (Duvall, 1957; Carter & McGoldrick, 1988, 1999, 2005; Laszloffy, 2002). It can also help family social workers understand how some families get derailed at certain points in time.

Understanding family development can also help the family social worker understand whether a family is meeting social expectations for child rearing (Holman, 1983). It can also predict issues and tasks that families will face down the road. Few families move seamlessly from one stage to another, and problems are especially likely to appear during vulnerable developmental stages such as coupling, the birth of the first child, or adolescence. For example, one well-known study depicted marital satisfaction as a roller coaster, with significant decreases in marital satisfaction beginning early in marriage and continuing a slide until children leave home (Olson, 1981). Nevertheless, individual variations in the family life cycle as well as marital satisfaction do occur.

We begin our discussion by outlining developmental stages that may be typical for middle-class families. This model is merely a template and is based on the assumption that families remain intact from formation to death. Yet, the model has been criticized for some fundamental weaknesses. The first is that it assumes that all families develop in the same way (Laszloffy, 2002), failing to account for diverse family forms such as never-married, childless couples; divorced parents; or gay and lesbian couples (who are legally denied the right to get married in many jurisdictions). The family life cycle fails to capture cultural nuances as well. Second, the model assumes that the stages are sequential and linear and that families enter and exit the cycle at the same points. We point out, however, that the sequential and linear model of family development is probably the exception to the rule. Rather than being a closed group, membership in a modern family is more fluid than the family life cycle portrays. No single list of stages is sufficient or inclusive, and the breakdown of stages is arbitrary (Carter & McGoldrick, 1999). Nor is the family life cycle the same for all kinds of families (Carter & McGoldrick, 2005).

This model is useful but has several other shortcomings. First, because each family is unique, family members' developmental stages vary greatly. Second, developmental models tend to focus only on the milestones of one family member, usually the eldest child (Becvar & Becvar, 1996). For example, how would we classify a family that included both a newborn child and a teenager who was ready to leave home? Where would a never-married single parent fit into the family developmental life cycle? Needless to say, there are many variations of the family life cycle. Breunlin (1988), for example, depicts family transitions as moving back and forth between stages rather than as a linear progression from one stage to the next.

Families therefore vary in the expression of each stage of development according to personal experiences, socioeconomic circumstances, culture, religion, sexual orientation, and historical context. Childbearing now often occurs later in life, many people do not remarry after a relationship ends, and others are choosing never to get married. Moreover, forces related to racism, sexism, homophobia, classism, and ageism also create differences in family life cycle patterns (Carter & McGoldrick, 1999, 2005). Finally, immigration to North America produces unique permutations in family life cycle patterns. The final criticism is that the model is biased toward a single generational level (Laszloffy, 2002). For example, the Launching Stage emphasizes the tasks of parents and focuses less on the young person who is leaving home.

We discuss variations of family development under these divergent themes. However, groups are not homogeneous, and creating immutable patterns risks pigeonholing families. We do not intend to present stereotypes, and we encourage the reader to recognize that cultures and subcultures have enormous internal diversity. Finally, we would like to emphasize that although the sequential, linear model of family development does not apply to all families, all families do evolve and develop over time and face developmental tasks and challenges, even though their order may differ.

A word of caution is in order. It has been our experience that when some students hear that the linear family life cycle model does not apply to most families, they decide that *nothing* about the family life cycle is applicable. This is simply not true. For sure, the ordering is not necessarily from Point A to Point B to Point C and so on. Nevertheless, all families experience transition points related to their development, and each transition point poses challenges. And, each challenge requires a concerted response on the part of the family.

FAMILY DIVERSITY ACROSS THE LIFE CYCLE

Culture

Culture has an enormous impact on how the family life cycle unfolds, starting with how a family defines itself. Differences in the processes that families go through include the weight given to each transition, the intergenerational struggles, determination of responsibilities and obligations based on gender roles, expectations about motherhood and fatherhood, and how children of different genders are treated (Moore Hines, Garcia Preto, McGoldrick, Almeida, & Weltma, 2005). In addition, the expectations of various cultural groups differ with regard to how much intergenerational sharing and dependence should occur between aging parents and adult children. When the cultural rules for dealing with these stages are devalued, the stresses on the family increase (p. 71). Culture also impacts how families are formed, the timing of when children leave their families, how close they remain to their families, how the generations relate, and the level of intimacy within the families. The underlying message of our discussion in this section is that all cultures are heterogeneous in terms of life cycle practices.

EXERCISE 4.1   Impact of Culture on Your Family

What is your cultural heritage? How is your cultural heritage expressed in terms of:

1. Definition of family
2. Gender roles
3. Family rituals during transitions
4. Relationship among generations
5. History of your culture

After you have described how your family expressed itself in terms of these five areas, try to sort out how much was unique to your particular family and how much culture influenced your family. What are the implications for family work?

Some cultures define family as the immediate nuclear family, whereas others incorporate extended kin, ancestors, and friends. The dominant Anglo definition focuses on the nuclear family, whereas African American families include an expanded kin network. Chinese families focus on ancestors, and Italians would say that there is no such thing as the nuclear family—as they include several generations of extended kin in their notion of family (McGoldrick & Giordano, 1996; Moore Hines, Garcia Preto, McGoldrick, Almeida, & Weltman, 2005). In some cultural groups, relationships with extended family and kin networks are based on interdependence, group orientation, and reliance on others. Similarly, Puerto Ricans believe so strongly in family obligation that it affects interaction with other groups (Lum, 1992).

Culture affects how families go through the family life cycle. They vary in how they break down the family life stages as well as in their definitions of the tasks at each stage. Moreover, even several generations after immigration, the family life cycle patterns of various groups are unique (Carter & McGoldrick, 2005, p. 3). For example, Mexican-American families experience a shorter adolescence, but longer courtship, period. For other cultures, the involvement of the extended family marks a unique relationship and different perspective on such stages as childbirth, launching young adults into the world, and the formation of family units. Additionally, a daughter from India is expected to live with her parents until she is married, and a grandmother in a Japanese family may take an active role in raising young grandchildren. Poor African American families experience a condensed life cycle in which the generational cycle seems to overlap (Moore Hines, Preto, McGoldrick, Almeida, & Weltman, 1999). In addition, the percentage of single-parent families has increased in these households (p. 72).

Cultural values about family practices that a member from another culture may label as "strange" or "unhealthy" also provide structure for families. Family activities and rituals will probably also diverge from the practices of the dominant culture, with evident differences in the importance of various transitions (Moore Hines, Garcia Preto, McGoldrick, Almeida, & Weltma, 2005). Both the Irish and African Americans, for example, view death as the most important life cycle transition whereas for Italian and Polish families, weddings are central to the family life cycle (p. 70). As mentioned in Chapter 2, culture affects how families acknowledge transitions such as weddings and deaths. *My Big Fat Greek Wedding*, although overstated, does point out the importance of the wedding tradition in Greek culture. What other movies can you think of that mark family transitions in culturally unique ways?

In terms of intergenerational struggles, Anglo families strongly believe in children leaving home and becoming independent, whereas Italian families work hard to keep their children at home (Moore Hines, Garcia Preto, McGoldrick, Almeida, & Weltman, 2005). Moreover, Indian values perceive adolescent struggles concerning independence as disloyalty to both family and culture (p. 82), and Jewish children often enter counseling because of difficulty with issues of enmeshment (p. 84)

Gender roles and expectations and how parents relate to their children also play out through culture. In Latino families, women are heavily pressured to assume caretaking roles, whereas men are expected to assume financial responsibility for elderly parents, younger siblings, and even nieces and nephews (Moore Hines, Garcia Preto, McGoldrick, Almeida, & Weltman, 2005). This pattern contrasts with Irish families in which fathers play a peripheral role in intergenerational family relationships while mothers are at the center (p. 78).

There is evidence that recent immigrants face unique challenges. They have higher rates of unemployment and underemployment, which combined with the process of adjusting to a new country and culture places additional burdens on the family. The process of immigration involves finding a job, housing, and services in addition to getting established in a community, obtaining culturally preferred food, registering children in school, and adapting to a different climate. Gender roles might also be different, and family and support networks may not be available. Families face issues related to acculturation as well as challenges to values, expectations, and norms.

Families from various ethnic groups show family life cycle variations not seen in the mainstream family life cycle. For example, the African American family may consist of an extensive kin network, often including more than one household. Several families may live under the same roof, and children may reside in a kinship household different from the one in which they were born. Recent immigrants to North America often show cultural variations in which the previous generation exerts control over the new family, and families function as collective units (Lum, 1992).

Social Class

Many families seen by family social workers lack necessary economic and social resources; often they are politically powerless, socially disenfranchised, and likely to experience unemployment or job instability. Many also experience oppression by more powerful groups, are members of an ethnic minority, and are prone— because of all these issues—to experience multiple difficulties. Kliman and Madsen (1999, 2005) refer to these groups as the "working class" or the "underclass." They live with little hope and struggle to get daily basic needs met. Social class is affected by factors such as culture, ethnicity, education, and gender. "Class weaves into personal, family, and community ties to local, national, and global economies" (p. 90). It can affect how one enters the labor market and the obstacles that inform this entry. Moreover, one of the defining characteristics of class concerns the options and resources available to families for addressing developmental challenges in the family life cycle (p. 93).

Poverty is a poor buffer against pressures in the family, particularly those imposed by issues in the family life cycle (Kliman & Madsen, 2005). Poverty decreases life span. It also collapses the time in which families experience life cycle stages, causes children to leave home earlier and set up their own families at younger ages, makes grandparenting occur earlier, decreases educational opportunities, and contributes to decreased employment opportunities. Economic conditions today are very different than those encountered by previous generations, making it more difficult for young adults to leave home, purchase their own homes, or even live independently when they are in their twenties. Young people who grow up in impoverished families risk dropping out of school early and encounter an elevated risk of unemployment. Early pregnancy among some teen girls means that they will start their life's journey on shaky ground. Moreover, "[c]ompressed intervals create role ambiguity and confusion for family members who must take on responsibilities before they are ready" (Kliman & Madsen, 2005, p. 94).

Conversely, in economically advantaged families, young people are extending the family life cycle by remaining financially dependent and continuing with their education.

They are marrying later and having children at older ages. Childhood in these families takes on a very different tone than for children who grow up in poor families. Children in economically advantaged families may leave and return home many times, leading to the term *boomerang children*. Issues related to social class are best dealt with ecologically when appropriate. In addition, family social workers need to be aware of their biases, many of which stem from a middle-class, privileged vantage point.

Family social workers who herald from economically advantaged and disadvantaged families will differ on how they view the family life cycle in terms of what is considered normal and expected behaviors and attitudes.

EXERCISE 4.2 Navigating Social Class

It is easy to overlook the values embedded in social class. These values might include beliefs about education, gender roles, and politics. Break into small groups and try to identify values that might be part of the underclass, working class, professional/managerial class, and business-owning class. Compare your answers with the rest of the class's. What are the implications for family work?

Gender

The conundrum of responsibility without power has long characterized women's lives.
—McGoldrick, 1999b, p. 107

We discuss gender in more detail in Chapter 13. Social changes affecting women are affecting their roles within the family and their movement through the family life cycle. Compared to thirty years ago, women are better educated and are marrying later. They are less likely to tolerate abuse when alternatives allowed by education and employment are available to them. Modern contraception ensures smaller families and less financial dependence on a partner. More education and greater involvement in the workforce ensures that having children is delayed and that the number of children in a family is smaller than in the previous generation. "Few families can afford to have children … unless both husband and wife have paying jobs" (McGoldrick, 2005c, p. 110). This has led fathers to be more involved with all aspects of child care (p. 111). Moreover, a growing phenomenon in the family life cycle concerns the "sandwich generation" of women who are concurrently taking care of both their children and aging parents. While responsibilities for child rearing have changed, women still assume most of the responsibility for the household. Furthermore, women continue to devote more time to childcare activities than their male partners, even when their partners are unemployed.

However, fathers are increasing their level of involvement in their children's lives. This involvement benefits the whole family (Lero, Ashbourne, & Whitehead, 2006). For example, studies reveal that when fathers are involved in child rearing in a major way, sons become more empathic than sons raised in traditional ways (McGoldrick & Carter, 2005, p. 32).

Some women stay out of the paid workforce to raise children, and others work outside the home throughout their lives. Each choice brings with it unique challenges. For example, the rise of women in the workforce has afforded some families more disposable income while families living on one income or on social assistance struggle to make ends meet. Yet, there may be more time in one-income families for at least one parent to be more involved in their children's lives by connecting with their school and other activities. The arrival of children announces a return to traditional gender roles (Rosen, 2005). While this return disadvantages women, it also disadvantages men, whose only option is to work (p. 128). Once old age beckons, men are more likely to die earlier than women, leaving many women isolated and financially destitute.

Similarly, males have unique challenges in the family life cycle. Women are becoming more financially independent, making marriage more dependent on the quality of the relationship rather than on financial dependency. Males are also facing threats including the erosion of male prerogative in marriage and increased demands to be more involved with child care (beyond just "helping out") and domestic chores. When a family experiences divorce, custody is usually awarded to the mother.

The role of fathers throughout the family life cycle is also changing. Their involvement with children should not be underestimated since they assume a unique role and account for more variation in certain types of positive child outcomes such as autonomous exploration and better academic performance, behavior, attitudes, and relationships in school (Ange, 2006). Moreover, fathers who are actively involved and supportive have children who are more prosocial, are psychologically well adjusted, perform better in school, and exhibit less antisocial behavior. When fathers, in particular, view the classroom teacher as a positive resource, the child has more satisfying and less conflictual relationships with teachers. Research has led Ange (2006) to conclude that fathers do matter, making it necessary to include them in family work. Our belief is that unless there are exceptional circumstances, such as abuse, children need their fathers. Another benefit of equal parenting is that "the road to a better marital relationship often goes through a shared, collegial parenthood in which both are active and mutually respected partners" (Rosen, 2005, p. 135).

For a number of reasons, such as military service, incarceration, or out-of-town employment, some fathers are not involved in the day-to-day activity of the family. They are therefore transitioning in and out of their children's lives to varying degrees with protracted absences in between. For those parents who are still in a partnership, the role of the mother is important when the father is absent, because she assumes the bulk of caregiving and must facilitate the father-child relationship. This makes the father vulnerable to experiencing tensions upon re-entry into the family. Mothers who have assumed the onus of child care will have developed routines, coping strategies, and disciplinary techniques on their own, which will be followed by a period of readjustment upon the spouse's return. When fathers are separated or divorced from their children's mother and are living and working at a geographic distance from their children, this distance may pose additional challenges to maintaining a post-separation father-child relationship (Lero, Ashbourne, & Whitehead, 2006).

Immigration

Globalization is creating unique circumstances for families who immigrate to North America. In the United States, one-fifth of the nation's children are growing up in immigrant homes (Suarez-Orozco, Todorova, & Louie, 2002). A common way of immigrating involves one family member moving ahead of other family members to get established in the new location. When it is the mother who initiates immigration, children are often left in the care of the extended family. All family relationships are affected by the upheaval; both children and spouses may become disengaged in the process. Reunification of the entire family unit can be complicated. If children are left behind, they may develop attachments to their caretakers in their home country.

Because full immigration can take many years and is impacted by the tasks of settling into a new environment, it affects the family life cycle in powerful ways. When working with an immigrant family, it is important that the family social worker first understand the reasons for immigration. The family social worker must also understand who came with the family and who remained behind. The final point is to understand the culture in the immigrants' homeland, especially the roles of women, attitudes toward minority groups, political situation, and religion. What were the hopes and expectations of the family? Did the family come to the new land because of positive or negative reasons? For example, did they flee political turmoil in their homeland or did they move for greater opportunity? It is important to remember that every group in North America except indigenous peoples is or has been immigrants at one time or another. People who flee war-torn homelands come to a new country for very different reasons than those seeking economic security.

Immigrating is one of the most stressful experiences that a family can undergo, altering the family life cycle in unique ways. For example, young adults might adapt to the new culture more easily (Hernandez & McGoldrick, 1999, 2005); the older the person, the more challenging the move may be. When people come as a couple, uneven levels of adaptation might cause tension in the home (p. 175). When families with children migrate, family structural hierarchies and traditional roles might be disrupted because young children tend to acculturate more quickly than their parents (p. 177). Sometimes immigration can precipitate role reversal, such as when children are expected to translate for their parents. Children can also be caught between their parents' culture and the new culture, producing unique stress points within the family.

EXERCISE 4.3 Three Generations of Men and Women

EP 2.1.4a

Break the class into small groups. Each student will take turns comparing gender roles in the family for the past three generations: grandparents, parents, and the present generation. How have these roles changed? How have these roles affected the family life cycle?

EP 2.1.7a

DEVELOPMENTAL STAGES

The family is the context within which individuals grow and develop throughout a lifetime. Relationships with parents, siblings, and other family members change as they move along the life cycle (Carter & McGoldrick, 1999, 2005). It is during transitional periods that relationships and the family system are more vulnerable to stress.

EP 2.1.7b

Stress is greatest at the transition points, when families are required to rebalance, redefine, and realign their relationships (Carter & McGoldrick, 2005, p. 3; Laszloffy, 2002). If a family becomes stuck in a transition, it is said to have experienced a "snag point" (Pittman, cited in Laszloffy, 2002). Moreover, when stressful family events co-occur and are not resolved, they can be the catalyst for future difficulties. Similarly, multigenerational issues surrounding particular individuals can intrude at any time.

Because family relationships and behavioral expectations in different stages progress in relatively predictable ways, one useful way to understand them is to examine each developmental stage. Although it is difficult to predict how a specific event will unfold within a family, it is possible to identify the general types of crises that families will experience over their life span. Although each family will react uniquely to family transitions, all families encounter a similar range of developmental crises such as the death of a member, necessitating adjustment to loss at times. Developmental processes are marked by identifiable transition events such as weddings, birth of the first child, or retirement of parents. Each stage challenges the family with specific pressures related to developmental issues, tasks, and potential crises to be resolved. Knowledge about the family life cycle can help social workers observe ways in which a family has become "stuck" and identify changes that will help the family to move on. Pinsof (2002) suggests that pair bonding (he challenges the notion of marriage as the only way to go) might begin with cohabitation and be followed by the birth of a child, which could then be followed by marriage because each of these three events is an independent choice.

Families shift attitudes and modify relationships to adapt to evolving family life stages (Holman, 1983). Family crises can be anticipated and are unavoidable. Life cycle transitions exacerbate family stress, and family problems that arise at certain points suggest that a family is having difficulty adjusting at a particular developmental stage. Some families have evolved excellent problem-solving skills and strategies and well-developed support systems. Others have not. Awareness of the developmental issues facing a family places the family social worker in a prime position to assess the family's issues, the crises that occur as a result, and the coping tools used by the family to address these issues. During developmental crises, family social workers can provide much-needed knowledge, skills, strategies, and support to families who are overwhelmed by developmental crises.

As early as 1956, Geismar and Krisberg proposed a direct relationship between social functioning and the family life cycle. They discovered that families with limited economic and social resources become more disorganized as they progress through the family cycle. Family disorganization suggests a bad fit between the family's *need* for services and resources and the *availability* of services and resources, as well as the family's ability to use them. The growing need for economic and social resources strains the family's economic, social, and emotional resources.

Certain tasks accompany each family stage. Transition to a new stage is usually accompanied by some kind of crisis, whether large or small (Petro & Travis, 1985). Moreover, rituals often mark transitions, such as baptisms, weddings, funerals, rites marking puberty, and so on, many of which are culturally dependent. For example, Latino families preserve life cycle markers and appropriate rituals such as birthdays, religious rituals, holidays, or Sunday picnics, which are usually opportunities for large family gatherings (Falicov, 1999). While transitions between stages are not discrete, each transition point exerts pressure on the family system to adapt.

Roles of family members transform as children mature and family boundaries adapt in response to the changing needs of family members. For example, as children enter adolescence, family boundaries should ideally become more flexible in response to the changing developmental and social needs of teenagers. If family boundaries are too rigid during adolescence, parent-child conflict may ensue. If the adolescent complies with overly restrictive boundaries, the teen may have problems developing the social skills and independence needed to survive as an adult. Conversely, if the boundaries are too loose during adolescence, the child may lack adequate monitoring of activities, become prematurely disengaged from the family, and fail to develop necessary survival skills to function as a competent social being.

The stages of family development presented in Figure 4.1 are adapted from three models: Carter and McGoldrick (1988, 1999, 2005), Becvar and Becvar (2005), and Duvall (1957). The stages of family development include marriage (or partnering, coupling, or pair bonding), birth of the first child, families with preschool children, families with school-aged children, families with teenagers, and families with young people leaving home. Later family stages are relevant to this text inasmuch as grandparents are an important part of family life for many families. To this list of stages, we add children returning home after they have been launched, colloquially called "boomerang children." In part, we are jesting about this being a significant transition; on the other hand, we believe that children who return home after being launched give rise to a significant social pattern for families that places extra demands on a family. This stage might interfere with parents dealing with their issues as a couple.

Moreover, the number of alternative family forms has grown in recent years, and strict adherence to the stage-to-stage progression through the family life cycle has loosened considerably. Some couples have children before marriage, and some never marry but have children. Others are involved in serial relationships that involve children. New reproductive technologies are making parenthood available to those who previously had little choice over whether to have children. North America is experiencing historically low birth rates. There are growing numbers of births to unmarried women or gay and lesbian couples. Unmarried women may have male partners with whom they conceive a child but choose not to marry; or in the case of lesbian couples, they may choose to become pregnant through artificial means.

Additionally, many families undergo life cycle disruption initiated by separation, divorce, and remarriage. Many children born in the United States will experience the divorce of their parents. Typically, mothers retain custody and fathers receive visitation status. In other families both parents work outside the home, making child care a necessity. Other couples remain childless or delay having children beyond age 40. Spousal roles are often no longer premised on strict traditional gender arrangements, and social changes have led to common family structures that at one point in our history were marginalized, such as parenting by gay or lesbian couples. We know of at least a few people who were gay or lesbian who became

Stage	Family tasks
1. Marriage/coupling/pair-bonding	• Committing to the relationship • Formulating roles and rules • Becoming a couple while separating from families of origin • Compromising and negotiating around concrete and personal needs
2. Families with young children	• Restabilizing the marital unit with a triangle • Bonding with the child and integrating that child into the family • Realigning relationships with one another, deciding on work or career and domestic chores
3. Families with school-aged children	• Allowing greater independence of children • Opening family boundaries to accommodate new social institutions and new people • Understanding and accepting role changes
4. Families with teenagers	• Dealing with teen demands for independence through appropriate boundary adjustments • Redefining personal autonomy • Rule changes, limit setting, and role negotiation
5. Launching	• Preparing young person for independent living • Leaving home through schooling and job skills • Accepting and promoting youth's self-sufficiency
6. Boomerang stage	• Readjusting family system to accommodate children returning home as adult children • Dealing with couple issues • Renegotiating personal and physical space • Renegotiating role responsibilities
7. Middle-aged parents	• Adjusting to new roles and relationships apart from children
8. Aging family members	• Involvement with grandchildren and partners of the children • Dealing with issues related to aging • Striving to maintain dignity, meaning, and independence

FIGURE 4.1 | Stages of the Family Life Cycle

Adapted from Becvar & Becvar, 2005; Carter & McGoldrick, 1988; Carter & McGoldrick, 2005; Duvall, 1957.

involved in heterosexual relationships because they had few socially acceptable options. Their eventual "coming out" was difficult for everyone involved. Finally, issues inherent in the changing family life cycle include grandparents' involvement as primary caretakers, parenting later in life, and intergenerational family configurations (Helton & Jackson, 1997).

These changes in family configuration have sparked changes in the family life cycle (Carter & McGoldrick, 2005). Many of the changes have affected and been effected by women—child rearing does not take up the amount of family space that it did decades ago. Women are working and men are participating more in housework and child care. Diversity in family development is discussed later in this chapter.

EXERCISE 4.4   Seeds of Conflict

Break into small groups. Take each of the potential areas of conflict embedded in each stage of the family life cycle, and identify examples of how conflict might break out in the relationship. Role-play a couple in conflict over one of these issues, and include a family social worker working with the couple to resolve the difficulty. Describe to the class what happened in the role-play.

EXERCISE 4.5   Homeostasis and the Family Life Cycle

Review the different phases of the family life cycle. Beside each stage, list two tasks that the family must do as well as potential crises that occur during that phase.

Marriage/Partnering/Pair Bonding/Affiliative Orientation

Of all dilemmas in the life cycle, the existential dilemma of coupling is probably the greatest.
—McGoldrick, 2005c, 205e, p. 231

Boy meets girl. Boy marries girl. Boy and girl angst over which family they visit at Thanksgiving and which one in December and whether or not it's best to serve turkey or goose for the family feast. When first faced with the reality that the family you married into does things differently, the warmth of tradition can take on a chill.
—Marge Kennedy (www.Bartleby.com)

EXERCISE 4.6   Marriage

Is marriage an outdated social institution? What are the benefits and disadvantages of getting married these days?

The nature of marriage, partnering, or coupling has changed enormously over the past several generations. We hesitate to use the term *marriage* exclusively to describe the various types of coupling or pair bonding (Pinsof, 2002) that can occur; Sanders and Kroll (2000) offer the alternative term *affiliative orientation*, which is a mouthful indeed. In fact, deciding not to enter into a state-sanctioned relationship is now a viable option for many intimate relationships. Some people live together before marriage, and others move from one partner to another. Children may or may not be part of the relationship. Before a new relationship can happen, young people usually leave their family of origin. However, young people seem to be leaving home later and marrying later, usually between the ages of 25 and 35. The younger the age at marriage, the more difficult it is to adjust to the tasks and the greater the likelihood for breakup; according to McGoldrick (1999c, 2005e), it is better to marry later than earlier. Moreover, having children early in the relationship offers little opportunity for couple adjustment. Others are involved in serial monogamy, a practice that was frowned on one or two generations previously. Indeed, Pinsoff (202) suggests that cohabitation gives two people the opportunity to "check one another out" (p. 148).

According to Coontz (2006), marriage as a relationship between two individuals is now taken more seriously and is accompanied by higher emotional expectations than ever before. However, she also contends that marriage as an institution exerts less power over people's lives than previously. It is no longer the main mechanism for regulating sexual behavior and conferring differential economic and political rights and obligations, especially in areas of reproduction and dependent care (p. 15). At the same time, fewer people now consider that they have failed to realize a life goal if they do not marry. In more than half of marriages, the couple lived together before the formal ceremony (McGoldrick, 1999c, 2005e). Internet dating, which sometimes leads to marriage, is more common among all adult age groups, a scenario unheard of two decades previously. The term *marriage* is now a culturally and politically laden term that supports the State definition of what is a family. (Again we see how the use of language can exclude alternative family arrangements.)

Discourse in North America now centers on whether to extend marriage rights to gay and lesbian people. Conservatives argue that doing so would erode the meaning and sanctity of the family. Others say that denying gay and lesbian people the opportunity to legally marry is discriminatory and is a basic human rights issue. Regardless of the legal right to marry, gay and lesbian coupling is a fact of life. McGoldrick (1999c) suggests that gay and lesbian unions may be freer of traditional gender roles but at the same time face social stigma. Some couples have not come out to members of their family of origin, making contact with them tenuous. Not coming out may even alienate young people from their parents.

In North American relationships, it is believed that people marry for romantic love, or at least because they want to (Pinsof, 2002). Nevertheless, reasons for getting involved in a romantic relationship involve a complex set of factors including personality, social and cultural expectations, family history, and economics, to name a few. McGoldrick (1999c, 2005e) suggests that more than any other life transition, marriage is regarded as a solution to life's problems. McGoldrick (2005) also tells us that both lesbian and gay couples tend to have more intimate, cohesive relationships than heterosexual couples (p. 235).

The wedding ceremony, if there is one, can constitute a major ritual in the family life cycle. Wedding ceremonies are also big business, and families might feel pressure to put on an elaborate wedding. Cultures also have unique rituals around weddings. Once the ceremony is over, the couple learns to relate to in-laws, guided by different rules and expectations. Interestingly, the Native American culture has no word for *in-law*, whereas in the mainstream culture the mother-in-law is the subject of jokes and derision.

Progression through the family life cycle hits speed bumps or pressure points and conflicts that must be resolved for the family to reach fulfillment and satisfaction. In this case, four major tasks of the newly partnered couple include establishing a mutually satisfying relationship, realigning relationships with extended families (who must accept the new partner), negotiating roles, and making decisions about parenthood. People bring to a relationship accustomed ways of living from their early family experience. On entering a new relationship, they encounter unfamiliar ways of living that may contrast sharply with what is familiar to them in all areas of family life. Most aspects of life will need to be negotiated. Areas of negotiation include:

- Economic decisions
- Emotional/intimacy, dependency, communication style, and so on
- Power arrangements within the relationship, including decision making, interpersonal power, abuse, and so on
- Interpersonal boundaries with each other and boundaries around the couple, such as with parents, family, and friends. Boundaries may be flexible or rigid, and controlled by one person or mutually negotiated.
- Sexuality
- Deciding whether to have children. If children become part of the relationship, this dimension involves how they are raised.
- Domestic responsibilities (McGoldrick, 1999c, 2005e, p. 232).

Forming a relationship with another person, whether in marriage or by cohabitation, requires adjustment, compromise, and hard work. Partners must adjust to the behaviors, feelings, habits, and values of another person. The realities of adjustment to extended family, shared finances, and conflicting wants, desires, and living patterns mean that the couple will experience pressures that must be resolved for the relationship to succeed. Tension can emerge as the couple navigates differences, making this stage quite difficult. The difficulty of this stage is overshadowed by the cultural stereotype of the newlyweds who are "joined as one for eternity in wedded bliss." On a realistic level, the family social worker must assess the couple's satisfaction with the nuances of their relationship, their relationships with extended family, and agreement concerning decisions about parenthood. In assessing the marital relationship, the family social worker will find a marital satisfaction scale to be helpful (see Corcoran & Fischer, 2007).

Several myths have infiltrated marriage. The first is that marriage is harmful to men and that marriage privileges females by providing security, happiness, and social status. In fact, the opposite is true (McGoldrick, 1999c, 2005e). Marriage, in fact, improves men's mental, social, and physical health, whereas married women tend to experience greater depression, career interruption, and longer hours spent on domestic chores. The second cultural myth arises because traditional nuclear marriage comes from a Judeo-Christian tradition that threatens to eclipse other traditions. One must therefore consider different cultural contexts when looking at marriage. For example, slavery undermined both African American marriages and gender roles (Pinderhughes, 2002), thereby demanding new traditions to get needs met. African American relationships have also been affected by immigration, socioeconomic conditions, and unequal gender ratios—factors that exert less influence among white populations.

CASE 4.1   Transition

The following case example illustrates some of the crises a family may face during a time of transition: The Lee family consists of Sam and Lark, both in their early forties, and their three daughters, ages 7, 9, and 14. Problems with Mary, age 14, have brought the couple to the family social work agency.

Sam and Lark were both born in mainland China, and they met while studying at the University of California. The Lees describe enjoying a traditional Chinese lifestyle. Both Sam and Lark are devoted parents who want their children to know and respect their Chinese background and culture.

The family's problems began when Mary entered junior high school. Although Mary had continued to receive high grades at her new school, her behavior had undergone a radical transition. Their previously compliant daughter had become defiant. She had cut school to be with her friends on several occasions, and she had been absent from several family celebrations against her parents' wishes. When her parents tried to correct Mary's misbehavior, she became agitated and started yelling at them.

The event that brought the family to the agency was Mary's reaction to an argument with her parents during the previous week. She had left home during the night, apparently climbing out an upstairs window. Mary stayed at the homes of various friends for five days, and her parents were frantic.

Mary, who has accompanied her parents to the family social worker's office, tells the social worker that she needs some freedom from her parents' autocratic parenting. She feels that her parents are old-fashioned and unfair in comparison to her friends' parents. She explains that although she loves her parents very much, she does not share their attachment to traditional Chinese culture. She wants to be like her friends.

The family social worker, assessing the Lees' situation from a developmental perspective, sees a family with intergenerational value conflicts as well as developmental issues that frequently arise when children enter adolescence.

Issues may arise on several fronts during this first phase of the family life cycle. A partner who has not successfully negotiated independence from his or her family of origin may be squeezed by divided loyalties that threaten the fragile, developing relationship. Similarly, a partner who wishes to continue the social life of a single person also imposes stress on the relationship. Moreover, if a couple has children early in the marriage, there may be insufficient time to sort out crucial tasks demanded by a new relationship. Perhaps Gottman said it the best (cited in McGoldrick, 2005e): marital success depends on the mundane "mindless moments" of everyday life that create the emotional climate that will make the marriage work in the long run.

Birth of the First Child and So On

Rearing a family is probably the most difficult job in the world. It resembles two business firms merging their respective resources to make a single product. All the potential headaches of that operation are present when an adult male and an adult female join to steer a child from infancy to adulthood.

—*Virginia Satir, Peoplemaking (www.Bartleby.com)*

Deep inside us, we know what every family therapist knows: the problems between the parents become the problems within the children.
—Roger Gould (www.Bartleby.com)

Let it be stated here at the outset that becoming a parent is one of the most definitive stages of life, a crossing of the Rubicon.
—Betty Carter, 2005

No refunds, no returns! Crossing the Rubicon is colloquial language for passing the point of no return! Thus, according to Carter, with whom we agree, once a couple has a child, there is no going back. Regardless of whether the decision was made in haste, arrived at with partial information or with fully considered options, or accidental, having a child will affect a web of people for many, many years to come. It is important that people go into child rearing with their eyes wide open and that they fully understand the implications and expectations. People who opt to have children and who go into the transition with fewer romantic and exaggerated expectations are more likely to be happier about their marriage (Carter, 2005, p. 250).

The sequence of marrying before having children is no longer normative—many couples are having children before committing to a legal relationship. One-quarter of Caucasian babies and two-thirds of African American babies are born to unmarried women. This compares with half of all babies born in Scandinavia (Pinsof, 2002). Some, but not all, couples will eventually marry. Others who are blocked from forming a legal relationship, such as gays and lesbians, are committing to a relationship outside the legal system and at the same time are having children. When pregnancy occurs during adolescence, young people face the decision about what to do about the pregnancy. Adoption? Abortion? Keep the child and raise him or her? If the child is raised by the mother, will she move in with her parents and finish her education or will she strike out on her own? Moreover, should young single mothers seek employment, they must also concern themselves with child care, transportation, housing, food, and clothing costs.

Again, our description of this stage in the family life cycle is based on "typical" situations. Children born with disabilities can stress families who may not have adequate resources and skills to care for children with special needs. Families with disabled children need the opportunity to share their grief and sadness (Carter, 1999, 2005). In other instances one partner may face infertility, requiring the couple to decide whether to undergo infertility treatments, adopt a child, or remain childless. Other children are unanticipated and sometimes unwanted.

Parenthood is a major life transition that brings with it drastic changes in lifestyle. In fact, if parents do not change in response to the birth of a child, the child will have difficulty surviving. Whether to have children is a question for many potential parents, and more people are deciding not to have children. Some researchers question, however, whether reproductive decisions are decisions at all (Peterson & Jenni, 2003). Satir (1967) suggests that there are many reasons for having children, including fulfilling social expectations, obtaining a feeling of immortality, and addressing issues from the parents' past. Even when having a child is a conscious decision, it may be made with ambivalence. Making the decision to have a child seldom occurs at a discrete and definable moment. For some, the negative consequences of having a child might be more potent than the positive consequences. Although it is assumed that men are disengaged from reproductive decisions, this is not usually the case. We are aware of relationships that have fallen apart because one partner did not want to have children, while the other did. Moreover, some couples enter into a relationship, both agreeing on having children, but later one of the partners changes his or her mind. And, some couples that want children of their own have difficulty conceiving. As much as having children can be stressful, not being able to conceive also creates strains for many couples. It can be helpful for the family social worker to explore with future parents the reasons for and expectations associated with having children.

Having children is romanticized in North American culture; yet it is a stage in family life that can be very demanding. Previously, child rearing was a family focus for most of parents' lives; now child rearing consumes much less of parents' time (Carter & McGoldrick, 1999a, p. 8). For some people, the birth of their first child is a crisis that initiates a critical (although usually temporary) family adjustment period (LeMasters, 1957). Research suggests that couples that have negotiated a successful relationship adapt more easily to having children (Lewis, 1988). Once people accept responsibility for a child, they are expected to continue to accept that responsibility for a long time, maintaining a joint commitment to their child as well as to each other. The stakes are high.

Many changes take place, including but not limited to disequilibrium resulting from new roles, circumstances, and demands as well as individual changes in self-perception, self-efficacy, affective states, personal maturity, and values (Glade, Bean, & Vira, 2005). Men experience a profound change in their sense of responsibility and their relationship with their partner (p. 321). The first crisis of this stage, then, is preparing for and adapting to the birth of the child and resolving conflicts regarding commitment, roles, and fears about becoming a parent. Conflict can first arise if the couple does not agree about whether to have a child. In addition, a newborn interacts with only one person at a time, most often the mother who has traditionally assumed responsibility for childcare and domestic responsibilities while husbands "help out" (Carter, 1999). In the early phases of a child's life, mothers typically assume most of the childcare responsibilities (Carter, 1999; Garbarino, 1992; Mackie, 1991).

The arrival of a child complicates family life, creating at least temporary upheaval. Researchers have consistently discovered a decrease in marital satisfaction and adjustment among first-time parents: conflict levels increase, and a decreased emphasis on the partner role is evident (Ramage, F. (2005); Spanier, Lewis, & Cole, 1975). The decrease is greater for women (Glade, Bean, & Vira, 2005). At the same time, the birth of a child creates the first triangle in two-parent families. The triangle develops out of necessity since the child's survival needs must be met. The parental relationship must be reconfigured. Moreover, parents are also charged with the task of consistency in parenting—no easy feat. Satir (1967) points out the pitfall of having a child to fulfill one's emotional needs, only to discover that the child's needs are more pressing than one's own. New parents may experience conflict about caretaking roles that may threaten the existence of the marriage.

With the birth of the first child, a range of new roles and responsibilities emerge. Cultures vary in the extent to which new parents receive support during this phase. For example, in Latino families, the birth of a child draws relatives into the family circle to celebrate (Falicov, 1999, 2005). The arrival of children can precipitate or entrench gender differences and gender inequalities in domestic life (Doucet, 2001). Prior to the birth of a child, couples usually have relatively egalitarian divisions of household labor but move toward a more traditional gender division after the child is born (Carter, 1999; Koivunen, Rothaupt, & Wolfgram, 2009; Ramage, F. (2005)). Research suggests a significant relationship between the amount of household work done by each spouse and the level of marital satisfaction (Glade, Bean, & Vira, 2005). "Men end up doing less child-care housework than they expected and women end up doing more than they planned" (p. 323).

Having children necessitates adjustment to loss of freedom in lifestyle, recreation, and career flexibility. One of the greatest losses is sleep! Before having children, parents had the opportunity for self-care, career development, and couple bonding. With the birth of a child, lifestyles change abruptly, even when the child is eagerly anticipated. The couple has less time for themselves and each other, less money, and greater responsibility. Parenting a newborn child absorbs time and energy and requires high levels of self-sacrifice and self-denial. The needs of children take precedence over those of the parents, and people who have difficulty getting their needs met also have a hard time meeting the needs of others, particularly those of young children. Adjusting to the demands of a newborn threatens to destabilize the family. Of particular importance is the shift in power between the parents with the arrival of children.

Much attention has been given to the concept of bonding, or attachment. Most hospitals now encourage ongoing contact between parents and the child immediately after birth to encourage parent-child bonding. Hospitals also encourage the father to be present during childbirth. The nature of involvement of the extended family, especially grandparents, will take on different hues depending on culture and the relationship the grandparents have with the new parents.

Being reasonable, patient, consistent, and cheerful is difficult when night feedings, colic, and diaper-changing disrupt sleep patterns. The subsequent strain on the couple's relationship may result in one or both parents feeling neglected or misunderstood by the other. Decisions about child care and work while learning how to meet personal and couple needs are paramount. Some work sites are supportive of working parents, whereas others create hurdles for working parents. For example, one of the authors was working in a hospital when her daughter's school called her because of her daughter's broken foot. She left work to take her child to the hospital but was docked a day's pay. (Her boss was a female!)

The transition to parenthood is complicated by the fact that parents are expected to automatically know and be able to meet the needs of children without having received any education in or experience with parenting skills and child development, leading many new parents to fall back on their own upbringing or parents for advice at a time when they are still trying to redefine that relationship as adult-to-adult. More than likely, the grandparents also had little preparation for parenthood. To help the child learn to trust, parents must be dependable in meeting the child's needs. It is necessary for both to feel good about the relationship, but reciprocity is difficult when the newborn does not reward the parents by smiling, laughing, talking, or cooperating. It is easy for new parents, especially parents who are overwhelmed by issues in their own lives, to become frustrated by the one-sided nature of the early relationship with a child. Social support exerts a protective influence on new parents, particularly in the form of other parents (Glade, Bean, & Vira, 2005). However, many mothers sacrifice their social outlets as a function of being at home for the child (p. 325). While many men would like to be more involved in their children's lives, they are frequently inhibited by family-unfriendly work places (Koivunen, Rothaupt, & Wolfgram, 2009).

If both parents are working, the couple must decide if one person will remain at home to care for the child. Childcare expenses can place added stress on low-income families and families such as single-parent families. Seventy percent of women with children under the age of 6 are in the full-time workforce. Carter (2005) identifies three unresolved problems of the work-family dilemma: (1) unequal participation of men in the work at home, (2) the inflexibility of the workplace, and (3) the growing number of hours of work in the lives of both men and women (p. 252). Nevertheless, two-income parents are reportedly healthier and happier in every way (p. 252).

Child care for working parents creates anxiety for them. Various childcare arrangements include organized facilities, mothers working at home, fathers, grandparents, other relatives, and non-relative providers. Social and cognitive stimulation of children in care arrangements is imperative. Carter (2005) cites research that suggests that children who attend high-quality day care centers have better intellectual and social skills than children who have not gone to day care (p. 251). Yet, many poor families struggle to locate and afford quality day care arrangements. Additionally, Carter outlines two other issues faced by couples. These include the resultant power imbalance in the relationship when children arrive on the scene and issues pertaining to child rearing and discipline.

Some cultural groups such as African American and Latino families rely on relatives for child care (Carter, 1999, 2005). Usually, the decision has a greater impact on the woman, regardless of whether she returns to work. If she returns to work, she still often assumes primary responsibility for the child. If she stays at home, her earning power lessens, career advancement is placed on hold, interpersonal power in her marriage drops, and she becomes more isolated. Support from friends and family exerts a protective influence, enabling new mothers and fathers to view themselves as more effective. Other parents are an important source of support. Many mothers had to sacrifice their social outlets as a function of being at home following delivery (Glade, Bean, & Vira, 2005, p. 325). A child born to an impoverished family or a family with many social problems may exacerbate the stress that the family already experiences.

As the child matures, his or her relationships gradually grow to include more people and more complex social situations. A child benefits from a varied family life that includes diversity of relationships. Families with rigid boundaries are less likely to introduce new people into children's lives and are also more likely to severely restrict contact with others outside the family. The "social riches" of a child's life are augmented when relationships are multifaceted, reciprocal, and lasting (Garbarino, 1992). When families with children are homeless—an unfortunate burgeoning phenomenon—children lack basic provisions, and only about half attend school. Many shelters cannot accommodate two-parent families, thereby contributing to family breakup.

Parents of children with special needs face a number of challenges. These challenges for the child may concern physical or cognitive abilities. Some challenges, such as balancing work and family responsibilities, are similar to those experienced in other families. Other challenges concern ensuring that the child has access to and appropriate support to participate in specialized community programs. A common concern is how mothers and fathers respond to the variety of stresses they experience as individuals and as a couple, and potentially as parents who may have other children in the home.

The experience of becoming a first-time parent is a critical point in the lives of individuals, couples, and families. Nearly 90 percent of all married couples and countless more cohabitating and single parents experience this transition. The transition can be difficult due to changes experienced in areas such as marital satisfaction, division of household labor, individual mental health, and social relationships (Glade, Bean, & Vira, 2005, p. 320). While the actual biological experience of becoming a parent occurs instantly, the psychosocial transition takes considerably longer, beginning with the initial contemplation of conception and continuing through the early years of a child's life. Definite changes that take place include disequilibrium resulting from new roles, circumstances, and demands. Individual changes occur in self-perception, self-efficacy, affective states, personal maturity, and values. Men experience a profound change in their sense of responsibility and their relationship with their partner (p. 321). Many men and women experience depression and low self-esteem, and mothers in particular appear to have a more difficult adjustment. One indicator of depression is social withdrawal that results in isolation.

Couples who are unable to conceive may resort to a number of options for having children. These include adoption (open and closed), infertility treatments, and surrogate parenting. In addition, couples have the option of turning to international adoption agencies. Regardless of the route they take, new parents encounter a standard set of issues that may be compounded by special circumstances.

Families with Preschool Children

Being in a family is like being in a play. Each birth order position is like a different part in the play, with a distinct and separate characteristic for each part. Therefore, if one sibling has already filled a part, such as the good child, other siblings may feel they have to find other parts to play, such as the rebellious child, academic child, athletic child, social child, and so on.

—Jane Nelson (www.Bartleby.com)

The child who was formerly dependent soon becomes more active, propelled toward greater independence. As motor skills improve, nothing may be too risky for the child to try, including hopping off the stairs or climbing into the toilet. Superman pajamas may transform the youngster into a superhero recklessly leaping off furniture. The child's energy seems inexhaustible. At the same time, the parents' energy may be sapped and their relationship strained by lack of privacy and time together along with increased work. A young child greets each new experience— the moon, a dog, or another child—with glee. The toddler absorbs the world with excited openness and sees what adults take for granted. New experiences contribute to the growing cognitive abilities of the child. Unfortunately, the exploratory skills of the child are a mismatch with the child's awareness of safety, making parents tense and on guard for disaster. Poor parental supervision during this time exacerbates risk for the child. So does the failure of a parent to provide sufficient opportunities for growth and learning.

Parents need to be concerned about the safety of their children during this stage and provide an acceptable amount of stimulation while carefully monitoring their activities. It may be difficult for parents to encourage independence and at the same time protect their children. Parents feel the tug between allowing too much independence, thereby placing their children at risk, and becoming too protective, discouraging exploration and development.

Parental energy levels can also be an issue. Sometimes parents become careless or impatient because they run out of energy. The energy drain can be compounded if a second child arrives while the first is still young and demanding. A second child more than doubles the work, and adding a third child increases the work and demands exponentially. Changes in family dynamics in response to the addition of more children might not be appreciated by older children and can result in sibling rivalry and increased parental stress and fatigue. The growing cognitive ability of the firstborn can intensify the stress as the first child strives to attract the parents' attention. For example, a 3-year-old may try to distract the parents' attention from the newborn by using creative strategies such as filling the kitchen sink to take a bath or urinating on a rug during the infant's feeding. These represent the child's attempts to recapture center stage of the parents' attention.

At this stage of family development, children continue to develop increasingly complex social relationships that emphasize work, play, and love (Garbarino, 1992). Optimal development requires that children have access to a variety of significant others, gradually expanding the web of relationships from parents and siblings to a peer group.

For grandparents, this can be a particularly pleasurable time. It is a time when family identity is solidified, and grandparents can revisit this time without the day-to-day responsibility of child care (Blacker, 2005). However, difficulties can emerge if the grandparents are divorced, if their adult children are divorced, or if the adult children are incapacitated by drug abuse or illness and the grandparents must step into the role of parenting (p. 301).

Families with School-Aged Children

The school should be the appendage of the family state, and modeled on its primary principle, which is to train the ignorant and weak by self-sacrificing labor and love, and to bestow the most on the weakest, the most undeveloped.
—Catherine Beecher (www.Bartleby.com)

Family adjustment is once again stretched when the oldest child reaches school age, because family members must plan schedules around school, child care, child socialization, and extracurricular activities. The daily process of separating from and reuniting with the parents usually is established by the time the child reaches school age, and most, but not all, kindergartners are ready to take their first major step away from home. Children and parents might have difficulty separating from the safety of the family. Family tasks in this stage involve supporting children's adjustment to a formal structured learning situation in which they learn to interact cooperatively with peers and authority figures other than parents. During this period, children learn to adapt to a regulated routine. As mentioned, children in homeless families are disadvantaged, for multiple reasons, one of which is lack of access to proper schooling.

Many children from ethnic minority families encounter social institutions in the dominant culture for the first time. They may have been shielded from discrimination, but going to school may expose them to the harshness of this reality for the first time. In immigrant families, children often learn more English than their parents, potentially leading to role reversal. For example, immigrant parents might rely on their children to translate and interpret situations. Competing cultural values squeeze children between two cultures, perhaps upsetting their parents who have grown up with a different system of values. Children who enter the school system knowing their native tongue are challenged to learn a new language in addition to having to learn "reading, writing, and arithmetic" (Falicov, 1999).

Some middle-class parents believe that having school-aged children resembles running a taxi service. Baseball practices, swimming lessons, school meetings, and a range of other activities are very time-consuming for all of the family members. Skills required to negotiate this phase include organizing, cooperating, and supporting family members. For children from more disadvantaged backgrounds, the story is very different. At this stage, differences in family income levels become strikingly apparent, and some children notice that their schoolmates have more possessions and engage in more activities. Classmates may have more clothes, toys, access to recreational services, and financial resources. Another difference that has an impact on families is the amount and type of nutrition available to children from different socioeconomic backgrounds. Children who have not had a nourishing breakfast or who do not have enough to eat for lunch are further disadvantaged in the classroom. Parents who cannot afford to provide children with the basics, let alone the luxuries, often feel inadequate when their children enter school. Both the parents and children suffer.

The effort involved in getting children to school requires an enormous amount of family organization and structure. Just getting children ready for school each morning includes preparing breakfast, organizing lunches and books, choosing clothes, and getting the children out the door; this makes for hectic mornings. It becomes even more complicated if parents also are trying to get themselves ready for work, particularly if they must leave home before the children do. Parents who work shifts are also further stretched during morning time.

Working parents also need to arrange adequate out-of-school care. These arrangements include care and supervision before and after school hours and during school vacations, holidays, other school closures, and child illnesses. If arrangements are inadequate, children are vulnerable to potential danger at home and on the street. Low-income parents may find out-of-school care too expensive and may be unable to make safe after-school arrangements because of inadequate income for child care and a lack of extended family support. Although a responsible adult should be with children when they are not in school, too many children, referred to as latchkey children, arrive home to an empty house.

The increasing number of women, and consequently parents, in the workforce is well documented and might even be described as a revolution that has taken place since the end of World War II. More than half of new mothers work, and the numbers have grown steadily. Younger new mothers are more likely to stay home with their children than are women over the age of 30. In addition, college-educated mothers are more likely to return to work, as are single parents. Finally, African American new mothers are more likely to return to work within the first year of a child's birth than are Hispanic mothers (Hunter College Women's Studies Collective, 1995).

This growing workforce participation has impacted family life. Parents are challenged as they juggle work responsibilities, child-rearing tasks, and household chores while attempting to meet their own personal needs. Imagine the demands on single parents who often have fewer economic resources and assume all household and childcare responsibilities alone. In single-parent or two-career families, children may be left at home unsupervised; such children are more likely to be injured when they are home alone (Peterson, 1989). Children may experience increased anxiety and fear about being left to fend on their own. The length of time a child can remain unsupervised depends on age and competence, as well as the risks that the child is likely to encounter. Failure to supervise a child adequately is a familiar complaint to Child Protective Services.

During this stage, children acquire skills and attitudes needed for success in school. School success is equated with life success. To help children succeed, parents must adopt an academic culture and convey a positive regard for schooling to their children (Garbarino, 1992). Parents can help children translate the new world of school, and accomplishments by children should be reinforced. The family can provide a safe and secure haven for children to escape the stress of school. Perhaps most importantly, parents can help children assume self-responsibility for learning. The ability to value knowledge is a gift that parents can give their children. One of the best ways to help a child do well in school is to create a predictable and structured evening routine during which time the child is expected to do homework. This means eliminating distractions such as the television and conflict and setting aside a quiet part of the home so the child can focus. Homework can become a battleground for children and parents alike, both of whom are exhausted from the day. Interestingly, some schools, especially those serving high-needs families, have become "homework-free zones."

During this phase, parents should establish strong connections with the institutions that work with their children since parents who value school have a greater chance of encouraging academic success than those who do not (Garbarino, 1992). Again, close involvement with the school will help a child develop competence and skills in preparation for later life. While schools would like the involvement of parents in their children's education, for example by helping out in the classroom, overburdened parents often find this time commitment difficult, especially when they have other children in the home.

Bullying among young children is a common and persistent problem; as many as 27 percent of children report being bullied (Sutton, Smith, & Swettenham, 1999). Both parents and schools need to form a coalition against bullying. This is only possible when there is a strong coalition between home and school.

Families with Teenagers

Adolescence is reputed to be a time of family turbulence. It is a period of rapid change for the teen and the family. The adolescent is moving toward adulthood, causing the family structure to change and emotions to intensify. Preto (1999, 2005) suggests that attempts to resolve conflict may reactivate unresolved conflicts about issues embedded in the previous generation. The family environment transforms from a crucible in which children are nurtured and sheltered into a springboard from which teens start to venture out on their own in an attempt to assume adult responsibilities and commitments (Preto, 1999, 2005). Parents may agonize over the changing world and increased threats outside the home. It is during this stage that families encounter increasing demands to change every fiber of family functioning such as expectations, relationships, finances, and responsibilities. Although letting go of some things is important, so is limit setting. The concurrent demands of letting go and maintaining limits challenges even the most flexible family.

Despite popular lore's suggestions that the teenage years are stressful, most teenagers endure this period with no more difficulty than previous stages of development. Problems, if any, are more likely to be the fruit of ongoing family stress and difficulty adjusting than an unavoidable consequence of puberty. Teenagers face issues regarding sexuality, dating, renegotiating relationships with family, making decisions about what direction to head in school or their future career, and navigating between social norms and family norms. Some alienated young people find acceptance through gang membership, which is distressing to both families and communities.

The family's task during this time is to help the young person reach maturity and learn skills that will enable her or him to eventually leave the family as a competent and independent adult. The task of the young person is to develop skills necessary for work, including assuming greater responsibility and dependability. The challenge is for the child to get through adolescence without making poor decisions that will haunt him or her for the rest of life.

Many adolescent problems represent the teenager's attempts at achieving independence and adult autonomy. Adolescents struggle to define themselves and make their own decisions. Some problem behaviors are part of normal development and may focus on inappropriate clothing or makeup, outrageous attitudes, and noncompliance with family rules. Other problem behaviors are indicative of major issues. Parents need the wisdom to know the difference and pick their battles carefully.

An adolescent can display emotional drama culminating in unpredictable behavior, one day playing ear-splitting music and the next day being silent, withdrawn, and brooding. Perhaps most threatening, parents find themselves being challenged and defied by their formerly manageable child (if they had such a child to begin with). Compliant children may suddenly develop an independent style of logic seemingly contradictory to the facts. Parents may feel uncomfortable when challenged by children who in the past were obedient, loving, and compliant with parental guidance and direction. Children from minority cultures face an escalation of issues because they are caught between the teachings and practices of their own culture and those of mainstream society.

Despite the strife that can accompany adolescence, teenagers can also be a joy. The process of growing up may be difficult to understand and even stranger to watch, but the outcome can be quite healthy. Teens require support and encouragement during this time, and the challenge for parents is to support the youngster's struggle for independence and maturity while providing necessary structure. One wise child protection worker told parents: "You do not need to come out of this as best friends, but at least you can learn to like one another!" Adolescence is also a time of contradiction. Adolescents review and repeat all of the previous developmental stages as they inch toward adulthood. Tasks include learning to trust others, acquiring a stable identity, and addressing the questions of their life. Intimacy, relationships, morality, peer associations, and life goals are important as young people assume new roles in an attempt to determine their future direction.

A significant but often sensitive developmental issue is sexual maturation, which is often accompanied by strong but conflicting feelings. All at once, it seems, the adolescent has grown into a different body, and sometimes the changes can be frightening. The task for the young person is to develop a new self-image, but this new view of the self can be distressingly fragile. It is no wonder that many young people think of adolescence as a period of embarrassing self-consciousness and self-reflection, rather than as the best time of their lives.

Teenagers expect more privileges and freedom than they enjoyed earlier, but they may still have little sense of responsibility for their actions. At this stage, much behavior is centered on peer standards because the approval of friends is preferable to parental approval. Parents are considered naïve and embarrassingly out of touch. The rapid changes suggest that parents take on new roles to provide support when needed but back away when they are not needed. Wise parents do not intrude except in cases of need, painful as this often may be to all concerned. The degree of parental intrusiveness depends on the severity of the issue.

As adolescents loosen family ties, they establish closer relationships with peers. While moving toward greater independence, freedom, and responsibility in preparation for leaving home, they are developing skills while remaining within the safety of the family unit. Unfortunately, some teens disengage from the family prematurely, before they have had the opportunity to develop skills needed for independence. Clearly, some homes are safer than others.

Adolescence is marked differently across cultures. In lower socioeconomic groups there is a narrow age difference between the generations (Petro, 1999, 2005), and becoming a grandparent before the age of 40 is not unusual. Burton (cited in Petro, 1999) offers an astonishing picture of a family in which the great-grandmother was 43. Alternatively, some ethnic groups struggle to keep teenagers at home (p. 281).

Riley, Greif, and McAuley (2004) looked at runaway youth and found a number of disturbing trends. Runaway youth, who present a profile distinct from that of delinquent youth, have a high risk of involvement in dangerous situations. Some youth who are considered "throwaway youth" have been forced out of their homes or encouraged to leave. They display behaviors that place them "at-risk." Many have ongoing conflictual relationships with their families, and their families are marked by strife and dysfunction including parental incompetence, financial problems, alcohol abuse, physical abuse, and marital instability. Before running away, such youth might be involved with substance abuse and may underperform in and drop out of school. The event of running away can precipitate a family crisis or make a covert crisis overt. Theses families are often paralyzed and depleted, having struggled with a myriad of family problems including but not limited to raising an oppositional adolescent (p. 142). For these young people, school was merely a social setting, rather than a springboard for future career and educational aspirations. Parents had difficulties raising a challenging child such that overseeing homework, which requires strong executive functioning skills, was too difficult for the parent (p. 146).

EXERCISE 4.7   Your Adolescence

Reflect on your own adolescence, and describe what was going on in your family and how your teen years (or those of your siblings) created changes in the family system. How did your family's values differ from values outside the home? How did you and your family navigate these differences?

EXERCISE 4.8   Letting Go and Limit-Setting

Break into groups of two. Role-play a parent and teenager negotiating where to let go and where to set limits. (For skill development, you might want to include a family social worker helping out the parent and child.) Write down the results of this negotiation and present them to the class.

EXERCISE 4.9   Teens in Conflict with Outside Authorities

Many families become involved in family social work for the first time because their teenagers' behaviors have come into conflict with outside authorities. Make a list of some of the issues that such teens might have. Present your list in class, and discuss the possible sources of these behaviors and what a family social worker might do to intervene.

Families with Young People Leaving Home: Launching

Once referred to as the *empty nest*, the term has now been mostly discarded in favor of "The Launching Stage." Fulmer (2005) refers to this stage as "Becoming an Adult." Notice how the various labels emphasize different individuals in the family—the first being the parents and Fulmer's being the individual young person. The earlier suggestion was that women's roles revolved around home and children and that mothers become depressed and their lives lack meaning when children leave home. This depiction is a myth for most women and was socially constructed with the political purpose of reinforcing the belief that women should remain at home by suggesting that their lives will forever exclusively revolve around family.

We now know that many parents celebrate when their children are *successfully* launched; there is less work, more time, fewer worries, and more money. Parents may also celebrate their children's achievements. Television commercials are starting to capitalize on this, such as when the child returns home only to find the parents using margarine instead of butter. The child packs his bags and leaves home in disgust. The parents pretend to be heartbroken. After the door shuts, the parents start to dance! Of course, parents want their children to leave home "the right way"—that is, with a solid plan in place, the resources to follow through on that plan, and the desire to come home to visit. Fulmer (2005) suggests that this stage might bring conflicting feelings for parents who have less ability to monitor, influence, and protect their children, despite a feeling of continued responsibility (p. 219). By comparison, Blacker (2005) suggests that couples in their midlife who have launched their children report more enjoyment of life and more happiness in their marriages (p. 287). Perhaps early theory placed too much emphasis on separation and independence, particularly for males (Fulmer, 1999), but we believe that an extreme opposite response is also not useful, as the boomerang phase suggests.

At this stage, children separate from their parents, develop intimate peer and love relationships, and move toward consolidating their education or lifework goals. During this stage, young people focus on establishing themselves as independent adults, capable of functioning on their own. They will focus on preparing for work and solidifying a few special relationships (Fulmer, 1999, 2005). In some cases, they will be starting their own families. If they left home early or had children early, this struggle can be difficult. On the other hand, difficulty finding meaningful employment or getting into post-secondary education means that many young people delay leaving home, and this also can be stressful. The move to independence is compromised by a continued dependence on parents. In fact, rumor has it that the experts have tagged another 10 years onto adolescence because of the longer time it takes for children to leave home and become established.

The time when young adults leave home depends, in part, on culture as well as occupational opportunities. Today, young people in middle-class families tend to live with their parents longer because of increased educational aspirations, lack of employment opportunities, and overall economic difficulties. In other families, young people leave prematurely, running away from home, dropping out of school, and working in low-paying, unskilled jobs. How individuals leave their family of origin will greatly affect the rest of their lives. Although people can return to school later in life, doing so becomes more difficult when they have fewer supports in place and greater responsibility. Thus, there are wide variations in how and when young people leave home and what educational and career skills they bring into relationships. They will also differ in the degree to which they have separated from their family of origin.

When young people leave home (permanently), the size of the family shrinks and parental responsibilities change. As each young person departs, parents are able to devote more attention to the younger children remaining at home (Fulmer, 2005). Parents, if they are still together, renegotiate their relationship without triangulating others. Parental reactions might range from ecstasy to grief or a combination, depending on the age of the child, the relationship with the child, and the process of how the child is leaving. Running away from home (discussed in the previous section) at the age of 16 can evoke quite different feelings in parents than the feelings that arise when an 18-year-old child leaves for college. Throughout this back-and-forth movement, young people are getting involved in serious relationships, working, or attending school, which requires flexibility of and stretches the parent-child relationship. However, an unfortunate (for parents) outcome of these activities is that if young people are working and remaining at home, some do not contribute to the family finances and instead use their money on personal expenses. Parents want to get out of debt at this point, and many are disappointed.

How parents assist with launching depends on several factors, including individual choice, socioeconomic status, culture, and family circumstances. For example, Anglo and Polish children might receive little parental assistance compared with the assistance given in Italian or Brazilian families (Blacker, 1999, p. 289). If children continue schooling, middle- or higher-class families provide more assistance. Nevertheless, parents provide a sense of continuity for adult children by maintaining the home base and hosting family celebrations such as for holidays and birthdays (Fulmer, 2005).

Parents face issues of their own as they experience their own aging process and changes in their relationship. They have a renewed opportunity to focus on their relationship. In fact, Blacker (2005) suggests that women report a better quality of life at midlife than any other time (p. 287). The parents can no longer deny that they are getting older since they now have adult children. When parents have focused much of their adult lives on their children, the last child's final departure from home demands a distinct kind of adjustment, requiring that parents find an alternative to their usual focus on their children. Some people pressure their children for grandchildren, whereas others develop new hobbies or pursue employment. Children leaving home can enhance marriages, as couples have more time to focus on one another. If parents' previous focus on and responsibilities toward children masked marital discord, children leaving home might present an opportune time for divorce. Additionally, men and women can have different priorities as they go through midlife, which usually coincides with launching (Blacker, 1999, 2005). That is, women become more autonomous and develop increased social commitments, whereas men wish for more leisure and travel time. The couple may make plans about their relationship with one another and regarding their work once their children have left. Moreover, once people retire, the power balance shifts in many homes, with men slowing down at work and developing other interests. On the other hand, women may reinvest in a career once family responsibilities abate. Another issue is that their own parents may be frail and elderly, demanding more attention from the couple. Women are usually the caregivers of parents.

At midlife, their tasks are to develop adult relationships with adult children, accept new family members through marriage and birth, and resolve issues with and provide care for their parents (Blacker, 2005, p. 287). Again, culture and class affect how people go through this stage, with the lower socioeconomic group encountering fewer job opportunities. Launching children is good for their relationships (p. 292).

Communication, sexual intimacy, money, and power are issues commonly faced by couples when their children leave home. Other issues include relatives, religion, recreation, friends, drugs and alcohol, children, and jealousy. In midlife, marriages face a number of unique transitions. This is when many couples face the responsibility of caring for elderly parents while caring for children. This is a time when there is both an increase in marital satisfaction and an increase in divorce rates (Blacker, 2005)! Henry and Miller (2004) found that the most common problem areas for midlife couples were financial issues, sexual issues, and ways of dealing with children.

Gender, ethnicity, social class, and sexual orientation mediate the timing and manner of how young people leave home (Blacker, 1999, 2005; Fulmer, 1999, 2005). Young men are expected to be independent and, because of this, might separate from their parents early. In the past, young women often left by getting married, although this is no longer usually the case. Nevertheless, females usually remain more connected to family relationships, although young women who receive higher education are now expected to delay marriage longer. Young men struggle with successful independence (Fulmer, 2005). Gays and lesbians usually come out in stages (e.g., self-definition, self-acceptance, and disclosure), although the process typically starts in young adulthood (p. 225). Coming out contributes to unique relationship dynamics with parents and extended kin, particularly if the person has been in a heterosexual relationship previously. Family support and family acceptance will affect the psychological adjustment of gay, lesbian, bisexual, and transsexual (GLBT) people (Elizur & Ziv, 2001). Low income and few work skills may keep members of low-socioeconomic groups at home for extended periods. This might be complicated by having children at a young age, criminal activities, and gang membership.

When is a young person ready to leave the home? This question is difficult to answer. While many young people are leaving home much later than children did a generation ago, some leave home before they are ready, perhaps to escape difficult family situations such as abuse, poverty, or chemical dependency. On the other hand, for middle-class families, adolescence is extending beyond the teenage years as children remain at home while they continue in school or become financially secure. Many middle-class parents can no longer afford to send their children away from home for college. However, young people in families where postsecondary education is not pursued face difficulty because blue-collar jobs are becoming increasingly scarce.

Young adults may leave the family in a series of slow steps culminating in permanently moving out of the home. This may be a back-and-forth process with the young person leaving and returning a number of times, creating mixed reactions to the transition on the part of the parents. The leaving and returning process is becoming so predictable and patterned that we suggest making it a distinct stage.

EXERCISE 4.10   Leaving Home

Break into groups of four or five. Have one of the group members report back to the class (without identifying names) on each group member's responses to the following questions:

1. At what age did you first leave home? How often have you moved back home since you left?
2. What were the circumstances behind your leaving home? If you returned home, what were the circumstances behind each return?
3. How did your parents respond to your departure? How did your parents respond to your return(s)?
4. How had your family changed if you returned home?

Boomerang Phase

As mentioned, we have taken the liberty to add this phase to the family life cycle. Young people leave and return home for different reasons. More sons than daughters appear to be moving back home (Blacker, 1999, 2005). They might return home from college for summer break. They might encounter relationship difficulties or financial setbacks. They might become ill and need the care of their parents. Some will bring pets. Sometimes, particularly when marriages have broken up, adult children might move back home and bring their children. Whatever the reason, the leaving-returning-leaving cycle requires flexibility and active negotiation to allow young people and their parents to keep relationships running smoothly and to allow everyone healthy personal, physical, financial, and emotional space. The challenge is for children to assume adult roles and not revert to earlier parent-child days when the parent was the authority. This phase should not mark the continuation of childhood dependence. Although the economy almost demands extended periods of financial dependency on parents, society still expects individual freedom (Fulmer, 1999, 2005).

Blacker (1999) suggests that the return of adult children is more likely to occur under three conditions: (1) if the parent-child relationship is positive, (2) if the family agrees to continue to provide support, and (3) if the parents have remained together rather than forming a new stepfamily or becoming a single-parent household (p. 299). Moreover, parent-child relationships become more affectionate after children leave home (p. 299). The challenge for parents is to recognize that their young person is an adult and capable of setting her or his own rules and guidelines without undue interference. On the other hand, young people must also realize that they have taken over their parents' space and should assume responsibilities such as chipping in financially (no matter how well off the parents are), respecting the personal space of others, and contributing to domestic chores, in addition to recognizing that at this point in their lives parents are not obligated to take care of them or their children.

EXERCISE 4.11   Boomeranging Home

Break into small groups. Discuss some of the difficulties in the family that might arise when children return home. Then devise some interventions for dealing with these difficulties.[1]

Issues for Older Parents

> One's family is the most important thing in life. I look at it this way: One of these days I'll be over in a hospital somewhere with four walls around me. And the only people who'll be with me will be my family.
>
> —Robert C. Byrd (www.Bartleby.com)

As societies age, the process of family development is becoming longer and more varied (Walsh, 2005). While some cultures value the input of elders, Western culture is notorious for devaluing such input. Nevertheless, Walsh claims that families provide most of the direct caregiving assistance, psychological support, and social interaction for elderly loved ones (p. 309). At this stage, parents are retiring and often becoming grandparents.

This stage includes middle-aged parents who no longer have their children living with them. Their major task is reestablishing themselves as a couple, and they may experience a new courtship stage as they redefine new roles and rules in their

---

[1] Please send your suggestions to the authors!

relationship. As mentioned, some couples find that they no longer have a reason to stay together without the children at home to bind them together. Children who have left home find themselves in a position where roles with their parents are reversed, as parents become more vulnerable due to failing health and increased dependence. Previous, unresolved issues might appear. If a parent had been abusive, for example, children might feel torn about the extent of support that they will provide to ailing parents. Given the mobility of many families, some children may move far away from their aging parents, leaving siblings who are closer to home to provide support.

This final stage, the aging family, lasts until the death of one of the partners. The couple must adjust to becoming older and facing inevitable death. Couples might become isolated during this stage as friends die or as they are forced by poor health to move to institutions such as nursing homes or hospitals. This stage is even more difficult if the couple has inadequate finances. Another area of potential stress for the couple is the trend of older parents moving into the residence of one of their adult children. This role reversal, whereby the adult child may take on a caregiving role for his or her parent, disrupts family homeostasis as new rules are made.

Middle-aged couples or singles may find themselves caring for their own children as well as their aging parents. With increasing longevity, many older people wish to remain at home for longer periods. Many do so, although some will have physical ailments that require ongoing support and services. Interestingly, if it is the male partner who is infirm, the female partner is likely to keep him at home and take care of him. On the other hand, if the infirm partner is female, she is more likely to be institutionalized. It is at this time that one of the adult children may step in. These adult caretaker children have been dubbed the "sandwich generation." The sandwich role was common in past years when society was less mobile and extended families stayed together. It is more difficult today, when both partners in a marriage often work full-time. If one parent is deceased, the adult children may provide extra support. While the child who provides this care is often female, it actually depends on who is near the aging parent. When there are cutbacks resulting in limited services to seniors, it is often adult female children who are expected to fill the gap.

Walsh (2005) provides a touching view of the grandparent-grandchild bond, which can be special and not necessarily infused with the responsibilities, obligations, and conflicts that might have troubled the parent-child relationship (p. 313). One note of caution raised by Walsh is that this pair needs to avoid triangulating against the parents.

Later, partners must face the possibility of chronic illness and demands for caregiving if one person becomes incapacitated. The proportion of women to men at this time increases quite dramatically. Women are more than four times as likely than men to be widowed. They are also widowed at earlier ages, and the resulting bereavement is a major life stressor.

We would like to remind you that the developmental stages discussed in this chapter are generalizations about families based on assumptions that all families have children, families remain intact over the lifetime of the parents, and children leave home in a logical and sequential way. Of course, this is not the case. Each of these factors creates special issues for the family that need to be taken into account when working with families. Every family, regardless of composition, is unique. In the context of uniqueness, however, the vast majority of families are similar in that families get bigger and then get smaller. Not only do children grow up to form their own families, but family size is affected by divorce and death. At each transition, the family experiences stresses and strains as its members attempt to respond to the changes.

EP 2.1.7a

VARIATIONS AFFECTING THE FAMILY LIFE CYCLE

Economic and cultural trends influence how families move through the life cycle (remember Person-In-Environment). More women are actively involved in the workforce now; in fact, married women in the workforce exceed the number of full-time homemakers (Eichler, 1997). Poverty is more prevalent among children and women. Female-led, single-parent families often experience more severe economic disadvantage than do two-parent families or male-led single-parent families. Moreover, approximately half of all marriages end in divorce. Live-in common-law relationships are now the norm. Death and desertion may disrupt the family life cycle. Eichler (1997) identified major demographic patterns in industrialized countries that have an impact on the family life cycle: the decline in fertility, postponement of marriage, a sharp rise in the incidence of divorce during the 1970s and 1980s, and a growing proportion of people living in small households. The diversity of family styles brings with it differences in family life cycle development. We examine life cycle disruptions here.

Separation and Divorce

A major challenge that is central to the destigmatization and cultural normalization of divorce is the creation of nontraumatic legal processes that do not become party to and inflame the acrimony and alienation that most families bring to the divorce process.
—Pinsof, 2002, p. 152

When I'm alone, I can sleep crossways in my bed without an argument.
—Zsa Zsa Gabor, on being between marriages (www.Bartleby.com)

Divorce is probably of nearly the same date as marriage. I believe, however, that marriage is some weeks the more ancient.
—Voltaire (www.Bartleby.com)

Divorce is a cultural, financial, legal, parental, emotional, and spiritual issue (Murray, 2002). While some religions are simplifying divorce, the degree to which divorced individuals feel supported and accepted will vary. Carter and McGoldrick (1999a) suggest that dissatisfaction with the traditional nuclear family produced the 50 percent divorce rate of the recent past. They (1999b, 2005b) also suggest that statistically, the pattern is now marriage, divorce, remarriage, and redivorce. Coontz (2006) tells us that our standards for what constitutes a "good" marriage have risen steadily.

Coontz (2006) also discovered that the belief that marriage should be based on love and companionship only began to be accepted and practiced in Western Europe and America under the influence of the Enlightenment and the individualistic doctrines of the French and American Revolutions. In response, conservatives of the day—defenders of what was then seen as "traditional" marriage—warned that love would be the death of marriage (p. 9). Later, the concern of the eighteenth-century conservatives was the danger of poor people claiming the right to marry ... similar to the claims of lesbians and gays today (p. 9).

It is now a cliché to suggest that marriage should be more difficult to enter into and divorce easier to obtain. Divorce and other forms of family dissolution have always been part of the family landscape, with rates varying depending upon the time and the legal and religious restrictions (Pinsof, 2002). Several factors have affected the current divorce rate: increased longevity of life, changing women's roles, changing cultural values, and changing legal restrictions. Although there are different types of coupling configurations, statistics represent only one kind of coupling—legal marriages. The statistics exclude relationships formed outside the parameters of legal and religious arrangements, and little is known about the permanence and stability of other types of relationships. Thus, divorce rates apply only to those who marry and for whom the state keeps a record. Moreover, statistics do not reveal how many people are actually living in satisfying relationships; they merely tell the story of how many remain together in a recorded marriage. We also need to point out that while divorce rates have risen, marriage rates have fallen. It appears as though marriage has lost some of its luster and is diminishing in importance as a life goal.

Historically, reasons for divorce have varied because the reasons for marriage were different. Our standards for what constitutes a "good" marriage have risen steadily (Coontz, 2006). While the divorce rate was only 10 percent during the mid-nineteenth century, by the mid-1980s, approximately half of all first marriages and 61 percent of remarriages ended in divorce (Nichols & Schwartz, 2004, p. 138). The divorce rate leveled off after 1980. In fact, one-quarter of all marriages last less than seven years, and about half will end before their twentieth year (Pinsof, 2002). The divorce rate depends on ethnicity, with African Americans having the highest divorce or separation rate (63 percent) for first marriages, compared with 48 percent for whites and 52 percent for Hispanics. For second marriages, the trend for whites is 39 percent (Pinsof, 2002). Several demographic characteristics increase the risk of divorce: marriage before the age of 20, lower income and education levels (with the exception of well-educated women with good incomes), African American ethnicity, Protestantism, and not living together before marriage (Ahrons, 1999).

Gottman (1999) contends that the dissolution of a marriage is often a bigger stressor than marital unhappiness. Divorce is associated with physical and psychological difficulties. Divorce affects all family members, but its effects can be mediated by coparenting and a sustained relationship with the noncustodial parent (easier said than done) (Pinsof, 2002). Trauma can be reduced by redefining divorce as normal and acceptable, increasing social connectedness and social support, and dealing with shame and stigmatization. Regardless of the philosophical debates about whether family social workers should work to keep *all* families together, "it is naïve to think that we can ever again reduce divorce to a minor part of the family terrain by tinkering with law and social policy" (Coontz, 2006, p. 14).

Gottman and Levenson (2002) point out two critical high-risk periods for divorce in the family life cycle. Nearly half of all divorces occur in the first seven years of marriage, which is seen as a volatile and emotional phase of marriage. The second high-risk time for divorce is midlife—a time when most families have adolescents. This latter risk occurs when marital satisfaction bottoms out. It appears that intense emotions, particularly anger leading to conflict, make it difficult to sustain the relationship. If this effect transforms into indifference, it may be easier to stay in the relationship. However, over time the indifference poses another risk in that it results in distance, leading to the demise of the marital relationship.

Major practical and emotional readjustments, as well as short-term distress, accompany separation and divorce (Carter & McGoldrick, 2005b), and it takes between two or three years for a family to adjust to its new structure (p. 374). Throughout the various stages of divorce, certain points are marked by peaks of emotional tension including when the decision is made and then announced, when money and custody arrangements are discussed, when the actual physical separation occurs, when there is contact about money and/or custody, when each child hits a transition point, and when the ex reaches a transition point such as remarriage, illness, or death (p. 376).

Why should someone be forced to remain in a relationship that is chronically troubled or riddled with addiction, abuse, unhappiness, intense conflict, or mental illness? Many family social workers enter families where intense unhappiness or severe conflict exists, and they set as a goal keeping the family intact because they believe that their work is a failure if the relationship dissolves. Yet, we encourage family workers to reexamine this position and develop attitudes that embrace divorce as a viable option for families they are working with.

Though divorce is not necessarily a failure, it punctuates the life cycle of the family in unique ways. Divorce lowers the economic status of family members and demands new coping skills. The major tasks during divorce are to end the relationship while also parenting the children cooperatively. It is as though some couples never really divorce; they keep their relationship alive through anger and use the children as guided missiles against one another. Issues involved in divorce include making the decision to divorce, planning the dissolution of the relationship, separating, and, finally, divorcing. During each stage, family members must come to terms with personal issues related to divorce. For example, upon reflection, partners need to acknowledge their roles in the dissolution of the relationship. If the decision to divorce appears imminent, partners must learn to accept the inevitable. Often, one partner is more reluctant to divorce than the other. Additional issues include forging new relationships with extended family members and mourning losses. Once the divorce is final, the partners must rebuild their lives as single people or adjust to life with a new partner.

The decision to separate and divorce is not made overnight. Rather, it is a *process* that occurs over several stages: the decision, the announcement, and dismantling the family (Ahrons, 1999, 2005). Murray (2002) broadens the process to seven stages: emotional divorce, legal divorce, economic divorce, coparental divorce and the problems of custody, disengagement from the divorce, psychic divorce, and religious divorce. It is apparent that some people may be divorced only legally but not with respect to the other stages.

It is not *what* couples argue about, but *how* they argue, that leads to divorce. Usually one person initiates the divorce. This person has probably been agonizing over the decision for a long time. The person who decides to leave (usually the woman) experiences mounting dissatisfaction coupled with accumulating evidence to justify the decision. Gradually, one person emotionally disengages. Sometimes a crisis will mark an announcement, but other times the move is more gradual. The movement toward divorce is often marked by feelings of guilt, anger, and betrayal. Once the announcement is made, separation occurs. Separations can be orderly or disorderly (Ahrons, 1999, p. 389).

Divorce brings long-standing baggage that affects every family member. Few divorces are without distress, regardless of how dissatisfying couple and family relationships were. Divorce affects families on many levels: family life cycle, finances, individual well-being, friendships and support networks, and relationships with extended kin, to name a few. Some authors claim that it takes up to three years to adjust to the issues posed by divorce. Moreover, divorce is not a binary process; it is not true that one day you are a couple and the next day you wake up divorced. The process of arriving at a divorce can be tumultuous and emotionally draining. Divorce as an emotionally stressful event brings with it many decisions. Within a year after a divorce, about 50 percent of men stop contact with their children and 40 percent do not pay child support (Rosen, 2005).

Wolfe (2001) uncovered a number of difficulties that children from divorced families faced. She found that children from divorced homes experienced more depression than children from nondivorced homes, with many of them experiencing a clinical level of depression. These children also suffered from low self-esteem and irritability. Many children also had sleep disturbances and somatic complaints, typically associated with depression, as well as problems in school. She also discovered overwhelming evidence of extreme parental stress among those who divorce, some of whom were so stressed that they were at risk for committing child abuse. While most parents viewed themselves as competent, many also experienced their parenting responsibilities as a burden, perhaps in part because they were not receiving sufficient emotional and practical support. Wolfe concluded that depression among children of divorce was linked with stressful and undesirable life events. Their parents had little emotional and practical support, and their families were unstable, characterized by emotional problems or drug and alcohol abuse. Families also experienced conflict between husband and wife, and perhaps conflict among the children. In other words, the parents were highly distressed. Wolfe concluded that the problem of depression is so pervasive in divorcing families that workers should make direct enquiries about it. Parents should also be assessed for stress.

Although the impact of divorce on children is a special concern, much of the research on the effects of divorce on children fails to make fair comparisons. For example, Pinsof (2002) suggests that a fairer comparison would be between children from unhappy and deeply troubled marriages. Most children cope emotionally with the separation or divorce of their parents, but for many it still exacts a psychological toll. For some children, divorce and marital separation may be comparable to losing a parent through death (Wallerstein, 1983). Wallerstein and Kelly (1980) suggest the major pitfall of divorce is the impact it has on child development. Parents undergoing a divorce often feel psychologically drained because they have to deal with their personal grief and stress, sapping available emotional energy needed to take care of the children's emotional, physical, and social needs. During postdivorce adjustment, custodial parents are less supportive, less nurturing, and more anxious in their relationship with their children than they were before the divorce

(Bolton & Bolton, 1987; Wallerstein, 1985). Children stand to benefit when the relationship between the parents is supportive of and sensitive to the children maintaining contact with the noncustodial parent. While such decisions should be based on what is best for the children, this is not always the case. Unfortunately, children may become pawns to get at the other parent, and children suffer in the process.

Children between the ages of 6 and 8 feel responsible for the marital breakup (Thompson, Rudolph, & Henderson, 2003), although guilt is not confined exclusively to this age group. Additionally, children may experience academic difficulties, anger, or other behavioral problems related to the divorce. It is not unusual for children to feel rejected and anxious following a divorce, but these emotions are not often acknowledged or dealt with by significant people in the child's life. Divorce is especially hard on young males, for whom it may take up to two years following a divorce to stabilize their lives (Hetherington, Cox, & Cox, 1978). Thus, children are often victims of divorce as they face possible long-term ramifications of marital dissolution (Wallerstein, 1985).

Family disruption depletes psychological resources available to the child (Garbarino, 1992). For example, many separations and divorces are acrimonious, and the child's dual loyalty to parents is threatened. The custodial parent (usually the mother) assumes much of the childcare and household responsibilities, and her financial resources often diminish. In addition, children who are unsupervised for extended periods of time are twice as likely to belong to single-parent families as to families with two parents (Garbarino, 1992). After divorce, fathers commonly feel that they have become unimportant in their children's lives (Ahrons, 2007), making it important for custodial mothers to recognize that children need the benefits of a continuing relationship with their father. When parents are divorced, the family social worker can help mothers examine their gatekeeping role with regard to paternal access to the children.

Separated and divorced fathers fare better financially after divorce. They also benefit financially from less childcare and fewer direct and indirect costs in the form of time away from work and time spent on caregiving. Some are reluctant to disturb children's living arrangements. Behaviors designed to alienate a child emotionally and physically from the noncustodial parent can lead to a breakdown in the parent-child relationship. Parental alienation through verbal, physical, and emotional means by either parent has the potential to negatively influence both the mother-child and father-child bond (Lero, Ashbourne, & Whitehead, 2006, p. 106). Overt and covert tactics may be utilized by a parent to alienate a child from the other parent, ranging from the child not being "available" for visitation to the more subtle, but equally injurious, act of speaking ill of the other parent or encouraging the child to choose between them. Custody and access arrangements may be sabotaged, child support payments may be evaded, and allegations of abuse may be made. Some allegations are real and some are not. The pattern of one parent alienating a child from the other is so common that it is now called the "alienation syndrome." Other noncustodial parents simply give up the battle and disengage completely from the children.

Children usually experience divided loyalties between the custodial and noncustodial parent, and in acrimonious divorces, children may be used as a pawn between parents (Ahrons, 2007). Hostile parental relationships can generate agonizing loyalty conflicts for the children. Parents forget that most children say that they want to have relationships with both parents. It is important for children that their parents are cordial with one another and do not triangulate the child into their conflict. Children find it stressful to maneuver between parents.

Thompson, Rudolph, and Henderson (2003) propose several tasks that children of divorce must successfully accomplish in order to move on with their lives:

- *Feelings of anxiety, abandonment, and denial*: Parental support is a crucial factor in helping a child overcome negative feelings. A parent must explain to the child what has happened without blaming the other partner.
- *Disengaging from parental conflict and distress and resuming their regular activities*: Divorce should not be allowed to encroach on the routine activities in which children have been involved.
- *Resolution of loss*: Children must grieve not only for the loss of a significant person in their lives but also for the loss of other important aspects of their lives such as familiar surroundings and neighborhood friends. Divorce involves coming to terms with many losses—including the loss of attachment (Bernstein, 2007).
- *Resolving anger and self-blame*: Children may feel responsible for the breakup or blame one parent for the divorce. They should be reassured about this.
- *Accepting the permanence of the divorce*: Children often do not consider divorce final. They may hold on to reconciliation fantasies long after the divorce. Some children may even scheme to reunite their parents or develop problems aimed at reuniting their parents. They may do so by developing a problem that both parents need to solve together.
- *Developing realistic hopes regarding relationships*: Children need to recognize that although their parents' relationship failed, positive marital relationships are still possible and that they cannot overgeneralize their parents' failure to all relationships.

Because divorce is laden with many potential land mines for all parties, a growing area of intervention has been in divorce mediation. Outcome studies of mediation suggest that a successful agreement is reached between 50 and 85 percent of the time (Hahn & Kleist, 2000). In some jurisdictions, divorce mediation is mandated. Mediation is most often used to settle disagreements involving the division of property, custody decisions, and visitation rights. Apparently, mediation results more often in joint legal custody than in adversarial processes (Hahn & Kleist, 2000, p. 166).

EXERCISE 4.12 Viable Divorce

Make a list of some circumstances that make divorce a viable and preferred option in families. What actions can a family social worker take with these families?

EXERCISE 4.13 Decisions Involved in Divorcing

Many decisions accompany the decision to divorce. List as many decisions as you can think of that a couple has to make when they divorce (including decisions that crop up as children get older). Compare your list with those of your classmates.

EXERCISE 4.14 Developmental Challenges from Divorce

Discuss the challenges you believe a family experiences immediately after a divorce. Contrast these with what you believe to be the challenges experienced by families who have lost a parent through death. In what ways can a social worker assist the family during and after these critical periods?

EXERCISE 4.15 Good and Bad Divorces

Describe the qualities of a "good" divorce. Describe the qualities of a "bad" divorce. Discuss in class and compare your list with the rest of the class. What can a worker do to help a divorce be "good"?

EXERCISE 4.16 Social Changes Affecting the Divorce Rate

How would the following social changes affect the divorce rate?

1. Longer life span
2. Changing women's roles
3. Changing cultural values
4. Changing legal restrictions

Single Parenting

More people are living single than at any other time in history. Nearly half of all children in the United States live in a single-parent home at some point during childhood, and most single-parent homes are mother-led. Many of the issues related to difficulties in single-parent families pertain to ecological issues rather than structural defects in the unit. Many of these issues revolve around finances, social and emotional support, and role-overload concerns. As stated by Anderson (2005): "Most single parents provide the structure, values, and nurturance that their children need, despite the hardships they experience and the bad press they receive" (p. 399). Moreover, poverty and its associated issues, the history of living in a dysfunctional family, and the stage of adjustment to divorce prevent drawing clear and direct conclusions about single-parent functioning (p. 400).

The number of people who never marry, although still a minority, is growing (Berliner, Jacob, & Schwartzberg, 1999), and never marrying is a viable option. People are also delaying the age at which they decide to marry. At the same time, the number of single-parent families rose from 12 percent in 1970 to 26 percent in 1995 (Mannis, 1999). In addition, the proportion of children born to mothers who have not married is also increasing. What do these statistics reveal? Many of our beliefs are derived from our culture. For example, some might suggest that these statistics are the result of feminism, the decline of religion, the diminished importance of the father, or the erosion of family values. In some quarters, single-parent families are depicted as deviant or as undermining male prerogative. Conversely, others suggest that rigid laws and patriarchal values leave vulnerable family members in untenable family situations. The profession of social work values client self-determination, and the option to divorce is one way self-determination is manifested.

This being said, children from single-parent households have been shown to experience more problems than children from two-parent homes (Blum, Boyle, & Offord, 1988). They have a greater incidence of behavior problems such as conduct disorders, attention deficit disorder, poor school performance, and emotional problems. This is not to suggest that every child from a single-parent family is destined to experience adjustment problems. The problems of single-parent families are compounded by economic difficulties (Eichler, 1997; Goldenberg & Goldenberg, 2000; Nichols & Schwartz, 2004; Pett, 1982) and fatigue (Okun, 1996). On the positive side of the equation, maternal education works to ameliorate the negative impact of these stresses (Tuzlak & Hillock, 1991).

Single parenting can occur for several different reasons: death, divorce, desertion, and never having been married through choice. The various pathways to single parenthood suggest that even single-parent-led families experience great diversity. Regardless of the reason for single-parent status, some but not all single parents might share feelings of loneliness, sadness, guilt, and anger (Goldenberg & Goldenberg, 2000). In addition, divorced parents need to decide whether to cooperate with and support contact of the child with the ex-spouse and his or her family (Carter & McGoldrick, 1999b).

It is important to recognize that children can and do grow up in healthy single-parent households and that not all women choose to share a household with a male partner. Nevertheless, raising children single-handedly is demanding for many people. Often, single-parent households are poor, primarily because of the feminization of poverty. In addition, single parents have difficulty finding time for self-care because few people can or will step in when the parent is tired or overloaded. Social support is important since it may buffer the effects of role strain, stress, conflict, and poverty for single-parent families (Gladow & Ray, 1986). Poverty also plays a role in many of the social and psychological difficulties associated with growing up in a single-parent household.

Both mothers and children in joint custody arrangements fare better than mothers with sole support (Hanson, 1986). Single parents can experience role overload as they are burdened with tasks that are usually shared between two people. (Even in some two-parent households, it is possible to be a single parent because the other partner does not carry his or her share.) Perhaps the burden is greatest when children are young and when they need the most care, attention, and supervision. Once the children become adolescents, parental power may dwindle with no one to back up the authority of the lone parent (Anderson, 1999). Task overload may be reflected in family disorganization, social isolation, and problems in the parent-child relationship. Single parents who have a rich network of kin and friends fare better than single parents who are socially isolated. The temptation might be to become romantically attached to another partner, a solution that works for some but not all.

Many interventions with single-parent families will and should be ecologically based. "Since the context of single-parent households is so vital, an assessment of the number and quality of supports available to single parents forms one of the cornerstones of the treatment" (Anderson, 2005, p. 403). Moreover, the support networks of the children must also be looked at, particularly the father (pp. 406–407). Issues related to provision of concrete resources and social support need to be built into interventions. In addition, single parents may need assistance with stress management, grief counseling, and skills related to effective child management. Finally, single parents will benefit from an enhanced informal support network including grandparents and friends.

The special tasks of parents in single-parent families are indicated in the following list:

- Develop adequate social support systems.
- Resolve feelings of sadness, anger, and loneliness.
- Cope with stress, fatigue, and role overload without taking it out on the children.
- Develop child management skills that do not result in anger directed at children.
- Develop time management skills that allow for meeting children's needs as well as personal needs.
- Access to concrete services, such as employment, housing, and respite care.

Remarriage, Stepparenting, and Blended Families: How Many Times Do You Hear About Ugly Stepfathers?

The privileged status of the biological nuclear family ... contributes to the stigmatization of all nonnuclear families, but especially that of stepfamilies.
—Anne Jones, 2003

"A second marriage involves the interweaving of three, four, or more families whose previous family life cycle courses have been disrupted by death or divorce" (McGoldrick & Carter, 2005e, p. 417). Stepfamilies are the fastest growing family configuration (Greeff & Du Toit, 2009). Negative stereotypes about stepfamilies abound in fairy tales and Hollywood; yet stepparenting is commonplace and not the exclusive domain of storytellers. Between one-third and one-half of families will be part of a stepfamily (Jones, 2003; McGoldrick & Carter, 1999, 2005e). Despite biases and myths, stepfamilies are neither problematic nor inferior. They do, however, face special challenges. As with all other families, some blended families function quite well, whereas others have difficulty navigating common issues. Mothers most often are awarded custody, making a stepfather family the most common arrangement.

The process of recreating a new family based on the experience and needs of multiple individuals can be complex. Remarriage involves a complex set of changing conditions starting with pre-divorce tensions and extending through separation and reorganization of a new household and parent-child relationships to remarriage and stepfamily integration. The process is complicated and can even be messy (Greeff & Du Toit, 2009). Furthermore, the issues related to adjustment are associated with the ages of the children at the time of the re-marriage. The process is made even more difficult if the ex-partner is uncooperative or tries to sabotage the new family unit. Embarking on a new relationship requires an emotional divorce from the first marriage (Holman, 1983). Remarriage demands dramatic changes to a new family's organization. The joining of two families is made more complex, given that the parent-child bond existed before the second marriage, which sometimes leads to stepparents competing with their stepchildren in the relationship (McGoldrick & Carter, 2005e). While many step relationships are at first tenuous, relationships with stepparents improve over time (Ahrons, 2007). When parents remarry, they often believe that their children will share their enthusiasm, but this is seldom the case.

Divorced adults must deal with their own fears about entering into a new relationship. In addition, remarried families experience common triangles that show up on genograms (McGoldrick, 1999a; McGoldrick, Gerson, & Petry, 2008); family social workers must be keenly attuned to these triangles because they can rapidly become ghosts that haunt current relationships. The first triangle consists of the two new partners and the previous partner. The second triangle includes the two new partners and one or more of the children. In fact, in previously divorced families, arguments about child rearing occur most often (Stanley, Markman, & Whitton, 2002). Each triangle is infused with *potential* conflict.

Blended relationships experience a higher risk of separation than relationships without children, in part because of negative communication and intergenerational issues related to divorce (Greeff & Du Toit, 2009; Halford, Nicholson, & Sanders, 2007). Things that can influence integration could be experiences in the previous marriage, continued contact with the former spouse, differences in personal maturity, life experiences, social status, and different norms and expectations (Greeff & Du Toit, 2009). Four tasks encountered by blended families include development of an effective new couple relationship, maintenance of parent-child bonds, formation of new step relationships, and the development of a sense of membership in the new unit. In stepfamilies, loneliness might be exchanged for conflict (Nichols & Schwartz, 2007), and parents may be engaged in a continuous struggle over child rearing. Conflict may occur over who assumes primary parenting responsibilities for the children and what type of parenting should occur. Rules in stepfamilies may be vaguely defined initially, with a lengthy period of time elapsing before roles, rules, and boundaries are reconfigured. Children may feel confused and harbor resentment toward the stepparent whom they consider has usurped the role of the noncustodial parent. Rivalry between stepsiblings may be intense (Thompson, Rudolph, & Henderson, 2003). In addition, children's need to maintain contact with the noncustodial parent can interfere with the custodial parent's desire for a complete emotional break.

Children sometimes have difficulty adjusting to life in a blended family. They may have trouble accepting the fact that their parents will never reconcile, and loyalty to both parents may be tested. Divided loyalties are likely when one parent uses the children to direct resentment at the former partner. In addition, children may fantasize about their parents eventually reuniting and may try to make this happen. When there are other stepchildren entering the relationship, adjustment is exacerbated since it might involve competing for affection, attention, and material possessions.

Stepfamilies face many tasks in order to accomplish successful integration:

- Mourning losses of previous relationships
- Arriving at a satisfactory stepparenting role
- Redefining financial and social obligations

- Agreeing on visitation and custody
- Establishing consistent leadership and discipline
- Ensuring that expectations for relationships are realistic
- Forming new emotional bonds in the family
- Developing new traditions
- Dealing with sexuality in the home
- Developing an effective new couple relationship
- Developing a sense of family membership (Greeff & Du Toit, 2009; Thompson, Rudolph, & Henderson, 2003; Visher & Visher, 1982).

Boundaries in newly blended families need to be negotiated. Not only must members establish boundaries concerning physical space (sharing, property), but they must also decide how much emotional closeness to develop with new family members and mutually agree on roles that will work. Adults involved in a marital dissolution often need a clean break from the relationship; yet the presence of children demands that contact with each parent be ongoing and consistent for access to be maintained. Additionally, joining family subsystems (mother-child or father-child) bring to the new system independent functioning. Changes and adaptations are needed to combine the new family subsystems adequately (Nichols & Schwartz, 2007).

In a review of research on remarried families, McGoldrick and Carter (1999, 2005e) suggest that children fare better when:

- Custodial parents function effectively, and children have regular contact with both parents.
- There is less parental conflict.
- The extended family approves of the relationship.
- The biological parent handles discipline and visitation arrangements.
- Conflicting role expectations between the stepmother and biological mother are avoided.
- Children visit regularly with their noncustodial parent.
- The relationship with the ex-partner is low-key and amicable.
- Nontraditional gender roles kick in.
- The extended family is cooperative.

In addition, family integration is easier initially when the children are not adolescents and there is not a new child in the new relationship. Blended families are capable of resilience in the face of these challenges. Greef and Du Toit (2009) suggest that resilience in blended family arrangements will be manifested through positive relationships and support, spirituality and religion, affirming family communication, conveyance of care and support, a sense of family control over outcomes, and development of social support.

EXERCISE 4.17   Developmental Tasks of Stepfamilies

A blended family must accomplish certain tasks as the family subsystems merge. List some concrete interventions the family social worker can carry out to help the family complete each of the tasks listed in this chapter.

Death of a Family Member

Historically, most marriages lasted only between 10 and 20 years. Death of one partner was the predominant reason for the end of a marriage (Pinsof, 2002). Divorce is now the main reason for the end of a marriage, bringing with it numerous issues. Some of the issues related to divorce also apply to families in which one of the parents has died (Wallerstein, 1983). Although the death of a parent in families with young children is rare (Eichler, 1997), it does happen. The circumstances of the death also affect adjustment. Death through suicide, for example, has a different effect on the family and its members than does death through natural causes.

Death in a family creates challenges related to adaptation and long- and short-term family reorganization (McGoldrick & Walsh, 2005). Adaptation requires that the family put the loss into perspective and move on (p. 185). It disrupts family equilibrium and patterns of interaction (p. 186). The extent and type of family disruption depends upon a number of things including the circumstances of the death, the relationship with the person (partner, parent, child), when in the family life cycle the death occurred, and other issues that may be going on with the family and individuals in the family.

Death of a loved one is the most stressful life event that families face (Greeff & Human, 2004). All families will encounter the death of an immediate family member at one point or another. McGoldrick and Walsh (2005) assert that five factors influence the impact of a loss:

- Timing of the death
- Concurrence of multiple losses or loss in conjunction with other major life cycle changes
- A history of traumatic loss and unresolved mourning
- The nature of the death
- The function of that person in the family (p. 186).

To children, losing a parent through divorce can seem almost as final as death. Although widowhood is less likely to be associated with the dramatic drop in income that often occurs among custodial parents after divorce, widowed parents are less likely than divorced parents to remarry (Fustenberg, 1980). In addition, families who experience the death of one parent are likely to maintain contact with the deceased parent's family and with members of the community. Losing a child is also devastating to parents and the rest of the family.

When widows and widowers with children do remarry, there is an increased likelihood of the new parent being accepted by the children if the new parent is a father. It appears that children have a harder time accepting new mothers (McGoldrick & Carter, 1999). At the same time, children need to be allowed space to grieve for the deceased parent. However, triangles involving ghosts are harder to deal with (p. 422). Regardless of the timing and nature of the death of a parent, grief is a long-standing issue that ripples through the family. Family dynamics will determine the course of the grieving process, and the family social worker can help family members grieve together and alone; both processes are necessary.

Greeff and Human (2004) outline two processes that need to be used in order for a family to deal with death:

1. Adjustment that includes the influence of protective factors in facilitating the family's ability to cope. Families must undergo efforts to maintain their integrity and functioning and fulfill developmental tasks in the face of risk factors.
2. Adaptation that involves the functioning of recovery factors that promote the family's ability to "bounce back" and adapt. Adapting involves altering the environment, the community, and the family's relationship to the community.

In the process, families need to draw upon all their resources to cope with the death. This involves drawing upon family characteristics, behavior patterns, and capabilities that cushion the impact of the death and help the family recover. The family can do this through sharing the experience of death, open and honest communication, adapting to change in the family structure, dealing with blurred boundaries and role expectations, empathy, and tolerance of conflict. To move on, family members need to reorganize and reinvest in other relationships and life pursuits and find a way to make meaning of death through cultural and religious beliefs and linkages to the social worlds. Spirituality is a fundamental resource for resilience in that it provides the individual with the ability to understand and overcome stressful situations (Greeff & Human, 2004, p. 30). Moreover, economic resources can buffer the family's experience of loss and influence their adaptation. Finally, tapping into social support from extended family and friends is most important, as is intrafamilial emotional and practical support. The key is when the family works collaboratively to confront their challenges.

Parenting by Grandparents

Despite the mobility of many families, grandparents often play a significant role in the lives of their grandchildren. For example, many grandparents care for their grandchildren when parents are at work (Gattai & Musatti, 1999). In past decades, parenting by grandparents was most common in African American families, but now is increasingly common in other ethnic groups (Okun, 1996). Increased drug and alcohol problems among young adults, increased divorce rates, harsher prison sentencing for criminal acts, the spread of HIV/AIDS, and increased teen pregnancy rates are causing many children to live without adequate parental care (Williamson, Softas-Nall, & Miller, 2001). When faced with a choice between seeing their grandchildren placed in foster care or caring for the grandchildren themselves, many grandparents feel obliged to take on parental responsibilities.

Child rearing by grandparents is not necessarily without stress and difficulty. For example, some child-rearing practices of grandparents may conflict with modern parenting techniques (Okun, 1996). Also, grandparents may worry about who will care for their grandchildren if they die or become incapacitated. In addition, many older people lack financial resources to care for their grandchildren, and adding another mouth to feed in an already financially strapped household may create additional burdens. Additionally, some grandparents may have looked forward to time on their own without any responsibilities for others. Grandparents, as parents, experience a disruption in the family life cycle because they are caring for children at a time when many peers are enjoying the benefits of spare time and relief from some of their financial obligations.

Grandparents who take on the role of parent for their grandchildren face emotional pressures when the grandchildren move in. These include loss of time and freedom and the resultant changes in lifestyle. Becoming a caretaker leads to increased physical, emotional, and economic vulnerability. Williamson, Softas-Nall, and Miller (2001) also related the following themes in their study on grandmothers assuming a parenting role (these themes probably apply across the board):

- Ongoing involvement of the parents was an important piece affecting adjustment to the situation. Lower stress was associated with the view that grandmothers' relationships were nonconflictual, supportive, and respectful of the grandparents' arrangements. When parents interfered with the placement, grandmothers may have felt anger and frustration, particularly when the absent parent raised expectations in the children and did not follow through. When parents collaborated, grandmothers were satisfied with the arrangement.
- Many grandmothers reported depression and feeling overwhelmed, often while trying to work and maintain a home. They also encountered financial and discipline issues.
- When the grandchildren arrived as a result of abuse and neglect, strong feelings of anger, anxiety, and general unhappiness were evoked among grandmothers.
- Health concerns and concerns about grandparent longevity arose. Grandparents hoped to live long enough for the grandchildren, and lack of health insurance for grandchildren was also a concern.
- Discipline issues were problematic, including changed behaviors after visiting parents, leading children to believe that they did not have to obey the grandmother.
- Grandparents reported on the time required to focus on learning problems, low grades, poor study habits, and behavioral problems in school.
- Changes to grandmothers' role and plans were indicated. Lives, self-images, and plans for growing older were altered by the arrival of the grandchildren. Grandparents had envisioned retirement as a time for leisure and travel.
- Positive emotions were also associated with grandparenting. Grandparents expressed pride at keeping children out of foster homes.
- Regardless of everything, grandparents did not regret their decision to take in the grandchildren.

Regardless of whether grandparents assume a primary or secondary caretaking responsibility for their grandchildren, they often develop a strong attachment with them and play a very important role in their development. Wilcoxon (1991) identified five important roles of grandparents:

- *Historian*, who can link children with the familial and cultural past
- *Role model*, or an example of older adulthood
- *Mentor*, or wise elder, who has experienced his or her own life transitions
- *Wizard*, who is a master storyteller
- *Nurturer*, who is the ultimate support person during familial crises and transitions.

CASE 4.2	Working with Diverse Family Structures

The family social worker prepares herself or himself to work with diverse family structures. Examples are a gay couple who coparent a child, a single parent, and grandparents parenting their grandchildren. Following is a case example of the latter:

Catherine and Walter are a retired couple who became involved with Child Protective Services when their daughter, Margie, dropped off her children at the CPS office and disappeared. Catherine and Walter agreed to take custody of the children, Amy (8), Harold (6), and Linda (3). All of the members of the newly constructed family have required counseling, which was arranged by referral from the family social worker to a family agency. Some of the issues experienced by the children are grief over the loss of their mother; adjustment to their new parents, Catherine and Walter; adjustment to a more structured style of parenting than they had previously experienced; and adjustment to a new neighborhood. Problems experienced by Catherine and Walter include adjustment to having young children, adjusting to societal norms about how to parent that have changed from when the couple were young parents years ago, and loss of the freedom of their previous retired lifestyle.

© Cengage Learning 2013

EXERCISE 4.18   Developmental Variations

If your family of origin or that of a friend's was not a traditional middle-class family, describe how the family's developmental stages differed from the stages described in this chapter.

EP 2.1.7a

CHAPTER SUMMARY

One way for social workers to understand families is to become familiar with issues that arise at various developmental stages. Stages of family development include marriage or partnering, birth of the first child, families with preschool children, families with school-aged children, families with teenagers, and families with young people leaving home.

The transition from each stage to the next is associated with a variety of stresses and strains for family members. Understanding these issues enables the family social worker to help families cope with changes that occur as the family matures.

KEY TERMS

Family Life Cycle Stages*
Marriage/Partnering/Pair Bonding/Affiliative Orientation
Birth of the First Child and So On
Families with Preschool Children
Families with School-Aged Children
Families with Teenagers
Families with Young People Leaving Home: Launching
Boomerang Phase
Issues for Older Parents

*Note: Stages may not be linear.

SUGGESTED READING

Carter, B., & McGoldrick, M. (Eds.). (2005). *The expanded family life cycle: Individual, family, and social perspectives* (3rd ed.). Boston, MA: Allyn & Bacon. This edited text is the bread and butter of understanding the family life cycle. Every chapter is replete with rich detail regarding the various life cycle phases. It also discusses the phases through the lens of diversity—diversity in terms of countering the linear model and also diversity in terms of family characteristics that impact the family life cycle.

COMPETENCY NOTES

E.P. 2.1.4a Recognize the extent to which a culture's structures and values may oppress, marginalize, alienate, or create or enhance privilege and power: Recognize the diverse structures including development stages, gender, culture, etc.

E.P. 2.1.7a Utilize conceptual frameworks to guide the processes of assessment, intervention, and evaluation: A developmental conceptual framework can be helpful in assessing individuals' development as well as families' developmental stages.

E.P. 2.1.7b Critique and apply knowledge to understand person and the environment: An additional assessment consideration is the families' social class.

If a family were a container, it would be a nest, an enduring nest, loosely woven, expansive, and open. If the family were a fruit, it would be an orange, a circle of sections, held together but separable—each segment distinct. If the family were a boat, it would be a canoe that makes no progress unless everyone paddles. If the family were a sport, it would be baseball: a long, slow, nonviolent game that is never over until the last out. If the family were a building, it would be an old, but solid structure that contains human history, and appeals to those who see the carved moldings under all the plaster, the wide plank floors under the linoleum, the possibilities.

— **Letty Pogrebin, 1983 (www.Bartleby.com)**

Family Strengths and Resilience

CHAPTER **5**

LEARNING OBJECTIVES

- Conceptual: Understand strengths-based practice. Students will also gain an understanding of family risk, culture, and resilience using a strengths-based lens.
- Perceptual: Observe family and community strengths.
- Valuational/Attitudinal: Value families' strengths and resilience. Believe in a strengths-based approach versus a pathologizing approach.
- Behavioral: Learn how to ask about family and community strengths.

STRENGTHS-BASED PRACTICE

Strengths based, resilience oriented approaches are needed to shift focus from how families have failed to how they can succeed.

—*Froma Walsh, 1998*

In this chapter, we introduce the concepts of strengths-based practice and family resilience, which become a beacon guiding our intervention with families. Traditionally, social workers have been educated pessimists! They have been pulled to the dark side through teachings about dysfunction and pathology so much that

147

they see them in many places. The focus of family social work historically has dealt with distress and adversity, dimming family social workers' vision to notice what is going right. The emphasis on what is going wrong can be all-consuming because it is problems that cause family pain and distress and are the reasons why families engage in family social work. The urgency to deal with pressing problems has relegated family strengths and health to the backseat of family work.

Pathologizing families has contributed to a practice in which family social workers get to know families on the basis of what is negative. The family social worker then sets out to "repair the damage" by eliminating or correcting certain behaviors. Nevertheless, the process of "correcting" is only part of the equation. The other part entails recognizing what is going right, reinforcing those behaviors, and then building on family strengths and competence—thereby creating a more wide-angled practice with families. Families appreciate the recognition of their positive attributes, and having a family social worker acknowledge them enhances the working relationship and builds confidence. It also establishes a foundation upon which families can fall back once family work is completed and new difficulties emerge in the future. Later, families can draw from these identified strengths to self-correct.

Over the past decade and a half, helping professionals have started to pay attention to resilience; it entails a complex process involving the biological, psychological, and social factors that neutralize the negative effects of stressful events and help individuals and families to overcome difficult life events. Through a focus on strengths and resilience, social workers can become educated optimists! Strengths-based practice and tuning into a family's resilience guide social workers to develop interventions from a positive perspective.

The strengths-based perspective reveals to family social workers how to discover and explore, embellish, and exploit families' strengths and resources in the journey of achieving their goals, realizing their dreams, and shedding the shackles of their own lack of confidence and misgivings (Saleebey, 2000). It trusts the creativity, courage, and innate courage of a family under intense pressure. Using this perspective, family social workers adopt a unique lens through which to view families, their environments, their difficulties, and their capacity to draw from existing internal and external resources. Rather than focusing exclusively on problems, family social work forms a strong foundation for family and environmental building blocks.

The shift to illuminating family abilities instead of solely concentrating on deficits and problems rebalances the long-standing overemphasis on pathology and assumptions of causality dominated by the medical model and psychoanalysis (Walsh, 2002). In the process of moving to an affirmative focus, the relationship between the family social worker and the family becomes more collaborative and empowering. Assessment and intervention are redirected from how problems were caused to how they can be resolved, amplifying and using extant and buried resources and abilities lurking under the surface.

Family strengths-based practice is defined as "the set of relationships and processes that support and protect families and family members, especially in times of adversity" (Myers, 2003). Sometimes clients may be competent and successful in facets of their lives that we fail to see, in part because families present with multiple problems that divert our attention (Gilligan, 2004). Working with family strengths is both an attitude and a skill. Saleebey hints that, "strengths may lie in unlikely places," making it imperative to develop an awareness and respect for positive qualities and abilities, talents, and resources.

Much has been written about how families get derailed. We know considerably less about what successful families do, and we are handicapped by a paucity of research and theory about healthy relationships (Young, 2004). Families are diverse and enjoy multiple domains of competent functioning in spite of specific problem areas (Benzies & Mychasuik, 2009). It is important, then, to tune into the strengths that families use to deal with everyday problems as well as larger life crises.

There is no universal model or definition of a healthy family (Walsh, 2006). Reflect on the following famous quote about families: "Happy families are all alike; every unhappy family is unhappy in its own way." Was Tolstoy correct in his depiction of happy families? If so, what are the qualities of happy families? Now substitute "healthy" for "happy." It is important to remember that while all families experience stress at one time or another, they all also share times that are joyful, intimate, and problem-free. Experiencing times that are stressful and problematic does not mean that families are dysfunctional or unhealthy. "The presence of risk factors does not imply a dysfunctional family but it does increase the likelihood that family problems will develop" (Greeff, Vansteenwegen, & Ide, 2006). Walsh (2006) agrees, saying that it is a myth that healthy families are problem-free.

DEFINITIONS OF RESILIENCE

A number of definitions for resilience exist. Consider the following definitions:

- Resilience involves the ability of a family to respond positively to an adverse event and emerge strengthened, more resourceful, and more confident (Benzies & Mychasuik, 2009, p. 104).
- Resilience refers to positive adaptation patterns in the context of significant risk or adversity and combines the interaction of risk factors and the presence of protective factors (Greeff & Du Toit, 2009).
- Resilience includes "[t]he characteristics that help families resist disruption in the face of change and adapt in the face of crisis. Resiliency is the family system's response to stress and involves the interaction of family problem solving and coping, family resistance resources, social support, and family coherence" (McCubbin, cited in Greeff, Vansteenwegen, & Ide, 2006).
- Resilience is the capacity to rebound from adversity strengthened and more resourceful. It is more than just hanging on (Walsh, 2006).
- Resilience is the family's ability to cultivate strengths to positively meet the challenges of life (National Network for Family Resiliency, 1995).
- Family resiliency includes characteristics, dimensions, and properties, which help families to be resistant to disruption in the face of change and adaptive in the face of crisis situations (McCubbin & McCubbin, 1988).

Other phrases capturing resilience include "self-righting capacity" and "responding with resourcefulness and tenacity when encountering extreme challenges." Challenges include normative (e.g., stages of the life cycle) and non-normative stressors (health problems or unemployment), ongoing family strains (e.g., marital conflict), and daily hassles (e.g., getting the children ready for school in the morning) (Patterson, 2002). "To be resilient, one must be exposed to risk and then respond successfully" (Fraser, Richman, & Galinsky, 1999, p. 137). A positive response to risk involves tapping into family resources as part of the family's coping behaviors.

In synthesizing these definitions, several features of resilience stand out. First, resilience is tested and revealed in the face of adversity. Second, resilience involves a constructive response to difficulties through mobilization of a unique set of available resources. The resources can include qualities and processes in the individual, family, and community. Probably no single set of resources works alone to bolster resilience; rather, a complex interaction of factors at multiple levels comes into play. Third, the family responds in such a way as to overcome the adverse event and arrive at the other end stronger than before.

Resilience is starting to move from being an abstract concept to one that has practical implications for social work practice. Resilience develops not through the ability to sidestep adverse events, but rather through a family's successful use of protective responses that help them cope with these events in such a way that the family is strengthened (Benzie & Mychasuik, 2009). Resiliency, then, is a dynamic process, not a destination. It is affected by a number of factors and varies in strength over time and circumstances. Families may be resilient during one crisis, but struggle during another vulnerable period. Resilience is boosted by protective factors and thwarted by risk factors.

Protective factors augment a response to a threatening event by arming the family with resources to defend against the deleterious effects of challenges and increase the probability of a positive outcome. Risk factors, on the other hand, threaten the probability of a positive outcome. Both risk and protective factors exist in all families and can include many things. By understanding resilience, family social workers will be more able to identify strengths alongside of assessing problems.

MEASURING RESILIENCE

A number of instruments and frameworks designed for assessment are available to help family social workers pinpoint sources of strength and difficulty.

Gardner and colleagues (2008) present the "Family Adaptive Model," which looks at the dynamic tension between protection and risk along five dimensions: demands (stressors), appraisals (how the family views the situation), social supports (from each other and from others outside the family), coping (what a family does about demands), and adaptation. Demands include major life challenges such as socioeconomic status, health problems, abuse, and so on. Multiple demands that pile up simultaneously are considered multiplicative rather than additive. Therefore, more than one stressor being exerted on the family increases vulnerability. Adaptive appraisals are beliefs and attitudes that the family draws into the situation about its ability to handle the demands and make sense out of what is happening to them. Social support has long been recognized as an important factor that cushions against negative life events and provides comfort. It comes from a number of sources such as extended kin, friends, community networks and institutions, work, and so on. The role of social support is broad in that it can offer support along a number of dimensions: emotional, psychological, informational, instrumental, economic, and so on.

In Chapter 8, we present the Family Categories Schema that can be used to identify how families are functioning in the areas of (1) problem solving, (2) affective responsiveness, (3) affective involvement, (4) communication, (5) role behavior, (6) autonomy, (7) modes of behavioral control, and (8) general functioning. This framework, while helpful in assessing difficulties, can also show family social workers where to look for a family's positive qualities by highlighting strengths in each category.

EXERCISE 5.1   Family Strengths

Break into eight groups. Each group is to take one of the eight areas of functioning in the Family Categories Schema and make a list of possible strengths that can be found in this schema. Present your list to the other groups in class. Discuss how a family social worker might work with the various strengths.

Family strengths and family health are closely interrelated. As such, Hettler (1984, cited in Myers, 2003) proposed a six-dimensional model of healthy family functioning: 1) physical, 2) emotional, 3) social, 4) intellectual, 5) occupational, and 6) spiritual. Each dimension points to an area of potential strength for a family and gives family social workers direction for where to look when working with a family.

EXERCISE 5.2   Potential Strengths

Make a list of potential sources of strength in Hettler's six-dimensional model of healthy functioning. Compare your list with the rest of the class.

Similarly, the Wheel of Wellness model posed by Sweeney and Witmer (1991, cited in Myers, 2003) describes health as stemming from interrelated and interconnected life tasks that include spirituality, work and leisure, friendship, love, and self-direction. These are all included in Hettler's model described above. Self-direction is subdivided into (1) self-worth, (2) sense of control, (3) realistic beliefs, (4) emotional responsiveness and management, (5) intellectual stimulation, (6) problem solving and creativity, (7) sense of humor, (8) exercise, (9) nutrition, (10) self-care, (11) gender identity, (12) cultural identity, and (13) stress management. These tasks interact dynamically with family, community, religion, education, government, media, and business or industry.

EXERCISE 5.3   Wheel of Wellness

Use the wheel to assess the wellness of your own family. Imagine a family social worker helping your family, and write down his or her appropriate strengths-based suggestions. These suggestions would be about building on your family's strengths.

McCubbin and McCubbin (1988) considered that resilience involves two family processes:

1. Adjustment that involves the influence of protective factors in facilitating the family's ability and efforts to maintain its integrity and functioning and how they fulfill developmental tasks in the face of risk factors, and
2. Adaptation that involves the functioning of recovery factors that promote the family's ability to "bounce back" and adapt in family crisis situations. Adapting involves altering the environment, the community, and the family's relationship to the community.

In their study of resilient families, McCubbin and McCubbin found a family type they called "Regenerative Families." These families cultivated trust and respect and worked to maintain emotional calm and stability. They had faith, accepted stressful events and difficulties, and worked together to solve problems. They also felt in control. Compared with other families, Regenerative Families were strongly bonded and flexible, had greater satisfaction with other members of the family and people outside the family, and enjoyed good physical and emotional health (p. 251).

In the Circumplex Model of Family Function, Olson and colleagues depict two dimensions: "cohesion" and "adaptability" of family functioning (Olson, Sprenkle, & Russell, 1989; Olson, Russell, & Sprenkle, 1989; Olson & Lavee, 1989). A balance of family cohesion and adaptability potentially captures some of the qualities of family resilience.

Family cohesion concerns the "emotional bonding that family members have toward one another" (Olson, Russell, Sprenkle, 1989, p. 60). It includes emotional bonding, boundaries, coalitions, time, space, friends, decision making, and interests and recreation. Family cohesion ranges from "disengaged" (very low) to "separated" (low to moderate) to "connected" (moderate to high) to "enmeshed" (very high). Families in the middle of the dimension ("separated" or "connected") are considered healthy because family members can be both connected to and independent of their family. Disengaged or enmeshed families are considered problematic.

"Adaptability," the second dimension of the model, is "the ability of the marital or family system to change its power structure, role relationships, and relationship rules in response to situational and developmental stress" (Olson, Russell, & Sprenkle, 1989, p. 60). Adaptability ranges from "rigid" (low) to "structured" (low to moderate) to "flexible" (moderate to high) to "chaotic" (very high). The middle ranges of "structured" and "flexible" adaptability characterize a well-functioning family as a matter of degree. A structured relationship is less rigid, less authoritarian, and more shared. A flexible relationship is even less rigid, and the leadership is more equally shared. A rigid (highly authoritarian leadership) or chaotic relationship (erratic or limited leadership) is considered problematic for the family and its members.

Based on the Circumplex Model of Family Functioning, one can conclude that families that are cohesive (in the "separated" or "connected" range) and families that are adaptable (in the "structured" or "flexible" range) are best equipped to tackle family difficulties.

EXERCISE 5.4   Resilience and You

Reflect on a difficult period in your life—a difficult time that you overcame. Using a strengths-based lens, identify four individual qualities, four family qualities, and four social qualities that helped you deal with this difficulty. Keep the nature of the difficulty to yourself, but provide the class with a list of the qualities that helped you.

EXERCISE 5.5   Exploring Resilience

Split into groups of two. Each student will recall a difficult time in his or her family of origin and share this experience with a partner. The student will then talk about the strengths within the family that helped the student and the family deal with the difficulty.

QUALITIES OF RESILIENCE

Professional helpers often view themselves as central to a family's life. Yet, Gilligan (2004) argues that positive influence flows from multiple sources. Sometimes resilience is based on competence in a particular domain such as parenting skills or family cohesion (Patterson, 2002). The role of the family social worker, then, is to help the family tap into and release positive energies that are trapped behind a wall of despair and feelings of being overwhelmed and to connect them with a supportive environment. Reflecting on the work from Miller, Hubble, and Duncan (1995), we point out that although the quality of the relationship with the worker is an important contributor to change, the most powerful influences on the change process are client factors. This means that as much as 40 percent of change can be attributed to the characteristics of the family. Focusing on the positive aspects of family functioning will optimize the probability of positive movement.

These positive factors include personal characteristics and belief systems as well as resources available within a strong social support network. This means that family social workers might not be the exclusive or even the primary source of help, but their egos can handle it! The worker's task, more than being the sole source of help, is to tap into reservoirs of strength in the family and its environment. As a starting point, he or she should ask, "What is the client doing well? What are other people doing well?" (Walsh, 2003).

A number of family qualities emerge when we speak of strengths and resilience. First, flexible families have the ability to move in a positive direction in spite of the need for outside assistance during rough periods. Parents in these families provide firm but flexible leadership during difficult times as well as nurturance, protection, and guidance. Second, these families have strong communication and problem-solving abilities that allow them to see crisis situations clearly. At the same time, the family is able to respond effectively to one another and problem solve together. Research also highlights the importance of supportive individuals. Researchers note the importance of warmth, affection, emotional support, and clear-cut reasonable structure and limits (Walsh, 1998, p. 11). Walsh adds other qualities to this list: crediting positive intentions, praising efforts and achievements, drawing out hidden resources and lost or hidden competence, locating strengths in the midst of adversity, and building empathic connections with and between family members. All these qualities fit well into the areas covered by the Family Categories Schema.

Benzies and Mychasuik (2009) posit that factors related to resilience have negative and positive poles, such as education, health, and income, which fall along a risk-protective continuum. For example, low educational levels pose a risk while higher educational levels serve as a protective factor. Strengths might also include such positive relational qualities as closeness, concern, caring, involvement, and positive communication. Resilient families are able to draw on successful coping strategies to meet their challenges and stresses. Moreover, factors related to positive child development are connected with parental well-being, including physical and mental health; shared family activities such as household chores, routines, and recreation; parental involvement in children's activities; and positive communication patterns. In response, we reiterate here that "In order to help children, you must first help parents."

EP 2.1.4b

The hallmarks of resilience are initiative and perseverance, both of which are fueled by hope and confidence. Individuals and systems can both be resilient. Qualities of resilience then include: (1) the ability to change or adapt to negative life circumstances—overcoming the odds, (2) the capacity to bounce back—sustained competence under stress, (3) the ability to mount a challenge against the risk factor under question (Hinton, 2003, p. 38), (4) recovery from trauma, and (5) successful adaptation despite adversity. Patterson (2002) considers family meaning as an important component of resilience that includes how families define their demands and abilities, their family identity, and their worldview.

EP 2.1.10b

EP 2.1.10e

FAMILY RESILIENCE

In the field of family therapy, we have come to realize that successful interventions depend as much on the resources of the family as on the skills of the therapist.
—Froma Walsh, 1999

It should be clear by now that a strengths-based and resilience-oriented family approach builds on the family's and community's capacity to master adversity. While most research on resilience has focused on individuals, Walsh (2003), among others, has been intrigued by the fact that some families are shattered by crisis whereas others emerge strengthened and more resourceful after a crisis. "The paradox of resilience is that the worst of times can also bring out our best" (Walsh, 1998, p. 10). Resilience therefore involves the ability to withstand and rebound from adversity, or to bounce forward. It refers to coping and adaptational processes within the family *as a functional unit* (Walsh, 1998, p. 14). Resilient families are able to achieve positive and even unexpected outcomes when challenged by adversity.

Resilience and stressors reverberate throughout a family. Stressors are problematic in that they affect children to the extent that they disrupt crucial family processes and relationships (Patterson, 2002, cited in Walsh, 1998). Luckily, resilient families are able to absorb these stressors. A strengths-based, resilience-oriented approach fundamentally alters the traditional deficit-based lens of viewing troubled families as pathological and beyond repair to seeing them as challenged by life's adversities (Walsh, 2002). It involves strengthening protective mechanisms that a family possesses in order to prevent poor outcomes (Patterson, 2002).

Resilience is a dynamic process that includes a broad "class of phenomena involving successful adaptation in the context of significant threats to development" (Fraser, Richman, & Galinsky, 1999, p. 138) and other life course events. It also entails meeting the demands and mounting capacity that stem from individuals within the family, the family unit as a whole, and the community.

Resilience is not a naïve minimization of difficult life experiences, pains, and hurts. Rather, it is the ability to trudge on in the face of these difficulties—believing that as much as trauma is unpleasant, it can also be instructive and transformative (Saleebey, 1996, p. 299). Resilient families believe in their abilities and also are aware of ongoing risks and what protects them. No family is ever free from stress or problems. If that were the case, there would be no healthy families since they all face demands, stresses, challenges, and opportunities. The family social worker must discard beliefs that the only trail left by problems is pathology and destruction and that a problem-laden environment will inevitably cause everlasting difficulties. By comparison, resilience embraces the belief that families have the capacity to self-correct, to overcome obstacles, and to become strengthened in response.

Resilient families, even when stressed and in crisis, have strengths and resources that propel them forward. Pathology-based models view families as contributors to risk but neglect to focus on their sources of strength. "Resilience came to be viewed in terms of an interplay of multiple risk and protective processes over time, involving individual, family, and larger sociocultural influences" (Walsh, 2003, p. 2). Resilient families function well *despite* the risk factors they face. Having an optimistic outlook and an unwavering belief in the existence of strength and resilience can help family social workers join with family members who are understandably defensive regarding labels of pathology.

When assessing a family from a resilience perspective, the family social worker blends ecological and developmental perspectives in order to understand family functioning within the broader context of the sociocultural environment. Because resilience is a *process* rather than a single characteristic or a laundry list of traits, it is best nurtured through supportive contexts and relationships. Family social workers who work with resilience are keenly attuned to the central importance of significant relationships with extended family, intimate partners, mentors (such as coaches or teachers), and friends who support efforts, believe in potential, and encourage family members to make the most of their lives (Walsh, 2003, p. 2). Strong community connections further amplify a family's capacity to respond favorably to difficult life events. A family resilience perspective also builds upon parental strengths while recognizing limitations as areas in which to grow. Recognizing both strengths and limitations realigns assessment and intervention and shifts from the deficit-based lens that views people as damaged or dysfunctional to viewing them as challenged by life situations, just as everyone else is.

Resilience is more than having the ability to manage difficult challenges, shouldering a burden, or surviving an ordeal (Walsh, 2003, p. 13). Embedded in resilience is the recognition of the potential for personal and relational change and growth that emerges from successfully dealing with adversity. A central tenet of both crisis theory and resilience theory is that families (and individuals) can emerge stronger and more resourceful after a crisis because dealing successfully with one situation generates the strength and ability to deal with similar difficulties in the future. In other words, skills garnered in one crisis can be transferred to similar situations in the future.

Walsh (1999, p. 24) offers a framework with which to understand family resilience:

Family Belief Systems

- Making meaning of adversity
- Positive outlook
- Transcendence and spirituality

Organizational Patterns

- Flexibility
- Connectedness
- Social and economic resources

Communication Processes

- Clarity
- Open emotional expression
- Collaborative problem solving

Family belief systems are the heart and soul of resilience (Walsh, 1998, pp. 45–78). In other words, the slogan is "It is not the problem; it is the attitude toward the problem!" Belief systems include making meaning of adversity, having a positive outlook, and transcendence and spirituality. We discuss each of these areas briefly in the following list:

- *Making meaning of adversity:* Families must believe in the importance of the family and its ability to care for its members. Crisis then becomes a shared challenge, with each family member contributing to the solution. Members have faith in one another and in the family. They also trust one another. Resilient families are in a continuous process of growth and change throughout the family life cycle and accept the fluid and changing nature of family life. Family social workers need to understand the meaning of family for each member. Through ongoing family transactions, members learn to make sense of adversity, and how they make sense of it will determine what they do about it. Difficulties emerge when families become locked into a rigid explanation of or belief about their problems. Positive beliefs include statements such as "This is a difficult time for us right now, but if we all pull our load, the future looks brighter." Negative beliefs include blaming an individual or thinking that family problems will be resolved if the "problem person" is removed from the family unit.

- *Positive outlook:* Resilient families consider crises as challenges that provide opportunities that can be defeated through perseverance. Such families endure hardship bravely and hold onto the belief that the situation will be better in the future. Mistakes then become a launching ground from which new learning springs. In addition, humor within the family enhances coping. Resilient families, as the Serenity Prayer teaches, take initiative to deal with their problems. They are motivated as a family.

EP 2.1.7a

- *Transcending beliefs:* Transcendent beliefs provide meaning and purpose beyond the individual, the family, and the adversity (Walsh, 1998, p. 68). As emphasized throughout this book, families fare best when they are connected to larger supportive social systems. Spirituality takes many forms and can also give families the tools and belief systems with which to deal with adversity. Finally, families can learn and grow through struggles and pain.

EP 2.1.10e

ECOLOGICAL RISK AND OPPORTUNITIES

Resilience falls under the umbrella of ecological, developmental, relational (Hernandez, 2002), and strengths-based perspectives. In this section, we explore risk and opportunities in the different levels of the ecosystem: the micro-, meso-, macro-, and exosystems.

> The family is the first school for young children, and parents are powerful models.
> —Alice Sterling Honig (www.Bartleby.com)

Microsystem

In the *microsystem*, the first layer of relationships is face-to-face relationships within the family. "We measure the social riches of a child by enduring, reciprocal, multifaceted relationships that emphasize playing, working, and loving" (Garbarino, 1992, p. 22). This set of relationships is initially small and starts with the primary caretaker, who is usually the mother. As the child develops, the number and range of relationships expands to embrace father, siblings, and extended kin, when available. As a child gets older, his or her skills also grow to embrace peers and family friends. In the words of Marianne Neifert:

> The family is both the fundamental unit of society as well as the route of culture. It represents a child's initial source of unconditional love and acceptance and provides lifelong connectedness with others. The family is the first setting in which socialization takes place and where children learn to live with mutual respect for one another. A family is where children learn to display affection, control their tempers, and pick up their toys. Finally, a family can be an ongoing source of encouragement, advocacy, assurance, and emotional refueling that allows children to grow and develop with competence into the larger world and to become all that they can. The family is a microcosm of the outside world where children learn about themselves and others. It is within the family that children learn about love, sex roles, relationships, competence, intimacy, autonomy, and trust.
> (www.Bartleby.com)

Garbarino (1992) advocates for a rich and diverse microsystem when he talks about the need for an expanding web of relatives, neighbors, and friends. A rich family is one where relationships are reciprocal, power is balanced, and the emotional climate is warm, responsive, positive, and affectionate (pp. 36–39). Within this context, social isolation is detrimental to growth and development.

Some families have built-in protective mechanisms, or "shock absorbers," that buffer them from the effects of negative experiences. Walsh (1998) also identifies a number of family "shock absorbers":

- Flexibility
- Stability
- Capacity for change
- Counterbalancing stability and change
- Connectedness
- Balancing unity and separateness
- Clear boundaries
- Shared leadership providing nurturance, protection, and guidance

These families display competence in the presence of intense pressure and extraordinary adversity. We are only now beginning to understand how some families are resilient in the face of such odds. Yet other families are not only able to overcome trauma; they are sometimes in better shape at the other end. Benzies and Mychasuik (2009) reviewed the research on protective factors to support family resilience and distilled 24 factors that have been shown to support family resilience. The protective factors ranged from individual protective factors, family protective factors, and community protective factors. We integrate their findings with those of others within the context of an ecosystems framework. To this list, we add factors proposed by others that play a protective role for families facing challenges and obstacles to their functioning.

A number of factors reside at the microsystem level to protect families and increase resilience. Since much of the research on resilience to date has focused on individuals, it is not surprising that many of the protective factors describe individuals. Benzies and Mychasuik described nine protective factors for individuals. However, given that these are individually based, it is still not clear how individual factors translate into family functioning, particularly when one member is highly functioning while others are more incapacitated. One might assume that a family consisting of resilient individuals would lead to resilience in the entire family unit. What is less clear is what happens in the family when one member is resilient while another is less so.

Individual Protective Factors

- *An internal locus of control*: People with a strong internal locus of control believe that they have control over their destiny and that they have the power and ability to either change their circumstances or create their own unique circumstances. In other words, they believe that the responsibility for control of their lives lies with them.

- *Good mental and physical health:* People with good physical and mental health have an increased capacity with which to deal with life's challenges. It gives them the strength, energy and perspective to move forward.
- *Temperament:* Temperament involves a predisposed style of emotional and behavioral responses to stimuli. Temperament is often stable over a lifetime.
- *Gender:* According to Benzies and Muchasuik, gender is a protective factor for young girls, who typically have better peer relationships and fewer externalizing behaviors than boys. One wonders about how protective these factors are in a patriarchal society as females become adults.
- *Emotional regulation:* Individuals with the ability to emotionally regulate are in control of their thoughts, emotions, and behaviors. They have good impulse control, can think clearly in stressful situations, and are able to delay gratification.
- *Belief systems:* A number of belief systems can serve as protective factors. These can include spiritual beliefs, as well as positive and optimistic attitudes.
- *Self-efficacy:* This involves an individual's belief that she or he is independent, self-reliant, and able to think and act autonomously.
- *Effective coping skills:* This involves the ability to respond to demands that are potentially overwhelming and taxing of available resources.
- *Education, skills, and training:* Having any of these qualities opens up more options for individuals in the form of job opportunities and income.

Family Protective Factors   A number of protective factors reside at the family level. These factors play out as the family works together as a team. They include:

- *A sense of belonging:* The most important social entity to belong to is the family. Members feel a connection to families through culture, shared religion, rituals, and a shared identity. Family cohesion, or having a sense of involvement, belonging, and caring, is also a potent protective factor (Benzies & Mychasuik, 2009). Cohesive families confront adversity together, demonstrating that resiliency is mobilized through cooperation, mutual support, and a family commitment to tackle problems together. With the ongoing valuing of social networks, family members can also strengthen strong bonds with community ties such that members are engaged in developmentally appropriate activities outside the family. The family social worker can work to strengthen ties between all family members as well as to community support systems.
- *Family structure:* Smaller families experience less financial strain, and children are more likely to complete high school. Moreover, mature, older mothers are more likely to have stable employment, while teen mothers are disadvantaged (Benzies & Mychasuik, 2009). Single-parent families may be more disadvantaged, primarily because of fewer financial resources and the burden of doing the work of two people.
- *A microsystem that expands and diversifies as the child develops:* A growing child develops a hierarchy of attachment relationships, first through a primary caretaker and then by embracing other members of the primary family, extended kin, neighbors, and friends. Sometimes parents can benefit from education about the developmental needs of their children. The family social

worker might help parents chart how their children's microsystems have grown over the life of the child. Adults in the family also need social outlets outside the home. Primary caretakers have a heightened risk of being isolated, particularly when children are young. For example, McGoldrick and colleagues found while doing a caretaking genogram that caretaking exerts a strain on families, particularly women (McGoldrick, Gerson, & Petry, 2008).

- *Sibling relationships as a potent source of support:* We spoke about the sibling subsystem in Chapter 3. The quality of sibling relationships varies from one family to another. One study, for example, noted that the sibling relationship was the most violent relationship in the family. Nevertheless, sibling relationships usually last a lifetime, and the family social worker can work with families to strengthen sibling ties. "...The more time siblings have with one another, the more intense their relationships are likely to be ... [close] siblings can rely on one another, particularly when parents are unavailable or unable to provide for their nurturing needs"(McGoldrick, Gerson, & Petry, 2008, p. 120).

- *Social skills and problem-solving abilities, emotional intelligence, coping abilities, tenacity, and a sense of humor at the individual level:* The family social worker can help family members identify these qualities and reinforce their development. While still controversial, Emotional Intelligence suggests that someone with a high EQ understands self and others, knows and manages his or her own emotions, is self-motivated, recognizes and understands the emotions of others, and can manage relationships (Goleman, 1998).

- *Family characteristics such as cohesion, good communication, and behavior management skills:* These families have warm and close interaction patterns. They are cooperative and provide mutual support (Benzies & Mychasuik, 2009). The Family Categories Schema further helps family social workers to identify and foster the qualities of positive family characteristics.

- *Family relationships:* Supportive relationships with parents who are sociable maximize child development. This provides positive and secure attachments, and parents are involved in their children's lives and set clear and consistent rules. Their personal characteristics, parenting styles, disciplinary techniques, interaction patterns, quality of the parent-child attachment, and parental support all affect the quality of peer relations. Family support predicts friendship quality, and both family support and friendship quality are associated with self-esteem. Extended family relations may also help.

- *Adequate and stable income:* Job loss takes a toll on breadwinners in the form of depression, loneliness, and emotional sensitivity (Benzies & Mychasuik, 2009). Employment enhances available resources and keeps people connected to networks outside the family.

- *Adequate housing:* This affects academic achievement because frequent moves disrupt schooling (Benzies & Mychasuik, 2009). A stable, organized home provides children with a safe and comfortable base.

- *Routines and rituals:* These practices are recognized as anchors of family resilience. They provide stability and predictability through daily, regular routines and rituals embedded in family and school. Routines and rituals reinforce family structure and predictability and make daily life safe and dependable.

Routines are observable, repetitive, and predictable family behaviors that regulate daily life. Family members know that meals are served regularly, the laundry is done, and parents are available at predictable times. Routines provide a secure base from which the child explores the world. They differ from rituals in that they do not have the same symbolic or emotional significance.

In truth a family is what you make it. It is made strong, not by the number of heads counted at the dinner table, but by the rituals you help family members create, by the memories you share, by the commitment of time, caring, and love you show to one another, and by the hopes for the future you have as individuals and as a unit.
—*Marge Kennedy (www.Bartleby.com)*

"Rituals have symbolic significance in that they signify ... collective identity and continuity" (Sandler et al., 1989, cited in Gilligan, 2004, p. 93). Rituals also help people tune into their spiritual core (Walsh, 1999). The following example illustrates the importance of a family's adherence to a ritual. While sitting in a hair salon, one of the authors overheard another patron speaking about her family rituals. She said, "I think I came from a pretty dysfunctional family, but what kept us going is that our parents took us on picnics every week. I am going to make sure that my kids also experience this ritual because it sure saved my family." What is interesting about this comment is that her family lived in a climate where temperatures can plummet to as low as 40 below zero, but the family still followed through on its picnic ritual in one form or another!

As shown by the previous example, rituals contribute to a family's identity. They also help families make sense of their existence. Children are better insulated from parental problems when the family plans and carries out traditional family rituals. Rituals include ceremonies, traditions, and routines, which all create order and predictability. Family social workers can value and promote opportunities for families to mark and celebrate their identity by establishing new or restoring lost rituals and routines. Family rituals not associated with a particular family problem (such as substance abuse) buffer a family from drowning in a problem-saturated identity.

The role of family rituals as a positive and protective family practice has become evident over the last decade. Originating in religious practices, a family ritual is "a symbolic form of communication that, owing to the satisfaction that family members experience through its repetition, is acted out in a systematic fashion over time" (Wolin & Bennett, 1984, cited in Viere, 2001). Similar to daily routines, family rituals contribute to family stability and predictability and give family members an identity such that they feel part of a unique family. They are anchors during a storm when family homeostasis is disrupted. Rituals can mark the loss of a life and a loved one (Walsh, 1998) and be used to bring family members together during difficult times. Rituals might also include ceremonies associated with weddings, births, food, and various rites of passage.

Families differ in the degree to which they adhere to rituals. Wolin (1993) suggests that rituals lie on a continuum, with one pole representing a family in which there are few rituals and the other pole representing a family in which rituals are rigidly adhered to. However, four types of rituals are universal to all families: family celebrations (connected to the larger culture, such as Christmas, Ramadan, or

Rosh Hashanah), family traditions (idiosyncratic to a particular family such as the picnic ritual described above), family life cycle rituals (funerals, weddings, graduations, etc.), and day-to-day life events (dinner, bedtime, etc.). Thus, family social workers can work with families around their rituals. Rituals might also be a source of humor about the family, which is an important source of resilience.

EXERCISE 5.6 Rituals

Break into small groups and discuss how each member's family practiced (1) universal rituals, (2) life cycle rituals, and (3) day-to-day rituals. Also discuss what the most important rituals were and why they were important to each member's family. Present the results of your discussions to the rest of the class.

EXERCISE 5.7 Idiosyncratic Rituals

Now for some fun! Break into small groups. Each person will take turns presenting one or two idiosyncratic rituals from their family that was experienced while growing up. What is unique about these rituals? How did these rituals define your family? Be creative and play a little with the idea.

Mesosystem

> *Parents need all the help they can get. The strongest as well as the most fragile family requires a vital network of social supports.*
> —*Bernice Weissbourd (www.Bartleby.com)*

The mesosystem is the quality of face-to-face relationships within the microsystem, such as how parents get along with each other or how they get along with their child's teacher. Sources of resilience in the *mesosystem* involve richness of relationships between microsystems. "We measure the richness of mesosystems for the child by the number and quality of connections" (Garbarino, 1992, p. 23). A number of factors exist at this level:

- *Strong social networks:* Networks can be a source of stress and hurt when relationships are stressed and troubled. Alternatively, they are a potent and preferred source of help, support, and connectedness. Recognizing the power of social connectedness, family social workers can work with families to strengthen ties with each other and with the community. Social support involves the comfort that interpersonal interactions with extended kin, friends, neighbors, co-workers, and the like provide. These people are reservoirs of emotional support, information, or tangible sources of support such as baby-sitting, financial support, assistance with household chores, and so on.
- *Peer acceptance:* Children develop an expanding group of friends as they develop. Adults in the family also need friendships outside the family.
- *Involvement in the community:* This includes access to larger social networks and information regarding health care, education, and resources. It also includes involvement in neighborhood activities, having a sense of belonging in the community, access to role models, and nonfamilial companionship (Benzies & Mychasuik, 2009).

- *Supportive mentors and role models:* This consists of involvement with people outside the family who are supportive and trustworthy (Benzies & Mychasuik, 2009). Strong relationships are those in which important people work together for the child's best interest to foster a friendly and caring world for the child. The stronger these mesosystems, the more the child will develop skills and abilities to navigate different systems. Despite the social value of independence, no family is an island. One of the most important initial mesosystems outside the family is that between the family and school. When a parent is supported at work, the security and contentment that grows within the parent is brought back home to the family. When a school values a child's input regardless of ability, the child is happier at home. When a congregation helps out a family when a member is ill, it relieves some of the family's burden. These relationships, according to Garbarino, launch children mindfully and gently into the wider world. Everyone benefits when the relationships are diverse, collaborative, and supportive.
- *Family of origin influences:* Benzies and Mychasuik (2009) suggest an association between cross-generational links and cognitive development, school performance, and transmission of risk factors. Grandparents and extended kin can enrich a child's development by providing support and diversity.

Communities can enhance family resilience by providing and promoting opportunities for informal networks, social networks, and intergenerational mentoring to create a safe space for the family to participate in community life, make meaningful social contributions, and take on the role of responsible citizens. Family social workers can help families identify and use available resources in order to assist them with their concerns. These resources can be traditional and formal (e.g., social service agencies, organized sports teams) or nontraditional and informal (e.g., social clubs, faith communities) (Dosser, Smith, Markowski, & Cain, 2001). Supportive networks are tailored to a particular family's requirements and resources. They are also culturally sensitive and sprinkled with natural and informal support networks within the family's community. Moreover, services are based on teamwork, with the family at the core, directing what is useful and meaningful.

Extended family and social support networks offer a lifeline during times of distress by providing practical and emotional support. They also serve as role models and mentors. The centrality of social support networks and ongoing positive relationships, both within and outside of the family, cannot be underestimated. As mentioned, it is imperative during an ecological assessment that family social workers tune into significant people in the family's social network, especially people who are positive and supportive. Important relationships that palliate the effect of stress include multiple layers of positive relationships starting with the microsystem and expanding to significant others outside the family. These relationships help cushion the damaging blows of difficulties.

Gilligan (2004) refers to this as the *scaffolding* of social support (p. 95). Scaffolding forms a supportive web or safety net that prevents someone from crashing to the ground. It might include:

- *A secure attachment to one significant other person:* In an ideal world, the significant person is at least one parent but can also be a teacher, sibling, grandparent, extended kin, or friend.

- *A sense of belonging to a community, culture, or other important group:* School provides developmental opportunities through academics, sports, and other positive social experiences that provide meaning and acceptance. Teachers can be powerful mentors. Neighborhood social organizations, faith communities, and cultural organizations are also invaluable sources of social support and provide mechanisms through which multiple social identities can play out.
- *An expansive social network that is compatible with individual developmental needs:* As children get older, their social network expands beyond the immediate family to embrace friends, extended family, and teachers. As mentioned, adults also need positive connections with social networks.
- *Positive role models:* These can include teachers, community workers, media figures, or important people in a person's life. If none are available to a child or parent, the family social worker can connect his or her to organized community supports such as Big Brothers and Big Sisters.

Family social workers work with a family's scaffolding to build and strengthen positive influences on the family. Ongoing positive relationships with the world beyond family walls will result in a multiplicity of roles and identities, as well as a great sense of self-satisfaction. By comparison, being trapped into monotonous and static roles stifles potential. Single and immutable roles such as mother, student, or breadwinner are overly restrictive and isolating because everyone needs to draw from a wide range of roles, social identities, and opportunities. In the process, the family social worker will explore and encourage family connectedness to the community. Resilience is about realizing potentials.

Impoverished neighborhoods can be strengthened through community capacity building. It is not that micro (direct practice) social work is superior to macro (community practice) social work, or the other way around. Both ambitions of the profession converge to work toward a common vision. From a social network perspective, family and peer relations are subsystems within a broader ecological system and have overlapping functions with respect to child development and well-being (Franco & Levitt, 1998, p. 315). Relationships with professionals may sometimes be necessary, but they should never replace natural networks in the family's environment. Hernandez (2002) depicts the importance of the "sheltering power of communities" when working with people from war-torn homelands.

Exosystem

The family does not participate directly in the *exosystem*, but its effects trickle down to the family and its members through social institutions in which families participate such as schools, places of employment, churches, the social service network, neighborhoods, the city council, and so on. For example, the city council may decide to separate mothers and fathers in different homeless shelters, build recreation centers for families, or provide before- and after-school programs in local facilities. Such policies can have either a negative or positive impact on families. Schools might provide extra tutoring for students who are struggling with homework or family difficulties. Schools can also develop a zero-tolerance program for bullying. They might have cultural heritage days on which ethnic and cultural diversity are celebrated. We are aware of some schools that have Bannock Days, on which Native American families share their history and food with the rest of the school community. All of these actions will positively affect the well-being of children and their families.

Above all, families need to live in safe neighborhoods,—neighborhoods that are free of poverty, crime, and violence and that provide sound infrastructure, basic services, and diminished environmental risks (Benzies & Mychasuik, 2009). They also need access to quality child care, schools, and health care.

EXERCISE 5.8   Exosystemic Support or Non-support of Families

Devise a field trip into your community to look at social agencies, civic laws and policies, schools, and any other infrastructure you can think of. Investigate one of these institutions to find out how it supports or does not support families. Report back to the class.

Macrosystem

In the *macrosystem*, broad social values are the social "blueprints" (Garbarino, 1992, p. 45) that permeate the various layers of the ecosystem and shape attitudes and behaviors. Social policies echo these larger social values and beliefs and can also influence social values and beliefs. Unfortunately, the politics of helping within many bureaucracies and organizations are often diametrically opposed to a strengths-based orientation (Saleebey, 1996, p. 297) due to the preferred language being disease and problems and policies failing to envision the wholeness of the family. "Pursuing a practice based on the ideas of resilience, rebound, possibility, and transformation is difficult because, oddly enough, it is not natural to the world of helping and service" (Garbarino, 1992, p. 297).

As an example of macrosystem values, The National Network for Family Resiliency outlined a number of social policies that can support family well-being and resilience. They include:

1. *Family support and responsibilities:* Policies should support and supplement family functioning and provide substitute services as a last resort. The underlying value of this declaration is that families fill some functions best and that substitutes are a last resort.
2. *Family membership and stability:* Policies should encourage and reinforce family commitment and stability, especially when children are involved. The underlying value is that removal of family members is justified only as protection from serious harm.
3. *Family involvement and interdependence:* Policies must recognize the interdependence of family relationships, the strength of family ties and obligations, and the resources families have to help their members. The underlying value is that solutions to individual problems should not harm other family members.
4. *Family partnership and empowerment:* Policies must encourage family members to collaborate as partners with professionals in service delivery. The underlying value is that policies are usually more relevant to family needs when families are involved in their development.

5. *Family diversity:* Policies must acknowledge and value the diversity of family life and recognize the different ways families may be impacted. The underlying value is that all families need support and should not be disadvantaged because of structure, cultural values, life stage, or circumstance.
6. *Family vulnerability:* Families with the greatest economic and social need should have first priority in government policies. The underlying value is that all families deserve support and that policies should give special consideration to those with the greatest social and economic limitations and to those most likely to break down.

These six statements provide a clear direction concerning what policies and values best support families. They advocate for the human rights of members of all families and strive for social justice. Similarly, different political parties embody unique social values: Should we invest in the army or should we invest in health care? Do we believe in the survival of the financially fittest? Does helping out disadvantaged families make them more dependent? Can providing help to families create a solid foundation for children to overcome the effects of an impoverished generation and environment? Take a look at the statements provided above, and decide what political philosophy best supports them.

The influence of the media is also pervasive, but we tend to overlook its influence. An important question about the media is: Whose interest does it serve? The media in many countries, even democratic ones, provide biased perspectives on the news. Inasmuch as a family is enriched by diversity and strength of the relationships it has with the surrounding environment, a macrosystem is also enriched by a respect for diversity of views and values. Diversity of perspectives respects pluralism. Yet, the media appears to have hijacked our beliefs. We need to be thin, sexy, married, heterosexual, successful, and patriotic to be a good citizen. Information is power, and those who influence the media are indeed the most powerful of all.

"The family and society are inextricably bound up with one another, each the condition for and the negative of the other" (Becvar, 1998, p. 1). Some of society's greatest social philosophies were fought for at the political level: work for welfare, birth control for teens, the sanctity of the family, birth control, the role of women, and so on. Yet, how informed are voters? Some seem to vote according to multigenerational or community patterns, rather than as the result of sincere reflection on the issues. According to Garbarino (1992), "the available data suggest that the greatest danger to children's moral development lies in the totalitarian society that commands total allegiance to the state" (p. 47). Yet, are we encouraged to critique the state? What are the forums for such a critique? Does a critique mean that someone is less patriotic?

EXERCISE 5.9 Macrosystem values

Discuss in class: What political ideology best supports the goals and objectives of family social work? Why? What is your evidence?

RISK

In the preceding section, we examined layers of the ecosystem and identified risks and opportunities for children and their families. *Risk,* referring to the probability that an individual or family will experience an adverse event (Fraser, Richman, & Galinsky, 1999), exists in each layer. A combination of factors contributes to the risk of a problem developing. For example, risk factors associated with child abuse might include caretaker depression, social isolation from friends and family, lack of parenting skills, high rates of stress, lack of parenting skills, loose family boundaries (for offenders outside the family), substance abuse, unemployment, and inappropriate expectations of children.

Risk and protective factors interact to determine how well a family will respond to a threatening event. Saleebey (1996) adds "generative factors" to the mix—factors that, taken together, dramatically increase learning, resource acquisition, and development, thereby accentuating resilience and hardiness. In summary, the ingredients of resilience include family competence or functioning over time, nature of adversities faced, individual and social assets, environmental protections and challenges, context in which stress is experienced, and individual perception and definitions of stressful situations. As mentioned, people are more motivated to change when their strengths are acknowledged and supported.

However, Fraser, Richman, and Galinsky (1999) strongly caution against counting exclusively on strengths or resilience to overcome adversity because they cannot completely counteract "the poisonous effects of extreme adversity" (p. 140). Their view advocates for fighting against the conditions that create adversity for families in the first place.

Let us now look at child sexual abuse as an example. Finklehor (1986) identifies four preconditions of child sexual abuse: motivation to sexually abuse, overcoming internal inhibitors, overcoming external inhibitors, and overcoming child resistance. Each of these factors contributes to the risk of sexual abuse happening and together work to increase the risk set within the microsystem of the family. Other risk factors exist outside of the microsystem.

1. The offender's *motivation to abuse* must be dealt with as an individual issue that is probably beyond the expertise of the family social worker. Deviant sexual arousal will be an important focus of intervention, as will issues such as the offender's own history as a victim of abuse. Motivation to sexually abuse can be a powerful factor in sexual abuse; in fact, it is the first and foremost risk factor. Not everyone who is motivated to abuse actually abuses.

2. Addressing the offender's likelihood of *overcoming internal inhibitors* falls under the purview of a specialist, particularly when the offender has problems with substance abuse, impulse control, or psychopathology. However, the family social worker can convey to the offender that the behavior is unacceptable and that the role of the family social worker is to protect the child. Potential offenders must overcome their inhibitions, and substance abuse is a powerful disinhibitor. However, someone who is not inclined to sexually abuse a child would not do so even when under the influence. We recall one stepfather who sexually abused his stepdaughter for a number of years.

In counseling, he claimed he was not responsible because he was drinking at the time. The family social worker told him, "I am really glad you told me that. We now have two problems to work with—your abuse of children and your drinking!"

3. The next precondition is *overcoming external inhibitors*; for example, another parent in the family might be present and prevent any opportunities from arising. Environmental impediments can be strengthened by building into the family necessary structures and mechanisms with which to interfere with the other predispositions. This can involve teaching family members to respect personal privacy and personal boundaries. Social isolation of the family should also be addressed. Other siblings in the family should be told about the abuse (when they are old enough to understand) in order to break the secret, to see if they have been abused also, and to add another dimension of monitoring in the family. Family members can be taught about healthy sexuality and respect for gender differences. Empowerment of the nonoffending parent also is crucial.

4. *Child resistance* is another point of intervention that can be targeted by the family social worker. Children can be taught about sexual abuse and taught how to be more assertive. Children can also learn to tell someone about the abuse (preferably the nonoffending parent or another person who will act on the information). The child's relationship with a nonoffending parent can also be strengthened to create an ally for the child.

This model is useful for identifying where the various layers of risk lie. The most potent risk factor is the motivation to abuse. Other factors revolve around this particular risk, such as social isolation of the family and closed family boundaries. Intervention for the last three factors will be rather weak and even dangerous if worked with singly when the first precondition has not been addressed. Some workers following particular theories have placed much of the responsibility further down the risk continuum—for example, blaming mothers for the abuse. In one case example, a family social worker was called by child protection. A young girl's mother had just started living with a man who was released from a forensic hospital with a diagnosis of pedophilia. A child welfare worker called the agency requesting that counselors see the young girl to build in protection and resistance skills. This was clearly not a viable plan when the young girl was living in the same household as a pedophile.

We need to be aware of the tendency to assign risk too narrowly. Instead, it is necessary to cast our nets wider, into the other levels of the ecosystem. For example, some families are cut off from relationships outside the family. In fact, some intrafamilial sexual abuse perpetrators and domestic violence abusers purposely control with whom members of the family have contact. This behavior has the effect of isolating family members from important relationships and information, shielding the abusers from detection. At the same time, social isolation removes the victims' potential sources of support. This is but one example of how important the mesosystem is. When a victim has a trusted teacher or coach outside the family, the opportunities for disclosure and safety are increased.

Several other examples of risk exist in the exo and macro levels. While much has been written about sexual abuse from all these different levels of the system, we give only a couple of examples here. Some exosystemic-level decisions might increase the risk of sexual abuse within the family. One is the decision by schools *not* to provide sex education to children, particularly when sex education includes a sexual abuse prevention component. We recall one community where the provision of sex education in the schools was proposed, to which one group was opposed. There were many heated meetings in the community about the proposed programs. One leading opponent of the program suggested that teaching children to say no would create anarchy in the family because parents would lose their authority over them. Eventually the program went ahead, but children were required to get parental permission to participate. This is only one example of risk in the exosystem. Can you think of other examples?

Much has also been written about the impact of macrosystemic values on sexual abuse of children. The sexualization of children in the media is but one example. Patriarchy—in which male power is embedded in the social structure, giving males authority over women and children—is another example. Perhaps when Freud wrote about the Oedipal and Electra complexes, he was speaking more about the society in which he lived and less about the children who were sexually abused.

Given this brief discussion about risks embedded in the ecosystem, it should be clear that assessment of risk can be quite complex. Every problem that a family social worker will see in family work will be associated with different levels of risk factors—and this is where theory, research, and critical thinking come into play. Family social workers see the world through a wide-angled lens and take into account all potential risks and strengths.

Fraser, Richman, and Galinsky (1999) caution that there is no single or direct path leading to the risk of something negative happening. However, the probability of a negative event occurring increases as the number of risk factors accumulates. Therefore, the family social worker might be able to lower the potential of an adverse event happening by intervening in some of the key risk factors that exist in a family. In the case of physical child abuse, the family social worker might be able to teach parents more effective child management techniques, increase the level of social support, and help parents manage stress better. In Chapter 12, we present ways to improve parenting skills through the use of behavioral management principles. By now, most people know about the television program *Super Nanny*, in which a professional nanny comes into the family home and teaches parenting techniques for very difficult child behavior. Improved parenting skills might decrease the risk of child abuse or more adverse outcomes when the child gets older. When one contributing factor is stress, the family social worker will work with the family to understand the source of the stress and then work with the family to alleviate the stress. This might occur through connecting them with support in the community, relaxation training, or helping an unemployed parent conduct a job search. The family social worker can also help the family understand when it handled stress successfully in the past so it can access the same skills as before.

The relative influence of a risk factor varies depending on the particular characteristics and resilience of the individuals and family. Some individuals have a high tolerance for risk whereas for others, the same risk factor might be crippling. Other families, for example, require large amounts of social support from formal social agencies to function, whereas others are successful when they receive the support of one or two people. Individualized assessment is the key. This is when it is particularly important for the family social worker to help the family tap into its existing resources. A child with a strong and supportive friendship network might be less vulnerable to family conflict than a child who is isolated or rejected by his or her peer group.

As with resilience, risk factors are embedded throughout the ecological levels: the micro-, meso-, macro-, and exosystems. When examining the family's ecological niche, it is important to recognize how risks and opportunities are also distributed throughout the family's ecological network. Problems arise in the interaction of family vulnerability and strengths and in the impact of stressful life experiences and social contexts. Distress occurs when attempts to deal with the situation become overwhelming. The levels of ecological systems are nested systems for nurturing and reinforcing resilience.

- *Risk factors may be time-limited or ongoing:* Risk involves many factors. As mentioned, risk is linked to harmful outcomes but not in a direct cause-and-effect way. Risk is relative and individualized, ranging from modestly harmful situations to those that are life-threatening. A child's pattern of temper tantrums may signify independence to one parent, whereas for another parent the same behavior may signal defiance, rejection, and parental incompetence. Each belief leads to very different parental responses.
- *Risk factors interrelate and are cumulative:* Parents who are worried about where the next meal will come from, how they are going to address their partner's substance abuse and violence, and how they are going to get a good night's sleep have cumulative risks compared with those who feel competent and secure in their life's niche.
- *Risk factors change with age:* Young children need to be protected from themselves, whereas teenagers often need protection from negative peer and social influences.
- *Risk may reflect structural qualities:* Living in a high-crime, high-risk community is vastly different than living in a gated, sheltered community.
- *Risk assessment is a predictive tool with limits:* Family social workers can be aware of the layers of risk within the ecological niche of a particular family. Nevertheless, an assessment of risk does not necessarily mean that a family is doomed. Accessing family buffers and strengths can counterbalance threats to family well-being.

On the basis of the preceding list, it is evident that some families are more buffered from risk than others who face the same adverse event. These buffers are better known as protective factors, and they help the individual or family compensate or overcome the negative impact of an event. In much the same way that risk factors can be cumulative, protective factors can also be cumulative.

EXERCISE 5.10 Family Risks and Buffers

Break into groups of three. Discuss areas of risk and buffers to those risks in your family while growing up. Make a class list of both risk and buffer factors.

EP 2.1.7b

CULTURE

Overcoming challenges is more difficult when families concurrently have to deal with racism or poverty (Hernandez, 2002). For too long, people have been discriminated against on the basis of ethnicity and culture. The history of societies around the world bears testament to unscrupulous regimes that have used culture as an excuse for oppression, discrimination, and genocide. The Holocaust, slavery, and the conquering and attempted genocide of indigenous peoples across the globe are but a few examples of "man's inhumanity to man." Oppression and discrimination exist both at home and in the present. In the face of these inhumanities, culture can provide a haven for those who have suffered at the hands of the powerful. An examination of the history of oppression and the response to it reveals that culture has buffered people through providing an identity, a community, a sense of belonging, and ways to manage and overcome oppression in the face of extreme adversity and oppression.

Culture is one of the most potent contexts for families. It provides them with a sense of identity, meaning, belonging, rituals, and continuity. Moreover, "Cultural identity has a profound impact on our sense of well-being ... and on our mental and physical health" (McGoldrick, Giordano, & Garcia-Preto, 2005, p. 1). Belonging to a particular culture opens the door to an immediate support network in times of distress. It is therefore vital that family social workers become aware of their biases and ethnocentric views so that they can fully tune into the strength available to culturally diverse families.

Culture and ethnicity are related but not interchangeable concepts: "Culture refers to the culmination of values, beliefs, customs, and norms that people have learned, usually in the context of their family and community. Ethnicity relates to a client's identity, commitment, and loyalty to an ethnic group" (Jordan & Franklin, 2009). Ethnicity applies to everyone and influences everyone's values, not only those who are at the margins...."(McGoldrick, Giordano, & Garcia-Preto, p. 2).

Historically, the approach to teaching cultural sensitivity and competence has been to create a laundry list of characteristics and traits of various ethnic and cultural groups. However, culture is too dynamic and complex to be understood in terms of checklists that reduce culture to a static stereotype and homogeneous entity rather than a dynamic and living entity affecting everything from worldview to communication styles to food preferences to beliefs about family to daily behavior and practices. In fact, culture has multiple dimensions. Elsewhere (Coleman, Collins, & Collins, 2005), we posed a number of different dimensions of culture. These dimensions contain potential gifts to families to help them tap into an identity, construct routines and rituals, and establish valuable social connections. Awareness of the historic background of different ethnic groups is important, as is knowledge of the customs and beliefs shared by members of each group. The task of the family social worker is to "see the limitations of our own view so we can open our minds to the experiences of others" (McGoldrick, Giordano, & Garcia-Preto, 2005, p. 11).

Some strengths within a culture according to these dimensions of culture include:

1. *Cultural identity:* Culture provides people with a sense of belonging to at least one particular cultural group. As mentioned, a sense of belonging is an integral feature of resilience.

2. *Belief systems:* McGoldrick and colleagues (2005) argue that it is impossible to understand the meaning of behavior unless one knows something of the cultural values of the family (p. 24). Beliefs govern actions, and we develop a worldview based on our belief systems that is transmitted in great part from our cultural heritage. Interestingly, most people in North America are also multicultural through intermarriage. Belief systems are also influenced by religion, social class and socioeconomic status, migration experience, and history, to name a few (McGoldrick, Giordano, & Garcia-Preto, 2005). It is crucial for the family social worker to locate key beliefs of a particular family and work with them as they cope in our modern society. On an ecological level, family social workers must critically evaluate the extent to which society appreciates the richness of diversity within it. Hernandez (2002) encourages workers to help people make sense out of their struggles through the development of consciousness and making meaning to inspire a sense of hope. Making meaning out of hope is also Walsh's (1998) focus.

3. *Worldview:* Worldview is closely aligned with beliefs. It gives people a way of understanding and operating in the world. For example, one prevailing belief system across North America is that of individualism, in which people are expected to be independent and self-reliant, compared with a communal view of community living. Individualism contributes to social policies that value people "making it on their own" without government assistance. Some cultures emphasize communal responsibility. For example, Moore Hines and Boyd-Franklin (2005) describe the African American family as stressing kinship bonds, religion and spirituality, and a belief in hard work. Similarly, while members of different Native American tribes hold different beliefs, there are certain common beliefs that distinguish Native Americans from members of other cultures (Sutton & Broken Nose, 2005). Another shared belief centers on the spiritual relationship between man and nature (Sutton & Broken Nose). (The current concern about the environment and climate change affirms the centrality of this belief to our survival!) Native Americans believe that they are one part of the whole, and they appreciate and maintain a balance with other living things. The respect for nature leads the Native American to view time in terms of natural cycles or seasons. Furthermore, sharing is a traditional practice, which includes bestowing one's belongings on others to honor them or to honor deceased relatives. In traditional Native American culture, children learn to respect others' rights to be or do as they wish, and not to interfere with others. Spiritual beliefs vary among the different tribes, but a similar emphasis is placed on rituals and ceremonies. Tribal medicine people, rather than physicians or other health professionals, may be consulted for treatment of physical and mental problems. Moreover, beliefs about community belonging and family support offer us much.

4. *History of a culture, including history of colonization:* Through a culture's history, people come to know who they are and how they took shape at various points in time. For example, African Americans were uprooted from their homelands and brought to the West involuntarily. "Africa lost about 50 million of her people to death and slavery during the 16th through

19th centuries ... and usually lived in horrible conditions at the hands of slave traders and plantation owners" (Black & Jackson, 2005, p. 78). In response to the harshness of their history, they developed skills to rise above difficulties imposed on them by their oppressors. Moore Hines and Boyd-Franklin point out survival skills utilized by African Americans in a hostile society:

a. Strong kinship bonds, which are broader than traditional bloodlines (Moore Hines & Boyd Franklin, 2005, p. 89).

b. Strong education and work achievement orientation. "African American parents generally expect their children to pursue careers offering security and to surpass them in achieving the comforts of life" (p. 94).

c. Flexibility in family roles, which can be accessed in times of crisis. It is quite common for a child to be informally adopted by grandparents (particularly the grandmother) or extended kin.

d. Commitment to religious values and church participation. Historically, African American families placed great emphasis on a strong spiritual orientation, which is still evident today. Spirituality connected families to a network of people and played a role in dealing with oppression.

e. A humanistic orientation. The strong spiritual base includes sensitivity to others' feelings, responsibility for one's own actions, personal fulfillment and satisfaction, self-discipline, forgiveness of others, healthy sexual fulfillment and satisfaction, and a striving for a sense of purpose (p. 93).

5. *Communicating meaning and the use of language, including self-expression:* Perhaps one of the major sources of intercultural misunderstanding occurs through the failure to understand what another person is communicating. Language reveals how we view the world. Cultural groups using social services from agencies where there is no bilingual helper risk being misunderstood or even assessed incorrectly. Use of interpreters can also lead to difficulties. McGoldrick (2005) introduces us to the use of language by the Irish, "who used their words to enrich a dismal reality... they have more expressions for coloring reality with exaggeration and humor than any other ethnic group" p. 598).

6. *History of migration:* It is interesting to explore with families the history of their family's migration to North America. Did the family come for new opportunities, or did it immigrate to escape intolerable conditions in the homeland? What were their hopes and expectations upon coming here? Have they been met? It takes courage to leave a country of origin to move to another country that is thousands of miles away. For many immigrants, there are few family relations, friends, and other natural social supports in their new community. Many have to overcome language barriers, job-skill challenges, and discrimination. The resilience of new immigrants needs to be celebrated and honored in family work. In summary, migration takes strength, vision, and resilience. "Allowing families respectful acknowledgment of their history and helping them translate adaptive strategies they used in other contexts to solve current problems" can highlight the strengths of recent immigrant families and families of color (Boyd-Franklin, 2006, in McGoldrick, Gerson, & Petry, p. 238).

EXERCISE 5.11   Migration

Break into dyads and interview each other, exploring the history of the other person's family's migration to this country. What hopes and expectations did they have, and were they met?

7. *Beliefs about family, family structure, and kinship bonds:* The concept of family is expressed differently in different cultures. Moore Hines and Boyd-Franklin (2005) suggest that African American women have assumed a central role in the lives of their children (p. 90). One reason might be the high unemployment and mortality rates of African American males. Consequently, families tend toward egalitarian sharing of roles. Mothers often shoulder the economic, breadwinner burden, as well as assuming responsibility for child care. The extended family network is likely to be involved in supporting the family, as is the church family.

    In Native American families, extended family networks (which may include nonkin namesakes) are important. These groups may or may not live together in one household, but extended family groups provide support for Native American families. Support may come in the form of modeling marital and parental roles. It is not uncommon for grandparents to parent their grandchildren (Mooradian, Cross, & Stutzky, 2006). Child welfare recognizes the value of this kinship care that allows children to grow up in their own culture. The level of acculturation influences marital relationships. Intermarriage is common between members of different Native American groups and between Native Americans and members of other racial groups. Divorce and remarriage are acceptable practices in Native American society.

8. *Beliefs about children and child rearing:* Every culture has a unique approach to child rearing. In African American families, children are treated in an egalitarian fashion and given responsibility on the basis of age. The oldest child may be responsible for looking after younger sisters and brothers. In Native American families, children are seen as important to the renewal of tribal life and historically have been highly valued. Children are disciplined and taught by extended family members in an egalitarian fashion, often through role modeling. Corporal punishment is not used; rather, role modeling is the preferred child-rearing technique (Coleman, Unrau, & Manyfingers, 2003). In the extended family environment, children are surrounded by siblings and cousins, with the older children often caring for and teaching the younger children.

9. *Family life cycle issues and cultural rituals related to life cycle:* Family rituals including rituals associated with cultural membership are important sources of family strength and resilience, giving a group identity. Some cultural rituals celebrate life cycle events such as weddings, funerals, and births. In addition, in some cultures, different expectations accompany the various phases of the family life cycle, such as when to leave home, whom to involve in child care, and so on.

10. *Partnering:* The subtle and not so subtle messages about how we find a partner often have a lot to do with our cultural background. For example, in Indian Hindu families, arranged marriages are often common; but according to Hinduism, women are to be respected and given equal rights as men (Pillari, 2005). It is worthwhile to explore not only a person's beliefs about with whom they

hope to partner but also the extended family's beliefs. Sometimes marrying outside a culture is frowned on.

EXERCISE 5.12 Partnering

What messages were you given as a teenager about whom you could or could not date? What beliefs do you have about this issue? Discuss with your classmates the different messages and beliefs.

11. *Gender roles:* In Chapter 13, we explore gender issues, including gender roles. Some cultures strictly adhere to traditional gender roles, which can be difficult for family social workers who operate from a position of equality of the genders. We form our beliefs about gender roles from our parents, culture, historical context, and current social attitudes, which are often propagated from the mass media. Do people take on traditional gender roles? Where did a person get her or his gender role beliefs? Is the person making changes to accommodate modern times? For example, although in Mexican families a patriarchal view of gender roles exists, complex dynamics are also evolving (Falicov, 2005, p. 229).

EXERCISE 5.13 Gender Equality vs. Cultural Diversity

Respect for cultural diversity is an important social work value. Respect for the equality of the sexes is also an important value. Imagine that you are working with a very traditional family in which women have less power and that you believe they are suffering as a result of this. Which value takes priority—gender equality or cultural diversity? Debate in class.

12. *Social values, sense of community, and social supports:* Some cultures support rugged individualism whereas others greatly value loyalty to the community. That is, some cultures are more communal in their orientation. For example, in Asian families sources of strength lie in support from the extended family, a sense of obligation, a strong focus on educational achievement, and support from religious and ethnic communities (Lee & Mock, 2005, p. 286).

13. *Religion and spirituality:* Religion and spirituality are important aspects of family life, and the literature is just beginning to acknowledge the importance of working with a family's religious and spiritual values. "People use religion as a means of coping with stress or powerlessness, as well as for spiritual fulfillment and emotional support (McGoldrick, Giordano, & Garcia-Preto, 2005, p. 22). Religious beliefs have had both a positive and negative effect on parenting. On the positive side, religiosity has also been helpful in providing assumptions critical to warm parent-child relationships, social support, and closeness. (For a more comprehensive discussion of religion and the family, see Walsh, 1998.) Religion and family life are often deeply intertwined, and a system of values and "shared beliefs that transcend the limits of a family's experience and knowledge enables family members to better accept the inevitable risks and losses in living and loving fully" (Walsh, 1999, p. 9). Religion helps families construct or enact rituals about marriage, birth, and death that mark progression through the family life cycle. Ethnicity and religion have a tenuous

link, and it is imperative that workers not assume that the two are interchangeable.

In working with the religious or spiritual dimensions of families, workers struggle with a number of ethical issues. Workers especially recognize that imposing religious beliefs on clients is a form of colonizing practice, and respect for families whose religious or spiritual teachings differ from their own is a basis of ethical practice. Family social workers are encouraged to work with the client's belief systems and, firstly, avoid making value judgments that are isolated from the client's reality (Thayne, 1998). They must find a balance in working with the family in a way that beliefs are respected but not at a cost to family members. Perhaps this latter issue underscores the historic reluctance of helpers to enter the religious world of clients. Religion may also take on a negative connotation for family workers who may have been taught that there is only one true religion (theirs!) or who may be skeptical about religion and how it has sown the seeds of national and international conflict. Others may struggle with the tenets of any religion, particularly the more conservative creeds, that discriminates or oppresses others such as women and gays.

Religion and spirituality, while related but distinct concepts, often go hand-in-hand within a particular culture. Religion is seen as extrinsic (being imposed from outside as through religious institutions), whereas spirituality is intrinsic (coming from within). Religious practices can support family cohesion through family rituals and customs associated with religious holidays. "If, as many social scientists argue, religion has to do with two major foci of concerns—*personal meaning* and *social belonging*—then most certainly it is around the first of these that religious energies revolve primarily today" (Roof, 1999, cited in Wendel, 2003, p. 172). The concept of *lived religion* tries to understand the space between official religions and the day-to-day experience of people and is considered to be the concrete expression of the personal and sacred dimensions of human life (pp. 173–175). In many ways, personal religion is a subjective and personal experience, although intricately tied into institutional expressions of religion.

In some ways, religion is an institutional manifestation of ethnic and cultural heritage. Even though people are free to convert, they usually follow the religious teaching of their parents. For many years, the helping professions viewed religion as either a form of pathology to treat or something that was best left outside the helping process (Wendel, 2003, p. 165). These days, spirituality is viewed from quite a different angle. In assessment and intervention, it is important to take both the religious and spiritual dimensions of a family into account. Addressing spirituality shows respect for a diversity of beliefs and practices. The key is to not impose religious beliefs on clients. This might be difficult since one of the tenets of many religions is to convert nonbelievers. Family social workers should keep their personal religious beliefs out of family social work. The purpose is not to determine how religious a particular family is; rather, the purpose of asking is to find out about the family's world and what beliefs, social networks, and rituals guide its passage through the life cycle (Wiggins Frame, 2001). Church, at times, might be considered part of the family's extended family.

Both religion and spirituality play a major role in clients' decisions, thoughts, and feelings about particular issues such as divorce, abortion, the role of women, and child rearing (Murray, 2002). According to Walsh (1998), "suffering invites us into the spiritual domain" (p. 71). For some families, divorce or death can be spiritual issues. Intermarriage of two people from different religious backgrounds can also challenge relationships.

Research indicates that religion is a prominent factor in family relationships (Marks, 2004). Three dimensions of religious experience—religious beliefs, religious practices, and religious community—correlate with higher marital quality, stability, satisfaction, and parental involvement. There is also a connection between certain expressions of religiosity and such undesirable outcomes as prejudice, authoritarianism, abuse, and tolerance for abuse. Nevertheless, shared religious activities can contribute to intimacy and commitment in marriage. Religious practices contribute to the creation of family rituals. "Acknowledging that religion is vital to some families is one issue, but arguing that therapists *should* include and address religion in a substantive way is another" (Marks, 2004, p. 228).

EXERCISE 5.14   When Religious Values Clash with Equality

We are all familiar with social values that go against the teachings of a particular religious group. Some examples include the role of women, the condemnation of gay and lesbian relationships, abortion, and so on. Select one such issue to debate. Divide the class randomly into two sections and debate the following statement: "It is more important to respect the religious beliefs of the family than it is to free a single family member from religious beliefs that oppress that individual." Then discuss how workers can respect and work with religious values in family social work.

Frame (2001) recommends developing a spiritual genogram with families for whom religion and spirituality play an important role. Such a genogram will depict a visual history of how spiritual and religious issues across generations shape and affect the client's beliefs and values in the present. When focusing a genogram on religion or spirituality, it is important to look at the family history of denomination, interfaith marriages, baptisms, first communions, events in religious communities, stable and unstable affiliations, religious closeness, divorces, religious messages, and so on. He cautions family workers to know their own religious beliefs and attitudes before working on religious beliefs and attitudes with others.

EXERCISE 5.15   A Spiritual Genogram

Do a three-generation genogram of your family, with particular emphasis on religious adherence and spirituality. What does this genogram say about you and your family? What are the implications for family social work?

Spirituality provides meaning and purpose beyond our families, our troubles, and us. Suffering can be a spiritual issue, and spirituality can construct meaning for human troubles. Spiritual rituals such as prayer and meditation or the support of a spiritual or religious community can provide strength during difficult times. Crisis can lead to the development of a clear moral compass and make relationships more meaningful. Creative changes arise out of a crisis—a true feature of resilience.

Discussing spirituality can create anxiety in students and seasoned practitioners about how to work with family spirituality, especially given the great diversity both within and between religions. We urge students to assume a humble and not-knowing stance, one that is equally applicable to working with cultural diversity and working with religious diversity. Griffith (1999) recommends the following stance in working with a family:

- Do not assume that you know what God means to a particular family, even if you are of the same religion.
- Do not assume that you know what a family's language about God means.
- Do not assume that a family must have the same image of God that you do.
- Do not use psychological theory to explain another's belief in God.

14. *Cultural expressions related to dress, food, music, and the arts:* Again, shared cultural expressions related to aesthetic concerns give families a sense of belonging and stability. In recent years, mainstream society has developed a greater appreciation for ethnic food. At the same time, clothing may be different and have religious or social significance.

15. *Work, education, and social class:* Social class (level of education, income, standing in the community) is important to assess, as higher status usually leads to a higher level of well-being and access to a greater range of resources. "Class intersects powerfully with ethnicity and must always be considered when one is trying to understand a family's problems (McGoldrick, Giordano, & Garcia-Preto, 2005, p. 23). Groups differ in the extent to which they value education or "getting ahead" (p. 23). In some cases, however, families may be discriminated against by the dominant culture despite their high social standing, while at the same time being rejected by members of their ethnic group because of their high level of acculturation into the mainstream culture. This places them in double jeopardy.

16. *Beliefs about social troubles and help-seeking behavior, including the use of indigenous and traditional healing practices:* Studies in ethnicity reveal that people differ in:

    - Their experience of emotional pain
    - What they label as a symptom
    - How they communicate about their pain or symptoms
    - Their beliefs about the cause of the difficulties
    - Their attitudes toward helpers
    - The intervention they expect (McGoldrick, Giordano, & Garcia-Preto, 2005, p. 28).

In this section, we talked about honoring the strengths bestowed by culture to enhance family resilience. However, sometimes family social workers will need to make some difficult choices. As McGoldrick and colleagues caution, "Just because a culture espouses certain values or beliefs does not make them sacrosanct. All cultural practices are not ethical" (McGoldrick, Giordano, & Garcia-Preto, 2005, p. 31). This caution applies to our own culture as well. Everyone has values—they are just ordered in a different hierarchy (Rokeach, 1973). This means that some cultures agree with the oppression or mistreatment of women and children. Some values are a "human rights issue" (p. 31), and family social workers must learn to pull out the values that respect basic human dignity and separate them from values that marginalize vulnerable populations within groups, including women, children, and those with marginalized sexualities.

EXERCISE 5.16   Impact of Diversity

Make a list of how diversity is discouraged and encouraged in your community, subculture, and country. What would be the impact on families with whom you might work? What can you do as a family social worker to neutralize or help families cope with these larger social issues?

EP 2.1.4a

PRACTICAL APPLICATIONS

To focus on a strengths-based practice, family social workers need four skill sets:

1. *The ability to identify and use strengths*: Identifying and using strengths is both an attitude and a behavior.
2. *Cultural competency*: Cultural competency provides family social workers with an openness and sensitivity to hidden reserves within a family's culture. It also involves knowing how to use cultural assets to benefit the family.
3. *Interpersonal sensitivity and knowledge*: This involves knowing where to look in the family's life for assets.
4. *Relationship-supportive behavior*: A cornerstone of social work practice is relationship building (Green, McAllister, & Tarte, 2004).

Family social workers can use the ideas of risk, protection, and resilience in their practice in several other ways. First, they can look at what risk factors are in play in a particular family. Recognizing risk factors is the first step toward removing them. If a parent is unemployed, for example, the social worker can assist that person to upgrade skills or improve job-search abilities. The next step is to help improve the coping mechanisms that have been blocked and become chain reactions that heighten stress levels. Next, family social workers can determine what factors are present to protect the individual or family in that particular circumstance and emphasize them in the work. Finally, the social worker can help improve family confidence in their abilities to master difficulties. The key is for the social worker to help the family gain a realistic perspective on their situation such that they are not overwhelmed by their problems and can see what skills they have to tackle their issues (Walsh, 2006).

In addition to asking family members what their problems are, the family social worker can inquire as to what strengths they bring to the family and what they think are the strengths of other family members. The worker creates a language of strength, hope, and movement (Kaplan & Girard, 1994, cited in Saleebey, 1996) instead of a problem-saturated conversation.

Cultural diagrams and time lines can be used for tracking nodal points in family history (McGoldrick, Giordano, & Garcia-Preto, 2005, p. 757). These diagrams can help place a family in a context of kinship network, culture, race, gender, religion, migration history, and so on. They can also be used to outline family resources and vulnerabilities. These authors provide a list of cultural genogram questions that can be asked in reminding families of their resilience "through the values of their heritage, their ability to transform their lives, and their ability to work toward long-range goals that fit with their cultural values" (p. 762). Moreover, using genograms can help families acknowledge their history and help them translate and reach for adaptive strategies they used in other contexts to solve current problems. (McGoldrick, Gerson, & Petry, 2008, p. 238).

CHAPTER SUMMARY

The focus of this chapter was to help the family social worker to start thinking about family strengths-based practice and resilience. Resilience is a dynamic process whereby families rally their resources and cooperate as a unit to meet their challenges. These strengths can be placed in an ecological approach along with risk factors, paying attention to micro-, meso-, macro-, and exosystems. It also emphasizes the need to examine family members' beliefs as a source of both strength and risk. Culture is not a straightforward concept but involves multiple dimensions. The contributions of culture and ethnicity to strengths and resilience is very important and must be understood by the family social worker. Finally, there is a growing recognition of the importance of religion and spirituality in family life, which can pose dilemmas and opportunities for family social workers. Social workers can broaden beliefs about working with families by embracing a family's strengths.

KEY TERMS

Family strengths-based practice is defined as "the set of relationships and processes that support and protect families and family members, especially in times of adversity" (Myers, 2003).

Levels of the ecosystem micro, meso, exosystem and macrosystems.

Microsystem: the first layer of relationships consisting of face-to-face relationships within the family.

Mesosystem: the relationship of the family with social systems such as a child's teacher.

Exosystem: the local policies and community beliefs that affect families.

Macrosystem: the larger social system of social policies, social values, and beliefs that affect families.

Resilience The ability of the family to respond positively to an adverse event and emerge strengthened, more resourceful, and more confident (Benzies & Mychasuik, 2009, p. 104). Resilience is tested and revealed in the face of adversity. Resilience involves a constructive response to difficulties through mobilization of a unique set of available resources. The family responds in such a way as to overcome the adverse event and arrive at the other end stronger than before.

Risk Risk refers to the probability that an individual or family will experience an adverse event (Fraser, Richman, & Galinsky, 1999).

SUGGESTED READINGS

Becvar, D. (2006). *Families that flourish: Facilitating resilience in clinical practice*. New York: Norton. This book will help students and workers understand how to integrate resilience into practice with a variety of families. Becvar does a good job of capturing the characteristics of families that do well despite obstacles.

Saleebey, D. (2000). *The strengths perspective in social work practice* (4th ed.). Boston, MA: Allyn & Bacon. Saleebey is a leader in the field of strengths-based social work practice. Rather than taking the traditional approach to viewing problems as pathology, the strengths perspective looks at client empowerment.

Walsh, F. (2006). *Strengthening family resilience* (2nd ed.). New York: Guillford. This book should be required reading in the classroom or offices as it forged a change in how we think about families by emphasizing that all families have strengths that can be tapped into to stimulate change. Walsh discusses the theory behind family resilience and presents belief systems, organizational processes, and communication processes as three factors in family resilience.

COMPETENCY NOTES

EP 2.1.4a Recognize the extent to which a culture's structures and values may oppress, marginalize, alienate, or create or enhance privilege and power: These include diversity, values, and life cycle issues.

EP 2.1.4b Gain sufficient self-awareness to eliminate the influence of personal biases and values in working with diverse groups: It is important for the family social worker to maintain cultural competence.

EP 2.1.7a Utilize conceptual frameworks to guide the processes of assessment, intervention, and evaluation: A person in environment perspective guides the family social worker; from this framework comes the concept of risk assessment.

EP 2.1.10b Use empathy and other interpersonal skills: In addition to empathy, the family social worker needs to be sensitive to family issues and concerns and to identify and use family strengths in the assessment and intervention process.

CHAPTER **6** | Practical Aspects of Family Social Work

CHAPTER CONTENTS

LEARNING OBJECTIVES

- Conceptual: Understand the importance of preparedness for family social work and recognize that the worker-family relationship is the foundation of family work.

- Perceptual: Be aware that clients appear anxious during their initial contact with a family social worker.

- Valuational/Attitudinal: Value a professional, caring, nonjudgmental relationship with families.

- Behavioral: Learn specific skills for initial contact with families.

There are many practical decisions to make in family social work. In this chapter, we look at some of these nuts-and-bolts issues. We discuss the importance of adhering to a regular schedule for family interviews but remaining flexible enough to accommodate unforeseen events. Suggestions are given for the preparation and care of materials used by family social workers. We discuss how to decide whether to include children in family meetings, and we offer tips for dealing with disruptions and maintaining contact with families who move frequently. Safety issues are also addressed. Within the context of the first family meeting, we introduce the topics of assessing a family's needs and engaging family members in the helping process. Finally, we describe ways to orient clients to family social work and to safeguard client confidentiality.

REFERRAL PROCESS

Families can be referred to family social workers through a number of ways. First, families might refer themselves after hearing about the service and deciding they need assistance. Second, families might be referred by another agency that believes your agency will appropriately meet their needs. Finally, families might be involuntarily mandated by the courts to receive family services from your agency. Case notes might accompany the family's referral, and there are benefits and disadvantages of reviewing case notes from previous workers prior to the first family interview.

EXERCISE 6.1   Reading Case Notes

Break into small groups and discuss the pros and cons of reading case notes prepared by previous workers. Discuss in class.

Benefits include learning what has been attempted and accomplished with the family previously. It might also alert the family social worker to special issues and risks of working with the particular family. However, reading prior case notes also comes with disadvantages. For example, the family might have progressed past where it was since being in family social work. In addition, the previous worker might have had biases or theoretical frameworks that will slant the new worker. Minimally, new workers can read the referral and previous case notes but are advised to keep an open mind regarding changes in the family and new ways of seeing it. Family workers might also benefit from having a discussion with the previous worker or referral agent.

EP 2.1.10a

SCHEDULING FAMILY MEETINGS

Prior to the first home visit with a family, the family social worker needs to accomplish the following tasks:

1. Determine the overall purpose of the meeting, as well as both short-term and longer-term purposes.
2. Outline specific issues to be addressed during each meeting.
3. Contact a family member to set up an appointment time.
4. Locate the family's home.
5. Decide how much time should be allotted for each meeting.

Sticking to a regular schedule benefits both the family social worker and the family. Changes in the schedule are almost inevitable, but establishing a proposed timetable for visits helps promote steady progress toward the family's goals.

Weekly appointments are usually sufficient, but frequency and duration of meetings depends on the goals and needs of each family. Time for related responsibilities such as meetings with colleagues and supervisors, community liaison and advocacy, documenting, case management, and other related tasks must be worked into the family social worker's schedule.

The established schedule for family meetings may have to be altered because of unexpected events that are beyond the control of either the family or the social worker. Family social workers must develop sufficient psychological flexibility to adapt to changes in plans without duress. A useful tip is to plan carefully but expect that circumstances may interfere with the execution of those plans. Attention to scheduling is especially important given that family social workers must meet the needs of all the families assigned to them.

Setting Up the First Appointment

In most cases, the social worker's initial contact with the family will be a telephone call to arrange the first meeting. Family social work begins with the first contact. For families who are unreachable by telephone, the family social worker will need to write a letter of introduction or drive to the home to make the first contact.

First impressions are important, and both the family social worker and the family will form first impressions of one another during the telephone call or visit (Goldenberg & Goldenberg, 2000). The social worker will get an idea of the family's readiness to work and start to take an inventory of how family members view the problem. From the family's perspective, first impressions are particularly important. The family social worker enters into practice "armed with theory and technique, experience and intuition, and the desire to be helpful. The client enters into the social work agreement with both the expectation and hope that they will be helped or at least not harmed!" (Graybeal, 2007, p. 513). Clients prefer a family social worker who is warm and understanding and who conveys hope and competence. The family will also size up the worker's dress and demeanor and form an opinion about whether they will want to trust and connect with the worker.

In preparation for the first interview, the family social worker makes an appointment to meet with the family. For this purpose, many family social workers prefer to meet with as many family members as possible. For various reasons, clients may try to exclude family members from this first appointment. They may request that the social worker see only the child with the problem, or they might try to exclude other family members such as the father or other children who do not have a "problem." The general rule is to include as many family members as possible in the first appointment because the number of family members present at the first session can predict who will be involved in future sessions (Brock & Barnard, 1992). The presence of more family members also means that multiple perspectives about the problem can be considered, but the social worker must be careful not to get caught up in one person's view of the problem (Nichols & Schwartz, 2007).

The social worker might also suggest that attendance by as many family members as possible will help him or her understand the problem more fully and that the presence of the entire family is important because the problem affects everyone.

EXERCISE 6.2 Including Family Members

Break into small groups. In these small groups, list all the reasons you can think of for including as many family members as possible in the interviews. Then list possible reasons that a family might give to exclude certain members. Role-play this initial discussion, with one person playing the role of the social worker and another person playing the role of the family gatekeeper.

Allowing for Travel Time

When scheduling home visits, the family social worker should be sure to allow enough time to become familiar with the neighborhood and to arrive at the agreed-on time. If time permits, the family social worker may make a trial run to a family's home before the first appointment to determine how much time is needed to arrive at the destination, the fastest routes, and issues related to parking and general safety. A rehearsal trip will ensure a timely arrival at the first family meeting and also orient the worker to the family's neighborhood.

Traffic patterns, construction delays, bridge openings and closures, one-way streets, and similar situations that affect travel time should be considered when planning for the meetings. A current city or county map is a simple but necessary tool for family social workers. As well, online resources such as MapQuest can help chart out the easiest route to the family's home. Additionally, many agencies now equip their workers with a GPS.

EXERCISE 6.3 Mapping an Address

Randomly select an address from a telephone book. Using an online resource, map out how you can get from where you are to that address.

Within an agency, the distance between families' homes might be the main criterion for assigning cases to social workers. To reduce travel time, supervisors of programs that cover large catchment areas may assign family social workers to cases on the basis of geographic location. This practice may not be as desirable as assigning workers on the basis of the best match with family needs, but it acknowledges the impact of travel time on workload planning. Allowing sufficient time between family meetings ensures that a delay in completing one meeting or an emerging crisis will not result in subsequent delays for other family interviews. Mileage sheets can be kept on a clipboard in the social worker's car and filled in immediately after every trip. Being well organized at the outset will prevent a lot of difficulties later on.

Many programs require the social worker to write up case notes after each meeting before beginning the next one. Thus, time and location of documentation should be considered when setting the daily schedule. Family social workers searching for suitable places to complete documentation often become regulars at coffee shops, libraries, and other convenient locations near the homes of client families.

Accommodating Family Needs

The scheduling of home meetings should reflect the mutual needs of the social worker and family members. For example, fluctuating energy levels should be taken into account to ensure productive visits. The level of difficulty involved in working with various families should also be taken into account. For example, family social workers may schedule meetings with their most challenging families early in the day or week. Flexible scheduling that accommodates personal preferences and needs will maximize the social worker's effectiveness and promote personal well-being. Managing a demanding caseload based on an inconvenient schedule can contribute to professional burnout. Although it is important for family social workers to be flexible about work hours, they must still find a balance so personal time is protected. An exhausted and unhappy family social worker cannot provide the quality of service that families deserve.

Families also have preferences for meeting times. Ultimately, their needs should be the most important consideration when scheduling home appointments. Families have varied lifestyles and routines that reflect their dynamics. Some have stable, predictable schedules and home lives that easily accommodate regularly scheduled home meetings. Others have less organized or chaotic lives that make regularly scheduled meetings difficult or even impossible. Parents can have varied work schedules, and the family social worker needs to set up meetings to fit within these schedules. Being sensitive to family preferences, habits, and lifestyles will help the social worker to schedule appointments appropriately and help in the engagement process.

Because family social work meetings often occur within the home, respect for privacy and accommodation to schedules is crucial. Some families, for example, may not want to meet when young children are napping, whereas others may prefer to meet while young children are asleep. Other people may drop in during a family work session. A family member or the family social worker should ask them to come back later, on the basis of a decision made by the parents in consultation with the children.

The dedication of some families to certain television or recreational programs is another factor worth considering when scheduling home appointments. Family social workers who arrive during these times may be welcomed into the house but might not expect to have the family's full attention during activities or discussions. Some social workers have found that briefly watching certain television programs with families before engaging in work provides a useful basis for building rapport, particularly with families who find opening up difficult.

Scheduling home interviews with parents who work outside the home can be quite complicated. After a day's work, the parents and the family social worker may be tired and feel the pressures of impending evening activities. Instead of scheduling every meeting during the evening, the family social worker might set up an occasional weekend visit. While disruptive to the family social worker's personal routine, meeting at odd hours may be best for some families. At the same time, part of the assessment process involves determining the difference between legitimate reasons for difficulty in setting up schedules and resistance to getting involved in family work.

To sum up, the key to scheduling family meetings is flexibility. The family social worker needs to find a balance between achieving specific program goals in every meeting, being responsive to the family's immediate needs, and taking care of personal needs to prevent burnout. Even after the social worker and family have decided on a mutually agreeable schedule, some meetings may have to be postponed or rescheduled. A family may be unable to benefit from the planned purpose of a meeting on a particular day because of crises such as the threat of eviction, loss of employment, or a child's illness. Under these circumstances, the family social worker should attend to the family's immediate concerns and discuss available resources. A crisis may require that the family social worker listen to the family's concerns, offer emotional support, encourage active problem solving, or help the family access resources from other agencies. Trying to impose a set agenda on an unreceptive family can block the helping relationship. As one family social worker phrased it, "Flexibility kept me sane. I had to remind myself that nothing was cast in stone, and that I could really trust my instincts." Nevertheless, workers can decide whether the scheduling difficulties are indicative of a deeper resistance to get involved in family work.

EP 2.1.10a

PREPARATION AND CARE OF MATERIALS

Another important aspect of planning is preparation and compilation of materials. Materials may be standardized, or they may be created or collected for each meeting and for each family. Materials can include activity cards, pamphlets, toys, coloring crayons or pencils with paper, books, recording instruments, evaluation measures, or referral forms. Parents might also volunteer toys, giving the family social worker the opportunity to assess the resources that the parents have for their children. Preparing for a family meeting will take time, particularly if materials must be gathered or made. The family social worker should bring extra copies of materials that have been left with the family in case they have been misplaced.

EXERCISE 6.4   Useful Materials

Develop a list of potential materials useful for family social work. Break down the materials used for different age groups.

Infant

Toddler

Preschooler

Public school child

Young adolescent

Older adolescent

Parent

Family as a whole

Materials should be organized and stored so that they can be located and used easily. This is an important part of planning for the family social worker who travels regularly between the agency and family homes. Because different sets of materials for several clients will be needed while traveling from home to home and because other forms or materials might also be kept at the office, an appropriate organizational system is needed. Disorganization can result in loss of time, missed opportunities for effective family interventions, and considerable frustration for both the worker and the family. A family social worker may want to keep a file box in the car trunk for case-by-case storage of recent and current paperwork. The family social worker can transfer older materials from the file box to the main office files and add new materials for upcoming meetings.

The family social worker must take care to protect confidential materials from being misplaced, damaged, stolen, or inadvertently combined with other materials that could be distributed during an appointment. Again, organizational skills are critical. A laptop computer makes it easy for the family social worker to record data, provide duplicates for office files, and protect case notes and other confidential information. Electronic files should be password-protected for extra security. If a laptop computer is unavailable, a separate container or secured portable file box can be used for storage of confidential materials both en route to and during home visits. After each family meeting, confidential materials should be filed immediately in the appropriate secure location. Special care must be taken to keep one family file separate from other family files. This will prevent the family social worker from accidentally mixing files.

EP 2.1.10a

WHAT TO WEAR

Each community and client population has its own standard of dress, and family social workers will learn to be sensitive to these standards. While clothing should be professional, the degree of formality will vary. In addition, clothing should match the planned activities in an interview. For example, if the meeting requires the family social worker to play on the floor with children or be physically active, clothing can be selected with these activities in mind. One of the authors recalls interviews she had with a family that had six dogs in the home. The author wore comfortable clothes to sit on the floor and play with the children. On her return home, she noticed red bite marks all over her body and discovered that she had been bitten by fleas during the visit! Nevertheless, the family appreciated the worker's effort to engage the children.

Moreover, expensive designer clothing might create a sense of social distance between the family social worker and the family and interfere with rapport building. We remember one worker who showed up for meetings in a Cadillac and a mink coat, and her families were reluctant to engage with her.

EP 2.1.10a

INCLUDING CHILDREN IN FAMILY INTERVIEWS

EXERCISE 6.5 Children in Family Interviews

Break into small groups and list situations for which children should and should not be present for family interviews. Share this list with the rest of the class and discuss.

Since home meetings are often initiated in response to the needs of an individual target child, sometimes referred to as the identified person (IP), children are often the focus of family social work. Although only one child may be the focus of intervention, other children in the home may also benefit from attention. The family social worker can join with the parents in devising a strategy for dealing with children during meetings. The plan might call for the children to play in another room, particularly when discussion centers on personal adult issues such as marital distress, sexuality, or financial difficulties. When the focus of the interview is a child, children can join in the interview. Obviously the inclusion of children depends on the purpose of the session. When no one is available to supervise children excluded from the meeting, special activities can be arranged in another room to occupy them. Materials provided by the social worker should include items that can occupy children productively. The family social worker should supply materials that will interest the children. Alternatively, the worker might want to spend special time playing with the children apart from the parents to get an idea of how the children play and what special issues are on their mind. In this situation, the worker will explain the purpose of this special time to both the parents and the children. The parents can be nearby in case either the children or the parents get anxious.

Generally, meetings with parents alone are easier to manage and control. As suggested by Satir (1967), "the presence of children might spell anarchy to the therapy process" (p. 136)! Nevertheless, the presence of children cannot be dictated by whether the interview will be easier without them. Children could be a part of the entire interview when they are old enough to contribute to family sessions. When they cannot contribute, their presence may also be important to see how the parents and children relate and to use the opportunity to teach parents skills in disciplining or relating to their children. Satir (1967) agrees, suggesting that social workers take an active role in interviews when there are children (p. 186). For example, the family social worker can model ways of communicating with children. Initially, the family social worker may want to assess how parents set limits and manage children's behavior. The bottom line is that the structure of family interviews is based on an intentional decision-making process.

Approaches to children during home meetings can include negotiating with them to occupy themselves productively, either with their own activities or with those brought by the worker, after which they are rewarded with special attention. In difficult situations, another family social worker may be available to work with the children apart from the meeting with the parents. A coworker can also help coordinate a meeting in which the entire family is present. Observing how parents interact with their children during a home visit helps the family social worker to assess the parent-child relationship and to design interventions that will promote positive change.

Sometimes, the family social worker may need to ask the parents to arrange for the children to be elsewhere during a home meeting; if this is not practical, the meeting can be conducted at another location such as the agency office. This may be necessary when the parents want to discuss something that children should not hear, such as marital difficulties or intimate personal problems, or when the needs of one or more children require almost constant adult attention. Parents may talk more freely with the social worker when the children are not present. Some agencies pay for child-care expenses during these times.

In one office-based meeting, for example, a parent sat passively while the child ravaged the worker's office, opening desk drawers and otherwise intruding on the worker's privacy. Rather than imposing limits on the child, the social worker asked the parent to intervene. The parent found this request difficult to follow through on. When asked by the worker why she did not intervene, the mother said she considered controlling and disciplining her child to be a form of abuse. In response, the worker suggested that *not* controlling her child was a form of abuse since the child would not learn how to respect the property of other people and would experience rejection by those around him when he was insensitive to others. To this, the mother replied, "That is already happening." This incident opened the door to a discussion of limit-setting and discipline. The mother had failed to recognize that her child had developed few social skills and was being rejected by his peers. In another family, the mother, a caring single parent with three rambunctious teens, harshly proceeded to pull her children's ears when they did not listen. Their ears became very red during the interview, and this situation also opened the door to a discussion of discipline and how to appropriately gain compliance from children.

Failure of parents to set limits with children during the family meeting therefore provides valuable information about what goes on in the family and how effective parents are in managing their children's behavior. In addition, the social worker can help parents devise limit-setting techniques with children on the spot, providing feedback as the parent practices newly learned parenting techniques. The presence of children can provide the social worker with information about family dynamics, parenting skills, and parent-child relationships. Therefore, when the presenting family problem involves children, observing the interaction between parent and child will be necessary for understanding the particular issue. The presence of children will also help determine how parents are implementing the changes made during the work.

When assessing the role of the children within a family, the family social worker keeps in mind that the family is a system in which each member is affected by dynamics that affect other members. The birth of a physically or mentally challenged child, for example, can influence parental interactions with other children and with one another. In addition, the existence of a serious problem such as delinquency or alcoholism will have a strong impact on family needs and interactions. Siblings of target children are often neglected, but they also need opportunities to talk about their feelings and have their questions answered honestly and directly. Parents often mistakenly assume that because a certain child is not the "problem," that child does not need to be included in the session. Asking a child a question such as "Can you tell me what you are worried about?" may unleash a barrage of concerns. Therefore, family social workers must be sensitive to the dynamics of the whole family and consider all members' needs when conducting meetings.

EP 2.1.10b

HANDLING DISRUPTIONS AND MAINTAINING CONTACT

Although most home meetings will run smoothly, the family social worker should be prepared for occasions when they do not. Disruptions such as blaring televisions, visits from friends and neighbors, and telephones are all a natural part of the home milieu, and finding creative ways of handling distractions, such as meeting on the front porch or at another private location or having older siblings entertain younger ones, will help make the interview run smoother. If distractions and chaos persist, the family social worker and family need to discuss these obstacles and decide on a reasonable method for resolving them.

It is also important for clients and the family social worker to know how to reach each other. Contact is aided if the client has a telephone; however, if clients do not have a phone, another method of reaching the family during unscheduled times can be worked out. This may involve using a neighbor's telephone or leaving notes at the home. One family worker, after many failed meeting attempts, found that providing the family with addressed, stamped envelopes and stationery to inform her of canceled meetings or unanticipated moves was an effective way to remain in contact. Agency policy and worker well-being will determine whether the family social worker provides a home phone number.

Frequently, the transience of clients can interfere with schedules. If a family's move is planned and the social worker is aware of it in advance, the appointment schedule can be adjusted. However, some families move without notifying the family social worker, who then has difficulty locating them. At the first meeting, the family social worker should request the name and phone number of a person who will always know the whereabouts of the family.

TELEPHONE FOLLOW-UP

Telephone follow-up between sessions can be a good idea because many parents have additional questions after reflecting on the interview. They also may have been in crisis, and a check-in phone call might prevent the crisis from deepening. If the family social worker initiates telephone contact, she or he can be more helpful to parents who worry about asking "dumb" questions and are reluctant to bother the family social worker with problems.

When information, teaching, and careful follow-up are insufficient to accomplish the agreed-on goals, the family social worker can determine what types of additional intervention may be useful to the parents. The goal is to help parents understand their problems and enable them to change their behavior in ways that will work for them and their children. It would be counterproductive to assign homework that parents cannot execute. The family social worker can judge what can be undertaken immediately, what should be delayed until appropriate preliminary goals have been achieved, and what can be postponed indefinitely. Consequently, the family social worker should be flexible enough to adopt alternative methods based on an assessment of the situation and of parental responses to intervention. Follow-up can reinforce new behaviors or help the family social worker to decide if further intervention is needed.

EP 2.1.10b

SAFETY CONSIDERATIONS

It will be impossible for social workers to achieve program goals when their safety is threatened. In some cases, the family social worker's safety is threatened by clients who become violent; in others, the risk is created by an unsafe neighborhood.

In other situations, drugs or weapons may be in the home or in the possession of one member of the family who has a history of violence. Awareness of the family history in such situations is useful. The best predictor of future violence is a history of previous violence. Knowing how to protect one's personal safety is essential in family social work.

Violence against social workers does not appear to be random. Rather, the person committing the violence will often have some complaint against an agency, whether real or imagined (Munson, 1993). For example, an aggressive parent who demands that the family social worker bypass waiting lists, provide special services or resources, or produce unrealistic results may be hostile to the family social worker. The family social worker must be ready to deal with clients' attempts to manipulate, cross boundaries, or attack verbally or physically. A part of the family social worker's effectiveness for parents depends on the ability to deflect personal intrusion and impending threat. For self-protection, social workers must be caring, yet capable of separating involvement on a professional level from involvement on a personal level.

EXERCISE 6.6 The Hostile Client

Some social workers are taken unaware by the verbal hostility of clients. For this role-play, we would like the class to break into groups of three to play a social worker, a hostile client, and an observer. Taking turns, role-play a situation in which the client is extremely angry with the social worker. The observer will take notes on what worked and what did not work. Switch roles until everyone has had a chance to role-play each part. Discuss in class the effective techniques for disarming the client, and make a list of these techniques.

Some parents may use threats or alliances to avert negative repercussions for themselves. The family social worker must be aware of and guard against client attempts to manipulate, attack, or cross boundaries. A part of the family social worker's usefulness to parents depends on the ability to deflect personal intrusion and impending threat.

Because families live in all types of neighborhoods, from rural areas to inner cities and suburbs, safety issues will vary within and across programs. However, several basic safety guidelines are relevant for all family social workers. To ensure the safest conditions for home meetings, we recommend the following guidelines:

1. Perhaps the most important safety guideline is not to dismiss a sense of danger. When social workers feel vulnerable or unsafe, they should take whatever precautions are necessary for protection. Sometimes family social workers feel awkward about being suspicious of clients' friends or feeling uncomfortable and apprehensive in certain neighborhoods. They might underplay the sense of feeling threatened. Ignoring these anxieties can place the social worker at risk. On the other hand, if family social workers are merely unfamiliar with the client's setting or are meeting in an unfamiliar cultural milieu, the source of apprehension needs to be examined before concluding that conditions are unsafe. Becoming acquainted with diverse cultures and neighborhoods allows family social workers to discern real from imaginary danger.

2. A related guideline for safety in home meetings is to become familiar with neighborhoods where home visits take place. Learning the layout of the immediate area around clients' homes and the usual types of activities that occur there will provide a baseline from which to assess risk.

3. Make certain that the program supervisor or other responsible agency personnel are aware of the family social worker's schedule of family meetings. Family social workers should also discuss issues of safety when they feel vulnerable. The schedule should include the name and location of the family, the date and scheduled times for the meeting, and the expected time of return. When a home meeting is scheduled in an unsafe environment, family social workers can develop a monitoring system such as a call-in procedure when the visit is complete. We recommend the use of a cellular telephone, and all family social work programs should consider using them. The following scenario demonstrates how a social worker's failure to let the agency know her whereabouts placed her at risk. She related a situation in which she was eight months pregnant and went into the home to apprehend the children. The father, not at all pleased with the purpose of her visit, held her hostage. The incident lasted eight hours, but no one from her agency knew that she was being held hostage or even where she was because there were no call-in tracking arrangements at her agency. She managed to leave the situation after keeping a cool head and talking fast, but after that episode she always let several people in her office know her schedule.

4. Avoid dangerous neighborhoods at night. If this is impossible, arrangements should be made for an escort. For example, one program hired an escort for late afternoon and early evening hours. Social workers in the program then scheduled appointments when the escort could accompany them. Another option is to ask a relative or friend to accompany the social worker into the home and to come back again when the family meeting is over.

5. Assess the safest route to and from the client's home in advance. If the most direct route does not have well-lit or well-patrolled streets, a safer route should be chosen. Parking in clients' neighborhoods may also present safety issues. The only available parking may be far from clients' homes or in a high-crime area. If safe parking cannot be found, using a paid driver may be worthwhile. One program serving a high-risk urban community hired a full-time driver who escorted family social workers to all of their meetings. If a social worker feels uncomfortable meeting a family in their home, making arrangements to meet in a public place is acceptable.

6. A social worker who feels unsafe during an interview should leave (Kinney, Haapala, & Booth, 1991).

Clients and communities can participate actively in planning for the safety of the family social worker, and this can be an important and useful component of an empowerment strategy. Also, safety planning within the family itself is an important aspect of the family social work process. Besides the preceding guidelines, several other safety factors should be considered. Since family social workers usually drive to appointments, they need to maintain their cars in good condition. One of the authors was using an agency vehicle, which was poorly maintained. The transmission fell out of the car on the way to a family visit. On another occasion, she locked her keys in her car and had to go back to the home and request to use the telephone. In other words, the rule of thumb is to be prepared for all possibilities! Family social workers who travel long distances through high-risk neighborhoods should also ensure that they have enough gasoline. Further, since confidential program materials may be kept in automobiles, it is imperative that they be secured against theft.

The security of personal possessions should be considered when meeting families in the community. The family social worker should avoid carrying more money than necessary. Accessories such as purses and jewelry are generally not appropriate for home meetings. Theft of money or other items from family social workers, while rare, can occur. One home-based worker wore expensive clothing and drove an expensive car to family meetings and was advised by the agency to avoid doing so. Preventing incidents from happening is better than having to deal with them once they have occurred. Worrying about confidential items left in a car may also prevent a social worker from devoting complete attention to a family during an appointment.

Most agencies provide training to family social workers on recognizing signs of potential violence among clients. Most agencies will also have clearly established safety protocols for social workers, in addition to offering training sessions on handling violence when it does occur. If a social worker feels frightened during a visit, he or she needs to assess the severity of the immediate risk and be unapologetic about leaving. Erring on the side of caution is best. As mentioned, circumstances that might require this response include violence in the home, drug use and drug dealing, the presence of weapons, or the presence of intoxicated or out-of-control individuals. If a social worker encounters any of these situations during family meetings, he or she must discuss the incident with supervisors and explore alternatives for ensuring safety during future appointments. In some circumstances, home appointments may be ended or situated in safer locations.

Another precaution concerns illness in the home. If a family member has an infectious disease, the social worker should use judgment about being exposed to the illness. When confronted with communicable illnesses such as hepatitis or influenza, the worker should consult with medical personnel about the advisability of meeting in the home. Sometimes rescheduling a home visit is the best option. For example, the Head Start home-visiting program has clearly defined procedures for social workers to follow when confronted with client illness.

Sometimes family members will offer the social worker refreshments such as coffee or cookies. Normally this will not be a problem. Eventually, however, most social workers will come across unsanitary conditions in some homes and will have to think of a graceful way to decline the offerings without offending the family. Within some cultures, offering food to a visitor is a sign of respect and hospitality. Families would be insulted if the social worker refused their offer. A brief but direct approach is suggested, such as thanking the family for their offer of food or coffee and explaining that the family social worker has just eaten or finished a cup of coffee before arriving for the meeting.

EP 2.1.10a

THE FIRST MEETING: ASSESSING CLIENTS' NEEDS

Social workers who are familiar with the skills of individual counseling can become overwhelmed when they begin working with families. They may be uncertain about what to expect or how to proceed. It is important to keep in mind that the purpose of the first meeting is to assess the problem and engage the family in problem solving.

EXERCISE 6.7   Difficult First Meetings

Write a list of potential situations for a first interview that would be difficult for you to deal with. For each situation, provide two alternative responses to overcome the difficulty.

The family social worker may offset the apprehension of seeing a family for the first time by obtaining as much information as possible before the meeting. Reading family files, if available, is a good starting point, as is reading literature about the family's specific problem. The supervisor can discuss how to apply specific theories to the family's problems. The family social worker should also examine personal values or biases that may affect her or his performance with a particular family and again consult the supervisor. Gaining understanding of any diversity issues is also very important before this first meeting.

Keeping the specific family in mind, new family social workers may review the principles and techniques of family interviewing. Topics to be explored include: How should this family be engaged? What particular techniques might be useful in engaging this family? How are goals set in a family meeting, and what specific goals might be set in the first meeting with this family? What are the special cultural issues for this family?

After the family social worker has formulated answers to these questions, the supervisor can provide practical feedback and direction. The supervisor and other agency colleagues may be willing to role-play the family so the family social worker can practice what to say first, where to sit, whether to accept coffee, and so forth. Role-playing provides the family social worker with the opportunity to develop new skills and obtain important feedback before meeting with the family. It is a form of dress rehearsal. The supervisor may encourage role-playing other tasks such as engagement and goal setting. Even though the reality may differ from the rehearsal, the family social worker will have developed a sense of what to expect during the initial meeting with the family.

Basic patterns to look for at the first meeting involve repetitive verbal and nonverbal communications among family members. The family social worker should pay attention to indications of conflict, who gets involved in disagreements, where family members sit in relationship to one another, who speaks for family members, and so on.

EXERCISE 6.8   Introducing Yourself

Write a list of opening instructions or statements that you can use to introduce yourself and the purpose of family social work.

At the start of the first interview, the family social worker should introduce himself or herself and explain the agency's purpose. Description of the agency is especially important if the client is not familiar with the agency. Once this has been done, the family social worker starts to engage the family and begins to assess its problems. Assessment involves understanding what the problem is, what is causing the problem, and what can be done to change the situation (Holman, 1983). Ideally, assessment will be a shared responsibility between the worker and family. The worker collects information by encouraging participation by every family member. This involves getting to know names and developing a sense of how each family member understands the problem, making it important for every member to speak. It is common for parents to speak for the children or for one adult to speak for another. This may be an example of a repetitive family pattern that the family social worker should note and address. Social workers learn to understand who is speaking for whom in the meeting and begin to get the spokesperson to allow others to speak for themselves. To do so, the family social worker may need to challenge family patterns, especially established patterns of family authority. Understanding cultural norms and ways of communicating is also important.

The process of identifying problems and learning about the family can be complex and time-consuming. The worker can gradually engage the family in activities such as drawing a genogram (family map) or an ecomap (diagram of social contacts). Genograms and ecomaps are described in detail in Chapter 8 on qualitative family assessment. These activities will assist in deepening the engagement of family members, facilitate balanced individual participation in the interview, and help the family to define the problem so that family members can accept the plan for future work. Assessments done from an ecological perspective that examines the interactions between the family and its environment are most comprehensive (Holman, 1983). An ecological assessment should be required for all problems.

Social workers should assess the family's living environment. A tour of the home can reveal much about the family, especially differences between public and private areas. Eating areas are another focal point for the family and give information also suggestive of family style and management. A family that dines together every night around a large table presents a different image from the family that eats dinner on TV trays in separate rooms in the house. Going to the "right part of the house" when assessing a family can be of great value in planning future work with the family, especially if the family social worker encourages parents and children to discuss perceptions of different spaces and to describe what the spaces mean to each family member.

Encouraging worker-family communication during a home interview includes sitting where everyone can be seen. Eye contact is critical in engaging family members. It is advisable not to begin an interview until all family members are present. Time-consuming social exchanges can be left to the end of the interview. The tone of the interview will help the family social worker decide whether refreshments are a distraction or a gift and whether they should be postponed to the end of the session.

Demarcating the physical space in the home interview is useful so everyone can participate. Someone may stomp out of the room in a rage, retreating to a section of the house where she or he can still listen to what is being discussed. If someone goes into the bathroom and locks the door, however, that is a clear indication that he or she has left the session and the family will have to problem solve about how to deal with the absence. Such events do not curtail work with the family. Instead, they are examples of natural events that can be used to learn more about the family. Additionally, they can provide opportunities for family members to learn new patterns of behavior.

Increasingly, social workers are becoming technique-driven, and various interventions and theories compete with one another. The growing interest in demonstrating intervention techniques can make social workers worry that they will be ineffective if they are not using the latest intervention. However, it seems that therapists are more impressed with techniques than are clients (Miller, Hubble, & Duncan, 1995). For instance, parents report valuing the most fundamental elements of service: support, listening, on-the-spot assistance, and availability of the social worker (Coleman & Collins, 1997).

Basic helping skills of empathy, warmth, and genuineness are crucial to intervention, as is the willingness to ask for clarification when meanings are unclear. Demonstrating these qualities will lay the groundwork for a strong worker-client relationship, often known as a therapeutic alliance. Family social workers secure with these basic skills can successfully negotiate both the first and subsequent family meetings with little apprehension. The second interview will be easier and the third interview easier yet. The fourth interview may be more difficult for new family social workers who are developing critical awareness of their own performance. However, this difficulty and self-consciousness should be welcomed as a positive sign of learning and growth.

EP 2.1.10b

BUILDING A RELATIONSHIP WITH CLIENTS

The core of family social work is the relationship between the family social worker and the family—a relationship that will make it possible for the family social worker to work productively with the family. The relationship is the vehicle that carries interventions and makes them palatable to the family. It contributes as much as 30 percent to the effectiveness of intervention (Miller, Hubble, & Duncan, 1995). The first family meeting marks the beginning of a helpful relationship between the family social worker and the family. This relationship may be quite brief or long term.

It is crucial for family social workers to recognize that when there is family conflict, family members may try to get the social worker to side with them in their particular view of the problem. The family social worker should anticipate this maneuver and avoid it by empathizing with individual viewpoints without colluding with them. Family work involves maintaining a delicate balance between neutrality and sensitivity to individual experiences. When neutrality does not occur, certain family members can feel alienated and judged (Coleman & Collins, 1997). Social workers struggle with issues of alliance with individual family members versus advocating for justice for family members who have been wronged or harmed by family dynamics, particularly those disadvantaged or harmed by family dynamics as in the case of abuse. Worden (1994) suggests three crucial elements for developing a strong relationship with clients:

1. A consensus between the worker and client on the goals of therapy
2. Worker-client agreement and collaboration on implementation of tasks
3. A strong, positive, affective bond between each member of the family and the worker.

Keeping these three elements in the forefront will assist the family worker to negotiate the complexities of the first family meeting. The relationship will be strengthened further by attending to issues involving ethnicity, gender, and stages in the family life cycle (Worden, 1994, p. 25).

The first family meeting requires special attention, not only because it lays the foundation of a positive relationship between the family social worker and family, but also because it will affect the quality and course of later work. Consequently, engaging the family's interest and developing rapport is crucial to the family social worker's continued work with the family. The family social worker will aim for the first family meeting to be time-limited, focused, and relaxed.

Another component of the first meeting is instilling a sense of trust to enable family members to express their concerns honestly. Trust is not automatic; it is constructed gradually as family meetings continue. The family social worker can encourage the development of trust by taking a sincere interest in family members' needs, conveying a willingness to help, and supporting the family during difficult times. Rapport may be achieved quickly with some families, while other families require patience and persistence. The nature of the family and its problems, the purposes of the family work, the personality of the family social worker, and life experiences of family members influence how quickly trust and rapport are achieved. How the family feels about dealing with a problem and their perceptions of the problem influence their receptiveness to family work. Remember, building a relationship with a family takes time.

It is important to foster a supportive atmosphere not only between the family and the family social worker but also among family members. A high level of rapport and trust facilitates problem identification and effective working relationships, which in turn contribute to positive solutions. Effective working relationships facilitate behavioral changes that stimulate family satisfaction and self-confidence. One role of the family social worker is to help clients clarify personal goals and develop a plan for reaching them. The relationship between social workers and clients is so important to family social work that program objectives cannot be met unless positive rapport is established. The worker-family relationship is strengthened as family priorities are assessed, information is conveyed, support and encouragement are provided, and self-reliance and effective coping are promoted.

Development of a trusting relationship is not always smooth. Clients who are disillusioned with helping systems will struggle with issues of trust. Thus, progress made in establishing trust during one meeting may be lost at the next appointment, depending on the family's interpretation of intervening events. These events may or may not involve the family social worker per se, but may include incidents from the family's life that create suspicion about motives. We know of one situation in which trust was undermined when a family received a visit by a children's protective services caseworker for suspected neglect or abuse of the children. Although the family social worker's involvement was not related to the investigation, the family projected its distrust and fear onto the family social worker.

In the first meeting, and also in later ones, the family social worker should be sensitive to the privacy of the family and avoid being intrusive. Conveying respect for the family's territory and showing appreciation to the family for allowing the worker onto their turf opens many doors. In other words, family social workers are guests in family homes (Kinney, Haapala, & Booth, 1991). Questions should focus on information needed to carry out program goals, especially during the first meeting. Some families may be eager to share information, but usually this will not be the case. If the family chooses to talk about personal matters, the family social worker may listen attentively and respond supportively. The family social worker may redirect the conversation to program-related topics if conversation becomes tangential or irrelevant. Probing into the personal life of family members during the early phases may undermine the development of a working relationship with a family. A family member who has shared information freely may later regret having shared so much. The family social worker should be supportive and non-probing early in the work.

EXERCISE 6.9   Giving Out Home Phone Number?

Divide the class into two groups for a debate. One side will argue for a policy that allows families to have the family social worker's home phone number. The other side will argue against the family having the family social worker's phone number. Write down the points argued on each side, and discuss after the debate has ended.

EXERCISE 6.10   Trust

Write down one family secret that you have never told anyone in your life. Include reasons why you have not told anyone this secret. Close your eyes, put your pencil down, and spend about five minutes imagining that you must now reveal this secret to a stranger who has just come into your house. What are your feelings about telling this stranger your secret? What must happen (concretely) before you would be prepared to talk to this stranger about your family secret?

EP 2.1.10b

ORIENTING CLIENTS TO FAMILY SOCIAL WORK

The intensity of the family social worker's involvement with family members and their problems can contribute to feelings of personal closeness; yet the relationship must remain at a professional level. Family social workers often work with families who are in severe crisis. Many have endured a lengthy history of family problems plus multiple episodes of prior service or treatment from various agencies. Because the family has probably experienced previous failures, it is important that the family social worker establish positive expectations for change and convey hope to the family at the beginning. Support can be provided through use of appropriate opportunities for family change.

Reviewing the purposes of family social work and the nature of the activities to be completed promotes work with families. Focusing on family goals can help make each meeting productive. Time may have passed since the family first agreed to participate in family work, and the family social worker will need to help the family remember the specific details originally agreed on. Reminding the family about these details may also stimulate enthusiasm, interest, and participation.

During the first family meeting, the family social worker explains clearly his or her role, including responsibilities and limitations of involvement. When the limits and structure of the relationship are clarified, the family social worker and the family can focus on productive work together. Clarification of roles may need to be repeated and reinforced frequently. Some family programs have narrowly defined roles for family social workers, whereas others permit and even encourage family social workers' flexibility and independence in establishing work-related boundaries. In either case, clarifying family social worker responsibilities and limitations helps prevent the possibility of confusion and disagreement concerning the social worker's role.

The family's role in the change process should also be made explicit. Enlisting the entire family as partners in the process, rather than as recipients of service, establishes the idea that family social work is a mutual responsibility of the family and the social worker. The most obvious contribution of the family is availability for the work. Without access and ongoing participation, the family social worker cannot perform the roles involved in the helping process.

The family's perceptions and expectations of family work also should be explored during the first meeting. Sometimes expectations are not realistic. The family social worker may discover that clients have misunderstood program objectives or were misinformed. Finding out what the family expects and correcting misperceptions during the first meeting eliminates misunderstanding later. Ultimately, the whole family should be encouraged to reach a consensus on expectations for family work.

The first home meeting might last between one and two hours, depending on the objectives. It should be ended when planned activities have been completed. If the meeting is proceeding smoothly and the family is becoming engaged, the family social worker may extend the meeting accordingly. A successful outcome of the first meeting means leaving the family feeling comfortable and looking forward to the next meeting.

EP 2.1.10c

PROTECTING CLIENTS' CONFIDENTIALITY

Family social work offers professional services to families on a potentially more personal level than other service-delivery systems. Because of the nature of the work, maintaining appropriate confidentiality is critical (Collins, Thomlison, & Grinnell, 1992). Case 6.1 illustrates the high risk of breaching client confidentiality.

CASE 6.1	Confidentiality

You receive the Simpson family case at a screening and referral. In the first meeting, you inform the Simpsons that you are their new family social worker. They seem a little reluctant to talk, so you encourage them by giving your assurance that anything they say will be held in the strictest confidence. At the time, you believe this implicitly. Later, while you are talking to your secretary, Romalda, you realize that she is typing case notes, including your information obtained about the Simpsons. Afterward, in the coffee room of your agency, workers are talking freely about their cases and ask you about your cases. You respond with details of the Simpson family case. Later, you learn that Mr. Simpson has asked for medical assistance, and your entry in his file has been shared with various government and medical service agencies. You think with dismay that you might as well have sent the record to the newspaper—and later discover that a sheet of your notes has fallen out of your briefcase and been picked up by a neighbor of the Simpsons. You search frantically for the audiotaped interview that you plan to share with your supervisor. Meanwhile, the Simpsons have discovered that what they said to you in strictest confidence is now common knowledge in the social service delivery system. On Friday, you meet with your supervisor and give a rundown of your cases. The Simpson family case is at the top of your list.

Filled with righteous indignation, the Simpsons complain to your supervisor. Your supervisor gently explains to you the difference between absolute confidentiality, in which nothing your client family says is shared with anyone in any form, and relative confidentiality, in which information is shared with colleagues as required. You realize you will never be able to promise absolute confidentiality as an agency worker and, probably, you will never be able to promise confidentiality at all.

Despite your supervisor's gentleness, you feel that she is convinced of your incompetence. You also feel vaguely resentful; she could have told you about relative confidentiality before.

Guidelines for Protecting Clients' Confidentiality

1. Do not discuss clients outside of the interview (e.g., an open office door, class, group, or restaurant) even with changed names and altered identifying details. Discussing details about clients with family or friends is not permitted. Family social work can be stressful, and social workers sometimes need to unwind by talking about their feelings and their stress. The only time it is appropriate to discuss clients is in a private setting with your supervisor or colleagues, for example, in a case conference. Discussions should occur at the office with supervisors and colleagues, not with family and friends who are not bound by the same rules of confidentiality as the family social worker. Nonprofessionals may listen with interest to a story about families or agencies, but, in the process, may lose respect for the social worker, the agency, or the profession. They could be thinking, "If I have a problem, I will never go to her or any other social worker; it would get all over town," and it might.

2. If a client is not at home when you call, leave only your first name and say nothing about the nature of the business. It may be acceptable to leave your phone number, depending on how recognizable it is.

3. Social workers must not become involved in discussions about clients with colleagues over lunch or coffee. At a restaurant or other public place, there is an obvious risk of the conversation being overheard. Even when names are not mentioned, people might identify the client or think they have. Overhearing personal conversations about work gives others the impression that the social worker is casual about confidentiality.

4. Arrange for phone calls to be taken by someone else when interviewing a client at your office. Interruptions lead to a break in rapport and inadvertent breaches of confidentiality. Also, the client may think, "She has more important things to do than listen to me." When in a family home, if using a pager, postpone returning the call so that there is no chance for the family to overhear your phone conversation.

5. Ensure that every interview is private and conducted in a private setting out of the hearing of others.

6. Do not leave case records, phone messages, or rough notes on your desk or in an unlocked car. Case records often have the name of the client prominently displayed on the file, and they may catch someone's attention. Secure records and files before leaving your desk, and make sure that client files are locked up overnight. Clients who observe that the family social worker is haphazard in managing files may assume that the family social worker will be haphazard in protecting their interests.

7. Clients should not be discussed at parties and social activities. Colleagues frequently socialize together, and it is tempting to discuss a difficult case or talk about a case to illustrate a common problem.

8. Even if a client seems unconcerned about confidentiality, it must be protected anyway. Some clients may want to begin the interview in a waiting room or initiate or continue a discussion in a public place. In such circumstances, the discussion should be deferred until a private setting can be arranged.

9. Confidentiality about the internal operation and politics of the agency is essential.

10. Before linking a family to other community services, the family social worker must obtain permission. When a family gives permission for confidential information to be shared with specific agencies or individuals, information should be limited to that which is essential. Most agencies have developed a release-of-information form to be used in these situations.

11. In most states, confidentiality must be breached if someone (particularly a child) is at risk of harm. Clients need to be informed of this ahead of time. (Items 1–11 reprinted from Collins, Thomlison, & Grinnell, 1992, pp. 186–187.)

EXERCISE 6.11 Confidentiality

Role-play with another student a discussion of confidentiality with a client.

EP 2.1.10b

CHAPTER SUMMARY

Considering the practical aspects of case planning helps the family social worker demonstrate the skills of a competent professional. Scheduling enough time for meetings and travel time and locating clients' homes helps instill client confidence.

| CASE 6.2 | Preparing for the First Visit |

Sharon and Geordie and their 6-month-old daughter, Jackie, were referred to the family social worker from Child Protective Services (CPS). The couple has been married for a year and a half, is experiencing marital problems, and was reported for the father's violent behavior toward his wife and child. The intake report said that Sharon is a stay-at-home wife and mother. Geordie has been employed at a pawnshop for five years. Neighbors have reported that the couple fight and scream almost nightly, while the baby cries loudly in the background.

To prepare for the initial visit, the family social worker reviewed the intake report and familiarized herself with directions to the couple's home since she had scheduled a home visit at night after Geordie's workday was over. She also prepared a folder with recording instruments and measures she believed would be useful, including a family violence index. Since the family social worker believed the neighborhood to be unsafe, she asked a colleague to accompany her to the visit. To prepare for her visit, the family social worker also reviewed guidelines for establishing a positive relationship, rules for confidentiality, and rules for interviewing a family.

Planning and preparing ahead for requisite materials and for dealing with children in the home also will alleviate stress for the family social worker.

Maintaining client contact may be challenging when working with multiproblem families, who are often seen in family social work. The family social worker will need to develop ways of dealing with disruptions and locating clients who move frequently.

Ensuring family social worker safety is essential, as most family social work is done in clients' homes. The family social worker must be aware of the working environment and take steps to avoid danger, such as refraining from wearing expensive clothes or jewelry in a poor neighborhood with a high crime rate.

The first family meeting sets the stage for all other meetings. A clear introduction of self, the agency, and the purposes of family meetings is crucial. Establishing rapport and trust is the cornerstone of family social work. Finally, client confidentiality is essential for a trusting client-worker relationship.

KEY TERMS

Ecological assessment An ecological assessment involves charting the relationship and interactions of the family with the larger social, ecological environment. These include, for example, interactions with social support groups, friends, and church.

Eco-map As part of an ecological assessment, an eco-map is a diagram of social contacts (see Chapter 8).

Genogram A genogram is a drawing of a family map (see Chapter 8).

Neutrality Initially it is important for the family social worker not to side with one family member over another's particular view of a family problem. They should empathize with individual viewpoints without colluding with them.

SUGGESTED READING

Coleman, H., & Collins, D. (1997). The voice of parents: A qualitative study of a family-centered, home-based program. *The Child and Youth Care Forum, 26*(4), 261–278.

COMPETENCY NOTES

EP 2.1.2b. **Make ethical decisions by applying standards of the National Association of Social Workers Code of Ethics and, as applicable, of the International Federation of Social Workers/International Association of Schools of Social Work Ethics in Social Work, Statement of Principles:** Guidelines for protecting clients' confidentiality include taking care regarding when and where you discuss clients' issues, privacy of client interviews, and sharing of client information with others.

EP 2.1.10a. **Substantively and affectively prepare for action with individuals, families, groups, organizations, and communities:** The family social worker prepares for family work including taking safety precautions, preparing materials, and wearing appropriate clothing.

EP 2.1.10b. **Use empathy and other interpersonal skills:** The family social worker has the skills necessary to successfully include children in the interview process.

EP 2.1.10c. **Develop a mutually agreed-on focus of work and desired outcomes:** Orienting families to family work involves educating families about what is involved, what they can expect, and what their role and yours will be.

The Beginning Phase

LEARNING OBJECTIVES

- Conceptual: Understand the necessity of engaging all family members without blaming any individual.

- Perceptual: Tune into the initial reactions of the family to being involved in family social work. Observe how the beginning relationship between family social worker and all family members unfolds.

- Valuational/Attitudinal: Work nonjudgmentally with all family members and the family as a unit.

- Behavioral: Develop skills of family social work necessary to engage, set goals, and contract with the family.

In the preceding chapters, we laid a foundation for understanding the phases of family social work. First, we looked at the historical underpinnings of family social work and explored the evolution of the meaning of "family" over time and across cultures. We then discussed the values, assumptions, and beliefs that underpin effective and fair family practice. Next, we applied systems theory to family social work. Chapter 4 examined family development and the family life cycle and Chapter 5 described family strengths and resilience. Finally, we explored practical aspects of working with families and offered guidelines for building a relationship with the family and for conducting an initial interview.

In this chapter, we continue our discussion of how to establish a positive working relationship with a family to set the stage for family change. We begin by describing principles of effective communication, focusing specifically on skills needed as the family social worker begins to work with a family.

Family social work unfolds over four phases: engagement (beginning), assessment (identification of problems and strengths), intervention (facilitating change), and termination. Each family meeting includes elements of these phases, paralleling family social work's overall involvement with a family. In the following chapters, we outline tasks and skills required of the family social worker in each phase. While the phases of helping are presented in a linear way as if they were mutually exclusive, in practice the phases overlap. Family social work begins at the moment of the referral. The family social worker begins assessment by reading the referral form or previous case record. The tasks involved in engaging with a family and assessing family needs and resources continue throughout the family social worker's involvement, but they are particularly crucial during the first meetings.

EXERCISE 7.1 Challenges Facing the Family Social Worker

Think about types of clients or types of problems you may find difficult to handle. List these, and write what you would do if faced with each.

TASKS FOR THE BEGINNING PHASE: ENGAGEMENT, ASSESSMENT, GOAL SETTING, AND CONTRACTING

New social workers long for a recipe of what to say and do in specific situations, particularly because spontaneity is an important skill. Unfortunately, no recipe exists. While it is now cliché to suggest starting where the client is, a more accurate statement might be to start where the social worker is (Hartman & Laird, 1983) because the knowledge, skills, and values of the family social worker influence how assessment and engagement will proceed. The family social worker also brings to the family an agency mission with which to carry out his or her role. As mentioned, perceptual, conceptual, and executive skills underpin all of family social work.

Engagement is the process of establishing and maintaining a meaningful working relationship between the family social worker and the family. It includes developing a convincing rationale for a family approach, establishing positive working relationships, conveying personal competence, maintaining a productive worker-family relationship, and establishing hope. In a very succinct way, you will know if the family members are engaged because they are talking to you! Hopefully, the family members will go beyond talking to the family worker at a superficial level to a level that presents deeper issues and feelings in the family.

Engagement of the family is an essential but insufficient skill in family social work. By this we mean that engagement lays the foundation and opens the door for further, more in-depth work. Indicators of successful engagement might include good attendance, completion of homework assignments, emotional investment in sessions, making progress toward meeting the goals of intervention (Cunningham & Heneggler, 1999), and, of course, family members continuing to talk in depth to you. Conversely, engagement problems might be revealed by difficulty scheduling appointments, missed appointments, intervention plans not being followed, goals of the family containing little substance, uneven progress, and family members lying about important issues and avoiding talking about anything in depth to you. Tomm and Wright (1979) offer tips for successful engagement of families, suggesting the use of empathy, gift-giving (strategies that provide the client with direct and immediate benefits during initial work), normalization of problems, anxiety or guilt reduction, and increased hope.

The first tasks of the family social worker in the beginning phase are engaging families in the helping process, assessing the problem that is troubling the family, goal setting, and contracting. It is important to recognize that family social workers do not "do" interventions "to" families. Families are neither passive nor helpless; they have a reservoir of strengths and abilities that can be tapped to allow them to take an active and productive role in the process. Let us now discuss these skills in more detail.

Several conditions must be met before a family is ready to become involved in family social work. First, the family has to agree *as a family* that a particular problem requires outside intervention. Some family members may feel the problem more acutely than others. Second, the family must connect with an appropriate agency. Finally, the agency must determine whether the family's issues fit its mandate. Each factor will influence the course of family work. In some cases, the court will mandate contact with the agency, erecting some hurdles to engagement. Even though work with some families may begin involuntarily, effective engagement will help the family to understand and accept the value of family social work so that they will agree to continue the work.

Engagement involves establishing a working relationship between the social worker and *all* members of the family; assessment involves identifying repetitive patterns and issues within the family that relate directly to the problem as well as identifying issues related to the nature of family relationships with the social environment. All members are involved. Rather than exclusively examining one person's role in the family, the social worker must actively connect with all family members. This is one benefit of the entire family being present at the first meeting. A strong worker-family relationship has the potential to transcend cultural differences (Beutler, Machado, & Allstetter Neufelt, 1994).

An integral part of engagement involves creating a safe environment where people can talk about themselves and about each other (Satir, 1967). A safe working atmosphere will diminish anxiety and increase confidence for everyone. The development of rapport with *all* family members underpins successful engagement. Parents may feel anxious and lack confidence by the time a family social worker enters their life space. Parents often report that intervention is stressful and that they feel blamed (Stern, 1999). Most families will feel defensive regardless of how agreeable they may appear on the surface (Haley, 1976, p. 16). They may believe that their need for family social work involvement is a sign of personal incompetence or failure. Many parents expect to be blamed for the problems that exist and may feel isolated, unsupported, and dejected after having tried to solve their issue for a long time before formal helper involvement. Feelings of hopelessness can be addressed by reframing the situation into a more positive conceptualization, positively reinforcing the family's courage, and highlighting family strengths to deal with their situation (Cunningham & Henggeler, 1999). Most families will have attempted previous solutions to their difficulties before entering the present work, and the worker can discover what these previous solutions were.

At the same time, the person with the "presenting problem" (who is often, but not always, a child) may feel blamed and ganged up on for causing the family distress. This person may worry about being blamed further or being removed from the family altogether. Hurt, anger, incompetence, fear, and rejection will be common feelings. In this early stage, family members will seldom agree about the cause of the problem.

It is important not to expect the family to trust the worker or the work immediately. Automatic trust in another person is not a typical feeling when embarking into new and scary territory. When workers sense a lack of trust, it should be discussed and validated when appropriate (Cunningham & Henggeler, 1999).

The tasks of the first couple of interviews can be broken down into five components:

1. Make Contact with Every Family Member

First, the social worker needs to create a setting in which the worker connects with the family and members start to feel comfortable. In this stage, social courtesies are observed without focusing on the problem. Introductions are made, and every family member is personally greeted. This stage can be used to observe the family, its mood, and the family relationships, behaviors, and attitude about receiving services. The family social worker can observe where members sit in relation to one another. Initial impressions and observations might be revisited with additional information, and it would be premature to share them with the family at this early time. This stage can last several minutes but if it lasts longer, the family social worker might have difficulty transitioning to a deeper discussion of family issues. The worker is aware of this when the interview focuses on superficial issues rather than trying to address the family's concerns.

A common term used for the engagement process is joining (Minuchin, 1974), by which the family social worker conveys to the family, "I am with you." Joining helps bridge the social distance between the social worker and family.

At this time, the family social worker connects with family members by actively seeking unique information about each member. Because each family is unique, no definitive rules prescribe which person the social worker should turn to first. However, critical reflection and thinking play a role in determining how to proceed, taking into account gender and cultural issues. The protocol of some cultures might dictate that the social worker address the father first. Nevertheless, the ordering of introductions should be deliberate. For example, turning first to the family member with the identified problem might single out that individual as "the problem." Starting with the "problem child" might put too much pressure on a child who already bears the brunt of the family's anger and blame. Another alternative is to start with the family member who appears to be most detached to ensure that this person becomes involved.

Alternatively, the social worker might wish to validate parental authority by turning to the parents first. Ideally, the process of introductions should match the presenting problem and the family culture. The family social worker will also need to make a personal introduction to the family, including her or his name, agency, how the family came to the agency's attention, and a tentative statement about her or his role.

The worker enters the family's world, noting family vocabulary and matching the family's style of language (Goldenberg & Goldenberg, 2000). How members address one another will influence how the social worker addresses them. Regardless of what names the social worker uses, names should be selected intentionally. For example, Satir (1967) suggests referring to the parents as "Mom" and "Dad" when discussing parental roles but otherwise using their first names. Additionally, minority families have certain relationship and cultural protocols that need to be respected by the worker. The social worker's manner of addressing individuals in minority families should adhere to the family's cultural practices. Thus, the social worker must be attuned to the cultural practices of the family's ethnic group and determine how traditional the family is in their cultural practices, remembering that there is much heterogeneity in every culture.

One approach to introductions might be to first address the family group as a whole in order to ameliorate personal biases. Leaving the question open will flesh out the family's typical ways of operating; this is what the family social worker wants to accomplish at this stage, without drawing premature conclusions. Remember that in Chapter 3, we discussed triangles and noted that it is easy for a family social worker to become triangulated into the family system. Vigilance and awareness about this possibility from the outset are important.

When deciding with whom to speak with first, the worker becomes attuned to issues of blame, gender, age, family structure and hierarchy, cultural patterns, and so on. The opportunity to address these factors in more detail will arise later so long as the worker is sensitive to them and understands, firsthand, how these issues come to play out in this particular family.

Several roadblocks, rooted in different sources, might derail successful engagement. For example, parents might be experiencing substance abuse, mental health problems (such as depression), limited intellectual ability, discomfort about being involved in services, and low expectations about self-efficacy. Other hurdles might stem from family and social factors such as poor parent-child bonding, marital discord, unemployment, poverty, lack of social support, and a history of coercive interactions with helpers. This cluster of factors will alert the worker to conditions that need to be addressed in the course of the work. Additionally, worker factors interfering with engagement might include collusion with one member of the family, excessive self-disclosure, poorly conceptualized client problems, stress, burnout, being child-centered vs. family-centered, discomfort about addressing certain issues, and a lack of understanding client cultural backgrounds or value systems (Cunningham & Heneggler, 1999; Stern, 1999).

Parental involvement and cooperation is particularly important to resolve problems associated with family difficulties because parents are the core of the family and parents are positioned to be primary contributors to the positive functioning of their children (Kindsvatter, Duba, & Dean, 2008). In addition, the social worker will become aware of the advantages and disadvantages of approaching the family from the perspective of an outsider (Hartman & Laird, 1983).

EXERCISE 7.2   Starting a Family Interview

Break into small groups and, using the case example below, have one person role-play the social worker and the rest of the group role-play family members. Role-play the start of a family interview several times, each time starting introductions with different family members and lastly with the entire family. Which introduction felt right? Why?

2. Define the Problem to Include Perceptions of All Members of the Family

In clarifying "the presenting problem," the social worker speaks with each family member to obtain his or her unique perspective on the problem. If infants are present, the family social worker can acknowledge their presence, noting who is responsible for the infants' well-being. The family social worker should allow each family member to offer an opinion of the problem without interference or influence from other family members. This might be the first challenge to the family social worker—to politely but firmly deal with disagreement and interruptions and allow the person who is speaking to have airtime. The social worker should then attempt to understand each member's perspective on why the family is receiving services.

The family social worker can also determine what family members have attempted previously to address the problem and what hopes they hold for the future. If anger and blame erupt, the family social worker is entrusted with the task of ensuring that no one is scapegoated for the conflict. The social worker should provide a clear rationale for offering assistance to all family members, as some members may not understand the social worker's presence.

During the initial phase, it is important for the worker to "base all his or her behaviors on understanding and showing respect for the family reality, which

CASE EXAMPLE 7.1

John, age 44, his wife Mary 43, and their three children, 14-year-old son Marvin, 13-year-old son Michael, and 11-year-old daughter Sharon, were referred to you by their family doctor due to the mother, Mary, feeling depressed and overwhelmed primarily related to family issues. These issues include poverty. The father works evenings as a pizza delivery person making minimum wage. He has a history of unemployment. The mother works a couple of days a week cleaning houses. Back problems and fatigue prevent her from working more hours. They live in a small, two-bedroom low-income housing unit.

They regularly attend church, and all three children attend a Christian-based school. Since this school is private, added expenses are involved for the family. There is no extra money for recreational activities for the children outside of the school. The children are doing reasonably well academically although Marvin is struggling in math. Daughter Sharon is overweight and also suffering from acute eczema.

Since this family lives in cramped quarters, there is little privacy in their home. The two boys often fight with each other as well as excessively tease their sister. Since the father is often at work in the evenings, discipline is left to the mother. None of the children pay much attention to the mother. They rarely help out with household chores.

includes the value system, cultural context, and experiential nature of all family members" (Alexander, Holtzworth-Munroe, & Jameson, 1994, p. 623). Eventually, the focus of problems will shift to the entire family. There are several different ways of teaching the family to view problems from a family context. One common metaphor of the family is that of a mobile to demonstrate how the behavior of one member affects other family members. Ultimately, the problem is framed by connecting family members' common experiences of distress within the context of what needs to be changed. Describing the problem as something that affects everyone and needs to be changed sets the stage for the mutual work that lies ahead.

In the problem identification stage, the conversation centers on the "presenting problem." At this point, social niceties take a backseat as the focus narrows to a discussion about the problem. It is a time when the family social worker assumes control of the process and gets down to business by asking family members why they think they are involved in family work. The family social worker will observe how each family member frames the problem, with special focus on the emotional quality of the presentation and individual responses to how the problem is described by others. At this point, it is common for family members to describe the problem in terms of a "problem" person.

3. Encourage Family Members to Interact with Each Other

During the problem definition stage, the family social worker encourages family members to interact about the problem by discussing it among themselves with the social worker observing. This stimulation of interaction occurs only after each family member has provided an individual opinion. At this juncture, the family social worker moves from being the center of the interview to being an observer and a director of the family conversation. Doing so will flesh out repetitive patterns that may have contributed to problem development and bring into focus why the social worker is seeing the family.

During this interaction period, the role of the family social worker becomes more of a conductor of the family orchestra, observing the family "music" that is produced. The melody includes family patterns and interactions as well as family structure, circular patterns, and other notable issues related to family relationships. At the end of this segment, the family and the family social worker should have a clearer idea of what needs to be worked on. Ask the family to specify just what changes they seek, which is a goal-setting stage.

Initially, the social worker maintains a neutral stance, avoiding premature confrontation and not making interpretations before more complete information is gathered (Gurman & Kniskern, 1981). Maintaining a neutral stance must be approached cautiously because sometimes the worker will need to take a stand, such as in the case of abuse and violence or other imminent threats to well-being. At the same time, the family social worker will help the family mediate when emotions become particularly heated, as in the blaming of a family member.

The problem needs to be packaged in such a way that something can be done about it. The problem can be connected to family strengths and abilities to convey a sense of hope and confidence to the family about their abilities to address the problem. Families, particularly ones who are burdened by multiple problems, should not become overwhelmed by the problems they are facing. The family social worker can help them partialize and prioritize what they would like to address first. Problems can also be defined in terms of actual behaviors and occurrences. The family social worker might be concerned that this discussion places too much emphasis on the "problem" person. One antidote to this is to help the family examine how these difficulties impact individual family members. Usually the common ground is worry and concern (and there is always hurt behind anger). It is probably not an overgeneralization to assume that every family member wants to feel better about the family; pointing out how worried, concerned, and hurt everyone is about the problem can help create a common ground from which every family member can work. Here is but one way of finding a common theme of family member concerns: "I can see that everyone in this family is feeling upset by what is going on. My sense is that everyone in the family feels angry and hurt about the situation, even though everyone might have different ways of understanding what is going on."

The stance of the family social worker is one of curiosity. The family social worker listens to the emotional content of the description as well as family responses when members are describing their individual perceptions. Also noteworthy is who is blamed for the problem and who takes responsibility. When one person is speaking, the family social worker is freed to observe the reactions of others (Haley, 1976, p. 30).

EXERCISE 7.3 Family Definition of the Problem

Using the same family role-play as in the previous exercise (Case 7.1), practice working with the family and arrive at the point of achieving a common family definition of the "problem."

In cases of suspected child abuse and neglect, assessing whether any child is at risk becomes a critical first task. Risk assessment of abuse can be difficult because the best information is obtained when trust is established and the relationship is strong. The social worker may be aware that the family was referred specifically for abuse. In other cases, abuse may be suspected as the work unfolds. In assessing whether a child is being abused, the social worker should first note any physical signs of abuse such as unexplained bruising and cuts, combined with the behavior of the child. While behavioral indicators of abuse might include timidity or aggressiveness, these signs could also indicate other, less serious problems. The behavior of the child in the presence of a parent will reveal much about the parent-child relationship. Does the child appear fearful of the parent? Finally, the nature of the parent-child relationship should be observed, especially how the parent interacts with the child. Is the parent irritable and impatient with the child? How much does the parent explain things to the child? Is there an affectionate relationship, or is physical contact avoided?

EXERCISE 7.4 A Family Issue

Break into groups of six. One person will play the role of a family social worker interviewing a family in which a teenaged child has been charged with possession of drugs (marijuana). The family consists of Katie (mother), Bobby (father), Phil (14-year-old charged with drug possession), Jackie (16-year-old "perfect" daughter), and Jimmy (typical 8-year-old). The court has ordered the family into family social work. All of the family members are angry with Phil for putting the family through this turmoil. Family members do think that they play a role in the problem.

Role-play this family with the goal of defining the problem as a family issue that each member owns a piece of. Stop when you reach your goal. Share with the rest of the class what happened in your role-play, and explain how you shifted the emphasis from Phil to the entire family unit.

4. Establish Goals and Clarify an Intervention Process

After key issues have been identified, the next step is setting goals. Clear, specific, concrete, and measurable goals, consistent with the family's beliefs and interests, can be itemized in contract form. Goals will be significant, achievable, realistic, and determined by the family's commitment and resources. A reasonable length of time for achieving goals should be established and an evaluation date set. An explicit understanding of approaches to be used and the responsibilities of various family members and of the family social worker also should be components of the contract. At this time, the importance of regular attendance at the family sessions should be reinforced because some family members may continue to resist the work (Nichols & Schwartz, 2007).

Agreeing on a goal requires cooperation between the family and family social worker, and this is facilitated if the prior two stages have been successfully completed. The social worker will develop a picture of the level of motivation in the family and what the family hopes will happen. Goals should involve the family as a whole, with all members agreeing to work toward the development of behaviors to eliminate the problem. Concrete ideas and plans can be proposed for problem solving, instilling in the family a renewed sense of optimism that problems can be resolved.

Self-determination—the principle that clients have the right and responsibility to agree to what they will do—is intrinsic to family social work. To arrive at a goal statement, the social worker and family must collaboratively determine the *desired end state*—that is, a description of how the family would like to get along with each other (Bandler, Grinder, & Satir, 1976). To arrive at the desired state, all must agree upon what the current state is, as well as what resources are necessary and available for arriving at the intended destination. Families should not be manipulated or coerced to accept goals that they do not believe are important. Goals, interventions, and responsibilities may be modified in response to changing circumstances.

To assist families with goal setting, family social workers need to:

1. Recognize that family members are most receptive to change during times of crisis.
2. Move from abstract, global goals to concrete and specific goals.
3. Define clear, concrete, and measurable goals.
4. Help the family identify goals that they would like to achieve first.
5. Assist family members to negotiate with each other regarding behavioral changes.
6. Identify skills and strengths of the family.
7. Obtain a commitment from the family.

The family work will move forward if goal setting is done with focus and purpose. Family social work goals stated in clear and specific terms forecast what will be happening once the goals are achieved. In other words, goals identify the end state that the family wishes to arrive at. Although goal setting is ongoing and continuous, the most productive time to set goals is after the problems have been identified and explored. Until the family social worker and the family have a shared understanding of the situation, goal setting will be premature.

5. Contract with the Family

In this phase, the social worker and family arrive at an agreement about concrete issues such as how often family meetings will be held, who needs to be present, the length of meetings, the proposed overall length of intervention, the motivation of family members, the goals that need to be accomplished, the input required of each family member, and the criteria for judging when goals have been achieved. A definition of the problem should be included in the contract, as well as what everyone can do to address the problem. The social worker and family should reach a consensus on goals and methods. A written contract lends clarity, formalizes the work that lies ahead, and places a demand for work on the family. Contracts will also cover concrete issues such as time and place of meetings and reflect the agreed-on changes in individual and family behaviors that need to be accomplished. An example of a family social work contract is provided in Case 7.1.

CASE 7.1 | **Family Social Work Contract**

The Rocheleau family has been encountering several difficulties in several areas of their lives, which are addressed in this contract. This contract is a formal agreement between Theresa and Ed Rocheleau, parents of 12-year-old Campbell and 6-year-old Jackie, and the family social worker, Ms. Gordon, who mutually agree to work on: (1) parenting skills, (2) the husband's unemployment, and (3) Campbell's absence from school.

1. All family members and the family social worker agree to meet each Monday in the Rocheleau home from 6 to 7:30 P.M. for the next six weeks.
2. They will discuss the homework assigned from the previous weeks.
3. Mr. and Mrs. Rocheleau agree to follow up on information on parenting classes and job training resources provided by Ms. Gordon. They will discuss their progress in these areas in each session.
4. Mr. and Mrs. Rocheleau agree to attend parenting classes and will work together to improve housekeeping skills.
5. Mr. Rocheleau agrees to participate in job training seminars and to follow up on suggestions made at these seminars.
6. Mr. and Mrs. Rocheleau both agree to be present with Campbell to meet with his teacher to develop a plan for him to make up missed work.
7. Campbell agrees to attend school regularly. He will be assisted by his parents every morning to get out of bed, eat breakfast, and bring his homework to school every day.
8. Jackie agrees to continue doing her homework and make her bed every day.
9. This contract will be reviewed on _____ (date) and renegotiated if necessary.

EXERCISE 7.5   The First Family Interview

Break into groups of six. One student will be the family social worker and another student will be the observer. Formulate a problem and create a family. Role-play the first family interview. Take ten minutes for each stage outlined above. Report back to the class on how the interview went, including what went right and what the difficulties were in this first interview. At the end of the discussion, brainstorm with the class how to overcome some of the obstacles that were encountered in the role-play.

From their first meeting, the family social worker and the family will have expectations about what they want to accomplish and how objectives will be met. Contracting can be done on a short-term and/or long-term basis. For example, short-term verbal or written contracts can help a family get through a crisis (Kinney, Haapala, & Booth, 1991), while long-term contracts focus on results that occur over an extended period of time, such as improved grades in school. The family social work contract is a concrete agreement that specifies goals of the intervention and the means by which to achieve them. The contract should state specific problems, the goals and strategies to alleviate them, and the roles and tasks of the participants. A contract is an explicit agreement concerning the target problems, the goals and strategies of family work, and the expected roles and tasks of family members. Families are experts on the nature of their challenges and on what they desire from a program. Contracts should also draw from the family's untapped strengths and expertise about their issues (Fraenkel, 2006).

Contracts may begin as recommendations from the social worker to the family about what needs to be done to resolve the problem (Nichols & Schwartz, 2007). It may take at least a couple of interviews for the family social worker to assess the situation and establish a bond with the family before a firm contract is set. Contracting should also cover important procedural details such as when and where meetings will take place, how long they will last, what records will be kept, rules governing confidentiality, and who will attend sessions.

Ongoing accountability between the family and the family social worker is intrinsic to a contract. Family members are active participants in the entire process, not passive recipients of service. Egan (1994) outlines four basic features of a family contract:

1. The contract is negotiated, not declared, by both the helper or family.
2. The contract will be understandable to all involved parties.
3. An oral or written commitment to the contract will be obtained.
4. The contract will be reviewed as the work progresses. If necessary, the contract will be revised.

The family social worker takes the lead in initiating and structuring discussion about contracting, first by identifying common ground between the needs of the family and the services that can be provided. Time constraints that limit the social worker's availability for work with a family must be taken into account. In addition, the mandate of an agency will place further constraints on how social workers enter into contracts with client families. Finally, family social workers should not contract to provide services that are beyond their competence or exceed the agency's capacity and resources.

As mentioned, contracts change as progress is made, reflecting the dynamic nature of family social work. Essentially, every time the family social worker and family agree on an activity, they have formulated a contract. As the work moves forward, the contract might become more complex and may even address issues in the family social worker-family relationship. A contract makes the family and the family social worker accountable to one another, ensuring that each assumes an active role and responsibility to fulfill agreed-on tasks and to work toward negotiated goals. The contract should identify reciprocal obligations and ways to evaluate change.

By the end of the first interview, the family social worker will have established a preliminary definition of the problem that does not hold one individual exclusively responsible for either its presence or the solution. This is known as broadening the focus, whereby the problem and the solution are both owned by all family members (Nichols & Schwartz, 2007). Even though some family members may frame the problem as belonging to one person, the family worker will make movement toward conceptualizing (silently at first) in terms of family dynamics involving every member of the family. Theory and research about a specific area can guide the way. For example, Satir and Haley both suggest that children develop problems when a generational boundary has been violated and a parent becomes overly involved and concerned with that child. Others (for example, Kindsvatter, Duba, & Dean, 2008) suggest that problems occur in one or more of three domains: the hierarchical organization of the parental subsystem within the family; the executive function of the parental subsystem; and the psychological proximity of family members to each other.

EP 2.1.10b

EP 2.1.10c

EP 2.1.10f

BASIC SKILLS NEEDED BY FAMILY SOCIAL WORKERS

As mentioned, a range of perceptual, conceptual, and executive skills are essential to be an effective family worker. For some, these skills may be a repeat of previous skills that have been learned. However, we would like to emphasize that in working with families, similar but not identical skills for working with individuals are needed. Not only will the skills be useful in accomplishing the tasks outlined in the preceding section, they will also model new behaviors to family members. Basic interviewing skills are necessary for family social work. These skills include:

- Listening carefully to expressed meanings of individuals and the family as a unit;
- Being sensitive to verbal and nonverbal communication about the meanings, desires, and goals from each family member;
- Recognizing family difficulties related to effective problem solving;
- Promoting skills, knowledge, attitudes, and environmental conditions that enhance family functioning.

The role of the family social worker is to assist parents to deal with their children more effectively through the enhancement of problem-solving, decision-making, and parenting skills.

Interviewing a group is more complicated than interviewing an individual. This is because the maze of problems has expanded to include each individual within the family unit as well as the multiple relationships between them. Interview dynamics increase exponentially in a family. Because of the number of people and subgroups involved in a family interview, the social worker has less control than in an individual interview (Munson, 1993). Social workers often report feeling overwhelmed by information, which is sometimes contradictory, coming from a number of sources and frequently at the same time. The complexities present in individual work are therefore amplified in family interviews. Understanding every family member simultaneously and avoiding aligning or colluding with individuals are especially crucial tasks. Other issues to heed include gender roles, ethnicity, and the number of dyadic relationships demanding attention (Alexander, Holtzworth-Munroe, & Jameson, 1994).

Before starting family social work, workers need to distinguish between a friendship and a professional relationship and between a social conversation and a task-centered family social work interview. If they are confused about these distinctions, family social workers risk losing focus with a family and fail to engage the family in problem solving. While family social work can be rather informal at times, clear boundaries between family social workers and families can be useful in ensuring that the work gets accomplished successfully. Moreover, clear boundaries can pave the way for ethical practice.

EP 2.1.10b

GUIDELINES FOR EFFECTIVE INTERVIEWS

The following guidelines can help family social workers develop professional relationships with clients (adapted from Kadushin & Kadushin, 1997):

- An interview is deliberate. That is, the social worker meets with a family to address clearly specified concerns; all the behaviors of the social worker are intentional.
- The content of an interview is related to an explicit purpose.
- The family social worker has the primary responsibility for the content and direction of the interview.
- Relationships are structured and time-limited.

A family interview is *deliberate* and has a purpose and set goals that are agreed on by all participants. Thus, the focus of a family interview is on the family and its issues, and the direction is toward a solution. To arrive at a solution, the family social worker overcomes the temptation to engage in conversations that detract from the task. For example, *extended* chitchat can be a waste of time or a way to avoid painful topics, although brief chitchat may be useful initially to allow the family to settle and become acquainted with the work. Chitchat may also be useful for engaging a resistant family member by establishing rapport. The caveat is to return to issues after a resistant member has become involved.

When working with members of a different culture, the family social worker can initially engage the family in friendly conversation rather than immediately focusing on the problem. Rules about relationships differ from culture to culture, and seasoned workers are attuned to the unique cultural nuances of engagement with members of different cultures. Western culture is often considered direct, rude, and even disrespectful by members of less aggressive cultures. Family social workers need to be sensitive to cultural variations in how relationships and rapport develop in cultures other than their own. When differences do arise (and even when they don't), discussion of differences will help to clarify and sort out misunderstanding.

Once rapport develops, the family social worker can pinpoint a specific focus for the work. The longer it takes to develop focus, the harder it will become to shift the focus onto a specific agenda and accomplish later work. Clients may drop out between the first and second meetings if they sense a lack of purpose and direction. Establishing a clear direction, focused on family needs and concerns, gets the family social worker's relationship with the family off to a positive start.

Some new workers may be confused about the difference between content and process. *Content* refers to what is being said and consists of information and ideas. *Process*, on the other hand, refers to "what is really going on" and how it is occurring. Process involves deeper levels of communication and is conveyed in a number of ways including the frequency and timing of talking, tone of voice, facial expressions, eye movements, gross body movements, body posture, and seating arrangements. Content, then, is the "what" whereas process is the "how."

The *content* of family meetings should flow from an agreed-on purpose and move in the direction of addressing the identified problems. Words and behaviors are directly connected to an agreed-on purpose. For example, a family social worker who initiates a family meeting with a general question such as "How are things going?" will lead the family in a less productive direction than the family social worker who begins by saying, "Tell me how the parenting techniques we discussed last week worked out," or, "I'd like to hear about the positive changes in the family over the past week."

In family work, the family social worker assumes *primary responsibility* for the process and direction of the interview. For example, the social worker is attuned to the various processes in the work, thus ensuring that engagement unfolds well. The family is an expert in the content of the work. Sometimes the family social worker may hesitate to use professional authority and expertise with a family, particularly if the parents are older or if the family social worker has no children. Parents who ask the family social worker if he or she has any children may really be asking whether the social worker is able to understand what they are going through (process versus content). They will also be assessing the social worker's experience, demeanor, and competence, which are legitimate concerns given the meaningfulness of the work to them. These questions might generate insecurity for new workers who do not have children and who do not want to appear incapable of understanding and helping. The best response to these questions may be to discuss the parents' concerns directly. For example, the family social worker can say, "No, I don't have any children myself. It sounds like you are worried that because I don't have any children, I will not be able to understand your situation or help you. Let's talk about this."

The relationship between the family social worker and the family is also *structured* and *time-limited*. This means that activities of family social work are intentional and centered around the identified task within an atmosphere in which family members are expected to work on identified problems. It also means that family social work has a beginning and an end. Thus, participants will be able to recognize when a family has achieved the specified goals and no longer requires intervention. Similarly, each individual session with the family is time-limited, depending on the nature of the work that needs to be accomplished. As much as family social workers try to achieve a partnership with the family, the relationship is a collaborative partnership but not really reciprocal. The family social worker provides leadership, knowledge, and direction to the family. The interests and needs of the clients are primary, demanding that the needs of the family social worker be set aside. For example, families may ask the family social worker personal questions. The social worker will decide how much information to share, remembering that the needs of the family and the work focus come first. Self-disclosure by the social worker to a client is a double-edged sword, and responses need to have a definite purpose.

Thus, every action of the family social worker is *intentional.* Words are selected mindfully, targeting an intended effect. For instance, the family social worker may select words on the basis of family interests: if the family is sports-minded, the family social worker may refer to the family as a team. Being deliberate with every word, motive, and action can be exhausting for the social worker, but our work is greatly improved because of it. Deliberateness by the worker occurs at several stages. On the basis of an assessment of here-and-now conditions in the family, the social worker decides what to say. Once the worker has intervened, she or he assesses the impact on the family of what she or he has said. If the impact is undesirable, the worker opts for a refined approach; if the impact produces desired results, the family social worker continues on the same track.

The family social worker-family relationship is guided by clear professional boundaries, ensuring that family needs take precedence over those of the social worker. New family social workers often struggle with the desire to be friendly and establish personal relationships with families. This is a natural inclination because family social workers become involved in intimate details of family life and because positive relationships are pivotal to the work. Family social workers work closely with people in intense and emotionally-laden situations. Moreover, the family social worker may sincerely like clients, and this liking is a crucial ingredient for the work that lies ahead. This is not to say that family social workers cannot get gratification from their work with families. It means, instead, that gratification should derive from work well done.

Despite temptation, it is important for family social workers to maintain a professional focus. The helping relationship is different from friendship because the family social worker wields authority in relation to the family, making a completely equal relationship impossible. Social work codes of ethics also dictate which behaviors are acceptable and which are breaches of professional conduct. For example, one family social worker arranged to purchase a vehicle from a family, with the family financing the purchase. This was a breach of professional conduct that had to be dealt with by the agency once the supervisor reported it. Other breaches include sexual involvement with clients, taking the family for vacations, or deciding to parent a child from the family in the social worker's home. We have witnessed seasoned workers who breached professional boundaries with clients; being vigilant about the issues and temptations is a lifelong journey. Social workers can refer to their code of ethics and discuss situations with supervisors when in doubt. In addition, workers must not withhold any information about a client family from a supervisor. A useful guideline is that if the social worker feels the need to hide information from the supervisor or the agency, it needs to be carefully examined.

Family social workers thus must be committed to putting the needs of the family first, as the family social worker's personal needs are not the focus of the relationship. It is natural for social workers to want to do their best and be appreciated, but they should resist comparisons to other social workers, regardless of how families may flatter them by saying "You are the best social worker we have ever had!" or tell them about the atrocities they experienced at the hands of other social workers. The social worker can accept a sincere or spontaneous compliment. However, compliments that draw negative comparisons with other workers need to be handled delicately.

EXERCISE 7.6 Friend versus Professional Interview

Divide the class into groups of three. Half of the groups role-play a situation in which a friend tells a problem to another friend. The rest of the groups role-play a client discussing problems with a social worker. At the end of the role-play, which will last about ten minutes, the class will discuss the differences between talking with a friend and having a professional interview.

EXERCISE 7.7 Worker Issues

All family workers have personal issues from their family of origin that they bring to family work. One key to effective family work is to be aware of these issues and stop them from playing out in family work. Issues might include having a parent who was an alcoholic, a history of sexual abuse, having turbulent teen years, and so on. Reflect on your family of origin, and list three or four issues from your past that might interfere with family work. Beside each issue, speculate on how this issue might play out in your work with families and then what you can do about your natural response. This can be a very personal issue, so do not feel compelled to share your responses with the rest of the class. However, if one or two members of the class are willing to share their responses, it might be useful for the rest of the class to hear about and discuss them.

EP 2.1.10d

PRINCIPLES OF EFFECTIVE COMMUNICATION

The interview is a special type of social conversation, and *everything* within this encounter conveys a message. Communication takes place between the social worker and the family, and also between family members. All communication by the family social worker is deliberate. The process of communication is complex, and experienced family social workers recognize the first axiom of human communication: "You cannot *not* communicate" (Watzlawick, Beavin, & Jackson, 1967). Communication involves more than speaking with words and includes facial expressions, gestures, posture, proximity, and tone of voice (Satir, 1967). Nonverbal communication is often a cue as to what processes are in play in the interview.

EXERCISE 7.8   Silence

Break into dyads. Try to communicate nothing to each other. How possible was not communicating?

Other axioms of communication include:

- All communication contains information and imposes an expectation of a response. Therefore, any time that communication is present, there is commitment and a relationship. All communication involves content and a message about the relationship—that is, communication has both a report and command component: data about the communication and how the communication is to be taken.
- All behavior is communication.
- Two levels of communication exist: content and relation.
- The nature of a relationship is contingent on the *punctuation* of the communicational sequences between the communicants. This punctuation organizes the sequencing of the interaction. Some relational conflicts revolve around disagreements about how to punctuate a series of events: who starts a conversation, who interrupts, who agrees, who disagrees, and so on are examples of punctuation. It is interesting, for example, that one definition of power is "who gets the final word."
- Communication is both digital and analogic (Suissa, 2005). Digital communication occurs when a word is spoken. Words are symbols of something, such as *cat*, and are connected with language syntax. Analogic communication, on the other hand, is more abstract. It refers to nonverbal components of meaning such as body movement; posture; gestures; facial expressions; voice inflections; the sequence, rhythm, and cadence of the words; and any other nonverbal communication, as well as subtle communicational clues evident when interaction takes place. The clarity of what analogic communication refers to can be ambiguous and unclear. Nonverbal communication, head nods, and "uhmms" are examples. In our communication classes, for example, we try to discourage "minimal prompts" because of this ambiguity. Many workers are notorious for their use of head nods and "uh huhs," which can convey a number of different messages, including "I agree," "Keep talking," or "I am asleep at the wheel and am operating on automatic pilot!" When digital and analogic communication styles coexist, they should be congruent. When they are not congruent, confusion and ambiguity arise.
- All communication interchanges are either symmetrical or complementary, depending on whether they are based on equality or difference (Watzlawick, Beavin, & Jackson, 1967, pp. 48–70).

Satir (1967, 1971, 1972) placed a great deal of emphasis on communication in her work with families and emphasized that communication needs to be *clear*, *direct*, and *honest*:

- *Clear* communication is not masked. The communicator says what he or she means.

- *Direct* communication is addressed to the person for whom the message was intended. (Indirect messages avoid conveying personal responsibility and expressing real feelings.)
- *Honest* communication conveys a genuine message.

Simple communication involves sending messages from one person to another as pictured below.

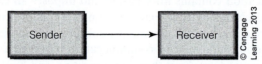

This diagram captures a simple linear communication that suggests content but no process, such as a parent telling a child, "Pick up your toys." In this message, the message is thought to be linear; the message implies an active sender and passive receiver. However, even in this seemingly straightforward example, additional meaning may be intended or inferred. Imagine that "Pick up your toys" is said by an exasperated parent who believes that the child is thoughtless or careless. The message will then be more than the simple instruction and may contain angry verbal tones and nonverbal behavioral clues revealing the parent's displeasure. The body language of the parent may also appear threatening. Yet, as we explored in Chapter 3, communication is not linear. Rather, most communication in ongoing relationships involves a circular, interactive process of involvement by participants (Tomm, 1988).

Many words contain more than one meaning, and the same word can mean different things to different people (Bandler, Grinder, & Satir, 1976). People seldom select words consciously and instead select words that are based on personal experience, vocabulary, culture, and how meaning is personally constructed.

The Communication Process

A transactional explanation of the communication process is given below. Note that these transactional patterns resemble circular causality in that they break down the sequence of circular interactions discussed in Chapter 3 into five distinct steps:

- Intentions, ideas, and feelings of the sender are formed before sending a message. The sender *encodes* a message by translating ideas, feelings, and intentions (thoughts and feelings) into a message appropriate for sending.
- The sender articulates and transmits the message to the receiver through a *channel*. Often the channel is provided by words, tone of voice, facial expressions, posture, and body language (Bandler, Grinder, & Satir, 1976).
- The receiver receives the message through relevant sensory channels such as sight, hearing, and touch.
- The receiver translates the message by *interpreting* its meaning. More than the content is translated. Meaning is derived from how the message is conveyed as well as the context within which the message is sent. The receiver's interpretation depends on how well she or he understands the content and context of the message and the intentions of the sender. It is also determined by the quality of the relationship between the communicators.

- The receiver processes and interprets this message. Meaning in a message can include the literal content of the message (denotative level) as well as what is inferred from the nature of the relationship between the sender and the receiver (metacommunication). In other words, metacommunication is a *message about a message* (Suissa, 2005; Satir, 1967, p. 76). Additionally, the receiver of the message will connect the message with past experiences (history, culture, etc.) that influence how the message is understood (Bandler, Grinder, & Satir, 1976). The life script or internalized self-image and expectations of the receiver also influences translation.
- The receiver then responds to the sender's verbal and nonverbal messages after encoding, interpreting, and transmitting.

For one exchange, all these processes can transpire in under a minute! Consider, then, a family interview that lasts an hour, which presents with a lot of information to translate. Many things interfere with the encoding, transmission, reception, and interpretation of messages. This is known as "noise." Noise includes anything that gets in the way of the communication process. Noise for the sender includes attitudes, frames of reference, emotions, and difficulty in choosing appropriate words. For the receiver, noise can include factors such as attitudes, background, and experiences that influence the decoding process. In the communication channel, noise may result from environmental sounds, speech problems such as stammering, annoying or distracting mannerisms such as mumbling, or difficulty hearing. Accurate communication is therefore complex and ultimately depends on the degree to which noise is overcome or controlled.

In family social work interviewing, many things are happening at the same time, making it challenging to know what to focus on and what to let go. Because of the complexity of communication, it is amazing that people understand each other to the extent that they do.

EP 2.1.10b

Influence of Cultural Background

A fundamental quality of an effective social worker is the ability to empathize with the experiences of a client despite potential cultural differences (Canfield, Low, & Hovestadt, 2009). Culture affects how people communicate with one another. It also creates unique noise. For example, ethnicity is often associated with differences in social class. This is because the percentage of nonwhites who are poor is larger than that of whites (Davis & Proctor, 1989). Studies in ethnicity have shown that people differ in:

- Their experience of emotional pain
- What they label as a symptom
- How they communicate about their pain or symptoms
- Their beliefs about its cause
- Their attitudes toward the social worker
- The intervention they expect (McGoldrick, Giordano, & Garcia-Preto, 2005, p. 28).

Given these differences, social workers from the dominant group may misunderstand when ethnic families communicate in unfamiliar ways.

The family social worker will carefully consider factors that affect both verbal and nonverbal behaviors. In family social work, we assume that the behavior of an individual occurs within a family context. Similarly, behavior also occurs within a cultural context. Personal, familial, cultural, and social background affect behavior and thus are factors that need to be taken into account when interpreting nonverbal or verbal behavior. For one person, lack of eye contact may suggest avoidance; for another, the same behavior may suggest that the person is listening but believes that eye contact is impolite. Similarly, talking face-to-face may be a sign of interest and concern in some cultures but a sign of disrespect in others.

Subtleties of cultural communication permeate every interaction, starting with how members of the same culture greet one another. Cultural communication is discussed in more detail in Chapter 2. Many are familiar with the different ways individuals greet each other. In some cultures, hugs and kisses are exchanged, whereas in others the same type of greeting would be uncomfortable. Family social worker interpretations of a client's nonverbal behavior should be tentative until the family social worker learns more about the personal, social, and cultural background of the client. The most effective way to become familiar with another culture is to ask questions conveying a respectful curiosity about the family's background. Most people will be pleased to educate workers about their culture. Some experts on culture offer the following advice: "Assume that no one can ever fully understand another's culture, but that curiosity, humility, and awareness of one's own cultural values and history will contribute to sensitive interviewing" (McGoldrick, Giordano, & Garcia-Preto, 2005, pp. 36–37).

Helping professions are increasingly becoming more sensitive to the impact of culture. Additionally, family issues may be filtered through the lens of gender, roles, expressiveness, birth order, separation, or the amount of autonomy that family members have. As mentioned, cultural background may also prescribe norms of communication. Beliefs about keeping things in the family or the manner of discussing (or not discussing) certain subjects learned between generations reflect individual and cultural influences. Beliefs and patterns by various ethnicities are discussed in Chapter 2. Interested readers are referred to McGoldrick, Giordano, and Garcia-Preto (2005).

EXERCISE 7.9 Cultural Background

Break the class into dyads. Members of each dyad will interview the other person about his or her cultural background. Reverse roles. Report back to the class on the cultural uniqueness of each individual. You can use the following questions as a starting point: How does the particular culture view the issues reported by McGoldrick and Giordano listed above? If you were to interview a person from a particular culture, what would be the key differences in how members of this culture interact? What is unique about families in this particular culture? What would be the best way to engage with the family? How well would a worker from another culture be accepted into this family?

EP 2.1.4a

Providing Information by the Worker

The most common intervention in all professional helping is giving and receiving information. The family social worker evaluates and decides what information to offer to parents and how to measure the parents' understanding of this information. If parents do not understand the material, it is the family social worker's responsibility to repackage the steps so that the parents either develop the understanding necessary to handle the issue or modify their behavior so that necessary goals are achieved.

The family social worker assesses the parents' levels of functioning, including how well they will work as a team. Understanding parents' backgrounds helps the family social worker decide how to convey the information and direct attention to areas of parental concern. Through an accurate assessment, the family social worker also gains an understanding of parental strengths and weaknesses that influence child management, understanding that child-rearing practices vary from culture to culture. Observing and listening to parents with child-related concerns are the most valid and reliable ways of developing this understanding. Even basic instructions to parents must be tailored to fit the parents' unique characteristics. A permissive parent, for example, may need to learn skills with which to adhere to a firm behavioral regime for an acting-out child, while an authoritarian parent may have to learn to negotiate house rules with the child. Between these two extremes are parents who do well with most instructions if the instructions are clear and specific. An individualized approach involves an accurate assessment of parenting styles and modification of tactics.

The family social worker is charged with understanding parents' personalized responses to stresses and their unique problem-solving abilities. This process applies even in the seemingly simple task of giving instructions. Thus, finding clear ways of instructing (teaching) and of determining whether the information is understood is central to the process.

More complex teaching instructions can be provided in written form to parents. The family social worker may suggest a place for the instructions, such as on the refrigerator door, so that parents can easily refer to them. Parents can be asked to repeat instructions to assess the accuracy of understanding. A verbal and behavioral rehearsal is one way to ensure that instructions are clearly and concisely presented and understood, allowing parents an opportunity to ask questions. However, the system is not foolproof, and other steps may be necessary as well.

Follow-up telephone calls can also be useful, as parents may have additional questions after they have reflected on an interview but be reluctant to ask questions that may make them feel incompetent. Alternatively, for various reasons, some may hesitate to bother the family social worker. Encouraging parents to telephone the family social worker freely may be needed (with a bookmark about how easy it can be to become triangulated into family dynamics). Reassessment of the situation and discussions with the parents at subsequent visits can be ongoing to reinforce the impact of the information.

When offering information, giving instructions, and following up are inadequate to accomplish the tasks, the family social worker can determine what further assistance is necessary. The goal is to find a practical way to help parents understand their problems and change their behavior if required. Competent family social workers can judge what can or needs to be undertaken, what should be delayed until intermediate goals have been achieved, and what must be postponed indefinitely. Consequently, the family social worker should be willing to adopt alternative procedures based on an assessment of the total situation.

When parents are unable to comprehend even simple directions, other forms of help can reinforce the intervention to enable supportive and preparatory intervention to occur. In this, as in all aspects of family support social work, the family social worker solicits feedback from parents so they may participate actively in the evaluation process.

Attending Behaviors

Attending behaviors help the family social worker to tune in and focus on all people in the interview. When one family member is speaking, the worker listens to what the individual is saying while subtly observing the behaviors of other family members. Many skills that family workers have learned about one-on-one interviewing are applicable to family work, although the complexity of these skills is amplified.

For example, active listening skills are fundamental to attending, indicated by conveying an accurate understanding of client messages. Attentive listening involves all the senses working in synchronicity, drawing clients into the conversation through appropriate body language and words conveying interest and curiosity about what clients are saying. Family members need to feel understood. Visual attending skills, eye contact, and responsive facial expressions also convey understanding. Maintaining eye contact involves keeping the client within the range of vision in a continuous, relaxed way rather than intense staring. The level of eye contact should echo the protocols of the culture of the family.

It is not only the client who is speaking who is in the visual field; others in the room are also observed. Family social workers also use physical attending skills. Ideally, throughout a meeting, the family social worker faces family members with a posture that is neither tense nor overly relaxed. Verbal attending skills involve listening closely to what others are stating verbally (content), paraverbally (voice tone and inflection), and nonverbally (body language). Leaning forward slightly, especially during vital parts of an interview, motivates clients to speak more, but keep in mind that cultures vary in comfort levels concerning proximity (distance), which should be understood and practiced. With practice, family social workers can isolate clients' metamessages (hidden messages), particularly messages about relationships. What is unique about family interviews is that the person who is speaking to family members conveys reactions to individual family members, to family patterns, to relationships, and so on.

These are suggestions rather than hard and fast rules. Sensitivity to cultural differences will require modification of attending behaviors. Members of some cultures consider direct eye contact disrespectful, others vary as to preferred distances between speakers, and yet others hesitate to speak about emotions. Ultimately, the social worker tailors attending skills to be culturally appropriate. Cross-cultural issues and skills are interspersed throughout this book since a laundry list of cultural qualities works to perpetuate stereotypes and fails to honor the heterogeneity within cultures.

Self-Awareness

Self-awareness is an important ingredient of family social work and indeed of any helping process. In Chapter 2, we discussed the influence that values and biases may have on work with families. Everyone has needs, values, feelings, and biases, but family social workers assess and adjust personal biases that interfere with effective family social work. In achieving self-awareness, the family social worker demonstrates nondefensive honesty and avoids unethical use of clients to fulfill personal and interpersonal needs. All people have unmet needs and quirks that must be examined to ensure that the work is focused and ethical. For example, clients who are experiencing issues similar to those of the family social worker can stimulate feelings of confusion or avoidance in the family social worker. They can also create blind spots for the family. There are several benefits of self-awareness:

1. Self-awareness strengthens interpersonal competence whereby the family social worker does not need to rely on clients to enhance self-esteem. Work with clients can be honest, without false reassurance from a family social worker attempting to elicit positive feedback from clients or fearing that clients may drop out of family social work.
2. Self-awareness encourages ethical use of the professional relationship. Family social workers have the potential and opportunity to misuse power, such as when a social worker is comfortable only when in control or when coercing a client to comply. Power can also be abused through compulsive advice giving or the need to feel superior.
3. Self-awareness works to regulate the *managed use* of intimacy. Family social workers with unmet intimacy needs or a poorly developed capacity for intimacy will have trouble building professional relationships. For example, the social worker that lacks self-awareness risks showing excessive distancing behaviors or over-involvement with the client.

Through self-awareness, the family social worker will understand when personal problems, unmet emotional needs, and critical life events interfere with effective work with clients. Transference and countertransference are important concepts related to self-awareness. Transference occurs when clients relate to family social workers as if they were another significant figure (e.g., parent or another authority figure). Feelings, fears, defenses, and reactions present in another relationship are then projected onto the family social worker. On the other hand, countertransference occurs when family social workers transfer their own feelings about significant others to clients. Such feelings are common within the context of helping, but self-awareness allows the family social worker to control these experiences rather than vice versa.

Steps can be taken to enhance worker self-awareness. First, workers can undergo personal counseling with the goal of expanding self-awareness. Issues also can be discussed with the worker's supervisor, and if they interfere with effectiveness or create difficulties in working with particular problems or clients, the caseload can be restricted to clients with whom the individual can work best. Reflective social work practice is critical, and social workers who continually reflect on minute parts of their practice are also able to improve their practice.

Effective family social workers are in touch with their personal experiences and feelings and have come to terms with a range of feelings and experiences. They are aware of personal values, beliefs, and needs and can develop warm and deep relationships with others. Effective family social workers feel secure enough to reveal who they genuinely are. They accept personal responsibility for their behaviors, receive feedback nondefensively, admit when they are wrong, accept limits placed on them, and are honest with themselves and others. They also strive for excellence instead of perfection and are sensitive to the impact they have on others. Becoming an effective family social worker is an ongoing process rather than a one-time endeavor. Thus, family social workers are committed to continuous learning throughout their careers.

EP 2.1.10b

EXERCISE 7.10 Skill Development

Think about what skills you need to develop as a family worker. List these skills below, starting with the most important skill. Then reflect on the strengths that you already have and list them.

EP 2.1.10d

CORE QUALITIES NEEDED BY FAMILY SOCIAL WORKERS

Research consistently supports the importance of the social worker's capacity to demonstrate empathy, warmth, and genuineness with clients. These qualities are known as the core conditions that are essential to most helping situations and together help the social worker create a climate of trust and safety in which family members can begin to view their problems in new ways (Kindsvatter, Duba, & Dean, 2008; Lambert & Bergin, 1994).

We find it reassuring to know that about 30 percent of change in counseling occurs because of the quality of the worker-client relationship, whereas model and technique contribute only about 15 percent. Strong working relationships develop when families *perceive* the social worker to be warm, trustworthy, nonjudgmental, and empathetic (Miller, Hubble, & Duncan, 1995). This opinion is supported through interviews of parents who took part in a home-based, family-centered program (Coleman & Collins, 1997). In this study, families reported valuing social workers' basic interviewing skills such as listening, supporting, and teaching. The researchers concluded that, "families did not remember the fancy techniques. Instead, they recalled the dignity and respect received in treatment" (p. 268). At the same time, it is important to realize that it is unrealistic for family workers to be liked or immediately respected. Another study validated these findings (McWhey, 2008) in that parents appreciated many worker characteristics such as personality, support, and focus on skill building.

Empathy

The family social worker uses empathy to communicate understanding of family members' experiences, behaviors, and feelings *from the client's point of view*. Empathy is a core ingredient in establishing and developing relationships with clients. Social workers need to maintain empathy and respect for the family's way of doing things. It means respecting where the client is, even when the client's perspective eventually needs to be challenged. Empathy involves seeing the world through another person's eyes and is not the same as sympathy or pity. It must be remembered, however, that some ethnic groups do not focus on feelings directly, requiring the worker to seek culturally unique ways of seeing the world through another's eyes.

When it is difficult to understand what a client feels, empathy cannot be faked. Admitting to a lack of understanding is preferable for family social workers, who can then ask for clarification. Asking for clarification gives the message that the social worker is listening and wants to understand the family. Poorly executed empathy includes parroting, verbatim repetition, insincerity, and inaccurate empathy. In addition, too much empathy can seem artificial and result in annoying people. A particularly complex situation for family social workers to navigate is how to be empathic when another person is being blamed. In these cases, the family social worker might say something like, "I can see that you are troubled by Phil's behavior. I can understand how you might be upset, and my hunch is that Phil is also troubled. Phil, can you tell us how you feel when you hear Katie say that she is upset with your gambling?" One trap of expressing empathy in a family interview occurs when the worker empathizes with one person, resulting in the development of a coalition against another family member. One way of avoiding collusion with a member of the family is to listen to everyone's feelings and then draw out common themes or point out differences among members within the family. Another option is for the family social worker to get family members to empathize with one another.

EXERCISE 7.11 Empathy

Continue role-playing a scenario from the case you have selected. Empathize with each person as she or he speaks, trying to avoid colluding with that person. After everyone has spoken, try to arrive at a common theme that all members feel.

Empathy can be expressed at different levels of depth and effectiveness. A five-level scale has been developed by Truax and Carkhuff (1967) to measure empathy:

Level 1: At Level 1, the responses of the social worker detract significantly from the verbal and behavioral expressions of the client. The response communicates less than the client expressed, and the social worker shows no awareness of even surface feelings. The social worker may be bored, uninterested, or operating from a preconceived frame of reference that does not recognize the client's individualism.

Level 2: The social worker responds, but not fully, and subtracts from the noticeable affect of the client. The social worker may show some awareness of obvious surface feelings, but detracts from the client's experience.

Level 3: The social worker mirrors client responses. Responses are interchangeable in that they express the same affect and meaning. The social worker responds with an accurate understanding of the client, but may overlook deeper feelings. The response does not add or detract and shows that the social worker is willing to know and understand more.

Level 4: The responses of the social worker enhance the client's expressions, taking client feelings to a deeper level than the client was able or willing to express.

Level 5: The social worker gives accurate responses to all of the client's deeper and surface feelings. The social worker is tuned in to the client, making it possible for the two to explore very deeply aspects of the client's existence.

Empathy below Level 3 suggests that the social worker has failed to pick up on key client feelings.

EXERCISE 7.12 Five Levels of Empathy

Break into small groups. Devise empathic responses at all five levels to the following quote:

I don't know what I am going to do. My son just got arrested for selling drugs, and my husband started drinking again. On top of everything else, my daughter was just diagnosed with bulimia, and I am about to lose my job.

Level 1:

Level 2:

Level 3:

Level 4:

Level 5:

Share the responses with the rest of the class.

The ability to understand the needs of parents forms the foundation of effective work with families. Family social workers often identify strongly with children, and at times this identification may be so strong as to come across as "anti-parent." This can lead to the view that parents are negative influences on the child, accompanied by an inclination to side with the child and work against the parents. Doing so risks alienating parents and halting family work prematurely.

Of vital importance is an empathic awareness of the challenges that parents experience in raising children, particularly parents of children with special needs or behavioral difficulties. In addition, it is helpful for the family social worker to recognize that parents may feel confused, hurt, and guilty by the time family problems have reached a level where professional help is needed. They might show this through anger and blame. Therefore, effective family social work entails a shift from a child-centered focus to a family-centered one, empathizing with both parents and children. While empathy is a necessary skill for the family social worker to master, family members would also benefit from strengthening empathy skills to use with one another.

A basic formula for making empathy statements is "You feel ___ (emotion) because ___ (restatement of client's experiences or behaviors)." While some often think that using sentence stems creates a mechanical approach to empathy, their use is merely a beginning in developing empathy skills. Once social workers get a feel for expressing empathy, they will be more prepared to branch out and create their own style of conveying empathy. It is important to vary the sentence stems used and to draw from a rich repertoire of feelings and words. The following sentence stem for packaging empathy statements has been developed to help in creating empathy statements:

1. "It seems like you feel ..." "It sounds like ..." "You seem to feel ..." "From your point of view ..." "It sounds like you are saying ..." "I am sensing that ..." "I am not sure I am with you, but...."
2. Feeling label (using a range of descriptors for feelings).
3. Place the feeling in a context.
4. Make the tense of the feeling *here and now*.
5. An added step in being empathic in family interviews is to check with other members of the family to locate their feelings about an issue.

EXERCISE 7.13   Empathy Responses

In small groups, one person role-plays the family social worker and another person role-plays the client. Using one of the examples in this book, role-play for approximately five minutes. The goal of the social worker is to use as many empathy responses as possible. Report back to the class.

Reflection of Feelings   Reflection of feelings is one way of showing empathy. Since client feelings may be masked or unknown, accurate reflection of feelings validates feelings and shows that the social worker is listening. A metaphor for this reflection process is that of a *mirror* that reflects both feelings and content. While several different feelings often coexist, an accurate reflection may help the client sort out conflicting or unclear feelings. Because feelings are expressed both verbally and nonverbally, it is important to observe the degree of congruence between verbal and nonverbal expression. For example, a client might verbally express comfort in the meeting with the family social worker, but at the same time, the family social worker may note nonverbal signs of discomfort such as a scowl, rigid closed posture, or a lack of eye contact.

While reflections help build rapport and trust, some clients may be uncomfortable about a strong and direct focus on feelings; for example, some people use intellectualization as a defense.

Examples of Five Levels of Empathy   Client (describing her husband's reaction to her decision to find a job): "He laughed at me. My own husband just sat there and laughed at me. I felt like such a fool, so put down."

Level 1: What did you say his name was?

Level 2: Uh huh, I see.

Level 3: You sound upset with your husband.

Level 4: You sound humiliated by his comments.

Level 5: I get a sense that your husband hurt you a lot. It seems to me that you are also feeling angry with him.

Advanced Empathy   Using advanced empathy, the family social worker shares *hunches* about clients in an attempt to understand the clients' underlying feelings and concerns more clearly. The goal is to facilitate client self-awareness, which, in turn, leads to new client goals and behaviors. Examples of advanced empathy through sharing of family social worker hunches include the following:

- Hunches that help clients develop a bigger picture. For example, "The problem doesn't seem to be just your attitude toward your husband anymore. Your resentment seems to have spread to the children as well. Could that be the case?"
- Hunches that help clients articulate what they are expressing indirectly or merely implying. For example, "I think I also might be hearing you say that you are more than disappointed, perhaps even hurt and angry."
- Hunches that help clients draw logical conclusions from what they are saying. For example, "From all that you've said about her, it seems to me you also are saying right now that you resent having to be with her. I realize you haven't said that directly, but I'm wondering if you are feeling that way about her."
- Hunches that help clients discuss topics about which they have hinted. For example, "You've brought up sexual matters a number of times, but you haven't followed up on them. My guess is that sex is a pretty important area for you but perhaps a pretty sensitive one, too."
- Hunches that help clients identify themes. For example, "If I'm not mistaken, you've mentioned in two or three different ways that it is sometimes difficult for you to stick up for your own rights. For instance, you let your husband decide that you would not return to college, though that is against your wishes."
- Hunches that help clients completely own their experiences, behaviors, and feelings. For example, "You sound as if you have already decided to marry him, but I don't hear you saying that directly."

EXERCISE 7.14   Reflection of Feelings

Break into small groups and create a list of at least 25 words that can be used to describe the following feelings as part of statements to clients:

Anger

Happiness

Sadness

Excitement

Anxiety

Fear

Worry

Share the list with the rest of the class.

Nonpossessive Warmth

A second quality of a strong family social worker-family relationship is the level of warmth and caring shown to the family and its members. Warmth exists when the social worker conveys acceptance, understanding, and interest in client well-being to make them feel safe regardless of factors such as problematic behavior, demeanor, or appearance. "Without warmth, some interventions may be technically correct but therapeutically impotent" (Hackney & Cormier, 1996, p. 65). Establishing a relationship based on feelings of warmth and understanding is the second foundation for successful client engagement and, ultimately, change.

Warmth is more than saying, "I care," although this is nonetheless important. While warmth can be conveyed *verbally* by one's choice of words, it is also displayed *nonverbally*. Examples include (Johnson, 1993, as cited in Hackney & Cormier, 1996, p. 66):

Tone of voice:	soft, soothing
Facial expression:	smiling (when appropriate), interested, concerned
Posture:	relaxed, leaning toward the other person
Eye contact:	looking directly into the other person's eyes (depending upon cultural rules)
Touching:	touching the other person softly and discreetly[1]
Gestures:	open, welcoming
Physical proximity:	close (depending on culture)

[1](Note: The issue of touch in family work or any other type of counseling is controversial. Virginia Satir, known for her strong expressions of warmth with clients, touched clients frequently. However, many clients have experienced "bad touch" through abuse and violence, and touch may upset them.)

EXERCISE 7.15 Touching

Break into small groups and discuss whether touch is acceptable in a helping relationship. Make a list of the reasons why touch could be useful, and make another list of why touch could be problematic. Then write out a rule about touch in a helping relationship. How does this list compare with the other groups?

Warmth or the lack of warmth can impact the client and the worker-client relationship. Without it, "a worker's words will sound hollow and insincere...." (Sheafor, Horejsi, & Horejsi, 1997, p. 149).

Five Levels of Nonpossessive Warmth Five levels of nonpossessive warmth are presented in the following list. Again, Level 3 is the minimal level to be achieved for the effective family social worker, whereas Levels 4 and 5 communicate deep warmth and regard. Levels of warmth that fall beneath Level 3 fail to convey adequate warmth.

Level 1: The family social worker's verbal and behavioral expression communicates lack of respect (negative regard) for the client. The family social worker conveys a total lack of respect.

Level 2: The family social worker communicates little respect for client's feelings, experiences, and potentials and may respond mechanically or passively.

Level 3: The family social worker minimally acknowledges regard for the client's abilities and capacities for improved functioning. The family social worker, at the least, communicates that the client matters.

Level 4: The family social worker communicates very deep respect and concern for the client. The family social worker's responses enable the client to feel free to be himself or herself and to feel valued.

Level 5: The family social worker communicates deepest respect for the client's worth as a person and for his or her potential and communicates deep caring and commitment to the client.

Examples of Five Levels of Nonpossessive Warmth (Tone of voice and nonverbal behavior are crucial in conveying warmth.)

The client says, "My daughter is a bright girl, but she's been getting bad grades in school. I'm not sure what to do.'"

Level 1: Uh huh. (No eye contact with the client, bored tone of voice.)

Level 2: That's tough. (Some eye contact, flat vocal tone.)

Level 3: You feel angry that your daughter is not living up to her potential. (Eye contact, leaning toward the client.)

Level 4: It is disappointing for you when your child is not doing well in school, and you are worried about her. (Family social worker looks into client's eyes. Tone of voice expresses concern.)

Level 5: It must be disappointing for you and your daughter that she is not doing well in school. I can see you are worried about her. Let's look at ways we can help your daughter have a more successful experience in school. (Good eye contact, relaxed and open posture, concerned yet optimistic tone of voice.)

EXERCISE 7.16 Five Levels of Warmth

Using your preferred role-play, break into small groups and role-play all five levels of warmth. Then role-play for five minutes demonstrating warmth toward the client.

Genuineness

Genuineness is perhaps the most difficult to describe. According to Truax and Carkhuff (1967), genuineness refers to a lack of defensiveness or artificiality in communications with the client. It also involves sincerity, honesty, and unpretentiousness. Being genuine can also involve the ability to convey negative feelings such as anger, impatience, and so on. Like empathy and warmth, genuineness is conveyed at different levels. Level 3 is the minimum for effective family social work.

Five Levels of Genuineness

Level 1: The family social worker's verbalizations are slightly unrelated to what he or she is feeling at the moment. Responses may be negative or destructive. The family social worker may convey defensiveness in words and actions and does not use these feelings to explore the helping relationship with the client.

Level 2: The family social worker's verbalizations are slightly unrelated to what she or he is feeling. The family social worker does not know how to manage negative reactions toward the client or how to use them constructively in the interview. The interviewing style may sound mechanical or rehearsed.

Level 3: There is no evidence of incongruence between what the family social worker says and feels in the interview. The social worker might take a neutral personal stance. The family social worker makes appropriate responses that seem sincere but do not reflect intense personal involvement.

Level 4: The family social worker presents cues suggesting genuine responses (both positive and negative) that are nondestructive. Responses are congruent, but the family social worker might hesitate to express them fully.

Level 5: The family social worker freely expresses self but is nonexploitative. The family social worker is spontaneous, open to all experiences, nondefensive, and uses interactions constructively to open further discussion and exploration for both the client and the family social worker.

Examples of Five Levels of Genuineness   The client says, "I'm ready to throw my daughter out of the house. She doesn't listen to a word I say, and she does whatever she pleases."

Level 1: You seem to be overreacting.

Level 2: You need to practice tough love.

Level 3: Teenagers are a handful.

Level 4: I know from personal experience that it can be very challenging to deal with teenagers.

Level 5: I know it can be challenging and difficult to communicate with teenagers. Sometimes when talking with my own teenager, I have felt frustrated because we were not communicating very well. Let's look at how we can help you and your daughter work toward a more satisfying relationship.

EXERCISE 7.17   Five Levels of Genuineness

Using your preferred role-play, break into small groups and provide examples of all five levels of genuineness. Then role-play for five minutes, demonstrating genuineness toward the client. Debrief in class what it was like to respond genuinely to clients. Also discuss the level of self-awareness required to be genuine with clients.

EXERCISE 7.18 Core Conditions

Provide examples of each of the core conditions: empathy, nonpossessive warmth, and genuineness. Create responses that fit into each of the five levels of response.

Client statement: "I don't know what to do. My husband just left me, my son got picked up for shoplifting, and my daughter just told me she is pregnant. If that is not enough, my boss told me that I might lose my job because there is not enough business at this time of year."

EP 2.1.10b

DYSFUNCTIONAL BEHAVIORS TO AVOID IN FAMILY SOCIAL WORK

Common Pitfalls of New Family Social Workers

In this chapter, we have described a number of beginning skills needed in the beginning phase of family social work. In addition to knowing what is helpful in an interview, the social worker can minimize dysfunctional behaviors that can interfere with effective helping. New family social workers fall into some common traps when seeing families for the first time (Collins, 1989; Gabor & Collins, 1985–86). These "traps" are a normal part of learning family work, and making them is part of the process. As mentioned, reflection and awareness are part of the process of readjusting your practice. Accordingly, we provide the following list of behaviors to avoid. These include:

1. Seeing the one with the difficulties as the primary focus of family social work.
2. Overemphasizing history at the expense of what is going on in the here and now.
3. Waiting until she or he has amassed a pile of information before intervening.
4. Being overly concerned with destructive underlying feelings and attitudes.
5. Fitting a family to a method instead of the method to the family.
6. Overlooking outcomes and goals as important reasons for the family interviews (Haley, 1971, pp. 228–236).
7. Developing alliances and colluding with certain people in the family at the expense of others (taking sides) or otherwise getting caught up in the struggle between family factions. This might be due to over identification with certain people in the family.
8. Giving false reassurance or agreement where inappropriate.
9. Ignoring cues about the family's subjective experience of the problem while dealing exclusively with objective material; failing to keep focus in the interview.
10. Judgmental responding.
11. Inappropriate use of humor or other responses that inhibit discussion or undermine trust. This might be due to difficulty dealing with emotionally-laden family processes.
12. Premature problem solving.
13. Over-reliance on chitchat.
14. Overprotecting family members by ignoring clear cues to implicit information.

A final pitfall for new workers is to get trapped into talking about someone outside the room. The family social worker knows when this is happening because engaging in such discussions starts to feel like gossip. Clients often do this to take the focus off themselves. Recognizing these feelings demonstrates that the social worker is paying close attention to what clients are saying and doing. Because family meetings are not social chats, the social worker will contain and be in control of himself or herself.

EXERCISE 7.19   Dysfunctional Behaviors

Using the example provided in Exercise 7.4, break into small groups and take turns role-playing the dysfunctional behaviors listed above. Discuss in the larger class the impact of these behaviors on work with families. Can you think of other behaviors that would be problematic in family social work?

EXERCISE 7.20   First 15 Minutes of an Interview

Using one of the cases (or creating your own), role-play the first 15 minutes of the first family interview. One member of the group is the observer. Be aware of when you or the family chitchats and when you make a demand for work with the family. If you find yourself involved with chitchat, stop and start to work with the family.

EP 2.1.1d

CHAPTER SUMMARY

Family social work takes place in five phases: beginning, assessment, intervention, evaluation, and termination. Specific skills are required of the family social worker in each of these phases. In this chapter, we looked at skills involved in the beginning phase when the social worker establishes rapport with families. The family social worker needs to understand the principles of effective communication and know how to interpret clients' verbal and nonverbal messages. Core qualities required of the family social worker include empathy, nonpossessive warmth, and genuineness. The skills and qualities required for effective social work are developed and refined throughout the social worker's career.

KEY TERMS

Attending Behaviors   helps the family social worker to tune in and focus on all people in the interview. Fundamental to attending is the development of active listening skills. Listening entails hearing, observing, encouraging, remembering, and understanding.

Communication   is both digital and analogic. Digital communication occurs when a work is spoken and refers to the content. Analogic communication is more abstract, as it often refers to nonverbal components of meaning or the relationship.

Empathy   is a way for the family social worker to communicate understanding of family members' experiences, behaviors, and feelings *from the family member's point of view*.

Genuineness refers to a lack of defensiveness or artificiality in the family social worker's communications with the family members. Genuineness is being sincere and honest.

Nonpossessive Warmth exists when the family social worker communicates with family members in ways that convey acceptance, understanding, and interest in their well-being and make them feel safe regardless of such external factors as the family member's problematic behavior, demeanor, or appearance.

Self-Awareness involves an understanding of your own needs, values, feelings, behaviors, thoughts, biases, and their effects on your work with families. The family social worker needs to be honest and avoid unethical use of clients to fulfill personal and interpersonal needs.

SUGGESTED READINGS

McGoldrick, M., Giordano, J., & Garcia-Preto, N. (2005). *Ethnicity and family therapy* (3rd ed.). New York: The Guilford Press.
    This book is a must-read for anyone working with families. It is a cornerstone for family work with diverse families.
Watzlawick, P., Beavin, J., & Jackson, D. (1967). *Pragmatics of human communication.* New York: W.W. Norton.
    This book is a classic. It provided the foundation for future work on communication, particularly in family therapy.

COMPETENCY NOTES

EP 2.1.1d Demonstrate professional demeanor in behavior, appearance, and communication: Common pitfalls for the family social worker to avoid include ignoring appropriate boundaries with the family, problem solving too early, and being judgmental, among others.

EP 2.1.4a Recognize the extent to which a culture's structures and values may oppress, marginalize, alienate, or create or enhance privilege and power: The family social worker recognizes issues related to family diversity.

EP 2.1.10b Use empathy and other interpersonal skills: Interpersonal skills such as genuineness and warmth are used by the family social worker.

EP 2.1.10c Develop a mutually agreed-on focus of work and desired outcomes: The family social worker negotiates the case focus and activities with the family so that casework will be meaningful to the family.

EP 2.1.10d Collect, organize, and interpret client data: The family social worker has skills in choosing what data about the family to collect, then to organize it for interpretation to the family. This provides the family with feedback about their strengths and limitations.

EP 2.1.10f Develop mutually agreed-on intervention goals and objectives: It is important that the family agree on moving forward with the specific intervention goals and objectives set. Otherwise, the family is likely to drop out of family work.

Qualitative Family Assessment

LEARNING OBJECTIVES

- Conceptual: Understand a structured way to assess families.
- Perceptual: Observe families through a structured lens.
- Valuational/Attitudinal: Appreciate the need to be more comprehensive in our understanding of families.
- Behavioral: Use concrete assessment tools.

INTRODUCTION TO QUALITATIVE ASSESSMENT

Assessment is an ongoing process of data collection aimed at understanding clients in the context of their environmental systems.

—*Jordan and Franklin, 2003, p. 1*

The next two chapters discuss how to conduct a family assessment, using family strengths and resilience as a core focus in the assessment process. Assessment starts with problem identification, and *both quantitative and qualitative methods may be used to create an ... approach that links assessment to intervention.*

A person-in-environment, systems approach underlies assessment from both qualitative and quantitative perspectives (Jordan & Franklin, p. 4). The process of devising an accurate definition and assessing the problem definition involves meeting
with the family and exploring, identifying, and defining dynamics both within and
external to the family that contribute to the family's problems *and* strengths.
Assessment is a *process* of collecting enough information about the family to
allow informed intervention decisions.

Mindful assessment also will lead to the creation of realistic and concrete goals
by charting out a road map for the family and the family social worker. For example, when an assessment determines that a child's problems are due to triangulation
within a conflicted marriage, the worker will target de-triangulation and marital
repair (see, for example, Chapters 3 and 13). If, on the other hand, the worker
determines that a child's difficulties are because the family has not mastered the
principles of successful behavioral management (see, for example, Chapter 12),
the intervention will target teaching parents about behavioral principles and child
management techniques to help them develop parenting skills that are consistent
and appropriate to the child's behavior.

Assessment is both flexible and fluid. As more information is gathered, the
family social worker is open to revising or broadening the assessment. In many
ways, assessment is never completed because new information is continually being
gathered and processed by the family social worker. During assessment, the family
social worker assists the family, ideally with all members participating, to explore
issues of concern. This exploration will lead to a deeper, more accurate understanding of the situation faced by the family. Each family member shares a unique perspective of the problem, and every individual perspective is important. For
example, a problem defined by the family as a child spending time hanging out
with friends may be a conforming issue for a parent, an independence issue for a
target child, and an exclusion issue for siblings. Problems usually span behavioral,
affective, cognitive, and experiential domains. In addition, some problems are
more likely to arise in particular families at crisis periods in the family life cycle
(Chapter 4).

Theoretical concepts will shape the assessment and the intervention. The
assessment of the family sets the stage for later interventions and is critical to the
success of work with the family. Three approaches are embedded in conducting a
comprehensive assessment of families:

- The interview
- Observations
- Checklists and instruments (Holman, 1983).

Two additional kinds of information necessary for assessment include *content*
and *process*. Content is the *what*, that is, information given to the family social
worker. Process refers to *how* family members interact with one another.

In this chapter, we describe approaches to qualitative assessment of families.
Qualitative assessment tools help the family worker to understand meaningful
events in the family's world using words, observations, pictures, and graphic analyses rather than numbers (numbers are used in quantitative assessment). Five unique

contributions of qualitative assessment measures were reviewed by Jordan and Franklin (2010, pp. 127–130):

1. Qualitative measures uncover realities that might be missed using only quantitative measures by adding context to the family picture. A family might keep a diary, for example.
2. Qualitative techniques are open-ended and process-oriented, providing people of color the opportunity to tell their stories by accentuating cultural scripts and meanings. (Quantitative techniques have not been verified with all populations.)
3. Qualitative assessments promote practitioner self-awareness and may contribute to development of a positive working relationship.
4. Qualitative assessments are holistic, thus encouraging a reciprocal client-social worker relationship.
5. Qualitative techniques fit with many theoretical and therapeutic perspectives. These include those commonly used by social workers including family systems approaches, ecosystems models, cognitive-constructivist therapies, feminist therapies, and so forth.

Typically, family workers will obtain an overview of the family's life and functioning. Qualitative techniques are particularly helpful in this process, as we have discussed. Next, a case example will be presented for thought as we proceed through the philosophy and techniques of qualitative assessment. Then we will describe the context of family assessment, present a number of qualitative techniques, and discuss issues related to assessment of diverse families. Finally, we will present special issues in qualitative assessment.

THE CONTEXT OF FAMILY ASSESSMENT

What is going on with Jasmyn in Case 8.1? Several issues are of concern in this family. The most pressing concern is that Jasmyn is threatening suicide and is harming herself right now through self-mutilation. Yet, there are many other issues facing this family. What issues should the family worker address? Where should a family worker start in working with this family? In this section, we

---

CASE 8.1 | Family Assessment

Fourteen-year-old Jasmyn and her 49-year-old mother, Jennie, were referred for counseling after Jasmyn started cutting her arms with razor blades and threatening suicide. She moved out of her family's home eight months previously in an act of what Jennie's common-law partner, Jack, described as adolescent rebellion. She lives with her best friend, Sarah. Jennie and Jack have been together for 10 years. Jennie divorced her first husband, Al, after Jasmyn's older sister Allison disclosed sexual abuse by Al. Allison, 25, lives in another part of the country and has little contact with them. Al was eventually convicted of sexually abusing Allison. There are two other children in the family: Graham, a 10-year-old boy, and John, who is 6.

(Continued)

CASE 8.1	Family Assessment (*Continued*)

Jennie has strong support from her sister Judy. Judy has worked hard to hold the family together and has encouraged both Jennie and Jasmyn to be open with each other about their experiences. Several losses have plagued the family in recent years. Judy's daughter died a couple of years ago. In addition, Jennie's mother also died several years ago and her father died one year later. The loss of her mother was very difficult for the family, and it does not appear that they have fully recovered from the loss.

Jasmyn just recently disclosed that she had been sexually abused by both her biological father and her mother's common-law partner. Jennie believed Jasmyn and immediately ended the relationship with Jack. Apart from dealing with Jasmyn's abuse, Jennie is also experiencing quite severe financial difficulties. The financial problems have worsened since she is now working only one job and since Jack is no longer in the home to add an extra income. Jennie is worried about Jasmyn and recognizes how stressful the disclosure and the abuse are on her. At the same time, Jennie has had a hard time "reading" and understanding her daughter. Because of these difficulties, Jennie is uncertain how to manage her daughter and discipline her. If Jasmyn's problems were merely "adolescent stuff," Jennie would be able to deal with the behaviors as such. On the other hand, if Jasmyn's difficulties stem from the sexual abuse, she would handle the behaviors more supportively and in a different way. Jennie needs assistance with understanding her daughter. She worries that once Jasmyn gets older, she will lose whatever leverage she has over her daughter's behavior. At the same time, she wants to be closer to her daughter.

Where would you start as a family social worker?

---

discuss the context of assessment including the purpose of assessment and ecological assessment.

EXERCISE 8.1 Brainstorm

Break into groups of three. Brainstorm about all the issues faced by the family discussed in Case 8.1. Develop hypotheses for what lies behind each of these difficulties. Then, beside each of these problems, suggest an intervention for it. Please note that each problem should have a unique intervention plan (unless the problems are all related). What further information do you need to collect in order to plan an intervention with this family? Reconvene into the larger class, where each group will share their answers with the rest of the class. What similarities and differences of opinion exist in the class? Discuss.

Austrain (cited in Jordan and Franklin, 2010) suggests that ongoing assessment involves five steps:

1. Exploration through multiple methods such as listening, observation, and other means of data collection
2. Inferential thinking, which leads to clinical judgments that are grounded in empirical knowledge and guide decision making about a case
3. Evaluation of the capacity of a client's functioning and skills, as well as of the stressors of social environments that may impede a client's (and we add families') optimal functioning

4. Problem definitions that are well defined and agreed on by the client and social worker

5. Intervention planning with the client, which leads to more effective outcomes (p. 4).

Deciding what information to gather in the first and subsequent meetings will be aided through knowledge of the range of available assessment tools. Whereas workers benefit from knowledge of theoretical concepts related to understanding the family and the presenting problem, different models of family intervention emphasize different factors in assessment. Some theories, for example, emphasize dyads and triangles, whereas others look at the entire family unit. Perhaps the most important advice in assessing a family is to treat every family as unique. A clear and accurate understanding of the problem is necessary for devising appropriate interventions. Family social workers can initially research the literature to see what experts in a specific area suggest in terms of contributors to the presenting problem. It will be necessary to understand the *duration* of the family's presenting problem (often concern or difficulties with a child) and *how the family has tried to resolve* the issue previously. As well, the family social workers will be interested in identifying the strengths and resources the family possesses. (Strengths, resources, and resiliency were discussed in Chapter 5.) Family social workers will be concerned with family roles, communication patterns, skills family members have to carry out required roles, family closeness, and family rules. They will also need to know how the family functions as a system and how various family subsystems such as the parental and child subsystems are operating.

Several qualitative tools are available for a family assessment. These include genograms, ecomaps, and family time lines. These tools capture important family information through visual depiction of the family information. They are symbols that provide a practical way of compiling an enormous amount of data about a family together on a single page. They organize the information collected in a coherent and understandable order and are connected with various components of family theory. At the same time, these graphic images can capture process data as families move through their life cycle in interaction with one another and with their environment. They also can be used to understand family dynamics and growth at different points in the intervention. In Chapter 3, for example, an image of a circular interaction pattern—circular causality—showed how the repetitive interactions in a dyad are embedded in familiar transactional patterns. This image is both dynamic and capable of capturing complex patterns of interaction in a single graphic image. Similarly, other graphic assessment tools have been developed to capture processes and complex sets of information.

One example is the genogram, a popular graphic tool commonly used in family work to capture process and content information about families. In fact, genograms are often a starting point for assessing family functioning. We also look at ecological information that is critical for successful assessment of a family. Ecological information is captured by ecomaps (sometimes known as ecograms). Another useful graphic tool includes the use of a family time line. These techniques are discussed later in this chapter. Next we discuss the purposes of family assessment, followed by ecological assessment.

EP 2.1.3a

Purpose of Family Assessment

Assessing family functioning is complex, and workers are challenged to determine what information is essential and what can be put aside. Although it is necessary to collect the content of family information from the family, the worker should also observe family interactions. In addition to information gathered through questions and answers and observing interactional patterns within the family in the here and now, concrete tools to organize information are indispensable. Aside from focusing on problems, it is also important to understand areas of family strength and resilience, discussed in more detail in Chapter 5.

Family assessment has several purposes:

1. To assess whether a family will profit from family work and, if so, decide what types of interventions will target their primary issues
2. To identify what specific changes in the family should be made
3. To create short-term and long-term goals of the intervention based on realistic objectives
4. To identify family strengths and resources as well as environmental and community resources available or needed to move the family toward desired changes
5. To understand and collect information on baseline family functioning so that the outcome of the intervention may be determined
6. To identify mutually agreed-on targets of change so that a termination point can be targeted and so that workers and families will be able to measure achievement of desired outcomes.

EP 2.1.3a

Ecological Assessment

As mentioned in Chapter 1, family social work often involves working with families whose basic needs are not getting met, often through no fault of their own. Consequently, family social workers seek to understand a family's relationship with their environment. This relationship is reciprocal; that is, families give and take from the community and the community gives and takes back. Nichols and Schwartz (2007) suggest that ecology is the study of relationships that connect all members of Earth's household. The environment plays a role in the development and maintenance of problems experienced by families. Many helping professionals have fallen into the trap of viewing problems exclusively from the perspective of sickness or pathology. In contrast, a family ecological assessment enhances the understanding of how a family operates within its environment; strengths and weaknesses are both considered. In Chapter 3, we discussed how each individual family member's behavior affects and is affected by the other members. One popular metaphor is to compare a family to a mobile hanging in the wind. Think of each piece of the mobile as a family member. When one piece moves, the others do also; such is the case with family members. One member's behavior produces corresponding changes or responses in all the other members. Issues in the environment such as racism, poverty, and negative attitudes about single parenthood reverberate throughout the family. Thus, the family's reactions are affected by the "atmospheric conditions" in their environment.

Individuals are nested in a set of larger social units, similar to Russian nesting dolls. The first nesting unit is the family, which is known as the microsystem. An ecological assessment identifies the social supports available to the family and the amount of reciprocity (give and take) between the family and society. Some families rely strongly on environmental supports without returning any resources back to the environment. Others experience severe gaps in environmental supports that prevent the meeting of needs. Generally, when a family has sufficient resources for coping with stress and demands, the overall functioning of family members will be adequate (Rothery, 1993). As children grow older, their ecological niches expand:

> "An assessment that considers all aspects of a child's life provides information that aids clinicians in developing an appropriate intervention and treatment plan" (Yalof & Abraham, cited in Jordan & Franklin, 2010, p. 181).

Most children attend school, and it is important for parents to nurture a supportive attitude toward their children's education. Yet, school difficulties can be particularly complex for families and social workers to navigate. Children suffer academically when their home life is too chaotic for them to develop competence in school. Others have difficulty when they are preoccupied with hunger pangs, when they are bullied, or when they are sleep-deprived because of worry. Children in school may be further challenged by learning disabilities, ADHD, Asperger's Syndrome, or any other type of mental health issue. Peer pressure and lack of structured and predictable family routines also take a toll on a child's educational success. When children exhibit antisocial behavior in school, everyone suffers. Family social workers can provide the necessary linkage between families and schools to help parents and teachers work together to address the issues that interfere with effective learning. School is but one example highlighting the importance of family social workers taking account of the impact of larger systems on individuals and families.

A family's support system is also an important piece of ecological assessment. Some families have an overrepresentation in formal networks such as child welfare, the criminal justice system, addictions, mental health, and so on. When a family is overloaded with formal support and lacking in informal supports such as kinships and friends, their lives may be chaotic as helpers may get in one another's way and work at cross-purposes. Culture plays a role in the nature of support networks as well. For example, diverse families may have strong kinship ties. In such cases, family social workers must understand what the community has to offer a family.

When working with diverse families, culturally competent family social workers must consider ethnicity and immigration status in assessment; the family social worker must be willing to advocate for change in the larger system (e.g., schools and communities) (Canino and Spurlock, cited in Jordan & Franklin, 2010, p. 192).

Another aspect of an ecological assessment is the direction of the energy flow. Is the community giving to the family exclusively, or does the family return something to the community? Relationships within neighborhoods are also an important indicator of how connected a family is to the community. How well do people know their neighbors? When given a choice, it is preferable that people rely on informal networks. That is, formal networks should never replace what a family can do for itself.

An ecological assessment is therefore multifaceted, and if the worker delves into the family's life in detail, the picture will become richly textured and complex. Almeida, Woods, Messineo, and Font (1998) suggest the cultural context model to incorporate the many facets of a family's life:

> Pulling threads from developmental theory, feminist theory, family theory, and cross-cultural studies to weave an integrated web, the cultural context model approaches the family from a multifaceted community-based perspective that addresses gender, ethnic background, and socialization factors. (p. 415)

A comprehensive ecological assessment, using the hierarchy of needs as a framework, involves recognizing concrete realities of a family's life such as food, clothing, shelter, medical care, employment, and social realities derived from social relationships (Holman, 1983). Because social networks involve informal or formal supportive persons or formal institutions, it is imperative to inquire about both. As mentioned, informal supportive persons are an important part of a family's network, and these individuals or groups are known as natural helpers. For some families, environmental resources are unavailable, whereas others may not be aware of them or, alternatively, either not know how to use them or refuse to use them. Therefore, an ecomap is a useful starting point to obtain information about the family's relationship with its environment. An ecomap can provide important information about how the family gets its needs met, informed by the structure of Maslow's (1968) hierarchy of needs.

Abraham Maslow developed a theory of human needs, placing the needs into a hierarchy that includes five broad layers: physiological, safety and security, love and belonging, esteem, and self-actualization (see Figure 8.1). The needs echo developmental needs as people progress through a lifetime.

Physiological needs are the most important and immediate, involving physical needs for food, water, and physical sustenance. It is troubling to realize that some people, children in particular, in the wealthiest nations on Earth fail to get their basic physical needs met. Children go to school hungry, and the elderly live on pet food. Both are vulnerable populations; you can tell a lot about a society by how it treats its most vulnerable members!

The second layer of needs, safety and security needs, come after the physical needs. Living in safe neighborhoods, feeling safe from physical and emotional danger, and feeling secure in their job are but a few of the safety and security needs that people require. The next level, belonging needs, includes the need for friendship, love, affection, and a sense of belonging to a community. Esteem needs include two components: the need to be respected and the need for self-respect. The former is derived from appreciation and dignity, whereas the latter comes from confidence, competence, achievement, independence, and freedom. Maslow saw these four layers of needs as deficit needs; that is, when we do not have these needs met, we have a deficit. However, when these needs are fulfilled, they do not motivate the person.

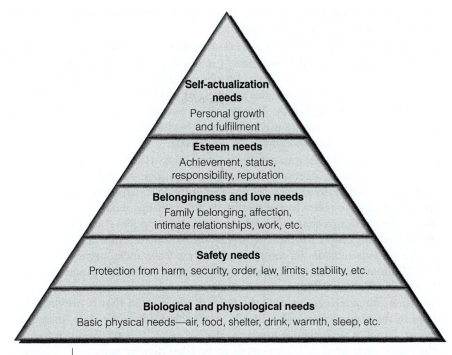

FIGURE 8.1 | Maslow's Hierarchy of Needs

The last level, self-actualization, includes the needs to grow and be one's best—to transcend. People who are self-actualized possess the qualities of the ideal human being: honest, good, just, playful, unique, and so on. Family social workers will probably not be seeing self-actualizing families in their practice, although they will get glimmers of these qualities in the families they are working with and will want to nurture these qualities when they do appear. Minuchin (1974) pointed out that most low-income families are entangled in a basic struggle for survival.

EXERCISE 8.2 Hierarchy of Needs

Using Maslow's (1968) hierarchy of needs, make a list of examples of these needs for individuals within your family, possible ways of getting these needs met, and how the needs might be threatened.

Relationships with significant others outside the family constitute an important source of emotional support. In assessing the quality of a family's social supports, it is useful to look at the dimensions of *reciprocity, density, complexity, sufficiency, emotional climate*, and, finally, *feedback characteristics* (Rothery, 1993):

- *Reciprocity* involves the extent to which social support is exchanged with others. Relationships with formal helpers are typically based on a one-way relationship in which the helper gives and the family takes since such relationships are seldom reciprocal. A preferable configuration occurs when the family both gives and receives support.

- *Density* involves the number of relationships family members have with others. Ideally, each family member will have a multiplicity of relationships outside the family with supportive individuals. Family members should also be free, depending on their developmental abilities, to form relationships with significant others outside the family. Parents often complain that the relationships of teenagers outside the family are too dense! On the other hand, relationships of abuse victims are often thought to be too sparse.
- *Complexity* refers to the capacity of a social support network to meet diverse individual and family needs. Social support networks are *sufficient* when social supports are adequate to meet family and individual demands and needs.
- *Emotional climate* refers to the quality of relationships with others outside the family. Relationships that are mostly caring and supportive are preferable to aversive relationships. Mothers who have *little* positive daily contact with supportive persons outside the family apparently behave more negatively with their children than those who have more frequent positive interactions outside the family (Wahler, 1980).
- *Feedback characteristics* involve the type of information that is provided by those in the support networks. Ideally, feedback needs to be clear, direct, and honest. Families with rigid boundaries do not receive corrective information when they most need it. It also needs to be corrective or supportive when needed.

The ecomap captures the nature of the relationship between the family and the world around them and how resources and needs match. Ecomaps are discussed in more detail in the techniques section which follows.

EP 2.1.10e

QUALITATIVE TECHNIQUES

Qualitative techniques, as mentioned at the beginning of this chapter, aim to describe and understand the meaning behind a family's functioning. The qualitative techniques discussed here include interviewing, observation, and visual techniques, including genograms and ecomaps.

The family social worker focuses with the family on a specific topic based on the following guidelines:

- *Severity or urgency:* Is this a topic that needs immediate attention because of the distress it causes, the danger it poses, or its frequency? Physically or emotionally threatening issues should be addressed first.
- *Importance:* Is this issue sufficiently important for the family to discuss and act on it? For the family to deal with issues, the problem must be meaningful enough to members.
- *Timing:* Is this a problem that can be managed at this time with available resources?
- *Complexity:* Is this concern a manageable piece of a larger or more complex problem? Can it be made more manageable if broken down into parts?

- *Hope of success:* If this issue is the focus, is there a chance that it can be managed successfully? If not, is this the right place to start?
- *Generalization effect:* Is this the kind of problem that, if handled correctly, might lead to improvement in other areas of the family's life?
- *Control:* Is this a problem under client control? To manage it more effectively, will the family have to act or influence others to act?
- *Willingness:* Is this a concern or problem that the family is willing to discuss and tackle?

During assessment, the family social worker will need to address the following topical areas:

Family History

A family history is another good place to start. A family history, similar to a social history for an individual, is broken down into specific categories and is concerned with the development of the family and its issues over time.

PROBLEM

1. What factors contributed to the need for the worker's involvement? Why does the family need help now? If the family is involved with an agency involuntarily, how did that happen? What are the conditions of involuntary involvement? How does the family feel about being mandated for service? What were the events that led the family to arrive on the doorstep of the agency?
2. What problems are the family currently experiencing, both short-term and long-term? What has the family done about the problems before seeing you?
3. How severe are the problems? What is the urgency with which these problems need to be dealt with? Are any members of the family at risk of harm—physical, emotional, sexual, or environmental?
4. Who is in this family? How are they involved with the presenting problems?
5. What is the family structure? Describe boundaries, circular exchanges, roles, communication, relationships, and coalitions and triangles.
6. What is the family's attitude and motivation concerning the worker's involvement? How motivated are individual family members for change compared with the other family members?
7. How do family members frame (define) the problems (e.g., shared responsibility versus one member being a problem)? Do they have a hypothesis or belief about what has caused the problems? If involvement of the entire family seems warranted, how motivated is each member to be involved in the resolution of the problems? What does the family expect to achieve from family intervention?
8. What other social systems outside the family are involved with the family? For what issues? What does each family member perceive the problems to be? What do other agencies perceive the problems to be? Are any family members physically or emotionally at risk if they remain in the family during work?

FAMILY INTERNAL FUNCTIONING

1. What are areas of family competence, strength, and resilience, especially psychological and social resources used for daily living and meeting crises as they emerge?
2. How would family members describe their family and their relationships with the various subsystems of the family? What is the nature of relationships within the family? What are the ongoing patterns and themes in this family? What are the patterns of interaction between family members? What interaction patterns seem to keep the problem going?
3. How is the family structured hierarchically? Who has power, and how is that power used? Who is disadvantaged by that power?
4. What are the strengths and resources of the family unit and of members within the family that can be mobilized to resolve the problems?
5. How does the family communicate? What are the circular patterns of interaction that have become repetitive? Is communication direct, open, and honest?
6. How are family members functioning in their informal and formal roles?
7. What are family boundaries like? How do these boundaries operate between individuals and subsystems and around the family as a whole?
8. Who is aligned with whom in the family and around which core issues?
9. What are the triangles in the family? Which triangles are hurting family members?
10. How well is the parental unit functioning? What is the level of marital satisfaction? Do parents support each other in the discipline and behavioral management of children?
11. How do parents manage child behavior? Do parents behave consistently with their children?
12. How involved are family members with one another?
13. Whose needs are getting met, and whose needs are neglected? What contributes to the differential meeting of these needs?
14. Who is hurting in this family? Who is blamed for the difficulties?

FAMILY LIFE CYCLE

1. What is the history of the family? How did the parents meet? What did they bring to their relationship? How did they decide to have children?
2. Where in the family life cycle is this family? How adequately does the family meet the developmental needs of members? What possible developmental issues is the family system facing at this particular point in time? How do these developmental issues fit with the presenting problem and overall family functioning?
3. How well are family members fulfilling their developmental roles and tasks?
4. What are the family's usual means, patterns, or mechanisms for resolving developmental crises?
5. What critical events and disruptions in the family life cycle has this family encountered? Divorce? Separation? Death? Birth of children? Illness? How has the family handled these disruptions?

FAMILY ECOLOGICAL ENVIRONMENT

1. What is the nature of the family's relationship with its environment? Do environmental factors nurture or hinder family functioning?
2. What is the quality of the family's interactions with the social environment, including the breadth and quality of outside relationships and the impact of external factors on the family?
3. How does the family get basic needs met? What is lacking, and what are strengths?
4. Who can family members rely on in time of need? What is the nature of contact with support people outside the family in terms of quantity and quality?
5. How dependent or self-sufficient is the family in terms of external resources?
6. How does the family relate to key people, including friends, family, school, work, religious institutions, health care, and so on?
7. What is the family's place in and relationship to their ethnocultural group?
8. What are the impacts and influences of religious beliefs and values on this family?
9. What is the family's cultural heritage, which can provide strengths and barriers?
10. What are the formal and informal supports for the family?
11. How is this family situated in terms of culture, ethnicity, and religion?
12. What is the extent of oppression and discrimination this family experiences? What is the impact of this oppression and discrimination on family functioning?
13. How many other agencies are involved with the family? For what reason?

Family social workers also need to observe the social functioning of the family. Social functioning is best understood by looking at the social roles family members perform. Individual behavior and adjustment reflects how well family members perform their social roles. Geismar and Ayres (1959) proposed four areas of role performance within the family and four outside the family. Internal roles include:

- Family relationships and family unity
- Child care and training
- Health practices
- Household practices.

External family roles include:

- Use of community resources
- Social activities
- Economic practices
- Relationship of the family to the social worker.

EXERCISE 8.3   Meeting Family Needs

The following list includes needs that all families have. Give examples of needs for each category. Beside each example, indicate possible available ecological

EP 2.1.3b

resources that can meet these needs. In the examples of ecological resources, provide a variety of formal and informal sources of support and indicate whether they are developmental or basic.

Needs	Example Formal	Example Informal
Physical needs		
Safety needs		
Belonging needs		
Esteem needs		
Self-actualization needs		

VISUAL TECHNIQUES

As mentioned, genograms and ecomaps are the preferred assessment tools for most family workers. Concrete and diagrammatic depictions of abstract concepts such as those found in genograms and ecomaps generate greater understanding and retention of material. Events and materials gleaned from genograms and ecomaps are integral to the development and support of the family assessment. They are also useful tools with which to establish rapport with families. From our experience, families are intrigued by these graphic symbols of their lives and are eager to see how their family life is depicted on paper. While the family is engaged in documenting their life history on paper, the pressure is removed from the presenting problem and family difficulties. The tools become a vehicle through which relationship building can develop with the family and with individual members. At the same time, both tools depict relationship patterns within and outside the family.

Other assessment devices such as family time lines may be used to supplement genograms and ecomaps. Family assessment devices serve dual purposes. Inasmuch as measurement instruments may be useful for diagnostic information about family functioning, they can also serve as the basis from which family members can examine family functioning themselves, discuss family problems, and set family goals in a focused, structured, and collaborative way.

Because family structures and family problems can be complex, graphic images are used to sift through detailed data. The availability of visual recording tools provides family social workers with practical tools for assessment and intervention. As mentioned, such tools are useful to organize information effectively and help workers develop a coherent plan for intervention. Social workers are relying on graphic tools more often in their work because they capture comprehensive details in complex cases. Because of the detail of graphic instruments, many problems and issues jump out. Nevertheless, this does not mean that every problem that arises becomes the target of intervention. Rather, graphics provide a backdrop against which a range of problems can be understood. These targeted problem areas may then be the focus of intervention. Family social workers will select interventions that have the greatest possibility of having an impact. The amount of material included in a single graphic depiction of a family depends on the worker's defined role. Graphics should include enough detail to capture the complexity but be simple enough that they can be easily understood.

Genogram

A genogram is a graphic family tree that can reveal who is included in the family. This family diagram can be utilized to depict the family's structure, the nature of relationships, and the appearance of issues across several generations. As mentioned, family members are often actively engaged in genogram construction as both the family social worker and family members gain insight into family patterns and interactions.

Genograms visually display family information to permit a quick overview, or gestalt, of complex family patterns (McGoldrick, Gerson, & Petry, 2008). Families often become animated as their input provides a detailed picture of significant family events such as births, marriages, separations, and deaths. Genograms can also convey social information such as racial group, social class, and religious status (Holman, 1983). Finally, genograms help the worker conceptualize the past and present family situation to unblock the system, clarify family patterns, reframe and detoxify family issues, and isolate multigenerational patterns.

This tool appeals to both families and family social workers because it is concrete. Genograms permit family social workers to map family structure clearly and update the family "picture" as it develops. Genograms often change as the family social worker and family members learn new information. As a record, the genogram provides a concise family summary, allowing those unfamiliar with a family to rapidly understand a vast amount of information about a family. Family issues also become evident. Patterns of behavior that occur across multiple generations are easily viewed with a genogram, which is an important benefit since patterns, events, relationships, and behaviors often repeat themselves over multiple generations. For example, in Freud's family, a number of relatives experienced mental illness and suicide (McGoldrick, 1999a; McGoldrick, Gerson, & Petry, 2008). Communication and relationship patterns are particularly important to observe because they are reproduced across generations.

Genograms may help prevent the discovery late into family work that a significant person or issue is missing from the intervention and can be used in early family work. Through genograms, family social workers can identify repetitive patterns experienced by a family. Although written information may become lost or submerged in the volumes of case files, information on a genogram is highly visible. One genogram can situate pages of narrative information on a single page. Genograms can be created to include any moment in the family's history, showing the ages and relationships at that moment to better understand family patterns as they evolve through time (McGoldrick, Gerson, & Petry, 2008).

Additionally, genogram construction creates opportunities to establish rapport between the family social worker and the family, rapidly engaging the family in the family work process. Working together in genogram construction sets the stage for the worker-family partnership and draws families into a participatory style of problem identification and solving.

How to Draw a Genogram

McGoldrick, Gerson, and Petry (2008) suggest that the process of genogram construction involves "casting an 'information net' from the presenting problem to the larger context, from the immediate to the extended, from the present to the historical, from easy nonthreatening to sensitive, and from facts to judgments and hypotheses" (p. 62).

To start, it is important to note that genograms capture individual perceptions of families and embedded relationships. Before starting a genogram, it is important to prepare for the possibility of differences in perception about the nature of relationships. For example, someone in the family might consider his or her relationship with another member extremely close, while the other person might see the relationship as conflicted. Usually such extremes are rare, but the potential exists for hurt feelings. Relationships are affected by the nature of the communication people have with one another. Some relationships may have communication that is marked by anger or conflict, whereas another relationship might have communication that is quite intimate, with the two parties telling each other their innermost secrets.

Although no standard method of genogram construction exists—despite the widespread use (see, for example, McGoldrick, Gerson, & Petry, 2008; Hartman & Laird, 1983; Wright & Leahey, 1994)—they all contain the same basic information: who is in the family, when children were born, significant relationships, and critical family events. Some genograms document medical ailments across generations. Others depict psychosocial problems such as mental illness, suicide, or alcoholism across generations. Another common use of genograms is to capture the nature of relationship patterns across generations—particularly conflicted, disengaged, or enmeshed patterns. Sometimes workers use color coding to make intergenerational patterns stand out, although this can take more time than necessary. However, currently there is only a loose consensus about what specific information to include, how to record information, and how to interpret it. Fortunately, the general structure of the genogram follows conventional genetic and genealogical charts. Since it is standard practice to include at least three generations in a genogram (i.e., grandparents, parents, and children), it is important to plan spacing ahead of time, particularly to accommodate diverse family structures. Many symbols are used because the core information of genograms is depicted in shorthand. Figure 8.2 shows examples of the more common symbols contained in a genogram.

Common Symbols in Genograms

The genogram shows family members in relation to each other. It also helps the worker understand who is involved with the presenting family issue and allows the worker to include that person in treatment planning. Genograms can be quite complex beyond the traditional nuclear family configuration. Divorce, common-law relationships, separations, blended families, affairs, and stepfamilies all should be placed on a genogram. Add stepsiblings, foster children, and adopted children to the mix, and you can have a complicated potpourri of relationships.

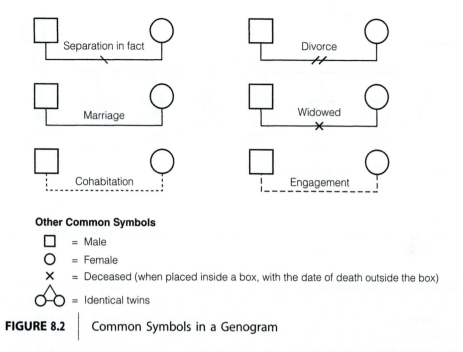

FIGURE 8.2 | Common Symbols in a Genogram

Genograms consist of a vertical and horizontal axis. In the vertical axis, family history and patterns of relating and functioning that are transmitted down the generations, primarily through the mechanism of emotional triangulating (McGoldrick, Gerson, & Petry, 2008, p.15), are represented. The horizontal flow includes both predictable developmental stresses and unpredictable events that may disrupt the family life cycle process (p. 16).

Individual Symbols

□ = Male
○ = Female
X = deceased (when placed inside a box, with the date of death outside the box)

Every family member is represented either by a box or a circle, on the basis of gender. Lines for the individual client (index person, or, alternatively, identified patient [IP]) for whom the genogram was constructed are doubled. A pregnancy is represented by a triangle, and a miscarriage is represented by a triangle with an X drawn through it. Males are depicted by squares, and females are depicted by circles o. Identical twins start at the same point on the horizontal line above but separate to form a triangle, with either circles or squares placed at the end of each arm. The same is true for fraternal twins, although the arms may have a circle and a square. Foster children are connected to the horizontal line via a dotted vertical line, and adopted children are designated by both a solid and dotted vertical line attached to the line above. Each individual in the family must be represented at a specific, strategic point on the genogram, regardless of whether that individual is currently alive or living in the household at that particular moment. If a person has ever existed, he or she belongs in the genogram. Depending on the number of

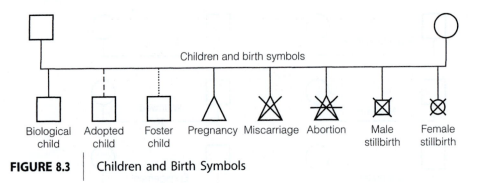

FIGURE 8.3 | Children and Birth Symbols

people and relationships involved, genogram construction can become quite involved. See Figures 8.3 and 8.4.

Relational and Generational Lines A horizontal line connecting people captures adults in a family. Children are placed below the parents' horizontal line, ordered by youngest to oldest from left to right. Family members of the same generation are placed in horizontal rows that signify generational lines. For example, a horizontal line denotes marital or common-law relationships. Divorce is shown by a double slashed line in the horizontal line (//) with the accompanying dates. Separation is indicated by a single slash (/). Affairs and common-law relationships are depicted by a dotted line (......) connecting the two people. When remarriage occurs, the ex-partner can be shown with a smaller shape. If there is more than one marriage, they are placed from left to right with the most recent marriage being placed last. Children of a union are placed on a different horizontal line underneath the parents and joined to the line of the parents by a vertical line. Triangular patterns are of particular importance to identify in the family. In addition, family social workers should look for descriptions rather than conclusions. This means asking about concrete activities and examples of behaviors rather than getting family members to evaluate relationships. See Figure 8.5.

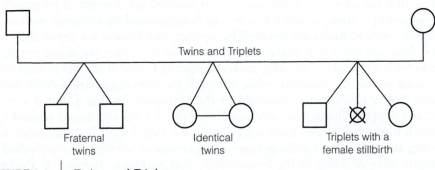

FIGURE 8.4 | Twins and Triplets

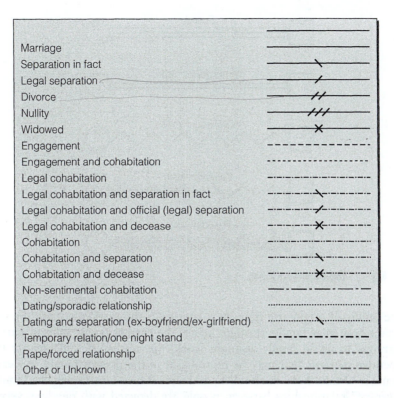

Marriage	
Separation in fact	
Legal separation	
Divorce	
Nullity	
Widowed	
Engagement	
Engagement and cohabitation	
Legal cohabitation	
Legal cohabitation and separation in fact	
Legal cohabitation and official (legal) separation	
Legal cohabitation and decease	
Cohabitation	
Cohabitation and separation	
Cohabitation and decease	
Non-sentimental cohabitation	
Dating/sporadic relationship	
Dating and separation (ex-boyfriend/ex-girlfriend)	
Temporary relation/one night stand	
Rape/forced relationship	
Other or Unknown	

FIGURE 8.5 | Relational and Generational Lines

Additional Detail   Each family member's name and age is placed inside the square or circle representing that person. The year of birth and date of death are recorded above the gender symbol. Birth dates are displayed horizontally, moving from left to right on the page. Sometimes, if birth dates are past the century mark and cannot be mistaken for another century, the first two numbers in a year can be provided. Outside each symbol, significant data and important events (for example, "travels a lot" or "school dropout") should be recorded. Some events send emotional shockwaves throughout the family, fostering or shutting down communication (Nichols & Schwartz, 2007). If a family member has died, the year of death, the person's age at death, and the cause of death should be recorded. When the symbol for miscarriage is used, the sex of the child should be identified, if known.

Relationship Lines   Once the important facts about the relationships captured by the genogram are recorded, the family worker can move on to describing relationships within the family. Adding lines to show the nature of relationships can make a genogram quite detailed, so it is important to plan ahead and target the most important relationships first. Lines between people in the genogram describe the nature and quality of relationships. Questions such as "What was the nature of your parents' relationship?" or "Who did you feel closest to in your family?" are useful to capture the quality of family relationships. The worker is advised to work

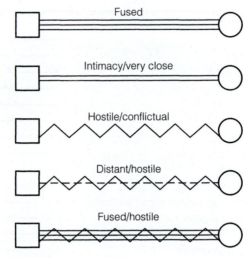

FIGURE 8.6 | Relationship Lines

with one family of origin at a time. At a later time, the worker can ask the spouses to interpret how their family of origin affects the current family unit, in particular, the marriage. In doing family-of-origin work, the worker should identify themes and repetitive patterns that may be reproduced in the present family. An example of a theme is "Males have the final say in major decisions affecting the family."

"Average" relationships between people are depicted with one line, very close relationships with two lines, and enmeshed relationships with three lines. A dotted line represents a distant or disengaged relationship between two people, and a jagged line shows a very conflicted or hostile relationship between two people. Broken relationships are indicated by a line with two slashes in it. See Figure 8.6.

In Chapter 3, we discussed triangles as being a very important family subsystem, particularly when a triangle involves the coalition of two people against another. It could be two parents against a child or a parent and child against another parent. Putting triangles in a genogram can be a very useful assessment tool.

The website www.genopro.com offers four rules to guide the construction of a genogram.[1]

1. The male is always to the left of the family, and the female is always to the right of the family.
2. In the case of ambiguity, assume a male-female relationship, rather than a male-male or female-female relationship (when more than two people are represented on the same horizontal line).
3. In the case of multiple marriages, a spouse is always drawn closest to his or her first marital partner. Next the second partner (if any) is drawn into the genogram, next is the third partner, and so on.

---

[1] The diagrams included in this chapter are from www.genopro.com/beta/. The diagrams are free to the public, and the website allows you to download, free of charge, a program that creates genograms. After one month, you must purchase the program if you are going to continue to use it.

4. The oldest child is always to the left of her or his family, and the youngest
    child is always to the right of her or his family.

As we have discussed in this chapter, genograms are most useful when multiple
family generations are of interest. Figure 8.7 is an example of such a genogram
using the family of Barack Obama, President of the United States of America.

Three generations are seen in the genogram. At the top of the figure are
Barack's maternal grandparents, Stanley Dunham and Madelyn Payne, both born
in Kansas. Sometimes birth and death location are included in a genogram as well
as other information such as occupation, relationship issues, or disease history.
Barack's mother, Ann, was born in Kansas and married two times. Her first hus-
band was Barack's father, Barack Obama, Sr.; the marriage lasted only two years.
Ann's second marriage, to Lolo Soetoro of Indonesia, produced a half-sister named
Maya for Barack. This marriage also ended in divorce after 14 years.

On the right side at the top of the figure are Barack's paternal grandparents,
Onyango Obama and Akuma from Kenya. Onyango had two other wives. Barack
Obama, Sr. had multiple wives as well. Ann Dunham was his second wife. With his
three other wives, Barack Sr. had seven children. One of the half-siblings is
deceased; the others live in Kenya, the United States, and the United Kingdom.

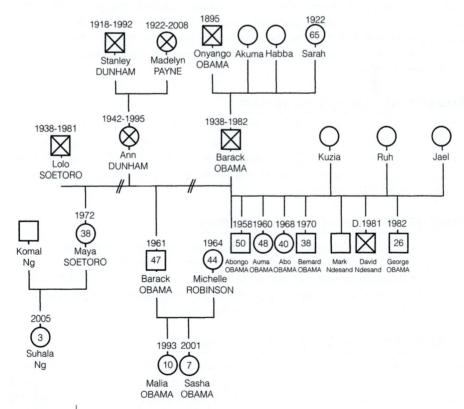

FIGURE 8.7 | Genogram of the Barack Obama Family

Barack Jr.'s parents met while students at the University of Hawaii. Ann's parents located there from Kansas; Barack Sr. was there as an exchange student. During their careers, Ann worked as an anthropologist in Hawaii and Indonesia, whereas Barack Sr. worked as a government economist in Kenya. Both parents are now deceased. Barack Sr. died in a car crash in Kenya; Ann died of ovarian cancer in Hawaii. There are no surviving grandparents as Madelyn Payne Durham, who lived in Hawaii, died shortly before her grandson was elected. She was secluded from the presidential election process due to her poor health. Madelyn passed away in Hawaii two days before Barack Obama, Jr. was elected President of the United States. Barack Jr.'s immediate family consists of his wife, Michelle, and their two children, Malia and Sasha.

EXERCISE 8.4   A Genogram of Your Family

Create a genogram of your family. Start by planning what information you want to obtain and how far back you want the generations to go. Part of this will depend on how much information you have at your disposal. If you would like to go back several generations but lack the necessary information, you might want to ask your parents (if they are available) some questions before you start. Questions might include important dates, names, relationships, and useful pieces of information such as occupations, education, and significant medical or mental health difficulties. It is easiest to draw the genogram by hand, although there are electronic resources available to purchase or download from the Web. Make yourself the IP in this genogram, and select one of your issues. See if you can trace the history of this issue through the generations or, alternatively, from your family of origin.

EXERCISE 8.5   Creating a Genogram

Select a movie or television family for which there is sufficient detail about the family and multiple generations. Construct a genogram based on this family. Share this genogram with the class. Then, break into small groups and analyze the information contained in this genogram. Develop a list of questions to ask this family about their genogram. Compare your answers with the other small groups'.

EXERCISE 8.6   Rules of Genogram Construction

Following the four rules of genogram construction provided in the chapter, map out a genogram for a woman who has been married four times. She had three children in her first relationship, no children with her second partner, two children with her third, and none with her fourth. However, her fourth husband brought two children from a previous relationship. Compare your genogram with the rest of the class.

EXERCISE 8.7   Role-Play Creating a Genogram

Break the class into groups of three. One person will serve as a coach/observer, one person will be the family social worker, and the third person will be the client. Respecting privacy and boundaries, create a genogram for the client. The client has the right, in this role-play, to refuse to answer specific questions.

Ecomap

While a genogram reveals the internal dynamics of the family, the family's external dynamics and relationships are represented on an ecomap. Some difficulties appear at the interface between the person and the environment. This map charts family relationships with the outside world (ecosystem) and captures the strength and quality of external connections and areas of conflict with the family. Ecomaps also demonstrate the flow of resources from the environment to the family, in addition to deprivations and unmet family needs (Holman, 1983). Ecomaps account for client transactions with the environment and are useful for assessing and conceptualizing families holistically and contextually. Important observations concerning family-community connections are cataloged through the ecomap.

As with the genogram, the primary function of an ecomap is the visual and conceptual impact of collating an extensive amount of information on a single page. The map is an easy-to-read depiction of family support systems. Family social work relies heavily on the information portrayed by an ecomap because needs and community resources are central to family work. Creating an ecomap with a family often occurs during assessment and planning, concentrating on crucial information about systemic formulations such as boundary issues and the direction, rate, and mutuality of social relationships. It should reduce the amount of narrative needed for case files. However, there are tradeoffs between the level of detail required and the time it takes to complete an ecomap. Ecomaps can also capture changes over time by doing one at assessment and others later in the intervention. They are now a standard part of agency recording, especially in agencies with high staff turnover and clients with many unmet social needs.

As with the genogram, constructing an ecomap can be beneficial to the family, particularly during the early stages of engagement. Because families of color have experienced societal discrimination, the effects of this discrimination can be depicted on the ecomap. Ecomaps capture transactions with systems outside the family, while genograms identify exchanges within the family. Sometimes the two are used together to develop an integrated picture of a family situation. Both workers and clients find these tools useful. Ecomaps also capitalize on gathering important religious and cultural ties to the community. For diverse clients, they can help identify the sources of oppression and financial well-being.

How to Draw the Ecomap   The ecomap is made up of a series of interconnected circles representing various systems extraneous to the family. Placing the previously constructed genogram in a center circle labeled as the family or household is one option, but many workers find the result too messy. Circles placed outside this center circle represent significant people, agencies, or organizations in the lives of the members of the family. The size of the circles is not important. Lines drawn between the inner and outer circles indicate the nature of the existing connections. Straight lines (--) show strong connections, dotted lines (.......) denote tenuous or weak connections, and slashed lines (-/-/-/) represent stressful or conflictual connections.

The thicker the line, the stronger the connection. Arrows drawn alongside the lines represent the flow of energy and resources. Additional circles can be drawn as

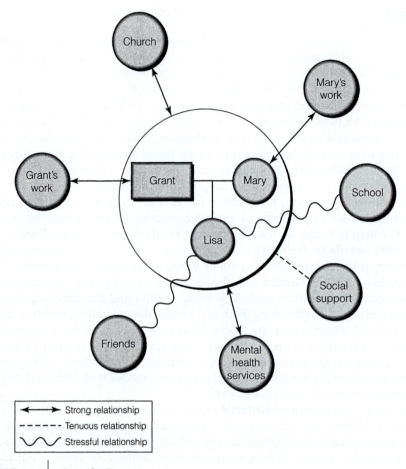

FIGURE 8.8 | Sample Ecomap

necessary, depending on the number of significant contacts. The ecomap may be modified as the family changes or as the family shares further information with the family social worker. An example of an ecomap is shown in Figure 8.8.

EXERCISE 8.8   Ecomap

Continue Exercise 8.7, but this time create the client's ecomap instead of a genogram. Discuss with the client what changes they would like to see if they could change their social system interactions.

Other Visual Techniques

Family Drawing   Another related technique for depicting family relationships is to ask a family to create a family drawing together. Family members can also draw their family separately, and the portraits of individual family members can later be compared and discussed. Another similar technique is to have families arrange a family photograph with family members posing for family pictures. How people are positioned for this photograph will generate information about family relationships. After each exercise, ask individual family members to discuss what they see in the family portrayal.

Family Sculpture   Alternatively, family members can be asked to "sculpt" their family (Satir & Baldwin, 1983); that is, have family members physically stand in a room posed in ways to depict a family sculpture of their relationships. Members take turns arranging family members in relationship with one another; body gestures, distance, and physical actions are captured through the sculpture. Each family member takes charge of his or her particular sculpture, instructing family members in the sculpture what position to assume. Essentially, the sculptor treats members as if they were made of clay. Sculptures of the same family will differ, depending on the perceptions of the one directing the sculpture. Sculpting is especially useful for nonverbal families to provide a means of expressing and understanding one another (Holman, 1983).

Family Time Line   Another interesting qualitative assessment tool is the family time line, which is represented on a grid. It is a simple grid designed to capture and rate important family events according to the dimension of time. Events unfold as the family moves across the life cycle; parents meeting, dating, marriages, deaths, births, periods of illness or unemployment, moves, divorces, and so on can all be rapidly captured on a single time line. A time line can help the family social worker quickly pick up enormous detail about a family's history as well as the significance of events in their history.

There are two ways to rate the impact of an event. The first is to place negative events below the line and positive events above the line. The second, and probably easiest, way is to rank the events on a scale of 1 to 10. A 1 indicates an extremely upsetting or stressful event, and a 10 indicates an event that is extremely positive. Numbers that fall in between indicate important experiences, with 5 being a somewhat neutral response. Points on the line are then connected to reveal highs and lows in the family's development. Events can be analyzed in terms of their impact on the family, starting with the first event and proceeding into the present time. Once the time line is completed, the family social worker can initiate discussion to analyze the events in the family's life. Fruitful discussion ensues if family members disagree about the importance of the events. When this happens, the family worker can help family members understand how different events are perceived differently by every member of the family.

Events that might be important to families include:

- Moving
- Birth of a child
- Divorce
- Marriage
- Death
- Arrival or death of a pet

- Family accomplishment
- New job
- Personal event of family members (e.g., graduation, getting a promotion, making a new friend)
- Family life cycle event such as when grandparents went into a nursing home, when Mom and Dad went on the Dr. Phil show, and so on.

EP 2.1.3b

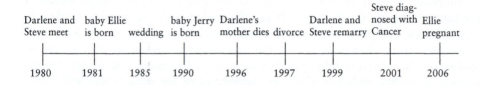

SPECIAL CONSIDERATIONS IN QUALITATIVE ASSESSMENT

Special considerations in qualitative assessment are considered in four areas: criteria for assessing family functioning, family categories schema, assessing parenting skills, and assessing diverse families.

CRITERIA FOR ASSESSING FAMILY FUNCTIONING

Many models are available with which to assess family functioning (see, for example, Corcoran & Fischer, 2007). Most of these models support one theoretical framework or another. For example, one family assessment tool, the Circumplex Model of family functioning, conceives of family functioning as falling on two continua: adaptability and cohesion (FACES III) (Olson, 1986). Another (Beavers-Timberlawn Family Evaluation Scale) developed by Beavers (1981) looks at family functioning on the basis of competence, structure, and flexibility. The Family Assessment Measure (McMaster Model), otherwise known as the Family Categories Schema, describes family functioning as involving basic tasks, developmental tasks, and hazardous tasks (Epstein, Baldwin, & Bishop, 1983), as well as specific areas of family functioning like problem solving, communication, roles, affective responses, affective involvement, and behavior control. It was designed to assess the need for family work (McMaster Clinical Rating Scale) (Epstein, Baldwin, & Bishop, 1983).

Workers can also develop their own checklists for predetermined purposes, and some agencies might have devised their own checklists that capture the specific purposes of their mandates. Checklists can be constructed to account for physical resources in the home. Conversely, a worker may want to focus on specific areas of role performance of family members. Checklists can also cover physical care of the children or a rating of the emotional climate of the family. The benefit of checklists such as these is that they can be specially tailored to families and their circumstances.

A very useful book for assessing problems not just with families but also with individuals is *Measures for Clinical Practice, 4th edition* (Corcoran & Fischer, 2007). This text includes many Family Categories Schema that examine a multitude of areas of family functioning. Some measures are concerned with specific family relationships such as parent-child functioning, whereas others target the functioning of a family unit as a whole. In this book, we present the Family Categories Schema because it comprehensively covers most areas of family functioning and was developed using a family systems framework. The measure can be used for a quantitative measure of family functioning, or alternatively, the family social worker can rely on the conceptual base with which to understand family functioning through interviews and observations.

FAMILY CATEGORIES SCHEMA

A helpful way to understand and assess family functioning is to use the framework provided by the Family Categories Schema based on the work of Epstein, Bishop, and Levin (1978). These authors designed an instrument for family social workers to complete after their initial meetings with families. The quantitative instrument is a 60-item self-report questionnaire containing eight categories: (1) problem solving, (2) affective responsiveness, (3) affective involvement, (4) communication, (5) role behavior, (6) autonomy, (7) modes of behavioral control, and (8) general functioning. If the family social worker decides not to use the specific instrument, she or he can, as mentioned, try to understand family functioning using the categories provided. After describing each category, we will present a sample item from the instrument.

Problem Solving

Problem solving is how a family copes with threats to emotional or physical well-being or to the family's survival as a functioning unit. Threats can be either instrumental or affective. *Instrumental* threats involve mechanical or concrete aspects of living, such as economic, physical, or health concerns. Thus, parental unemployment or the physical abuse of a child are two examples of instrumental threats to the family. *Affective* threats endanger the emotional well-being of family life; examples include a depressed child, an overwhelmed parent, or a maladaptive circular interaction. Frequently, instrumental and affective problems overlap. A parent feeling depressed because of unemployment is one such example. Walsh (1998), in describing resilient families, suggests that although well-functioning families are not characterized by the absence of problems, what distinguishes resilient families is their ability to manage conflict well. In addition, there are several steps in effective problem-solving processes: first, recognize the problem; second, communicate about it; third, collaborate in brainstorming; and fourth, initiate and carry out action, monitor efforts, and evaluate success (Epstein, 1983, cited in Walsh, 1998).

An example of a self-report statement related to problem solving is, "We resolve most everyday problems around the house." Other questions to ask include "Give me an example of a family problem that you have had. How did you handle this problem? What are the problems that make life difficult or stressful for the family?"

Affective Responsiveness

Family members should be able to express a variety of emotions within a supportive family environment. The range of emotions can be divided into two major categories: *welfare emotions* such as happiness, joy, tenderness, love, and sympathy, and *emergency emotions* such as rage, fear, anger, and depression.

The family social worker should assess the family's ability to respond with the appropriate quality and quantity of feelings to affect-provoking stimuli. Family social workers are concerned with the welfare and emergency emotions expressed in the family, as well as with the pattern of their expression. This involves whether the expression of emotions is clear, direct, open, and honest or indirect, masked, and dishonest. The degree to which individual family members participate in the affective interchange is also important. Walsh (1998) suggests that empathic sharing of emotions, combined with loving tolerance for differences and negative emotions, is an important aspect of resilient family processes.

An example of a statement related to affective responsiveness is "Some of us just don't respond emotionally" (Corcoran & Fischer, 2007).

Affective Involvement

To what extent are family members emotionally involved with one another in activities and interests that go beyond those needed for instrumental family functions? Involvement transcends mere expression of affect and captures the amount and quality of the emotional involvement that family members have with each other. It is one thing to praise a child for doing homework, and it is something else to sit down with the child and discuss the homework. We strongly endorse the need for parents to support children; thus, parents need to be actively involved in their children's interests and activities.

One example of a statement related to affective involvement is "It is difficult to talk to each other about tender feelings" (Corcoran & Fischer, 2006). Questions to ask might include: What are you involved in or interested in?, Who shares your interests?, How do they show this interest?, Do you feel in your family that family members go their own way and do not care about what you do?, How do you relate to the children?, and How would you describe your relationship with so-and-so?

Communication

Communication can be quite complex. An adage of communication theory is "*You cannot not communicate.*" Hence, the verbal and nonverbal communications that occur within a family are both important. Communication serves two functions: to communicate content and to define the nature of the relationship between the speaker and listener. The second function is called *metacommunication*. Listening carefully to how family members communicate with one another will give the family social worker important clues about a family's relationships. A message conveyed out of care will come across differently than a message conveyed out of anger, even if the content of the messages is the same.

Healthy family communication is clear, direct, open, and honest. As with problem solving, communication can be categorized into affective and instrumental areas. *Affective communication* is defined as that in which the communicated message is mostly emotional in nature, whereas *instrumental communication* occurs when the message is primarily mechanical. An instrumental message is related to the mechanics of getting things done and involves the regular, ongoing tasks of family living.

Communication is both verbal and nonverbal, including such behaviors as posture, voice tone, gestures, and facial expressions. If a person says "I'm listening" while making eye contact and smiling, the words are interpreted differently than how they would be perceived if the speaker were hiding behind a newspaper. Ideally, verbal and nonverbal communication should be congruent. Additionally, information that is exchanged should ideally be reciprocal and positive.

An example of a statement related to communication is "When someone is upset, the others know why" (Corcoran & Fischer, 2006). Other questions to ask might include: Do people talk much in this family? Who talks to whom? and Who do you speak with in your family when you are feeling upset? To find out whether communication is masked, you can ask: How did so-and-so let you know that he or she was upset? How did you get the message?, What was so-and-so getting at when she or he said 'It's up to you'?, What did so-and-so just say?, and So-and-so, is that what you just said?

Walsh (1998) elaborates on communication processes within the family.

CLARITY

- Clear, consistent messages (words and actions)
- Clarification of ambiguous information: Truth seeking/truth speaking

OPEN EMOTIONAL EXPRESSION

- Sharing a wide range of feelings (joy and pain; hopes and fears)
- Mutual empathy; tolerance for differences
- Responsibility for own feelings and behavior; avoiding blaming
- Pleasurable interactions; humor

COLLABORATIVE PROBLEM SOLVING

- Identifying problems, stressors, options, and constraints
- Creative brainstorming; resourcefulness
- Shared decision making; negotiation, fairness, reciprocity
- Conflict resolution
- Focusing on goals; taking concrete steps
- Building on success; learning from failure
- Proactive stance; preventing problems, averting crises, preparing for future challenges (p. 107)

Role Behavior

Every family faces daily pressures, tasks, and obligations. To cope, each family member plays roles that develop into established and predictable patterns of behavior. *Roles* are repetitive patterns of behavior that serve a function in day-to-day family life. They can take many forms, such as those that follow traditional role definitions (such as gender roles) and roles that deviate from traditional roles, known as idiosyncratic roles.

Traditional roles involve those of mother, father, husband, wife, son, or daughter as traditionally defined by a culture. Roles based on gender are much less clear today than they used to be, as are spousal and parental roles. However, most people still regard children as more the mother's responsibility than the father's (Eichler, 1997). Roles that are not always clearly agreed on include the parental role to socialize children and the assumption of responsibility for their emotional and physical well-being. Idiosyncratic roles fall outside traditional social prescriptions. For example, a mother may assume the role of primary financial provider (traditionally the male role) while the father cares for the children and takes care of household tasks. Some idiosyncratic roles are related to the family's presenting problem, as when one child takes the role of scapegoat. Other idiosyncratic roles, such as the clown and the hero, are seen in alcoholic families.

Optimal family roles include:

- Clearly differentiated roles of parents and children
- Flexibility of roles when the situation demands it
- Roles that are performed competently (Brock & Barnard, 1999).

An example of a statement related to role behavior is "Each of us has particular duties and responsibilities." Questions to ask include: How do you decide who does something in the family?, Who does a particular role in the family?, and What if a job doesn't get done?

Autonomy

Autonomy concerns the ability of family members to act independently and to make individual, responsible choices based on their age and abilities. Autonomy is demonstrated when each member has a sense of identity as a separate person rather than as an extension of others, is able to make choices in selecting or rejecting outside influences, and is willing to take responsibility for making personal choices. Autonomy should be assessed in light of each member's age, developmental abilities, and potential. Also of importance is the degree of *individuation* that occurs in the sphere of the family unit and in the individual members' lives beyond the family unit. *Individuation* refers to the sense of being a unique individual, distinct from others.

An example of a statement related to autonomy is "Mom is always telling me what clothes I should wear."

Modes of Behavioral Control

Behavioral control involves the family's way of dealing with impulses, maintaining standards of behavior, and coping with threatening situations. Four modes of behavioral control are described in the following list:

- *Rigid:* A fixed pattern of familial behavior that is intolerant of individual variation (e.g., children are never allowed to sleep over at a friend's home).
- *Flexible:* A familial pattern of behavior that is firmly and clearly defined but at the same time involves a flexible style allowing for individual variation (e.g., agreed-on family rules are present but may be bent in the case of special circumstances; i.e., children usually are not allowed to have sleepovers on weeknights, but the rule is bent to celebrate a birthday).
- *Laissez-faire:* A pattern in which no effective or established patterns of behavioral control exist (e.g., the rule might be that no sleepovers are allowed on a school night, but the rule is altered inconsistently, such as when a child pleads).
- *Chaotic:* A pattern of complete inconsistency in modes of behavioral control within the family (e.g., there is no rule about sleepovers during a school night, and on one occasion the child is permitted to sleep over, but on other similar occasions the child is denied a sleepover; thus, the child is not aware what rules regulate sleepovers).

These four modes of behavioral control can be evaluated with regard to whether they are consistent or inconsistent, that is, whether the mode of behavioral control is predictable or unpredictable.

An example of a statement related to behavioral control is "We have rules about hitting people."

EXERCISE 8.9   Family Functioning

Compose four questions, each relating to one of the seven areas of family functioning discussed above. Be especially aware of any sexist, ageist, or cultural biases that enter into the questions you formulate.

ASSESSING PARENTING SKILLS

Family social workers will be required to assess parenting skills, especially if a child's safety is at risk. The following criteria can be used to assess parenting (Steinhauer, 1991):

1. *Level of attachment:* Healthy attachment is a prerequisite for the formation of trust, self-esteem, and the ability to develop future intimate relationships. The child's primary attachment should be with the parents. Parents must be sensitive to their child's needs and respond accordingly. Parents with personal problems such as immaturity or self-absorption are often unable to accurately understand their children's needs. In addition, parent-child relationships should be neither enmeshed nor disengaged.
2. *Transmission of a moral code:* Parents are responsible for teaching their children to distinguish between right and wrong. Through parental teaching and

modeling, children learn to respect the rights of others and to control their impulses. Morality should be congruent with that of the larger culture with respect for distinct cultural patterns.

3. *Absence of rejection, overt or covert:* Neglect and abuse are examples of overt rejection, whereas covert rejection is more difficult to identify. It may involve subtle or blatant emotional abuse.

4. *Continuity of care:* A continuous relationship between parents and child is crucial, and the care should match the developmental needs of the child.

Sometimes the court or a custody lawyer will ask the family social worker to assess the ability of parents to care for their children. At other times, the social worker will have to decide whether children can safely remain within their families or they should be placed in foster care, at least temporarily. Making these decisions can be extremely difficult. In assessing parenting ability, the family social worker will need to look at the child's development as well as the history of the parent-child relationship. Sometimes the family social worker will need to consult a specialist for an expert assessment of child development or diagnosis of psychiatric disabilities in a parent or child. The starting point for assessment, however, should be to determine the quality of the parent-child relationship over time.

Assessment of Child Development

Information on the child's development, including cognitive, emotional, physical, and social abilities, should be included in the assessment. Social workers should have knowledge of normative child development to supplement their observations. According to Steinhauer (1991), child assessment should include information about the following topics:

- Behavior in the areas of cognitive, behavioral, emotional, or academic functioning
- Parental attitudes toward the child
- Attachment issues pertinent to parent-child relationships, including a history of separations and parental abuse
- History of psychiatric or social disabilities on the part of the parents, including evidence of substance abuse or antisocial/criminal behavior
- History of involvement with social service systems and agencies
- Risk assessment of child safety in the areas of abuse (emotional, physical, or sexual) and neglect
- Attainment of developmental milestones
- Medical/physical history
- Attitude of parents toward the child and indications of current or past parental rejection or hostility
- Corroboration from external sources regarding the above-mentioned areas
- School and friendship history
- The development of the child based on one or more theories of child development: psychosocial, cognitive, psychosexual, and so on.

EXERCISE 8.10   Assessment of a Child

Select one child you know and conduct an assessment of that child using Steinhauer's ten-point child assessment areas.

Assessment of Parent-Child Relationship

A central concern of the family social worker is parent-child interactions. Observations should occur over a period of time, looking at how the parent and child relate to one another and noting normative, age-appropriate information. Especially important are the amount and quality of physical and emotional contact that parents and children have with one another. The family social worker should observe the parent's disciplinary style and ability to set boundaries. Play skills can be useful as children often express opinions indirectly through play rather than directly through verbalizations. In addition to relationship issues, the social worker should assess how well the child's physical, social and intellectual needs are being met (i.e., whether the child receives adequate nourishment, clothing, shelter, and supervision and whether the child receives adequate social and intellectual stimulation). Further, the social worker may refer clients to other professionals for specialized assessment or psychological tests of the parent or child.

Steinhauer (1991) reports that there are three levels of parenting capacity. At the highest level are families who are functioning well, in which child development is proceeding normally and any help provided will be at the request of the parents. In the middle group, child development has become impaired as the result of a temporary crisis rather than a long-standing, chronic problem. A child-related crisis may have destabilized the family so much that it temporarily lacks the resources to cope. Parents in this category appear to have no chronic emotional or social disabilities and are cooperative with the assistance offered. These parents accept responsibility for their role in the development of the problem and also show willingness to deal with the problem. In the third group, there may be significant impairment in child development and functioning. The family's problems appear to be chronic, and lack of parenting abilities is long-standing. Children display significant disturbance in one or several areas of their lives. Parents are significantly disabled socially or emotionally and have a history of unsuccessful social service involvement. Parents in this category appear to be uncooperative and do not accept personal responsibility for their role in problems.

ASSESSING DIVERSE FAMILIES

"Racial/ethnic trends in the United States point to a society that is increasing in ethnic diversity and developing a growing awareness of ethnic identity. By the year 2050, racial and ethnic minorities will represent nearly 49.9 percent of the population" (Gilbert, 2011, p. 360).

Mapping techniques such as genograms, ecomaps, and time lines are particularly helpful in assessing diverse families because they emphasize assessment of the extended family. The family social worker will also observe family interactions during home visits. In assessing diverse families, we would like to point out that there is a great deal of heterogeneity within cultures. The danger of offering a checklist of qualities and experiences might be stereotypical and ultimately lead to biased conclusions. It is with this caveat that we discuss some of the issues that groups of diverse families might experience. All families, diverse families included, benefit from ecomap and genogram construction. If measures and questions from mainstream society are used, the family social worker must be attuned to the possibility of cultural biases.

Assessment Issues for African American and Black Families

Socioeconomic status, educational level, cultural identity, family structure, and reactions to racism are important variables in assessing African American families (Gilbert, 2011). Gilbert reviews alternative methods of assessment for this population including use of revised tests and newly devised ethnic specific tests, assessment of cultural and ethnic identity acculturation and related stress, and use of qualitative methods such as genograms and other maps.

Assessment Issues for Hispanic American Families

American families may experience discrimination, underemployment, and lack of housing or other resources, and these problems should not be overlooked in the assessment (Jordan, Lewellen, & Vandiver, 1994). The level of acculturation, or assimilation into the ways of the dominant culture, is a major issue for Hispanic families as with most other cultural and ethnic groups. Three levels of acculturation are commonly found among Hispanic American families: immigrant families who have just arrived, immigrant-American families, and immigrant-descent families (Padella, et al. and Casas & Keefe, cited in Jordan, Lewellen, & Vandiver, 1994).

The first group, newly arrived immigrant families, has yet to be acculturated into the new country's values and ways. Family members usually speak little or no English. Immigrant-American families, the second group, consist of parents born in the old country and children born in the new country. This may result in a clash between oldsters and youth as children are acculturated more rapidly into the new country. The third group, immigrant-descent families, consists of all generations born in the new country. Members of this group are likely to be fully acculturated into the new country.

Assessment Issues for Asian American Families

Acculturation to the dominant society is a concern when assessing Asian American families. Barriers to service provision may include unfamiliarity with the health care system in a new country, language difficulties, and cultural traditions and values that conflict with those of the dominant culture (Jordan, Lewellen, & Vandiver, 1994). Vietnamese and Laotian families may have spent time as refugees in resettlement camps and thus been exposed to great traumas. The family social worker should be sensitive to this possibility and assess the family's need to obtain appropriate services for stress-related illnesses. The history of immigration, including the reasons for it, is a helpful area to explore.

Assessment Issues for Native American Families

Red Horse (1980) describes three types of Native American families that require different kinds of assistance. The first type is the traditional family governed by tribal customs and beliefs. Older members speak the native language, and the extended family network is influential. The second type is the nontraditional or bicultural family. Though the extended family network is important and the older generation may speak the native tongue, English is primarily spoken. The family interacts freely and comfortably with members of the dominant culture. The third type is the pan-traditional family. These families are seeking to reconnect with their cultural heritage. Bicultural families are most apt to seek services from mental health professionals. When traditional or pan-traditional families require help, they are likely to consult tribal community helpers or religious leaders.

In addition to considering the family type when assessing Native American families, the family social worker should be aware of their history as victims of discrimination, colonization, and genocide. Historically, Native Americans were coerced into signing unfavorable treaties that stripped them of their land and way of life. In many cases, children were separated from their parents. Consequently, Native Americans have experienced poverty, unemployment, alcoholism, family disruption, and other effects of discrimination. In addition, Native Americans may have a distrust of social institutions, which is understandable given the trickery involved in signing treaties and the mass removal of their children into residential schools and the foster care system.

Psychosocial Adjustment

The family social worker must be sensitive to ethnic and cultural factors when doing a psychosocial assessment of a child from an ethnically diverse family. The social worker must have knowledge of the family's ethnic group, including familiarity with its beliefs, customs, and values. Again, and we cannot emphasize this enough, the family social worker must recognize that within each ethnic group, much individual variation exists. Therefore, it is important for the social worker to learn as much as possible about each family's beliefs, customs, and patterns of interaction. Areas to be covered in the psychosocial assessment include:

1. *Physical assessment:* Low-income, ethnically diverse children may be experiencing physical problems—due to malnutrition and lack of proper medical care such as routine checkups and vaccinations—as a direct result of poverty. A physical (or eye or dental) exam may be needed.

2. *Emotional assessment:* Feelings of self-esteem, competence, and other aspects influencing children's affect may be a product of the children's ethnic background. The family social worker should verify his or her assumptions to ascertain cultural norms.

3. *Behavioral assessment:* Behavioral factors such as aggression and achievement may be culturally determined and different from the dominant culture. For instance, achievement in sports or music may be valued more highly than academic performance. Different parenting techniques—guilt, shame, behavioral modeling, and so on—may be used by the family to manage aggression.
4. *Coping and defense mechanisms:* The child may learn either externalizing or internalizing behaviors as coping and defense mechanisms to deal with anxiety or fear. In response, acting-out behaviors such as fighting or talking back or, alternatively, internalizing behaviors may appear.

Relationships with Family Members

The family's view of appropriate child behavior is a critical element for assessment. Areas to look at include:

1. *Parent-child relationship:* Ethnically diverse families often differ from the dominant culture with respect to the nature of the relationship between parents and children. Variations range from hierarchical and patriarchal relationships, such as those seen in some Asian American families, to the egalitarian parent-child relationships of some Native American tribes.
2. *Birth order:* Families characterized by hierarchical structures may have rigid role prescriptions for the children. For example, the youngest daughter in an Asian American family may be charged with caring for her elderly parents.
3. *Age:* Sibling relationships may be prescribed by age; for instance, older children in Native American families may provide teaching and role modeling for younger siblings and cousins.
4. *Sex:* Male and female family members may be expected to perform different roles and may hold higher or lower family status.
5. *Family expectations:* Other expectations may be imposed on family members, such as dictates about whom children should marry or who will care for children or elderly relatives.

EXERCISE 8.11   Relationships with Family Members

Break into small groups and discuss the five areas presented above in terms of each group member's personal experience in her or his culture. Make a list and report back to the class.

School Adjustment and Achievement

School is the environment in which children spend the most time outside the family. Factors related to school performance provide important indicators of well-being, but assessments must include attention to ethnicity and culture. Four important indicators of school adjustment and achievement are psychological adjustment, behavioral adjustment, academic achievement, and relationships with peers.

1. *Psychological adjustment:* Ethnically diverse parents and children may fear school or view it negatively if the values of the dominant culture differ

drastically from those of the family. Alternatively, some groups emphasize the importance of education as a way of succeeding.

2. *Behavioral adjustment:* Ethnically diverse families may teach their children externalizing or internalizing behaviors to cope with or to solve problems. Use of these types of behaviors may pose difficulties for children in the school setting. It is also important for family social workers to recognize that behavioral problems may reflect underlying health problems such as attention deficit disorder, fetal alcohol syndrome, vision problems, hunger, or lack of sleep.

3. *Academic achievement:* If an ethnically diverse child's grades in school are below average, the child may be having trouble with books and tests that are culturally insensitive. Parents who are unfamiliar with the school system may not provide appropriate support or modeling of efficient study skills.

4. *Relationships with peers:* Children may fear appearing different from their peers and thus may exclude themselves (or be expelled) from peer group activities. Peer support from children of their own cultural or ethnic group may be unavailable.

The example in Case 8.2 illustrates some of the issues faced by children who belong to ethnic minorities.

CASE 8.2 | ### Ethnic Minorities

Sally Redmond, a 7-year-old second grader, came to the family social work agency with her parents because of problems at school. Sally told the family social worker that she did not like her school and did not care if she ever went back. Her teacher has reported that Sally is quiet and withdrawn at school, has no friends, and does not take part in most activities.

Sally's parents, Lou and Darlene, adopted their daughter when she was 2 years old. Sally's birth parents were both Korean, and she was placed in a Korean orphanage at birth. The little girl has black hair, black eyes, and dark skin, unlike Lou and Darlene who are fair-skinned blondes.

The family social worker visited with Sally on the school playground, where she also had the opportunity to observe Sally's behavior during recess. The other children ignored Sally for the most part, but when she got in the way of some boys playing football, they called her dumb. Later, when asked about the boys, Sally said they always talk to her like that and often make fun of the way she looks. She said she feels best when playing with the African American children "because they have skin like mine." Sally told the family social worker that she wished she looked more like her (adoptive) mother and that if she did, she would have more friends. Her teacher mentioned to the family social worker that Sally does not do well in school because "She does not give me eye contact when I talk." After talking with Sally, her parents, and her teacher, the family social worker began to realize that none of the adults had much knowledge about Korean culture.

Peer Relationships

Assessment of the ethnically diverse child's peer interactions gives the family social worker an important indicator of the child's level of acculturation into the majority culture.

1. *Peer interactions:* Children's relationships with peers may be an indicator of their well-being. Fitting in with others and having a peer support group are important to the child's self-esteem and sense of belonging. Indicators include the child's report of friendships as well as involvement in group activities.
2. *Degree of involvement:* The family social worker can assess the level of involvement by asking questions about the child's hobbies and other activities. Examples include sports or other team memberships, Girl or Boy Scouts, and clubs. Also, does the child have a close friend among his or her schoolmates?
3. *Opposite-sex relationships:* For adolescents who are beginning to think about opposite-sex relationships, assessment considerations include availability of partners. For instance, does the ethnically diverse adolescent feel accepted by others at school dances and in dating relationships?

Adaptation to the Community

Indicators of community involvement are important to the assessment of the ethnically diverse child's fit into the broader social environment. The family social worker can assess group and work involvements, as well as family members' reactions to the child's community activities.

1. *Group involvement:* The family social worker may need to assess formal groups in which the child participates such as church, recreation centers, and clubs. Also, the level of involvement is an important indicator of the child's successful participation. For instance, how often does the child attend church, does she or he have friends there, and in what church-sponsored activities does the child participate?
2. *Work involvement:* Adolescents may hold jobs in the community that must be assessed for their appropriateness. Concomitantly, adolescents may want jobs but need help in finding appropriate employment.
3. *Family members' reactions to the child's community involvement:* Family members' level of acculturation may affect their reactions to the child's group or work activities. The family social worker may need to help families understand their children's interactions outside of the family; or he or she may need to help the family to allow children freedom to explore relationships in the community.
4. *Child's special interests or abilities:* Identifying children's special interests, and especially their special abilities, is important to the development of a successful intervention plan. The family social worker may build on the child's strengths to help promote adjustment to a culture different from that of the family of origin. For instance, some children may excel in sports or music rather than academic endeavors. Successful performance in these areas may mitigate poor school performance and increase the child's self-esteem.

CASE 8.3 | Genogram

The family social worker received an assignment to investigate a large family living on the edge of town in a small house. The family was new to the little community, and neighbors reported a chaotic situation with multiple generations coming and going at all hours, as well as several small children who seemed unsupervised.

When the family social worker arrived at the home, she found that the neighbors were correct about the confusing number of family members living in the home. She decided to interview the family and fill in a genogram to better understand the family composition. She was able to arrive at a time when most family members were present and could participate in the activity. The genogram the family social worker put together is shown in Figure 8.9. The family social worker found that three generations were living together in the grandparents' (Ellen and Ted) home; their daughter (Bonnie) with her husband (Al) and Bonnie's children (Ben, Jake, Sue, and Ann) were also in the home.

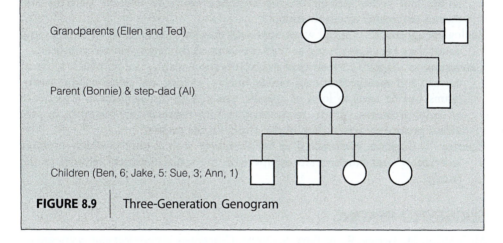

Grandparents (Ellen and Ted)

Parent (Bonnie) & step-dad (Al)

Children (Ben, 6; Jake, 5: Sue, 3; Ann, 1)

FIGURE 8.9 | Three-Generation Genogram

EXERCISE 8.12 Targeting Issues

The lists in this chapter of issues to focus on in a family assessment interview cover several of many possibilities. Break the class into groups of three and brainstorm what other issues and questions might be asked. Report back to the main group. Assign a class member to collate the lists given by all the groups. This list can be distributed to the entire class for future reference.

CHAPTER SUMMARY

Chapter 8 gives an overview of assessment and then presents the area of qualitative assessment. Qualitative assessment uses words, pictures, and observations to understand the client family. In contrast, quantitative assessment uses numerical tests and scales to quantify client strengths and weaknesses (see Chapter 9).

Families are social groupings that grow and contract depending on constantly changing membership. No family remains static. Family dynamics are shaped by how members define them rather than by a rigid, predetermined formula. Genograms and ecomaps assist the family social worker to understand fluid family dynamics and provide a visual overview of family membership, relationships, and environmental connections.

The context of family assessment was first addressed and included the purposes of family assessment, models of family functioning, and ecological assessment. Then qualitative techniques were discussed. These included communication techniques and visual techniques such as genograms and ecomaps. Finally, special issues in assessment were discussed including criteria for assessing family functioning, family categories schema, assessing parenting skills, and assessing diverse families.

KEY TERMS

Qualitative technique   a research and information-gathering technique that uses words and verbal descriptions of identified issues to uncover patterns and themes embedded in information.

Ecological approach   a social work approach that looks holistically at families and issues they are experiencing as they are situated in their social environment.

Genogram   a diagram, constructed in collaboration with a family, which looks at current and multigenerational family history, events, and relationships. Genograms can be used to look at specific issues (e.g., disengagement, experience of social problems, culture, spirituality, and intergenerational issues) or to provide a general understanding of the family in the present.

Ecomap   a diagram, constructed in collaboration with a family, which captures individuals' and family relationships with the social network external to the family.

SUGGESTED READING

McGoldrick, M., Gerson, R., & Petry, S. (2008). *Genograms: Assessment and intervention.* New York, NY: Norton.

COMPETENCY NOTES

EP 2.1.3a. Distinguish, appraise, and integrate multiple sources of knowledge, including research-based knowledge and practice wisdom: In qualitative assessment, it is important to get an in-depth understanding in four areas: the family problems (and strengths), the family system, the family environment, and the family life cycle.

EP 2.1.3b. Analyze models of assessment, prevention, intervention, and evaluation: Qualitative tools, such as the genogram or ecomap, help the family social worker to describe and understand the meaning behind a family's functioning. Guidelines such as severity, importance, and timing of the problem help the family social worker to focus on a specific topic with the client.

EP 2.1.4c. Recognize and communicate their understanding of the importance of difference in shaping life experiences: The differing experiences of diverse populations, as opposed to the white, middle-class majority population, help to shape differential life experiences.

The family social worker must aim to understand the client's characteristics and experiences that influence their life, strengths, and problems.

EP 2.1.10e. Assess client strengths and limitations: Looking at the family as a system in their environmental context helps the family social worker to understand what is happening at the various levels of the client's life. In turn, this helps to identify strengths and weaknesses at all levels.

9 | Quantitative Assessment

LEARNING OBJECTIVES

- Conceptual: Understand a structured approach to family assessment.
- Understand concepts related to quantitative measurement.
- Perceptual: Observe and record concrete behaviors.
- Valuational/Attitudinal: Appreciate a rigorous means of assessment.
- Behavioral: Use concrete assessment tools.

We discussed qualitative family assessment in Chapter 8. Qualitative assessment refers to using descriptive methods to compile and make sense of family information; these include mapping techniques and focused open-ended interviewing. Chapter 9 introduces the use of quantitative measures to inform the organization of information leading to assessment. Quantitative assessment includes using measures to arrive at "numerical indicators of a particular aspect of client functioning" (Franklin & Corcoran, 2006, p. 71). "Today's assessment is an evidence-based approach (McNeece & Thyer; Gibbs & Gambrill, cited in Jordan, 2008, p. #1396). "Evidence-based approaches assume that the best evidence is used along with critical thinking skills, knowledge of best practices, and client input" (p. 1396).

The rationale for including quantitative measures in assessment includes the following four reasons (Franklin & Sanchez in Jordan & Franklin, 2011, pp. 53–54):

1. Quantitative measures help the practitioner to improve treatment.
2. Quantitative methods enable the practitioner to contribute to clinical research.
3. Quantitative measures provide a basis for practice evaluation and accountability.
4. Quantitative measures increase the practitioner's skills repertoire.

This chapter discusses the purposes of quantitative assessment, provides a framework for incorporating quantitative assessment, describes commonly used measurement instruments, and discusses the use of measurement to link assessment and intervention.

PURPOSES OF QUANTITATIVE MEASUREMENT

Our approach to quantitative family assessment and measurement includes the following requirements (Jordan & Franklin, 2011). First, assessment must be evidence-based; that is, it must make use of the best techniques based on a literature search. From this perspective, measures shown to be highly valid and reliable for family assessment should be used. A second requirement is that assessment should be systems-oriented. In other words, problems should not be narrowly defined and measured in isolation from the family context in which the problems occur, although measures of individual family members can be used. We consider families from a systemic perspective, taking into account the multiple contexts within which they live, work, and interact.

A third requirement is that assessment should be based on multiple measures of client strengths and problems. *Triangulation* (different from the family dynamic discussed in Chapter 3) is a term that describes approaches to multiple measures. Triangulation encourages use of a three-prong measurement system for any client problem or strength: (1) client self-report, (2) client behavioral observation, and (3) external report or observation. Using this approach allows the family social worker to develop a fuller and more accurate view of what is going on with the family.

Fourth, the use of quantitative assessment allows for a better grasp of the extent of the family's problems. It also places family difficulties within the context of a larger population so they can be understood and compared. Valid and reliable instruments (discussed in more detail in this chapter) have been tested on "normal" and clinical populations. Through quantitative assessment, monitoring and evaluation of practice activities are ensured—an approach required in today's managed care environment. Measuring change in the family adds to professional accountability.

Additional benefits of quantitative assessment include the potential for improving treatment because of the ongoing monitoring of family social work practice, for contributing to the family research literature, and for giving feedback to the family social worker to increase skills, competence, and accountability.

EP 2.1.3a

SELECTING A MEASUREMENT INSTRUMENT

When selecting a measurement instrument, it is important that it be both *valid* and *reliable*. These terms are discussed in greater detail in the following sections. In *Measures for Clinical Practice*, Corcoran and Fischer (2007) provide information about the psychometric properties of the instruments included in their book. We offer some examples from their book in the Exercises in this chapter. By the end of this discussion, it is hoped that you will understand the concepts of reliability and validity and use this understanding to select the best instrument for your work with your families. Be prepared—the discussion is quite technical! However, this information is necessary for family social workers to make informed decisions in selecting a quantitative measuring instrument.

Empirically-based practice is an important component of professional social work. The growing recognition that the profession needs to be accountable has led to the development of measures to monitor and evaluate clinical practice (Corcoran & Fischer, 2007). The effectiveness of social work intervention is primarily determined by available instruments, and it is important to develop systematic approaches to measurement.

Many of the issues demanding the attention of social workers are abstract, making measurement a difficult exercise at times. The science of measurement has become an essential component in the development of a professional knowledge base and evaluation of clinical practice. Measurement involves the "process of linking abstract concepts to empirical indicators" (Carmines & Zeller, 1979, p. 10), or the "process of quantifying a variable" (i.e., assigning numbers to a variable). Quantitative measurement therefore involves assigning a number to something that someone is evaluating such as self-esteem, the quality of family relationships, or family conflict. By definition, measurement is often an empirical process of linking observable events (e.g., a family regularly having dinner together) with concepts that are theoretical but frequently not observable (e.g., healthy family functioning). Usually an instrument consists of a variety of items that can be scored and summed, resulting in a score for each family. As mentioned, the cornerstone of measurement is the establishment of reliability and validity. These terms are defined in the following sections.

Instruments should also be culturally sensitive. This means that the instruments selected can be appropriately used with a particular culture and that the concepts being measured are culturally sensitive. Sometimes in the development stage, instruments are tested with only one culture. Applying untested instruments uncritically to other cultures is problematic and will affect both the validity and reliability of the instrument. Moreover, the criteria measured in the particular instrument need to be able to capture the unique nuances of a culture. For instance, the Index of Family Relationships Scale (see Figure 9.8) has been tested on people with various cultural backgrounds so can be reliably used with diverse populations.

Standardized Measures

Standardized measures have been prepared and tested by experts in their areas. The testing is most useful when it has been done on populations similar to client families and when it best captures the problem being targeted. In selecting a measure to use with your clients, the reliability (accuracy) and validity (truth) of a measure are necessary considerations. Also, the types of questions asked are important because there are multiple ways to measure any problem or client characteristic. For instance, one family satisfaction scale may focus on behavioral interactions of family members whereas a different family satisfaction scale may measure family dynamics, communication, or overall family functioning. We recommend that the family social worker become familiar with a scale's questions, scoring, ease of completion, and so forth before getting a family member to take it. Take it yourself first to really learn about it!

A handbook containing multiple measures that may be useful for the family social worker is the two-volume set called *Measures for Clinical Practice: A Sourcebook* by Kevin Corcoran and Joel Fischer (2007). The book includes two volumes; one measures child and family issues, while the other measures individual issues. In these volumes, standardized tests can be found that measure many different types of client problems from both intrapersonal and interpersonal perspectives and that offer a good example of the range of scales available (Corcoran & Fischer, 2007). As mentioned previously, these measures are particularly useful when they have cutting scores or norms to which we can compare our clients' scores. Figure 9.8 (Index of Family Relationships—IFR) measures family relations; when computed, this index provides cutting scores. For example, the cutting score for the IFR is plus or minus 25. This indicates that anyone scoring above plus or minus 25 on the measure probably has a significant problem with family issues. A score lower than plus or minus 25 indicates little chance of a clinically significant problem with family.

EP 2.1.3a

QUALITIES OF A GOOD INSTRUMENT: RELIABILITY AND VALIDITY

We mentioned reliability (accuracy) and validity (truth) in the previous section of this chapter. We will now describe these in more detail.

Reliability

A good instrument is one that produces stable results and minimizes error. Reliability is concerned with the "extent to which an experiment, test, or any measuring procedure yields the same results on repeated trials" (Carmines & Zeller, 1979, p. 11). Thus, the consistency and stability of a measurement over time are the focus in the determination of reliability. The measurement precision and consistency of reliability lend themselves more easily to mathematical calculations than do measures of validity. Although it is virtually impossible to completely eliminate error, the aim of attaining reliable measures is to eliminate as much error as possible. Adequate measures that tend toward consistency from one measurement occasion to another indicate high reliability. Reliability of a test score is the freedom of the test from errors of measurement and is essentially a theory of error. A reliable instrument yields a small amount of error since reliability is based on the amount of error that is contained in the observed scores. The resultant score is known as the reliability coefficient. If the reliability coefficient is large, the instrument is considered reliable, whereas smaller coefficients are indicative of less reliability.

Test construction theory evolved primarily from classical test theory, a large part of which emphasizes the elimination of error (Pedhazur & Pedhazur, 1991) and is expressed by the equation $O = T + E$, where O stands for the observed score, which consists of T, the true score, plus E, some type of error. While it is virtually impossible to obtain absolute true scores, a good measurement instrument eliminates error as much as possible. Measurement error may be either systematic or random or both. Good measurement practices dictate the elimination of both types of error. True scores are hypothetical, unobservable quantities that cannot be directly measured. Any particular observed score will not be identical to its real score because of noise (the interference of some factor). It is assumed that the fluctuations due to the various occurrences of errors are random and cancel each other out with a mean of zero.

All measurement devices contain both random (unsystematic) and nonrandom (systematic) measurement error. An instrument is reliable when repeated measurements are not influenced by random error. Random error is caused by factors that randomly affect measurement of the variable. Since random error is unsystematic, the errors are thought to cancel each other out. Random error includes all those chance factors that confound measurement, and it may evolve from several sources such as clerical mistakes, interviewer fatigue, and the respondent's failure to follow instructions. Reliability is inversely related to the amount of random error present in the measurement process. By comparison, nonrandom error systematically biases the results of measurement and is a problem for the determination of validity because such error prevents indicators from representing the theoretical concept under study (Carmines & Zeller, 1979). Validity therefore depends on the extent of nonrandom error present in the measurement process.

The reliability of a measure varies between the values of 0 and 1. Thus, reliability can easily be expressed in terms of the variances of true scores and random scores. Some disagreement exists regarding the range of acceptability of a reliability coefficient (Pedhazur & Pedhazur, 1991). However, a reliability coefficient of .60 or greater is generally acceptable for science, whereas .80 or greater is advocated for clinical practice (Corcoran & Fischer, 2007). For the purposes of interpretation, a score of .80 indicates that 80 percent of the variance of observed scores is systematic (Pedhazur & Pedhazur, 1991, p. 86) while 1–.80 refers to the proportion of variance due to random errors. The difference in acceptability levels between science and clinical practice stems from the fact that science can average out errors by using large samples.

The four basic methods for estimating reliability of empirical measurement include (1) the test-retest method, (2) the alternative form method, (3) the split-halves method, and (4) the internal consistency method.

Test-Retest Method In the test-retest method, the same group is measured twice using the same instrument. Reliability is computed as the correlation between a set of scores obtained by a single scale on two separate occasions (Hudson, 1982). This procedure is based on the assumption that the underlying observable scores are constant (i.e., that there has been no change in scores from time 1 to time 2).

The lower the correlation, the greater the random error of measurement. (Correlations range between 0 and 1.) This method attempts to capture the stability of a device over time. Corcoran and Fischer (2007) suggest that a coefficient value of .69 is acceptable if the tests are conducted one month apart and a coefficient of .80 is acceptable for shorter periods between testing.

Equivalent Form, Alternative Form, or Parallel Form Method   This procedure involves the administration of an alternative form of the same test designed to measure the same construct. It reflects reliability to the extent to which the two forms used are a measure of the same attribute. The correlation (again, varying between 0 and 1) between the two parallel forms serves as the estimate of reliability of either. It is a direct estimate of the alternative form of reliability that would be attained if an equally good alternative form of a particular scale were available.

Carmines and Zeller (1979) suggest that the parallel form method is superior to the test-retest estimate, although its fundamental flaw is that the reliability may be contaminated by true change, which may become indistinguishable from unreliability. This is particularly true if the two measures are taken over wide spans of time. Additionally, the use of parallel forms may be a problem in that it may be difficult to construct or obtain another instrument that measures exactly the same concept.

Again, the range of acceptable coefficient values for this approach to validity varies, but Corcoran and Fischer (2007) recommend at least a coefficient of .80.

The Split-Halves Method   This approach to estimating reliability involves splitting the scale into two parts and examining the correlation between them. The split-halves method is conducted on a single occasion, thereby eliminating some of the problems involved in both the parallel and test-retest methods. It is a convenient form of testing for reliability and is based on the fundamental assumptions of classical test theory, that is, that the traits measured are constant and the errors are random. In other words, the errors are equal to zero.

In this method of testing, the total set of items is divided in half and the scores on the halves are correlated to produce an estimate of reliability. Each half of the test is correlated with the other rather than with the total score. A statistical correction for length is introduced (Spearman-Brown prophecy formula) to enable the researcher to determine reliability with the total test. A corrected reliability coefficient is necessary because the reliability of a test increases as the number of items increases, provided that the average correlation between items does not change (Norusis, 1990).

Internal Consistency   An instrument has internal consistency if the items are consistent with one another and are judged to measure the same variable (Corcoran & Fischer, 2007). Internal consistency is garnered usually from a single test administration, and Cronbach's alpha is a commonly used estimate of reliability. Alpha is based on the internal consistency of a test. The values of Cronbach's alpha depend on both the length of the test and the correlation of the items in the test. Theoretically, it is possible to have a large reliability coefficient even when the average inter-item correlation is small, provided the number of items in the scale is large enough. Acceptable values for Cronbach's alpha vary, and some suggest that it needs to be .80 or more for widely used scales (Carmines & Zeller, 1979; Corcoran & Fischer, 2007).

For measures with dichotomous (e.g., yes or no responses) rather than ordinal (based on order, such as 1 = strongly disagree, 2 = disagree, 3 = neither agree nor disagree, 4 = agree, 5 = strongly agree) items, Kuder-Richardsons Formula 20 is the preferred statistic to measure internal consistency. In this method, dichotomous items are dummy coded (e.g., 0 = no and 1 = yes) depending on whether the respondent has the characteristic under study. The KR-20 is a special case of alpha that is interpreted the same way as alpha. Ordinal or continuous variables should not be collapsed to dichotomous variables since valuable information is lost in the process.

Validity

You cannot have a valid instrument unless the instrument is reliable. Validity reflects the extent to which any measuring instrument measures what it is designed to measure (Corcoran & Fischer, 2007; Carmines & Zeller, 1979). There are not different types of validity. Rather, there are different approaches to ascertaining validity. Thus, the following classification system of validity does not imply a set of mutually exclusive and exhaustive categories, much less different types of validity; the methods are interrelated facets describing the same idea. *Validation* refers to inferences made on the basis of scores obtained on a measure. One therefore validates not the measuring instrument itself but the measuring instrument in relation to the purpose for which it is being used (Carmines & Zeller, 1979). Thus, an instrument may be valid for measuring one kind of phenomenon but invalid for assessing another.

Validity is predicated on two expectations: that it measures the concept in question and that the concept is measured accurately (Bostwick & Kyte, 1988). Approaches to validity are applicable both in the measurement context and the research design context. As with reliability, validity is a matter of magnitude and there are often shades of gray. Although reliability is necessary for validity, the converse does not hold. Additionally, validity is determined or limited by its reliability, and we thus need to guard existing validity by protecting reliabilities. The upper limit of the validity of any scale is established as the square root of its reliability (Hudson, 1982). The several approaches to validity include (1) content, (2) criterion-related, (3) construct, and (4) factorial.

Content Validity This approach to validity refers to a domain of content, covering relevant and sufficient content to capture the content of the concept. Therefore, the content of the measure must be consistent with the definition of the construct (Pedhazur & Pedhazur, 1991, p. 80) and contain an adequate sample of items that represent the concept. It therefore needs to completely include all the components that are thought to represent the content in a way that can be measured. Items must reflect the meaning associated with each dimension of the concept.

Unfortunately, in the social sciences there is often widespread disagreement regarding the domain, and the determination of content validity becomes somewhat dependent on subjective judgment and is vulnerable to error. Since it is virtually impossible to create a total list of items to represent different measures of a single construct, a sample of items is therefore used. Overall, the total domain should be specified and then items should be sampled from the domain and put into a testable form. At the beginning of deciding which items to include, too many items are preferable to too few, and inadequate items can be eliminated from the instrument at a later date.

Content validity is frequently accomplished through critical thinking combined with the consensus of experts in the field, aiming for a high degree of consensus. A measure that is not content valid is unlikely to survive other tests of validity. Concepts in the social sciences are usually abstract, making it difficult to comprehensively capture the content.

EXERCISE 9.1   Content Items

Select one of the following concepts, and make a list of possible content items that best describe it:

Healthy family functioning

Good mothering

Good fathering

Sibling rivalry

Triangulation

Severity of physical abuse

Now share your list with the rest of the class.

Face validity   This is considered the weakest approach to determining validity; it becomes a matter of judgment based on the *appearance* of the idea the instrument is designed to measure. An underlying problem in determining face validity is that there is often little consensus about the definition of the concept to be measured. Furthermore, the concept may be a multidimensional one consisting of several subconcepts, for which the measure becomes lengthy and complex. Although face validity may be important to the respondents and lack of it may adversely affect responses, it becomes a necessary but not sufficient form of validity.

Criterion-Related Validity   The criterion-related validity approach involves comparing scores with external criteria that have been previously validated and shown to be reliable. This approach "is at issue when the purpose is to use an instrument to estimate some important form of behavior that is external to the measuring instrument itself, the latter being referred to as the criterion" (Nunnally, 1978, p. 87). This method is empirically based. The degree of criterion-related validity depends on the extent of correspondence between the test and event or criterion. Validity coefficients are usually much smaller than their theoretical upper limit, and "good" coefficients range from .40 to .60 (Hudson, 1982).

Criterion-related validity is further subdivided into two categories: *concurrent* and *predictive*. Concurrent validity is useful for diagnostic purposes in the here and now, whereas predictive validity is concerned with the prediction of a criterion (Anastasi, 1988). Predictive validity involves the ability of an instrument to measure (predict) a future event. It entails administering the instrument to relevant subjects and then correlating the results with a criterion at some future date to obtain the validity coefficient. It is concerned with how successfully the instrument can make a prediction, regardless of whether it is possible to explain the process leading to the phenomenon that is being predicted (Pedhazur & Pedhazur, 1991, p. 32). Statistics can be used to predict the criterion out of which a cutting score (e.g., a score that demarcates the existence of a problem) emerges. Cutting scores are imperfect indicators due to measurement error. For example, some instruments in the Clinical Measurement Package (CMP) (Hudson, 1982) have a Standard Error of Measurement of about 5, making the cutting score of 30 open to interpretation.

Concurrent validity correlates the test scores with the *criterion* scores at the same time. It distinguishes between one group that displays the criterion being measured and another group that does not. Concurrent validity is determined by correlating a measure and the criterion at the same point in time (Carmines & Zeller, 1990) and requires independent evidence of the extent to which the measurement of the criterion is valid. In the known groups method, groups are selected and subdivided on the basis of whether they have the same trait, attribute, and so on under consideration. On the basis of a comparison of the two cumulative frequency distributions, cutting scores are determined that minimize both false negatives and false positives. A valid instrument will detect statistically significant differences between the two groups.

Construct Validity This approach to validity is often considered the strongest validation procedure and the most useful. It refers to the degree to which an instrument measures the construct or trait that it was designed to measure (Allen & Yen, 1979). The process of construct validation is driven by theory and involves specification of the theoretical relationship between the concepts, determination of the empirical relationship between concepts, and then the interpretation of the empirical evidence. Kerlinger (1979) suggests that construct validity is central to validity. It is "concerned with the extent to which a particular measure relates to other measures consistent with theoretically derived hypotheses concerning the concepts (or constructs) that are being measured" (Carmines & Zeller, 1979, p. 23). It thus involves both the validation of the instrument and of the underlying theory (Bostwick & Kyte, 1988). This is often accomplished by correlating a scale device with another piece of evidence to obtain support for the construct.

Construct validation requires a consistent pattern of findings from different researchers using a variety of theoretical structures. When the process yields negative evidence, the theory may be flawed and the testing procedure may either lack construct validity or reliability. Multiple indicators should ideally yield results that are consistent, of the same direction, and of similar strengths. Testing hypotheses generated by construct validation can involve either convergent or discriminant validation. Some authors subsume factor validity under construct validity, while others view it as a distinct category.

1. If two independent measures of the criterion under study produce similar results, a measure is deemed to possess *convergent* validity. "Convergent validity is demonstrated by high correlations between scores on a test measuring the same trait by different methods" (Nunnally, 1978, p. 111). For example, if a newly constructed instrument designed to measure healthy family functioning yielded similar results to those of previously validated instruments designed to measure healthy family functioning, the new instrument could be said to possess convergent validity.

2. If the construct is independent of other unrelated constructs, it is considered to possess *discriminant* validity. It therefore positively correlates with other measures that have been validated but does not correlate with measures the instrument is not intended to measure. Using the preceding example, the newly constructed instrument to measure healthy family functioning may be uncorrelated to a measure designed to measure family wealth and therefore is said to possess discriminant validity.

Factorial Validity   The factor composition of measures plays a part in the aforementioned approaches to validity. Factor analysis (an advanced statistic tool) can be used to determine internal consistency and is based on the assumption that the items in the scale are parallel and measure a phenomenon equally. When items measure a single phenomenon unequally or when items measure more than one concept equally or unequally, then factor analysis is a useful tool. Factor loadings (results of the statistic) are used to determine the extent to which each item is correlated with each factor. Items from other scales can also be factored together to determine if each item measures the construct under examination or another construct. A factorially valid measure will exhibit high correlations with similar measures of the construct and low correlations with unrelated items.

EXERCISE 9.2   Selecting an Instrument

The following are two excerpts from *Measures for Clinical Practice* (Corcoran & Fischer, 2007) describing two separate instruments. Using the information provided at the beginning of this chapter, select the instrument with the best psychometric properties. You might want to work in groups for this exercise.

1. *FACES III is a 20-item instrument designed to measure two main dimensions of family functioning: cohesion and adaptability. Reliability: FACES III has only fair internal consistency, with an overall alpha of .8 for the total instrument, .77 for cohesion, and .62 for adaptability. Test-retest data are not available, but for FACES-II there was a four- to five-week test-retest correlation of .83 for cohesion and .80 for adaptability. Validity: FACES-III appears to have good face validity, but data are not available demonstrating other types of validity. On the other hand, a number of studies have shown FACES-II to have fair known-groups validity in being able to discriminate among extreme, mid-range, and unbalanced families in several problem categories. A good deal of research is being*

conducted on FACES-III, which might generate more information on validity. (Corcoran & Fischer, 2007)

2. *Family Assessment Device:* The FAD is a 60-item questionnaire designed to evaluate family functioning according to the McMaster Model.... It identifies six dimensions of family functioning: problem solving, communication, roles, affective responsiveness, affective involvement, and behavior control. *Reliability:* The FAD demonstrates fairly good internal consistency, with alphas for the subscales ranging from .72 to .92. No reliability figures are reported for the overall measure; test-retest reliability data are not available. *Validity:* When the general functioning subscale is removed from the analysis, the six other subscales appear to be relatively independent. The FAD demonstrates some degree of concurrent and predictive validity.

 In a separate study ... the FAS was moderately correlated with the Lock-Wallace Marital Satisfaction Scale and showed a fair ability to predict scores on the Philadelphia Geriatric Morale Scale. Further, the FAD has good known-groups validity, with all seven subscales significantly distinguishing between individuals from clinical families and those from nonclinical families. (Corcoran & Fischer, 2007, pp. 250–251)

EXERCISE 9.3 Family Issue Measure

Select a specific family issue. Then locate a family instrument designed to measure this issue. What are its psychometric properties? How well do you think the instrument measures what you would like to measure?

FRAMEWORKS FOR INCORPORATING QUANTITATIVE MEASUREMENT

Two frameworks for incorporating quantitative measurement into the family social work practice are presented here. They include case-level design and goal attainment scaling.

Case-Level Design

Case-level design, also known as single-subject design, provides a framework for setting up a quantitative measurement system to monitor and evaluate family social work practice and family programs. In our discussion, this design can be used to study an individual or a family. Either the individual or the family is considered the case. This approach to monitoring and evaluating practice is designed for social workers working in direct practice and gives the social worker information about how well the family work is progressing. If it is not progressing well, the family social worker might want to change the intervention to include something more effective. Case-level designs can also be used to combine the data from all the clients in a program to see how effective the program is in achieving its goals (Grinnell, Williams, & Unrau, 2009). A, B, C, and D are the usual designs.

 Here we provide you with a summary of the different designs and indicate what the various letters entail in terms of the case-level designs.

A design   A baseline of the family's or individual's problem is established. Baseline data is collected before intervention starts. Some researchers suggest collecting between three and seven data measurements before beginning intervention (Grinnell, Williams, & Unrau, 2009). An A design asks (1) if the problem exists at different levels over time, and (2) if the problem is changing by itself (p. 124). However, in terms of family intervention, family social workers are often called into crisis situations, making it difficult and at times unethical not to intervene.

B design   This design addresses the question of whether the problem is changing as a result of the family intervention (Grinnell, Williams, & Unrau, 2009). The problem is measured with a standardized instrument at the beginning of treatment, and the family social worker administers the same instrument at regular intervals during intervention. In this type of design, the family social worker does not know whether the change occurs as a result of the family intervention or whether the intervention is producing the changes.

AB design   This design incorporates a baseline phase with a B phase. Again, ethical considerations and urgency will determine whether the social worker will incorporate a baseline (A) phase in the intervention.

BB design   In a BB design, the family social worker administers an intervention and uses an instrument as described above, but at some point during intervention (particularly when the family social worker decides that the intervention is not working), an adaptation of the B intervention is attempted to see if the new intervention is creating change.

BC design   The BC design continues as above, but rather than just tweaking the intervention, the family social worker incorporates an entirely new intervention (C) that is different from the B intervention. In a BC design, the family social worker cannot attribute change to the C intervention since she or he does not know if it was caused by a delayed reaction to the B intervention, whether it was caused by how B and C worked in tandem, or whether C alone was the catalyst for change.

ABC design   This design is similar to the previous BC design, but incorporates a baseline phase. You can create an ABCD design by adding yet another new type of intervention.

EXERCISE 9.4   Frameworks for Assessment

How would you suggest to an agency director that a single-subject framework be employed? Next, describe how a goal attainment scaling framework could be used.

The following seven steps are adapted from Bloom, Fischer, and Orme (2009):

Step 1. Measure the problem. During this step, the family social worker is concerned with beginning the relationship with the family, gaining entry into the system, establishing rapport, and beginning assessment, including collecting data. At this step, the data collection may be qualitative (see Chapter 8).

Qualitative tools such as genograms or ecomaps may help to engage the family while also helping the family social worker to view the range of the family's problems and strengths. A clear, measurable problem needs to be defined.

Step 2. Perform repeated measures over the course of assessment and treatment. Step 2 moves into the use of quantitative measurement to further capture information about specific client problems and strengths. A specific measurement instrument to measure the targets of the intervention is identified, and these measures will be used consistently over the course of the intervention. For example, if the client is depressed, a parent-child relationship scale may be used on a weekly basis to monitor the client's progress during the intervention.

Step 3. Decide on the unique design. The various types of designs were discussed above. A common single-subject design is the AB design, in which A refers to the baseline phase of treatment and B refers to the intervention phase. The A phase of intervention is the period before treatment starts. It is the baseline phase when quantitative information is collected before the intervention. This data can then be compared with the data collected regularly from the intervention phase during the administration of the intervention.

Step 4. Collect baseline data. Step four involves collecting baseline data during the initial assessment meetings. The data is then graphed as in Figure 9.1. Note that in Figure 9.1, the baseline data (A phase) was collected for three weeks prior to beginning the intervention (B phase). The intervention should be clearly defined so that the family social worker can learn what treatments work with specific clients as she builds up her repertoire of graphs from various families. The family social worker then continues collecting data after the baseline phase is over and intervention begins.

Step 5. Analyze the data. Simple analysis of the data may be done by "eyeballing" it. For example, what is the trend and slope of the data in both phases? Note that in Figure 9.1, the slope and trend of the baseline data are in an upward direction. In the case of the Beck Depression Inventory (BDI) captured in Figure 9.1, higher scores indicate more significant levels of depression; by examining the slope and trend of the data during the intervention, we see that the scores are improving as they move downward to a non-clinically significant

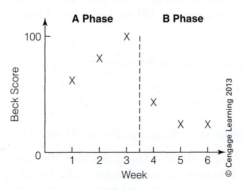

FIGURE 9.1 | Single-Subject AB Design Graph

level. The BDI is a standardized measure with cutting scores and norms. These refer to scores that can be used for comparison with our clients' scores. Using these, we can look at the specific score obtained on the test and determine whether our client is depressed by comparing with scores from clinical populations. This is one of the advantages of using *standardized* tests that have such comparison information.

In some cases, such as when using direct behavioral observations and worker-constructed measures, we do not have comparison scores. Statistical procedures are available to compare baseline scores with intervention scores. These include the Shewhart chart, the celeration line, and the t-test. For more information about these, see Bloom, Fischer, and Orme (2009).

Step 6. Perform follow-up measurement. Follow-up is an important phase of family social work practice. Tracking clients to keep up with their whereabouts can be challenging. It is important, however, especially when families are troubled and likely to need continuing services from the family social worker and the agency. Many agencies find it useful to continue to monitor the families after the services have ended to ensure continuing positive progress and maintenance of the changes from family intervention. Effective follow-up can ensure that families do not fall into old patterns that necessitate more intensive services later on. Tracking is easier when mechanisms for tracking are built into the assessment from the beginning. Some strategies include getting names, addresses, and phone numbers of extended family members or friends of the family in treatment in the initial meetings. It is important to get the names of those with whom the family will keep in touch in the event that they move away. Another strategy is for the person doing the assessment and treatment to also be the tracker since rapport has been built and the family will likely respond to a family social worker with whom they have a warm relationship.

Step 7. Present the results. Finally, we have discussed how the results of single-subject data collection are valuable to the client and to the family social worker. Others who may be interested in this data are supervisors, community members, and funding sources. The data can also be used for the larger purpose of program evaluation and applying for funding, particularly when the data from multiple families are aggregated to capture program effectiveness.

If we used a single case design to measure a family's issues with their relationships, we might use the Index of Family Relationships—IFR (see Figure 9.8)—mentioned earlier. The IFR could be administered to all family members so that their scores could be compared. You might expect to see one family member who is more distressed than the others; or perhaps they are all unhappy with their family relationships. Using a single-subject design methodology would then require that all members fill out the measure on a regular basis across the course of treatment in order to monitor progress for all family members. Since the IFR has a cutting score, it is easy to see which family members are significantly distressed. The IFR also will give some guidance to the family social worker as to when the family is ready to terminate.

Goal Attainment Scaling (GAS)

Another way of evaluating your practice is to use goal attainment scaling. In goal attainment scaling the family social worker, in collaboration with the family, describes areas of change along with identifying the range of possible outcomes, ranging from the most unfavorable outcome to the most favorable outcome (Jordan, Franklin, & Corcoran, 2005). The advantage of GAS is that areas of focus can be completely individualized for the particular family once the goal has been selected. The least favorable outcome is rated as minus 2, while the most favorable outcome is given a score of plus 2. Figure 9.2 shows a completed GAS. The figure below is a blank form for three possible client problems. For example, the first column might target parent-child arguing, the second column might target a parent seeking employment, and the third column might target parents sitting down for 30 minutes to discuss the day's events.

Goal attainment scaling has several benefits. First, goals are individualized for each unique family and can be altered if needed. The client family participates in goal setting and through this develops a concrete understanding of what possible outcomes might look like and what is required of them. It is important to remember, however, not to select an overwhelming number of goals for the family. Goals also need to be realistic and manageable based on time and abilities.

Setting up a GAS involves the four steps listed below:

1. Identifying the prioritizing goals to be attained.
2. Identifying possible outcomes for each selected goal. Outcomes need to be specific and identified as a specific observable behavior. (The most likely outcome is listed as 0; higher levels of success would be either +1 or +2. Similarly, lower levels of success are denoted by either −1 or −2.)
3. Sitting down with the family to score the scale every session.
4. Discussing what needs to happen further to improve the score, if necessary, or, alternatively, what needs to happen to keep the positive changes going.

See the case example at the end of this chapter for an example of using goal attainment scaling with a teenager who is doing poorly in school and exhibiting suicidal thoughts and attempts at hurting herself. You will see that Figure 9.3 is a measure of this girl's treatment goals: (1) to improve school attendance and performance, and (2) to reduce suicidal thoughts and attempts.

EP 2.1.3b

Goal Attainment Scaling for

Levels of Predicted Attainment	Scale 1 (Wt.)	Scale 2 (Wt.)	Scale 3 (Wt.)
−2 Much less than expected outcome	1 2 3 4 5 6 7 8	1 2 3 4 5 6 7 8	1 2 3 4 5 6 7 8
−1 Less than expected outcome	1 2 3 4 5 6 7 8	1 2 3 4 5 6 7 8	1 2 3 4 5 6 7 8
0 Expected outcome	1 2 3 4 5 6 7 8	1 2 3 4 5 6 7 8	1 2 3 4 5 6 7 8
+1 More than expected outcome	1 2 3 4 5 6 7 8	1 2 3 4 5 6 7 8	1 2 3 4 5 6 7 8
+2 Much more than expected outcome	1 2 3 4 5 6 7 8	1 2 3 4 5 6 7 8	1 2 3 4 5 6 7 8

FIGURE 9.2 Example of a Blank GAS Form for Three Identified Problems

Goals: To attend classes and to rid self of suicidal thoughts/attempts. Check whether or not the scale has been mutually negotiated between client and CIC interviewers.

Yes _____ No _____

SCALE HEADINGS AND SCALE WEIGHTS

SCALE ATTAINMENT LEVEL	SCALE 1: EDUCATION (W1 = 20)	SCALE 2: SUICIDE (W2 = 30)
a. Most unfavorable treatment outcome thought likely (−2)	Patient has made no attempt to enroll in high school X	Patient has committed suicide
b. Less expected success w/treatment (−1)	Patient has enrolled in high school, but at time of follow-up has dropped out	Patient has acted on at least one suicidal impulse since her first contact w/CIC, attempt(s) unsuccessful
c. Expected level of treatment success (0)	Patient has enrolled and is in school at follow-up, but is attending class sporadically (misses an average of more than a third of her class during a week)	Patient reports she has had at least 4 suicidal impulses since her first contact with the CIC but has not acted on any of them
d. More than expected success w/treatment (+1)	Patient has enrolled, is in school at follow-up, and is attending classes consistently but has no vocational goal*	
e. Best anticipated success w/treatment (+2)	Patient has enrolled, is in school at follow-up, is attending classes consistently, and has some vocational goal	Patient reports she has had no suicidal impulses since her first contact with CIC

X = level at intake
* = level at follow-up

FIGURE 9.3 | Goal Attainment Scale

From: Reid, W., & Smith, A. (1981). *Research in social work.* New York: Columbia University Press.

MEASUREMENT INSTRUMENTS

The section on single-subject design discussed how to evaluate work with families using quantitative assessment. Types of quantified measures are presented in this section. These include client self-anchored and rating scales, direct behavioral observation, and standardized measures. Other ways of quantifying client data also are presented. This section is from Franklin and Corcoran (2007).

Self-Anchored and Self-Monitoring Instruments

Self-anchored and self-monitoring instruments are the most common type of quantitative measure used in practice. These are generally very high in validity because they are designed for the specific client or family and take into account their unique issues. The client and the family social worker usually design these instruments together. They may be a combination of qualitative and quantitative techniques. Figure 9.3 is an example of this. Note the combination of anger diary (qualitative) and rating scale (quantitative) in Figure 9.4. In this measure, the client takes both home and fills them out as situations emerge. An example of a quantitative question is "How many arguments have you had this week?" The client provides a discrete number. A qualitative question from the diary is, "Which intervention steps did you use?" The clients are asked to narrate in their own words what happened when they had an argument. Adding this qualitative dimension to quantitative measurement gives the family social worker more information to know what went right and what went wrong about the treatment. Further refinements or adjustments can then be made. Note that we can assign several family members to complete an anger diary, thereby giving us the triangulated system we discussed earlier in this chapter.

Name _____   Date _____

How many arguments this week? _____

Rate (1–10) how angry you were? _____

What were your internal signals?

_____

Which of the intervention steps did you use?

_____

What happened afterwards?

_____

FIGURE 9.4 | Anger Diary and Rating Scale

From: Jordan and Franklin (2003). *Clinical assessment for social workers: Qualitative and quantitative methods.* Chicago: Lyceum.

EXERCISE 9.5 Measurement Instruments

Think of a client family you have worked with or might work with in the future. Design a self-anchored scale to measure one of its problems. Can the same problem be measured by direct behavioral observation? How would you, for example, record the data of a client role-play?

Do a literature search for standardized measures that might be used to measure the same client problem.

Figure 9.5 is an example of a self-anchored scale designed by the family social worker and the client together. This self-anchored scale measures depression, but almost anything can be measured in this simple way (e.g., client resistance to treatment). Note that the self-anchored scale usually has 7 points and is anchored on both the high and low end of the scale. These anchors are developed from the client's unique responses to depression, in the case of Figure 9.5. Other clients would have different anchors. For another self-anchored scale, see Figure 9.6, which measures conflict avoidance. Note that many client issues or problems might be measured in this simple way. The rater could be the client, a family member, the family social worker, or some other participant (e.g., school teacher or other professional).

Direct Behavioral Observation

Figure 9.7 is an example of a chart for recording information obtained from direct behavioral observation. In other words, the family social worker, in discussion with

---

Instructions: Circle the number that applies every day before 8 A.M.

| 1 | 2 | 3 | 4 | 5 | 6 | 7 |

Energetic,   Tired, no energy

feel alive   feel like lying down

and ready to go to work   and never getting up

FIGURE 9.5 | Self-Anchored Scale for Depression

From: Jordan and Franklin (2003). *Clinical assessment for social workers: Quantitative and qualitative methods.* Chicago: Lyceum.

Inadequate 1 2 3 4 5 6 7 8 9 10 Adequate

Changes the subject,   Stays on topic,

Leaves the room,   Engages in

Refuses to talk about issues   conversation about

                                                              conflictual issues

---

FIGURE 9.6 | Conflict Avoidance Self-Anchored Scale

From: Jordan and Franklin (2003). *Clinical assessment for social workers: Qualitative and quantitative methods.* Chicago: Lyceum.

COUPLE'S RATING SCALE TO RATE COMMUNICATION ROLE-PLAY

Inadequate 1   2   3   4   5   6   7   8   9   10   Adequate

- Speak for self
- Send I messages
- Use a stop action
- Ask for feedback
- Listen
- Summarize
- Validate
- Ask open questions
- Check out

FIGURE 9.7 | Behavioral Observation Rating Scale

the parents and target child, broke down the steps involved in completing homework, and then the parents and child jointly filled in the form every evening after the homework was completed. The scale in Figure 9.7 itemizes the behaviors necessary for completing the daily homework. The parents observed the child and rated each of the elements on the scale, discussing with the child what happened to achieve each score. These types of rating scales for direct observation are easily made, especially if the elements of the intervention are easily broken down or the goals easily operationalized. Other aspects of family members' behavior, for example, child behavior problems, may also be observed and documented in this way. The family social worker may observe the child in a classroom and count the number of times that the child gets out of his or her seat, talks out of turn, and so on. Teachers are sometimes good adjuncts to treatment and can record this information for the family social worker. Figure 9.8 is the IFR mentioned previously in this chapter.

Other Quantified Measures

Other ways of quantifying clients' problems and strengths include behavioral by-products and psychophysiological measures. Behavioral by-products are material symbols of the problem. For example, a client trying to quit smoking might count his cigarette butts in the ashtray. In the instance of a child who gets in trouble in school, a behavioral by-product might include the number of times a parent is called for behavioral difficulties.

EP 2.1.10e

USING MEASUREMENT TO LINK ASSESSMENT AND INTERVENTION

This section provides guidelines for assessing when clients are ready to move from the assessment phase to intervention. It is taken from Jordan and Franklin (2011).

This questionnaire is designed to measure the way you feel about your family as a whole. It is not a test, so there are no right or wrong answers. Answer each item as carefully and as accurately as you can by placing a number beside each one as follows:

1 = none of the time

2 = very rarely

3 = a little of the time

4 = some of the time

5 = a good part of the time

1. ____ The members of my family really care about each other.

2. ____ I think my family is terrific.

3. ____ My family gets on my nerves.

4. ____ I really enjoy my family.

5. ____ I can really depend on my family.

6. ____ I really do not care to be around my family.

7. ____ I wish I was not part of this family.

8. ____ I get along well with my family.

9. ____ Members of my family argue too much.

10. ____ There is no sense of closeness in my family.

11. ____ I feel like a stranger in my family.

12. ____ My family does not understand me.

13. ____ There is too much hatred in my family.

14. ____ Members of my family are really good to one another.

15. ____ My family is well respected by those who know us.

16. ____ There seems to be a lot of friction in my family.

17. ____ There is a lot of love in my family.

18. ____ Members of my family get along well together.

19. ____ Life in my family is generally unpleasant.

20. ____ My family is a great joy to me.

21. ____ I feel proud of my family.

22. ____ Other families seem to get along better than ours.

23. ____ My family is a real source of comfort to me.

24. ____ I feel left out of my family.

25. ____ My family is an unhappy one.

Copyright © 1992, Walter W. Hudson

1, 2, 4, 5, 8, 14, 15, 17, 18, 20, 21, 23

FIGURE 9.8 | Standardized Measure: Index of Family Relationships (IFR)

From: W. Hudson in Jordan and Franklin (2003). *Clinical assessment for social workers: Qualitative and quantitative methods.* Chicago: Lyceum.

Client Readiness for Intervention

It is important *not* to push the client toward intervention if she or he is not ready. This is a surefire way to ensure failure! Following are ways of telling if clients are ready to move forward in the family social work process. As discussed in Chapter 5 clients fall along a continuum in their readiness to make changes in their lives. We have mentioned several times throughout this book that clients need to be partners in the family social work process.

> *Client indicators:* An important question to ask is, "Has the family social worker established rapport with the family"? Practitioner ability to influence the client in a positive direction is an important indicator for success of the intervention.
>
> *Data collection:* It is important that the family social worker completely understand the client's problems and strengths. The quantitative and qualitative data collection is critical.
>
> *Agency/social worker variables:* Another key consideration is whether the agency or the family social worker can provide the intervention that the client requires. If not, referral should be considered.

EP 2.1.3a

EXERCISE 9.6   Linking Assessment to Intervention

Describe some of the client and agency variables that you might use at your agency to select an intervention.

Make up a treatment plan for problems that one of your clients is likely to experience.

TREATMENT PLANNING

Treatment planning involves defining measurable goals, objectives, and outcomes, as well as evidence-based treatments known to be effective with specific client problems and populations. Jordan and Franklin (2011) detail five steps involved in the treatment planning process:

> **Step 1. Problem selection.** Problem selection involves understanding the problem from both a qualitative and a quantitative perspective, taking into account the context within which the family lives and the family's definition or understanding of the problem.
>
> **Step 2. Problem definition.** Quantitative methods in particular help to define and operationalize problems so that they can be measured and tracked.
>
> **Step 3. Goal development.** The goal statement is a broadly stated description of what successful outcome is expected. There should be a goal statement for each problem. Goals may be long-term expectations.
>
> **Step 4. Objective Construction.** Objectives are the measurable steps that must occur for the goals to be met. Each goal should have at least two objectives. Objectives are operationalized in measurable terms. Target dates may be assigned to each objective.

Problem: Behavior problems

Definitions: Distractibility, inattentiveness, angry outbursts, and occasional aggression

Goals: To improve attentiveness at home and at school

To eliminate angry outbursts

Objectives:	Interventions:
1. Parents and teachers learn how to help Anthony stay on task.	1. Teach parents and teachers develop a reward system for Anthony's staying on task.
2. Anthony learns to control anger.	1. Teach Anthony anger management.

Diagnosis: 314.01 Attention-Deficit/Hyperactivity Disorder, Combined Type

---

FIGURE 9.9 | Example Treatment Plan

From: Jordan and Franklin (2003). *Clinical assessment for social workers: Qualitative and quantitative methods.* Chicago: Lyceum.

Step 5. Intervention creation. Interventions should be matched with each objective. Interventions are selected on the basis of the family worker's skill and the family's need; however, the trend is toward brief, evidence-based methods that have proven efficacy for specific individuals, families, or problems. Also, manualized interventions and treatment planners are recommended. Figure 9.9 gives an example of a treatment plan.

EP 2.1.3a

CASE 9.1 | Quantitative Assessment

Sharon, age 14, her mother, Joy, and stepfather, Otto, were reported to Child Protective Services by Sharon's school. According to her teacher, Sharon has been playing hooky at least once a week and her grades have dropped from an A average to a C level this semester. Sharon also confided to her teacher that she was having suicidal thoughts and had even cut on herself once. At the home visit, the family social worker found that Joy and Otto are at a loss to know what to do about Sharon's behavior. Joy said that Sharon "had never acted this way before." Otto, the stepfather, is a new entry to the family, and Sharon's problems started when Joy and Otto married about four months ago, according to Joy. Otto said that he had decided Sharon needed a "firm hand" and that Joy is "too easy" on her. His disciplinary techniques are not working, as the parents reported that Sharon is misbehaving at home in addition to her school problems. They gave an example of Sharon jumping out of a second-story window to stay out all night at a rock concert with friends.

The family social worker recommended that the parents make a contract with Sharon according to which appropriate behavior (staying at school and maintaining at least a B on school assignments) would be rewarded. Sharon was referred for an evaluation for her suicidal behavior. Measurement of the two goals: (1) increase school attendance and performance, and (2) reduce suicidal thoughts and actions would be by goal attainment scaling. Figure 9.3 is an example of the goal attainment measure used.

EXERCISE 9.7   Purposes of Quantitative Assessment

Consider an agency where you have worked or where you have done a field placement. What purposes of quantitative assessment and measures could serve the particular agency that you have in mind?

CHAPTER SUMMARY

This chapter presented the area of quantitative assessment. Its purposes are to help the practitioner to improve intervention and to contribute to social work research. Quantitative measures also provide a basis for practice evaluation and accountability, as well as increase the practitioner's skills repertoire. Finally, they can be used as tools with the family to demonstrate concrete changes that they have made as the work has progressed.

Frameworks for incorporating quantitative measurement in the family social workers' practice were presented. Single-subject design can help to target client problems and monitor progress throughout the course of the family work. Standardized measures frequently are used to collect the quantified data. Another method, goal attainment scaling, is frequently used in agency settings. Any problem can be quantified using this system.

Types of quantified measures were presented. These included self-anchored and self-monitoring scales, direct behavioral observation, standardized measures, and other measures. Finally, guidelines for using measurement to link assessment and intervention were presented.

KEY TERMS

Quantitative measurement   a form of measurement that uses numbers that are assigned to variables. In referring to family assessment, it involves the use of valid and reliable scales that have been subjected to extensive testing and are designed to measure a specific aspect of family functioning.

Reliability   the property of an instrument to consistently produce the same results, given the same value of the variable being investigated, over time. Ways to determine reliability include test-retest, split-halves, and internal consistency.

Validity   the extent to which an instrument accurately measures the concept under investigation. Approaches to validity include content, face, criterion-related (concurrent and predictive), construct, and factorial.

SUGGESTED READINGS

Bloom, M., Fischer, J., & Orme, J. (2009). *Evaluating practice: Guidelines for the accountable professional* (6th ed.). Boston, MA: Pearson.

Corcoran, K., & Fischer, J. (2007). *Measures for clinical practice: A sourcebook* (Vols. 1–2). New York: Oxford Press.

Franklin, C., & Sanchez, K. (2011). Quantitative clinical assessment methods. In C. Jordan & C. Franklin (Eds.), *Clinical assessment for social workers: Quantitative and qualitative methods* (pp. 51–79). Chicago, IL: Lyceum Books.

COMPETENCY NOTES

EP 2.1.3a. Distinguish, appraise, and integrate multiple sources of knowledge, including research-based knowledge and practice wisdom: Quantitative assessment requires knowledge of assessment instruments that can be used to measure client problems. These are used for evaluation of case outcomes as well.

EP 2.1.3b. Analyze models of assessment, prevention, intervention, and evaluation: Quantitative measurement requires having a repertoire of instruments that can be used to measure and evaluate client problems, and the ability to choose the correct instrument for individual clients and client problems.

EP 2.1.10e. Assess client strengths and limitations: Examples of instruments that assess client strengths and limitations are self-anchored scales and self-monitoring instruments.

LEARNING OBJECTIVES

- Conceptual: Understand the need for comprehensive family assessment.

- Perceptual: View family problems from many different angles (six different problem definitions as well as a strengths-based lens).

- Valuational/Attitudinal: Value many different ways to understand problems, as well as value families' strengths in coping with day-to-day and life problems. Shift from pathologizing families to a strengths-based perspective.

- Behavioral: Complete a comprehensive family assessment, and work with systemic dynamics as well as circular causality.

In Chapter 10, we present guidelines for effective family systems interventions. We also present a very different lens to understand a family problem—in particular, the different ways that family members, in collaboration with the family social worker, can view and define a problem. We continue our strengths-based approach by assessing families' abilities to problem solve using their strengths. We discuss some of the change facilitation skills with particular emphasis on working with circular patterns in a family and problematic triangles.

EP 2.1.10g

EFFECTIVE ASSESSMENT AND INTERVENTION

What does assessment and intervention look like from a strengths-based perspective? First, workers must develop an attitude that values the potential of families to change. It means using interventions that empower families to take action on their own behalf. The process of empowerment should minimize feelings of family and community powerlessness and maximize beliefs that the family has the motivation, skills, and resources to work on their issues. In the process, family social workers help families uncover their latent strength and mobilize the strengths within their community. All clients possess a repository of strengths; helping professionals have often overlooked the massive and frequently unappreciated resources and competencies that families possess. Nurturing client strengths instills a sense of confidence in families and sparks their motivation. Moreover, families will be more likely to continue autonomous change and growth when family work capitalizes on existing family abilities, knowledge, and skills. Working with strengths draws social workers into a collaborative relationship with clients because family workers recognize that clients are experts on their own lives. Because family social workers' work with families uses an ecological angle, they are aware of resources in the environment that can help them.

EXERCISE 10.1 Targeting Assessment Issues

Break the class into groups of three and brainstorm issues and questions that might be asked in an assessment interview. Report back to the main group. Assign a class member to collate the lists given by all the groups. This list can be distributed to the entire class for future reference.

Assessment and mobilization of family strengths should focus on the positives related to many areas, including:

- *Family relationships* involves caring for members, gender roles that are respected and valued, parent-child relationships based on what is best for the child, physical and emotional self-care, the presence of positive family events and successes, supportive couple relationships, family history of previous successes in conflict management, and a strong family identity.
- *Individual family member skills* looks at cognitive and intellectual abilities, a positive attitude, hope and optimism, assuming self-responsibility and accountability, competent parenting, positive role-modeling, and an ability to build and access supportive social environments.
- *Personal qualities* includes motivation, goal directedness, self-esteem and competence, an ability to laugh at oneself, inner strengths and resources, strong relational abilities, nondefensiveness, and willingness to work on issues despite challenges.
- *Availability of community resources* includes friends and caring others outside the family, supportive relatives, health care, education, recreation, a spiritual community, social services, and the skills to navigate in these community resources.

- *Seeing and learning* entails the ability to recognize difficult life experiences and to learn from these experiences.

The family social worker pays particular attention to the multigenerational family system as it moves through the life cycle. At each stage, family homeostasis vacillates between stressful events that exacerbate vulnerability and protective factors that stimulate resilience through the support and caring of family, peers, and other social forces. A family resilience framework focuses on family adaptation around key events, including both predictable, normative transitions and unexpected untimely events (Walsh, 2003, p. 4).

At the same time, it is important to observe when problems and symptoms coincide with recent or looming events that have disrupted or threatened the family. Frequently, difficulties accompany stressful transitions. In discussing stressful events, it will be necessary to explore how the family has handled its difficulties previously, including anticipatory responses, immediate responses, and long-term survival strategies. Effective family processes play a central role in dealing with adversity. When strengths and resilience are not accounted for, models of family assessment become static and remove a family from its context. Static perspectives provide only a snapshot of interaction patterns and fail to capture contextual issues in relation to the family's resources and constraints. Without a focus on strengths and the successful resolution of problems, family strengths are negated.

EP 2.1.10g

KEY STRATEGIES IN WORKING WITH STRENGTHS

The first strategy involves drawing out family belief systems through family and social transactions. These beliefs influence how a family perceives and understands its problems and what it does about them because perceptions shape family processes and responses to crises. "Adversity generates a crisis of meaning and potential disruption of integration" (Walsh, 2003, p. 6). The family social worker can support family beliefs that capitalize on opportunities to resolve problems and encourage personal and family growth. Two questions capture important family beliefs: 1) asking family members to discuss what caused their particular difficulty, and 2) asking what family members believe needs to happen for their difficulties to be resolved.

The family social worker works with the family to find meaning embedded in family difficulties. Strong attachments in the family enable members to approach problems as a shared venture. Family members who recognize and place problems within a larger life course context are better equipped to understand and accept how their family continually adapts, changes, and grows. They can be helped to understand challenges posed by family life cycle transitions and view these as meaningful and unavoidable influences that are anticipated and met head-on instead of being viewed as problematic family events that sow the seeds of family destruction. Families can learn that blaming, shaming, or pathologizing individuals drags the entire family down, and instead learn to view their problems as both understandable and manageable. At this time, the family worker's role is to reframe the nature of problems, direct the family to available resources, and enhance family connectedness for ongoing support. Resilience thrives in climates of mutual support and collaboration, where respect for differences, personal autonomy, and clear boundaries are valued.

Optimistic beliefs play a role in how a family functions. Stories and narratives about difficulties form the building blocks of how families construct meaning and reveal how a family perceives itself and its difficulties. Family stories connect core beliefs to who the family is. Families need the space to tell their stories. "Groups who suffer the domination of broader social institutions or suppression of their own cultural devices under the dominant culture frequently do not have their stories heard, not only in the wider world, but also in their own world" (Saleebey, 1996, p. 301). Certainly one feature of oppression is having stories and beliefs negated by ignorance, stereotypes, and indifference.

A realistic perspective concerning the problem is a necessary component of helping, even when working from a strengths-based perspective. Families' difficulties and the associated pain and distress are real; disregarding them is disrespectful. The challenge is to acknowledge problems without allowing them to become all consuming. It is for this reason that family social workers should incorporate a balance of strengths and problems into family assessment and intervention plans to capitalize on the power and will of the family to self-correct with the help of appropriate environmental supports. The worker injects hope into the work, accompanied by a belief that family difficulties can be overcome through a spirit of worker-family collaboration. Together they develop knowledge, access tools, and set out goals within an environment of respect. Saleebey (1996) contends that practicing from a strengths-based perspective does not mean ignoring the real difficulties that families face:

> In the lexicon of strengths, it is as wrong to deny the possible as it is to deny the problem.... It does deny the overwheening reign of psychopathology as civic, moral, and medical categorical imperative. It does deny that most people are victims of abuse or of their own rampant appetites. It denies that all people who face trauma and pain in their lives inevitably are wounded or incapacitated or become less than they might.... The appreciations and understandings of the strengths perspective are an attempt to correct this overwrought and, in some instances, destructive emphasis on what is wrong, what is missing, and what is abnormal. (p. 297)

The family social worker can help the families by injecting positive messages concerning their difficulties, intended to instill hope and a belief that the future holds promise. This means not allowing the family to be suffocated by feelings of futility and failure since hopelessness erodes motivation and spawns passivity and pessimism. Optimism, nurtured through a positive outlook, acknowledges and honors strengths and promises that new options for solving problems will appear. At the same time, family social workers cannot minimize or dismiss a family's justifiable despair; the family social worker can empathize with despair and at the same time validate family strengths and potential.

Balance is the key. Assessment takes on a richer texture when it includes what is doable and what is possible: capacities, talents, competencies, possibilities, visions, beliefs, hopes, and potentials. It means broadening the lens by focusing on family capacity. It also means flexible interventions that readily embrace the possibility of using individual, family, and community resources. Strengths-based practice involves paying close attention to the use of language during family work. "Words create worlds." Words have power. Pathology-based words darken the vista by imposing problems, while strengths-based words impose solutions and hope. Saleebey (1996) encourages us to "use a dictionary of helping," a dictionary that includes the use of such words as *empowerment, skills, hope, support, ability, and knowledge.* Re-languaging, through the mindful selection of positive words, equips family social workers with new and powerful tools that include such ideas as change, power, and hope. A new lexicon tells us what is going right, what the possibilities are, and how to get there. Instead of just talking about what is going wrong in a family's life, the family social worker adds to the repertoire of what is going right. At the same time, the worker and the family can use humor, foster healthy loyalty within the family, support independence, and encourage insight so families can learn and grow from their difficulties.

The family social worker assesses and intervenes in ways that help the family system change for the better. This change often targets not only change in internal family interactions but also changes in the family's interactions with larger systems. Change is not always a steady process, and the family social worker's interventions

---

CASE 10.1 | ## Looking for Strengths

Sometimes family social workers must focus on family problems because these problems create a dangerous situation within the family. However, even families with the most serious problems also have strengths, and it is important that the family social worker acknowledge these.

Connie and Dave were referred to the family social worker of the CPS because of the neglect and possible abuse of their two small children, Campbell (3) and Ashley (2). The mother was a stay-at-home mom and the father worked as a mechanic's assistant in a garage until the garage closed and left him unemployed. At the time of the report, he'd been unemployed for six months, and the couple's meager savings was almost gone. Both parents were feeling the stress of the situation and were fearful of being evicted from their small, two-bedroom apartment. This situation resulted in Dave being depressed and withdrawn and Connie being angry at her husband for not getting up and going job hunting every day. This created an environment where the children were left unattended, as well as an unconfirmed report from a neighbor that the children were being spanked too frequently and too severely.

During the assessment, the family social worker looked for strengths as well as problem areas. She knew that finding the couples' strengths would indicate areas that could be used to shore up the couple's coping responses. Some of the strengths she reported were social supports, including extended family members nearby who were willing to help, and church attendance with caring members and friends willing to help. The church also had a mother's-day-out program that could offer respite care for the children. A local community center offered parenting courses that could work with the parents on appropriate parenting and disciplinary techniques. Individual strengths of the parents noted in the assessment included Dave's good work record and training to be a mechanic. Both Dave and Connie were willing to come in to work with the family social worker and looked forward to the help they would receive.

with a family can be obstructed in various ways. Assessment and intervention will be more effective if the family social worker keeps the following considerations in mind:

1. Be attuned to culture and adhere to culturally sensitive practices.
2. Focus on family needs.
3. Respect client autonomy.
4. Avoid fostering unnecessary dependency.
5. Reassess and reinterpret client resistance as avoidance of pain.
6. Keep healthy professional boundaries while remaining emotionally available.
7. Set realistic expectations.
8. Work at all levels of the ecosystem, particularly the micro and meso levels.

Culturally Sensitive Practice

This book does not debate whether workers from a specific culture should work only with families of their culture. Instead, we advocate for cultural competence for all workers—competence that avoids the application of stereotypical checklists to families from minority cultures. The reality is that agencies hire the best workers for the job, and until there are sufficient numbers of minority group workers in the field of social work, workers from a variety of backgrounds will work with all families. Minority and nonminority people can collaborate to improve the quality of life for families living in a range of cultural groups. Family social work can be individualized and adapted to work with minority families, being respectful of the unique customs of each family. The bottom line is family social workers' sensitivity and understanding that the best way to help children is to help their families and that an effective way of helping families is to ensure that social resources are available to enhance successful parenthood (Garbarino, 1992).

North America is comprised of every culture on Earth, and each culture contains much heterogeneity. Suggesting that a *single* program model or intervention can meet the needs of *all* cultural families risks stereotyping and reducing each culture to a single entity (Gross, 1998). Family social workers must pay close attention to the spirituality, language, social structure, and family differences across cultural communities. In other words, they cannot overgeneralize cultural knowledge or use this knowledge inappropriately and ineffectively with multicultural families (Sue & Zane, 1987; Weaver, 1997). Programs must be flexible. Gross (1998) was aware of the dangers when he cautioned "all the study in the world about a given culture or subculture might not lend a hint of explanation of the behavior or attitudes of a single member of that culture or subculture" (p. 9). He also discussed the importance of understanding "grand narratives" of a culture from the perspective of individuals or "micronarratives." For example, grand narratives of native people include respect for people, land, and creatures, which results in high esteem for elders; noninterference in the lives of others, including in child-rearing efforts; and interconnectedness and interdependency (Coleman, Unrau, & Manyfingers, 2001). Workers therefore need to understand families on societal and individual levels. Outsiders often misunderstand cultural narratives.

Moreover, family social workers can learn to understand and communicate with families on both cultural grand narratives and micronarratives. Micronarratives deserve their own place in intervention, and they can be uncovered only by listening to people and not by reading about diversity (Gross, 1998). Thus, family social workers can listen to individual families, "using the grand narratives as a cultural backdrop" (Coleman, Unrau, & Manyfingers, 2001). It is impossible to know everything about a specific cultural group or family, but assessment and interviewing skills are indispensable in locating critical information about different groups.

The history of a particular culture has implications for how members of a group respond to family social work intervention. Some groups may see family workers as untrustworthy and coercive authority figures. Moreover, not all members of a cultural group are connected in the same way to their cultural heritage. Enormous differences exist within cultures, depending on the level of assimilation or acculturation and the particular family history. Some groups will have blended traditional and nontraditional practices in their daily living. "Acculturation can be seen as a mosaic, blending traditional native ways with dominant cultural ways. While it might be tempting to characterize all families by the wholeness of the mosaic, or a favored part of it, the richness of a mosaic is in the multiple perspectives it offers" (Coleman, Unrau, & Manyfingers, 2001).

Coleman, Unrau, and Manyfingers proposed five program structures that can be incorporated into family social work in order to work appropriately with families from different cultures:

1. Workers must have a sincere interest in learning and accepting different cultures. Doing so creates better chances of evening out existing power differences within helper-client relationships. Family social workers must feel free to admit cultural ignorance when it occurs, and agencies can assist workers to develop strategies to learn about client families.
2. Workers can challenge their ethnocentric beliefs as an integral part of family social work. Supervision can focus on workers' universal assumptions regarding "normal" or "healthy" families as well as examine popular theories in terms of their fit for a particular culture and expectations of change. Reflection skills allow workers to be self-critical and aware of their practice so they can understand families as cultural beings. It reduces the risk of imposing unwanted values on clients and further oppressing clients during vulnerable times.
3. Family social workers can be open to collaboration with traditional cultural healers and leaders and support family choices about traditional sources of help that parallel, supplement, or replace interventions that are more common (Weaver, 1997b). Natural helpers in communities can be included in the service delivery system.
4. Family social workers should be familiar with and be prepared to use existing client support systems, following the appropriate cultural protocols.
5. The intervention skills used by family social workers can be adapted to specific cultures.
6. Family social workers can seek specific cultural knowledge, which includes awareness of communication patterns, worldviews, belief systems, and values

(Weaver, 1999). Communication patterns are central because miscommunication leads to misunderstanding or mislabeling. Communication awareness includes knowledge of verbal and nonverbal communication patterns, how a culture interprets problems and expresses emotions, and what services they think will be helpful.

7. Knowing how to gain entrance into a cultural community is important if a worker is to access culturally appropriate resources for a family.

Even given these seven recommendations, we argue that it is impossible to fully understand other cultures. Initial family work techniques are those that promote bonding and trust between the social worker and the family. It is extremely helpful for the family social worker to start from a position of not knowing and showing genuine interest about cultural issues for the family. This involves asking questions about the family's background in a curious and empathic manner and being non-defensive about stories of oppression and wrongs perpetrated by the dominant culture. We find that most families are willing and comfortable in teaching family social workers about their cultural background and appreciate family social workers who show this kind of interest.

Focus on the Family's Needs

The heart and soul of family social work involves keeping family needs front and center in the work. As mentioned in Chapter 4, family needs are categorized according to their importance and urgency, starting with basic physical needs, safety needs, belonging needs, esteem needs, and actualization needs. Working from this framework, family social workers take note of what families need and incorporate this as a focus of their work. At times, family social workers must forgo personal needs for the sake of the family, such as in the case of scheduling. However, we caution that an erratic and self-sacrificing approach to work contributes to worker burnout. Signs of burnout include fatigue, lack of interest in the work, and apathy about client concerns. Burned out workers may also feel angry toward clients and discouraged and cynical about their work. Burnout is often the result of prolonged stress. Workers who are burned out cannot provide a high-quality service to families. At the same time, the client's behavior or choices may be inconvenient or at odds with the family social worker's beliefs. For example, one client insisted on living with her unemployed boyfriend in a high-crime area rather than moving in with her mother in a safer neighborhood. The client got more emotional support from her boyfriend than from her mother. Even though the family social worker would have preferred to meet with the client in a safer location, she recognized that her client fared better with her boyfriend than with her mother.

Respect Clients' Autonomy

Self-determination is a core social work value, and family social workers recognize that clients have a right to make their own choices. All choices, of course, are associated with consequences, but the consequences belong to the client. The role of the family social worker is to sustain and encourage clients to make deeply personal decisions. It can be difficult for the family social worker to avoid moving in and taking over for the client, particularly if the client's choices are self-destructive, such as refusing to leave a dangerously abusive relationship. Encouraging people to make their own decisions increases their competence and control over their lives because people learn by experience. As one family social worker said, "When we support clients by helping them access community resources and by continuing to help them improve their skills, clients become increasingly able to make appropriate decisions and to change destructive life patterns."

In accepting clients' right to make their own decisions, the family social worker must always remember that the client is autonomous with the right to self-determination. The family social worker cannot accept responsibility for client actions. The real issue involved concerns who is affected by another person's autonomy and self-determination. If a child is being hurt by a parent's substance abuse, the consequence might be the removal of the child from the home until the substance abuse is dealt with. The family social worker also must differentiate between his or her personal values and life goals and those of the family, remembering that the goal ultimately is for the family to learn skills and make the best decisions. Indeed, effective professionals encourage self-exploration and self-direction. If the family social worker has trouble separating his or her personal needs from those of the family, a supervisor can assist in the self-examination process. For example, the family social worker may highly value college education and the client may not. It is important for the client to choose her or his own life direction.

Avoid Fostering Dependency

A third consideration for family social workers involves independence and autonomy. Sometimes family members might rely on the social worker, but excessive dependency can be counterproductive, especially if it is long term. During periods of stress and crisis, they may rely on family social workers to support them in making and carrying out decisions. For example, one family social worker helped a depressed parent obtain professional counseling. The parent asked for assistance in finding an appropriate therapist and setting up an appointment. The social worker responded by spending most of a home visit phoning therapists and scheduling the first appointment, though the family social worker would usually just provide information and support to encourage the client to initiate contact.

While temporary and time-limited dependency is acceptable, the family social worker avoids fostering unnecessary dependency. Encouraging clients' independence strengthens existing abilities and helps them develop additional competencies. Family social workers who regularly allow clients to become dependent will harm rather than help them in the long run. One family social worker left a family party when a client called her and asked her for a ride. This was not an emergency, and the family social worker did not place appropriate limits on her professional role. Helping the client find her own transportation would have been more valuable for this client, encouraging her to develop her problem-solving capacities. During the family social worker's working relationship, the type and amount of dependency varies. The goal is for clients to become self-reliant apart from the family social worker. Keeping this goal in mind helps the social worker judge when dependency is appropriate and when it is not.

Reassess Clients' Resistance

A fourth consideration for family social workers involves client motivation. Some clients may appear unmotivated to comply with program expectations or to work toward other life goals that are important. Often social workers label this behavior as resistance, but the behavior may occur because of avoidance of pain or conflict between the family social worker and the client over the goals to be accomplished. The family social worker who feels frustrated about a client's low motivation should ask, "Are these the client's goals, my goals, or goals of the agency? Is this client appearing resistant because in reality she is feeling extreme pain over facing the situation?" Perhaps the goals are not culturally appropriate or personally meaningful to the client. If so and if the selected goal will benefit the client, the family social worker may try to present it in a way that is acceptable to the client. If the goal does not appear to be of benefit to the client, the expectation should be dropped. This means that the family—instead of the family social worker—guides the direction of the intervention, taking the urgency of the issue into account.

Resistance may be a message from the client that the family social worker is overstepping the boundaries of the relationship. Resistance can also signal that the issues being discussed are sensitive to the client. If the family is not making progress toward establishing goals, the family social worker attempts to discover what barriers may be preventing it from trying to achieve these goals. Two major barriers to goal attainment include lack of resources and skills or a direction that is too painful. Perhaps helping the client problem solve to overcome or work through the barriers will propel the family to move toward its goals.

If the family is not complying with a required goal in an involuntary program, such as court-ordered treatment for child abusers, program policy and legal procedures will guide the family social worker's response. Workers are advised to be up-front with clients about pending consequences of client decisions. If a client in a voluntary program does not want to attend parent meetings, however, the family social worker may change her or his expectations for this family. Alternatively, the family social worker may occasionally encourage the client to attend the meetings while focusing attention on other aspects of the program to which the family is attracted. Resistance to a court order can be addressed by discussing the difficulties. "I can see that this court order gets your back up. Why don't we start by discussing the court order?"

Maintain Professional Distance

A fifth consideration for family social workers is the nature of their relationships with families. Over time, professional relationships change. For example, as positive feelings develop between the family social worker and the family, boundaries may become blurred and the relationship may resemble a personal friendship. The family social worker may become truly fond of the family and deeply committed to working with them through thick and thin. Although positive regard for clients is essential for a good working relationship, it should not become confused with friendship. Maintaining this close distance is important for several reasons.

The family social worker needs to remain objective and goal-focused to help the family become independent and effective. Appropriate distance between family members and the social worker encourages the family to view the family social worker as a role model for behavioral change. On another level, maintaining a professional relationship with a family will protect the family social worker and the family from future complications. The circumstances of the family's life could become overwhelming for a family social worker who becomes emotionally involved or takes personal responsibility for solving the family's problems. Failure to establish clear boundaries can leave the family social worker feeling burdened by distressing family situations. Focusing on understanding how the family may feel, without overidentifying, helps the family social worker function professionally and effectively.

Set Realistic Expectations

A sixth guideline for family social workers is to foster families' feelings of competence, rather than inadequacy. Families often feel that bringing the social worker into their home places them in a vulnerable position, regardless of the purpose of the program. Additionally, families may feel overwhelmed by expectations that they think they cannot meet. Although the family social worker focuses on encouraging and positively reinforcing family strengths, as mentioned, family limitations and despair must also be acknowledged. At the same time, the family social worker takes care to avoid creating feelings of inadequacy by exclusively empathizing with negative feelings and circumstances.

Maintaining a Dual Micro and Macro Focus: Ecological Intervention

The family social worker layers his or her focus, moving beyond solely focusing on internal family interactions. Keeping both macro and micro focuses on the radar screen, the family social worker also works with macro-level interactions by working with the interactions a family has with systems outside the family. Ecological theory is helpful for this. The type of ecological intervention required arises from an assessment of the family's relationship with its environment, as portrayed in an ecomap. The ecomap is the blueprint for planned change and is the first stage in deciding on an action (Hartman & Laird, 1983). Not only does an ecomap organize information visually, it also outlines family themes and targets for change. As mentioned in Chapter 8, the family must be involved in creating the ecomap. The family social worker can ask family members "What does the ecomap mean to you?" Focusing on the ecosystem will also extract the problem from the level of individual blame. We should point out here that the goal of ecological intervention is to teach clients how to problem solve for themselves, rather than relying on the family social worker to do it for them.

Kaplan (1986) suggested that the social worker focus on environmental problems to help the family deal first with less-threatening issues, while assisting them in locating community supports. The type of ecological interventions used depends on the issues, skills, and available resources. For example, one family social worker reported that the following resources were either not available to clients or difficult for them to locate: mental health treatment, housing, day care, low-skill jobs, transportation, legal services, and employment (Goldstein, 1981). Social workers in a different program found that emergency housing, homemaker services, group homes, parent aides, in-patient drug and alcohol treatment, and respite care were difficult to access (Kohlert & Pecora, 1991). The social worker helps families develop creative ways to use formal and informal resources. Sometimes families lack information about where resources exist. Other times, family members may have the knowledge but lack the skills to get connected to resources. In such cases, the family social worker will have to help the family get connected. The ultimate goal is for clients to learn to get needs met on their own, even if it often is tempting and perhaps easier to take care of clients' needs rather than encouraging self-sufficiency (Kinney, Haapala, & Booth, 1991).

Hepworth and Larsen (1993) list the following ecological interventions that family social workers can perform for families:

- Supplementing resources in the home environment
- Developing and enhancing support systems
- Moving clients to a new environment
- Increasing the responsiveness of organizations to people's needs
- Enhancing interactions between organizations and institutions
- Improving institutional environments
- Enhancing agency environments
- Developing new resources

EP 2.1.4b

DEFINING PROBLEMS

The goal of problem definition is to explore, identify, and define dynamics within and beyond the family to open up possibilities for change. Problem definition is important because the way we define problems can open up very different directions for family work. Using a strengths-based perspective alongside problem definition opens up positive directions for change. Each member of the family has a unique perspective on the problem and family strengths, and every perspective is important. For example, a problem defined by the family as a child spending too much time hanging out with friends may be a conforming issue for the parents, an independence issue for the target child, and an exclusion issue for siblings.

EXERCISE 10.2   Reframing a Problem from Individual to Family Focus

Select one possible family problem that a family social worker might see in family work. How might this problem be considered an individual problem? Now create a scenario in which you reframe this problem as a family problem. How might family members resist this reformulation of the problem?

Painting a clear picture of family problems is a prerequisite for devising interventions. Thus, how the family social worker and the family *jointly* view a problem is crucial. This viewpoint or definition of the problem directs intervention. Most problem definitions adhere to a systemic view. Yet these systemic views can be radically different. The following list describes six ways to view problems, along with related intervention models, most of which are discussed later in this book. The way a problem is defined often depends on:

- How the family initially defines the problem.
- The theoretical perspective the family social worker uses.
- The mandate of the agency and how the agency views problems. For example, some agencies embrace solution-focused counseling and define problems to fit this theory.
- How the problem is defined *jointly* between the family and worker in a way that both feel offers the most opportunities to create positive change.

Let us now examine six unique ways of viewing a problem:

1. A traditional analytic view is that *the symptomatic person is the problem*. This traditional analytic view has its roots in individual psychopathology, in which problems are viewed as being inside people. Nearly all workers involved in individual counseling subscribe to this view to some extent. However, the influence of a more generalist, ecological view has expanded the exclusive focus on individual psychopathology to embrace the effect of larger social systems on an individual's well-being.

   Imagine you have the Smith family referred to you because of concerns about their 13-year-old child being noncompliant, argumentative, and throwing temper tantrums. The traditional analytic view would say, for example, that the child has anger management problems and self-esteem issues. Because of this individually oriented assessment of the problem, the preferred treatment approach would be individual counseling for the child, focusing on anger management techniques and discussion of self-esteem issues.

2. The social systems assumption is that *the family is the problem* (the systems view). Family systems theory reframed the way many workers viewed problems. Instead of viewing problems as being within an individual, problems were seen as systems problems, that is, problems evolving from relationship patterns within the family. The primary system of concern and influence on a person is the family. Thus, the social systems assumption is that the family, particularly the way family members relate to each other, contains the roots of the problem. Major family work models that ascribed to this view included the communicative approach and structural family work approach.

   For example, the Smith family has difficulties in dealing with anger and relating to each other in ways that give each other support. By defining the anger as a family systems problem, the treatment approach would involve family counseling, focusing on how the family as a whole supports one of its members to deal with anger. More appropriate ways for the family to express anger and its accompanying hurt would be put into place.

3. The assumption of the Mental Research Institute in Palo Alto is that *the attempted solution is the problem* (an interactional view). This is an interesting view that could be simplified by saying, "If what you are doing does not work, stop doing it and try something different!" If yelling at the children to do their homework is not working, try something different. If nagging to get your partner to help with household chores is not working, try something different. Thus, if what you considered to be the solution to a problem (that is, yelling as a solution to not doing homework or nagging as a solution to not doing household chores) is not working, then these "solutions" become the problem that need to be changed. Behavioral family therapy becomes a helpful model to look at alternative behaviors (solutions) to help achieve desired family changes.

   For example, a family yelling and arguing (their attempted solution) increases the family members' anger instead of decreasing it. Family work would be provided, but the focus would be on changing the family behavioral and relational patterns of yelling and arguing to more adaptive behaviors. A typical maladaptive pattern occurs when parents are experiencing a child with temper tantrums. Parents arguing or yelling at the child only fuels the temper tantrum. Yelling increases tension in the room, although parents might discharge energy initially. Instead, the parents need to "starve" temper tantrums. A radical approach would be, instead of yelling or arguing, parents physically hugging (comforting) the child and then giving the child a choice of continuing to be hugged, talking nicely about what is bothering him or her, or going to his or her room to get control of the temper tantrum. Thus, instead of yelling at or arguing with the child, the parents learn to take control by giving choices to help the child learn more appropriate ways of seeking attention and taking control of temper tantrums.

4. The Milan group suggests *the problem is the solution* (a functional cybernetic view). The Milan group is one major school of strategic family work approaches. It views problems as having a *function* in the family system. Thus, within the family relationships or systems there is some reason or function for the problem. It is therefore important to assess and hypothesize what function the problem is having and then turn this function around to make the problem the solution.

   For example, by being angry, the Smith family will learn the value of affective closeness; that is, family anger will lead to forgiveness and force the family to become affectively close. Again, given this definition of the problem, family counseling would occur. The family would be made aware of the payoff, or function, the anger has in the family, which involves attempting to force the family to be more affectively close. The family would be supported in becoming routinely affectively close without the need for anger to force them to be so.

5. The late Michael White, a social worker from Australia, and his colleague David Epson (1990) from New Zealand offer a very unique narrative model view of a problem in which *the symptom (problem) is a restraint* (evolutionary cybernetic view; i.e., the direction of interaction between the problem and solution is important).

   For example, the Smith family at times allows anger to take control of the family and needs to become more vigilant as a family unit to keep anger away.

(Anger or yelling is verbalized as an external entity.) The focus in family counseling would be to help the family become aware of the power or influence anger or yelling has on the family. The family may be encouraged to exercise behaviors that have been successful in minimizing the impact anger has on them. Family recreational activities, family talk times, and during a member's temper tantrums may provide opportunities to practice this.

6. Maturana sees *the distinction as the problem* (the structured determined view). Anger or yelling can be seen as overwhelming or as a challenge. Whether the family defines anger as a negative (i.e. overwhelming) or as a positive (e.g., a call for affective attention), challenges open possibilities for change. It is similar to whether you view yourself as an optimist or as a pessimist. Do you make the distinction that the glass is half empty or half full? When you wake up in the morning, do you say to yourself, "I do not want to get out of bed; I hate going to work," which may lead to a more negative approach to the day, or do you get up in the morning and say, "What a beautiful morning; I am going to have a great day!" The latter may lead to a positive approach to the rest of the day.

   In the process of family social work, the family is encouraged to redefine anger in a way that opens up opportunities for them. For example, anger can help people appreciate the times in the family when anger is not present. The adolescent girl feeling angry could be defined differently (restoried) to reflect that she is a very sensitive, caring child, who is deeply involved and moved by what is happening in the family. By no longer viewing herself as an angry person but as a very sensitive, caring child who is deeply involved and moved by what is happening in her family, she can receive the support she needs to continue to try to be a respectful, compliant, and confident adolescent without self-doubt and blaming others.

   In the Smith family, anger can be viewed as a call (a loud one) for attention. By providing immediate affective support, positive attention is given, and the need to receive affective support in response to continued anger decreases. The hope is that family members will learn that if they want affective support they just need to ask for it instead of having to yell or get angry to receive it. Thus, when adolescents feel angry or hurt or are struggling with self-doubt, they do not need to resort to anger outbursts but instead can just ask for the support and comfort they so often need.

EP 2.1.10e

STRENGTHS-BASED ASSESSMENT

Through a strengths-based assessment, the family social worker works to relegate problems to a secondary position behind strengths. This may seem difficult when the problem appears to be too serious to be ignored, such as behaviors that might cause injury to a family member or to others. When a family member is at risk of suicide or of hurting others, the problem situation demands immediate attention by securing the safety of those involved. Unfortunately, because the behavior might be expected to reappear, these critical problems tend to dominate assessment and case planning even after the crisis situation has abated. However, it is important for the family worker to move beyond an exclusive crisis intervention into a strengths-based, longer-term family intervention approach. Although some risks are too critical to be ignored, they can be assigned to a position secondary to the family members' strengths once the immediate threat is gone.

The dilemma for both the family member and the social worker is determining whether the risk is sufficiently urgent and so overwhelming that the details of daily life seem to be of little significance by comparison. The paradox appears to be that the problem will not be under control until the family member feels gratified enough to make it worth the effort of overcoming a risk as powerful as suicidal thoughts or family violence (Saleebey, D. 1992). Problems may even be exacerbated through the use of a problem-focused model. Listing problems can stifle family enthusiasm and discourage family members who acknowledge that they have problems, but did not realize the extent of them. Focusing on problems puts one at risk of creating problems. "The longer one stays with a problem-focused assessment, the more likely it is that the problem will dominate the stage. However, problems do have a role to play. Just as actors with a few lines are important in a larger drama, problems produce uncomfortable emotions such as pain, anger, shame, and confusion, which serve to get our attention and put us on notice. Theses are signs that something needs to change" (Saleebey, D. 1992, p. 45). Complicated assessments concerning family problems can eclipse more potent areas of strengths, as well as small victories that family members experience.

By focusing work on family members' strengths in the assessment, planning, and intervention process, problems are less likely to be invented or exacerbated. When a problem does appear, it is framed as an obstacle to the attainment of a goal that is important to the family members, increasing its relevance. Problems can be presented in a way that allows family members and the family social worker to tackle them. As the family social worker examines the orientation to problems, buffered by the strengths-based perspective, problems no longer assume center stage as family members grow to understand that a problem neither defines nor consumes the family's identity. Whether the name of the problem is substance abuse, child abuse, or troubled family relations, a family is always greater than its problem (see Chapter 3, systems theory)!

EP 2.1.10e

CIRCULAR PATTERNS

In addition to the preceding ways of defining and working with problems, another practical way to assess and intervene with families is to understand and work with circular repetitive patterns. (Repetitive circular patterns were discussed in detail in Chapter 3.) In working with circular patterns, the family social worker intervenes with these patterns by stimulating interaction and by using lineal, circular, strategic, and reflexive questions. Repetitive patterns are particularly relevant when we see problems within the social systems assumption that the family is the problem.

Recognizing repetitive and problematic patterns is the cornerstone of family systems theory. The term *patterns* means that the same behavior happens repeatedly and is predictable. Families function in both predictable and patterned ways. In particular, the family social worker pays attention to the ongoing, repetitive patterns of communication between family members. These predictable patterns contribute to family system stability so that the energy of family members is not wasted on mundane tasks. Behavior is explained and shaped through ongoing, repetitive patterns, which both trigger and maintain behavior. When systems are stable (i.e., in homeostasis), familiar patterns within a family play an important role in keeping the family on an even keel. Family patterns also reveal patterns of affiliations, tensions, and hierarchies within the system (Minuchin, Colapinto, & Minuchin, 1998). Some family patterns are shaped by ethnicity and culture.

When a family is mired in problems, it may be because their repetitive patterns have produced gridlock without providing an adequate response to the issue at hand. In this way, *the solution becomes the problem.* Because the patterns are habits, family members feel secure in the stability they provide. The habitual patterns might be hurtful to individuals and harmful to the family system, but because family members are unaware of or unskilled in other ways of responding, they are unable to change, and the family is described as being stuck.

EXERCISE 10.3 Circular Causality

Reflect on a well-established relationship in which you are currently participating or one from your childhood. Try to identify an ongoing circular pattern of interaction between you and the other person. Label your own thoughts, feelings, and behaviors; then try to do the same for the other person. How does circular causality work when there seems to be a power imbalance?

EXERCISE 10.4 Ongoing Personal Circular Causality

Examine one of your ongoing relationships. Identify an ongoing circular pattern of interaction with that significant other. It does not matter where you start to identify the pattern. (You might want to work together with this person.) Start with one individual and identify thoughts, feelings, and behaviors, and then move to a second person and do the same. Draw the pattern on a piece of paper one step at a time. How does circular causality work?

Not only does the family social worker need to assess maladaptive patterns, it is also equally important to identify *adaptive* patterns (Healthy Interaction Patterns or HIPs) from a strengths-based lens. Indeed the goal of family work is to increase the adaptive patterns within families. Intervention includes both changing maladaptive patterns to adaptive ones and reinforcing existing adaptive ones.

Step 1. Stimulating Interaction. To assess circular patterns, it is necessary to observe a repetitive circular pattern as it appears during the family interview. We do this by stimulating interaction (similar to enactment). A practical definition of a pattern is a circular sequence of communication that occurs three times. The family social worker waits for spontaneous family events to emerge where a pattern evolves. Alternatively, the worker may set the stage to encourage family members to play out their usual family patterns. "Effective enactments empower the family, allowing them to express their usual ways of functioning and to explore new pathways on their own" (Minuchin, Colapinto, & Minuchin, 1998, p. 49).

The family social worker asks two people in the family to face each other and stimulates interaction by inviting them to discuss a particular issue. For example, with the Smith family, the worker might introduce the interaction by asking the mother and father to face each other and try to resolve the problem they had last evening about disciplining the children.

The family social worker then sits back and closely observes their communication for approximately five minutes (which is the usual length of time to observe a pattern of communication). The Smith couple begins communicating, and the family worker might notice Mrs. Smith looking more depressed, quiet, and withdrawn and Mr. Smith appearing uncertain, anxious, and wanting to be quiet and withdraw. Working with one person at a time, the worker elicits from each member his or her thoughts, feelings, and behaviors. It is important for the three to be connected. As one person describes his or her thoughts, feelings, and behaviors, the other person in the dyad must sit and listen without saying anything. After the family social worker has a cognitive understanding of the pattern (after the repetitive cycle is repeated three times or over a five-minute interval), it is important to stop the maladaptive pattern and work with the dyad.

If, on the other hand, the couple is communicating in an adaptive way, let them continue! Adaptive communication is what they need to do, and they should be encouraged in their efforts. For example, if the Smith couple is able to share their parenting concerns, listen to each other, and develop realistic plans, let them do so! After they complete an adaptive interchange, commend the efforts of the dyad and help them become aware of their adaptive circular communication. The worker can point out what they were doing correctly—hence a focus on strength. It is then important to contract with the family if they want to change the maladaptive pattern. Once the family social worker walks the couple through the process, they learn to understand where they misunderstood one another. They also learn about how they have been gridlocked in a maladaptive pattern and are then encouraged to problem solve by replacing maladaptive patterns with more positive behaviors. They are asked what needs to be changed, with each individual assuming responsibility for creating change in the pattern. "What can you do differently to change what happened?" They are then asked to practice the new way of communication, with the family social worker coaching them when they become stuck. When they complete the exercise successfully, the family social worker positively reinforces the change—a process known as commendation.

Step 2. Intervening in Maladaptive Circular Patterns. In order to work with circular causality, it is important to isolate recurring behavior and interactions involving circular interaction patterns. (Refer to examples in Chapter 3 and to Figure 3.1.) It is often helpful for the worker to draw the pattern of the family's circular patterns on a piece of paper, especially the patterns that revolve around a selected issue. A flip chart may be especially useful so everyone in the family will have the same visualization of the circular pattern. Remember, the simplest patterns consist of feelings–thoughts–behavior–feelings–thoughts–behavior and around and around.

1. Clarify with the family these patterns, pointing out the relationship between affect, or feelings, and behavior. For example, father scolds child, child feels

hurt, child pouts, father feels frustrated, and father scolds, and around and around the pattern goes. It is helpful for a family to see how they go around and around in these maladaptive circles.

2. When this is done, help clarify any family rules or myths that perpetuate these patterns, for example, a myth that the only way a child will listen to a parent is when the parent yells at the child.
3. When clarifying a circular pattern with a family, it is necessary to explore underlying feelings and any additional behaviors.
4. Point out evidence of emotional distress, and get members to label specific feelings. When feelings are out in the open, particularly fears and hurts, they can be directly faced.
5. Encourage the family to provide each member with reassurance and support.
6. Help the family develop understanding of each other by bringing their circular patterns out in the open and including underlying feelings.
7. After the dysfunctional patterns have been identified, the worker should then get the family to think of helpful *adaptive* patterns to deal with problem situations.
8. Help the family negotiate simultaneous change.
9. Reinforce family members' constructive suggestions.
10. Coach family members in trying out new adaptive behaviors, and assign realistic tasks explicitly as homework. (Tomm & Wright, 1979)

Lineal, Circular, Strategic, and Reflexive Questions

Beyond stimulating interaction, the family social worker can also assess circular patterns through the use of questioning (Collins, Coleman, & Barlow, 2006). Karl Tomm (1987a, 1987b, 1988) describes four types of questions that are appropriate for family interviewing: lineal, circular, strategic, and reflexive. According to Tomm, different types of questions can be used for therapeutic and assessment purposes. Tomm (1987a) cautions that selecting an area for examination needs to be done carefully, and "every question and every comment may be evaluated with respect to whether it constitutes an affirmation or challenge to one or more behavior patterns of the client or family" (p. 4). For example, starting an interview by asking "What problems would you like to discuss today?" will elicit different responses than asking "What positive things have happened to you over the past week?" The family social worker must carefully note clients' reactions to the questions being posed.

Lineal questions ask for basic information and assume a cause-and-effect sequence. Lineal questions attempt to define problems and seek explanation. Examples of lineal questions include:

- What brings you in today?
- How long have you been experiencing these problems?
- What is making you depressed?

Circular questions, on the other hand, are based on circular causality and the connections among family members. Circular questions help the family social worker to learn about ongoing patterns of family interaction and the effects that family members' behaviors have on one another. Circular questions demonstrate to the family that issues do not belong to individual members; everyone is connected to the problem regardless of whether or not they have a symptom themselves.

Circular questions are intended to create change, whereas lineal questions are intended to draw out information (Wright & Leahey, 1994). Circular questions are aimed at developing explanations for problems and identifying relationships between individuals, ideas, beliefs, and events. They can be used to change cognitive, affective, and behavioral domains of family functioning. Circular questions are useful for assessing the role of the presenting problem within the family. Each person is asked questions related to the definition of the problem, including who says what to whom. Examples of circular questioning include:

- When Melissa said that she was upset with you, how did you react?
- When you hear your husband yelling at the kids, how does that make you feel?

Strategic questions are directed at change, on the basis of the family social worker's assessment of the situation. The underlying intent of strategic questions is to correct behavior. Such questions challenge or confront patterns within the family. Examples of strategic questioning include:

- Can you try to see it his way?
- When are you going to tell her what you think?

Reflexive questions ask clients to become self-observers. Reflexive questioning is based on the belief that change depends on the efforts of clients, not the social worker. Examples of reflexive questioning include:

- What do you plan on doing about finding a new job?
- What do you think you can do to improve your school grades?
- When your mother gets into a fight with your sister, what does your father usually do?

EXERCISE 10.5   Circular Causality Role Play

Role-play with two other students who are to play two people in a family who are having a problematic pattern of communication. The family social worker should instruct the dyad by saying, "I would like to see how the two of you resolve differences." Members of the dyad then turn and face each other and start to interact over an issue (select an issue relevant to the dyad). This should take at least 5 to 10 minutes to explore. The family social worker then clarifies what the first person in the dyad is feeling and thinking and the resultant behavior. The worker then focuses on the second person's thoughts, beliefs, and feelings, ending with a description of the behavior of the second person.

The next step is to connect the behaviors to the thoughts, beliefs, and feelings of the first person. Once this is done, the worker can start the pattern anew until people understand how they impact the other person. The next step is to ask, "Well, how is this ever going to change?" and let the individuals develop a concrete approach to what they are going to do to solve their difficulties.

EP 2.1.10g

INTERVENTION SKILLS: FACILITATING CHANGE OF MALADAPTIVE CIRCULAR PATTERNS

Tomm and Wright (1979) identify six skills necessary to make changes regarding maladaptive circular patterns, which are now referred to by Karl Tomm as pathological interactive patterns or PIPs (Tomm, 1991).

1. **Break Maladaptive Patterns.**
   - Refrain from introducing changes that exceed the capabilities of the family or its members.
   - Initiate those changes that at least one member of the executive subsystem is liable to recognize as useful.
   - Interrupt maladaptive patterns of behavior, and take control of the immediate interaction.
   - Intervene to control maladaptive patterns by restructuring family interaction verbally or physically.
   - Instruct family members to clarify behavioral expectations for one another and to follow through on the limits set. Model if they are unable to do so.
   - When appropriate, facilitate the adaptive expression of anger of one family member in order to block the recurrent problematic behavior of another.

2. **Clarify Problematic Consequences.**
   - Ask the family to describe the problematic behavior that is occurring in the immediate process, and reinforce their articulated awareness when it is accurate.
   - Label the pattern for the family by detailing the preceding moments of maladaptive interaction, and seek the family's recognition of the sequence and its recurrent pattern.
   - Stimulate family members to reflect on the eventual outcome if problematic patterns were to continue.
   - Stimulate each family member to evaluate his or her own contributions to the problems by exploring the impact of his or her behavior on the cognition, affect, and behavior of other family members.
   - Confront family members on the problematic consequences of their own behaviors.
   - Provide verbal or nonverbal support before and after direct confrontation whenever possible.

3. **Alter Affective Blocks.**
   - Convey the importance of expressing and clarifying affective experience in order to better comprehend the maintenance of overt behavior patterns.
   - Remove inappropriate affective blocks by encouraging open discussion of the emotional turmoil of family members; validate their experience, clarify the content, and provide support.
   - Stimulate family members to further self-reflection and verbalization of specific affective experiences by entertaining alternative possibilities.
   - Explore catastrophic expectations with a view toward desensitizing inappropriate and unrealistic fears.

- After facilitating the overt expression of covert anger, curtail the projective aspect and stimulate self-reflection by exploring the underlying frustration.
- Facilitate and legitimize crying as a healthy response to loss, but differentiate the controlling aspect of whining from the psychological release of weeping when necessary.
- Mobilize family members to provide validation and support verbally or nonverbally; model if the family is unable or unwilling to do so.
- Provide support and slow the therapeutic process when an issue is too stressful and disorganizing, and help other family members to alter their expectations as well.
- While the affect is aroused, elicit verbal expression of immediate cognitive associations relevant to the (earlier) experience that is being reenacted.

4. **Initiate Cognitive Restructuring.**
   - Encourage verbalization by family members in order to expose relevant personal constructs and family belief systems.
   - Clarify issues by repeating salient points and carefully linking concepts and events.
   - Call into question collective beliefs, values, or goals that appear to be problematic, and initiate open discussion and reevaluation of relevant issues.
   - Challenge maladaptive ideas, stimulate the individual's willingness to hear other views, and facilitate corrective feedback from other family members.
   - To prevent new affect from blocking further progress, encourage the expression and discharge of emotion (especially through laughing or crying) while modifying a previous cognitive set.
   - Use metaphor, simile, overstatement, paradoxical statement, and so on to clarify, distill, and emphasize concepts that have adaptive potential.
   - Provide appropriate new information or a reformulation as required to develop more adaptive comprehension.
   - When possible, reframe preexisting negative concepts that are problematic in more positive constructive terms.
   - Describe and define relevant issues at different conceptual levels to stimulate new family understanding.
   - Encourage family members to consider new ideas further and to continue to discuss specific issues at home in order to reach a reality-based consensus.

5. **Implement New Adaptive Patterns.**
   - Using behavioral principles, apply social reinforcements to strengthen appropriate behaviors at any time during the sessions and encourage family members to do the same.
   - Stimulate each family member's willingness to identify new adaptive behaviors for herself or himself, and support her or his suggestions when they are constructive.
   - Elicit family members' willingness to be receptive to suggestions, and invite specific behavioral suggestions from other family members (or offer some).
   - Coach the family in implementing changes that are compatible with appropriate developmental tasks for the whole family as well as individual family members.

- Introduce adaptive changes in behavior during the interview by redirecting interaction patterns and altering spatial and seating arrangements to rearrange subsystems.
- Help family members negotiate and implement simultaneous changes, and, when appropriate, direct them to initiate the new behaviors in the session.
- When required, focus on preexisting or underlying conflictual issues in order to stimulate motivation for behavioral change.
- To achieve optimal anxiety levels for different family members, intensify or diminish the degree of crisis experienced by specific individuals through confrontation and support, respectively.
- Relinquish control of the interaction, and avoid interrupting when adaptive patterns of family interaction emerge.
- Elicit verbalization of the positive experience, and stimulate feedback to one another concerning the constructive event.
- Assign realistic and concrete behavioral tasks as homework. Seek explicit commitments to carry them out within a specific time period.
- Facilitate hope by stimulating interaction between family members to clarify the future consequences of adaptive change.

6. **Mobilize External Resources as Required.**
   - Openly admit to lack of progress, and explore possible inhibiting factors both inside and outside the family.
   - Coach family members to mobilize external resources and to influence them to be constructive; when indicated, ask the family to invite friends or relatives to sessions.
   - Seek immediate supervisory, consultative, or co-therapy counsel, or consider transferring to another therapist when there is unexplained deterioration in the family.
   - Carefully select and refer particular family members to other professional resources for appropriate treatment as required.
   - Articulate realistic tasks or natural resources to provide adequate controls and supports.

EP 2.1.10g

DETRIANGULATION

In Chapter 3, we discussed how triangulation often occurs in families. See also Figure 10.1. What is important now is for the family social worker to stop problematic triangulation by detriangulating involved family members. One of the authors was conducting a family session and noted that the child with the "problem" was seated between two angry parents yelling at one another. The child looked as though he were watching a ping-pong match, and it was evident that he was triangulated into the marital conflict. The author got up and invited him to move to another part of the room, saying, "I see that you are caught in the middle of your parents' argument. I'd like you to sit in a safer place on your own so you do not get caught in the middle anymore." Detriangulation involves developing strategies through which the family worker disrupts one triangle and opens up the family members to new, more functional alliances or triangles.

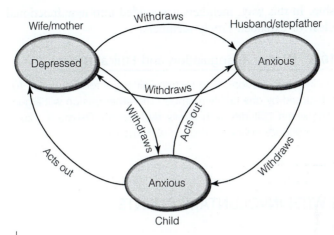

FIGURE 10.1 | Triangulation

Carter and McGoldrick (1999) point out that detriangulating involves "unlocking compulsory loyalties so that three dyadic relationships can emerge from the enmeshed threesome" (p. 441). Often dysfunctional triangles are revealed through an intense relationship between a parent and a child, often in opposition to the other parent. Four possible methods of detriangulation are available for the family social worker:

1. One way of detriangulating is to point the triangle out to the three people. People cannot change what they do not know about. Therefore, labeling the process brings to awareness what is happening.
2. Another method of detriangulation is ensuring that family members interact as dyads. This involves making certain that a third person does not jump into conflictual relationships, but instead allows the two other family members to work out the conflict on their own.
3. Another method is through reversal, or getting one person in the triangle to do the opposite of the pattern. For example, if a teenager acts out every time the parents begin an argument, the teenager would be instructed to instead go to his or her bedroom to study for an hour and let the parents work out their issue.
4. Detriangulation also can occur by shifting alliances (i.e., who does what with whom). If the mother is always the one trying to get a child to comply with a command, change can be accomplished by having the father gain the child's compliance. When a couple is triangulated with a child as a means of avoiding issues in their relationship, they might be instructed to spend a certain amount of time together talking about whatever is on their minds that day without the third party present. If they need the assistance of a third party to bring an issue to resolution, they might be encouraged to talk with a different adult, including the family social worker. Ideally, the couple should learn to deal with their issues directly and honestly. Alternatively, another adult family member could act as a supportive advice giver, removing the children from the conflictual

relationship. In this way, members are guided into new functional attachments with nuclear or extended family members.

EXERCISE 10.6   Worker Triangulation and Ethical Issues

EP 2.1.10g

Divide the class into two sections. One section will argue for the worker to keep a secret disclosed by one family member. The other section will argue that keeping the secret colludes with family dysfunction. Debate in class. Then formulate an agency policy for dealing with the issue.

WORKING WITH INVOLUNTARY CLIENTS

EXERCISE 10.7   Resistance in Problem Definition

Identify one possible problem where an individual in a family is the reason for initiating family work. How can the family social worker redefine the problem into a family issue without stimulating resistance in the family?

Involuntary clients typically receive services from an agency without requesting them. They may not be motivated to engage in family social work, and they may refuse to work toward the goals that the family social worker, the agency, or another outside authority has identified. They often arrive at an agency because they have been forced to receive help by public officials and are mandated to receive agency intervention because of problems involving child welfare, mental health, or criminal justice. Substance abuse is often an overarching issue. For all these categories of problems, laws exist to force clients into treatment against their will. When clients enter treatment against their will, they are likely to resist the efforts of the family social worker. In this light, assessment of involuntary clients should be done carefully because of the possibility that the problems are dangerous, illegal, or both. The family social worker might have to appear in court to testify or write a report for court.

Such families enter family work reluctantly, and some are visibly resistant. Clients who are experiencing problems such as sexual abuse, family violence, or substance abuse often exhibit strong resistance at the outset of family social work, and some continue to resist throughout the time spent in family work. Resistance should not be surprising, since many people enter family social work feeling anxious, frightened, or ashamed. In addition, parents often feel like failures when a problem attracts attention from agencies outside the family. Family members often show varying degrees of reluctance toward acknowledging a problem and engaging in the necessary work to produce change. An especially complex and sensitive situation occurs when there is victimization within the family and the perpetrator resists acknowledging the problem and does not show a desire for change. In child protection, for example, parental motivation and readiness for change are of considerable interest (Littell & Girvin, 2004).

Families may also be resistant to the actions of a particular agency because of past experience or because of what the agency represents to them. Some families may have been involved with other agencies without seeing any change in their problems. Clients may be concerned about possible breaches of confidentiality or anticipated lack of agency understanding of their situation. As a result, they may choose to be minimally compliant, doing only enough work to get by. Most involuntary clients are resistant clients, but not all resistant clients are involuntary. The degree of willingness to become involved in family work varies from one family to another. At one extreme end of the continuum are clients who are legally mandated to receive service and who do not believe they have a problem. Somewhere in the middle are those who believe they have a problem but do not want to enter family work to make the necessary changes. The ideal clients recognize that they have a problem and want to change their circumstances to eliminate the problem and work nondefensively toward a solution.

Even when there is no legal mandate forcing clients into family work, some clients become involved because of pressure from family members or friends. For example, the spouse of a substance abuser may threaten to leave unless the person starts treatment. Children usually have little leverage to force the family into work unless the child's behavior becomes so problematic that it is difficult to ignore, as when a child becomes suicidal or runs away from home. When some family members are resistant to family work, they are likely to hamper the progress of the rest of the family. In another common scenario, some family members agree that there is a problem, but they believe that the problem belongs to someone else in the family. This is a very common stance among families in which teenagers are acting out. The challenge for the social worker is to help all family members understand their roles in the development of the problem.

Clients usually look for one of two outcomes from family social work. Some just want to eliminate the pain created by the problem, and in the process want to be nurtured. These clients may be satisfied once the initial stress has been alleviated, and they may avoid making difficult or lasting changes. Other clients want to change their lives in concrete ways. They are willing to work hard to achieve needed changes in their lives. These are the most rewarding clients for family social workers.

EXERCISE 10.8   Role-Play

Break into groups of six. One person will play the role of family social worker to interview a family in which a teenaged child has been charged with possession of drugs (marijuana). The family consists of Katie (mother), Bobbie (father), Phil (14-year-old charged with drug possession), Jackie (16-year-old perfect daughter), and Jimmy (typical 8-year-old). The court has ordered the family into therapy. All family members are angry with Phil for putting the family through this turmoil. Family members do think that they play a role in the problem. First, role-play to deliberately create resistance in the family. After 5 to 10 minutes, work with this resistance to diminish it and engage to work with their problems. Compare the two approaches. What is different between the two role plays? Report back to the class.

Littell and Girvin (2004) connect resistant families with Prochaska and DiClemente's Stages of Change model (1992). They suggest that this model can be useful in assessing the risk of future harm to children. Conceivably, many involuntary clients are precontemplators. In other words, they do not believe they have a problem. Others may acknowledge they have a problem but are not prepared to work on it. Depending on where parents lie on the continuum of change, family workers will need to adapt their interventions accordingly. For some families, engagement skills become paramount, as moving too quickly into intervention will not be productive. Realistic expectations for families are critical to moving forward.

Involuntary or otherwise resistant families usually benefit from a clear contract stating the expected outcomes of their actions. The family social worker's task is to convey that despite the involuntary nature of their involvement in the work, some choices remain, and every choice is associated with an anticipated outcome. For example, those who are ordered into work for reasons of abuse but refuse to become involved may find that the family social worker has written a letter to the court or that their children have been placed in foster care. Ultimately, the social worker can empathize with clients' anger and fears about family social work and discuss how the involuntary nature of the work affects everyone.

Families need to know that participating in family social work is their choice. When families understand that there are certain issues over which they have control, their resistance may decrease. The family social worker should emphasize that freedom from unwanted agency intervention will occur when the conditions of the court order or contracted work are met. The contract should contain some recognition of client self-determination and state the conditions under which the family will become free from agency and legal intrusion. Work with involuntary clients begins by finding out what it is like for them to be ordered into family work. This question is one way of showing empathy and starting where the client is. Once the family social worker understands what it is like for the family to be receiving services involuntarily, the work can then focus on specific, concrete changes.

When clients are court-ordered, they should be informed that some conditions of the work are not negotiable and they need to understand the specific conditions for termination. As uncomfortable as it may be, family social workers must clearly describe the conditions linked to involuntary family social work. For example, if the social worker is required to prepare a court report, families should know about this at the outset. Clients must know what is expected of them as well as what is negotiable. When clients do not want to work, the family social worker can point out that the family has a right not to participate but that nonparticipation involves some consequences. In summary, the family social worker must discuss the nature of the problem, his or her role, nonnegotiable requirements, procedures mandated by the referral source, negotiable requirements, and choices available to the clients (Hepworth & Larson, 1993).

Motivation is the flip side of resistance. Motivation is present when families have a sincere desire to change something in their lives. Resentment and negativity undermine motivation. When clients feel blamed for their problems, without any concomitant understanding or empathy, the family social worker becomes a threat. Family social workers must be prepared to face clients' feelings of hostility and anger and to respond openly to the negative feelings. Arguing accomplishes little and can escalate clients' hostility and resentment. Since resistance to work may be part of a family's general style of dealing with outsiders, empathic responses by the family social worker can role-model appropriate behavior. We suggest not confronting client perceptions until trust and acceptance have developed. Direct confrontation about responsibility for problems during the assessment phase is likely to produce defensiveness rather than lead to change (Ivanoff, Blythe, & Tripodi, 1994). Instead, using empathy and rolling with resistance might be most productive. The family social worker can start by opening up the topic of how it is apparent that the family does not want to be involved in the work and then leading a discussion of what is going on with the family.

By recommending that family social workers not confront client perceptions early in the work, we are not saying that family social workers should collude with client dysfunction. The single most important skill for working with family resistance is being able to identify when it may be counterproductive to push an issue with the family (Brock & Barnard, 1992). Appropriate work with resistant clients entails opening up windows of opportunity to induce change. Sometimes clients may block the development of a working contract by insisting on pushing through their own definition of the problem. Family social workers may be able to find a common ground somewhere between the family social worker's and the client's definitions of the problem. Once the initial barriers are broken, many family social workers discover that clients gradually drop their defensiveness in defining the problem. Social workers need to remember that defensiveness serves a protective function for clients, and this protective stance can be dropped only after clients feel safe.

CASE 10.2 | ## Working with Other Helpers

Wanda and Kenneth came to the family social worker because Kenneth's ex-wife had moved out of the state with his 2-year-old son, Johnny, and refused to allow Kenneth to see the boy. Kenneth reported that his ex-wife, Nola, was angry with him about their divorce and was jealous of his new wife, Wanda. Nola had envisioned that she and Kenneth would remarry until Wanda came on the scene. Wanda reported that not only was Nola angry with the couple but that both of their families (and some of their friends) were upset about the union. Wanda said this is because she is somewhat older than Kenneth and divorced herself. Both families have religious beliefs against divorce, and they have had much difficulty accepting the untraditional age difference between the newlyweds.

The family social worker's assessment revealed a need for legal aid to deal with the custody and visitation issues, as well as family counseling for the extended family issue. Since Wanda and Kenneth did not have a great deal of money, the family social worker referred the couple to an attorney service that provided help on a sliding-fee scale according to family income. The family social worker then referred the couple to a family counseling center associated with their religious denomination to help with the family issues.

Overcoming resistance usually involves finding out about the family social worker and evaluating her or him (Lum, 1996).

Work with involuntary clients can be just as effective as work with voluntary clients (Ivanoff, Blythe, & Tripodi, 1994, p. 57). The most positive results seem to be related to the quality of worker-client interaction. One last word of advice is in order: A wise worker must be able to recognize the difference between a resistant family and an ineffectual intervention.

EP 2.1.10g

INTERVENTION WITH MINORITY FAMILIES

Family work techniques for family social workers to use with minorities are those that promote bonding between the social worker and the family. In order to engage the family, the social worker may adopt the family's verbal and nonverbal communication style and relevant metaphors. This is sometimes referred to as *joining*. Other family systems techniques that may be used include behavioral methods such as social skills training. For instance, specialized treatment packages are available to help families learn better communication, problem-solving, or anger management techniques (see Franklin & Jordan, 1999).

Intervention with African American Families

Feelings of family empowerment and satisfaction with services were related to successful family intervention (Lewellen & Jordan, 1994). Further, trust and communication style were important variables. African Americans, in comparison to other ethnic groups, reportedly were more sensitive to such matters as insensitivity of the family worker. Members of this group reported less trust in the establishment, including mental health service providers. Lack of trust may result in guarded communications and defensive interactions with the family social worker. Specific recommendations for working with African American families include the following:

1. Offer services to the extended family network or to groups of families who support each other.
2. Take into account the needs of single, female heads of households, including transportation problems, accommodation to work schedules, and babysitting needs.
3. Consider flexible hours for meetings so that extended family members may attend. Also, consider transportation and lodging needs for the extended family.
4. Services should be brief and time limited to encourage attendance of families who may distrust the mental health system.
5. Treatment focusing on psychoeducational and social skills methodology may be used, as well as direct communication with the family about treatment issues.
6. The family social worker must be willing and able to acknowledge racism and issues that may impede self-disclosure by African American family members.
7. African American family members value mutuality and egalitarianism; thus, the family social worker should provide services that respect the client family

and include the family in the decision-making process. (Jordan, Lewellen, & Vandiver, 1994, p. 32)

Intervention with Hispanic American Families

Intervention issues for Hispanic American families may be identified by looking at families according to their level of acculturation. Newly arrived immigrant families need concrete services such as language instruction, information, referral, and advocacy. Efforts must be made to reach out to these families, as they may not access services on their own due to language and cultural barriers. Immigrant-American families may require conflict resolution, problem-solving, or anger management training due to intergenerational conflicts. Immigrant-descent families are more comfortable seeking traditional mental health services. They likely speak both Spanish and English in the home and are acculturated into the dominant culture (Padella et al. and Casas & Keefe in Jordan, Lewellen, & Vandiver, 1994, p. 33).

The family social worker may be considered as equal to a healer, priest, or physician by the Hispanic American family, depending on the family's level of acculturation. In fact, the family may have consulted a priest or folk healer before seeking services from an agency.

Jordan, Lewellen, and Vandiver (1994) make the following recommendations for work with Hispanic American families:

1. Time-limited intervention that includes the family and extended family, due to the importance and insularity of the family
2. Content sensitivity to the family's level of acculturation, beliefs, hierarchy, and traditions
3. Sensitivity to role confusion and conflict the newly arrived family may be experiencing (Thus, techniques including communication skills, negotiation training, and role clarification may be important.)
4. Sensitivity to the family's need for education, information, and referral services
5. Inclusion of folk healers, priests, or other nonrelative helpers. (p. 34)

Intervention with Asian American Families

Jordan, Lewellen, and Vandiver (1994) suggest techniques to enhance service provision to Asian American families. Because hierarchy is important to Asian American families, treatment plans should include high-status members of the family or community. The family social worker may be seen as an authority figure and can use this status to implement positive family changes. The social worker must be sure to show respect for members of the family. Services offered within the family's neighborhood are believed to increase client participation in treatment.

Clear communication between the family social worker and family members is essential. The social worker should avoid using slang, jargon, or regional expressions. Also, if an interpreter must be used, he or she should be sensitive to the family's culture and social class. Treatment should include psychoeducational techniques. The entire family may be included in the treatment, with deference shown by the family social worker to the elderly members. Other families in the community (in centers, churches, or temples) may be utilized in support, or social groups for treatment of problems such as severe and persistent mental illness may be joined.

Intervention with Native American Families

Ho (1987) makes the following recommendations for treating Native American families in a sensitive manner:

1. Provision of concrete services may be necessary for Native American families experiencing difficulties due to lack of food, housing, or other necessities. Provision of necessities helps the social worker to engage with family members.
2. The family social worker's communication with the Native American family should be "open, caring, and congruent … (and delivered) in a simple, precise, slow, and calm" manner (Ho, 1987, p. 94).
3. To get to know the Native American family, the family social worker should observe their communication patterns and styles and note how members of the extended family network interact with one another. "To do this, the family social worker needs to be attentive, talk less, observe more, and listen actively" (Ho, 1987, p. 95).
4. Mapping techniques may be used to learn about the extended family.
5. The Native American value of the collective indicates the need for mutual establishment of treatment goals.
6. Problem solving may be facilitated by "(a) social, moral, organic reframing/ relabeling; (b) mobilizing and restructuring the extended family network; (c) promoting interdependence as a family restructuring technique; (d) employing role model, educator role, and advocate role; (e) restructuring taboos for problem solving; and (f) collaborative work with medicine person, paraprofessional, and therapist helper." (p. 99)

Overall, the family social worker should be sensitive to individual families and let the family be the guide in learning about the family culture. Differences are seen within groups due to differential levels of acculturation, regional differences, and so forth.

EP 2.1.10g

CHAPTER SUMMARY

In this chapter, we focused on assessment of the entire family, moving into six different ways to define family problems. Of particular importance is for the family social worker to be continually culturally sensitive. Intervention targeted changing circular patterns through stimulating interaction; the use of lineal, circular, strategic, and reflexive questions; and detriangulation. We also discussed working with involuntary clients, including the need for the family social worker to develop goals and set contracts with all family members.

The family social work relationship is established to achieve certain goals. Goal setting allows the work to develop and retain its purpose. Goals should specify what the client wishes to achieve through family social work, as well as the methods that will be used. Goals should be measurable, set within a reasonable time limit, consistent with the client's values and abilities, and under the client's control. Strategies for setting goals include identifying general intentions, defining the specifics of the goal, and setting goals that can be reached within a measurable period.

Contracting occurs at the end of the assessment phase. The contract is an agreement between the client and the family social worker outlining the goals of the relationship and the means to be used to achieve these goals. The contract can be oral or written and should be negotiated early in the work, but it may change as the work progresses. Without a contract, there is often confusion because the family social worker and the family are proceeding without a shared understanding of the work to be accomplished. Contracts are limited by time constraints and agency mandates. Effective contracts specify what needs to be accomplished and how, the roles of the family social worker and the client, and procedural details such as when and where meetings will take place.

KEY TERMS

Adaptive patterns or healthy interactive patterns (HIPs)   circular interactive patterns that are both congruent with family members' feelings, thoughts, and behaviors and foster growth, caring, and healthy communication and interactions between these family members.

Affective blocks   get in the way of circular interactive patterns to change. They are usually a fear of some sort, for example, fear of an anger outburst or fear of being abandoned.

Circular patterns   interactions or communications between two people that over time become repetitive. They are either adaptive or maladaptive.

Culturally sensitive practice   Social work practice that is aware, sensitive, and respectful of a culture other than the social worker's culture. The social worker is able to incorporate and use features of the family's culture in family social work.

Detriangulation   The process of removing a third party from a dysfunctional triangle, with the aim of getting a problematic dyad to address its issues without the need to draw in a third person.

Lineal, circular, and reflective questioning   forms of questioning that are designed to draw out various types of information. Some questions (e.g., lineal) are designed to draw out facts, while others (e.g., circular) draw out connections between family members, create change (e.g., strategic), or stimulate clients to reflect on their life (e.g., reflexive).

Maladaptive patterns or pathological interactive patterns (PIPs)   circular interactive patterns that are incongruent with feelings, thoughts, and behaviors between two people and tend to spiral downward to prevent problem solving and caring between family members.

SUGGESTED READINGS

Tomm, K. (1991). Beginning of a HIPs and PIPs approach to psychiatric assessment. *The Calgary Participator*, 1(2), 21–24.

Tomm, K., & Wright, L. (1979). Training in family therapy: Perceptual, conceptual, and executive skills. *Family Process*, 18, 250–277.

COMPETENCY NOTES

EP 2.1.4b. Gain sufficient self-awareness to eliminate the influence of personal biases and values in working with diverse groups: An ecological focus helps the family social worker to consider and be sensitive to diverse family structures and needs, thus eliminating personal biases in family work.

EP 2.1.10e. Assess client strengths and limitations: The family social worker's use of a strengths-based framework helps to view families' strengths as well as problem areas.

EP 2.1.10g. Select appropriate intervention strategies: Family systems interventions, such as circular questions and detriangulation techniques, help the family social worker to intervene at the family systems level. These techniques can be helpful with involuntary families.

The Intervention Phase | CHAPTER 11

LEARNING OBJECTIVES

- Conceptual: Understand different intervention roles of the family social worker as well as different techniques useful in intervention.

- Perceptual: Observe different roles and techniques, being mindful of their impact on families.

- Valuational/Attitudinal: Recognize that families have innate strengths to solve problems and that family social work intervention is a partnership with families.

- Behavioral: Use basic intervention techniques including problem-solving skills as part of the strengths-based approach.

INTERVENTION PHASES

Many family social workers feel most comfortable in the engagement, relationship-building, and assessment phases of family work but may experience the most self-doubt when specific family changes have been targeted. In Chapter 10, we discussed many practical change-inducing skills that family social workers can use with families. These skills are not to be used mechanically by family social workers. Rather, they must be used intentionally and selectively on the basis of the assessment of a particular family. The intervention phase formally starts after the family social worker has engaged the family and completed a thorough assessment, goals have been set, and a clear contract has been agreed upon.

In this chapter, we first look at the micro skills that can be used on a moment-to-moment basis to help families and their members alter behaviors and repetitive ways of functioning. These skills include focusing, using examples, confronting, enacting, externalizing the problem, and using metaphor. We then examine sub-phases of intervention, which include contracting, crisis intervention, ecological intervention, and problem solving. We believe these combined approaches offer a basis for a beginning generalist approach to family social work. We also go beyond these intervention approaches to briefly describe approaches helpful in dealing with the resolution of immediate problems, enhancement of family communication, dealing with boundary issues, and using a form of cognitive approach—namely the narrative approach. We believe that at a beginning level these approaches and specific techniques can be a useful enhancement of the generalist family approach. The approaches briefly described are the solution-focused approach, communicative/experiential approach, structural family therapy approach, and the narrative approach.

Choosing the Family Approach

How do you know which approach to use? It really depends on how the family and the family social worker define the problem(s) they wish to work on, including the language families use to describe problems or issues. The family worker has to listen very carefully to the subtle "nuances" of language the family members use (Collins & Tomm, 2010). If the primary nuance is around feelings, a communicative/experiential approach may be a good starting approach. For example, "I am feeling quite depressed today." If the key nuance is around lack of behavioral change, then a behavioral approach, problem-solving, or solution-focused approach may be a good starting model. For example, "I am finding it very difficult to deal with my son's temper tantrums." Nuances around oppression or powerlessness may point toward a feminist approach: "I feel that expectations of me as a mother and wife are unrealistic." "I am expected to do all of the housework as well as deal with the parenting of the children." Nuances around irrational thinking could lead to a cognitive or narrative approach. For example, "I think that I am a failure at everything I do."

EP 2.1.10g

ROLES AND OBJECTIVES OF THE FAMILY SOCIAL WORKER

Historically, professional helpers have approached families and individual clients from an expert position. With presumably greater knowledge and experience than clients, professionals worked with families to solve problems, make decisions, and show parents ways to become more effective. As an expert, the helping professional carried out this role as an authority, detached from the family. Families were not considered partners in a change process and power and knowledge were the domain of the professional helper. In the process, the helper gave and the family received. This giving-receiving pattern reflected power imbalances between the family worker and the family that interfered with motivation, commitment, and goals.

Changes in social workers' roles and expectations evolved out of shifts in the perception of the family and of effective helping. Today, the family is not a passive recipient of intervention but is an active partner and participant throughout the entire change process. Nor does the family social worker know better than the family (Wood & Geismar, 1986). The family, within parameters determined by society, must define its own needs, set priorities, and state preferences for services. Consequently, the family social worker is a collaborator, facilitator, and negotiator. These multiple roles demand that workers be well educated. Indeed, to fulfill these roles, family social workers must use multiple helping skills and be competent in a range of domains pertinent to their role. The role of family collaborator and partner requires that workers reject canned or manualized expert solutions to predefined problems. Families have both the right and the responsibility to identify their special concerns and goals in relation to their family situation and to play an active role in their resolution.

To better help families, family social workers must understand their own family issues and interpersonal relationships in order to develop mutual respect and partnership with the individual families. Broadening the focus beyond the individual to embrace the entire family unit is a profound shift in perspective for many professionals whose educational background and inclination motivate them to advocate for children and at times assume an *adversarial* role for the family. The shift from an individual to a family perspective requires family social workers to incorporate a belief in family competence into the decision-making and problem-solving process.

The role of expert or professional may not provide the best vantage point from which to appreciate family members' strengths and assets, since the underlying message in the expert role is that the family does not know what is happening. Family members and the family social worker are freed to connect with family stories and narratives, their hopes and fears, and resources rather than trying to fit them into the narrow confines of a diagnostic category or treatment protocol. "Ultimately a collaborative stance may make us less vulnerable to some of the more political elements of helping: paternalism, victim-blaming, and preemption of client views" (Saleebey, 1992, p.15).

In partnership with families, family social workers use seven roles as a springboard from which to stimulate change: empathic supporter, teacher or trainer, consultant, enabler, mobilizer, mediator, and advocate.

1. In the role of *empathic supporter*, the guiding philosophy of a family social worker is to identify and reinforce family strengths while recognizing family limitations and lack of resources. Acknowledging strengths enables the family social worker to join with the family and develop a bond that will increase trust, motivation, and optimism to work toward change. While every family has strengths, social workers have unfortunately often been preoccupied with dysfunction and pathology and have even reinforced dysfunction by focusing primarily on problems. It is important to remember that, despite negative parenting practices, most parents care deeply about their children. Such familial caring should be highlighted to create the foundation for dealing with targeted problems.

2. The *teacher* or *trainer* role allows the family social worker to cultivate areas where the family is deficient or lacking in skills or knowledge. Viewing family difficulties as stemming from skill deficits (or, more palatably, as the result of skills needed to be learned), rather than as evidence of pathology (which needs to be eliminated or corrected), makes families more open to working on problems nondefensively. Problem areas may include deficits in communication, parenting skills, problem solving, anger management, conflict resolution, values clarification, money management, and skills of daily living.

    The teaching role often plays out in parent training interventions. Sometimes the teaching role involves helping parents substitute verbal and physical punishment with more positive and constructive parent-child interactions. Other times, the family social worker teaches parents to work more effectively with difficult child behavior by reinforcing positive behavior and discouraging negative or annoying behavior. Through such teaching activities, parents can become "therapists" for their children.

3. The family social worker as *consultant* is an adviser to the family for specific problems that arise. For instance, the family generally may function well but may find adolescence a particularly trying time for which they need specialized help. The family social worker, as a consultant, can offer valuable information to parents about typical or "normal" teenage behavior. In the process, parents gain deeper insight about their adolescent's needs and will be less inclined to consider their child a problem in future interactions. The family social worker can also provide ongoing feedback to parents and children who may be isolated or otherwise lack mechanisms to obtain such feedback from other sources.

4. The *enabler* role allows the family social worker to expand opportunities for the family that might not otherwise be accessible. For instance, an immigrant family may not be familiar with the various services appropriate for their special needs. Informing a family about available services and helping them to use these services will empower the family. The empowerment that family members experience when accomplishing a task can pave the way for future successes.

5. The family social worker as *mobilizer* captures the worker's unique position in the social network of helping resources. A social worker, knowledgeable about helping systems and community support networks, activates and manages the involvement of various community groups and resources that serve families. The family social worker can mobilize and coordinate community agencies to work with a family. When school poses challenges to children, for example, the family social worker can coordinate with school and family and foster communication to gather additional resources for a struggling student.

6. In the *mediator* role, the family social worker addresses stress and conflict between individuals and systems. Mediation can occur at any level of the system. The family social worker can mediate solutions when the family is in conflict with the community or, at a narrower level, can mediate between family members who are in conflict. When a family member has an antagonistic relationship with a landlord or neighbor, for example, the family social worker can also work with all parties to resolve the conflict.

7. The family social worker also acts as an *advocate,* a role that requires activism on behalf of client families. The family social worker is in a unique position to understand how family problems are often rooted in conditions within the broader societal context. Consequently, community activism and political action give family social workers the means with which to work for social and legislative reform benefiting clients. Part of the strengths perspective in the role of advocacy is the importance of getting the stories and views of family members out to those who need to hear them—schools, agencies, employers, local governments, churches, or businesses. The policies and regulations affecting many families are crafted by governments that are often far removed from the daily reality of clients. Furthermore, these policies do not take advantage of the wisdom and resources of their intended beneficiaries and recipients. One current example is the recent change in California allowing same-sex marriage. However, if a couple decides to divorce, one of the partners needs to have been a resident of California for at least six months for this to occur. This, of course, discriminates against all couples not residing in California who had obtained their marital license in that state. (Note: As of January 2009, same-sex marriages are not recognized in California; however, legal challenges to Proposition 8 make the future status of same-sex marriage in California uncertain at the time of this writing.)

EXERCISE 11.1 Roles of Family Social Workers

Family social workers can assist families in a variety of circumstances. Consider each of the seven roles that a family social worker might assume. Give an example of a situation where each role might be used, and provide an example of what the family social worker can do to fill the role.

EP 2.1.10k

INTERVENTION TECHNIQUES

Family social workers can use a variety of techniques to assist client families to gain new insights and, ultimately, to practice new behaviors. Some useful techniques to help families gain new insights and create change include observing, focusing, using examples, confronting, reframing, using metaphors, and contracting.

Observing

Structured observation, a formal procedure used both in research and in practice to record behavior, may be used when objective information about the presence of events is needed (Polster & Collins, 2011). The family may be helped by seeing the frequency data collected about a particular problem, such as frequency of tantrums. Systematic observation helps parents learn to manage children with behavior problems and may be employed to help abusive parents develop positive, effective behavior-management techniques. Changing from a punitive, aversive parenting style to a more positive, reinforcing way of responding can be facilitated by self-monitoring procedures, such as teaching parents to count the number of times they respond positively or negatively to their child. Helping a parent learn to record a child's words during part of the day may be an important part of an assessment of speech difficulties. Having a parent learn to record the number of times a particular physical therapy routine is carried out could be very important for increasing compliance with a treatment program.

Listening and observing form the foundation of qualitative family assessments. Observation as a necessary skill for a family social worker cannot be overemphasized. Without open and accurate observation, the activities that follow will have no substance. Observation allows the worker to obtain accurate information essential for understanding families—some of which is not explicit. However, unless mindful use is made of the information, much can be lost. Descriptions of family events and dynamics by family members may be contradictory; other times, family members may be unable to describe what is going on because they lack verbal skills or because they do not understand what is happening. Additionally, through independent observation of what is happening in a particular family, the family social worker can piece together independent viewpoints into a unified whole. Thus, through observing, or "listening with the eyes," the family social worker notices the physical characteristics and nonverbal behaviors, energy level, emotions, and congruence between verbal and nonverbal expression.

Observation enables the family social worker to develop a comprehensive understanding of the ways the family experiences the world. The worker must listen to both the content and the process in the family. The worker observes, for example, subtle issues related to themes of power, authority, and ambivalence about seeking or receiving help. Difficulties in discussing socially stigmatized topics and inhibitions concerning the direct and full expression of powerful feelings are particularly crucial to look out for (Shulman, 1992). Since family social workers are likely to pick up indirect communication from nonverbal rather than verbal communications, they must observe these closely. Observations of family dynamics supplement information obtained from the verbal flow of an interview as well as from any assessment tools used by the family worker.

Family social work provides special opportunities for observation. In contrast to an office setting, family social workers have the opportunity to conduct an ecological assessment of the individual, the family, and the community. The worker makes mental notes about the community by becoming aware of the broader environment where the family lives, noting such things as access to community services (including transportation and medical and educational agencies), neighborhood safety, and recreational and cultural opportunities. Such information helps place into perspective discussions with the family and also provides a knowledge base to draw on when making linkages to resources.

Once in a home, observation has enhanced significance because the family worker is witness to the physical environment of the family. Seeing the organization of the home and resources available to meet basic needs allows the worker to understand more about client strengths and coping strategies, resources, and limitations imposed by the home environment. Before entering the home, the worker might construct a mental checklist for what to look for, given the special circumstances of the family. Certainly, observations of the physical environment will be affected by special circumstances (Holman, 1983). A family in severe economic crisis may live in a dilapidated house, with inadequate plumbing, mattresses on the floor, or an infestation of vermin. For example, one family worker worked in a small home where the family owned six large dogs. The day after each visit, the worker noticed multiple marks on her body, suggesting flea bites. Alternatively, an impoverished house may suggest depression and apathy. Similarly, when working with parents of an active child, the family social worker may observe that there are few children's materials available and wonder about parental knowledge of child development or their ability to purchase stimulating toys. The worker will also note that the family lives on the tenth floor of a high-rise public housing development, making access to fresh air and outdoor activities very difficult. Family social workers formulate hypotheses about families and work to validate or refute them. In the preceding example, a hypothesis about parents' lack of knowledge of child development might be discarded if the home was equipped with child-appropriate materials, including books, toys, and play equipment. Asking about recreational opportunities and access to playground equipment might validate a hypothesis about living arrangements in an apartment building.

Besides informing the family social worker about environmental and physical resources, home observation provides opportunities for observing how family members interact in their daily routine. In office meetings, professionals may interact with only one member of the family, whereas in-home sessions allow family social workers to speak with the entire family. Contributions to individual family members' well-being or dysfunction may be noticed and clues obtained for what assistance is needed. Careful observation also strengthens documentation and other record-keeping demanded by many programs.

Overall, observation skills lay the foundation for many intervention decisions. Cultural and ethnic differences also need to be factored into observations of the family. Information should be obtained in a way that remains sensitive to and respectful of the fact that the worker is a visitor in the home of the family. Such information should not be used to condemn or make value judgments about lifestyles.

Family social workers will also make note of the social functioning of the family. Social functioning is best understood by looking at the social roles that family members perform. Individual behavior and adjustment reflects how well family members perform their social roles. As mentioned, Geismar and Ayres (1959) proposed four areas of role performance within the family and four outside the family. These observations are still valid today. Internal roles include:

- Family relationships and family unity
- Child care and training
- Health practices
- Household practices.

External family roles include:

- Use of community resources
- Social activities
- Economic practices
- Relationship of the family to the social worker.

Focusing

After the family worker has made observations of the family and its environment, the worker then focuses on particular issues. Focusing involves paying attention. To do this, both the client and the family social worker must ensure that time is used productively. While tangents can sometimes be productive, most often they are unproductive. It is therefore important to recognize when clients shift topics or steer the discussion elsewhere. It is possible to focus on the client, on the main theme or problem, on others, on mutual issues, on the interviewer, or on cultural, environmental, or contextual issues. On the basis of prior knowledge of the problem and the client, the family social worker can develop a list of relevant and promising areas to be explored. However, anticipating problem areas is not always possible. Sometimes clients are scattered or overwhelmed.

EXERCISE 11.2   Focusing on the Client

Think of a specific person with whom you have had difficulty interacting (not necessarily in the context of social work). List some things you could do to establish rapport with this person. Next, list some ways you could show this person that you are focusing on him or her, rather than on yourself.

Using Examples

Examples help the family social worker explain, describe, or teach a concept to a family. Generally, examples should be compatible with experiences of the family's life. Examples can be used to accomplish several objectives. They offer reassurance that others have faced the same challenges. A family social worker may tell a worried parent whose child is about to begin kindergarten, "Many parents have these concerns. One mother told me that with each of her five children, she felt some worry as they began kindergarten." Examples can illustrate alternative ways of dealing with a difficult situation. The family social worker may tell a parent, "Once when I talked with another mother about a similar situation, she told me that she had tried letting her child take a nap in the afternoon. Your situation sounds similar. Does her decision seem as though it would work for you, too?"

Examples can help clients feel at ease with something that has made them uncomfortable. The family social worker may say, "I remember a mother who tried three different ways to help her child learn to use the toilet before the child was trained. Like her, you may find that the second or third effort will work, even though the first one did not." Examples in the form of interesting stories can be valuable teaching aids because they are likely to be remembered longer than generalized statements.

EXERCISE 11.3   Using Examples

Develop three examples that would help you to explain a concept or practice to a client. With a partner, practice using examples to explain one of these concepts (such as using time-outs) to a client.

Confronting

Confrontation is a useful skill for family social workers, but its effectiveness has been questioned because it can be either growth-promoting or damaging to a client. Confrontation often is viewed as hostile, unpleasant, demeaning, and anxiety-provoking. Family social workers may be reluctant to use confrontation because of potentially harmful consequences, such as the client pulling out of counseling or escalating anger. Yet confrontation can be helpful under some circumstances. The level of confrontation should be chosen carefully: "Don't use a cannon when a pea shooter would suffice!" Similarly, confrontation is not a verbal hit-and-run; rather, it is used constructively to bring about change.

The goal of confrontation is to raise awareness by presenting information that the client is overlooking or failing to identify. The family social worker must find a way to make new information palatable or acceptable to the person being confronted. While confrontation can be a difficult skill to master, particularly for family social workers who are ambivalent about its use, it can also generate change quickly.

A useful guideline in deciding whether to confront clients is to determine what purpose confrontation will serve. Is confrontation planned because the family social worker is impatient and unwilling to allow the client to move at his or her own pace? Does the worker enjoy confrontation or want to impose her or his personal values on the client? Conversely, is confrontation desirable because the worker is attuned to client feelings and wants to create change? Confrontation often is most useful only after other skills have failed.

Confrontation requires tenacity and tact on the part of the family social worker, who must be willing to bring into the open an unexpressed feeling, idea, or issue. Without confrontation by the worker, family members may persist in behavior that is self-destructive or harmful to others. Confrontation, when used appropriately and in a caring manner, benefits the client. Brock and Barnard (1992) suggest that the difference between a well-executed confrontation and a confrontation that is demeaning or hostile can be perceived in the social worker's tone of voice.

Confrontation is appropriate in addressing repetitive client problematic behavior that is not amenable to change through other efforts. For example, the client may be avoiding a basic issue that is troubling or creating dysfunction within the family. Confrontation may assist a family member to recognize self-destructive or self-defeating behaviors or to acknowledge the possible consequences of behaving in a particular way. Further examples of appropriate situations for confrontation include incongruent behavior during an interview that affects the quality of the family-worker relationship, failure to assume self-responsibility, visible discrepancies between thoughts or feelings and words or behaviors, and unrealistic or distorted perceptions of a situation.

The purpose of confrontation is to point out discrepant aspects of the client's verbal and nonverbal behavior, bringing them to awareness. The primary function of confrontation is to provoke disequilibrium in order to permit new behaviors to develop. Although confrontation does not solve the problem, it can motivate the client to work on the problem.

Confrontation is most effective when a strong client–family social worker relationship has been established. A general guideline is that the stronger the relationship, the more effective the confrontation. One positive outcome of effective confrontation is a deepening of the client-worker relationship. By using attentive listening and empathy skills to tune in to the client's reaction to confrontation, the worker may help the client to gain greater insight and motivation for change. For example, a worker might say, "I get a sense that you are bothered by what I just said." Because of the emotional intensity of confrontation, it should not be used at the end of a session, when feelings should approach a more even keel.

Confrontation has varied effects, depending on whether the client has the personal and social resources to cope with the information being presented. A client with well-developed defenses may block the impact of confrontation, and the family social worker should recognize these defenses and discuss them. Even though some people react poorly to feedback, a social worker who is not honest is colluding with maladaptive behavior.

Successful confrontation occurs in two stages: formulating the confrontation statement and addressing the response of the client. The social worker should prepare for possible reactions such as withdrawal, defensiveness about the family social worker's observations, denial, discrediting the feedback, arguing, or finding someone else to collude with.

The following sentence shells can be used for formulating confrontational statements:

"On the one hand, you say ___, and on the other hand you do ___." (used to confront discrepancies between words and actions)

"I am puzzled (confused) about what you just said/did. Would you please help me understand?"

"I don't get it...."

Effective confrontation requires that the social worker point out discrepancies, inconsistencies, or contradictions between the client's words and actions. In describing these discrepancies, the family social worker must avoid judgmental or evaluative speculations and conclusions. Following a confrontation with an empathic response will increase its effectiveness as a motivator for change.

Levels of Confrontation

Level 1: Giving in to the client. At this level, the family social worker either ignores the problematic behavior or makes a feeble attempt to confront and then backs off at the first sign of resistance. The worker may be overly concerned about being liked or being attacked or may not be committed enough to the relationship to invest emotional intensity.

Level 2: Scolding. The social worker attempts to coerce the client into changing by shaming, attempting to induce guilt, or nagging. The family social worker risks losing self-control and may even give the client a lecture about acceptable behavior. At this level, confrontation can be demeaning and manipulative.

Level 3: Describing ineffective behavior. The social worker describes the behavior that is hurting the client or others and identifies possible reasons for the behavior. The worker may attempt to empathize by conveying a message about how difficult it is to face and take responsibility for the behavior; yet the message is straightforward and does not involve lecturing or conceding.

Level 4: Identifying negative consequences of behavior. The family social worker identifies ineffective behavior patterns and examines feelings. The worker also helps the client to identify possible negative consequences of continuing the behavior.

Level 5: Levels 3 and 4, plus soliciting commitment to change. This level incorporates components of Levels 3 and 4 but also challenges the client to accept responsibility for the problem and for making changes. Changes will occur only if the client honestly agrees with the social worker.

EXERCISE 11.4   Confronting

List three situations in which confrontation would be a helpful intervention. With a partner, role-play the use of confrontation with a client.

Reframing

Reframing removes a situation from an old context (set of rules) and places it in a new context (set of rules) that defines it equally well (Becvar & Becvar, 1996). In a reframe, positive interpretations are assigned to problematic behaviors and responses (Satir & Baldwin, 1983). The technique is most successful if the family social worker is able to persuade the family that the reframe is plausible and more than the former interpretation (Brock & Barnard, 1992). When problems are understood in a more positive light, new responses are likely. For example, a reframe of a teenager's behavior is given to a family when they are asked by the worker to see the teen's arguments with the parents over curfew as attempts to grow up and be independent (positive) rather than rebellions against parental authority (negative).

What makes reframing such an effective tool of change is that it is almost impossible to revert to our previous helplessness and especially our original hopelessness about the possibility of a solution (Watzlawick, Weakland, & Fisch, 1974). Social workers should use reframing selectively because not all issues should be reframed. For example, sexual abuse should never be reframed as the perpetrator's attempt to show affection.

Example of Reframing   A hyperactive child can be reframed as a challenging, energetic child. Instead of exclusively relying on medication, parents may plan more physical activities to help the child burn off excessive energy.

EXERCISE 11.5   Reframe the Problem

Use the case of the hyperactive child and develop other reframes that might be used. Think of two other case examples with which you are familiar that might benefit from reframing. Write down the negative statement and the possible positive reframe that might be used instead in each case. Share with the class.

Using Metaphor

A metaphor is "a figure of speech in which a word or phrase literally denoting one kind of object or idea is used in place of another to suggest a likeness or analogy between them" (Satir & Baldwin, 1983, p. 244). Metaphors are used to help clients understand abstract concepts. They provide information in a nonthreatening way and give families some distance from a threatening situation.

Example of Use of Metaphor To help families understand how a crisis can destabilize the family system, the family social worker may compare the family to a mobile that gets out of balance when objects are added or moved around.

EXERCISE 11.6   Family Metaphor Example

Divide into groups of three or four and develop a family role-play. Write a short script of a family in crisis and then develop a metaphor, which will help the family to stabilize during the time of crisis. Share with the class.

Contracting

Contracting can include contracts between family members. Two types of commonly used contracts are *quid pro quo* (QPQ) and good faith (Jackson, 1972). In the QPQ contract, one person agrees to exchange a behavior for one desired by another family member. For example, a mother might agree to drive her daughter and friends to the mall if the daughter washes the dishes without being told. The good faith contract, by contrast, is not dependent on the behavior of another family member. A person is rewarded after contract conditions are met. For instance, if a child completes her homework all week, she can invite a friend over to spend the night on the weekend. In both types of contracts, the family social worker can help family members to make the conditions of the contract as clear and specific as possible.

EXERCISE 11.7   Contracts

Divide into groups of four or five. Decide on a child behavior that a family might like to see changed. Make two contracts, a QPQ and good faith contract, addressing this behavior. Which does your group prefer? Share your experience with the class.

EP 2.1.10g

Next we present three forms of intervention, all of which the generalist family social worker needs to be comfortable using with families. The three are crisis intervention, problem-solving intervention, and ecological intervention.

CRISIS INTERVENTION

There are many types of crises that a family social worker may encounter when working with a family, and sometimes a crisis can be used to the advantage of the family. At times this means that the worker might want to provoke a crisis, and at other times the worker will want to defuse one (Brock & Barnard, 1992). Crises provide opportunities for change because they disrupt family homeostasis and families feel a certain amount of pain and anxiety, making them want to change. Two methods exist to defuse a crisis: the family social worker can become triangulated into a relationship, and the worker can return the family to the past. One way for the worker to become triangulated is to get the member to direct exclusive attention toward the worker by using empathic statements. Taking the family into the past helps the family to recall similar crises and helps them to realize that despite the present crisis being consuming, they have experienced crises in the past and have used skills to get themselves out of those crises.

Regardless of the situation, it is crucial that the worker remain calm and reassuring throughout the interview. The best approach toward clients in crisis is a straightforward approach. It is very important that the family worker help the family to resolve the immediate crisis in order to provide both a safe environment and hope for family change, thus setting the stage for future longer-term family work.

There are many different models of crisis intervention, and we present a common model below (Gilliland & James, 1993):

1. *Defining the problem:* In defining the problem, the skills discussed in Chapter 10 provide a requisite base on which to do crisis intervention.
2. *Ensuring client safety:* The immediate needs of the client must be attended to.
3. *Providing support:* Sometimes the support will be in the form of referral to other helping sources.
4. *Examining alternatives:* Alternatives should build on the strengths of the clients.
5. *Making plans:* Plans involve creating short term and long term goals.
6. *Obtaining a commitment:* Obtain either a verbal or written commitment to do the tasks need to accomplish the short term and long term goals.

Workers will not always want to avoid a crisis. For example, family workers may sometimes want to induce a crisis to destabilize families. There are many ways of doing this, such as removing a child from the home. At times, families may be too complacent or may lack the motivational anxiety necessary to create change. One method of creating a crisis is by amplifying an issue in the family (Brock & Barnard, 1992; Minuchin, 1974). The worker might draw attention to a piece of interaction from an interview and magnify its significance. Alternatively, the worker might be able to change the meaning a family member attaches to a particular experience and work from the assumption that a change in how a client sees a problem will also promote a change in behavior (Brock & Barnard, 1992).

PROBLEM-SOLVING INTERVENTION

Family social work focuses on systemic interventions with the family as a unit rather than on individual members. Systemic intervention is linked with a problem-solving and communicative intervention. Because the systemic intervention focuses on the family as a unit, the problem-solving intervention teaches members to negotiate solutions to their problems that are acceptable to all. Seven steps in problem solving include problem definition, goal selection, solution generation, consideration of consequences, decision making, implementation, and evaluation. Teaching clients to problem solve requires a shift on the part of the family social worker, who is now no longer the expert but the facilitator. As facilitator and consultant, the worker teaches the family to develop solutions to their own problems rather than relying on outside help.

Stages of Problem Solving

1. Problem definition describes a problem situation. A situation is a problem when its resolution is not automatic. It also involves discovering how each person contributes to the problem.
2. Goal selection describes what each person wants to happen.
3. Generation of solutions as a result of brainstorming will lead to identification of a number of alternative responses that may lead to resolution of the specific problem.
4. Consideration of positive and negative consequences of any solution could relate to time; money; and personal, emotional, and social effects; it may also include possible immediate and long-term effects.
5. Decision making is based on weighing the proposed solutions and consequences and deciding which one is best for the individual at that time. Decision making involves consideration of a person's priorities and values and contracting a solution.
6. Implementation requires carrying out actions called for by the proposed solution.
7. Evaluation must review the results of problem solving and decide if it met the goals, if changes are necessary, or if another response to resolve the problem must be identified (go back to stage 3).

Developing Problem-Solving Skills

Disorganized and unskilled families often lack skills to be able to solve problems adequately. Families must learn how to deal with immediate problems and develop skills to solve problems in the future when the worker is no longer around. Problem solving entails seven steps to help families arrive at solutions to their problems.

The problem-solving approach not only focuses on helping people resolve present difficulty; it also involves teaching clients the skills to solve problems by learning strategies for dealing with present and future concerns. Thus, a problem-solving emphasis is on helping families learn more effective ways of becoming independent and self-reliant.

Teaching clients to problem solve requires that the family social worker serve as a facilitator rather than an expert. The shift from expert to facilitator starts at the point of problem and goal definition. Previously, workers defined client problems for them and then imposed solutions. Conversely, the current problem-solving model empowers clients and families to actively identify their own needs and goals. When a family has difficulty doing so, the family social worker simplifies the process. In some situations, if a family can only vaguely define a difficult situation, the worker may initially take a more active role in identifying a problem, gradually involving the family. The overarching goal is to empower the family to assume this responsibility as they develop the skills to do so.

In considering solutions to problems, however, family social workers will often have more knowledge about topics than the family does, thus placing the family social worker in a position to offer help. The shift in philosophy to facilitator does not mean that such information will not be shared. Rather, it means that clients will be encouraged to generate unique solutions on their own and consider consequences. In decision making, the worker will at times need to state an opinion or even ask specifically that something be done; usually, however, the worker encourages the family to decide. Clients develop more independence as they improve their coping and decision-making skills.

In the early stages of problem solving, more direction from the family social worker may be necessary. Later, the family social worker becomes less directive as the client assumes more responsibility. One program described how services to families changed over time: at first, "doing for;" then "doing with;" and, finally, "cheering on." A related technique is contracting (Jordan & Cobb, 2001).

EXERCISE 11.8   Problem-Solving Approach

Caitlyn Jones is a 15-year-old girl who is having trouble in school. Her older brother and sister left home before they had finished high school. Her brother, Ryan, got into trouble with the law, and her sister, Jamie, became pregnant at age 17 and moved in with her boyfriend's family. Caitlyn's parents, Bob and Kerrie, are worried that Caitlyn will also leave home early and drop out of school. Caitlyn feels she has been pressured by her parents to do well in school. She has been struggling with her classes and is fearful of failure. Write some "I" statements Caitlyn could use to communicate her feelings to her parents, as well as some active listening responses her parents could offer. With three other students, role-play a session with the Jones family (one student should play the family social worker and the other three should play Caitlyn, Bob, and Kerrie). Outline the steps of a problem-solving intervention for this family.

ECOLOGICAL INTERVENTION

The type of ecological interventions required will arise from an assessment of the ecomap described in Chapter 8. As mentioned, the ecomap is the blueprint for planned change and is the first stage in deciding on an action (Hartman & Laird, 1983). Not only does an ecomap organize information visually, it also outlines family themes and targets for change. The ecomap should be created with the family. Family attention can be directed to address the question: What kind of relationship do you have with a particular person/group or institution in their social system ecomap, and do you want to make changes to this relationship? Focusing on the ecosystem will also remove the problem from the level of individual blame. We should point out at this point that the goal of ecological intervention is to teach clients how to do for themselves, rather than rely on the family social worker to do it for them (Kinney, Haapala, & Booth, 1991).

Typically, the worker should focus on environmental problems first (Kaplan, 1986). This will help the family problem solve around less threatening issues while at the same time build in supports for the family. The type of ecological interventions used depends on the issues, client skills, and resources available in the community. For example, one author reported that the following resources are either not available or are difficult to access for family-centered workers: mental health care, housing, day care, low-skill basic jobs, transportation, legal services, and religious programs (Goldstein, 1981). In another report, workers found that emergency housing, homemaker services, group homes, parent aides, inpatient drug and alcohol treatment, and respite care were difficult to obtain (Kohlert & Pecora, 1991). The worker must also help families develop creative ways to use formal and informal resources. Sometimes families will merely lack information about where resources exist. Other times, family members may have the knowledge but lack the skills to get connected to resources. In this case, the family worker will have to help the family get connected (Helton & Jackson, 1997). The ultimate goal is to help clients learn how to get needs met on their own. It is tempting and perhaps easier to do for the clients instead of teaching them to do for themselves (Kinney, Haapala, & Booth, 1991).

Hepworth and Larsen (1993) presented a range of ecological interventions for families. They include:

- Supplementing resources in the home environment
- Developing and enhancing support systems
- Moving clients to a new environment
- Increasing the responsiveness of organizations to people's needs
- Enhancing interactions between organizations and institutions
- Improving institutional environments
- Enhancing agency environments
- Developing new resources.

EP 2.1.10g

SPECIALIZED FAMILY WORK APPROACHES

Keeping in mind differences due to diversity, we now present some approaches that can complement and expand upon crisis, problem-solving, and ecological interventions. The following approaches can be very useful depending on how the family and family worker define family problems as well as the specific goals of the family work.

Solution-Focused Approach

The solution-focused approach provides some very useful questions that can be asked to help families solve their problems (DeJong & Berg, 2002). It is particularly helpful during family crises when a family wants to develop rapid solutions to problems to help them to move out of the crisis and back to a healthier family functioning state.

Background The solution-focused approach is committed to brevity, de-emphasizes history, and gets the family to concentrate on solutions that have worked for members in the past. From its roots in strategic therapy, it has grown away from a focus on problems. The primary developer of this approach was the late Steve de Shazer, whose background included working in Palo Alto with the MRI group and who was influenced by their brief approach. Insoo Berg substantially contributed to the theory, training most of its leaders (de Shazer, 1983, 1991).

Major Concepts

1. *Focus on Solutions:* Rather than overexplaining problems or describing family dynamics, this theory focuses on solutions. It is based on the assumption that clients have a sincere interest in changing. Family social workers use techniques that steer clients away from "problem talk" to "solution talk," as language is reality. Thus, the family identifies their own goals, resources, and exceptions to their problem.

   Solution-focused family workers premise their work on the belief that people already have the skills to solve their problems but have lost sight of this ability. Their problems loom large, which saps their strength in dealing with them. This calls for a simple shift to what they are already doing that works, and searching for abilities that they are not currently using in dealing with life's difficulties.

2. *Modest Goals:* The family worker works from the client's understanding of the problem. Therefore, the concern is only with the client's presented complaint. Because the solution-focused approach is not designed to reorganize personality or family structure, modest goals are the desired standard. A small change is usually all that's needed because that change tends to snowball.

3. *Brevity:* It is not necessary for the entire family to attend the meeting—just those interested in coming. Intake information is limited, as solution-focused family workers prefer to focus on the future. The intervention itself is brief, which makes it preferred by the managed care industry.

Techniques   In the first meeting, the family worker asks, "What can I do that would be helpful to you?" This question directs the family to identify what they want help with specifically. It also sets the stage for the negotiation of an achievable goal. During meetings, several techniques are used to initiate and maintain problem-solving faculties in clients:

- "Miracle Question": Suppose one night while you are asleep, a miracle happens and the problem is solved. What would this look like? How would you know? What would be different? By asking these questions, people are producing a clear definition of their goal.
- "Exception Question": During times in the past or present when the problem wasn't present when it ordinarily would be, what was different? This produces clues in order to expand those times of exception. It conveys the message that the problem can be changed, controlled, or eliminated.
- "Scaling Question": On a scale of 1 to 10, with 10 being the best you can feel, how far along are you today on your way to 10? What do you need to do to get to (the next number)? This nurtures small changes and disarms resistance. It also identifies and measures concrete changes and goals when dealing with vague topics such as depression and communication.

- "Coping Question": When a client describes having surmounted difficult situations in the past, the family worker will ask how they did so. This question seeks out demonstrations of a client's competence and coping skills.
- "Formula First Session Task": At the end of the first meeting, the family is instructed to observe and write down what happens in their life or relationships that they would want to continue. This helps them focus on their strengths, creating a more positive outlook. This is the "Formula First Session Task."

Transcript Demonstrating Solution-Focused Therapy Techniques Scenario: Barbara, the mother (age 45), and Susanna, her daughter (age 22), are referred for family work by their family doctor regarding Susanna's depression. The family social worker will conduct the process of introductions and also explain to the family his or her expectations of what will transpire (6–8 sessions).

The following are examples of questions that could be asked of this family:

- "What can I do to be helpful to you?" (stimulates the client to identify what they want help with specifically)
- "How did you cope with your depression?" ("Coping Question" seeking a demonstration of competence)
- "Have you experienced anything like this before?" (looking for past success to build on)
- "On a scale of 1 to 10, with 10 being not worried at all, what number would you say represents the worry you feel for Susanna at this moment?" (using a "Scaling Question" for measuring steps toward a goal and change)
- "Now I would like you to think of what would need to happen in order for that 4 to be bumped up to a 5 or even a 6." (encourages development of concrete goals)
- "Susanna, let's look at what number, on a scale of 1 to 10 with 10 being not depressed, you feel best represents you today, right now." ("Scaling Questions" are especially effective in identifying change; the goal here is ending depression.)
- "And what steps would move that 3 to a 4? Or even a 5?" (again encouraging concrete steps toward the goal of ending depression)
- "It is important to concentrate on just one step at a time. You both have mentioned a goal of improving Susanna's sleeping patterns. That's a good first step for what we can begin to work on. Susanna, I'm glad you're here trying to do something about your depression. It shows me that you, like your mom, know when to go for help. It shows me strength on your part, and that's very good. Can you recall a time in, say, the last six months that you didn't feel depressed?" (encouraging incremental goals and small changes; affirmation of first steps toward a solution followed by an "Exception Question" to demonstrate the client's ability to change, control, or eliminate a problem)
- "If one night a miracle happened and you awoke the next morning with your depression gone, how would you know? What would that be like? Tell me about that." ("Miracle Question" used to produce a fine-tuned definition of Susanna's goal)
- (Turning to Barbara) "Now the same questions for you. One night a miracle happens in your life and you wake up the next morning with your worry

over Susanna gone. How would you know? And what would that be like?" ("Miracle Question" to seek Barbara's definition of the goal)

- "I want to compliment you both on how well you are able to share what's been going on. Your communication skills are great, and I sense tremendous warmth and caring between the two of you. Our time is coming to a close now, so I would like to suggest that each of you begin thinking about something in the next week before we meet again. I want you to write down what it is in your lives and in your relationships that you would want to continue. Then we'll discuss these things when I see you again." (Session is ended on an affirmative note highlighting their resources. The "Formula First Session Task" will help them focus on their strengths, which will then create more hope that a solution is not far away and that they are capable of finding it.)

Summary of Solution-Focused Questions

The following are some of these questions the family social worker could ask a family:

1. What resources does your family have right now?
2. What would you like to stay the same?
3. What will you notice in your family when things are getting better?
4. What will each family member be doing differently?
5. Are there times when the above is already happening to some (even a small) extent, and what is different about these times?
6. What would be the first sign that the family is moving in that direction?
7. How will your family know that they are making progress?

These questions can help a family discover that small changes lead to larger changes in a positive problem-solving process.

Communication/Experiential Approach

In this section, we present the communication/experiential approach primarily developed in practice by the late social worker Virginia Satir. If the main problem identified by the family is one of poor communication skills, particularly the communication of feelings in a supportive, caring manner, then skills from the communication approach can be very helpful. The emphasis of this approach is clear, direct, open, and honest communication, particularly of feelings of caring to each other in the family (Satir 1967, 1972; Satir & Baldwin, 1983).

The experiential approach is a form of family work that is based on becoming aware of feelings through focusing on experience. Families are viewed more as groups of individuals than as a system. The experiential approach focuses on the "here and now" interaction of family members in an attempt to help with the problems the family has brought to the family social worker. The underlying belief is that the expression of honest feelings will lead to personal and family fulfillment (Nichols & Schwartz, 2004, p. 200). That is, individuals who feel cared for and loved will have a high sense of self-esteem and will act in worthwhile ways. The major system for individuals to receive these messages of caring and love is the family system.

Historical Background   The experiential approach arose from the humanistic psychology of Gestalt and client-centered interventions. The two main developers of the experiential approach include Virginia Satir and Carl Whitaker. Satir strongly believed in the healing power of love and the importance of communication. Whitaker emphasized that self-fulfillment depends on family cohesiveness. Both are remembered for their use of spontaneity, creativity, and risk-taking as a means to conflict resolution. The communication/experiential approach is effective in helping family members get in touch with their affective blocks so that a healthier family unit can exist. Techniques such as family sculpting, role-play, and body contact (discussed in the next section) are particularly effective in helping family members get in touch with their feelings. Various techniques may be utilized in order to reach the family's goals. These techniques provide the family the opportunity to become aware of unhealthy and dysfunctional communication patterns and move on to more healthy and functional patterns of behavior.

Satir attempted to connect with people (establish an empathic relationship), for she believed that all people have the basic need to feel loved and valued. The experiential approach attempts to get to the core of people's unhappiness and move toward healthier functioning. In this approach, the family social worker is an active change agent and acts as a role model to teach clear and direct communication. Hence, family social workers need to be aware of their own emotions as well as be in tune with the family's emotions.

Major Concepts   Five concepts are fundamental to the communication/experiential approach of family work: (1) focusing on affect or feelings, (2) the family social worker as an important change agent, (3) self-worth, (4) communication, and (5) the marital relationship.

1. *Focus on affect or feelings:* People have a basic need to feel valued and loved. For example, the family worker wants to ask each member of the family, "What do you want?" or "What problems do you see in the family?" (Satir & Baldwin, 1983, p. 35); symptoms are caused by lack of emotional expression (dysfunctional families are often disengaged). For example, "It seems to me like the members in this family don't feel comfortable with expressing how they feel and this might be part of the reason the family is having difficulties."
2. *Family worker as an important change agent:* Family social workers should utilize and voice their own reactions and personal experience in helping the family reach their goals. This can be done primarily through appropriate self-disclosure. For example, if a member of the family is talking about a death, the family worker may want to state they themselves have also experienced the death of a loved one or that the family worker knows of someone who has gone through a similar painful experience.
3. *Self-worth:* Communication style and overall functioning is closely linked to self-concept and self-esteem. The premise is that if one gets in touch with one's emotions, change will occur. The family worker wants to increase awareness

through labeling. For example, "John, I noticed that when you talk about your father you become sad; are you aware you do this?" The family worker wants to listen carefully and normalize feelings and stay away from blaming. For example, the phrase "whenever we get mad" implies anger is a universal feeling (Satir & Baldwin, 1983, p. 23).

4. *Communication:* The focus on communication emphasizes clear and direct face-to-face interaction (with a focus on the present). For example, "I want to make sure I understand what you are saying right now; are you saying....?" Openness and honesty lay the foundation for trust, and the family social worker wants to emphasize that family work is a safe environment by stating "when the family comes into this room, I will do all I can to make sure everyone feels safe." Congruent messages should be both verbal and nonverbal. The family worker needs to teach the family to check on nonverbal cues when they are communicating; for example, "you have a look on your face ... I am not sure what you are feeling right now." (Satir, *Step by Step*, 1983, p. 48).

   Indirect communication tends to signal greater dysfunction (Satir, 1967, p. 17). In some families, there are implicit rules regarding talking about one's pain. For example, "I knew I couldn't tell my mother I was feeling sad; these things just weren't talked about."

5. *The marital relationship*: Partners are considered to be the "architects" of the family and influence family homeostasis (Satir, 1967, p. 1). It is believed that if the marriage or couple relationship is strong and healthy, the family unit becomes stable, whereas dysfunctional parenting tends to be a result of marital difficulties. For example, "I am sensing that Mary and Dan as a couple are not relating to each other as they would like, and this may cause a conflict when parenting decisions need to be made."

Goals of the Communication/Experiential Approach

1. *Growth of family members:* The communication/experiential approach aims to increase the family's awareness by taking risks. It is believed that maintaining the status quo generally does not lead to a stronger family unit. For example, a family social worker might say, "I am aware that you would solve this problem at home differently; however, I would like you to think of another way you can let Sally know you are upset with her."

2. *Enhancing family "comfortability"*: This goal emphasizes helping families feel at ease with talking and expressing their feelings. This can be done by using appropriate humor, which helps defuse the tension and attempts to connect people. For example, "There seems to be a lot of fighting going on in this family; I wonder if sometimes it doesn't feel like a wrestling match." Another belief is to enhance sensitivity to individual and family needs and encourage appropriate sharing. It is important to let each person speak for themselves whenever possible. For example, "Mary, I noticed you haven't said anything; I am wondering how the fighting between your brothers makes you feel." It is also important for the family social worker to encourage a sense of hope for the family. For example, "If everyone is willing to support each other, the situation will get better."

3. *Directive family worker role*: The family social worker's style is described as involved, active, and directive. For example, "I am going to have the family stand up and show me what happens at home." The family worker must model clear and open communication. For example, "Is it clear what I am asking you to do?" Relationship building with and maintaining respect for each family member can be done through reframing for a more positive understanding or, hopefully, a less negative connotation. For example, "The word *temper* has been changed to 'the way of bringing out his thoughts'" (Satir, *Step by Step*, 1983, p. 37).

Techniques

1. *Role-Playing*: Family enactment of roles and situations. When possible, try to move chairs so that they are facing each other and encourage interaction by asking, "Can you show me, Jane and Sally, how you talk to each other when you are at home?" It is believed that true feelings are revealed through acting out realistic issues. For example, "I never knew you felt that way."
2. *Family Sculpting*: A physical arrangement of the family by a family member or by the family worker in order to graphically depict an interpretation of what is going on within the family. If the family social worker is directing the session, it is important that the participants are aware of what the family worker is doing. For example, "I am going to physically arrange the different family members into positions I see them having within this family." Family sculpting helps provide further insight into family dynamics and interactions through visual illustration. Again, it is important to confirm if the picture is an accurate perception of the family. "Is this how you view yourself in the family?" Additionally, family art therapy or drawing is commonly used to stimulate unexpressed feelings, particularly when working with younger children.
3. *Body Contact and the Use of Touch*: To become in contact with deep emotions of love and affection through physical touch, as well as being physically close. For example, "Would you please move your chairs closer, and I would like Mary and Kathy to hold hands." (However, it is important for the family worker to assess if physical touch would be helpful for this family.) For example, when issues of sexual abuse are present, the family worker would want to try to help family members distinguish between "good" and "bad" touch.
4. *Family Life Chronology*: More focus on the marital relationship than on the "identified person." There is an assumption that the marital system needs to be healthy in order for people to be good parents (this is often the case with families who come in for therapy, but is not necessarily always true). For example, a child sucking his or her thumb may provoke the parents to fight. The underlying issue may be that the couple does not want to talk about (or admit) problems in their marriage; therefore, the focus is shifted onto the child. The family worker gets an idea of how decisions are made by asking the parents what their relationship was like with their own parents (to determine what beliefs were learned). For example, "It seems to me Mary's relationship with her father was very healthy and positive and as a result, Mary expects her marriage to Bill to be the same."

Exercise: Have two people in the class play a married couple. Remember the concept of detriangulating as forcing the two people to talk to each other directly, preventing triangulation. Start the role-play by saying, "I would like the two of you to turn your chairs facing each other and for the two of you to talk directing to each other about the feelings you are having about your relationship. I know this may be difficult but I would like to see if you can share your feelings." As the family social worker in this role-play, you want to look for circular communication patterns being mindful of the range of feelings shared. Eventually you will model and coach the couple to share feelings in a clear, direct, open, honest, and supportive manner if they are unable to do so.

Summary

The communication/experiential model is effective in getting family members in touch with their affective blocks so that a healthier family unit can exist. Techniques such as family sculpting, role-play, and body contact are particularly effective in helping families get in touch with their feelings. Various techniques may be utilized in order to reach the family's goals. These techniques provide the family the opportunity to physically become cognizant of unhealthy and dysfunctional patterns and move through to healthy functional patterns of behavior.

Satir attempted to personally connect with people, demonstrating her belief that people have the basic need to feel loved and valued. The experiential model attempts to get to the core of people's unhappiness and move toward a healthier functioning. In this therapy, the family worker is an active change agent and acts as a role model to teach clear and concise communication. Hence, the family worker must be aware of his or her own emotions as well as be in tune with the family's emotions.

Structural Family Approach

The Structural Family Therapy can be very useful when the family is having problems with developing appropriate rules and consequences in the family.

Historical Background   Salvador Minuchin began to develop structural family therapy in the 1960s through his work at the Wiltwyck School for Boys. In the 1970s, structural family therapy became one of the most practiced forms of family therapy in North America (Minuchin, 1974, 1981, 1992).

Major Concepts   There are three concepts fundamental to structural family therapy: 1) Family Structure and Hierarchies, 2) Subsystems, and 3) Boundaries.

1. *Family Structure and Hierarchies:* Rules create a family structure that determines how, when, and to whom family members relate. Functional families have a structure that places the parents at the top of the hierarchy, in a position of power and authority over their children.
2. *Subsystem:* "Units within a family, based upon characteristics such as sex, age, or interest" (Piercy and Sprenkle, 1986, p. 31) constitute subsystems. The three

major subsystems include the spousal/marital, the parental/executive, and the sibling subsystems. The spousal/marital subsystem includes the two individuals who have come together as a couple. The parental subsystem is made up of those persons in the family who have authority over the children. People can be part of both the parental subsystem and the spousal subsystem.

3. *Boundaries:* Boundaries are the "invisible barriers that regulate the amount of contact" (Nichols and Schwartz, 1998, p. 245) that individuals, subsystems, and the entire family unit have with each other. Boundaries can be visualized on a continuum ranging from rigid to diffuse, with "clear" being the midpoint:

   Rigid-------Clear---------Diffuse
   Disengaged-----------Enmeshed

Rigid boundaries are restrictive and inflexible. They limit transactions between different family subsystems, creating "disengaged" families. In disengaged families, "members are so separate, they seem oblivious to the effects of their actions on each other" (Piercy & Sprenkle, 1986, p. 31). Family members may be cold or indifferent to each other and uninvolved with each other's lives. Clear boundaries are firm, flexible, and allow for autonomy, yet they also support and nurture family members (Becvar and Becvar, 2005). For example, family members may be close to each other while having healthy and age-appropriate levels of individual freedom. Diffuse boundaries are blurred, and family members are overinvolved with each other, which results in "enmeshment." Enmeshed families have "family members who are so tightly locked that autonomy is impossible" (Piercy & Sprenkle, 1986, p. 31). For example, the family members are not allowed to be involved in any activities outside of the home.

Goals of the Structural Family Approach   The goal of the Structural Family Approach is "to change dysfunctional aspects of a family system to a more adequate family organization structure, one that will maximize the growth potential of each family member" (Minuchin, 1981, p. 446). Goals with the following types of families include:

- With enmeshed families, the goal is to clearly define and strengthen individual and subsystem boundaries to allow for individual autonomy. For example, the family worker may ask each family member how he or she perceives who makes the rules in the family: "Who decides where this family will go on vacation?" "Do the children have some say in vacation planning?"
- In disengaged families, the goal is to increase closeness and involvement of family members with each other. "The goal of 'family work' is structural change; problem-solving is a by-product of the systemic goal" (Nichols & Schwartz, 1998, p. 253). That is, the family worker is not there to solve the family's presenting problem, but is there to teach the family new interactions so that the family can solve its own problems.

The family worker works on changing the structure to allow the family to access their repertoire of underused problem-solving skills. It is important that the family worker understand interactions between *all* members of the family. The family worker might sit quietly and observe family patterns. When an interaction occurs three times, this usually indicates a family pattern. However, in dealing with "life-threatening symptoms," the structural family worker might employ techniques from other approaches. For example, in the case of anorexia, the family worker might use a behavioral technique such as reinforcement to get the person to eat.

Interventions/Techniques The following are the most commonly used techniques in the Structural Family Approach:

1. Accommodation: Accommodation involves using the skills necessary for the family social worker to achieve a helpful working relationship with the family. Keep in mind from the research of Miller and Hubble that probably the most helpful thing the family social worker does in family work is the establishment of a caring relationship with clients. There are a number of ways to accommodate (establish this positive relationship with) and work with a family:

   i) Joining: "The 'family worker' establishes rapport with family members and temporarily becomes part of the family system" (Piercy & Sprenkle, 1986, p. 33). For example, the family worker might try to understand the family members' feelings by saying: "I hear you are feeling very angry. I wonder if there might be sadness underneath that, too."

   ii) Maintenance: The family worker supports a part of the family structure while analyzing it (Kilpatrick & Holland, 1999; Piercy & Sprenkle, 1986). For example, the family worker will watch how the family acts toward each other while trying to get an understanding of what is really going on.

   iii) Mimesis: "The paralleling of a family's mood or behavior" (Piercy & Sprenkle, p. 34). Often the family worker mimics the way a client sits and matches his or her tone of voice and pacing of speech momentarily to "join" with the client. For example, the family worker may temporarily suck her or his thumb if a child is engaging in thumb-sucking.

   iv) Boundary Marking: "Structural 'family workers' intervene to realign boundaries, increasing either proximity or distance between family subsystems" (Nichols & Schwartz, 2004, p. 262). For example, in a family with a seating arrangement in which the parents were not beside each other, the family worker would have the parents move beside each other. The family worker would say: "Frank, I notice that you are sitting with the children and Gayle is here by herself. I would like you to move your chair over next to Gayle." Through "regulation of affect, repetition, and duration," family social workers push families out of their dysfunctional patterns of equilibrium. (Nichols & Schwartz, 2004, p. 260). For example, if a parent and child were having a discussion and the parent kept speaking with the family worker instead of with the child, the family worker might direct the parent by saying: "I want you to tell Jasmine, not me."

   v) Intensity: The family worker focuses on bringing out underlying feelings to intensify family patterns.

   vi) Unbalancing: "In unbalancing, the 'family worker' joins and supports one individual or subsystem at the expense of others" (Nichols & Schwartz, 1998, p. 263). For example, the family worker may momentarily take sides with one family member against another, usually done by stopping a family member who is interrupting the family worker and having the family worker continue to pay more attention to one family member over another.

vii) Perhaps the most important intervention used with families is *enactment*. An enactment is "the acting out of dysfunctional transactional patterns within the family session, encouraged by the 'family social worker'" (Piercy & Sprenkle, 1986, p. 33). For example, the family worker may instruct a family to discuss a certain topic in front of him or her. Family workers do this in order to analyze dysfunctional transactions between family members and to provide an environment conducive to practicing functional ways of interacting. "Once an enactment breaks down, the family social worker intervenes in one of two ways: commenting on what went wrong, or simply pushing them to keep going" (Nichols & Schwartz, 1998, p. 255).

Case Vignette Demonstrating Structural Approach The Brown family consists of Bill Brown (40), who is a single father, his twin 15-year-old daughters, Lisa and Lori, and his 8-year-old daughter, Susan. This family was referred to family social work by the principal of Lisa's high school because in the past three months Lisa has been highly truant from school, she has been failing most of her classes, and it was recently discovered that she has been stashing marijuana and magic mushrooms in her locker at school. Bill reports that he is extremely concerned about Lisa's behavior and the negative effects that it is having on himself and his two other daughters. As a result of Lisa's behavior, Lori has become withdrawn from her peers. She often talks about how worried she is about her twin sister and demonstrates such by trying to parent Lisa. Susan has started to act out at home by yelling a lot and by being hyperactive. Bill reports that he can't control Lisa anymore because she refuses to listen to anything he says and that he has given up trying to discipline her because this only makes her more defiant. He is at the end of his rope.

Structural Family Model Applied to Case Vignette Based on the information received about this family, a structural family worker would try to understand the family's structure, boundaries, and subsystems. The worker might interpret Lisa's actions as a symptom of this family's structure that is no longer working and suspect that Lori sees herself as a part of the parental subsystem with her dad. This is because Bill has said that she has been trying to parent Lisa and is no longer doing things that people her age normally do. If this proves to be the case, the family social worker would need to remove her from the parental subsystem, which is the wrong part of the family hierarchy for her to be in, and make her a part of the sibling subsystem.

Techniques

1. *Enactment:* I would first get the family to engage in an enactment in order to determine their interactional patterns. For example, I could say: "I would like to see how you problem solve. Dad and Lisa, could you talk to each other about Lisa's skipping school and the drugs found in her locker?"

2. *Manipulating Physical Space:* In family work, the family social worker could manipulate physical space by placing Lori with her sisters and seating Bill by himself, signifying that he is the one authority in the family. "Bill, I want you and Lisa to switch chairs so you, Bill, are by yourself in a position of authority. Lisa, I want you to be sitting with your sisters."

3. *Unbalancing:* The family social worker could side with Bill to support him in showing all of the children that he is the single authority in this family. For example, Lori is trying to parent Lisa and interrupts Bill when he is talking to the social worker. The family social worker might say: "Lori keeps jumping into the conversation. Bill, let her know that this conversation is between you and me." Bill: "Lori, the family worker and I are talking." Family Worker: "Bill, tell her again." Bill: "Lori, the family worker and I are talking. Keep quiet."

By using these techniques, the family social worker would aim to help re-establish clear and appropriate boundaries, structure, and subsystems in the Brown family. Once this is achieved, the family should be able to problem solve on its own.

Narrative Family Approach

Techniques from the narrative family approach can be useful for the family social worker to employ when a family uses words to describe a problem as a stressor or hindrance to their well-being. For example, family members may refer to being overwhelmed with stress, overwhelmed with nightmares, or allowing anger to dominate their communication. These problems are described like a story dominating their lives.

We are born into stories: the stories of our parents, our families, and our culture. These made meanings, which predate us and envelop us upon our arrival into the world, can be constraining, even imprisoning, or they can be freeing and liberating.... Born into the cradle of familial and cultural stories, we begin to construct personal narratives not long afterward, with all the idiosyncratic features that this many entail. (Epston, White, & Murray, 1992)

Historical Background   Narrative therapy is one of the latest approaches to family work embracing North America. The late Michael White and David Epston are two principal contributors to the development of narrative family work. At its most basic level, it involves the listening to and telling or retelling of stories about people and the problems that they identify they are experiencing (White, 1990, 1995).

Major Concepts   *Focus on Stories.* Stories are the reality in which we exist. There is no reality, only stories we tell about reality. The role of the family social worker is to listen to the family members' stories and identify openings for them to rewrite their stories into the preferred outcome. Through the process of telling their stories, family members are able to examine their lived experiences in a meaningful and fulfilling way (Freedman & Combs, 1966). The past can be changed by constructing new narratives or stories.

Goals of the Narrative Approach   The narrative approach assumes that the person is not the problem. *The problem is the problem.* (See Chapter 10 regarding definitions of problems.) This means that the problem is seen as separate from the individual, rather than as part of the individual. In the narrative approach, it is believed that each person's experience can be interpreted in many different ways, as there is no single 'truth.' Through family members sharing their interpretation of a situation, the family social worker is able to draw upon exceptions and use these exceptions to reshape the client's story. Although somewhat of an individual focus, the narrative approach not only encourages individual stories, but also invites the family to listen and rewrite the stories together—as they are the experts on their family experience.

Steps and Techniques

1. *Beginning the Family Session:* Family social workers first find out from family members how they usually spend their time in order to get an idea of how they view themselves. The family worker may also use circular questioning (see Chapter 10), which is used to create interdependence between the client and their stories. When doing this, the family worker pays much attention to talents and competencies. This is often accomplished through placing exaggerated importance on these things when they are mentioned by the client. For example, a family worker may say such things as, "Oh, that's so great that you are able to spend time with your son!!" or "That's wonderful that you are able to balance all the things in your life so well!!"

2. *Externalizing the Problem:* Externalizing the problem as an intervention is credited to the late Michael White, an Australian social worker, and his colleague David Epston from New Zealand. The technique involves separating the problem from the person to allow the problem to be viewed outside the person. "Externalizing is an approach to 'family work' that encourages people to objectify and at the same time personify the problems that they experience as oppressive. In the process, the problem becomes a separate entity and thus external to the person or relationship that was ascribed as the problem" (White & Epston, 1990, p. 38), affording the family a better opportunity to gain control over the problem. The process of separating the person from the oppressive problem is achieved by using externalizing language or activities to locate the problem outside the person.

    The family social worker begins the intervention by asking the family to describe how much influence they have over the problem and how much influence the problem has over them. This is called a relative influencing question (White, 1989). "The problem becomes the problem, and then the person's relationship with the problem becomes the problem" (White & Epston, 1990, p. 40). When families view problems from this vantage point (i.e., a double description), their perspective widens. By changing the perception and meanings attached to the problem, there is a greater potential to arrive at a solution (Brock & Barnard, 1992).

Example of Externalizing the Problem   Instead of the stress being perceived as an internal problem, it can instead be defined as an external stress monster that occasionally enters one's life. The family worker can then explore when the family member is most vulnerable to this stress monster and also when the family member is able to keep the stress monster out of his or her life. Externalizing the problem can be used in a number of situations. Brock and Barnard (1992) suggest that externalizing the problem is an especially effective tool in working with addictions in the family. Thus, alcohol becomes the enemy that the family confronts together.

EXERCISE 11.9   Externalizing

Divide into groups of three or four and develop a scenario to help a family experiencing an alcohol problem. In the scenario, students will demonstrate how externalizing might help to make alcohol the "enemy." Share your scenario with the class.

3. *Mapping Influence:* Next, the family social worker maps the influence of the problem by examining how the problem has affected the family members' lives and relationships. This may be done using a relative influence question such as, "How does the Anger Monster affect your life, Tanya?" or "What does Anger make you do?" As well, the family worker maps the influence of the person, which involves examining how the client has been able to control the problem. An example of a relative influence question here may be, "Can you remember a time when Anger tried to control you but you didn't let it?" or "Is Anger with you in the shower? Does Anger follow you to the gym?" Questions such as this may uncover unique outcomes that do not fit the client's presented pattern, as the problem is not present.

4. *Re-Authoring the Story of Lives and Relationships:* At this stage, the family social worker uses unique outcomes as a starting point from which to develop a new story of the client's life. By focusing on these victories over the problem, the client will realize that they do have options and that they are able to control the problem. Eventually, the client's entire identity will be reshaped around a new, more positive story.

5. *Reinforcing the New Story:* The client's new story is celebrated and affirmed. In order to maintain this new story, outside support is needed; thus, the client may be asked such questions as "Is there anyone that you would like to tell about this new direction you are taking?" to encourage the development of such support. As well, the family worker may get the client involved in letter writing, in which they formally document the changes in the client's life story. After the final session, the family worker may also use this technique by writing the client a letter to commend the client for the control they have over things in their life, in order to again reaffirm the client's new life story.

6. *Questions (see also Chapter 10 regarding circular patterns):* Family social workers using a narrative approach ask questions to generate experience rather than to gather information (Freedman & Combs, 1996). From the narrative perspective, the purpose of using questions is to elicit, clarify, and enhance

descriptions of times the problem is not influential in the family members' lives (Chang & Phillips, 1993). In asking questions, the family social worker is attempting to highlight times in the family members' lives when they have been able to cope successfully with adverse situations due to their own experiences. This process allows family members to highlight the abilities and competencies they are drawing to assist them with the presenting problem(s) (Morgan, 2000). For example, the worker may ask' "When in your life have you experienced happiness?" By using externalizing questions and uncovering unique outcomes, the tactics and strategies can be more readily understood and, therefore, more likely to support the client in finding the answers to disable the problem's influence on their lives. Although somewhat an individual focus, the narrative approach not only encourages individual stories but also invites the family members to listen and rewrite the stories together—as they are the experts on their family experience.

Case Vignette Demonstrating the Narrative Approach

Tanya is the single mother of 5-year-old Jason. She has told you that she is concerned about her inability to control the anger she sometimes feels. She says that her anger is often directed at Jason and that she ends up yelling at him, saying things that she does not mean and sending him to his room for the smallest reasons. She is worried about the impact this is having on their relationship, as she has noticed that Jason appears to be getting more timid and scared of her.

Narrative Intervention

Working from a narrative perspective, the family worker would first spend some time finding out how Tanya sees an angry episode as occurring. From this, the family worker would be able to determine Tanya's perception of the events. The family worker would encourage Tanya to tell her story, including her problems, after which the family worker would start to ask questions that would help externalize the problem. Examples of such questions would include, "Can you tell me what happens when you feel Anger taking hold of you?" or "How do you think Anger is coming between you and your son?"

Questions such as these demonstrate how the problem has influenced Tanya and Jason's lives, while reaffirming that Anger is a separate entity, outside of them both. The family worker would also look for unique outcomes to determine how Tanya has been able to take control of Anger in the past. This would be done through posing questions such as, "Can you think of a time when Anger tried to get a hold of you but you didn't let it?" Examining these victories over Anger allow Tanya to realize that she is able to control Anger. Proving Tanya's competencies allows the authoring of a new narrative to begin.

EP 2.1.10g

CHAPTER SUMMARY

This chapter introduced the family intervention phase. During the intervention phase of family social work, the family social worker provides support, education, and concrete assistance. Effective intervention requires that the social worker focus on the family's needs, respect client autonomy, avoid fostering dependency, reassess client resistance, maintain professional distance, and set reasonable expectations.

Specific intervention techniques available to the family social worker include use of examples, confrontation, reframing, enactment, use of metaphors, and contracting. Intervention techniques should be chosen to meet the needs of the family. The worker recalls the assessment phase and uses the ecomap when presenting ecological interventions.

Family social workers frequently encounter families who are experiencing crisis. It is important that the worker remain calm and help the family sort out its challenges.

Systemic interventions help family social workers and families to think about the family as a whole. Systemic interventions are particularly helpful in teaching problem-solving and communication skills to families.

We examined sub-phases of intervention, which included contracting, crisis intervention, ecological intervention, and problem solving. We believe these combined approaches offer a basis for a beginning generalist approach to family social work. We also went beyond these intervention approaches to briefly describe approaches helpful in dealing with the resolution of immediate problems, enhancing family communication, dealing with boundary issues, and using a form of cognitive approach—namely the narrative approach. We believe at a beginning level these approaches and specific techniques can be a useful enhancement of the generalist family approach. The approaches that were briefly described the solution-focused approach, communicative/experiential approach, structural family therapy approach, and the narrative approach.

KEY TERMS

Communicative/Experiential approach Emphasis is on clear, direct, open, and honest communication, particularly of feelings of caring to each other in the family.

Crisis intervention Helping families solve immediate threatening problems to a family's well-being in order to give families safety and hope and create the conditions for further longer-term family work.

Ecological intervention Based on an assessment of the family ecomap. Looks primarily at enabling the family to access and receive more support from community resources.

Narrative approach Based on taking a family's negative story about their family and having them reframe or re-story their negative story to one that opens up positive possibilities for empowerment and change.

Problem-solving intervention Teaches problem-solving skills that can be applied to a wide range of family problems.

Solution-focused approach Useful to help families find immediate solutions to problems. This approach avoids problem talk, instead focusing on "solution talk."

Structural approach Looks at rules that govern how, when, and to whom family members relate, including relating around resolving conflicts.

SUGGESTED READINGS

Garbarino, J. (1992). *Children and families in the social environment* (2nd ed.). New York: Aldine. An easy-to-read book targeting undergraduates that blends child development with ecosystems theory within a family context. It is user-friendly and includes research on each layer of the ecosystem, building upon Urie Bronfenbrenner's ecosystems theory. It takes a humane approach to working with families at every level of the ecosystem.

Minuchin, P., Colapinto, J., & Minuchin, S. (2006). *Working with families of the poor* (2nd ed.). New York: Guilford. A good undergraduate resource that describes how to work with poor families who are experiencing multiple crises. It differs from other books in this genre in that it looks at institutions and systems of care, particularly focusing on foster care, mental health issues, and substance abuse. The book makes good use of case studies.

Satir, V., & Baldwin, M. (1983). *Satir step by step: A guide to creating change in families*. Palo Alto, CA: Science and Behavior. This book advances Satir's communication model through a step-by-step analysis of a counseling session with a family accompanied by a presentation of the beliefs underlying her approach. Recommended for those who already have a foundation in general principles of family work.

COMPETENCY NOTES

EPAS 2.1.10g Select appropriate intervention strategies: The family social worker must have a repertoire of intervention skills at her fingertips that are appropriate for various client populations and client problems. In this chapter, interventions presented include crises intervention, ecological interventions, and others.

EPAS 2.1.10k Negotiate, mediate, and advocate for clients: We have mentioned in previous chapters that family social work is different than family therapy. The family social worker may use clinical skills, but is also a negotiator, mediator, and advocate for the family.

Interventions at the Child and Parental Levels

CHAPTER CONTENTS

A Behavioral Family Approach

Parenting Skills Training

Behavior Problems and Parent-Child Conflict

Assisting Parents in Setting Rules

Avoiding Pitfalls in Behavioral Interventions

Family Psychoeducational Interventions

Substance Abuse

Chapter Summary

Key Terms

Suggested Reading

Competency Notes

LEARNING OBJECTIVES

- Conceptual: To develop an understanding of behavioral principles as they apply to working with children in the family.

- Perceptual: To be able to observe concrete child behaviors as well as parenting behaviors.

- Valuational/Attitudinal: To value parents as instrumental in changing children's behaviors.

- Behavioral: To be able to teach and structure behavioral principles in working with parents and children.

A BEHAVIORAL FAMILY APPROACH

Interventions at the family and parental level are the focus of Chapter 12. These interventions are based on principles of behavioral intervention. A behavioral family approach is compatible with the family life cycle in that phases of family development require that members adapt to a continuously changing and maturing family system. The behavioral approach emphasizes ongoing reeducation or relearning and is particularly effective with younger children (Thompson & Henderson, 2011). However, the basic premises of behavioral intervention are also appropriate for later stages of the family life cycle and child development. Reeducation requires that parents develop a positive relationship with their children so that they can guide the children through challenging developmental phases. For instance, adolescence is a time when teens are moving toward adulthood.

The teen is an adult one minute and a child the next, requiring flexibility, sensitivity, and guidance by the parent. Teens also benefit from positive teachings from their parents.

Behavioral family social work has several advantages over traditional intervention. It is useful for chaotic families that require a structured series of intervention strategies for parents to carry out in their daily family life (Kilpatrick & Holland, 1995). In office settings, the behavior or events may appear too briefly, infrequently, or too removed from the child and family's other life experiences (Gordon & Davidson, 1981). It also avoids pathologizing families. Rather, behavioral family social work casts problems as due to a lack of skill that can be learned.

Behavioral family work grew out of the observation that behaviors are shaped and maintained by relationships in the environment, particularly those in the family. It therefore follows that behavior can be changed by changing environmental contingencies (rewards and punishment) that maintain the problematic behavior and prevent the emergence of prosocial behaviors. Since parents are most in control of significant contingencies in the child's environment, particularly when the child is young, they are in the best position to create behavior change with the child. Thus, change occurs first with the parent and later with the child. Essentially, parents are their child's therapists.

A family social worker (FSW) consults with parents, teaching them to intervene directly and immediately in the child's behavior. Parents live with the child and are a stable, continuous treatment resource. If parents learn to deal consistently with their child even when the FSW is not present, an environmental context for ongoing behavior change will be established. This fundamental principle of social learning theory can be used by parents with varying degrees of parenting skills.

Assumptions

Behavioral family interventions look at ongoing family relationships and interactional patterns rather than the intrapsychic life of individual family members. In behavioral terms, communication can be a powerful consequence of behavior, either positive or negative. Through a positive worker-family relationship, the worker models appropriate social behavior, coaches parents in developing positive communication skills, and helps them structure a set of behavioral contingencies to be used consistently in family interactions (Thompson & Henderson, 2011; Bloomquist, 1996; Kilpatrick & Holland, 1995). Given the premise that parents are the best therapists for their children, planned changes in parental behavior are expected to be followed by changes in child behavior and vice versa.

Behavior problems, then, are seen as learned responses that become set and intensified with ongoing reinforcement. Much of the reinforcement in families is unintentional because family members are seldom aware of how they reinforce and maintain the behavior of others. Being self-aware and tracking child behavior is difficult for many parents to do for extended periods. Without awareness, however, imposed consequences may produce unintended effects. For example, scolding may inadvertently reinforce a child's behavior because the child receives attention from an otherwise distant or removed parent. Other times, parents might ignore or reinforce behavior inconsistently, making it difficult to extinguish or eliminate a particular child behavior. Many parents do not know how to use behavioral consequences effectively and in such instances, parents fail to follow through on threats. Punishment may be delayed, defusing its effectiveness and confusing the child; other times, the level of punishment fails to match the level of the problematic behavior by being either too mild or too severe.

Echoing the circular interactions described in Chapter 3, parents who respond negatively toward their children are also most likely to have children behave negatively in return. In some families, negative behavior receives more attention than prosocial behavior. Thus, behavioral intervention targets the modification of problem interaction to alleviate presenting symptoms. Ideally, changes in negative behavior by either the parent or the child will begin a spiral of positive family interactions. Ultimately, treatment needs to be tailored to fit the specific circumstances of individual families. The goal is to increase rewarding interactions by producing positive behavior change, decrease the rate of coercion and aversive control, and teach effective communication and problem-solving skills.

Under the premise of behavioral family work, behavior should change when contingencies or reinforcements are altered. Before this can happen, family social workers must do a careful, detailed assessment with the family to understand the specifics of the problem and to find out how often (i.e., the baseline frequency) the problem behavior occurs before change is attempted. Then the FSW must devise strategies to change the contingencies of behavior in each family. During information gathering, the task is to identify *antecedents* and *consequences* of the problem behavior. Problems must be defined in concrete, observable, and measurable ways. Based on this information, strategies are then designed to alter the antecedents or consequences of the behavior. It is important to remember to measure the problem behavior before the intervention and after.

Figures 12.1 and 12.2 illustrate other types of measurements: time sampling (percent of time), behavior frequency recording, and duration recording (see Jordan et al. in Grinnell & Unrau, 2011).

Frequency of behavior shown in Week 1 by _____

Problem behavior _____

Date	Frequency	Total	Time	Comments

© Cengage Learning 2013

FIGURE 12.1 | Time Sampling and Behavior Frequency Recording

Duration of behavior shown in Week 1 by _____

Problem behavior _____

Date	Length of time behavior observed	Total time	Additional observations

© Cengage Learning 2013

FIGURE 12.2 | Behavior Duration Recording

Principles and Procedures

The behavioral family approach is based upon the principles of behavior modification and social learning theory, which explain how behavior can be increased, decreased, or maintained and how new behaviors can be learned, respectively. We believe that understanding these principles is essential for anyone who works with families. The social learning approach offers families a structured method for dealing with a range of family problems. Family workers who are unfamiliar with social learning approaches will not be as effective as they could be when working with parents.

The basic principles of behavior analysis address the effects on behavior of its antecedents and consequences. Though most attention has been focused on consequences of behavior, especially on the positive consequences or reinforcement, it also is important to recognize the effects of changing the immediate environment. This environmental focus can be used to make homes safe for young children. For instance, we put fences around playgrounds to keep children safe, and we remove dangerous objects from their reach. A FSW who brings toys or other activities to keep one child entertained while she talks to the parent and sibling changes the child's environment positively. What we say to each other can also be an antecedent condition that increases the likelihood that a behavior will occur. Parents who know how to give clear and unambiguous directions and follow through on them, for example, will likely see more cooperation on the part of their children than parents who give confusing, conflicting directions.

Behavior also is influenced by its consequences. Positive, reinforcing consequences *increase* the likelihood that behavior will be repeated, while negative consequences *decrease* the likelihood of recurrence. Many parents naturally use positive consequences, for example, when they praise and encourage a child who is learning to walk or talk. But as child behavior becomes more complex or problematic, parents often need help in knowing which behaviors require attention and which should be ignored or even punished. Parents may unintentionally become negative in their interactions with children because of lack of skill or frustration and may need help in learning to change unpleasant interactions into more positive and enjoyable ones.

Teaching parents to use reinforcement effectively is important in parent training, after parents learn to judge the appropriateness of the child's behavior by integrating knowledge of child development and behavior principles. Furthermore, the general family work guidelines discussed earlier also are important to include when teaching parenting skills. For example, the FSW may discover that the parents' needs and problems may interfere with their ability to parent and must be addressed. Also, the systems perspective presented earlier reminds the FSW to consider the effects of intervention on other family members. Similarly, the child's behavior is influenced by family subsystems, such as the widowed grandmother who lives with the family and is trying to take over the parental role; such subsystems must be considered when intervening in parent-child relationships. A broader ecological view goes beyond asking what consequences could change a child's behavior to asking questions about environmental conditions. For example, does the physical environment (including the interfering grandmother) make it possible for the child to comply with parental requests? Are there distractions in the environment that would interfere with the successful implementation of behavior change in the family?

Just as behavioral management principles are important to both family social work and to parent training, so are problem-solving skills. Problem-solving skills are necessary for competence in parenting. Also important is conducting parent training in the parents' home rather than in a clinic or other institutional setting.

EP 2.1.10.a

Techniques

Because we cannot present in this book every detail necessary for family social workers to master the knowledge and skills for using behavioral management principles, we urge the reader to obtain further information elsewhere as preparation for family work. Several excellent, comprehensive parent-training programs exist to help parents deal with many child-management problems. The procedures are especially important for parents of children with handicapping conditions and parents who abuse or neglect their children. The central premise of behavioral family social work is that behavior is maintained by its consequences, and rewards strengthen the connection between a stimulus and a response. This means that negative behaviors should not be reinforced, but positive behavior should be. Following are a few of the many behavioral techniques that families find helpful.

Teaching is a tool that can be used successfully with many families. In one study, a parent reported liking learning the different ideas on how to handle behaviors—for example, breaking power struggles by offering choices. In the same study, another parent said, "I learned how to intervene, trying different techniques of discipline" (Coleman & Collins, 1997).

Teaching should be based on an assessment of each situation and used to show families how to use a specific skill. Steps involved in teaching include:

1. Giving the members a rationale for learning the skill
2. Demonstrating the skill
3. Having clients practice the skill, after which they receive feedback. (Brock & Barnard, 1999)

Teaching Family Communication Skills   Family communication is a skill that underpins almost every aspect of family functioning. Bloomquist (1996) suggests a three-step model in teaching communication skills:

1. Introduce family communication skills to the family (e.g., being direct, honest, and open; focusing on the here-and-now; attentive listening; using "I" statements; not interrupting; not yelling; not being verbally abusive).
2. Practice the skills in the family. One way is to role-play both the "do's" and the "don'ts" so everyone knows the difference and can readily identify the skills that are acceptable. The family worker can model these skills before the family role-plays. All members of the family should take turns practicing these skills. A videotape can be used to help the family observe what they are doing.
3. Use the family communication skills in real life. The worker might want to enact or stage the "real" problem initially—that is, select a problem pertinent to the family—and then have the family demonstrate their new communication skills while talking about it.

Teaching Child Compliance   Bloomquist (1996) also provides a step-by-step method to obtain child compliance. A child is compliant when he or she listens to and obeys parents' directives. Both parents and children learn new behaviors:

1. *Give effective commands.* The commands should be specific and one-step so that the child knows exactly what is being asked of him or her. Commands that are vague, in the form of questions, multiple, or accompanied by a rationale, are to be discouraged.
2. *Use effective warnings.* If the child is not compliant with the command, the parent can issue a warning that takes the form "If ..., then...." The warning should be given only once.
3. *Give effective positive or negative consequences* to the child for compliant or noncompliant behavior. Praise can be used for compliant behavior, and negative consequences can be used for noncompliant behavior.
4. *Parents are to try and stay cool and avoid power struggles* if the child is not compliant.
5. *Persevere* until the child knows that the parent means business. Perseverance is necessary because compliance is seldom secured the first time a parent uses these techniques. In fact, it may take a long and exhausting time before the pattern of behaviors becomes engrained.
6. *Be consistent.* Make certain that the parents respond the same way each time the child shows a particular behavior.
7. *A chart can be used* for younger children.

The idea of learning new skills can be offered as a new way of overcoming problems. For many families, this will be new because the stereotype of counseling is to analyze and talk about the past.

There are several ways to teach clients. In *direct instruction*, the worker presents information directly to clients. In *modeling*, the worker performs the behavior in front of the clients, and in *contingency management*, clients are taught to manage contingencies of reinforcement—that is, to support change through rewarding behaviors they want to retain and by ignoring or punishing behaviors that they want to change (Kinney, Haapala, & Booth, 1991).

People will be more prepared to learn once they recognize that learning occurs every day. However, they may want to understand the rationale, particularly how using a particular skill will help them in their particular situation. Once the family has understood these issues, they will be prepared to have the skill broken down into manageable pieces. Demonstration of the skill needs to be accurate. After the worker shows the skill, the family members should be asked to describe what they observed step-by-step. Because a skill often involves a series of complex behaviors, the worker should break down the skill into manageable parts and have the clients learn components of the skill one step at a time. Teaching and demonstrating skills can be identified "on-the-spot" in the home. Workers can capitalize on teachable moments and use a crisis or other timely events to inject a teaching moment. Parents make use of teaching and report that it is a helpful intervention (Coleman & Collins, 1997). The final stage of teaching involves having the individual or family practice the skill and then receiving feedback on the performance. At this stage, the worker should offer positive comments and corrective feedback to the client.

Positive reinforcement is the process whereby appropriate behaviors are recognized and reinforced, thus *increasing* the probability of these behaviors occurring in the future. Unfortunately, many parents often notice only inappropriate behaviors and do not take the time to recognize "good" or prosocial behavior, thus failing to positively reinforce these good behaviors with praise and sometimes even a type of enjoyable reward. For example, a child who just spent one hour completing his or her homework and reading should be praised for the effort and invited to spend time with his or her parents in a mutually enjoyable activity. It is often helpful to have children select what they would like to have as a reinforcement and then create a chart to map progress. Ideas for reinforcement, apart from spending time with a parent (discussed in the following paragraph), might include being allowed to do a favorite activity, staying up later, praise, or having a friend sleep over. We recommend using social reinforcers (such as praise or time spent with a parent doing a favorite activity) over material reinforcers (such as money or a new bike).

An important form of positive reinforcement is the parent spending time with a child and being involved. Such social and privilege reinforcers are quite effective with children. Parental involvement fulfills the dual purpose of positively rewarding children for their behaviors *and* increasing affective involvement of family members: "positive reinforcement of good behaviors is related to well-behaved children" (Bloomquist, 1996, p. 52). Scheduling a positive activity with a child involves listing activities that parents and children enjoy doing together, opening up time together, and having the parent "notice" good behavior by praising, describing good behavior, and touching (p. 53). In order for behavior to be rewarded, *it must first be noticed!* To do so, parents must be aware of their own minute-to-minute reactions to and behaviors with the child. Parents must also understand the concept of positive reinforcement before they can use it. They must also be willing to put their own responses under a microscope so that they know what they need to change and how.

Negative reinforcement involves the use of consequences that strengthen or maintain a behavior through their *removal*. For example, a parent might yell to get a child to comply. Compliance in this case might be to do homework. If the parent *stops* yelling *before* the child complies and the child continues to avoid doing homework, the parent has taught the child that avoiding homework is acceptable and that she or he has won. Alternatively, if a child stops a particular behavior (in this case avoiding homework) in order to avoid more aversive parental behavior, the parent learns that yelling is effective. It is important that parents learn to ask children for compliance appropriately and to follow through on their commands. Negative reinforcement is not to be confused with punishment.

Punishment involves the use of an aversive punishment *immediately* after the behavior occurs. However, we strongly believe that positive consequences are preferable to punishment and should be used whenever possible. Examples of punishment include taking away privileges, grounding, or time-outs. We do not recommend the use of spanking as a form of punishment. Spanking teaches children that physical violence is acceptable to get one's way. It also creates fear of the parent.

Extinction is a behavioral technique designed to *eliminate* undesirable behavior. Clients are instructed to withhold attention from the individual who is behaving inappropriately and not reinforce the problematic behavior through inadvertent types of reinforcement. Extinction is useful for behaviors such as whining, crying, temper tantrums, and sleep disorders (Thompson & Rudolph, 1992). Extinction is a slow method. The annoying behavior must be *consistently* ignored, all family members must cooperate with the extinction plan, and parents must persist even when the method does not produce immediate results (Davis, 1996).

Time-out is an indispensable parenting technique used to weaken problematic behaviors of children. When used effectively, parents substitute time-out for physical discipline. Parents often observe that children's behavior tends to spin out-of-control, paralleling the loss of parental patience. Time-out entails removing the child from a stimulating environment and placing the child into a setting that is low stimulation. During time-out, parents have a chance to regain composure while the child calms down. A quiet place for children can be a chair or a quiet room. The child's bedroom should be avoided for time-out—its use as a time-out space can contribute to bedtime difficulties because the child associates the bedroom with upsetting incidents.

Time-out is useful when children fail to follow rules set by parents and can be a consequence of breaking a rule. At the moment when the rule has been broken and the consequence is imposed, the parent should immediately place the child in the time-out spot. The length of time in the spot will depend upon the child's age, but should range between 5 and 15 minutes at one time. Workers might want to use the following teaching sequence before implementing the time-out procedure. Davis (1996) recommends the following tips in using time-outs:

- Decide which behaviors qualify for time-outs. Then, parental expectations should be specified as clearly as possible to the child. Typically, time-outs can be used for temper tantrums or other noncompliant behavior.
- Determine in advance which quiet settings would be the most appropriate for time-out.
- Decide at what point the time-out will be used. We recommend that a time-out be used after the child has been warned about the impending consequence if the parent's orders are not complied with. If the child violates the order, the time-out should be imposed immediately, even if the child protests and backs down.

- Let the child know in advance what behaviors are acceptable and which ones are unacceptable. Then calmly explain to the child the purpose of the time-out.
- Do not argue with the child when imposing a time-out. Do not talk with the child except to explain the purpose of the time-out and why it is happening.
- At times, particularly at the beginning of using time-outs, the child may have to be physically taken to the time-out spot. The parent must be prepared to take the child back if he or she leaves prematurely. Parents should realize children often resist the time-out procedure when it is first implemented, and ensuring that the child remains in the quiet spot can be both frustrating and a drain of energy for the parent. Thus, parents may have to remain physically close to the child but distant enough not to stimulate the child's behavior further. Parents need to be assured that once the child becomes accustomed to the consistent use of time-outs, the child will become more compliant.

Role-playing allows the client to enact a real-life situation and develop skill and confidence with difficult situations. It is appropriate for times when the client has difficulty being assertive because of the newness of the situation. For instance, a parent offended by the abrupt manner of her child's school teacher may be reluctant to ask the teacher questions about the child's school performance. During the role-play, the FSW may take on the role of school teacher while the mother asks the teacher questions. The mother may then try out both roles. For instance, she can be the mother asking the teacher pertinent questions; she can then take the role of teacher while the FSW models some additional questions the mother could ask. In the process, the family social worker can coach the parent in developing a strong response.

Role-playing is used often with families. Through a role-play, clients start to see how their behavior is viewed by others and receive feedback about these behaviors (Thompson & Rudolph, 1992). Role-playing is useful for skill development and for playing out a scenario to determine the consequences of a particular behavior. Role-playing can also be used to depict problem situations outside the here-and-now setting, such as a problem with a neighbor or a boss.

There are several ways of using role-playing with a family. One way of staging a role-play is for the worker to play a role with the person playing themselves. Another method is to have people reverse roles and play a problem scenario. The latter method is useful to help people understand the other person and develop empathy skills. Finally, role-playing can be used to rehearse skills relevant to a situation, much the same as rehearsing for a play before performing in front of a live audience.

To role-play, clients are asked to bring a problematic situation into the interview and are asked to re-create it in the interview. Feedback can then be given to the family member about the scenario.

Role-play is a safe form of behavioral rehearsal, involving practicing a new behavior without the fear of consequences. During behavioral rehearsal, the worker and significant others provide feedback to the client. After the behavior is practiced in a safe environment, the client will then do the actual behavior in the real world (Davis, 1996).

EXERCISE 12.1 Practice a Role-Play

List some appropriate situations for which role-playing would be a helpful technique. Pick one of these and practice it with a partner.

Rule setting involves parents setting rules for their children, knowing what situations to set rules for, and learning how to enforce these rules when children are not compliant. Parents must learn a set of procedures for setting rules that ensures that they *consistently* follow through with rules and establish *consequences* for children who are noncompliant. Rule setting and enforcement can be broken down into several manageable steps:

- First, parents must convey to the children specifically what the rules are and the rationale for each rule. The explanation must match the cognitive ability of the child.
- Then parents should offer an alternative to the child's behavior, and the child should be informed of the consequences of not following through on the rules.
- If the behavior persists, the parent must firmly tell the child that if the behavior occurs again, there will be a consequence (the consequence should be clearly spelled out).
- If the behavior continues, the parent must then stop the child and impose the consequence *immediately*. This procedure must be followed every time the child breaks a particular rule. Consistency is imperative. Imposing a consequence one time but not another will only confuse the child. Additionally, inconsistent enforcement of rules does not produce behavior change with children.

Modeling is demonstration of a specific behavior for family members. This technique is particularly useful when the family cannot imagine themselves carrying out a particular action or when they cannot begin an activity. It is also useful when a family member lacks necessary skills to take action or is hesitant to try out a new behavior. Examples of situations appropriate for modeling include demonstrating a job interview, asking a spouse to help with child care, or comforting a sad child.

Family workers can model effective behaviors for parents. Other models may occur through videotapes or peers and adults who have experienced similar problems but have developed the skills to deal with those problems. In Chapter 7 we discussed a range of communication skills that workers can use to work with families. The family social worker can model these skills to the family with the expectation that the family will start to identify with the worker's communication style and use the skills with one another in the family.

After modeling the behavior, the worker should encourage the client to perform and practice the behavior. Doing so assures that the client understood what was modeled and that the client can imitate the behavior of the family social worker. The FSW can provide corrective feedback if necessary. Such practice helps ensure that the client will remember the behavior and provides the worker the opportunity to correct any errors in the client's performance as well as to reinforce and encourage the client's behavior.

EXERCISE 12.2   Modeling

List three situations in which modeling would be a helpful technique. Pick one of these and practice it with a partner.

Self-control training is useful for individuals who are able to assume some responsibility for their own behavior. Self-control training is useful for anxiety reduction, school refusals, stuttering, and, to some extent, hyperactivity. Steps involved include:

1. Selecting the behavior to be changed
2. Recording for approximately one week when the behavior occurs, the setting, and the antecedents and the consequences
3. Setting a realistic goal
4. Changing the antecedents and the setting related to the behavior
5. Altering the consequences that reinforce the behavior
6. Recording what happens
7. Devising a plan to ensure that the changes continue.

Assigning homework involves sending an assignment home with families. Change begun in family interviews does not stop when an interview ends—families should continue to change after the interview. One way of doing this is for the family to be given homework to work on between sessions. Assignments can take many forms but have a threefold purpose:

1. To get family members to behave differently
2. To collect information about family behavior outside the interview
3. To emphasize self-responsibility to create change.

Assignments should be based on the assessment and the work done in an interview and are useful in bridging gaps between sessions. They should be geared toward the ability and motivation of the family and must be clearly spelled out. Assigning homework to families will get them used to being responsible for behavior change and will prepare the family for when the worker is no longer available to nudge them along. Examples of homework include letter writing, making telephone calls, charting behavior, and continuing to use an agreed-upon parenting technique. Another example of a homework assignment is having family members keep track of how often a certain behavior occurs. Keeping track of the behavior can help family members become aware of how often a behavior occurs and, in doing so, the family will be involved in monitoring progress made in family work (Kinney, Haapala, & Booth, 1991). For example, if the family is socially isolated, a homework assignment could be for the family or any number of its members to use a community resource or nurture an outside relationship.

For homework to be effective, the FSW must start the next interview with a review of how the homework went. Occasionally, workers will discover that the family did not do the homework assignment. In this case, it will be necessary to find out what prevented the family from doing the assignment. Reasons may range from open resistance to not understanding the instructions. When homework is assigned regularly, families eventually learn to expect assignments at the end of every interview (Hartman & Laird, 1983).

Stress reduction includes progressive relaxation, a useful technique to deal with generalized anxiety or anxiety that is situation-specific. For generalized anxiety, the person is taught the skills of relaxation. For situation-specific anxiety, the person learns to relax while visualizing anxiety-provoking situations. In deep muscle relaxation, the individual relaxes the muscles, one group after another, until a state of deep relaxation is achieved. Typically, people are instructed to start by tensing and releasing their toes, and then gradually move the tension and relaxation to major and minor muscle groups up the body. Muscle tension should occur for about 5 to 10 seconds at a time. There are tapes or scripts that can teach progressive relaxation. Alternatively, the worker can script a relaxation session.

Contingency contracting is useful in working with children because it relies heavily upon input by all concerned parties. Through negotiation, a mutually agreed upon contract is developed indicating the behaviors that individuals will perform and when. Usually the contract is formally written and involves who is to do what for whom, under what circumstances, when, and where. Rewards are then placed in the contract to ensure that if the contract is successfully carried out by all parties, they will follow through on mutually positive rewards specified. All parties in the contract must be clear on what they will give and what they will get if the contract is followed.

Contingency contracting can be broken down into five steps (Thompson & Rudolph, 1992):

1. Problem to be solved is identified.
2. Data are collected to find out baseline frequency.
3. The counselor and client set mutually agreed-upon goals.
4. Methods for obtaining the goals are selected.
5. Techniques are evaluated for observable, measurable change.

Teenagers in particular may find contingency contracting useful (see Figure 12.3). The contract is used for families to specify appropriate behaviors and corresponding rewards and consequences. Both the teen and parent have input into what behaviors they want included, and disputes may be negotiated. When first beginning to use contracting, simple issues should be selected.

Assertiveness training teaches family members how to say what they need to say in an appropriate manner—that is, they are neither aggressive nor passive. Conflicts in families often occur because members do not know how to be assertive or do not know how to disagree appropriately, resulting in either passive or aggressive behavior. When members are passive, others can easily intrude on their rights. Aggressive members intrude on the rights of passive members and often learn to get their needs met through anger. Teaching assertiveness skills helps family members deal with one another, and the skills are also useful outside the family.

EP 2.1.10g

Evidence Base of Behavioral Family Interventions

Children usually behave differently from setting to setting, suggesting that adults determine what type of behavior is permissible in each setting. An exception is aggressiveness that remains constant wherever the child is; that is, a child who is aggressive at home will more likely be aggressive with peers. Interventions when

Ryan's Homework Program

Mon. Tues. Wed. Thurs. Fri.

Brings books home from school.

Starts homework at 7:00 P.M. without arguing.

Keeps television off during homework.

Stays in one room to do homework until 8:00 P.M.

Ryan gets:

    1 point for bringing home books from school

    3 points for starting homework without arguing

    2 points for keeping television off during homework time

    1 point for remaining in one room to complete homework

Total points

I, _____ agree to do my homework regularly based on the conditions set above. I understand that I will earn points based on the agreement above. When I earn _____ points, I will be able to cash them in for _____.

Mother's signature   Father's signature

Child's signature

FIGURE 12.3 | Example of a Contract Negotiated Between a Parent and Child to Complete Homework

children are young are most successful. Children with behavior problems also exert an enormous amount of control over their environment. They have difficulty "faking" good behavior and develop habitual patterns of problem behavior.

Behavioral family work has been used for such diverse problems as temper tantrums, hyperactivity, homework problems, bed-wetting, disobedience, delinquency, and aggressive behavior (Alexander & Parsons, 1973; Baum & Forehand, 1981; Foster, Prinz, & O'Leary, 1983; Webster-Stratton & Hammond, 1990). Others have used behavioral family work to teach parenting and child management skills to parents who physically abuse their children (Sandler, VanDercar, & Milhoan, 1978; Wolfe, Sandler, & Kaufman, 1981) and self-control techniques (Denicola & Sandler, 1980; Isaacs, 1982).

Parents of children with behavior problems have poorly developed parenting skills compared with parents of children who are functioning adequately (Patterson, 1982). However, it is more positive to view parents as having skill deficits rather than as pathological, because parents can learn new skills.

Intervention with child problems requires careful assessment and evaluation and clearly operationalized techniques. Behavioral family work is an educative experience in which parents are taught to understand and consistently apply behavioral skills with their children.

Besides teaching new skills, family social workers must pay attention to the environment in which families live. Some families experience more stress than others, and stress is disproportionately distributed among poorer families. They differ from other families in the ability to access resources that help them mediate stress and have fewer community, financial, and personal resources. Accordingly, they may feel alienated and distrust formal helpers. When they do connect with community supports, the experience is likely to be negative. Lack of support networks allows problems to grow because the resources are lacking to handle crises on the spot. Information, concrete resources, and emotional support may be absent. These families tend to have limited contact with people outside the family and aversive events dominate family life in these families, making it difficult for them to tune into daily family events effectively. Unless an ecological approach is undertaken to eliminate this "noise," parent training may be undermined.

In coercive families, both positive and negative reinforcement mechanisms are present, but most seem to reinforce the wrong thing in that parents of aggressive children appear to reward deviant behavior and punish prosocial behavior (Patterson, 1982; Patterson & Fleischman, 1979). In addition, abusive parents rely excessively on aversive methods of behavior control and fail to use consistent and positive child management techniques (Denicola & Sandler, 1980). Modifying "microanalytic" interactions between parents and children may reduce the risk of child abuse and other negative behaviors.

Currently, much of the behavioral family work is derived from the Oregon Social Learning Center where G. R. Patterson and colleagues (1982) examined microanalytic interactions within families and noted how responses shape the interaction. Microanalytic interactions resemble the circular patterns of interaction described in Chapter 3 although the model is more linear in that it sees a difference between an antecedent event and consequences. It primarily focuses on the here-and-now and makes minimal use of history.

Antisocial children have fewer house rules, and parental permissiveness is often related to aggressive behavior. Aversive parental behavior suppresses prosocial behavior and accelerates ongoing coercive behavior. Parents of antisocial children are more likely to give aversive consequences for coercive child behaviors (i.e., spanking, yelling). Thus, abused children have higher rates of coercive behavior than other children. Negative reinforcement increases the likelihood of high-intensity negative responses. For example, the child stops throwing a tantrum in the grocery store when the parent agrees to buy her candy.

EXERCISE 12.3 Behavioral Family Approach

Imagine that your supervisor asks you to see a client family named Smith. The Smiths are experiencing problems with a teenage daughter, Christina, age 13. The problems center around Christina's desire for more independence. She would like to go to the mall and stay out late with her friends on Saturday, but her parents (Tom and Julie) are worried that she is not old enough for this responsibility. Additionally, Christina feels that her father is too bossy and domineering, while her mother is a "doormat." Christina reports that her father actually spanked her when she sneaked out of school early to go to the mall with her friends. Christina also tells you that her brother Thomas, age 14, is allowed to go to the football game with friends without adult supervision every Friday night. She does not believe this to be fair.

Team up with a partner and use the steps of the behavioral family approach to address the Smith family's issues.

Step 1: Problem definition

Step 2: Behavioral observation

Step 3: Design of intervention

EP 2.1.6b

PARENTING SKILLS TRAINING

Parent training, unlike other models of family work, accepts parents' definition of the child as the problem. Parent training assumes that the problem identified by the parents should be targeted for change. However, while the model explicitly states that the child is the focus of change, parents are expected to learn to respond differently to their children. Thus, as mentioned, parent training helps parents to become aware of antecedents and consequences of their child's behavior and to exert control over them. Parent training can occur in a group session outside the home or with individual families either in the home or the office.

Assumptions

Parent training is based on the behavioral principles reviewed earlier in this chapter and can help parents in the following ways:

1. It can help parents learn to anticipate the needs and rhythms of a child. For example, stimulating a child before bedtime is unwise for the parent. Similarly, taking the child for his or her baby pictures while the infant would normally be napping is not recommended. The stimulation must be age-appropriate.
2. It can help new parents to understand how much self-sacrifice parenting requires. Parents must recognize that their previous lifestyle is changed forever once children arrive. Each stage of child development also requires a change in parental lifestyles. One cannot parent and party at the same time. Sleep may become scarce.
3. Parents can learn to understand the stresses on their relationship that come with raising children. While the parents' relationship may become closer, there will be times when they feel unloved, unwanted, isolated, or rejected. The couple must be helped to discuss the effects on their relationship openly—including changes in their energy levels and sex life. They also need to openly discuss concerns about being effective parents. Financial worries also have to be addressed rather than ignored.
4. Parents should recognize that some of their concerns may not be addressed immediately. Waking up four times a night to feed the baby decreases the likelihood of an active sex life for the parents. Similarly, staying awake waiting for a teenager to come in at night can also be draining. Sleeping patterns will

probably not change until the baby begins to sleep through the night. However, despite the inability of parents to change the situation, being able to talk about their frustrations and needs is still necessary for them.

5. Parents should recognize that frustrations, financial worries, and lack of sleep can result in many conflicts and feelings of frustration. Thoughts of hitting the child or leaving a partner are common. If they remain just thoughts, they are normal. However, these become problematic if acted upon.

6. Parents must recognize that they need to learn to love their children. The bond between parents and their children is not automatic; it takes time and work to make it happen. An important aspect of the parent-child relationship is the match of temperaments. An active baby is a challenge for calm, slow-moving parents. Conflict with an older child may also create much resentment in the parent-child relationship.

7. Parents should recognize that they may need assistance to appreciate the joys of parenthood. When parents are bogged down in the daily stress of parenting, they may miss some pleasures that a child can give to his or her parents. Thus, parents must learn to balance the work and responsibility of child care with the ability to play with their children.

8. Parents must recognize that unresolved personal issues will create additional stress. Distinguishing between ongoing personal or couple issues is important. Naturally, different issues will require different interventions. For example, a woman who has suppressed childhood memories of sexual abuse may suddenly have flashbacks and bouts of anxiety when a daughter is born or when the daughter reaches a certain age. These types of stresses cannot be dealt with in the context of a developmental crisis.

Principles and Procedures

Parent training relies on checklists, observation in the home, and interviews. Following is a suggested step-by-step plan for implementation of parent training.

Step 1: Develop a clear definition of the problem. In problem identification, behavior related to the presenting problem is broken down into concrete, observable, and measurable terms. Problem definition looks at three phases in relation to the problem. First, workers and parents identify what events precede the behavior. These are known as *antecedents,* and they provide important information about the cues that occur immediately before the behavior. Second, assessment of the problem describes behavior concretely. Third, assessment involves the *consequences* of the behavior such as the parental response, identifying responses that keep the behavior going.

The entire family should be included in problem identification and understand the role they play in provoking or reinforcing the behavior. However, it is advisable that input by parents be the focus of the first interview. Should the child be included in this first information collecting interview? Initially, the presence of the child may interfere with finding out critical pieces of information (Gordon & Davidson, 1981). Until parents understand the problem differently, having the child present for the initial problem identification may be detrimental to the child. Parents may also want to speak in private or refer to the child negatively during this first interview. Thus, until the behavior is reframed and understood by the parents as a learned behavior, the child may be labeled as "bad" or as the "problem." Video taping behavior in the home, with the family's permission, is also a useful method of breaking down the antecedents and consequences of a problematic behavior. The family social worker can then partner with the parents in examining the components of the problem.

A useful starting point in understanding the behavior would be to ask parents to describe a typical day, asking for detailed and concrete information. Checklists or charts may be used to capture the family's behaviors. At the second meeting, including the child might be useful so that parent-child interactions may be observed. When assessment is conducted in the agency, some agencies have observation rooms with two-way mirrors where colleagues can form a team to help in observing family interactional patterns.

Parents can identify a problem child easily but might have more difficulty identifying antecedents to the behavior. In other words, the parents may have labeled the child as "bad" but be unable to provide specific examples of when the behaviors occur. The FSW must help parents describe the specific problematic behavior; for example, if the child throws tantrums, what specifically does he do when he throws a tantrum (cry, yell, hit, throw things, etc.), and how often (per day, week, etc.) does a tantrum occur? The behavior must be understood in terms of frequency, intensity, duration, consequences, and social context. Parents should describe what they consider to be the sequences of interactions that contribute to problematic behavior. It is important that the behavioral sequences in the problem be described by concrete behavioral descriptions followed by a concrete description of the interactions between parent and child.

Step 2: Observe and measure behavior. After the specific behavior targeted for change is identified, the FSW must establish ways to observe and record the frequency and duration of the behavior. It is important that everyone involved know the baseline frequency of the behavior (i.e., the frequency of the behavior before intervention) to determine if there has been improvement. In this stage, the family social worker must teach the parents to observe and record the actual behavior as well as the antecedents and consequences. The FSW and the parents can use behavior checklists and questionnaires.

Observing and recording the behavior must occur with every family on the worker's caseload. Parents require training to recognize when the behavior is occurring and especially when the behavior is *not* occurring. Parents must also examine their own behaviors that occur before and after the behavior of the child—that is, occasions when they provide positive and negative attention to the child or when they ignore the child. Ultimately, the FSW wants to make certain that the behavior of the child matches the behavior of the parent and vice versa. Once parents are taught to observe and count child behaviors and to be aware of their subsequent responses to these behaviors, parents will become more "self-conscious" and understand their contributions to the child's misbehavior.

Family social workers that work in client homes are able to do this. It must be remembered that the manner in which problems are reinforced can be complicated because of remote reinforcers that keep behavior going. For example, parents may model aggressive behaviors to their children but spank the child for aggressive behavior, producing confusing messages. Events that occur outside the family home may also reinforce the child's problem behavior—for example, peer encouragement to skip school. Problems outside the home will require meetings and planning with significant others to make certain that the response to the behavior is consistent. The focus of family intervention is on changing the parent-child interactions. Focusing on efforts that the families are making is important rather than criticizing what they are doing wrong.

Material reinforcers (toys, coins) can be used in addition to social reinforcers (praise or time spent together). Determining what reinforcers should be used for the family is important because not everyone responds to the same rewards. However, many families that family social workers see lack material resources to use as reinforcers. In addition, when social reinforcers are used, the child learns to value relationships.

In sum, parents are instructed to conduct a "three-term contingency" measurement (Gordon & Davidson, 1981) that includes (1) observing the antecedents of the behavior (that is, the events that set the stage for the behavior), (2) describing the behavior, and (3) observing the consequences of the behavior (that is, the specific events that follow the behavior). Parents should record observations over a one-week period, during which time they will develop insight into the events. Insights gained by the family during this information-gathering phase will be an impetus for change.

Step 3: Design an intervention. Measurement should not be limited to assessment but must continue throughout intervention to determine whether the intervention is being applied correctly and to see if the intervention is producing the desired results. The intervention must match the circumstances of the family and be flexible and individualized for every family and every problem. The following four guidelines will help in designing an intervention plan (Gordon & Davidson, 1981): (1) Decide how realistic environmental control is, given parental resources; (2) Assess the quality of the marital relationship for parents' ability to work as a team; (3) Identify personal issues for the parents, such as depression or substance abuse, that could interfere with the ability to follow through on a treatment plan; and (4) Assess the child's ability to cooperate with the intervention plan. Be aware that "environmental noise" (stress) may interfere with the intervention.

Then, decide which behaviors should be increased and which should be decreased. Positive reinforcement accelerates behaviors that might not occur frequently. Reinforcers selected must be valued by the child, and family workers will find that children are remarkably willing to let parents know what reinforcers should be used in their program. During intervention, parents must learn to respond *immediately* (with positive reinforcement, punishment, ignoring, etc., depending on whether the behavior is to be increased or decreased) to the child's display of the problem behavior. When reinforcing behaviors are to be increased, reinforcements might be gradually withdrawn over time with the expectation that the desired behavior will become more durable once it is well established. Changes in child behavior will be the parents' own reward. However, the FSW may ask parents to think of ways to reward themselves also (a night out without the children, for example); parents of children with behavior problems often experience little joy because they are overfocused on the children and their own relationship.

Behavior can be diminished by applying contingent punishment and extinction. One example is time-out, in which the child is isolated at the point a problem behavior is shown. Other ways of diminishing behavior include verbal reprimands or ignoring the behavior. Time-out can be replaced by positive reinforcement—for instance, children can earn tokens or points for good behavior.

Step 4: Prepare the family to encourage the new behaviors to continue. Evaluations of most interventions have usually looked at whether treatment creates initial changes but seldom consider whether improvements persist (i.e., maintenance). Many therapists rely upon a "train-and-hope" approach, assuming that changes made during intervention will remain intact long after treatment has stopped or even permanently (Stokes & Baer, 1977). For parents to continue their new techniques over time, they must learn to use skills in different settings and in new contexts or situations (Foster, Prinz, & O'Leary, 1983). Parents must also learn to maintain these new changes despite facing environmental stressors that could erode gains made in treatment (Steffen & Karoly, 1980). Thus, an important part of the intervention should account for keeping the positive changes going when the FSW is no longer present. Parents can be asked directly about what they have learned and how they expect to keep the changes going.

The family social worker can work with parents to devise a checklist specific to the child's problem behavior. Observed behavior could include temper tantrums, working on homework, completing household chores, or staying dry at night, just to name a few. Many of the observed behaviors will occur at home and often in the parents' presence.

Parents should be taught how to observe and record the following aspects of their child's behavior:

- Count how many times a behavior occurred within a particular time period. The time period selected can be short or long, depending upon the problem. For example, if a child is to do homework between 7:00 and 8:00 every evening but avoids homework by leaving the room, going to the bathroom, or playing with pets, the parent can observe and record the avoidant behavior during the one-hour period. Alternatively, if the parent has been instructed to record the occurrence of a child's temper tantrums, the length of time needed to observe the child's behavior could be as long as a day or more. The family social worker and the parent can develop a chart for recording frequency of behavior.
- Note how long a behavior lasted. Some behaviors can be measured by how long they last. For example, a parent may record how long it takes a child to comply with the parent's request to do the dishes.
- Record the severity of the behavior. In this type of observation, the family social worker must help the parent devise a scale to measure a particular behavior. Examples could include how well a child washes the dishes or how loud a child's whining is in reaction to a parent's denial of a privilege.

Parents also need to become aware of events that precede the target behavior, as well as how they respond to the behavior.

Case 12.1 addresses parent training used with Harry and Lisa Fryer, a young couple with three-year-old twins.

EP 2.1.10a.

CASE 12.1	Parent Training

Harry and Lisa were 16-year-old high school juniors when their twins were born. Their inexperience at parenting was addressed by the family social worker (FSW), Joyce Perdue. Mrs. Perdue's assessment revealed that Lisa was the primary caregiver, while Harry worked in a local grocery store. Lisa reported that the twins were unmanageable much of the time. She reported that the children refused to take naps or go to bed at night without a tantrum. When they were awake, the twins either fought with each other or teamed up against their mother to get into mischief, according to Lisa. For instance, while Lisa talked on the phone one day last week, Tina drew pictures on the living room wall with crayons while Tommy climbed the bookcase, sending books and knickknacks crashing to the floor.

Harry tried to provide Lisa with some relief after he got home from work, but he was frustrated by the twins' lack of compliance with their parents. Harry said that the twins were "basically healthy and happy but totally out of control."

Mrs. Perdue helped the couple apply rewards for compliant behavior. For example, the twins could earn a Popsicle for dessert after lunch, or a trip to the park. The couple learned that rewarding the twins' good behavior was likely to increase it. The FSW also helped Lisa and Harry learn to use extinction whenever possible, discouraging negative behavior by ignoring it. In situations when extinction was not possible, the Fryers learned to use time-out. For instance, when Tina and Tommy fought with each other, the parents were to redirect their behavior by putting each child in a time-out chair.

The Fryers learned these new parenting behaviors by observing Mrs. Perdue as she modeled them. Lisa and Harry then practiced the behaviors while Mrs. Perdue observed and offered feedback. As the couple's parenting skills improved, Mrs. Perdue warned the couple that they might see an increase in the twins' undesirable behaviors before positive changes occurred. This was exactly what happened. But the Fryers continued using their new skills and gradually observed an improvement in the twins' behavior. Mrs. Perdue then helped the parents to establish a few simple rules to provide a routine for the twins and to guide their behavior. These rules included no hitting others or destroying others' property, bedtime at 8:30, and so on. The Fryers reported a much calmer and happier family life as their parenting skills improved.

Techniques

The following are some parenting skills that the family social worker can help parents learn:

1. Help parents learn to provide a variety of stimulating experiences for their children. The experiences must be age- and context-appropriate and involve shared parent-child activities such as reading, playing games, and recreational activities.
2. Help parents learn to reinforce a child's attempts to be independent. The child's development of a positive identity should be supported by the parents. The overarching developmental task of childhood is to separate from the parents and move toward maturity. Parents may find this developmental phase difficult to handle as they fear for the child's safety. Other parents may believe that attempts at independence are a sign of rejection. Also, studies suggest that

parents allow more independence to male children than they do to female children, so parents must be aware of gender differences.

3. Help parents recognize that the demands on them do not decrease during early family developmental stages; rather, the demands increase. For instance, having a second child is not just twice the work of having one child, but seems to increase the amount of work exponentially.

4. Help the parents recognize that the child has a need to be both independent and dependent at the same time. This can be confusing for parents and children alike. Family life can be quite confusing because of this.

5. Help parents recognize that if they work outside the home, they may feel torn between the needs and demands of their job and those of their family. Guilt is a common feeling for parents who are in this situation, especially mothers who may feel pressures from their husband, extended family, and neighbors to sacrifice their personal life for their child and family. Men do not usually experience this type of pressure.

EP 2.1.10g

BEHAVIOR PROBLEMS AND PARENT-CHILD CONFLICT

Parent-child conflict is often encountered by family social workers. Between one-third and one-half of all family social work referrals for children and adolescents may involve behavioral problems (Kadzin, 2004). Parent-child conflict may be symptomatic of a child with behavior problems or indicative of general family distress and poor parenting skills. Behavior problems take different forms, depending on the age of the child and situational and personality factors, but can include noncompliant behavior, temper tantrums, aggression, argumentativeness, refusing to obey curfews, running away from home, engaging in criminal behavior, or abusing alcohol and other drugs. Parents of acting-out children often feel alone and exhausted.

Generally, intervention in families with parent-child conflict involves a five-phase process (Forgatch, 1991):

1. *Tracking behavior:* Parents should pay close attention to child behaviors. In particular, they should learn to distinguish between compliant and noncompliant child behaviors. The parents need to respond appropriately to desirable behaviors and avoid reinforcing problematic behaviors.

2. *Positive reinforcement:* When the child behaves acceptably, the parents should respond with praise or rewards such as increased privileges.

3. *Teaching appropriate discipline:* If the child's behavior is not appropriate, the parents can apply a consequence such as time-out or loss of privileges.

4. *Monitoring children:* Parents should be taught to monitor their children's whereabouts, companions, and activities.

5. *Problem solving:* Problem-solving intervention strategies are discussed in Chapter 10. Use of problem-solving skills can help parents find solutions for their current difficulties and prevent the occurrence of future problems.

Parent-child conflict is often associated with children's behavior problems. Severity of conflict depends on the issues and personalities involved. In conflictual situations, parents are often desperate and children may be angry, rebellious, or sad.

Baynard and Baynard (1983) outline a three-step program to assist families who are experiencing parent-child conflict:

1. Have each parent make a list of the child's behaviors that are causing conflict. If there are two parents, they should make separate lists and then combine them.
2. Ask parents to cut the lists apart and separate the items into piles: one for the child, one for the parent(s), and one for items that overlap. Into the child's pile go the behaviors that will not affect the future life of the parents, even though they may have consequences for the child. Into the parent's pile go the behaviors that could have consequences for the parents. Items for the child's pile could include watching too much television, dressing sloppily, and fighting with siblings. Items for the parent's pile could include criminal activities by the child such as theft, vandalism, or assault. Items from the overlapping pile should be sorted and moved to either the child's pile or the parent's pile. In sorting through the child's problematic behaviors, parents need to consider which ones they can control and which ones they cannot.
3. Help parents learn not to take responsibility for items in the child's pile. Parents must convey to their children a sense of trust that children can make the right decisions.

EP 2.1.10a

ASSISTING PARENTS IN SETTING RULES

The following principles of natural and logical consequences have been identified by Grunwald and McAbee (1985):

1. The consequence should be directly related to the behavior.
2. The consequence should be meaningful to the child.
3. The consequence should be known ahead of time.
4. The child should be aware that there is a choice between appropriate behavior and behavior that will lead to negative consequences.
5. The consequence should take place as soon as possible after the behavior has occurred.
6. The consequence should usually be of short duration.
7. The consequence should not be a lecture; rather, it should involve some action.
8. As many family members as possible should agree to the action.

EXERCISE 12.4 Parent Training

Design a plan for intervening with a single-parent mother who is having trouble with her acting-out teenage son.

EP 2.1.10j

AVOIDING PITFALLS IN BEHAVIORAL INTERVENTIONS

In applying behavioral interventions, family social workers must be careful to avoid some common pitfalls. For example, Johnson (1986) suggests that defining problems as interactional may cause some clients to feel that the entire family is an object of blame. Also, certain interventions may seem to favor one family member over another, rather than treating family members equally.

In one study, parents discussed their perceptions of alliances and power imbalances that may develop during family social work. First, parents expressed concern about the possibility of having their parental power undermined by the FSW. Second, alliances between the social worker and family members were sometimes viewed as problematic; for example, if the FSW formed alliances with children, parents perceived these alliances as collusion against parental authority. Conversely, other parents were pleased when the FSW developed a working relationship with a child, because they felt that the child was receiving special attention (Coleman & Collins, 1997). Family social workers must be prepared to discuss alliances and power issues openly with clients so that potential problems can be avoided.

The following behaviors can interfere with the success of behavioral interventions and should be avoided:

- Blaming individual family members or the entire family for difficulties
- Taking sides or aligning with individual family members
- Telling clients what to do instead of helping them arrive at their own solutions
- Relying on negative consequences rather than positive reinforcement
- Using technical language that the family cannot understand.

By becoming familiar with how people learn and by developing skill in balancing family and individual needs, family social workers can help create an atmosphere in which all family members feel heard and understood, expectations are expressed in straightforward language, and family members participate actively in the process of change.

EP 2.1.10a

FAMILY PSYCHOEDUCATIONAL INTERVENTIONS

Family psychoeducation is included here because of its emphasis on family behavioral skills techniques combined with education and social support interventions. The following material is from *Family Treatment* (Janzen, Harris, Jordan, & Franklin, 2006, pp. 57–59).

Assumptions

The goals of family psychoeducation are to educate families about their problems and to improve families' interactions with each other and with their community. Family psychoeducation was developed to intervene with individuals diagnosed with a mental illness and their families. An educational component was combined with other skills techniques and social support interventions to round out the model. Skills such as communication or problem-solving training are included to improve the families' functioning. Support is included to identify and connect families with other individuals experiencing similar problems. Since its initial use with individuals with a DSM (Diagnostic and Statistical Manual, 4th edition) diagnosis, family psychoeducation has been used with many other problems and types of families. Examples of problems for which psychoeducational intervention has been used include child ADHD, anorexia, diabetes, and other health problems. The intervention also is used with family problems such as anger control and conflict resolution.

Family psychoeducation assumes that the family is healthy and functional and has strengths to bring to the table that will help the family improve. This is in contrast to previous theories that blamed family members for their ill member's problems. Names associated with the development of this model are Falloon, Hogarty, Anderson, Reiss, and Johnson. These clinician-researchers theorized that families could successfully learn to cope in the face of problems. Their research shows that families who react to a family problem with criticism, hostility, and over-involvement make the problem worse; conversely, families who have good communication and problem-solving skills will help the family and its members to successfully solve their problems.

Principles and Procedures

The FSW's role in family psychoeducation is to educate families, to provide skills training, and connect families with resources in the community. Roles needed therefore include educator, therapist, case manager, and advocate. The FSW also is charged with motivating and encouraging families, modeling new skills, and assigning homework for family practice. Family psychoeducation may be done with one family at a time or with groups of families meeting together.

EP 2.1.10a

Techniques

Assessment in family psychoeducation focuses on identifying the level of skills in the family (i.e., communication, conflict resolution, etc.). Qualitative and quantitative techniques may be used to further explore areas of family functioning. For instance, a genogram may help to explore family patterns of an illness that may be the focus of the family psychoeducational treatment. Alcoholism, for example, may be a dysfunctional family pattern that can be revealed by a mapping technique. Quantitative techniques may help to operationalize problems further. Using the example of alcoholism, a standardized scale to measure alcohol and drug usage may be helpful.

Education is the delivery of information in a didactic way. This component is often delivered in groups by the FSW or another expert (i.e., physician or other professional). The educational component may be offered prior to or simultaneously with other components of family psychoeducation.

Case management involves connecting families to appropriate community resources. Examples include job training, housing, support groups (e.g., AA), or any other resource that may meet the families' needs. The FSW must have a comprehensive knowledge of resources in his or her community.

Family therapy techniques used by the FSW are usually skills-oriented. Examples of particularly useful skills are communication, conflict resolution, anger management, marital enhancement, and problem solving. Some family members may require skills such as job training and other life skills such as medication maintenance.

EP 2.1.10g

Evidence Base for Family Psychoeducation

The many family psychoeducation research studies have focused on families involved with the mental health system. Lambert's meta-analysis shows the effectiveness of family psychoeducation with affective disorders, major depression, and anorexia (2004). A review by Franklin and Jordan (1999) showed this model to be effective, with improved family and patient outcomes with all family types regardless of background.

EP 2.1.6b

EXERCISE 12.5   Family Psychoeducation

Identify a client you know about and design a family psychoeducational plan including education, skills training, and identification of supportive resources.

CASE 12.2	Psychoeducation

The FSW received an intake on a family facing the mother's diagnosis of HIV. The mother, Elena, had watched as her husband Alejandro's health deteriorated from AIDS. He died two years ago, leaving Elena with one son, Joaquin, age 12. The FSW made a home visit to interview Elena and Joaquin after reviewing the steps of family psychoeducation. The FSW felt this intervention model to be appropriate because the intake indicated that the family was suffering with both health and psychological issues; the evidence-based literature she reviewed confirmed the efficacy of this approach with HIV-AIDS. Following is a brief review of the family social work in each phase of psychoeducation:

Assessment: The FSW focused on identifying the family's level of skills (e.g., communication, conflict-resolution). Qualitative and quantitative techniques were used to further explore areas of family functioning. An ecomap (qualitative technique) was used to assess the family's level of community and family support. A health inventory and social support inventory (quantitative techniques) were used to operationalize problems further.

Education: Elena and Joaquin attended a three-session workshop on HIV-AIDS along with other families.

Case management: The FSW served as the case manager for Elena and Joaquin, connecting them with appropriate community resources. The FSW connected Elena and Joaquin with medical resources and an HIV-AIDS family support group that meets monthly.

Family therapy techniques: The family therapy techniques used by the FSW were determined from the assessment, which revealed Joaquin's anger and Elena's need for parent training. This family may eventually need skills training such as medication maintenance, depending on the course of Elena's illness.

CASE 12.3 | Focusing on Children

The FSW made a visit to the home of Cliff and Claire, a middle-aged African American couple, and their four children. The children were Able (14), Fontana (12), Selena (6), and Foster (4). The family was reported for suspected child abuse by neighbors. The FSW found the couple to be somewhat suspicious of the FSW and the agency; they said that they had been reported before and that the neighbors were "out to get them."

In doing her assessment, the FSW looked for risk factors of child abuse/neglect to confirm or disconfirm the report. Some of the factors she looked for included isolation from family or other support systems; negative interactions within the family; inappropriate parental expectations of the children and/or lack of parenting skills; and high rates of stress. In her investigation of these issues, the FSW found that Cliff and Claire had very little knowledge of child developmental stages or parenting skills. The teenagers, typically, were testing boundaries. The two younger children were acting out, possibly because of the stress between the teens and their parents. Intervention focused on these issues.

CASE 12.4 | Incorporating Everyone's Perspective

Alice and Ray are part of the "sandwich generation." They are parenting Ray's two children from a previous marriage, twins Kathy and Ricky who are 14 years old. Together the couple has a six-month-old baby, Heather. The twins came to live with the family when their biological mother's alcoholism was revealed; she is currently in a treatment facility. Soon after the twins came to live with Alice and Ray, Alice's mother moved in with the family. Bess, 78 years old, fell and broke her hip. After surgery and rehabilitation, she was unable to live alone; thus she moved in with her son's family.

It is important when doing family social work to obtain the perspectives of all family members. Using this family as an example, the FSW found that Alice feels the twins have been spoiled by their mother and that they are undisciplined. She is angry with Ray for not being stricter with the two children. Alice is also angry with Grandma Bess's interference with parenting and other matters. Ray, on the other hand, feels that the children have been through a difficult time with their alcoholic mother and that they need a gentle hand. He also feels that his mother is elderly and harmless. He is mostly amused and just ignores her when she "meddles." The twins' perspective on the family situation is that their new stepmother is "wicked" and that she is "out to get them," clearly preferring the baby over them and their interests. They feel their father is weak for not standing up to Alice, and they miss their mom. They see Grandma Bess as the only adult who will stand up for them.

It will be the FSW's role to help the family negotiate these differences in perspective. Techniques such as problem-solving, conflict resolution, and communication training, as well as anger control, may be useful.

SUBSTANCE ABUSE

Substance abuse can exist in families regardless of the age, gender, culture, educational attainment, or occupational status of family members. In addition, within some client groups, polydrug use (use of more than one substance) may also be prevalent.

Until recently, interventions with addicted individuals have paid scant attention to the family or community context (Nichols & Schwartz, 2007). Although many therapists still prefer an individual approach, some addiction specialists have begun to use a family systems approach in working with substance abusers. Family systems theorists propose that substance abuse causes family dysfunction and conflict. Some also assert that family dysfunction causes substance abuse. Substance abuse can also mask underlying family problems such as sexual abuse or family violence.

Families of substance abusers share common characteristics, particularly family functioning that revolves around the addict's behavior. All areas of family life adapt to the addiction. It is common for family members to deny that addiction is the problem and also feel shame about it. The substance abuse is not discussed among family members or with anyone outside the family. All families have family secrets, but families of substance abusers seem to have more of them. These secrets are the source of much emotional pain for all family members.

Further, family members may inadvertently support the continuation of substance abuse because chemical dependency maintains the status quo. Family members become accustomed to living with inconsistency, insecurity, and fear concerning the routine parts of daily life.

Mealtimes change from day to day, and family members cannot rely on one another. In addition, family relationships are not very cohesive, an important issue because family cohesiveness can delay or reduce the use of substances by children. Besides diminishing the likelihood of addiction, strong family bonds can also promote children's self-esteem and positive attitudes toward school.

The open expression of feelings is often difficult in these families, especially feelings of sadness, love, and tenderness. Family members may not feel close, yet they worry about each other. They may also use family conflict to mask feelings of vulnerability, and such conflict may occur between parent and child or between partners. Anger and hatred may lurk beneath the surface. More typically, the family social worker will observe guilt and blame among family members. In families of substance abusers, parents speak to each other less but children speak with one another more. In addition, daily chores take considerably longer to complete in families troubled by substance abuse. Parents are disengaged emotionally from their children, and family members avoid conflict and confrontation (Aponte & VanDeusen, 1981).

When one partner in a marriage is a substance abuser, the other partner may blame and resent the spouse. Moreover, the entire family may resist treatment. Thus, getting the partner of a substance abuser into treatment may be difficult. The partner may be reluctant to examine his or her own behavior and attitudes in relation to the substance abuse. The family social worker should recognize patterns of blame, avoidance, and resistance.

Substance abuse infiltrates all parts of family life. The erratic and unpredictable behavior of the addict creates a predictable response from family members. Family structures evolve through a process in which family members' behaviors adjust to avoid stress and conflict associated with substance abuse. Eventually, the family adapts to the addict's dysfunctional behaviors to achieve homeostasis, and at the same time homeostasis increases the likelihood that substance abuse will continue because the system organizes to keep the addiction going.

Chemical dependency is debilitating to families, especially in the area of effective parenting. It may also accompany violent behavior in families. While some suggest that substance abuse causes family violence, it is more probable that it impairs judgment and self-control and gives an excuse for the behavior. For example, one of the authors was working with a family in which the daughter had been sexually abused repeatedly by her stepfather. When the stepfather was confronted about his behavior, his defense was, "But I had too much to drink." The social worker's response was, "I am really glad you told me that. You have two problems to work on: the sexual abuse of your daughter and your drinking!" Other family social workers have had clients who reported, "He does hit me and the kids, but only when he has been drinking. When he is sober, he is a great guy." Unfortunately, this excuse can hide a potentially dangerous and dysfunctional family style.

Family members use many defense mechanisms, and both the family and the addict often deny and minimize the addiction. Often the wall of denial can be impenetrable. Additionally, family members may believe that substance abuse is not a family problem but is the exclusive responsibility of the addicted family member. The stepfather mentioned above was more willing to admit to his sexually abusive behavior than he was to admit that he had a substance abuse problem. Family social workers must realize that substance abusers typically deny being addicted and have learned to camouflage the problem. Until people admit having a problem, they will not accept help. Social workers often must make extraordinary efforts to get clients into treatment and to prevent them from dropping out prematurely (Aponte & VanDeusen, 1981).

If attempts to get clients into treatment fail and the children are endangered because of the addiction, further action will be necessary. The family social worker will need to notify child welfare authorities, particularly if the children are being neglected, abused, or placed at risk through lack of supervision. Children of substance abusers often do not get their physical or emotional needs met, and parenting is inconsistent. Further, children of addicts are more likely to be delinquent, depressed, or suicidal (Wegscheider, 1981).

EXERCISE 12.6 Family Dynamics with Substance Abuse

Review the assumptions of family systems theory (in Chapter 3). Then get together in small groups and make a list of how family dynamics might have become set when a family member drinks to problematic proportions. Describe the dynamics that a family social worker will have to pay attention to when the family member stops abusing substances. Then select another family problem and repeat the exercise. Report back to the class.

Interventions with Children of Substance Abusers

Children of substance abusers face an increased risk of chemical dependency. Nevertheless, children are remarkably resilient, and having a substance-abusing parent does not necessarily doom children to enter a life of addiction. Between 70 and 92 percent of children of substance abusers do not become chemically dependent (Bernard, 1992). Unfortunately, children of substance abusers may become preoccupied with how to bring predictability into their lives (Gilliland & James, 1993).

Children of substance abusers show distress in various ways. Besides assuming characteristic roles discussed later, a child may develop problem behaviors in response to the parent's addiction. Although the behaviors described may stem from reasons not directly related to chemical dependency, the role of substance abuse should be considered. All these problems argue strongly in favor of working with every family member and thereby improving the lives of future generations.

The following behaviors may indicate that children are being affected by a parent's addiction:

- Lateness for school or frequent school absenteeism
- Concern expressed by the child about arriving home late from school or other activities
- Children wearing improper clothing, having poor hygiene, being ill frequently, or being fatigued most of the time
- Immature behavior such as bed-wetting, daytime soiling, and thumb-sucking
- Avoidance of arguments and conflict
- Fear that peers will have contact with his or her parents
- Temper outbursts, agitation, or aggression
- Exaggerated concern with achievement or the need to please authority figures. (Northwest Indian Child Welfare, 1984)

Even when children of addicts do not become substance abusers themselves, they can experience difficulties related to their parents' substance abuse. Children of substance abusers may face the following problems:

- *Fetal alcohol syndrome:* Fetal alcohol syndrome (FAS) results from maternal consumption of alcohol during pregnancy. Symptoms can include physical deformity or mental retardation. Children with FAS often require specialized medical attention. (Children with fetal alcohol effects [FAE] show some of the problems associated with FAS.)
- *Bonding difficulties:* Children of substance abusers often lack healthy attachment to caretakers because of caretaker unavailability, both physically and emotionally. Infants may be diagnosed with failure to thrive, and older children may have difficulty forming healthy social attachments.
- *Health problems:* Children of substance abusers tend to suffer more frequent illnesses than other children because of lack of proper nutrition, hygiene, and medical attention.
- *Educational problems:* Because basic survival consumes a lot of energy, children may have little energy available for learning. Social factors may also interfere with learning, including school absenteeism, tardiness, and missing

after-school activities because of worry about getting home on time. Children of substance abusers may be reluctant to have their teachers meet parents. In addition, substance-abusing parents are unlikely to help children with school-related problems. These children can be unpopular at school because of their relationship difficulties and because they are dirty or badly dressed. They may also alienate peers by being aggressive, having temper tantrums, or reverting to infantile behavior. Negative social experiences at school can damage children's self-esteem and make them more vulnerable to substance abuse.

- *Social problems:* Children of substance abusers often show many problems with their social functioning. They may be isolated and, because of peer rejection, may not have adequate opportunities to interact with other children or develop good social skills. Children of substance abusers are more likely than other children to become substance abusers themselves. Children of substance abusers face an increased risk of physical, sexual, or psychological abuse; dropping out of school; unwed pregnancy; delinquency; mental health problems; and attempted suicide. (Johnson, 1990–1991)

In addition to suffering from personal problems, children of substance abusers often assume distinctive roles (Maisto, Galizio, & Connors, 1995). These roles include the following:

- The responsible one (the family hero) is frequently the oldest child. This child is likely to be a high achiever but feel inadequate. "Parentification" of the child may be reinforced by alcoholic parents who praise the child for achieving high levels of mastery and self-control. This behavior response seems to be related to the alcoholic's issue of dealing with a lack of willpower.
- The scapegoat (the acting-out child) is often at the center of family chaos, distracting family members' attention from the substance abuser. The child may act angry and defiant, but is actually hurting inside.
- The lost child (the adjuster) relinquishes personal needs and accommodates to situations by suppressing these needs. The child does not question the family system but is often lonely or quiet. These children are often middle children who, because of their lack of presenting problems, may be overlooked by social workers.
- The placater (the leveler) is a sensitive child who copes by trying to make everyone feel better, solving disputes, carrying messages, and blaming himself or herself for problems. These children are "pleasers" who appear very polite. Many placaters grow up to be professional helpers.
- The family mascot (the distracter), often the youngest child, provides comic relief for the family. The child behaves immaturely and is seen as the baby of the family, in need of protection. This child may feel fearful and anxious and may also be hyperactive. (Bean-Bayog & Stimmel, 1987; Northwest Indian Child Welfare Institute, 1984)

These roles are also seen in families with other types of difficulties as well as addiction. The roles interfere with "normal" childhood behavior and may continue long past childhood, creating difficulties in later life.

Interventions in Families with Substance Abusers

If a family social worker suspects that a client has a problem with substance abuse, she or he should carry out the following tasks:

- Identify and assess the problem.
- Openly discuss the addiction with the family.
- Provide support while the family changes.
- Connect the family with specialized professional services.
- Provide case coordination and management after specialized treatment begins.

Social work with families of substance abusers often involves trying to alter family dynamics so that members no longer camouflage or collude with the substance abuse (Aponte & VanDeusen, 1981). Although family intervention often involves interviews with all family members, its aims may also be accomplished with one person or a family subsystem such as the couple (Bowen, 1973). A family approach to addictions is useful because it assists the entire family by changing family structure and dynamics to help members refuse to facilitate the addiction. A family approach looks at circular causality because the behavior of each person in the family affects everyone else. In alcoholism, where negative stereotypes and attitudes are prevalent, family social workers can convey a nonjudgmental attitude toward the family. Connecting family members with Alcoholics Anonymous and Al-Anon can also help them alleviate their feelings of blame and guilt.

When assessment of the family occurs in the home, the family social worker can observe daily routines and determine how substance abuse affects mealtimes, homework, and bedtimes. The social worker can also assess the family's resources such as competencies of each member and support from relatives. Families need to learn about the effects of substance abuse and to become aware that the problems they are experiencing are related to the addiction.

In working with families of substance abusers, the family social worker should validate family and individual strengths and guide the family toward problem solving. Obtaining a comprehensive assessment of the family helps the worker to understand effects of the addiction on individual family members and identify behaviors that perpetuate the addiction.

Engaging the family must precede all other interventions. The family must accept help in order to work toward change. The social worker usually must overcome the family's initial resistance. Getting past denial is a pressing task for the family social worker because denial prevents effective intervention. Confrontation should be used skillfully (Gilliland & James, 1993). In addition, family routines, individual differences, interaction, behaviors, coping patterns, and disciplinary procedures should be analyzed. Observation of family interactions at different times of the day may be necessary to obtain a comprehensive picture of family functioning. Conflicts and problems should be noted. Contact with schools, addiction specialists, doctors, and church leaders should be made during the assessment phase. It may be necessary to provide concrete assistance, such as ensuring that the family has sufficient financial resources to survive while the addicted family member is receiving inpatient treatment. Because families often will acknowledge the severity of the problem only during periods of severe chaos and disorganization, social workers should not expect the family to readily volunteer information about the problem. Family social workers should instead rely on indirect cues. Gradually, as alcoholism progresses through stages, the spouse and the older children are likely to acknowledge the problem and refuse to camouflage it.

Roles of the Family Social Worker

Addiction requires treatment by specialists. Nevertheless, family social workers can play several crucial roles while assisting families of substance abusers: nurturer, teacher, coordinator, and advocate. By carrying out these roles, workers can help to reduce family dysfunction and improve family communication.

Nurturer   A strong worker-family relationship is important for successful family work. Intense and frequent contact with the family helps the family social worker to develop a helping relationship. Families in crisis depend on the worker to stimulate hope, which will give them the courage to make the necessary changes. Unfortunately, families referred for service usually are people who have trouble developing relationships. Because of negative life experiences, these families have developed a mistrust of authority, institutions, and helping professionals. A close relationship with the worker can encourage families to use appropriate services.

Teacher   The family social worker is a teacher and trainer who can help family members learn a variety of skills: home management and life skills, communication and relationship skills, parenting and child management skills, assertiveness skills and self-advocacy, problem-solving skills, utilization of community resources, and, finally, constructive coping. The social worker can teach skills by explaining, modeling, role-playing, coaching, and encouraging. He or she can help the family to work out a budget, find housing, plan nutritious meals, or divide housekeeping tasks. Teaching practical skills is often necessary because families of substance abusers may have difficulty performing routine tasks. It is important to find out what the family does well and what they want to learn, using the helping relationship as the vehicle that facilitates that learning.

Coordinator   Family social work requires frequent family contact, and the family social worker should be aware of coordination needs and problems. The goals of service coordination are to develop joint treatment plans whenever possible, to spell out the roles and functions of all involved agencies and team members, and to assure that the efforts of all agencies are directed toward common goals. The methods and techniques used should not conflict with each other or confuse family members. The social worker will need to monitor services provided by other helpers and determine when the efforts of various agencies are at cross-purposes. It may be necessary to act as the family's advocate when services are not forthcoming, but the family social worker should support the efforts of other agencies. In addition, each service provider will need accurate information about the family and about other services that are being provided. The social worker should assist family members to develop their own support network that will remain in place after the intensive work is done. Sources of alternative support can be as varied as the circumstances of family members and can include community organizations, religious organizations, cultural groups and activities, parenting classes, and groups who share special interests (e.g., athletics, culture, karate, or gardening). Resolution of strained relationships between the client family and members of the extended family may be necessary before the involvement of extended family can be constructive.

The family social worker often intervenes or fights for the family but should also teach the family how to advocate for themselves. Immediate intervention on behalf of the family or one of its members generates hope, validates the social worker's credibility, and shows caring and commitment. However, before acting on the client's behalf, the worker should ask the following questions: Could my client accomplish this without my support? Could we attempt it jointly? Does she or he merely need the impetus to begin? Does she or he need a sounding board to evaluate options and plan strategies? By advocating and teaching self-advocacy, the family social worker empowers family members.

CHAPTER SUMMARY

This chapter presented some techniques for helping families to better handle the stresses and problems of day-to-day living and strategies to develop a positive family climate. Interventions included behavioral family therapy, family psychoeducation, and parent training. As couples transition through normal developmental stages, they can help the family maturation process by creating a positive parent-child relationship and learning techniques to shape their child's behavior in a positive direction.

KEY TERMS

Reinforcement a reward that keeps a behavior going.

Positive reinforcement the process whereby appropriate behaviors are recognized and reinforced, thereby increasing the probability that the behaviors will continue in the future.

Negative reinforcement the use of consequences that strengthen or maintain a behavior through their removal.

Punishment the use of aversive consequences immediately after the behavior occurs. Punishment is designed to eliminate a particular behavior.

Extinction a technique designed to eliminate behavior through the lack of any consequence (e.g., attention).

Time-out a child discipline technique designed to weaken problematic behaviors. It involves removing the child from the stimulating environment and placing the child in a low-stimulus environment.

SUGGESTED READING

Thompson, C., & Henderson, D. (2011). *Counseling children* (8th ed.). Belmont, CA: Brooks/Cole, Cengage.

COMPETENCY NOTES

EP 2.1.6b. Social workers use research evidence to inform practice: Part of an evidence-informed approach is to look to the literature to see which interventions and techniques work with which client populations and problems. This helps social workers to make informed treatment decisions.

EP 2.1.10a. Social workers substantively and affectively prepare for action with individuals, families, groups, organizations, and communities: Social workers prepare to intervene with clients by having knowledge of intervention models, the research base of these, and the underlying assumptions. Social workers must also have knowledge of the pitfalls of various interventions in order to prepare for eventualities as the case progresses.

EP 2.1.10g. Social workers select appropriate intervention strategies: Social workers must have a repertoire of interventions in order to choose the best ones for their clients.

EP 2.1.10j. Social workers help clients resolve problems: Social workers match up appropriate intervention techniques with the clients' problems in order to help clients solve their problems.

Interventions with Couples and Gender-Sensitive Intervention

LEARNING OBJECTIVES

- Conceptual: Observe and understand sources of inequality in the family.
- Perceptual: Recognize how inequality contributes to abuse within the family.
- Valuational/Attitudinal: Work nonjudgmentally with families and recognize how sources of gender oppression from the larger community impact gender relations in the family.
- Behavioral: Work nonoppressively with family members so that all family members are empowered.

COUPLE WORK

When working with families, the family social worker often will become aware that couple issues are directly impacting parenting. Moreover, couple issues can affect children's well-being. "There is convincing evidence that marital distress, conflict, and disruption are associated with a wide range of deleterious effects on children in families" (Gottman, 1999, p. 4). The focus of this book is on family work, not family therapy or couple therapy, and we suggest that beginning family social workers refer couples to a couples therapist if they require marriage counseling. However, in our work as family social workers, we still need to be able to focus on the couple dyad to help the couple become more supportive of each other in their conjoint parenting efforts.

Satir (1967) considered the parents the "architects of the family" (p. 2). Quite simply, this means that parents define and determine many of the characteristics of the family unit. Parents create the family structure and rules that govern a family. Parents need to teach children healthy ways of functioning, a major way of which is for the parents to model these healthy behaviors. If parents expect children to cooperate, it is important for parents to model cooperation between themselves.

Satir (1967) identified two central themes about parents within a family: 1) "The marital relationship is the axis around which all other family relationships are formed. The mates are the architects of the family, and 2) A pained marital relationship tends to produce dysfunctional parenting" (p. 2). Often the family social worker will meet just with the couple and focus on their relationship and how they communicate with each other and support each other to be consistent in their parenting. Parenting skill training with just the couple present (see Chapter 12) is also a role the worker performs. Family social work with couples is fairly basic, and more advanced couples work needs to be done by a family therapist. Basic family work is primarily educational and supports couples to model the behaviors they expect from their children.

Family rules created to help the family function also need to be followed by the parents. For example, if a rule is that children should not hit each other, this rule should be extended to prohibit hitting among *any* family members, including between parents. If a rule is no swearing by the children, the parents should model a no-swearing policy. Likewise, a family rule of no yelling may be put into place, and it is very important for the parents to model this no-yelling behavior. The overarching rule should echo the adage "Practice what you preach." We are aware that at times there are different rules and behavioral expectations for adults than for children, but many rules and behavioral expectations can be applied to the family as a whole and modeled by the parents. Children learn to share feelings, deal with anger and stress, and solve problems by observing the parents. Parents need to demonstrate healthy ways of communicating and problem solving to act as models of these behaviors to their children.

Two people with personal problems who get together hoping that these problems will get better because of the relationship often discover that their children develop difficulties. They might expect that a certain child will fulfill personal needs, or, alternatively, they might need a child to satisfy their relationship (refer to Chapters 3 and 10 on triangulation). It is important to get an idea of the history of the marriage (or relationship). How did they meet? What did they like about one another? How did they make decisions about their relationship? What was their relationship like before children came along? Eventually, the worker can find out about significant people in their lives and perhaps even locate issues that have been passed down the generations. Family social workers should be attuned to negative interactions between the parents because these interactions lead to negative child outcomes (Stanley, Markman, & Whitton, 2002).

Few people have studied what makes a healthy relationship, and many assume that health is the absence of problems or the absence of pathology. Yet as family social workers, we need to stress the importance of sharing love and caring in a family and minimizing—and especially stopping—criticism, defensiveness, contempt, and stonewalling in order to have healthy families. Parents have to be the leaders and models in this regard.

John Gottman (1999), in his extensive study of marriages, identified the following behaviors that predict divorce with a high degree of accuracy. These predictors exist in all relationships; however, in happy relationships, the behaviors occur less often. On the basis of his research, Gottman identified the following threats to marriages:

- Negativity outweighing positivity during disagreement.
- **Four Horsemen of the Apocalypse**: criticism, defensiveness, contempt, and stonewalling. These Four Horsemen are particularly corrosive to relationships. Contempt does not exist in satisfying relationships.
- Emotional disengagement, underlying tension and sadness, and the absence of positive affect.
- Conflict over perpetual issues is gridlocked or characterized by emotional disengagement.
- Repair attempts fail.
- Harsh start-up of conflict discussions.
- Refusal of husband to accept influence by the wife. (Wives typically accept influence from the husband.)
- Absence of de-escalation attempts.
- Little positive affect. (p. 68)

EXERCISE 13.1   A Healthy Marriage

Break into groups of four. List the qualities of a healthy marriage. Compare the qualities to the red flags identified by Gottman. Present your findings in class.

EP 2.1.7a

HOW TO TEACH COMMUNICATION SKILLS

Healthy communication is an important aspect of couple work because dysfunctional communication can interfere with effective problem solving (Kaplan, 1986). Effective problem solving requires that healthy communication between couples be congruent, direct, honest, and clear (Satir, 1967). (Refer to Chapter 11 for information on the specialized communication/experiential approach.) By examining communication, workers will be able to understand how couples experience their relationships with one another, how they express intimacy, and how they convey information (Satir & Baldwin, 1983).

Thus, work with communication in families entails fostering new skills. These skills may be taught by instruction or through worker modeling (Bodin, 1981).

Changing dysfunctional communication is a three-step process:

1. Partners should discuss communication.
2. The next step is to analyze their behaviors and emotional responses.
3. Finally, they should examine the impact of the interaction on their relationships with each other, their children, extended family members, and so forth (Watzlawick, Beavin, & Jackson, 1967).

EXERCISE 13.2   Understanding Intimacy

Describe the components of a healthy intimate relationship. Divide the class into groups of four. Each group is instructed to locate two marital satisfaction inventories. What does each inventory suggest are the qualities of a satisfactory marriage? Compare the qualities and discuss in class.

Metacommunication is "communication about communication" or a "message about a message" (Satir, 1967, p. 76). Communication entails either conveying information or making a demand. However, most communication is a request (Satir, 1967, p. 77). Metacommunication is useful to check out the meaning of what another has just said and is particularly useful in working with couples. While couples communicate a lot, they seldom spend time looking at underlying messages to one another (Hepworth & Larsen, 1993). Discussions of metacommunication are most effective if done in the here and now when the interaction is fresh in the minds of the couple. The family social worker will have to pay close attention to the ongoing couple interaction, stop the communication process, and then engage the couple in a discussion of the events that just occurred. The goal is to get the couple to replace dysfunctional patterns of communication with healthier and more appropriate communication.

EXERCISE 13.3   Communication Intervention with a Couple

Break into groups of three or four students. Divide a piece of paper into two columns. On the top of one column, write Dos and on the top of the second column write Don'ts. Devise a list of skills that can be used in communication skills training with a couple. Compare your list with those of the rest of the class, discuss the lists, and then compile a complete list based on everyone's responses.

Systemic intervention also focuses on the couple's interaction, particularly communication strengths and deficits. Training to improve a couple's communication emphasizes both verbal and nonverbal skills (Granvold & Jordan, 1994). Verbal communication skills include listening and empathizing, "I" statements.

Listening and Empathizing

Couples can be taught to actively listen, or paraphrase, what the speaker said in order to communicate that the message was received. For instance, a wife says to her spouse, "I feel angry right now because you were late and did not call."

Her husband, using active listening, says, "You are angry because I did not telephone to say I would be late." Problems could arise if instead the husband said, "You are always trying to control me by nagging. Get off my back." Compare the two different responses. Which response demonstrates more healthy and functional communication? Rather than getting in an argument, the listener in the first example has restated the angry message and communicated to his wife that he heard what she said, thus supporting her communication. Also, if the paraphrase is incorrect, the speaker has an opportunity to give feedback and clarify her message. This type of listening communicates empathy to the speaker.

Use of "I" Statements

Use of "I" statements to communicate a message, especially a message unlikely to put the listener on the defensive, can help members reduce couple conflicts. The angry spouse in the previous paragraph might say, "You are a thoughtless bum; you come home late all the time and never call!" Alternatively, she could use an "I" statement to express the effect of her husband's behavior on her feelings. For example, "When you come home late and don't call me, I feel angry and frightened because I worry about your safety." The general format for making "I" statements is "I feel (speaker's feeling) when you (family member's behavior) because (compelling rationale)."

Developers of one family-centered, home-based model provide the following guidelines for using "I" messages (Kinney, Haapala & Booth, 1991):

- Describe behavior, not persons.
- Use observations, not inferences.
- Use behavioral descriptors, not judgments.
- Avoid the use of generalizations such as never, always, and so on.
- Speak for the moment.
- Share ideas, and do not give advice.

If the listener uses active listening to be empathetic, the speaker might offer a solution, such as "Could we make a deal that I won't worry if you are less than an hour late and that you agree to call if you will be more than an hour late getting home?" The listener might modify the solution or offer an alternative one until a mutually agreeable solution is found. Active listening and use of "I" statements can be modeled and practiced, with the family social worker giving feedback.

The family social worker also may be alert to communication deficits in the interaction. For instance, one member of the couple may talk too loudly or softly, too quickly or slowly, or use a tone of voice that is monotonous and boring or excitable or hostile (Gambrill & Richey, 1988). The worker also may watch for ways to help members improve their nonverbal communication. For example, members may practice communicating with relaxed posture, with a warm and smiling facial expression, and appropriate eye contact (Hepworth & Larsen, 1986).

EXERCISE 13.4   *Communication Skills Training*

Kerrie Jones is angry about the lack of participation of her husband, Bob, with the family, including the time it seems he'd rather spend away from home "playing with his buddies." Write some "I" statements Kerrie could use to communicate her feelings to her husband, as well as some active listening responses her husband could offer. With two other students, role-play a session with the Jones couple (one student should play the family social worker and the other two should play Bob and Kerrie Jones). Negotiate some solutions to Kerrie's problem.

EP 2.1.10g

SAME-SEX COUPLES

A communication skills approach can work well for same-sex couples. However, it is important for the family social worker to be mindful of some of the key issues faced by same-sex couples and their families. The communication approach helps the couple to clearly and directly talk to each other about the issues they are experiencing as a same-sex couple or as parents if they have children. Below are some of the background and issues important for the worker to understand.

Sexual Orientation

In this book, we emphasize that families come in many sizes, shapes, and forms, making the definition of *family* broad. Here we look at an emerging and growing family form: gay and lesbian families. Patterson (1995) suggests that "the phenomenon of large numbers of openly lesbian and gay parents raising children represents a sociocultural innovation that is unique to the current historical era" (p. 263).

Gay and lesbian people face oppression as the result of homophobia and heterosexism (Adams, Jaques, & May, 2004). In addition, gay and lesbian parents encounter multiple oppressions because they are members of a minority group. Because of social work's unique anti-oppressive and person-in-environment perspectives, social workers are well positioned to challenge the status quo and advocate for social justice for all clients, including gay and lesbian families. To do so, they must be informed and open-minded. They must also think critically and analytically about social messages from their own particular sociocultural subgroups such as their family, religious groups, or their community's value systems. Our beliefs about gay and lesbian families reflect the political or social climate; the lack of social and institutional support; and personal beliefs, attitudes, and prejudices (Adams, Jaques, & May, 2004). This means becoming sensitized to heterosexist and antigay language and also advising that policies and practices be inclusive.

The actual number of gay and lesbian families is unknown, in part because they are not granted legal legitimacy in many jurisdictions. To date, only a few nations and states have legally recognized gay and lesbian intimate relationships, although the number is growing. Because of discrimination and stigmatization, gays and lesbians fear that they will lose custody or visitation rights regarding their children if the children were conceived in a heterosexual union. They therefore worry about how and to whom they should reveal their sexual orientation. In addition to custody disputes, fear about family-of-origin reaction, negative peer reaction, and decisions about when and whom to tell affect how open the families decide to be (Adams, Jaques, & May, 2004).

Gay and lesbian people can become parents in a number of ways. Reproductive technologies such as artificial insemination and surrogate parenting are providing gay and lesbian people with more options for becoming parents. Lesbian women have the option of artificial insemination of one of the partners. Gay men are now able to enter into surrogate parenting relationships with the assistance of artificial insemination. What stands out about these latter two arrangements is that parenting is a *choice* for these people. Pregnancy and parenting is not an accident as it might be in heterosexual relationships. Despite the fact that the decision is well thought out, and often extremely expensive, gay and lesbian parents are often the subject of legal discrimination based on negative assumptions about the outcomes of gay and lesbian parenting. Unfortunately, these assumptions have been aided and abetted by the social sciences. Early versions of the *Diagnostic and Statistical Manual* originally classified homosexuality as psychopathology, and social biases suggest that gay and lesbian parents are mentally ill or that lesbian mothers are not maternal. However, emergent research is proving otherwise.

Lambert (2005) summarized the research on gay and lesbian parenting. In this discussion, we remind students that much diversity exists in any social grouping and suggest that information that supposedly represents all groupings within a particular social grouping fails to capture the richness and diversity within groups. We encourage students to carefully synthesize the studies contained in Lambert's article. The review of research is summarized in the following list:

1. Lesbian mothers divorced from male fathers score at least as high as divorced heterosexual mothers on measures of psychological functioning.
2. There are no differences in parental sexual role behavior, interest in child rearing, responses to child behavior, or ratings of warmth toward children.
3. Divorced lesbian mothers are more fearful of losing children in custody disputes.
4. Lesbian mothers are more likely to provide children with toys relating to both genders.
5. Divorced lesbian mothers are more likely than divorced heterosexual mothers to be living with a romantic partner.
6. The extent to which lesbian mothers are "out" and involved with feminist activism has a positive relationship with children's psychological health.
7. Less information exists on gay custodial fathers. Gay fathers report higher incomes than do lesbian mothers and are more likely to encourage children to play with gender-specific toys than are lesbian mothers.
8. There are no significant differences in sexual orientation, gender identification, or gender role behavior in young adults from lesbian relationships.
9. Children in lesbian relationships are more likely to consider the possibility of having lesbian or gay relationships. This might be due to the climate of acceptance in which they lived.
10. Most children of gay or lesbian relationships identify themselves as heterosexual.
11. Children of gay and lesbian relationships have normal peer relations.
12. Children of gay and lesbian relationships report more teasing and bullying about their parents' sexuality. If parents fear safety (Adams, Jaques, & May, 2004), children also have a legitimate fear.
13. Early studies of divorced lesbian mothers report that their children are more likely to have contact with their fathers (the divorced husband) than are children of divorced heterosexual mothers.

14. Children in gay and lesbian families experience more stress in their daily lives.
15. Gay and lesbian families maintain an egalitarian division of labor.

Because of imposed marginalization from mainstream society, many gay and lesbian couples have had to make their own mark on the family life cycle. Johnson and Colucci (1999) note that for many gay and lesbian people, their friendship network is considered a family unit, partly in response to the mainstream definition of family as blood or legal ties. However, these authors argue that rather than dismissing the existing family life cycle model, the model can be amended. Challenges during each phase become quite complicated, given that the world is primarily based on heterosexual issues. Unique issues emerge at every juncture of the life cycle, including coming out and disclosing to family, dating, moving onto a job or career, setting up a romantic relationship, and parenting. What typically comes easily for heterosexual counterparts comes at a high cost for gay and lesbian people. Their struggles are exacerbated by homophobia and oppressive or insensitive reactions from the larger society.

EXERCISE 13.5 Inclusiveness

Select one example of heterosexism in society around you. Describe this heterosexism. Now select a policy or practice to revise this inherent heterosexism.

EXERCISE 13.6 How You Learned

What are your unique messages and learning about gay and lesbian families? Where did these messages come from? Whose interests do they serve? Where do you stand in regard to what you were taught growing up? How do these teachings diverge from or converge with the profession of social work? How do your beliefs reflect the political or social climate; the lack of social and institutional support; and personal beliefs, attitudes, and prejudices?

EXERCISE 13.7 Climate

Describe how each of the following influences public attitudes toward gay and lesbian families:

1. Politics
2. Religion
3. Patriarchy
4. Feminism
5. Social sciences
6. Research
7. Therapy and counseling

EXERCISE 13.8 Making the Right to Marry More Inclusive

Divide the class into three sections. One group will develop an argument that only blue-eyed people should be allowed to legally marry. The second group will argue for the right of brown-eyed and blue-eyed people to marry. The third group will argue that every adult should be allowed to marry, regardless of his or her eye color. Make note of some of the arguments. What points that were presented were solely value-based? What points had scientific merit? If research were more influential in the argument, which side would win?

Specific Issues That May Need to be Discussed in a Communications Approach

Gay and lesbian couples face the same and also unique issues as heterosexual couples. In addition, if levels of "outness" of the members of the relationship differ, it may cause strain in the relationship. They face special stressors because of the judgmental attitudes of society toward them. Laws are also discriminatory, and discrimination in health care regulations may mean that one person may not be able to put the same-sex partner on the other's work health care plan. In communicating with the couple, the family social worker can focus on their reactions to homophobia as responses in the community, the legal system, schools, religion, and other institutions and agencies to see if they feel accepted. Newly formed couples have to consider legal issues such as property rights, inheritance laws, and issues related to living wills, power of attorney, and medical decision making. Prenuptial agreements may also be an issue to be discussed.

Children in the relationships also encounter special issues. They may be bullied in school. If the child is from a previous heterosexual relationship, the gay or lesbian parent may face custodial issues, depending on the degree of "outness." Moreover, same-sex couples who have adopted children from other countries may face double discrimination, one related to sexual orientation and the other related to cultural issues. Children adopted from orphanages may have mental health issues, be HIV-positive, or have behavioral problems. Children of same-sex couples may not be entitled to both parents' work benefits. Parents face extra pressure to succeed with their raising of children, and involvement of grandparents becomes complicated if the couple is not "out" or if the grandparents do not accept the relationship.

The family social worker also needs to learn to be sensitive to language used in family social work. Even though there is some disagreement in gay and lesbian communities about language, it is important for the worker to learn what terms the couple is comfortable with. It is quite acceptable, if you do not know how to ask questions, to start with the comment, "If I am offensive, it is not intentional. Please help me out." For example, a gay couple may refer to themselves as two dads, whereas another gay couple may refer to themselves as a daddy and a papa. Terms are changing. A term heard in the sixties for a partner was *lover*; now, depending on the level of outness or comfort with whom the couple is speaking, terms used can range from *my friend* to *my roommate, partner, spouse, husband,* or *wife*. Also, the family social worker needs to be comfortable with and accepting of the range of gender expression. Where there is domestic violence, the worker needs to be aware of not making assumptions about size or gender.

The family social worker can also help the family get connected to community groups. These groups can be a helping system for same-sex couples to offer social support as well as useful educational experiences. Some of these groups include "coming out" groups, parenting groups, and gay and lesbian professional groups, to name a few.

EP 2.1.4a

GENDER-SENSITIVE PERSPECTIVE

An underpinning philosophy we now employ when working with families as well as couples is a gender-sensitive perspective. We let families and couples know that it is a philosophy and approach we strongly believe is important in today's Western society. We are aware that we are imposing our bias and not all couples or families will accept this view, but we believe the concept of equality is still important to share with families and couples.

We believe a gender-sensitive perspective is useful for the couple and parenting subsystems as well as the family as a whole. Our rationale for a gender-sensitive perspective is that we have found it highly conducive to understanding and engaging couples in family social work. It helps us be very sensitive to people's feelings and who they are.

We first present issues in work with couples and the gender-sensitive conceptual framework. The latter part of the chapter is somewhat an extension of behaviorally focused interventions from Chapter 12, in which we focus in greater depth on parenting skill training within a gender-sensitive context.

EP 2.1.4a

GENDER-SENSITIVE INTERVENTION

Gender-sensitive intervention is linked with support and education, as well as problem solving. Key elements of this approach involve helping families to:

- Recognize and change the destructive consequences of stereotyped roles and expectations.
- Avoid the promotion of dependency and submissiveness for women and children.
- Encourage women to build positive self-esteem, and encourage men to become actively involved in child and household duties.

Intervention using a gender-sensitive lens does not advocate neutrality for the family social worker, as does traditional family therapy. Gender-sensitive family work occurs with worker and family being on an equal footing. Family members are empowered to gain a positive understanding of their skills and abilities, changing the whole family in a positive way. This is congruent with the overall approach taken throughout this book, that the family worker actively supports family members. Support and education, as well as problem solving and contracting, support the goals of feminism.

Applying this supportive approach while utilizing a gender-sensitive perspective helps families through education about gender issues and gender realities. Young girls still grow up in a world that gives them very different messages from the ones that boys receive about their value, roles, and life opportunities. Yet traditional family work often fails to take this social context into account when dealing with women's (and girls') problems. One worker may treat a woman's depression and anger in response to an abusive relationship as a symptom of an individual psychiatric problem, encouraging her to adapt to the problems rather than to change her situation. It is important that family social workers understand families, and women in particular, in a modern social context and not from a traditional psychiatric model. The family social worker can teach a woman to differentiate between her problem and someone else's problem, helping her to realize that every failed relationship in her life is not her fault. Women have been socialized to take responsibility for family relationships and the well-being of individual family members.

Family social work helps families recognize and change the destructive consequences of stereotyped roles and expectations in the family. Traditional workers have assessed the mental health of women and men differently. Healthy women are often expected to be more submissive, less independent, more easily influenced, less competitive, more excitable and emotional, more conceited about their appearance, less objective, and less interested in math and science than are healthy men. For women, the most significant barrier to finding a good worker has been the male standard of behavior that traditionally guides what is "healthy" and "normal." It is imperative that family social workers present themselves in the beginning stage of family work as not following traditional views, but as defining adult relationships as egalitarian. In the intervention phase, this translates to having adults equally participate in child rearing and household tasks.

Gender-sensitive family work avoids promoting dependency and submissiveness for women and children. Women often believe that their role is to nurture and support others rather than to express themselves; they have been taught to take care of others first. As a result, they often have difficulty recognizing their own needs. Exhausted, working women are trying to keep up with all the demands of work as well as of home, resulting in stress and burnout. At the same time, gender-sensitive family work recognizes the importance of relationships to women on the one hand and the need that relationships not oppress women or allow others to manipulate them on the other.

For women who have been abused, health and well-being starts with recognizing their will to survive. Placing women's issues within a larger social context also boosts women's self-esteem. Effective family social work helps women build self-esteem, stand up for themselves, and assume greater control over their lives. It gives women choices and opens up opportunities otherwise denied to them and at the same time encourages men to value their roles of equal partner and parent. Men, in the process, are encouraged to become actively involved in parenting and household responsibilities. Strengths and competence are emphasized. Indeed, the key to helping women and families is to focus on strengths rather than weaknesses. In family or couple work, this means giving equal consideration to the skills, aspirations, and careers of women.

A gender-sensitive family social worker working with couples who are experiencing a troubled couple relationship should describe the two key ingredients for a successful marriage:

1. A good partnership requires a supportive, nurturing relationship involving genuine commitment and caring for each other. This is an indirect way of saying that partners need to develop intimacy to achieve couple satisfaction. As mentioned earlier, the major reason given for couple divorce was feeling unloved in the relationship.

2. A satisfying partnership also requires equal or at least a negotiated sharing of instrumental tasks within the household. When children are present, there should be equal sharing of parenting tasks such as assisting children with homework, taking children to dental appointments, and spending creative playtime with children. Both parents need to understand that the time and energy they invest in child care pays big dividends in terms of family functioning. Furthermore, the male's role in raising children has to be enhanced to that of an equal partnership with the female. This means that women also need to avoid making men feel incompetent when caring for children, and men need to become active partners in doing household tasks such as cooking and laundry.

EXERCISE 13.9   Different Perspectives on Family Problems

Think of a family with whom you are familiar. How would you assess this family's problems? Redefine the problems to include dimensions of power and gender.

EP 2.1.10g

PROBLEM SOLVING WITHIN A GENDER-SENSITIVE INTERVENTION PERSPECTIVE

A problem-solving approach complements a gender-sensitive perspective. Because gender sensitivity assumes equality of family members within the context of developmental and personal capacities, problem solving encourages participation of all members in solving common family problems. What affects one member affects everyone. Problem solving helps members negotiate solutions to problems that are acceptable to everyone in the family.

In teaching families problem-solving skills, family social workers help families identify concerns and goals, set priorities, and develop a plan for working toward resolution. Problem solving is an essential component of individuals' and family members' well-being, and the use of this model can enhance a family's ability to independently address its own needs. In the course of personal and work life, family members have goals as well as problems or stresses. Problem-solving strategies can be used to reach goals, meet challenges, or deal with stresses and problems and is one way of coping with life's events. Given the same stressful circumstances, one person may cope by denial or avoidance, whereas another may cope through effective problem solving. Parents may be taught the problem-solving process so that they will have a better understanding of the processes and strategies involved in thinking through a problem and carrying out proposed solutions.

The social work profession has a long history of using a problem-solving approach. The problem-solving model is based, in part, on an assumption that parents' day-to-day situations are often as complex and demanding as those of many professionals. Therefore, the preparation and training given to many professionals in problem solving is appropriate for parents. Problem-solving skills are an important part of social work education as workers are taught how to identify, assess, and intervene with client problems. A second assumption is that teaching parents problem-solving skills helps assure that parents have the necessary skills for developing positive parent-child relationships.

EP 2.1.10g

HISTORICAL CONTEXT

Historically, men have held more public and private power than women. Men wrote laws, controlled property and money, and were recognized as heads of households, whereas women did most of the work within the home and received little recognition, power, or respect for their contributions. These patterns have been changing within the last few decades as growing numbers of women have entered the workforce and the political arena, but imbalances of power remain. Because of long-standing patterns of gender inequity, family social workers are likely to encounter situations in which women are oppressed and abused.

Expecting women to adapt to oppressive situations is inappropriate; instead, family social workers should empower them to assume greater control over their lives. Empowering women might entail helping them find ways to change or leave oppressive and abusive relationships and to gain a broader awareness of the options available to them. Accordingly, gender-sensitive interventions are well suited to family social work, particularly work with families in which women have been oppressed or abused by their partners.

Gender-sensitive family social workers question some of the views held by traditional family therapists, including their emphasis on circular causality, particularly when applied to power imbalances. They disagree with the idea that women contribute to their own abuse. Instead, they attribute the abuse to imbalance and misuse of power.

To implement a gender-sensitive approach with clients, family social workers must be willing to question their personal assumptions about men and women and gender roles. They need to become familiar with the ways in which society reinforces unequal treatment based on gender. Gender-sensitive social workers wear an ecological lens when understanding family dynamics, recognizing the influence of a family's social environment on its internal functioning. Many families have uncritically absorbed messages about gender stereotypes and inequalities from the larger society. Finally, gender-sensitive social workers recognize that changes in families can slowly lead to changes in society and that social change can improve life for families.

EP 2.1.4a

A FEMINIST CRITIQUE OF FAMILY SYSTEMS THEORY

Gender-sensitive family social work uses a feminist perspective to understand how families function. The feminist perspective has been described as "an attitude, a lens, a body of ideas about gender hierarchy and its impact rather than a specific model or a grab-bag of clinical techniques" (Carter, 1992, p. 66). Feminist theory is a philosophical foundation on which family social workers can base gender-sensitive interventions without perpetuating patriarchal assumptions about the role of women in families and in society. Feminist theory, as it applies to family social work, advocates sensitivity to the problems created when rigid, traditional gender roles are assigned to family members (to the woman's detriment) or when power is not balanced or is abused. It also sheds light on the fact that gender has an influence in male-female relationships (Ramage, F. (2005)). Feminist social workers recognize the detrimental effects of power imbalances and gender-based inequality in family relationships.

Feminists have challenged some of the basic assumptions of traditional family therapists, noting the influence of cultural and historical biases on the development of family theory (Nichols & Schwartz, 2004). Feminist theorists have criticized sexist biases of the pioneers of family therapy and individual psychology, who failed to question the value of characteristics in which males are socialized (rationality, independence) while discounting characteristics (such as nurturing and interconnectedness) typically associated with female socialization. Early family theorists also endorsed a "normal family structure," often based on gender inequality. For example, they spoke about instrumental roles (which should be assumed by males) and affective roles (typically assumed by women). When the roles were reversed, family workers advocated "putting the pants back on the men" (Collins & Tomm, 2009, p. 3). Advocates of feminist social work practice believe this male-constructed view of the world associates female characteristics with weakness, passivity, masochism, and inferiority.

During the 1980s, feminists began to criticize family systems theory for some of its sexist biases, particularly the assumption that if all participants in the system contribute to a problem, they do so from positions of equal power. In particular, feminists challenged family systems concepts of circular causality, neutrality, complementarity, and homeostasis. Most of these concepts were discussed in Chapter 3. Feminists consider circular causality (implying that members are locked in an equal and never-ending, repetitive pattern of mutually reinforcing behaviors) to be a sophisticated way of blaming victims and rationalizing the status quo (Goldner, 1985a). Circular causality was considered particularly problematic in its explanation of abuse or other problems associated with power imbalances. Indeed, McGoldrick (1999b) noted "the conundrum of responsibility without power has long characterized women's lives" (p. 107).

When used to explain family violence, circular causality implies that the perpetrator and victim are equally involved in producing and maintaining "the problem." The most sexist use of circular causality was to "punctuate" the circular pattern by suggesting that the antecedent to wife abuse often starts with the woman nagging the man. Not only were women blamed for the abuse, they were also blamed for initiating the sequence of events that culminated in their abuse. Feminists took a different stance, challenging mainstream family theory by insisting that women are not equally responsible for their own abuse because they have little power in the family system. They argue that using circular causality to explain abuse subtly removes responsibility from the abuser while implying that the victim contributes to the problem by playing into the interaction pattern resulting in abuse.

Similarly, the family systems' idea of the worker being neutral during family work ignores and even condones differences in family members' power. Feminists disagree with the idea that social workers should avoid holding one family member responsible for a problem and suggest that those who abuse power are ultimately responsible. Through neutrality, they argue, traditional helpers contribute to the maintenance of the status quo.

Feminists also challenge complementarity—the belief that gender difference is acceptable because men and women play separate but equal roles in family life. According to traditional views, men are responsible for the economic well-being of the family, whereas women are responsible for the caregiving of family members. In other words, under the traditional model, wives are responsible for almost everything that keeps the family operating smoothly, such as housework and child care (Eichler, 1997). Feminists point out that while the homemaker role is valued in the abstract, the work is denigrated (Pogrebin, 1980). Moreover, women are socialized to assume responsibility for the emotional well-being of the family. Goldner (1985a) alerts us to this bias: "We think of mothers as gatekeepers, regulating the interaction between the family and the outside world, and also as switchboards, regulating communication patterns within the family" (p. 39).

A major concern about gender bias in family work is the long-standing tendency of the helping professions to blame mothers for the problems of other members or the family as a whole because family well-being is considered the responsibility of women. Ironically, they are responsible for family well-being even though they lack power. Mothers have been considered the central (and often only) socialization agent of children (Mackie, 1991), ignoring the role of fathers in child care. Because of this ascribed responsibility, when sexual abuse happens, it is the mother's responsibility. Mother blaming is both pervasive and disturbing (Caplan & Hall-McCorquodale, 1985). Difficulties such as attachment disorders (Bowlby, 1969), schizophrenia (Weakland & Fry, 1974), and sexual abuse (Trepper & Barrett, 1986) have all been placed on the doorstep of poor "mothering." Mothers have also been blamed for participating in their own abuse. In the literature, mothers are described as either overinvolved or remote. They are either incompetent or over-competent. They are either overemotional or cold. Women cannot win. Whichever way, women are responsible for the ills of the family. In the development of child problems, mothers are described as contributors to the disorders, but, repeatedly, fathers are ignored, even when the problems originate from them, as is frequently the case in sexual abuse (Coleman & Collins, 1990). Mothers have also been blamed for the difficulties of adult men (Caplan & Hall-McCorquodale, 1991).

Another fundamental tenet of family systems theory is that the family, as a living organism, attempts to maintain a balance or homeostasis. This view of family functioning obscures or eliminates individual responsibility because all behavior is seen as an attempt by the family as a unit to maintain homeostasis. Family homeostasis and mother blaming work together to maintain the gender power imbalance evident in family systems theory. On one hand, mothers are responsible for the problems of the family, but homeostasis is used to excuse or obscure power abuses by male family members.

Family social workers should take special note of how homeostasis has explained family problems, particularly when a problem involves victimization. For example, family systems theorists who discuss the causes of intrafamilial sexual abuse have interpreted the father's behavior in positive terms (i.e., a misguided attempt to show affection), while suggesting that mothers should be assessed for inhibited sexual desire. Such theories reveal a not so subtle gender bias. Not only are fathers given positive intent for the abuse, mothers become responsible for maintaining homeostasis. Again, in the words of Goldner (1985a), "Insofar as all roads lead to Mom, her excesses and deficiencies will indeed make an enormous difference in how life flows around her and how the children develop" (p. 40).

EXERCISE 13.10 Feminism

EP 2.1.4a

Many conservative thinkers argue that feminism has destroyed the family. Split the class into "agree" and "disagree" sections and debate this argument.

POWER IMBALANCES IN FAMILY RELATIONSHIPS

One of the strongest critiques of family intervention by feminists is the assertion that by failing to challenge the imbalance of power in families, family work has sanctioned this imbalance (Dye Holten, 1990). Because feminist practice is primarily concerned with power and how it is distributed, feminist theory is particularly concerned with inequality in family relationships. A fundamental aim of feminism is to ensure that power in family relations is fairly distributed.

One source of unequal power is the law, which gives husbands, wives, mothers, fathers, and children certain rights and obligations. A second source of power is the gender norms established by society. Although gender power is changing as traditional role definitions change, these changes seem to be more apparent in well-educated, middle-class households. Changes in gender roles may create confusion in families, and members may face conflicts as roles change. A third source of power involves access to knowledge and resources. People can increase their personal power base by improving their formal education and obtaining more resources such as money, information, or social support. Women usually have less economic power than men, and economic dependency becomes especially potent with the arrival of children (Mackie, 1991; McGoldrick, 2002). However, when wives have greater status or money than their husbands, divorce is more likely to occur.

Personality differences influence the distribution of power in family life. Members with high self-esteem, for example, are likely to have more power than those with low self-esteem. People who are outgoing, talkative, and assertive are also considered to have greater power and control than those who are not.

Another important source of power involves factors such as age and the life stage. Changes in life situations that affect personal power are sometimes difficult to understand and constitute potentially stressful life events. For instance, an unemployed husband may not have the same status and power he enjoyed while working. Sadness, anger, or both may accompany the loss of power from a change in life situations. Power differences may also shift at retirement when men lose social power because they are no longer as involved in public spheres of life.

A final source of power influencing family members concerns emotional factors. Family members vary in their ability and willingness to give or withhold love and affection. Motives also vary on this dimension, with some family members exerting control with manifestations of love, affection, dominance, force, denial, or rejection.

Not all power discrepancies in families are destructive or undesirable. For example, parents should have more power than their children. We see many families these days in which children have much more power in their families than they can responsibly handle. Ineffective parenting and failure to discipline appropriately leave many children with inappropriate power. The challenge to possessing personal power in a relationship is to use this power responsibly and not just assume that because it comes with a particular family role, power can be used in any way one wants. Every family has unique configurations of power based on age, sex, education, personality, and life situation. Couples need to be acutely aware of these factors in exercising power with each other. In addition, family workers should be keenly attuned to power issues within the families with whom they are working.

Power is neither diminished nor lost when shared. In fact, shared power helps to balance families, and family satisfaction is highest when all family members get to share in the family's power. Gottman and Notarius (cited in Ramage, F. (2005) p. 264) observe that a balance of husband-wife power is related to couple quality and couple satisfaction. A family council or regular couple review is one way families can equalize power distribution. Emotionally healthy families use power to support one another, whereas troubled families use power to distort, control, or dominate. Appropriate use of power helps members reach their potential and provides maximum benefit to family members.

Regardless of how power relates to gender in the family, social workers need to be sensitive to issues of power. Gender-sensitive family social workers strive to model egalitarian relationships with families. Rather than taking an authoritarian role, they work to empower family members, modeling the benefits of sharing power rather than appropriating it for oneself.

The Ecological Orientation of Gender-Sensitive Practice

In assessing family problems, gender-sensitive family social workers recognize the influence of the economic, political, and social environments in which people live, as well as the prevailing social attitudes and expectations that frame gender roles. By recognizing the social context of gender roles and associated traits, workers can better understand why men abuse their partners emotionally and physically. Additionally, they realize that women may remain in abusive relationships because of feelings of powerlessness, helplessness, and lack of control over their lives.

Until recently, traditional family systems workers failed to connect family problems to socially prescribed gender roles and power imbalances, and thus have not acknowledged how the interactions between family members are affected by the larger social system (Goodrich, Rampage, Ellman, & Halstead, 1988, p. 12). Feminists point out that trying to assess a family's problems without regard to ecological embeddedness "is like watching a parade through a key hole" (Goldner, 1985a, p. 34).

The larger social context needs to be considered when looking at family dysfunction. Feminists suggest that cultural values and beliefs about gender influence how families function, with the larger cultural context playing a role in wife battering and child abuse.

EXERCISE 13.11 Critique Systems Theory

On the basis of your personal experience, critique systems theory. What principles do not make sense to you? What principles make sense to you? How well do the principles fit for different cultures? For different genders?

EP 2.1.7a

FAMILY VALUES AND FAMILY VIOLENCE: A CRITIQUE

Why is an understanding of values and beliefs about families important? Don't families just exist independently from other families? Shouldn't families just do the best they can and face the consequences of not fulfilling social obligations? As with any social work practice, workers must understand the wider social context of their practice and how larger social values might influence their practice. In this critique, we use the example of family violence to show how workers have colluded with three social values and how this collusion has skewed workers' understanding of abuse in the family. In a study of family violence from colonial times to the present, Pleck (1987) suggested that three central societal values have hindered attempts to eliminate family violence. These values include beliefs about family privacy, family stability, and conjugal and parental rights.

Family Privacy

Over time, there has been lack of agreement about how much families should be left to their own devices without outside intervention from the state. This fundamental question concerns all family social workers who must grapple with the intrusiveness of their work. Many family social workers work for state-based agencies and have a legal mandate to enter homes. Some of the value placed on family privacy is based on the belief that intimate family relationships should be free from state intrusion and interference. As stated by Pleck (1987), "Modern defenders are likely to argue that the family has a constitutional right to privacy or insist that the home is the only setting where intimacy can flourish, providing meaning, coherence and stability in personal life" (p. 8). To what extent should family social workers intrude into resistant families?

In the same fashion, behavior within families is often viewed differently from behavior outside of families. "When we think of the family, and then think of the world that surrounds it, we tend to think in terms of contrasts" (Goldner, 1988, p. 24). For example, abuse of family members is sometimes attributed to family dynamics, but similar behavior directed toward a neighbor is considered criminal assault. Separate government agencies exist to deal with abuse inside and outside of the family, and one cluster of theories explains violence outside the home whereas another cluster describes violence within the home.

Social isolation has become the downside of family privacy. Many families seen by family social workers are socially isolated, making access to social resources difficult. Privacy removes them from scrutiny and keeps family members from potential sources of social support and information. Family social workers must identify their personal beliefs about family privacy and decide what impact their beliefs and agency mandates may have on working with families. When families are involuntary, the family social worker must cross the line concerning privacy.

If a family social worker is uncertain about how to deal with issues of privacy, he or she may be governed by politeness and apology instead of dealing with family problems. Drawing artificial boundaries around the family inhibits family work. Efforts to safeguard family privacy affect social work practice, especially when abuse is suspected. Notions about privacy may protect abusers from legal consequences and prevent victims of family violence from using resources to escape the abuse.

Family Stability

Keeping families together is a central goal of family social workers. When working with people involved in abuse, however, workers may be forced to choose between two basic values: the autonomy of the family and the protection of children (Giovanonni, 1982). Making this choice is difficult because the measure of success for family social workers is often keeping the family together. However, family social workers frequently face the difficult choice of protecting vulnerable family members, necessitating that children be removed from the home. Maintaining family autonomy becomes a line-drawing exercise, and the mandate of the agency might determine where family workers draw the line.

Traditionally, one way of ensuring family stability has been to reinforce established gender roles by keeping the male as the head of the household. Encouraging the independence of women has been viewed as a threat to the family unit (Cherlin, 1983). Strong women have the resources to manage on their own, and they are not economically dependent. Gordon (1985) contends, "the concept of the autonomous family, in fact, as it is manipulated in contemporary political discourse, is generally used in opposition to women's rights as autonomous citizens" (p. 218). Family social workers need to examine their personal biases about gender roles to consider what it means to empower every member of the family unit. Family social workers must decide whether the goal of preserving family stability meets the needs of every family member, particularly those who are vulnerable. Does failure to preserve the family make the intervention a failure?

The desire to maintain family stability has frequently led family social workers to make mothers the focal point of intervention, because traditionally women have assumed responsibility for family well-being. A mother may feel pressured to keep the family together even at great personal emotional cost. Moreover, the family's economic welfare may be at risk. As recounted by Goldner (1985a), "She knows that she has much more at stake and much more to lose if things don't work out than the man she married.... The breakdown of the traditional family has too often meant a new kind of freedom for men and a new kind of trap for women" (p. 41).

Conjugal and Parental Rights

From a feminist perspective, marriage is a relationship based on an unequal distribution of power, usually with the male as the dominant partner. "Truly, position is power" (Munson, 1993, p. 362). The husband is often the primary wage earner, and his position is validated politically, socially, and economically. He is usually physically more powerful, a fact that makes potential abuse of his power threatening to other family members. In patriarchal societies such as ours, both women and children have historically been considered possessions of the father, making them vulnerable to boundary violations and violence (Armstrong, 1987; Nelson, 1987). Feminists consider the traditional husband as the benefactor of the couple relationship at the expense of the wife.

Power hierarchies within families are influenced by both gender and age. These factors play an important role in how families are structured (Goldner, 1988), providing fundamental organizing principles of family life. Power comes from socially endorsed conjugal and parental rights. Just as there are special privileges and power imbalances outside the family, there are "private" power imbalances and special privileges inside the family. Women have power over children, and men have power over women (Mackie, 1991).

EXERCISE 13.12   Family Values

Define what is meant by family values. Where did this definition come from? Who benefits from this definition? Who is disadvantaged by this definition? How would social life be different if only one monolithic family form existed?

EXERCISE 13.13   Effects of Societal Values on Family Social Workers and Clients

Three central societal values influence the family social worker's role: family privacy, family stability, and conjugal or parental rights. List three of your beliefs concerning each value. Describe some of the effects these beliefs may have on your work with clients.

EP 2.1.7a

SOCIALIZATION AND GENDER ROLES

Families provide a socializing environment for children. Influences on children's gender role socialization are pervasive. Some of the influences are subtle, whereas others are blatant. Family social workers need to be attuned to biases involved in child rearing and to recognize how sexist biases handicap both male and female development. Mothers and fathers interact with their children differently. For example, mothers are more likely to feed, clean, and protect children, whereas fathers tend to play with them more (Mackie, 1991). Similarly, mothers often are more involved in the daily routine of child care and discipline, even when women work outside the home. Nevertheless, fathers are most responsible for the sex typing of the children. Researchers have noted that fathers are more likely than mothers to reinforce stereotypical gender behavior in children.

Children are often treated differently on the basis of gender. Parents cuddle female infants and talk to them, and they handle male infants less gently and play with them more. Boys are more likely to be spanked as a form of discipline, whereas girls are more likely to be verbally reprimanded. Achievement is expected more from male children than from female children. Parents are also more likely to punish behavior that deviates from social expectations of the child's gender and reward behavior that fits the mold of the specific gender. For example, parents are more likely to discourage independent activities of female children and to discourage dependence in male children. If parents observe a male child struggling with a problem, they are inclined to let him find his own solution. With a female child, they are more likely to take over and solve the problem instead of letting her develop the skills of doing it alone. Boys are often pressured to cover up or deny feelings of sadness and vulnerability (Pollack, 2000).

How parents relate to one another also affects children's perceptions of their own gender. For example, Pogrebin (1980) suggests that how the family allocates roles regarding household tasks and paid employment affects children's competence, their ability to overcome stereotypical notions, and their occupational choices.

Feminists note that despite the fact that many families are headed by dual career couples, role arrangements within the family often have remained static or at best have progressed very slowly. Most people acknowledge that men should contribute equally to domestic duties, but the reality is different. In the words of Eichler (1997), "There is an amazing inelasticity in men's contributions to household tasks; no matter how much there is to do, men do the same amount" (p. 60). Thus, women often continue to shoulder the burden of family and household responsibilities even when they also hold jobs outside the home.

To be gender-sensitive is to be aware of the different behaviors, attitudes, and socialization experiences associated with growing up male or female, especially differences in power, status, position, and privilege within the family and in society in general. Gender-sensitive family social workers strive to empower clients and enable them to move beyond prescribed sex roles to roles in which they have expanded options.

EXERCISE 13.14   Gender Roles

Think about your family of origin. How did your family encourage traditional gender roles for its members? How was flexibility of roles encouraged?

EXERCISE 13.15   Nonsexist Child Rearing

Describe behaviors that you consider inappropriate for girls but appropriate for boys, and vice versa. For example, some people would find it inappropriate for male children to play with dolls. Indicate why each behavior is inappropriate.

EP 2.1.7a

DIVISION OF LABOR IN FAMILIES

Relationships between men and women often shift after the birth of the first child. A woman who remains at home with an infant, even for a short period, often lags behind her partner with regard to career advancement and salary. The man becomes the primary breadwinner, whereas the woman slips into the traditional role of housekeeper and mother. Child rearing removes women from public roles whereas men gain public power, and public power is easily translated into private power.

Marriage and parenthood have different effects on men and women. Regardless of the labor status of the partners, females continue to do most of the work within the home. Domestic involvement encompasses housework, child care, emotional support of family members, and maintenance of the family's social status (Mackie, 1991). Traditional norms dictate that the first priority of women will be the family.

Domestic responsibilities are often not distributed evenly in families. This appears to be related to conjugal power. Housework and child care limit the amount of time in which a parent can pursue personal interests and career development. Men "help out" with the housework, whereas women have the primary responsibility for ensuring that jobs get done. In addition, men are said to "babysit" their own children. There are indications, however, that women's movement into the workforce has increased their conjugal power (Mackie, 1991).

Men's lives can be broadened and enriched when they participate in nurturing children and assume responsibility in family relationships. Unfortunately, some men resist changes in their roles. One explanation for the increase in divorce rates over the past two decades is that more women have been refusing to take sole responsibility for familial nurturing and communication, household tasks, and child care. Instead, they expect their partners to share these duties. Only when a male assumes equal responsibility for these tasks can the couple and parental relationship evolve into an equal partnership. At the very least, the distribution of roles needs to be negotiated between the two people. Dissatisfaction develops when a woman anticipates an equal partnership, with which her partner may verbally agree, but little change actually occurs.

The challenge of getting men to take housework and parenting seriously has been described as "troublesome, problematic, and complex" (Braverman, 1991, p. 25). In the 1990s, most wives worked approximately 1.5 hours more each day than their husbands, including part-time jobs, housework, and child care. This amounts to an extra month of 24-hour days per year. Only about 20 percent of husbands share equally in housework and child care (Carter, 1992). In order to preserve marriages, husbands and wives have constructed myths that support the egalitarian ideal of marriage, while in reality playing stereotypical, traditional roles (Carter, 1992, p. 64). For example, the female is responsible for laundry, whereas the male tends the car—hardly an equitable arrangement. Laundry consumes approximately four hours per week, whereas responsibility for the car demands only four hours a month (Collins, 1992). Women have changed their roles drastically, but male roles seem to have remained static.

Gender-sensitive social work seeks to empower women to assume greater control over their lives, rather than to adapt to oppressive circumstances. The following example illustrates a gender-sensitive approach to assisting a family:

EP 2.1.7a

CASE 13.1	The Martinez Family, Equalizing Family Roles

Jorge and Liz Martinez have four children, ages 9, 7, 5, and 3. The family came to the attention of the family social work agency when neighbors reported that the oldest child, 9-year-old Anabella, was left home as primary caretaker while both parents worked. The family social worker, John Preston, learned that Mr. Martinez worked as a city employee and Mrs. Martinez was employed full-time as a legal secretary. Both were required to work long hours, putting in overtime several nights a week. Mrs. Martinez reported feeling overwhelmed by her schedule. In addition to her job, she was responsible for the care of home and family. She turned to her daughter Anabella for help.

Mr. Martinez felt that his wife should take care of the household, as his mother had done when he was growing up. He believed that his contribution to the family was to keep a stable job and bring home a weekly paycheck, as well as maintain the yard and make car repairs. After all, Mr. Martinez explained, his own mother had raised nine children, kept a spotless home, and never complained.

Mr. Preston asked Mr. and Mrs. Martinez to make a list of the tasks they performed and the amount of time involved in each. Mr. Martinez was surprised to discover that doing the laundry took his wife four hours per week, while maintaining the cars took him only four hours per month. Mr. Preston also helped Mr. Martinez reassess his traditional expectations of family life in the context of a nontraditional household with a full-time working mother. Although Mr. Martinez still did not feel comfortable doing "women's work," he began to understand the bind his wife was in. The family did not have much extra money, but they decided to pay Mr. Martinez's 16-year-old niece to babysit and do light housekeeping after school.

EXERCISE 13.16 Division of Labor Based on Gender

On the basis of your own family of origin, complete the following list of household chores, allocating percentages to each parent. Put a check mark next to each task that you feel should be assigned on the basis of gender.

Task	Percent Done by Mother	Percent Done by Father
Buy groceries.		
Prepare meals.		
Discipline children.		
Stay home when children are sick.		
Shop for children's clothes.		
Vacuum the house.		
Take children to the doctor.		
Attend school functions.		
Volunteer at the school.		
Attend parent-teacher interviews.		
Help children with homework.		

Task	Percent Done by Mother	Percent Done by Father
Manage finances.		
Do the dishes.		
Do the laundry.		
Clean bathrooms.		
Discipline children.		
Change beds.		
Feed pets.		
Maintain lawn.		
Maintain car.		
Put children to bed.		
Other (describe).		

RECOMMENDATIONS FOR GENDER-SENSITIVE FAMILY SOCIAL WORK

Gender-sensitive practice promotes equality between the sexes. Its principles can also be generalized to include anti-oppressive practice regardless of the gender, ethnicity, and social class of a family. The family social worker strives to help family members examine their assumptions about gender roles (and other forms of oppression) as a prerequisite for deciding which aspects to keep and which to discard.

Within the context of conjugal relationships, a gender-sensitive philosophy embraces equality in decision making and shared participation in household tasks and child care. Family social workers help families to understand the connection between socially constructed gender roles and family dynamics. Family social work that is gender-sensitive is action-oriented, not merely nonsexist. Whereas nonsexist counselors attempt to avoid reinforcing stereotypical thinking about gender roles, proactive gender-sensitive family social workers help clients to recognize how their own perceptions have been affected by internalizing these stereotypes. Families are better helped when they have an opportunity to perceive and overcome social and political barriers.

The following guidelines will be helpful for family social workers who aim for gender-sensitive practice:

- Do not focus solely on mother-child interactions. Doing so reinforces the belief that children's problems are the mother's responsibility. Instead, make every effort to include the father in the intervention to ensure that both parents are actively involved in the lives of the children.
- Do not make mothers responsible for the only change that occurs in the family. Integrate intervention to include both parents when looking at parenting, taking histories, and changing individual behaviors. Fathers must be included in all aspects of assessment and intervention. If you are concerned about how receptive fathers will be to the intervention, especially that they may not participate in making changes, discuss the situation with your supervisor and with the family.

- Make gender-related issues with families explicit. Help clients negotiate the division of household and childcare tasks between parents (Goldenberg & Goldenberg, 1996).
- Explore the distribution of power within the family, and be especially alert to signs of abuse of power, such as evidence of domestic violence. When abuse exists, take every precaution to first protect the victim before working with family dynamics.
- Look for the strengths of women, rather than concentrating on pathology.
- Integrate the sociopolitical status of gender into family work (Good, Gilbert, & Scher, 1990). Do not merely assume that any family member should or should not do something just because of gender. Males can do laundry, just as females can work outside the home. Male children can be as involved in household chores as female children.
- Be attuned to your personal biases. This involves confronting personal agendas and becoming aware of blind spots related to gender (Brock & Barnard, 1992). Remember that some of your opinions were formed subtly over a lifetime of socialization. You might not even be aware of what your gender biases are.
- Families improve more when social workers are warm and actively structure interventions with families (Green & Herget, 1991).
- Realize that family structures take different forms and that no monolithic family structure is superior to all others. Single-parent families are not deformed, and children can thrive just as well in these family structures as in two-parent families. Judgments about the desirability of family structure and composition must be made in terms of the effects on family members, rather than adherence to rigidly prescribed gender roles.
- Recognize that increasing equality will require that one family member relinquish some power and privilege. The member who benefited the most from the inequality may resist relinquishing power.
- Despite all we discussed above, recognize that some families may prefer adhering to traditional gender roles. This may be based on religious or cultural beliefs. In working with these families, the family social worker should not impose different beliefs on them. However, the family social worker must be certain that family members are satisfied with the current role division, rather than having it forced on them by the most powerful family member.
- Encourage individual family members to take pride in their contributions to family life. Women's contributions are as essential as men's contributions. Look for the positives and build on them. If a man assumes a nurturing role, even for a short period, notice it and make positive comments, connecting his behavior with the well-being of other family members.

Intervention Steps

Couple and gender-sensitive intervention seems complicated because a large part of it involves the family social worker integrating the philosophy and concepts presented in this chapter into practice. Yet there are some concrete skills that will help in applying these interventions:

1. Introduce yourself to the couple or family and, during a window of opportunity, explain that you believe in a gender-sensitive perspective in your practice.

Explain what this means: specifically, you believe that family members should be treated equally and with respect and that couples should be a partnership of equals rather than one person dominating another due to past societal norms. Ask for questions, and respond to them as best as you can.

2. Model treating the couple or family members as equals, making sure that you try to spend equal time listening to each family member, not allowing one member to dominate the family work.

3. It is very important that the family social worker take the time to engage all family members, asking what it is like to be who they are because of their gender. Take the time to listen to and understand the client on gender issues. What is it like to be a woman in the year 2012? What is it like to be a man? How do gender roles play out in this particular family, and how satisfied are family members with these gender roles? What particular pressures are they feeling today given their gender? What roles and expectations do they have of each other, and how do they feel about these roles and expectations? Be aware of the language you use in discussing gender-sensitive practice. Some family members, for example, may dislike or feel threatened by the term *feminism*.

4. Encourage the couple to openly talk about gender roles and expectations with each other. Coach them in the discussion. Topics they may need to negotiate include issues such as money, control, equity, sex, sharing of feelings, couple time together, housekeeping, discipline, and child care.

5. Create structure in assigning housekeeping chores and expectations to help the couple negotiate getting these chores done. Do the same with childcare responsibilities. This might involve challenging the traditional arrangements of child-rearing and housekeeping tasks and negotiating a more balanced distribution of these tasks.

6. Use teachable moments to educate the couple about gender equality, including shifting the power balance between men and women. Some family or couple problems may be defined in such a way as to include dimensions of power and gender.

7. Support positive changes, particularly changes that alter gender roles—for example, a husband taking responsibility for helping children with schoolwork. We need to support the move away from gender-specific rules and roles.

EP 2.1.10g

DOMESTIC VIOLENCE

A major problem that families face is domestic violence. Abuse may occur in the same family or in conjunction with other difficulties. As with other problems of this severity, the family social worker should refer clients to professionals who specialize in this area. At the same time, the family social worker needs to help design the intervention, coordinate services with the specialist, and reinforce the treatment plan during home visits. Often the intervention process is complicated by the fact that clients are involved in family social work because the court system requires it, not because they have decided to seek help for their problems.

EP 2.1.7a

CASE 13.2	Evaluating Couple Work

Johnny and June had been married for 10 years, with no children born into the family, when June was diagnosed with depression. The family social worker determined that a psychoeducational approach was best for this particular case. The intervention focused on educating June and Johnny about the wife's illness and arranging support systems, medication, and cognitive therapy for June's depression, as well as marital counseling for the couple. A single-subject design was used to evaluate the case.

Measurement included weekly monitoring using a social support inventory completed by both members of the couple, a medication maintenance chart and a depression inventory for June, and a marital satisfaction inventory for the couple. The family social worker also used a 10-point rating scale to do independent ratings of June's mood as well as the couple's rating scale at the weekly treatment sessions. The measures allowed for ongoing monitoring and evaluation of treatment progress so that treatment modifications could be made as needed.

ABUSIVE RELATIONSHIPS

Straus and Gelles (1988), in their earlier study of domestic violence in the United States, found that one in six couples had experienced an incident of physical assault during the previous year. Although most incidents were minor, a substantial number were serious assaults. At least 3 percent of women in the United States were severely assaulted during the same period. Severe assault is defined as acts that have a high probability of causing an injury, such as kicking, biting, punching, hitting with an object, choking, beating up, and threatening to use (or using) a knife or gun (Straus & Gelles, 1988). An equal incidence of female-to-male assault has been reported; however, many of the latter assaults may have been acts of retaliation or self-defense (Gelles & Straus, 1988; Straus, 1993).

Children are not just bystanders when their mothers are abused (Wolfe, Jaffe, Wilson, & Zak, 1988). They may show a range of behavioral problems in response to witnessing violence in their homes, and some child protection authorities have been mandated to intervene when there is conjugal violence even when there is no apparent abuse of children. Male children are more likely to manifest problems immediately, but the effects on female children may appear years later. The negative impact of family violence on children is an important consideration for family social workers.

EP 2.1.7a

Factors Contributing to Domestic Violence

Just as family social workers may see or suspect child abuse in a family, they may also suspect other kinds of family violence. Whereas men can be the victims in spouse abuse, we focus on women because men often hurt their partners more severely. Men usually are physically stronger than women. There is currently much debate about whether or not females batter as frequently as males. Spouse abuse is often referred to as wife battering. Because the behavior occurs in private, domestic violence may go unrecognized. Few incidents are reported to the police, and because it is mostly female victims who have come forward, early work did not reveal much about perpetrators (Dutton, 1991).

Traditionally, domestic violence was analyzed through a family systems lens. That is, it was widely believed that abuse resulted from circular causality, homeostasis, and related family dynamics. Several problems exist due to explaining abusive relationships from a family systems perspective (Bograd, 1992; Dell, 1989; Myers-Avis, 1992). For example, traditional descriptions of the precursors to an assault often implied that the victim was nagging or otherwise provoking an assault. Clearly, these depictions are sexist and harmful. Today, conjoint partner work for domestic abuse is not recommended since victim safety cannot be guaranteed.

Physical abuse is a way for the batterer to establish and maintain control in an interpersonal relationship (Dutton, 1991; Gilliland & James, 1993). Usually the perpetrator does not suffer from mental illness, nor does the victim have a masochistic personality. Obviously, interpersonal violence is influenced by factors that include, but are not limited to, individual dynamics, family dynamics, and beliefs shared by peer and cultural groups.

Walker (1984) identified a cycle of violence within battering relationships (see Figure 13.1). The pattern is predictable and repetitive, and as the cycle is repeated, the phases get shorter and shorter. The cycle consists of four phases that increase in severity over time. The social worker has the best opportunity for intervention shortly after a battering incident has occurred and before the reconciliation phase begins.

Many battered women who stay in abusive relationships lack the economic resources to survive on their own. They tolerate abuse as long as it does not become too severe or involve the children. Often these women are strongly committed to making the relationship last. However, increased employment opportunities for women have provided the resources for women to remove themselves from violent relationships (Gelles, 1987). Battered women often lack education or work experience that would allow independent support of themselves and their children. They may therefore feel that the alternative to staying with abusive partners is poverty and loneliness. Some may remain in abusive relationships because they believe that all relationships are abusive. Others may fear the consequences of leaving,

---

1.   The first phase is characterized by calmness, often described as a honeymoon period.
2.   Tension slowly starts to build in the relationship.
3.   A battering episode occurs. Often the perpetrator causes the victim to feel responsible for the beating because of some alleged transgression.
4.   The abuser usually feels remorse and asks forgiveness. Often the victim forgives the abuser, and a period of calm in the relationship starts again.

FIGURE 13.1 | The Cycle of Violence in an Abusive Relationship

particularly if they have tried to leave in the past and have suffered repercussions from vengeful husbands or boyfriends. This fear may be real. Finally, women often see themselves (and are perceived by society) as being primarily responsible for the well-being of family relationships and hence view the failure of the relationships as their fault. They may feel too ashamed and guilty to seek help or to leave.

There are several reasons why a battered woman may remain in an abusive relationship (Gelles & Straus, 1988):

- Poor self-concept
- Belief that the partner will change
- Concern for children
- Fear of coping alone
- Fear of stigmatization
- Problems in developing a career.

Social isolation, combined with economic dependence, can create a sense of powerlessness and leave a woman feeling that she has no ability to free herself from a violent situation. Victims of abuse may have strong beliefs about marriage and commitment, often based on cultural or religious teachings, and may therefore be reluctant to end the partnership. Finally, there are women who out of love, dependence, fear, or desperation cling to the hope that things will change. Dutton (1991) sums up the trap of the battered woman: "When self-blame, dependency, depression and powerlessness are coupled with economic dependency, criminal justice system apathy, and the belief that she cannot escape, the net effect is to produce a victim who is psychologically ill-equipped for either self-defense or escape" (p. 212).

Intervention in Families Suffering from Domestic Violence

Before trying to intervene, the family social worker needs to understand abusive situations and look for ways to protect victims of family violence. Clearly, a family social worker cannot impose her or his own solution. The victim must make her own decision about what to do, and then the worker can help her follow through on her plans. Unfortunately, few abused women seek help; when they do seek help, they are likely to turn first to relatives, friends, and neighbors rather than to an agency (Gelles & Straus, 1988). The family social worker may talk to an abused woman about the violence, but pushing a premature solution may undermine the worker-client relationship and rule out the possibility of finding a solution later, when the time is right. To assist women who live with violent men, family social workers must be able to recognize signs of abuse. A woman probably will not disclose abusive behavior except in the context of a long-standing, trusting relationship with the social worker. The family social worker must be sensitive to the following clues suggesting violence in the home:

- Physical signs of violence, including bruises, cuts, burns, scratches, and blackened eyes of the victim
- Frequent physical complaints and illnesses on the part of the victim

- Children with physical injuries and illnesses, behavioral problems, and emotional disturbances
- Anxiety, fearfulness, apprehension, and depression of the victim
- Self-destructive behavior, including suicidal ideation and self-deprecation of the victim
- Insomnia and nightmares of the victim.

The above indicators are not absolute proof of abuse, but they should alert the family social worker to the possibility that something is wrong. When social workers see evidence that arouses suspicion, they are obliged to pursue the subject with their clients, albeit carefully.

Family social workers should be aware that homicide may result immediately after the victim has tried to leave an abusive relationship. In addition, homicides occur with greater frequency in families in which previous disturbances have been reported to the police, perhaps because the assaults are more severe. Nevertheless, the safety of the woman and children must be of utmost concern to the family social worker. Police recognize that intervening in domestic disputes can be extremely hazardous, and most police officers have received special training to deal with such situations. Family social workers should take steps to protect themselves when violence in a home escalates. Family social workers who have had the opportunity to learn about domestic violence as part of their professional education and to share their thoughts and experiences with colleagues and supervisors will be better equipped to handle situations involving abuse.

When a woman admits to a family social worker that she is in a battering relationship, the most important thing the social worker can do is to believe her and start intervention immediately (Walker, 1984). Once safety is assured, a multiplicity of issues can be addressed. Ensuring safety may entail moving the woman and her children to another location. Most communities have emergency shelters for battered women and their children. Shelters offer battered women immediate refuge and protection but, unfortunately, are not likely to be used (Gelles & Straus, 1988). Most communities have crisis telephone lines. Women who have admitted that they are in an abusive relationship often start there. Figure 13.2 provides a checklist for family social workers who are working with victims of domestic violence.

- Ensure safety by connecting the woman and children to an emergency shelter.
- Listen and support the woman's story.
- Be aware that it is difficult for most battered women to leave an abusive relationship.
- Determine whether medical attention is necessary.
- Acknowledge the woman's ambivalence.
- Help the battered woman examine her alternatives.
- Help the woman access community resources to enable independent living.
- Become familiar with resources available in the community.
- Work with the woman to find ways of diminishing her social isolation.

FIGURE 13.2 | Checklist for Working with a Battered Woman

In the process of deciding to leave, many abused women vacillate between staying and leaving. The social worker must be patient with the woman's ambivalence, keeping in mind that abused women are often dependent on their abusers and have low self-esteem. They may also be depressed and move through stages of mourning. Family social workers need to examine their personal reactions to abuse and to be aware that they bring their own orientation toward family violence into the helping relationship. Self-examination prepares social workers for their own reactions when confronted with the possibility of spouse abuse, thereby enabling them to express their reactions in a way that will be helpful to their clients.

EXERCISE 13.17   Interviewing a Battered Wife

With another student, role-play a social worker interviewing a woman who shows signs of having been beaten by her husband. Take turns playing the social worker and the battered wife. The social worker must make it clear that she or he is willing to talk about the abuse. As a part of the trusting relationship that the family social worker and client have established, the client needs to know that the worker is aware of the potential for violence in people's lives (not just in this particular situation) and is open to addressing it. This approach is very different from confronting a client with one's suspicions.

If an abused woman discloses to a family social worker that she is being harmed, the social worker should respond by validating her disclosure and encouraging the client to talk about the situation. After the client has talked about the abuse, the worker may address several factors if the client is willing. These include her safety, resources available to her, and coping strategies. Victims of domestic violence may be unaware of available resources such as emergency shelters, police, and agencies that specialize in assisting victims of domestic violence.

To help the abused woman, the family social worker will need to obtain information about the type, severity, frequency, and context of the violent episodes. For example, is the woman in imminent danger of severe harm? If so, precautions must be taken to protect her safety and that of her children. If the violence is predictable, is there any way to avoid it? What resources are available to help the client? These may include police, shelters, legal assistance, counseling, and sources of financial relief. What plans can the client make for escaping violence when she senses an episode is imminent? How can she deal with violence once it has begun? These are all practical avenues to explore and can be very helpful, perhaps lifesaving, in emergencies.

Often, a battered woman has become isolated physically, emotionally, economically, and socially. The ongoing presence of a family social worker can help diminish that isolation.

In addition to linking a battered woman to community agencies for practical relief, the family social worker may be able to help the client join a support group for battered women. Most battered women are unaware that other women have similar problems (Bolton & Bolton, 1987; Gelles & Straus, 1988). Learning that others have experienced the same things, have had the same feelings, and have dealt with the same realities can decrease a woman's feelings of isolation. By hearing about other women's experiences and sharing her own, a woman may also be better able to recognize alternatives to her situation. Learning that they are not alone also tends to help battered women become less self-critical and decreases their perception of themselves as being mentally unstable. Battered women often feel relieved to discover that their reactions are "normal" under the circumstances and that others have also felt afraid, helpless, angry, guilty, ashamed, and responsible for the violence.

Another way to help is to engage the abused woman in active problem solving on her own behalf. Helping her discover what she really wants, helping her identify her options and resources, and then discussing the consequences of various choices can help the client become aware of the strengths and options that she does possess. This problem-solving approach is particularly suitable for battered women because people under extreme stress tend to have difficulty thinking through their concerns and often have lost hope. Increasing an individual's sense of self-control through successful problem solving is an obvious goal for effective family social work. Possibly the most important concept for an abused woman to accept is the fact that she does not deserve to be abused, no matter what the circumstances. It is critical that victims do not blame themselves for the brutality they suffer. Popular stereotypes and myths, though changing, have perpetuated the belief that women provoke violence and even enjoy it. Battered women often agree with these ideas; this increases their sense of shame and makes it more difficult for them to seek help. Family social workers can do much to correct these misconceptions. A battered woman who receives outside support is better able to access help and make changes within her family (Giles-Sims, 1983). Family social workers can provide some of the support that abused clients require to eventually leave their abusive partners.

If the family social worker is working with a woman who does not want to talk about the abuse she is receiving, the social worker initially should express concern and offer to listen when she is ready. The worker may need to repeat this message many times. If the client does not respond to this approach, the social worker must not insist on pursuing the subject; doing so could alienate the client. Family social workers have found that most abused women eventually want to talk about abusive incidents.

If family social workers feel that they are in danger when visiting a violent household, they should leave quickly and notify the police. When threats to the family social worker's personal safety are serious, home visits should be terminated until the danger abates. Every family social work agency should establish clear policies and procedures for handling dangerous situations, and these should be covered in each social worker's training. If family social work is stopped, the agency should strive to maintain contact with the abused spouse, perhaps by having the worker meet with her in another, safer environment, or attempt to reach her by telephone. It is critical for the worker to leave the lines of communication open and offer the abused woman ongoing support.

It is not the role of the family social worker to tell a battered woman what she should do. The woman will bear the consequences of whatever action she chooses to take (or not to take). Another reason to refrain from giving direct advice is that only the battered woman knows how she feels. In spite of the most sincere and skillful efforts at understanding, the worker cannot experience the client's actual feelings. Finally, making decisions for the woman may reinforce the client's sense of powerlessness and inability to control her own life.

When working with families troubled by violence, family social workers must not allow themselves to harbor unrealistic expectations about what they can accomplish.

With violent families, as with other stressful client situations, social workers should appraise their own knowledge and skills and also consult supervisors and colleagues for the information and emotional support they need to make decisions. Further, in dealing with violence, family social workers must be well informed about existing community resources and understand how to help families access them.

Abusive relationships may remain hidden from public view. The following example illustrates characteristics of an abusive relationship.

EP 2.1.10g

CASE 13.3	Lilly, A Battered Wife

Lilly Foster spoke with the family social worker, Tonya Lovett, about her situation. Lilly contacted the family social worker after learning that she was pregnant. Her husband, Phil, whom Lilly described as physically and verbally abusive to her, was out of town. Lilly said that she would be "in trouble" if Phil learned that she had contacted outsiders for help. Lilly said she was concerned for the safety of their unborn child. She feared that Phil would harm the child.

Lilly reported having been married to Phil for three years. She said this was the second marriage for both, and that she was committed to "making this one work." Lilly described the courtship before her marriage as "perfect." She said Phil had seemed to be her "knight in shining armor." He didn't want Lilly to have to work, so he encouraged her to quit her job and stay home. Phil said he would always take care of Lilly, whom he called "his beautiful princess." However, in the first months after they were married, Phil became very possessive and controlling toward Lilly. He didn't want her to leave the house without telling him where she was going. He also became jealous of Lilly and imagined that she was having affairs with other men. Lilly said this accusation was ridiculous because she rarely left home without Phil. Phil eventually wouldn't allow Lilly to go out without him, though Phil reportedly stopped in a local bar for drinks with his office buddies most days after work. Lilly said that Phil usually came home after having several drinks and that drinking made him more abusive.

The first time Lilly went out on her own against his wishes, Phil became so angry that he hit her numerous times, blackening her eye and bruising her face, arms, and legs. This occurred after the couple had been married for six months. Phil was very apologetic afterward, but the beatings increased as time passed. Lilly reported that Phil was most likely to hit her if he felt jealous or if Lilly argued with him. Phil traveled as part of his job, and when he left on these trips, he took Lilly's car keys, her wedding rings, and anything else of value that she might sell to obtain money. Lilly never was given any cash; Phil accompanied her wherever she went and paid for groceries and other purchases. Lilly reported that Phil gradually kept her away from her family and friends and that she had become isolated.

Mrs. Lovett, the family social worker, realized that Lilly had no social support or financial resources. She believed that Lilly had sought help only because of her concern for the safety of the baby she was expecting and that Lilly greatly feared the wrath of her husband if he were to find out she had asked for help. Mrs. Lovett began to intervene immediately by connecting Lilly to an emergency shelter where experts in family violence could listen to her story and support her. As a resident of the shelter, Lilly would receive medical and financial help and counseling to examine her alternatives.

CHAPTER SUMMARY

A family social worker must be gender-sensitive, working with the family in a supportive and educational role. Gender-sensitive and problem-solving approaches can be implemented simultaneously for effective interventions with families.

The gender-sensitive perspective is sensitive to the impact of traditional gender roles on problems experienced by families. Traditional family therapists endorse a systems view of family functioning in which members share equal responsibility for family problems, but gender-sensitive family social workers recognize unequal power distribution and strive to empower women and children who have been victimized by inequitable family power arrangements.

Family social workers seek to understand gender roles within the families' economic, political, and social contexts. Gender-sensitive workers strive for political, economic, and social justice for women and children, whom they perceive as unequal partners in family life.

Feminist theory acknowledges the core inequality that is inherent in most spousal relationships. Sources of gender-based power include the legal system, societal norms, educational and financial resources, personality differences, life circumstances (age, location, or life stage), and emotional factors.

Gender-sensitive social workers seek to empower families by increasing their awareness of available options. Parents can be encouraged to share equally in childcare and household tasks, raising their children in a nonsexist atmosphere that recognizes each individual's capabilities and contributions to family life.

KEY TERMS

Four Horsemen of the Apocalypse criticism, defensiveness, contempt, and stonewalling. These Four Horsemen are particularly corrosive to relationships.
Healthy communication communication that is congruent, direct, honest, and clear.
Metacommunication communication about communication, or a message about a message.

SUGGESTED READING

Gottman J. (1999). *The marriage clinic*. New York: W.W. Norton & Company.
This book is required reading for anyone interested in a research-based book on couple dynamics. The work is based on years of studying interactions between couples. The most notable point is "The Four Horsemen of the Apocalypse," which Gottman describes as significant predictors of divorce.

COMPETENCY NOTES

EPAS 2.1.4a Recognize the extent to which a culture's structures and values may oppress, marginalize, alienate, or create or enhance privilege and power: In this chapter, we focus on a feminist critique describing how women may be oppressed and marginalized in a system that does not consider women to be equal with men.

EPAS 2.1.7a Utilize conceptual frameworks to guide the processes of assessment, intervention, and evaluation: A feminist conceptual framework is used to guide family assessment and intervention, particularly in instances of family violence.

EPAS 2.1.10g Select appropriate intervention strategies: The family social worker must be able to identify and treat violent family situations. In this chapter, we present intervention guided by a feminist orientation.

CHAPTER CONTENTS

LEARNING OBJECTIVES

- Conceptual: Recognize that termination is the ending of a relationship, which will occur many times in people's lives, thus making it important to understand the need to terminate well with families.

- Perceptual: Recognize that the termination process will affect individual family members differently.

- Valuational/Attitudinal: Be aware that termination is a form of loss, and the family social worker needs to empathize with this loss. Value the families' grief over the ending of the worker-family relationship.

- Behavioral: Use specific behavioral skills for the termination process.

In this chapter, we examine issues related to termination, including who takes the initiative to terminate—the family, the family social worker, or both. Because the decision to end family work does not necessarily mean that the family will stop contact with all agencies, referral is an important component of the termination process. Specific suggestions for phasing out and concluding family social work follow.

EXERCISE 14.1   Reasons for Termination

List some reasons for advising a family to terminate family social work.

Ideally, termination is the final phase of family social work. We say ideally because sometimes families do not reach the final phase of the helping process with the worker but end family work before a mutually agreed-on time has been reached. Sometimes even the most realistic and sensible goals have not been met because of premature termination.

While ending family work constructively sets the stage for continued positive change, termination is often overlooked as an essential part of the helping process (Kaplan, 1986). The cornerstone of termination is evaluating whether work with the family has resolved the presenting problem. A related purpose is ensuring that progress will be sustained—a process that can occur only if the family has developed the skills they need to resolve future problems independently after the family social worker's involvement has ended.

The length of family social work varies depending on agency mandate, family motivation, or the extent to which goals have been accomplished. Family social work is often short-term (sometimes between four and ten sessions) because many families seek assistance during periods of crisis and are motivated to solve only their immediate problems. Other families allow the family social worker into their home because they have been mandated to work on specific issues, but are at best reluctant or ambivalent about receiving help.

If the family work is terminating because the worker is leaving the agency, the family will need to understand this. Plans for termination or transfer to another worker should be negotiated with the family early in the helping process in the contracting and goal-setting phases. Some agencies automatically impose time limits on family social work, making the termination date clear and explicit. The family social worker will need to initiate the countdown to the final appointment in advance of the last scheduled contact by periodically reviewing with the family the progress to date, letting the family know about the termination date, and asking the family what it wants to accomplish in the interim. The family may also need the social worker's help to work through a number of important issues during the termination stage: denial, anger, sadness, and letting go.

The most ideal time to terminate family work is when the presenting problem has been resolved and both the family and the social worker are satisfied with the outcome. In practice, however, termination often occurs in unanticipated ways. Some families drop out of a program or terminate before the desired outcome has been achieved. Moreover, when work is unsatisfactory or is not going anywhere, despite repeated efforts to rekindle the process, the family social worker end the relationship after holding a final session to discuss and review what happened.

When the work has been successful, clients may experience a range of emotions as they approach termination. Most authors emphasize feelings of separation and loss, implying that a planned termination ignites a grief reaction. While we believe that this case may be overstated, many social workers may find that some families are reluctant to terminate. They may bring up new problems or claim that old problems have worsened. One the other hand, other families, especially involuntary ones, may welcome the end of the working relationship.

Social workers also react to termination in a variety of ways. Some may be hesitant to terminate services. Termination for these social workers will be easier when they acknowledge limits to their responsibility for people's lives (Gambrill, 1983). Family social workers should accept that after the end of family work, responsibility for decision making rests with the family. Other times, a social worker may have become quite close to the family and feel saddened that the relationship is coming to an end. It is important for family social workers to reflect on their feelings about terminating with a particular family. These feelings will reveal a lot about the nature of the relationship and the work that was achieved.

EXERCISE 14.2   Feelings about Moving On

Imagine you have just left a place that was difficult and where you worked very hard (e.g., high school). Make a list of your feelings about moving on. How might these feelings resemble termination in family social work?

PLANNING FOR TERMINATION

Tomm and Wright (1979) outline three actions that a family social worker must take at termination:

1. Assess family initiative to terminate.
2. Initiate termination when necessary.
3. Conclude family work constructively.

Successful termination requires skill on the part of the family social worker. The first step is for the worker to discuss impending termination with the family at the *outset* of the work, usually during contracting and goal setting, which provide a good opportunity to discuss the time frame and tasks required to accomplish the goals. It is important for the worker to recognize limitations and functions of family social work, including understanding differences between family social work and family therapy. Defining clear goals at the outset will help clarify when termination should occur.

In the initial contact with the family, the family social worker might give them an agency phone number and request that they phone if for any reason they cannot be present for a scheduled appointment or if they wish to terminate family work at any time. Although some worker-client relationships may end abruptly or unexpectedly, the best time for termination is when it is anticipated and planned for from the beginning of the work. The manner in which termination is handled can influence how well the family maintains changes and improvements made during the helping relationship. Satisfactory termination of a helping experience also may predispose a family to seek help again if they need it. The worker needs to help the family identify goals to be achieved after family social work ends and to explain the different roles of other helpers compared with those of the family social worker. Identifying community resources that can support the family after termination and helping the family link to these resources also occurs at this time.

Generally, the process of termination should parallel the end of each family meeting. For example, about 10 minutes before ending an interview, the family social worker can tell the family that 10 minutes remain and that they should address unfinished or pressing business and use the remaining time to summarize the session. At this time, the worker can identify the strengths of the family and its members. Arrangements for the next session can then be made. Again, remind the family to phone the agency number if for any reason they cannot keep a scheduled appointment. Every week the social worker and family will repeat the process of reviewing what family members have achieved and how the family can continue making progress (Kinney, Haapala, & Booth, 1991). Termination of the overall working relationship follows similar steps, except that there will be no further sessions. Summarization should cover what happened in family work from the beginning to the end. At this time, the family worker should encourage the sharing of feelings concerning termination.

EP 2.1.10l

POSSIBLE REACTIONS TO TERMINATION

Much has been written about ending helping relationships, most of it focusing on negative aspects. For the majority of clients and their social workers, however, termination is essentially positive because it is often used to focus on accomplishments. Positive reflection increases self-confidence and reinforces feelings of personal competence. The family social worker uses the opportunity to commend the family for its efforts in resolving problems. Families may be eager to try out new skills learned in the helping relationship. Similarly, when the social worker believes that the designated goals with clients have been accomplished, the worker's self-esteem increases, invigorating the worker for future work. The family social worker can recognize signs suggestive of difficulty with terminating; for example, a client may predictably cancel appointments as the date of each appointment draws closer. It may be difficult to schedule a final meeting when family members have canceled several times previously. Sometimes the worker will need to remind the family that time is running out before conducting one final appointment.

Problems with termination can emerge if the family social worker is reluctant to discuss termination with the family or avoids discussion of family members' feelings about stopping the family work. Problems can also emerge when the worker has not maintained clear boundaries with the family. For a family social worker who has become over-involved, termination may spark anxiety. The worker may grieve the loss of the relationship or worry about the family's future welfare. Although most terminations produce a mixture of feelings, family social workers who have maintained professional objectivity and boundaries will be able to deal with their emotions more effectively than those who have not. Of course, it is inappropriate for a social worker to end a professional relationship only to strike up a personal relationship with a family.

Effective family social workers establish intense and meaningful relationships with families, and many may feel hesitant about initiating termination. Termination means letting go and moving on. The worker's feelings can range from grief to joy or include a mixture of both. The worker should not minimize the role that family social work played in creating change. Terminating with some families may bring relief, whereas with others it may elicit feelings of sadness and loss. Through experience, the family social worker will anticipate feelings to address at the time of termination. Family members' feelings can range from pride and satisfaction to anger, sadness, or regret.

Clients may try to stop termination in the following ways:

- They may become overly dependent on the social worker.
- They may report that former problems are starting to reappear.
- They may introduce new problems.
- They may find substitutes for the social worker. (Hepworth & Larsen, 1993)

Most of these concerns can be anticipated by contracting at the beginning of the family work and by exploring the family's feelings about termination near the end. Referrals to other agencies and nurturing informal support networks are two important ways of easing termination. Families may be especially reluctant to terminate when goals have not been met. Short-term programs seem especially vulnerable to family dissatisfaction with the services. For example, a parent in one short-term program stated, "I disliked the shortness of it. We're quite dysfunctional. In order to get a habit established, we needed long-term help" (Coleman & Collins, 1997).

Alternatively, termination can be a time of celebration, especially when concrete, positive change has occurred. The family social worker should be aware of the limits of family social work and encourage the family to transfer to another helper if and when appropriate. Rituals associated with closure and evaluation should promote a sense of satisfaction with progress made.

EP 2.1.10l

PREMATURE TERMINATION AND DROPOUTS

Sometimes families terminate indirectly. Some may simply not be at home for a scheduled meeting, and others may call and cancel at the last minute. They may be difficult to contact after a failed appointment, leading the family social worker to suspect that the family is avoiding further contact. Other times individual family members do not show up with the rest of the family for a scheduled meeting with the family social worker. Another hint that families are considering dropping out is when, instead of expressing dissatisfaction with family social work, they talk about practical problems of participating in family sessions, such as missing work, having to reschedule other appointments, and so on. When the social worker begins to notice a pattern developing (e.g., two consecutive missed appointments), we suggest raising the topic for discussion if the worker is able to make contact. Termination can also be discussed at the beginning of family work. The family social worker can contract with the family, suggesting that if they feel like terminating, one final session will be necessary to review the course of work and to end productively.

The difference between families who stop work prematurely and those who merely drop out is that premature terminators try to give the social worker notice and a reason for leaving. It should be remembered that as many as 40 percent of families terminate work after six to ten sessions (Worden, 1994), but this percentage is perhaps lower for home-based services. Premature termination may be associated with ecological challenges such as lower household income and ethnicity (Clarkin & Levy, 2004; Kadzin, 2004). It is thus very important during the initial stages of family work for the worker to explore income issues as well as ethnicity with the family. Throughout the book, we have emphasized the importance of a worker being keenly attuned to cultural differences throughout the family work and understanding the impact of cultural differences on family work as issues emerge. Indeed, a major thrust of this book has been the micro and macro ecological systems approach as well as the importance of diversity, ethnicity, culture, and spirituality in a family's life (see Chapter 5). The worker needs to show understanding of these factors and discuss them with the family at the outset of family work in order to engage a family. These factors also need to be raised with sensitivity and understanding in the termination process.

When a family announces its decision to terminate, the family social worker should acknowledge the decision and elicit information about the rationale for termination. In such cases, the work may be stopped because of client absences, resistance, the social worker's inability to take the family further, or personality conflicts between family members and the social worker. Information garnered from clients will help the worker differentiate between timely, appropriate termination and inappropriate or premature termination.

One type of premature termination occurs when clients display sudden improvement; this is referred to as a flight into health (Tomm & Wright, 1979) or faking good. Families may fake good when they view change as threatening and make superficial changes to get the worker out of their lives. They may tell the family social worker that their problems have been resolved, and there may even be a temporary cessation of problems lasting for a short period of time. If the family specifically states that they would like to end work, but the worker believes that termination would be premature, the worker should move into the *recital* step of termination to review problems and even renegotiate a new contract. In doing so, the worker and family can encapsulate the changes, identify problems that still exist, and sort out what goals need to be achieved. Drawing out specifics of the family decision may be helpful. The family social worker can try to find out when the family decided to quit and what factors prompted the decision. What is most important is that the goals of the family worker be congruent with those of the family.

Although termination can sometimes be averted, at other times premature termination may be unavoidable. In such cases, the family social worker must accept the decision to terminate without applying inappropriate pressure, even though the worker disagrees with the family's decision (Tomm & Wright, 1979).

Avoiding premature termination can be more difficult with court-mandated clients, who often wish to avoid any work beyond what has been required by the court. They may rapidly become resistant the day a court order ceases to exert authority over them. One way to prevent this outcome is to encourage family members to discuss at the outset their reaction to being ordered into treatment. Court-mandated families who drop out of family work must also face the consequences of their decision. Premature termination may mean that child welfare authorities or the courts will have to be notified.

The family's ability to cope with problems, not avoid them, is an important indicator of readiness to terminate. Movement toward termination occurs smoothly if the beginning and middle stages of treatment have concluded successfully. Effective family social workers often set mini goal and suggest that progress toward a goal be evaluated within a specified number of interviews. However, the most important decision for family social workers concerns when to end work with a family. Ideally, termination should occur after goals have been met. In some agencies, the family social worker must assess whether the family needs further help or whether they can resolve problems on their own. Regardless of how termination occurs, the social worker should initiate an honest discussion of everyone's perceptions of what was achieved during family social work.

EP 2.1.10l

PRACTICAL TERMINATION STEPS

Termination can occur in several ways, ranging from early or premature termination to a completed mutually agreed-on termination.

1. Clients decide not to follow through with an initial meeting or do not show up for the initial meeting.
2. The family structure has changed since referral due to, for example, separation of parents or removal of the identified child client into care.
3. The family attends an initial family meeting but does not return.
4. The client withdraws directly, usually via a telephone call stating the client's decision to terminate with or without giving reasons.
5. One or more family members resist attending family sessions.
6. Clients actively resist family work, questioning the process and outcomes. One or more clients may be openly uncooperative or hostile.
7. Sessions seem to reflect no progress. Termination should be by mutual consent.
8. Clients repeatedly cancel appointments or fail to keep them without formal withdrawal.
9. Termination is by mutual agreement following successful resolution of presenting problem(s).
10. Termination is due to clients' initiative at the end of a contractual period of specified length. Contracting for a specified period provides a time framework that may make intervention efficient.

Let's look at each of the termination types presented in this list.

1. Clients decide not to follow through with an initial meeting or do not show up for the initial meeting.

    Some clients have been on a waiting list for weeks or even months prior to your initial contact and may have found an alternative agency to obtain their counseling needs. For some, the situation has improved (a crisis has passed), and the family no longer desires family work. Alternatively, when an appointment has been set up, one or more of the family members convinces the family they no longer require counseling. Some families use counseling as a threat to get members to change their behaviors! It is still important to terminate appropriately with these families. This is done by informing the family that if they would like your services in the future, they should recontact the agency (thus keeping the door open for them).

2. The family structure has changed since referral due to, for example, separation of parents or removal of the identified child client into care.

Some family structures can change significantly; this affects the initial referral problems. Separation of parents, removal of the identified child client into care, or an adolescent child moving out of the home to live with relatives or live on his or her own are all examples we have come across. It may be useful for the family social worker to invite the remaining family members to a family meeting to discuss the changes in the family structure as well as any other family concerns they may have. However, the family worker should let the family know that if in the future they would like family work, they may recontact the agency. The worker should also provide phone numbers of other agencies that an identified child who has left the home could contact if he or she wishes to receive some help.

3. The family attends an initial family meeting but does not return.

It is important to have a follow-up phone call with the family, or you will be left wondering if you did something wrong in your initial meeting. Indeed, you may not have engaged the family into the family social work process and may not have connected with the family. It is important to find this out and either to invite the family to return to discuss your role and their expectations of you and the process or to refer the family to another resource for help. Family social workers must be open and nondefensive about the feedback they receive from families. New workers might find feedback difficult. Nevertheless, family social workers can learn a lot about their skills and how they connect with families if they sincerely and whole-heartedly invite such feedback from families. The family's failure to return after an initial family meeting may not be due to the family social worker failing to connect with the family; instead, the family may state that the one session was enough.

There are many potential reasons for not returning after the initial sessions. One or more family members may feel that the family worker did not connect with them and thus believe that the counseling would not be helpful. Others may state that the family situation has changed and they do not feel further family work is necessary. Some families say that the particular service does not meet their specific needs, that another service would meet their needs better, and that they have sought help elsewhere. Again, in the follow-up phone call, the family social worker can support the position the family takes and can offer services at another time if they so desire it.

4. The client withdraws directly, usually via a telephone call stating the client's decision to terminate, with or without giving reasons.

Again, it is helpful to family workers and to the agency to find out the reasons behind the termination. If it is because the agency does not meet the needs of the family, the agency mandate might have to change to accommodate this particular family. If clients feel they did not connect with you, you may need to look at your engagement skills. It also could signal that the family crisis has passed. Whatever the reasons, it is important to invite the family to return if they so wish at a later date.

5. One or more family members resist attending family sessions.

Although it is more difficult to work with a family without all members living in the home involved, it is not impossible to still be helpful. Remember from Chapter 3 on systems theory that a change in one part of the system will effect change on other parts of the system. Thus, even if one family member does not want to attend, system changes may still positively affect this member. Nevertheless, the family social worker needs to explore with the family the reasons for one or more family members not wanting to attend family sessions. Again, openness and nondefensiveness are important components in doing so. This may prove to be a very helpful focus of a family meeting because it does say something about how the family organizes itself as well as how it solves problems. In this case, the central problem becomes one or more family members not wanting to attend family sessions. How does the rest of the family feel about this? How do they communicate their concerns with each other? What commitment do they have to work on family issues and to each other? How does this family plan to resolve this issue? These questions can lead to a most interesting and helpful family social work meeting.

6. Clients actively resist family work, questioning the process and outcomes. One or more clients may be openly uncooperative or hostile.

Sometimes clients become resistant when they have not felt understood and have felt that their feelings, such as fear and anger, have not been validated. It is important to spend the time joining (see Chapter 7 on beginning family work), not just at the content level but also at a feeling level. At the content level, it is important to clarify family expectations and hopes for family work as well as your role with them. It is also equally important to show all family members that you understand their frustrations, fears, concerns, and reluctance regarding this work. Feelings need to be brought out into the open and validated. It is helpful to try to normalize family issues (see Chapter 4 on developmental issues) and to point out the family's strengths to convey hope (see Chapter 5 on the strengths-based perspective). Any time in the family social work process when a client seems resistant, it is very important to immediately address their underlying concerns and feelings; otherwise, you risk losing the family to premature termination.

7. Sessions seem to reflect no progress. Termination should be by mutual consent.

It is important to routinely ask the family for feedback about whether they see progress being made or not (a form of formative evaluation 8). Family workers can adopt "change talk" at the end of each session by asking the family what has improved and what they have done to make those changes happen. At the end of every family meeting, you can "check in" with the family by asking what was helpful and what was not helpful to them. We suggest that in at least every fourth family meeting, time should be spent discussing the progress that has been made. Again, using "change talk" will put the focus on the positive aspects of change that the family has made, rather than emphasizing only the difficulties that still need to be addressed. If the family believes that no progress is being made, either a new contract of problems and goals needs to be made (see Chapter 7 on problem definition and contracting) or a mutually agreed-on termination should be considered. Remember that if you and the family decide to terminate, you should offer your services at a later date and inform the family of other services that may be of help to them.

8. Clients repeatedly cancel appointments or fail to keep them without formal withdrawal.

Canceled appointments can be very frustrating for family social workers because they have set aside the time to meet with the family. When a pattern occurs (we define a pattern as something that happens at least three times), we suggest phoning the family and openly discussing whether being involved in family work is really realistic at this period in the family's life. At this time, the family social worker can "normalize" the difficulties some families have in their very busy lives in committing themselves to the often time-consuming family work process and can graciously suggest that family work be terminated until the family feels they are in a better position to agree to regular appointments.

9. Termination is by mutual agreement following successful resolution of presenting problem(s).

There is little to be gained by continuing family work when the presenting problem has been successfully resolved. A major focus of family work is to teach families problem-solving skills (Chapter 11). It is hoped that the experience and skills gained in solving the presenting problem will not only positively affect other problems and family dynamics, but also can be applied to other problems in the present and in the future.

10. Termination is due to clients' initiative at the end of a contractual period of specified length. Contracting for a specified period provides a time framework that may make intervention efficient.

Termination at this time is the ideal. It is when we have an opportunity to terminate with the family that the family social work process has come to an end constructively.

EP 2.1.10l

STEPS FOR TERMINATION

Five steps are required for constructive termination: (1) recital, (2) inducing awareness of change, (3) consolidating gains, (4) providing feedback to the FSW, and (5) preparing the family to handle future problems.

1. *Recital:* As the helping process draws to a close, the social worker and each family member should be given an opportunity to comment on their experience in family work with an emphasis on discussing what has changed (Bandler, Grinder, & Satir, 1976; Worden, 1994). Doing so will help family members understand what changes have been made and what has happened to produce these changes. *Recital* is a technique that involves reviewing significant learning, events, and incidents that have occurred over the course of family work. Recital resembles summarization.

If negotiated goals have not been achieved or additional problems have emerged, the recital may point to the need for referral to a different agency or to another social worker within the same agency. In either case, the family should summarize their perceived progress to date so that they will be able to help the new social worker understand the situation. In a planned referral, the family social worker will speak personally with the new social worker after receiving the family's permission.

As mentioned earlier, routine and ongoing review of the family's progress throughout intervention will make the final summarization easier (Barker, 1981; Tomm & Wright, 1979). Negotiating for a predetermined number of sessions alerts families to the eventual end of intervention and sets a contract to track change. While an open-ended contract may be more typical, we suggest a time-limited, well-developed focus for work, allowing for flexibility with regard to the frequency and duration of sessions. Periodic reviews provide family members an opportunity to express satisfaction or dissatisfaction with the progress and also allow the family and the social worker to make changes as the work proceeds.

2. *Inducing awareness of change:* After family members have discussed their reactions to the social work process, they can receive feedback from the family worker's perspective. As the worker and family compare their perceptions of the process, family members will develop both a conceptual understanding and the tools with which to produce further change. These reflections can be a powerful source of self-esteem for family members.

Professional helpers want to be effective, and many have entered social work to fulfill a sincere desire to promote healthy social and family functioning. Because of this, they may believe that credit for the change belongs primarily to the social worker. It is unfortunate that failures are usually attributed to clients, whereas successes are claimed by social workers. Pinpointing the source of the change can be difficult because change often involves being in the right place at the right time and doing the right things with the right people.

In fact, for years researchers have been trying to isolate factors that create change. Regardless of where the family social worker believes the change originated, it is essential for the family to receive credit for making the change (Wright & Leahey, 1994). To accomplish this, the worker can ask family members what *they* did to create the change (Brock & Barnard, 1991). Social workers need to be humble in discussing their contributions. When family members are reminded of their own part in creating change, they will feel competent to meet future challenges.

It is natural for social workers to accept praise; success is a major source of professional gratification. Nevertheless, the family social worker's professional responsibility to the family is not complete until termination has been conducted satisfactorily. Families struggle with the pain, conflict, and pressure of their problems and deserve credit for making changes. When change occurs with a child, parents need to know that they are primary caretakers for the child in the present and future. Giving recognition for progress increases the chance that the positive effects of family social work will persist. To do otherwise conveys the message that the family cannot manage without the social worker.

If a family is distressed by lack of progress at termination, social workers must find a balance when discussing negative and positive aspects of the work. Negatives can be presented as goals to work toward in the future. Social workers may also want to explore with their supervisors possible reasons why the sessions were less successful than anticipated. Perhaps the goals were too high or unrealistic. Resistance to change may have been increased by the family social worker's inability to understand the family members' hesitancy. In many cases, social workers have explained lack of movement by claiming that families were unmotivated, rather than trying to understand how they themselves may have contributed to the problem.

Social workers need to acknowledge difficulties in working with families. Overburdened families sometimes will not benefit from complex or fancy interventions. It is important that the family social worker convey the opinion that the family has worked hard despite making little change. It is also important for the social worker to reinforce family strengths. Even though we are encouraging family social workers to credit families for change, the worker can also relish successes. Family social work is rewarding when the family social worker is a partner in the change process.

In Figure 14.1, we present a checklist for termination. Social workers and client families can complete the checklist together to determine whether termination issues have been addressed. The checklist consists of 16 factors that are useful in evaluating clients' readiness for ending family social work. If a family, together with the family social worker, can answer yes to most of these statements, then termination is appropriate and timely.

3. *Consolidating gains:* The third step of termination is talking about the future, emphasizing how to maintain and build on the goals achieved. Helping the family develop strategies for attaining future goals is an excellent method for consolidating gains (Lambert & Ogles, 2004). When appropriate, the family social worker can help the family make a transition to other community supports.

Reviewing family accomplishments is also an important component of the family social worker's self-evaluation. Client behavior is one factor in determining a successful outcome, but other factors are also important. The worker can note the professional learning accomplished while working with the family. The worker's professional development is advanced through learning new skills or improving existing skills, regardless of whether the case outcome is positive or negative. The worker may articulate the learning in various ways: "I persevered," "I learned how to work with a suicidal individual," or "I have developed more skills in teaching parents how to manage difficult child behavior."

Termination should be viewed as a transition, not an end. Describing termination in this way to clients produces the sense of a new beginning and a recognition of all that has been accomplished. Participating in a helping relationship requires faith in oneself, in families, and in the helping process. Family social workers may not witness clear evidence that they have helped families change or achieve desired goals, but their efforts may nevertheless make some important differences in their clients' lives. Additionally, some interventions may have no immediate impact but may exert an influence in the future. Some of the greatest benefits to families may come in the form of increased confidence, new skills, or supportive social networks that enable the clients to see themselves differently and help them respond to future

	Yes	No
The presenting problem has been eliminated	❏	❏
The presenting problem has been made manageable or tolerable for the family	❏	❏
The changes made can be measured effectively	❏	❏
Positive changes have been made in psychosocial functioning	❏	❏
Family members are communicating more effectively	❏	❏
Family members are safe from abuse	❏	❏
Formal support networks are available, and the family knows how to use them	❏	❏
The family has an adequate informal network on which to call when in need	❏	❏
Family or individual members have been referred for specialized services in the community	❏	❏
The family has agreed to be referred to specialized services	❏	❏
The family has learned skills to function in their daily routine	❏	❏
Basic physical needs of all family members are being met	❏	❏
The social worker and family have evaluated the family's progress to date	❏	❏
The family is satisfied with the service rendered	❏	❏
All family members are better off as a result of the work	❏	❏
The family has gone through recital of the changes they have made	❏	❏
Family members have acknowledged the role they have played in creating change	❏	❏

© Cengage Learning 2013

FIGURE 14.1 | Checklist for Terminating Family Social Work

challenges. Believing that their efforts have not been in vain diminishes the regrets family social workers feel about ending their work with a family.

4. *Providing feedback to the family social worker:* It is important to provide formal closure to the intervention by holding a face-to-face discussion. During the final session, evaluation of case outcomes may be conducted. Gurman and Kniskern (1981) recommend evaluating the progress of the entire family unit, as well as the subsystems that may have been experiencing problems (e.g., the marital subsystem and individual family members' functioning). The first step involves evaluating with the family their perceptions of success. The family social worker can ask family members, "What did you find most helpful during our work together?" and "What did you want to happen that did not occur?" It gives the family an opportunity to highlight the highs and lows of the process and also shows them that the social worker is receptive to feedback. The social worker should not react defensively to feedback but should express appreciation and inform family members that their contributions will help the worker in future work with families.

Additionally, measurement instruments or other assessment tools may be used one last time to provide comparative data to add to the evaluation.

5. *Preparing the family to handle future problems:* A final step in termination is to ask the family to anticipate upcoming changes or challenges that could cause setbacks (Nichols & Schwartz, 2008). The social worker should ask the family to describe how they plan to handle such situations. The family social worker can also use this theme to reinforce family strengths and newly developed skills. Another method of preparing families for the future is to gradually extend the time between family meetings and thereby encourage the family to lessen their reliance on the program.

Some agencies expect social workers to make a follow-up visit to clients after termination. Such a follow-up can provide a "booster shot" during a time when the family is vulnerable to relapse. Follow-up services can help families through transitional periods. During vulnerable periods, the family social worker may become re-involved with a family for a brief period of time to prevent the family from slipping into old patterns. Vulnerable periods depend on family characteristics and the type of problem experienced.

EXERCISE 14.3   Suggestions for the Future

Using a family from your field placement or work setting as an example, list some suggestions you could make to help the family maintain positive gains after termination.

Case 14.1 illustrates a successful termination of family social work.

CASE 14.1 | Termination

Lindy Stein and her parents, Mary and Todd, participated in family social work with their family social worker, Betty Chess. The family initially became involved with the family social work agency when 15-year-old Lindy ran away from home and was gone for a week. Prior to running away, Lindy was truant from school on numerous occasions and rebellious toward her parents and her teachers. Her grades had dropped from an A average to Cs and Ds, and she had been charged as a minor in possession of alcohol.

Mrs. Chess determined during the assessment that Lindy was reacting to her parents' separation and subsequent divorce. The divorce was difficult for the couple, who were angry at each other and had put Lindy in the middle of their fighting. Lindy's behavior was a response to her frustration and inability to communicate her needs and feelings to her parents.

Mrs. Chess intervened by helping Lindy learn to communicate her feelings to her parents. As Mary and Todd began to realize how their conflicts were affecting their daughter and contributing to her problems at school and at home, they recognized the need to arrive at a truce. Mary and Todd consequently agreed to allow Mrs. Chess to refer them for family counseling so that they could effectively co-parent Lindy.

As Mrs. Chess prepared the family for termination, she set aside time for the Steins to provide a recital of their experience in family work, followed by her own summary of the family's gains. Holding a termination session allowed Mrs. Chess to provide closure and to receive feedback from the family. She asked them to evaluate what had been most

(Continued)

CASE 14.1	Termination (*Continued*)

and least helpful during family social work. At the end of the termination session, Mrs. Chess asked the family to anticipate future problems and to describe how they planned to address them. This review of the skills learned allowed Mrs. Chess the opportunity to congratulate the family on their improved communication skills. Mrs. Chess referred the family for counseling to enable the Steins to consolidate their gains and to continue to improve their interactions. She also reminded the Steins that they could schedule booster sessions with her whenever they felt the need for follow-up services.

When becoming involved at a later date with families, the family social worker can refer to follow-up contacts as consultations or booster shots. Family members are likely to work through their problems more quickly if they feel that they are in charge of the changes, with the family social worker serving as an information provider and encourager on a short-term basis. The social worker must take care to identify the consultation as a sign of health rather than an indication of failure.

TIMING OF TERMINATION

The best time to decrease the frequency of sessions is when progress has been made, goals have been reached, and the family shows signs of stability. Most families agree to termination when they can identify improvement in their problem-solving capacity. If families find termination difficult to accept, the family social worker may ask a paradoxical question such as "What would each of you have to do to bring the problem back?" to give family members a better awareness of the changes made (Tomm & Wright, 1979).

The frequency of sessions may need to be decreased when a family seems overly dependent on the social worker. At times, paraprofessionals have acted in a supportive capacity with family members only to become their major support system because other supports have not been nurtured. To avoid fostering dependency, the family social worker can mobilize formal and informal supports for the family while concurrently decreasing the frequency of sessions. If the family resists decreasing the frequency of sessions, the worker should discuss concerns and solicit support from all family members (Tomm & Wright, 1979). Family members may worry that if appointments are discontinued altogether, they will be unable to cope. By asking "What do you think will happen if we stop meeting?" and by openly discussing family members' anxieties, the family social worker can often prevent the worst-case scenario from occurring.

EP 2.1.10l

HOW AND WHEN TO REFER CLIENTS TO OTHER PROFESSIONALS

Referral to other professionals may be necessary for a variety of reasons. Specific skills are needed by the family social worker to assist families in making a smooth transition from one professional to another. Major reasons for referring families to other professionals include:

- A family may need assistance from a specialist. It is unrealistic to expect family social workers to be experts in all areas. Assistance from other professionals may be needed when problems are complex. Referral can be either for consultation or for in-depth treatment. The role of the family social worker after referral will vary from a treatment collaborator to a former helper. For example, if an adult within a family is sexually abusing a child, it is important that specialists in offender treatment be consulted. The worker may refer the family for consultation with a psychiatrist but may continue to meet with the family until the consultation is complete.

- A family member may have a problem that should be assessed at an institution with the resources available to assess and treat the particular problem.
- A family moves out of the social worker's catchment area but needs continued assistance. Referral to a social worker in the new area may be indicated.

Family social workers should not think of themselves as inadequate if they must refer a family. Referral requires extensive knowledge of resources within the community as well as good counseling skills with families.

Clients need to be prepared prior to referrals. The family social worker must explain the reasons for referral and how the family may benefit from it. For example, if the worker has determined that the family's problems include a family member's alcoholism, the family social worker can refer the individual alcoholic and the family for addiction treatment. To facilitate the referral, the family social worker can provide a summary for the new helper and possibly give a copy to the family. Selecting an appropriate referral source is essential, and colleagues and supervisors can offer suggestions about which agencies can best meet the family's needs.

For families who have established rapport with their social workers, referral to other helpers may be difficult. The comments of a mother about what she did not like about a family social work agency illustrate this difficulty:

> We did not like being turned over to someone else. We are not machines; we are people. [The family social worker] had established an excellent rapport, she was trusted, she was effective, and when they thought she was done, she was pulled out without consultation. Not any consideration to the workability of the dynamic. These are intimate, profoundly personal issues.... If I don't like them, I don't want them in my family.... I want to accept help, but I'm simply not a case; I'm a human being.... It's really detrimental to take out someone who is working well with a family.... If [the family social worker] had stayed six months, [our child] would never have been in placement for a year and it would have saved [the agency] thousands of dollars. (Coleman & Collins, 1997)

As this mother's comments show, switching to a different family social worker can be difficult for some families. They may be emotionally attached to the first social worker and not want to go through the stages of trust building and engagement again. Referral may be more effective if the worker participates in the family's first meeting with the new social worker. This personalizes the referral and helps alleviate family members' anxieties about starting with someone they do not know and must learn to trust. Before the actual referral, family social workers should encourage family members to express concern or ask questions about the upcoming referral. Likewise, the new helper should clarify with the family why the referral was made and attempt to clear up any misconceptions the family may have. Thus, referral is smoothest if both the family and the new helper are given adequate explanations.

EP 2.1.10l

Checklist of Tasks for Termination[1]

Perceptual, Conceptual, and Executive Termination Schema

Tomm and Wright (1979) developed a very helpful paper on family skills, which is adapted below to be relevant for the termination stage of family work.

Assess Family Initiative to Terminate

1. Explore family members' rationale for termination to differentiate reasonable from inappropriate motives. (__)
2. Initiate a review of family problems and family strengths and offer to renegotiate the family work contract. (__)
3. When appropriate, point out unresolved issues and emphasize the general benefits of continuing family work to strengthen their interpersonal, problem-solving skills. (__)
4. When warranted, strongly encourage the family to reconsider their desire to discontinue sessions, and mobilize a spokesperson inside or outside the family who is most likely to anticipate potential benefits of further family work. (__)
5. Accept family initiation to terminate, and respect their right to do so without undue pressure or prejudice. (__)

Initiate Termination When Necessary

1. Stimulate the family to review the present status of their problems and their strengths and to consider termination when problematic issues have been resolved or adequate progress has been made and new strengths gained. (__)
2. Seek family members' perceptions of their own strengths and contributions toward the constructive changes that have occurred, and reduce the frequency of sessions. (__)
3. Encourage disclosure of fears related to the termination process, and elicit support from other family members. For example, "What do you think would happen if we stopped sessions now?" "Could you respond to her concerns?" (__)
4. Clarify the family social work limitations and initiate termination, pointing out that family members may become more receptive to change at a later date. (__)
5. Clarify emergent problems, and confront the family on the inappropriateness of relying too heavily on the family social worker to implement change and for general interpersonal support. (__)

Conclude Family Work Constructively

1. Review unresolved family problems by suggesting directions for future change, and strive to conclude most interviews and the overall family work on a positive note. (__)
2. Summarize strengths, positive efforts, and constructive intent of family members whether or not substantial improvement has occurred. Make clear commendations of these strengths. (__)

---

[1] Part of this checklist was adapted from Tomm and Wright (1979).

3. End the family work process with a face-to-face discussion when possible; otherwise, follow up by phone or letter. Again, remember to commend family strengths. (__)
4. Express personal appreciation for the family's openness and for the opportunity to have worked with them to solve problems and build on their strengths. (__)
5. Leave the family with an open invitation for further family work should crises recur. (__)

EVALUATING RESULTS OF FAMILY SOCIAL WORK

Although positive and even dramatic results may be obtained during family social work, success is measured by the positive changes that are maintained or continue to evolve weeks and months after termination. We encourage social workers to obtain follow-up information from the family. A focus on outcome directs the family social worker to orient work toward change, to focus on problems that can be realistically changed, and to think of how the family will cope on their own (Haley, 1976). In a follow-up contact, the worker should explain that this is a normal pattern of practice (e.g., "We always contact families with whom we have worked to get information on how they are doing"). It is also important to follow up with a clear and specific purpose in mind, such as reinforcing changes made in family work. To reinforce an emphasis on outcome, we suggest conducting follow-up sessions face-to-face.

The degree of change achieved in family social work should be assessed at all levels: individual, parent-child, marital, and family system. Gurman and Kniskern (1981) suggest that a "higher level of positive change has occurred when improvement is evidenced in systemic (total family) or relationship (dyadic) interactions than when it is evidenced in individuals alone" (p. 765). That is, change in individual family members does not logically require change in the family system, but stable change in the system does require both individual change and relationship change; relationship change also requires individual change.

Another measure of outcome is evaluation of practitioner performance. The competence of the family social worker is central to the success of family social work. Just as setting goals for family behavioral change assists in the change process, so too does setting goals for one's professional performance assist in your change process to becoming a more skilled worker (see Figure 14.2).

EXERCISE 14.4   Reevaluation and Follow-Up Procedures

List some procedures that would help you evaluate the effectiveness of your work with a family.

EXERCISE 14.5   Transfer of Learning

Break into small groups and discuss ways students can make sure that they transfer their learning from their social work program (1) after they graduate and start working with families, and (2) into their daily lives. Share responses with the rest of the class. What are the similarities about transfer of learning with families?

CASE 14.2	Termination

Johnny and June were seen by the family social worker for 12 weeks after June was diagnosed with depression. The couple also required marital counseling. A psychosocial intervention was introduced; the treatment plan included education for the couple about depression, arrangement of social support systems, establishment of regular medication and cognitive treatment for June, and marital counseling for the couple. The data collected during the treatment allowed the family social worker to make a judgment about termination of the treatment.

Measurement included weekly monitoring using a social support inventory completed by both of the couple, a medication maintenance chart and a depression inventory for June, and a marital satisfaction inventory for the couple. The family social worker also used a 10-point rating scale to do independent ratings of June's mood and the couple's rating scale at the weekly treatment sessions.

The scores on the inventory were recorded on a graph (see Chapter 9, and treatment was terminated when scores were at a satisfactory level.

I developed the following new skills in working with this family:

Skills in working with specific problems areas:

New techniques of intervention:

Self-awareness of strengths and problem areas:

With this family, my best work involved:

With this family, I could have done the following better:

I learned the following about my family practice:

Things I learned in working with this family that will help me in future family work:

© Cengage Learning 2013

FIGURE 14.2 | Family Social Worker's Self-Evaluation Form

EP 2.1.6b

EXERCISE 14.6 Negative and Positive Learning

Reflect back on what you have learned in your social work program. Make a list of the positive and negative things you have learned about people and families. How do the two different lists compare?

EP 2.1.6b

FUTURE TRENDS

It is imperative that social workers keep up with trends and changes in populations, policy, and the social work profession. In terms of populations, a major trend is the aging of the people. People are healthier and living longer but not without associated issues (Jordan, et al., 2011). Baby boomers are called the "sandwich generation" because they are squeezed between their not-yet-independent children (boomerangs, so called because they move out and then move back in to the parental home) and their elderly parents (Jordan & Cory, 2010). Boomerangs need help figuring out work (especially in today's economy) as well as life issues. The oldest baby boomers are nearing retirement age and facing a transition that this youth-oriented generation is ill prepared to face. Elders are living longer but facing loss of friends and family, potential health concerns, and possibly isolation. In schools, one of five children need mental health services but is not receiving needed help (Franklin, 2005). Another important population trend is the increasing diversity of the population (NASW Center for Workforce Studies, 2011). Social workers will need skills in responding in culturally sensitive ways.

Policy guides social work practice at the micro and macro levels. The widening gap between the richest and the poorest individuals is a concern for social workers. In the United States, a debate is ongoing about providing monies for social services versus balancing the budget in hard economic times. Tax money spent for military efforts is controversial as well. Participate in this debate online at http://debates.juggle.com/should-the-us-government-increase-social-services-for-the-poor.

The social work Profession has changed over time from the first "friendly visitors" who were for the most part wealthy "lady" volunteers. Recruiting the next generation of social workers into the profession is a concern because of increasing job stress and low salaries (NASW Center for Workforce Studies, 2011). While younger individuals may be reluctant to enter the social work profession, social work jobs are expected to increase more than the average of other jobs between 2008 and 2018 (Social Worker, 2011). Social work practice itself is changing due to technological advances and the trend toward evidence-based practice. Technology in the form of Social Networks and Online Worlds (SNOWS) is increasingly being used and has the potential to make service provision more efficient (i.e., professional SNOWS like LinkedIn). Technology also may be used to reduce isolation (i.e., SNOWS such as Facebook) and even to treat problems (i.e., SNOWS such as Lumosity, which offers games to improve the brain) (Jordan et al., 2011). The trend toward evidence-based practice "reflects a nationwide effort to build quality and accountability in health and behavioral health care service delivery" (Huang et al., 2003, cited in Franklin, 2005).

EP 2.1.9a

MEETING STANDARDS FOR ACCREDITATION

We have infused the standards from the Council on Social Work Education (CSWE) throughout the chapters, with competency notes at the end of each chapter elaborating on the standards. At this point, we present accreditation standards from the Canadian Association of Social Work Education (CASWE) that we believe can be achieved by the mastery of knowledge and skills learned from this text. As part of the termination process of this class on family social work, it would be useful for the students to review the standards presented throughout and in the next section and discuss as a class whether they have met these standards.

CASWE Standards for Accreditation

Curriculum Standards Curriculum at the first university level will ensure that graduates will be broadly educated and prepared for general practice and have sufficient competence for an entry level social work position. Competence is evidenced by an ability to arrive at professional judgments and practice actions, based on integration of theory and practice within the context of professional values and the relevant social work code of ethics.

The curriculum shall reflect social work values that promote a professional commitment:

- To optimize the dignity and potential of all people;
- To analyze and eradicate oppressive social conditions;
- To develop self-awareness which includes an understanding of the effect of one's ethnic, cultural, and racial background on client-worker relationships;
- To promote equal access to resources, services, and opportunities for the accomplishment of life tasks; and
- To promote the alleviation of distress, and the realization of aspirations and values in relation to oneself and others.

The curriculum shall ensure that the students will have:

- Intellectual abilities and skills of critical thinking and scholarly attitudes of curiosity, open-mindedness and reasoning and commitment to lifelong learning.
- Knowledge base related to human development and behavior in the social environment.
- Beginning level analysis and practice skills pertaining to the origins and manifestations of social injustices in Canada, and the multiple and intersecting bases of oppression, domination, and exploitation.
- Practice methods and professional skills required for generalist practice (i.e. analysis of situations, establishing accountable relationships, intervening appropriately and evaluating one's own social work interventions) at a beginning level of competence.
- A beginning competence for direct intervention with clients of diverse ethnic, cultural and racial backgrounds within the context of general practice.
- Understanding of social work's origins, purposes, and practices.
- Understanding of and ability to apply social work values and ethics in order to make professional judgments consistent with a commitment to address inequality and the eradication of oppressive social conditions.
- Awareness of self in terms of values, beliefs, and experiences as these impact upon social work practice.
- Ability to undertake systematic inquiry and critical evaluation related to social work knowledge and practice.
- Knowledge of multiple theoretical and conceptual bases of social work knowledge and practice including the social construction of theory and practices that may reflect injustices.

- An understanding of oppressions and healing of Aboriginal peoples and implications for social policy and social work practice with Aboriginal peoples in the Canadian context.
- Opportunities to develop an appreciation of social work purposes and ethics and to develop her/his social work values and professional judgment.
- Preparation to practice in a range of geographical regions and with diverse ethnic, cultural, and racial populations.

CHAPTER SUMMARY

In this chapter, we described the process of terminating the family social worker's relationship with a client family. Termination involves summarizing the family's accomplishments, reviewing problems that remain, and making decisions about further work, follow-up, or referral. Termination may occur for three reasons: termination is predetermined and time-limited, the family's goals have been accomplished, or the family or the family social worker decides not to continue.

Steps for successful termination include (1) recital of the family social work process with the client family, (2) inducing an awareness of change, (3) consolidating gains for the social worker and the family, (4) providing feedback from the family to the family social worker, and (5) preparing the family to handle future problems. If termination is described as a transition rather than an ending, it may seem more palatable both to the family and to the family social worker.

Contracting for a specific number of sessions at the beginning of family work sets time limits to encourage completion of goals. When adequate progress has been made, the family social worker can begin to decrease the frequency of sessions as a way to help the family prepare for termination. Referral to another professional may be necessary in some cases.

Giving families credit for the positive changes they have made is an excellent way to increase clients' self-esteem, feelings of competence, and motivation for independence. When families have made little progress during family work, the family social worker can acknowledge family members' positive efforts toward solving their problems. The worker may seek supervision or consultation for help in determining the causes of a lack of progress. Implementing systematic evaluation and follow-up procedures helps the family social worker to analyze her or his performance and set goals for improvement.

Future trends in social work include changes in populations, policies, and the social work profession. Social workers must be aware, informed, and flexible in order to best serve their clients.

KEY TERM

Termination the final phase of family social work. Ideally, this phase is completed after negotiation and discussion between the social worker and family and after the contracted goals have been accomplished.

COMPETENCY NOTES

EP 2.1.6b Use research evidence to inform practice: The degree of change achieved in family social work should be evaluated at all levels: individual, parent-child, marital, and family system.

EP 2.1.9a Continuously discover, appraise, and attend to changing locales, populations, scientific and technological developments, and emerging societal trends to provide relevant services: Social work must keep abreast of current changes at all systemic levels in order to be of use. People and societies are not stagnant; therefore, social work must be fluid and flexible and keep up with new trends as well.

EP 2.1.10l Facilitate transitions and endings: In order to best serve clients, social workers must be aware of the issues surrounding termination in order to plan. These issues include possible reactions to termination, as well as timing and steps of termination.

References

Abudabbeh, N. (2005). Arab families: An overview. In M. McGoldrick, J. Giordano, & N. Garcia-Petro (Eds.), *Ethnicity and family therapy* (3rd ed.) (pp. 423–436). New York: Guilford Press.

Ackerman, N. (1958). *The psychodynamics of family life.* New York: Basic Books.

Adams, J., Jaques, J., & May, K. (2004). Counseling gay and lesbian families: Theoretical considerations. *Family Journal: Counseling and Therapy for Couples and Families, 12*(1), 40–42.

Adler, A. (2003). Psychodynamic therapies. In J. Prochaska & J. Norcross (Eds.), *Systems of psychotherapy: A transtheoretical analysis* (pp. 63–100). Pacific Grove, CA: Brooks/Cole.

Ahrons, C. (1999). Divorce: An unscheduled family transition. In B. Carter & M. McGoldrick (Eds.), *The expanded family life cycle: Individual, family, and social perspectives* (3rd ed.) (pp. 381–398). Needham Heights, MA: Allyn & Bacon.

Ahrons, C., (2005). Divorce: An unscheduled family transition. In B. Carter & M. McGoldrick (eds). *The expanded family life cycle: Individual, family, and social perspectives* (pp. 381–398). New York: Allyn & Bacon.

Ahrons, C. (2007). Family ties after divorce: Long-term implications for children. *Family Process, 46*(1), 53–65.

Alessandria, K. (2002). Acknowledging white ethnic groups in multicultural counseling. *Family Journal: Counseling and Therapy for Couples and Families, 10*(1), 57–60.

Alexander, J., Holtzworth-Munroe, A., & Jameson, P. (1994). The process and outcome of marital and family therapy: Research review and evaluation. In A. Bergin & S. Garfield (Eds.), *Handbook of psychotherapy and behavior change* (4th ed.) (pp. 595–630). Toronto: Wiley.

Alexander, J., & Parsons, B. (1973). Short-term behavioral intervention with delinquent families: Impact on family process and recidivism. *Journal of Abnormal Psychology, 81*(3), 219–225.

Alexander, J., & Parsons, B. (1982). *Functional family therapy.* Monterey, CA: Brooks/Cole.

Allen, M., & Yen, W. (1979). *Introduction to measurement theory.* Monterey, CA: Brooks/Cole.

Almeida, R., Woods, R., Messineo, T., & Font, R. (1998). The cultural context model: An overview. In M. McGoldrick (Ed.), *Re-visioning family therapy: Race, culture, and gender in clinical practice* (pp. 414–431). New York: Guilford Press.

Anastasi, A. (1988). *Psychological testing.* New York: Macmillan.

Anderson, C. (1999). Single-parent families: Strengths, vulnerabilities, and interventions. In B. Carter & M. McGoldrick (Eds.), *The expanded family life cycle: Individual, family, and social perspectives* (3rd ed.) (pp. 399–416). Needham Heights, MA: Allyn & Bacon.

Anderson, C. (2005). Single-parent families: Strengths, vulnerabilities, and interventions. In B. Carter & M. McGoldrick (Eds.), *The expanded family life cycle: Individual, family and social perspectives* (3rd ed.) (pp. 399–416). Boston, MA: Allyn & Bacon.

Anderson, S., Russell, C., & Schumm, W. (1983). Perceived marital quality and family life cycle categories: A further analysis. *Journal of Marriage and the Family, 45*, 127–139.

Ange, R. (2006). Fathers do matter: Evidence from an Asian school-based aggressive sample. *The American Journal of Family Therapy, 34*(1), 79–83.

Aponte, H., & VanDeusen, J. (1981). Structural family therapy. In A. S. Gurman & D. P. Kniskern (Eds.), *Handbook of family therapy* (pp. 310–336). New York: Brunner/Mazel.

Arad, D. (2004). If your mother were an animal, what animal would she be? Creating play-stories in family therapy: The animal attribution storytelling technique (AASTT). *Family Process, 43*(2), 249–263.

Armstrong, L. (1987). *Kiss daddy goodnight: Ten years later.* New York: Pocket Books.

Arnold, J., Levine, A., & Patterson, G. (1975). Changes in sibling behavior following family intervention. *Journal of Consulting and Clinical Psychology, 43*(5), 683–688.

Assembly of First Nations. (1994). *Breaking the silence: An interpretive study of residential school impact and healing as illustrated by the stories of First Nations individuals.* Ottawa, ON: First Nations Health Commission.

AuClare, P., & Schwartz, I. (1987). Are home-based services effective? A public child welfare agency's experiment. *Children Today, 16*, 6–9.

Bailey, K. (1987). *Methods of social research.* New York: Free Press.

Balaguer, A., Dunn, M., & Levitt, M. (2000). The genogram: From diagnostics to mutual collaboration. *Family Journal: Counseling and Therapy for Couples and Families, 8*(3), 236–244.

Baltimore, M. (2000). Ethical considerations in the use of technology for marriage and family counselors. *Family Journal: Counseling and Therapy for Couples and Families, 8*(4), 390–393.

Bandler, R., Grinder, J., & Satir, V. (1976). *Changing with families.* Palo Alto, CA: Science and Behavior Books.

Bardill, D., & Saunders, B. (1988). Marriage and family therapy in graduate social work education. In H. Liddle, D. Breunlin, & R. Schwartz (Eds.), *Handbook of family therapy training and supervision* (pp. 316–330). New York: Guilford Press.

Barker, R. (1981). *Basic family therapy.* Baltimore: University Park Press.

Barker, R. (1995). *The social work dictionary* (3rd ed.). Washington, DC: NASW.

Barlow, C., & Coleman, H. (2003). Suicide and families: Considerations for therapy. *Guidance and Counseling, 18*(2), 67–73.

Barlow, C., & Coleman, H. (2004). After suicide: Family responses to social support. *Omega: Journal of Death and Dying, 47*(3), 187–201.

Barsky, A. (2001). Understanding family mediation from a social work perspective. *Canadian Social Work Review, 18*(1), 25–46.

Barth, R. P. (1990). Theories guiding home-based intensive family preservation services. In J. K. Whittaker, J. Kinney, E. Tracey, & C. Booth (Eds.), *Reaching high-risk families: Intensive family preservation services* (pp. 89–112). New York: Aldine de Gruyter.

Bateson, G., & Jackson, D. (1974). Some varieties of pathogenic organization. In D. Jackson (Ed.), *Communication, family, and marriage* (pp. 200–216). Palo Alto, CA: Science and Behavior Books.

Baum, C., & Forehand, R. (1981). Long-term follow-up assessment of parent training by use of multiple outcome measures. *Behavior Therapy, 12*, 643–652.

Baum, N. (2003). Divorce process variables and the co-parental relationship and parental role fulfillment of divorced parents. *Family Process, 42*(1), 117–131.

Baynard, R., & Baynard, J. (1983). *How to deal with your acting-up teenager.* New York: M. Evans.

Bean-Bayog, M., & Stimmel, B. (Eds.). (1987). *Children of alcoholics.* New York: Haworth Press.

Beavers, W. (1981). A systems model of family for family therapists. *Journal of Marriage and Family Therapy, 7*, 299–307.

Beavers, W. (1988). Attributes of a healthy couple. *Family Therapy Today, 3*(1), 1–4.

Beavers, W., Hampson, R., & Hulgas, Y. (1985). Commentary: The Beavers System Approach to family assessment. *Family Process, 22*, 85–98.

Becker, K., Carson, D., Seto, A., & Becker, C. (2002). Negotiating the dance: Consulting with adoptive systems. *Family Journal: Counseling and Therapy for Couples and Families, 10*(1), 80–86.

Becvar, D. (1998). *Family, spirituality and social work.* Binningham, NY: Haworth.

Becvar, D. (2006). *Families that flourish: Facilitating resilience in clinical practice.* NY: Norton & Company.

Becvar, D., & Becvar, R. (1996). *Family therapy: A systemic integration.* Boston: Allyn & Bacon.

Becvar, D., & Becvar, R. (2005). *Family therapy: A systemic integration* (7th ed.). Boston: Allyn & Bacon.

Beels, C. (2002). Notes for a cultural history of family therapy. *Family Process, 41*(1), 67–82.

Bending, R. (1997). Training child welfare workers to meet the requirements of the Indian Child Welfare Act. *Journal of Multicultural Social Work, 5*(3/4), 151–164.

Benzies, K., & Mychasuik, R. (2009). Fostering family resiliency. *Child and Family Social Work, 14*(1), 103–114.

Berliner, K., Jacob, D., & Schwartzberg, N. (1999). The single adult and the family life cycle. In B. Carter & M. McGoldrick (Eds.), *The expanded family life cycle: Individual, family, and social perspectives* (3rd ed.) (pp. 362–380). Needham Heights, MA: Allyn & Bacon.

Bernal, G., & Shapiro, E. (2005). Cuban families. In M. McGoldrick, J. Giordano, & N. Garcia-Petro (Eds.), *Ethnicity and family therapy* (3rd ed.) (pp. 166–177). New York: Guilford Press.

Bernard, D. (1992). The dark side of family preservation. *Afflia, 7*(2), 156–159.

Berry, M. (1997). *The family at risk.* Columbia, SC: University of South Carolina Press.

Besa, D. (1994). Evaluating narrative family therapy using single-system research designs. *Research on Social Work Practice, 4*(4), 309–325.

Beutler, L., Machado, P., & Allstetter Neufelt, A. (1994). Therapist variables. In A. Bergin & S. Garfield (Eds.), *Handbook of psychotherapy and behavior change* (4th ed.) (pp. 229–269). Toronto: Wiley.

Bitter, J. (2004). Two approaches to counseling a parent alone: Toward a Gestalt–Adlerian integration. *Family Journal: Counseling and Therapy for Couples and Families, 12*(4), 358–367.

Black, L., & Jackson, V. (2005). Families of African origin. In M. McGoldrick, J. Giordano, & N. Garcia-Petro (Eds.), *Ethnicity and family therapy* (3rd ed.) (pp. 202–215). New York: Guilford Press.

Blacker, L. (1999). The launching phase of the family life cycle. In B. Carter & M. McGoldrick (Eds.), *The expanded family life cycle: Individual, family, and social perspectives* (3rd ed.) (pp. 287–306). Needham Heights, MA: sAllyn & Bacon.

Blacker, L. (2005). The launching phase of the family life cycle. In B. Carter & M. McGoldrick (Eds.), *The expanded family life cycle: Individual, family and social perspectives* (3rd ed.) (pp. 287–306). Boston, MA: Allyn & Bacon.

Bloom, M., Fischer, J., & Orme, J. (2005). *Evaluating practice: Guidelines for the accountable professional* (5th ed.). Boston: Allyn & Bacon.

Bloomquist, M. (1996). *Skills training for children with behavior disorders.* New York: Guilford Press.

Blum, H., Boyle, M., & Offord, D. (1988). Single-parent families: Child psychiatric disorder and school performance. *Journal of the American Academy of Child and Adolescent Psychiatry, 27,* 214–219.

Bodin, A. (1981). The interactional view: Family therapy approaches of the Mental Research Institute. In A. S. Gurman & D. P. Kniskern (Eds.), *Handbook of family therapy* (pp. 267–309). New York: Brunner/Mazel.

Bograd, M. (1992). Changes to family therapists' thinking. *Journal of Marital and Family Therapy, 18,* 243–253.

Bolton, F., & Bolton, S. (1987). *Working with violent families: A guide for clinical and legal practitioners.* Beverly Hills, CA: Sage Publications.

Borstnar, J., Mocnik Bucar, M., Rus Makovec, M., Burck, C., & Daniel, G. (2005). Co-constructing a cross-cultural course: Resisting and replicating colonizing practices. *Family Process, 44*(1), 121–132.

Bostwick, G., & Kyte, N. (1988). Validity and reliability. In R. Grinnell (Ed.), *Social work research and evaluation* (3rd ed.) (pp. 111–126). Itasca, IL: F. E. Peacock.

Bowen, M. (1971). The use of family theory in clinical practice. In J. Haley (Ed.), *Changing families: A family therapy reader* (pp. 159–192). New York: Grune & Straton.

Bowen, M. (1973). Alcoholism and the family system. *Family: Journal of the Center for Family Learning,* 20–25.

Bowen, M. (1978). *Family therapy in clinical practice.* New York: Jason Aronson.

Bowlby, J. (1969). *Attachment.* New York: Basic Books.

Brant, C. (1990). Native ethics and rules of behaviour. *Canadian Journal of Psychiatry, 35,* 534–539.

Braverman, L. (1991). The dilemma of homework: A feminist response to Gottman, Napier, and Pittman. *Journal of Marital and Family Therapy, 17,* 25–28.

Bredehoft, D. (2001). The framework for life span family life education revisited and revised. *Family Journal: Counseling and Therapy for Couples and Families, 9*(2), 134–139.

Brendel, J., & Nelson, K. (1999). The stream of family secrets: Navigating the islands of confidentiality and triangulation involving family therapists. *Family Journal: Counseling and Therapy for Couples and Families, 7*(2), 112–117.

Breunlin, D. (1988). Oscillation theory and family development. In C. Falicov (Ed.), *Family transitions: Continuity and change over the life cycle.* New York: Guilford Press.

Brice-Baker, J. (2005). British West Indian families. In M. McGoldrick, J. Giordano, & N. Garcia-Petro (Eds.), *Ethnicity and family therapy* (3rd ed.) (pp. 117–126). New York: Guilford Press.

Brock, G., & Barnard, C. (1992). *Procedures in marriage and family therapy.* Boston: Allyn & Bacon.

Brock & Barnard (1999). *Procedures in marriage and family therapy* (3rd ed.). Allyn & Bacon.

Burden, D. (1986). Single parents and the work setting: The impact of multiple job and homelife responsibilities. *Family Relations, 35,* 37–43.

Burnett, G., Jones, R., Bliwise, N., & Thomson Ross, L. (2006). Family unpredictability, parental alcoholism, and the development of parentification. *The American Journal of Family Therapy, 34,* 181–189.

Butler, J. (2009). The family diagram and genogram: Comparisons and contrasts. *The American Journal of Family Therapy, 36,* 169–180.

Caffrey, T., & Erdman, P. (2000). Conceptualizing parent-adolescent conflict: Applications from systems and attachment theories. *Family Journal: Counseling and Therapy for Couples and Families, 8*(1), 14–21.

Caffrey, T., Erdman, P., & Cook, D. (2000). Two systems/one client: Bringing families and schools together. *Family Journal: Counseling and Therapy for Couples and Families, 8*(2), 154–160.

Callard, E., & Morin, P. (Eds.). (1979). *Parents and children together: An alternative to foster care.* Detroit: Wayne State University, Department of Family and Consumer Studies.

Canfield, B., Low, L., & Hovestadt, A. (2009). Cultural immersion as a learning method for expanding intercultural competence. *The Family Journal, 17*(4), 318–322.

Canino, I. & Spurlock, J. (1994). Culturally diverse children and adolescents. New York: Guildford.

Caplan, P., & Hall-McCorquodale, I. (1985). Mother-blaming in major clinical journals. *American Journal of Orthopsychiatry, 55,* 345–353.

Caplan, P., & Hall-McCorquodale, I. (1991). The scapegoating of mothers: A call for change. In J. Veevers (Ed.), *Continuity and change in marriage and the family* (pp. 295–302). Toronto: Holt, Rinehart & Winston of Canada.

Carich, M., & Spilman, K. (2004). Basic principles of intervention. *Family Journal: Counseling and Therapy for Couples and Families, 12*(4), 405–410.

Carlson, J., Kurato, Y., Ruiz, E., Ng, K., & Yang, J. (2004). A multicultural discussion about personality development. *Family Journal: Counseling and Therapy for Couples and Families, 12*(2), 111–121.

Carmines, E., & Zeller, R. (1979). *Reliability and validity assessment.* Sage University Paper Series on Quantitative Applications in the Social Sciences, 07–017. Beverly Hills, CA: Sage.

Carter, B. (1992). Stonewalling feminism. *Family Therapy Network, 16*(1), 64–69.

Carter, B. (1999). Becoming parents: The family with young children. In B. Carter and M. McGoldrick (Eds.), *The expanded family life cycle: Individual, family, and social perspectives* (3rd ed.) (pp. 249–273). Needham Heights, MA: Allyn & Bacon.

Carter, B. (2005). Becoming parents: The family with young children. In B. Carter & M. McGoldrick (Eds.), *The expanded family life cycle: Individual, family, and social perspectives* (4th ed.) (pp. 249–273). Boston, MA: Allyn & Bacon.

Carter, B., & McGoldrick, M. (1988). *The changing family life cycle: A framework for family therapy* (2nd ed.). New York: Gardner Press.

Carter, B., & McGoldrick, M. (Eds.). (1999). *The expanded family life cycle: Individual, family, and social perspectives* (3rd ed.). Needham Heights, MA: Allyn & Bacon.

Carter, B., & McGoldrick, M. (1999a). Overview: The expanded family life cycle. In B. Carter & M. McGoldrick (Eds.), *The expanded family life cycle: Individual, family, and social perspectives* (3rd ed.) (pp. 1–26). Needham Heights, MA: Allyn & Bacon.

Carter, B., & McGoldrick, M. (1999b). The divorce cycle: A major variation in the American family life cycle. In B. Carter & M. McGoldrick (Eds.), *The expanded family life cycle: Individual, family, and social perspectives* (3rd ed.) (pp. 373–380). Needham Heights, MA: Allyn & Bacon.

Carter, B., & McGoldrick, M. (2005a). Overview: The expanded family life cycle: Individuals, family, and social perspectives. In B. Carter & M. McGoldrick (Eds.), *The expanded family life cycle: Individual, family, and social perspectives* (3rd ed.) (pp. 1–26). Boston, MA: Allyn & Bacon.

Carter, B., & McGoldrick, M. (2005b). The divorce cycle: A major variation in the American family life cycle. In B. Carter & M. McGoldrick (Eds.), *The expanded family life cycle: Individual, family, and social perspectives* (3rd ed.) (pp. 373–398). Boston, MA: Allyn & Bacon.

Carter, B., & McGoldrick, M. (2005c). *The expanded family life cycle: Individual, family, and social perspectives* (3rd ed.). Boston: Allyn & Bacon.

Carter, C. S. (1997). Using African-centered principles in family preservation services. *Families in Society: The Journal of Contemporary Human Services, 78*(5), 531–538.

Catao de Korin, E., & de Carvalho Petry, S. (2005). Brazilian families. In M. McGoldrick, J. Giordano, & N. Garcia-Petro (Eds.), *Ethnicity and family therapy* (3rd ed.) (pp. 166–177). New York: Guilford Press.

Chang, J., & Phillips, M. (1993). Michael White and Steve de Shazer: New Directions in family therapy. In S. Gilligan & R. Price (eds). (1993). *Therapeutic conversations* (pp. 95–135). New York: W.W. Norton & Company, Inc.

Cherlin, A. (1983). Family policy: The conservative challenge to the progressive response. *Journal of Family Issues, 4*(3), 417–438.

Clarkin, J., & Levy, K. (2004). The influence of client variables on psychotherapy. In M. Lambert (Ed.), *Handbook of psychotherapy and behavior change* (pp. 194–226). New York: John Wiley & Sons.

Clements, W. (2001, March 14). The evolution of the word 'ethnic.' *The Globe and Mail*. Retrieved from http://www.theglobeandmail. com/news/arts/warren-clements/the-evolution-of-the-word-ethnic/article1936798/?utm_source=Shared+Article+Sent+to+User&utm_medium=E-mail:+Newsletters+/+E-Blasts+/+etc.&utm_content=1936798&utm_campaign=Shared+Web+Article+Links

Cobb, N., & Jordan, C. (2001). Competency-based treatment of marital discord. In H. Briggs & K. Corcoran (Eds.), *Social work practice* (pp. 169–198). Chicago: Lyceum.

Coleman, H., & Collins, D. (1990). The treatment trilogy of father-daughter incest. *Child and Adolescent Social Work Journal*, 7(40), 339–355.

Coleman, H. D. J. (1995). A longitudinal student of a family preservation program. Doctoral dissertation, School of Social Work. Salt Lake City, Utah: University of Utah.

Coleman, H., & Collins, D. (1997). The voice of parents: A qualitative study of a family-centered, home-based program. *The Child and Youth Care Forum (Special Edition on Research in the Field of Child and Youth Care)*, 26(4), 261–278.

Coleman, H., & Collins, D. (2002). Problem-based learning and social work education. *International Journal of Learning*, 9, 689–703.

Coleman, H., Collins, D., & Baylis, P. (2007). "You didn't throw us to the wolves": Using problem-based learning in a social work family class. *The Journal of Baccalaureate Social Work*, 12(2), 98–113.

Coleman, H., Collins, D., & Collins, T. (2005). *Family practice: A problem-based learning approach*. Peosta, IA: Eddie Bowers.

Coleman, H., Unrau, Y., & Manyfingers, B. (2001). Revamping family preservation services for Native families. *Journal of Ethnic & Cultural Diversity in Social Work*, Vol. 10(1), 49–68.

Collins, D. (1989). Child care workers and family therapists: Getting connected. *Journal of Child and Youth Care*, 4(3), 23–31.

Collins, D. (1992). Thoughts of a male counselor attempting a feminist approach. *Journal of Child and Youth Care*, 7(2), 69–74.

Collins, D., Coleman, H., & Barlow, C. (2006). Not an ordinary conversation. *International Journal of Learning*, 13(7), 21–29.

Collins, D., Thomlison, B., & Grinnell, R. (1992). *The social work practicum: An access guide*. Itasca, IL: F. E. Peacock.

Collins, D., & Tomm, K. (2009). A historical look at the change of family therapy over 30 years. *Journal of Marriage and Family Counseling* (in press).

Coltrane, S. (1998). *Gender and families*. Thousand Oaks, CA: Pine Forge Press.

Conoley, C., Graham, J., Neu, T., Craig, M., O'Pry, A., Cardin, S., Brossart, D., & Parker, R. (2003). Solution- focused family therapy with three aggressive and oppositional-acting children: An N=1 empirical study. *Family Process*, 42(3), 361–374.

Coontz, S. (1996). The way we weren't: The myth and reality of the "Traditional Family." *National Forum*, 76(4), 45–48.

Coontz, S. (2006). The origins of modern divorce. *Family Process*, 46(1), 7–16.

Corcoran, K., & Fischer, J. (2000). *Measures for clinical practice, Volume 1: Couples, families, and children* (3rd ed.). New York: Free Press.

Courtney, M. (1997). Reconsidering family preservation: A review of Putting Families First. *Child and Youth Services Review*, 19, 61–76.

Crichton, M. (1995). *The lost world*. New York: Ballantine.

Cross, T. (1986). Drawing on cultural tradition in Indian child welfare practice. *Social Casework*, 67(5), 283–289.

Cunningham, P., & Henggeler, S. (1999). Engaging multiproblem families in treatment: Lessons learned throughout the development of multisystemic therapy. *Family Process*, 38(3), 265–280.

Curtner-Smith, M. (1995). Assessing children's visitation needs with divorced noncustodial fathers. *Families in Society*, 76(6), 34–348.

Davis, K. (1996). *Families: A handbook of concepts and techniques for the helping professional*. Pacific Grove, CA: Brooks/Cole.

Davis, L., & Proctor, E. (1989). *Race, gender, and class: Guidelines for practice with individuals, families, and groups*. Englewood Cliffs, NJ: Prentice Hall.

Debates.juggle.com. (2011). *Should the US Government increase social services for the poor?* Retrieved from http://debates.juggle.com/should-the-us-government-increase-social-services-for-the-poor

DeJong, P., & Berg, I. (2002). *Interviewing for solutions*. Pacific Grove, CA: Brooks/Cole.

Dekovic, M., Janssens, J., & VanAs, N. (2003). Family predictors of antisocial behavior in adolescence. *Family Process*, 42(2), 223–235.

Dell, P. (1989). Violence and the systemic view: The problem of power. *Family Process*, 23, 1–14.

De Master, D., & Dros Giordano, M.A. (2005). Dutch families. In M. McGoldrick, J. Giordano, & N. Garcia-Petro (Eds.), *Ethnicity and family therapy* (3rd ed.) (pp. 534–544). New York: Guilford Press.

Denby, R., Curtis, C., & Alford, K. (1998). Family preservation services and special populations: The invisible target. *Families in Society, 79*(1), 3–14.

Denicola, J., & Sandler, J. (1980). Training abusive parents in child management and self-control skills. *Behavior Therapy, 11*, 263–270.

deShazer, S. (1983). Patterns of brief family therapy: An ecosystemic approach. New York: Guilford.

deShazer, S. (1991). Putting difference to work. New York: Norton.

Dickerson, A., & Crase, S. (2005). Parent-adolescent relationships: The influence of multi-family therapy group on communication and closeness. *The American Journal of Family Therapy, 33*, 45–59.

Doherty, W. (2003). A wake up call: Comment on "Lived Religion and Family Therapy." *Family Process, 42*(1), 181–183.

Donley, M., & Likins, L. (2010). The multigenerational impact of sibling relationships. *The American Journal of Family Therapy, 38*, 383–396.

Dosser, P., Smith, A., Markowski, E., & Cain, H. (2001). Including families' spiritual beliefs and their faith communities in systems of care. *Journal of Family Social Work, 5*(3), 63–78.

Doucet, A. (2001). "You see the need perhaps more clearly than I have": Exploring gendered processes of domestic responsibility. *Journal of Family Issues, 22*(3), 328–357.

Dunbar, N., Van Dulmen, M., Ayers-Lopez, S., Berge, J., Christian, C., Gossman, G., Henney, S., Mendenhall, T., Grotevant, H., & McRoy, R. (2006). Processes linked to contact changes in adoptive kinship networks. *Family Process, 45*(4), 449–464.

Dutton, D. (1991). Interventions into the problem of wife assault: Therapeutic, policy, and research implications. In J. Veevers (Ed.), *Continuity and change in marriage and the family* (pp. 203–215). Toronto: Holt, Rinehart & Winston of Canada.

Duvall, E. (1957). *Family transitions.* Philadelphia: Lippincott.

Dye Holten, J. (1990). When do we stop mother-blaming? *Journal of Feminist Family Therapy, 2*(1), 53–60.

Early, T., & Glen Maye, I. (2000). Valuing families: Social work practice with families from a strengths perspective. *Social Work, 45*(2), 118–130.

Eckstein, D. (2001). Counseling is the answer … counseling is the answer … But what is the question? 25 questions for couples and families. *Family Journal: Counseling and Therapy for Couples and Families, 9*(4), 463–476.

Eckstein, D. (2002). Walls and windows: Closing and opening behaviors for couples and families. *Family Journal: Counseling and Therapy for Couples and Families, 10*(3), 344–345.

Efron, D., & Rowe, B. (1987). *Strategic parenting manual.* London, Ontario: J.S.S.T.

Egan, G. (1994). *The skilled helper.* Pacific Grove, CA: Brooks/Cole.

Eichler, M. (1988). *Nonsexist research methods: A practical guide.* Boston: Allen & Unwin.

Eichler, M. (1997). *Family shifts: Families, policies, and gender equality.* Toronto: Oxford University Press.

Eisenstein-Naveh, A. (2003). The center for children and families at risk: A facilitating environment. *Family Journal: Counseling and Therapy for Couples and Families, 11*(2), 191–201.

Elizur, Y., & Ziv, M. (2001). Family support and acceptance, gay male identity formation, and psychological adjustment: A path model. *Family Process, 40*(2), 125–144.

Ellis, K., & Eriksen, K. (2002). Transsexual and transgenderist experiences and treatment options. *Family Journal: Counseling and Therapy for Couples and Families, 10*(3), 289–299.

Ellenwood, A., & Jenkins, J. (2007). Implementation of the intervention-based family assessment procedure: A case study. *The American Journal of Family Therapy, 35*, 403–415.

Epstein, N., Baldwin, D., & Bishop, D. (1983). The McMaster family assessment device. *Journal of Marital and Family Therapy, 9*, 171–180.

Epstein, N., Bishop, D., & Levin, S. (1978). The McMaster model of family functioning. *Journal of Marriage and Family Counseling, 4*, 19–31.

Epston, D., White, M., & Murray, K. (1992). A proposal for re-authoring therapy: Rose's revisioning of her life and a commentary. In S. MacNamee & K. Gergen (eds). *Therapy as social construction.* (pp. 96–113). Thousand Oaks, CA: Sage

Erickson, B. (2005). Scandinavian families: Plain and simple. In M. McGoldrick, J. Giordano, & N. Garcia-Petro (Eds.), *Ethnicity and family therapy* (3rd ed.) (pp. 641–653). New York: Guilford Press.

Etchison, M., & Kleist, D. (2000). Review of narrative therapy: Research and utility. *Family Journal: Counseling and Therapy for Couples and Families, 8*(1), 61–66.

Falicov, C. (1999). The Latino family life cycle. In B. Carter & M. McGoldrick (Eds.), *The expanded family life cycle: Individual, family, and social perspectives* (3rd ed.) (pp. 141–152). Needham Heights, MA: Allyn & Bacon.

Falicov, C. (2005a). Mexican families. In M. McGoldrick, J. Giordano & N. Garcia-Petro (Eds.), *Ethnicity and family therapy* (3rd ed.) (pp. 229–241). New York: Guilford Press.

Falicov, C. (2005b). The Latino family life cycle. In B. Carter & M. McGoldrick (Eds.), *The* expanded family life cycle: Individual, family, and social perspectives (3rd ed.) (pp. 141–152). Boston, MA: Allyn & Bacon.

Finkelhor, D. (1986). Sexual abuse: Beyond the family systems approach. In T. Trepper & M. Barrett (Eds.), Treating incest: A multiple systems perspective (pp. 53–66). New York: Haworth.

Fischer, J., & Corcoran, K. (2007) Measures for clinical practice and research (4th ed.). New York: Oxford University Press.

Fischer, J., & Corcoran, K. (1994). Measures for clinical practice. New York: Free Press.

Fischler, R. (1985). Child abuse and neglect in American Indian communities. Child Abuse & Neglect, 9, 95–106.

Fitzpatrick, M., & Reeve, P. (2003). Grandparents raising grandchildren—a new class of disadvantaged Australians. Family Matters, 66, 54–57.

Fong, R. (1994). Family preservation: Making it work for Asians. Child Welfare, 73, 331–341.

Ford, J., Nalbone, D., Wetchler, J., & Sutton, P. (2008). Fatherhood: How differentiation and identity status affect attachment to children. The American Journal of Family Therapy, 36, 284–299.

Forehand, R., Sturgis, E., McMahon, R., et al. (1979). Parent behavioral training to modify child noncompliance: Treatment generalization across time and from home to school. Behavior Modification, 3(1), 3–25.

Forgatch, M. (1991). The clinical science vortex: A developing theory of antisocial behavior. In D. Pepler & K. Rubin (Eds.), The development and treatment of child aggression (pp. 291–315). Hillsdale, NJ: Lawrence Erlbaum Associates.

Foster, C. (1993). The family patterns workbook. New York: Jeremy P. Tarcher/Perigree Books.

Foster, S., Prinz, R., & O'Leary, D. (1983). Impact of problem-solving communication training and generalization procedures on family conflict. Child and Family Behavior Therapy, 5(1), 1–23.

Fraenkel, P. (2006). Engaging families as experts: Collaborative family progam development. Family Process, 45(2), 237–257.

Frame, M. (2001). The spiritual genogram in training and supervision. Family Journal: Counseling and Therapy for Couples and Families, 8(1), 72–74.

Franco, N., & Levitt, M. (1998). The social ecology of middle childhood: Family support, friendship quality, and self-esteem. Family Relations, 47, 315–321.

Frankel, H., & Frankel, S. (2006). Family therapy, family practice and child and family poverty: Historical perspectives. Journal of Family Social Work, 10(4), 43–80.

Franklin, C., & Corcoran, K. (2006). Clinical Assessment for Social Workers: Quantitative and Qualitative Methods. 2nd Editon. Chicago: Lyceum Books. p. 71.

Franklin, C., & Corcoran, K. (2011). Quantitative clinical assessment methods. In C. Franklin & C. Jordan (Eds.), Clinical assessment for social workers: Quantitative and qualitative methods (3rd ed.) (pp. 71–94). Chicago: Lyceum.

Franklin, C., & Jordan, C. (1992). Teaching students to perform assessments. Journal of Social Work Education, 28(2), 222–243.

Franklin, C., & Jordan, C. (1999). Family practice: Brief systems methods for social work. Belmont, CA: Brooks/Cole.

Fraser, M. (1997). Risk and resilience in childhood: An ecological perspective. Washington: NASW Press.

Fraser, M., Richman, J., & Galinsky, M. (1999). Risk, protection, and resilience: Toward a conceptual framework for social work practice. Social Work Research, 23(3), 131–143.

Fraser, M., Pecora, P., & Haapala, D. (1991). Families in crisis. Hawthorne, NY: Aldine de Gruyter.

Freedman, J., & Combs, (1996). Narrative therapy: The preferred construction of preferred realities. W.W. Norton

Fulmer, R. (1999). Becoming an adult: Leaving home and staying connected. In B. Carter & M. McGoldrick (Eds.), The expanded family life cycle: Individual, family, and social perspectives (3rd ed.) (pp. 215–230). Needham Heights, MA: Allyn & Bacon.

Fulmer, R. (2005). Becoming an adult: Leaving home and staying connected. In B. Carter & M. McGoldrick (Eds.), The expanded family life cycle: Individual, family, and social perspectives (3rd ed.) (pp. 215–230). Boston, MA: Allyn & Bacon.

Furstenberg, E. (1980). Reflections on marriage. Journal of Family Issues, 1, 443–453.

Gabor, P., & Collins, D. (1985–86). Family work in child care. Journal of Child Care, 2(5), 15–27.

Gabor, P., & Grinnell, R. (1995). Evaluation and quality improvement. Boston, MA: Allyn & Bacon.

Gallagher, S. Contemporary Evangelicals, Families & Gender. http://hirr.hartsem.edu/research/evangelicalroles. (Downloaded June 2, 2008).

Gambrill, E. (1983). Casework: A competency-based approach. Englewood Cliffs, NJ: Prentice-Hall.

Gambrill, E. (2006). Social work practice: A critical thinker's guide (2nd ed.). New York: Oxford.

Gambrill, E., & Richey, C. (1988). Taking charge of your social life. Belmont, CA: Behavioral Options.

Garbarino, J. (1992). Children and families in their social environment (2nd ed.). New York: Aldine de Gruyter.

Garbarino, J., & Gilliam, G. (1987). Understanding abusive families. Lexington, MA: D.C. Heath and Company.

Garcia-Preto, N. (2005). Transformation of the family system during adolescence. In Carter, B. & McGoldrick, M. (Eds), *The expanded family life cycle: Individual, family, and social perspectives* (3rd ed.) (pp. 274–286). Boston, MA: Allyn & Bacon.

Garcia-Preto, N. (2005a). Puerto Rican families. In M. McGoldrick, J. Giordano, & N. Garcia-Petro (Eds.), *Ethnicity and family therapy* (3rd ed.) (pp. 242–256). New York: Guilford Press.

Garcia-Preto, N. (2005b). Latino families: An overview. In M. McGoldrick, J. Giordano, & N. Garcia-Petro (Eds.), *Ethnicity and family therapy* (3rd ed.) (pp. 153–165). New York: Guilford Press.

Gardner, D., Huber, C., Steiner, R., Vazquez, L., & Savage, T. (2008). The development and validation of the inventory of family protective factors: A brief assessment for family counseling. *The Family Journal, 16*(2), 107–117.

Gattai, F., & Musatti, T. (1999). Grandmothers' involvement in grandchildren's care: Attitudes, feelings, and emotions. *Family Relations, 48,* 35–42.

Gavin, K., & Bramble, B. (1996). *Family communication: Cohesion and change.* New York: Harper Collins.

Geismar, L. (1978). Family disorganization: A sociological perspective. *Social Casework, 69,* 545–550.

Geismar, L., & Ayres, B. (1959). A method for evaluating the social functioning of families under treatment. *Social Work, 4*(1), 102–108.

Geismar, L., & Krisberg, J. (1956). The Family Life Improvement Project: An experiment in preventive intervention. *Social Casework, 47,* 563–570.

Gelles, R. (1987). Family violence. Newbury Park, CA: Sage Publications.

Gelles, R. (1989). Child abuse and violence in single-parent families: Parent absence and economic deprivation. *American Journal of Ortho-psychiatry, 59*(4), 492–503.

Gelles, R., & Straus, M. (1988). *Intimate violence: The causes and consequences of abuse in the American family.* New York: Simon & Schuster.

George, L. (1997). Why the need for the Indian Child Welfare Act? *Journal of Multicultural Social Work, 5*(3/4), 65–175.

Germain, C. B., & Gitterman, A. (1996). *The Life Model of Social Work Practice* (2nd ed.). New York: Columbia University Press.

Gibbs, L., and Gambrill, E. (1996). Critical thinking for social workers: A workbook. Thousand Oaks, CA: Pine Forge Press.

Gilbert, D. (2011). Multicultural Assessment. In Jordan, C. & Franklin, C. (2011), *Clinical Assessment for Social Workers: Quantitative and Qualitative Methods.* 3rd edition. Chicago: Lyceum Books. p. 361.

Giles-Sims, J. (1983). Wife-beating: A systems theory approach. New York: Guilford Press.

Gilligan, R. (2004). Promoting resilience in child and family social work: Issues for social work practice, education, and policy. *Social Work Education, 23*(1), 93–104.

Gilliland, B., & James, R. (1993). *Crisis intervention strategies.* Pacific Grove, CA: Brooks/Cole.

Gillis, J. (1996). A world of their own making: Myth, ritual, and the quest for family values. New York: Basic Books.

Giordano, J., & McGoldrick, M. (2005). Families of European origin. In M. McGoldrick, J. Giordano, & N. Garcia-Petro (Eds.), *Ethnicity and family therapy* (3rd ed.) (pp. 501–519). New York: Guilford Press.

Giordano, J., McGoldrick, M., & Guarino Klages, J. (2005). Italian families. In M. McGoldrick, J. Giordano, & N. Garcia-Petro (Eds.), *Ethnicity and family therapy* (3rd ed.) (pp. 616–628). New York: Guilford Press.

Giovanonni, J. (1982). Mistreated children. In S. Yelaja (Ed.), *Ethical issues in social work.* Springfield, IL: Charles C. Thomas.

Gladding, S. & Cox, E. (2008). Family snapshots: A descriptive classroom exercise in memory and insight. *The Family Journal, 16*(4), 381–383.

Glade, A., Bean, R., & Vira, R. (2005). A prime time for marital/relational intervention: A review of the transition to parenthood literature with treatment recommendations. *The American Journal of Family Therapy, 33,* 319–336.

Gladow, N., & Ray, M. (1986). The impact of informal support systems on the well-being of low-income single-parent families. *Family Relations, 35,* 57–62.

Gold, J., & Hartnett, L. (2003). Confronting the hierarchy of a child-focused family: Implications for family counselors. *Family Journal: Counseling and Therapy for Couples and Families, 12*(3), 271–274.

Gold, J., & Morris, G. (2003). Family resistance to counseling: The initial agenda for intergenerational and narrative approaches. *Family Journal: Counseling and Therapy for Couples and Families, 11*(4), 374–379.

Gold, L. (2003). A critical analysis of fusion in lesbian relationships. *Canadian Social Work Review, 20*(2), 259–271.

Golden, L. (1999). Therapeutic stories with an ethnic flavor. *Family Journal: Counseling and Therapy for Couples and Families, 7*(4), 406–407.

Goldenberg, H., & Goldenberg, I. (1994). *Counseling today's families.* Pacific Grove, CA: Brooks/Cole.

Goldenberg, I., & Goldenberg, H. (1996). *Family therapy: An overview* (4th ed.). Pacific Grove, CA: Brooks/Cole.

Goldenberg, I., & Goldenberg, H. (2000). *Family therapy: An overview* (5th ed.). Belmont, CA: Brooks/Cole.

Goleman, D. (1998). *Working with emotional intelligence.* New York: Bantam Books.

Goldner, V. (1985a). Feminism and family therapy. *Family Process, 24*(1), 31–47.

Goldner, V. (1985b). Warning: Family therapy may be hazardous to your health. *The Family Therapy Networker, 9*(6), 18–23.

Goldner, V. (1988). Generation and hierarchy: Normative and covert hierarchies. *Family Process, 27*(1), 17–31.

Goldstein, H. (1981). Home-based services and the worker. In M. Bryce & J. Lloyd (Eds.), *Treating families in the home: An alternative to placement*. Springfield, IL: Charles C. Thomas.

Good, G., Gilbert, L., & Scher, M. (1990). Gender-aware therapy: A synthesis of feminist therapy and knowledge about gender. *Journal of Counseling and Development, 68*, 227–234.

Goodrich, T., Rampage, C., Ellman, B., & Halstead, K. (1988). *Feminist family therapy: A casebook*. New York: W. W. Norton & Company.

Gordon, L. (1985). Child abuse, gender, and the myth of family independence: A historical critique. *Child Welfare, 64*(3), 213–224.

Gordon, S., & Davidson, N. (1981). Behavioral parent training. In A. Gurman & D. Kniskern (Eds.), *Handbook of family therapy* (pp. 517–553). New York: Brunner/Mazel.

Gottman, J. (1999). *The marriage clinic*. New York: W. W. Norton & Company.

Gottman, J., & Levenson, R. (2002). A two-factor model for predicting when a couple will divorce: Exploratory analyses using 14-year longitudinal data. *Family Process, 41*(1), 83–96.

Granvold, D., & Jordan, C., (1994). The cognitive-behavioral treatment of marital distress. In D. Granvold (Ed.), *Cognitive and behavioral treatment: Methods and applications* (pp. 174–201). Pacific Grove, CA: Brooks/Cole.

Graybeal, C. (2007). The evidence for the art in social work. *Families in Society, 88*(4), 513–523.

Greeff, A. & Du Toit, C. (2009). Resilience in remarried families. *The American Journal of Family Therapy, 37*, 114–126.

Greeff, A., Vansteenwegen, A., & Ide, M. (2006). Resiliency in families with a member with a psychological disorder. *The American Journal of Family Therapy, 34*, 285–300.

Greeff, A., & Human, B. (2004). Resilience in families in which a parent has died. *The American Journal of Family Therapy, 32*, 27–42.

Green, B., McAllister, C., & Tarte, J. (2004). The strengths-based practices inventory: A tool for measuring strengths-based service delivery in early childhood and family support programs. *Families in Society, 85*(3), 326–335.

Green, R., & Hergret, M. (1991). Outcomes of systemic/strategic team consultation: III. The importance of therapist warmth and active structuring. *Family Process, 30*, 321–336.

Greeno, C. (2003). Measurement, or how do we know what we know? Topic one: Validity. *Family Process, 42*(3), 433–434.

Griffith, M. (1999). Opening therapy to conversations with a personal God. In F. Walsh (Ed.), *Spiritual resources in family therapy* (pp. 209–222). New York: Guilford Press.

Grinnell, R., & Unrau, Y. (Eds). (2005). *Social work research and evaluation: Quantitative and qualitative approaches* (7th ed.). New York: Oxford.

Grinnell, R., Williams, M., & Unrau, Y. (2009). *Research methods for BSW students*. Kalamazoo, MI: Pair Bond Publications.

Grold, K. (2000). The openness to therapy assessment. *Family Journal: Counseling and Therapy for Couples and Families, 8*(1), 85–90.

Gross, E. (1995). Deconstructing politically correct practice literature: The American Indian case. *Social Work, 40*(2), 206–213.

Gross, G. (1998). *Gatekeeping for cultural competence: Ready or not? Some post and modernist doubts*. Paper presented at the 16th Annual BPD Conference, Albuquerque, New Mexico.

Grunwald, B., & McAbee, H. (1985). *Guiding the family: Practical counseling techniques*. Muncie, IN: Accelerated Development.

Guillermo, B. (2006). Intervention development and cultural adaptation research with diverse families. *Family Process, 45*(2), 143–151.

Gurman, A. S., & Kniskern, D. P. (1981). Family therapy outcome research: Knowns and unknowns. In A. S. Gurman & D. P. Kniskern (Eds.), *Handbook of family therapy* (pp. 742–776). New York: Brunner/Mazel.

Haboush, K. (2005). Lebanese and Syrian families. In M. McGoldrick, J. Giordano, & N. Garcia-Petro (Eds.), *Ethnicity and family therapy* (3rd ed.) (pp. 468–486). New York: Guilford Press.

Hackney, H., & Cormier, L. (1996). *The professional counselor: A process guide to helping* (3rd ed.). Toronto: Allyn & Bacon.

Hahn, R., & Kleist, D. (2000). Divorce mediation: Research and implications for family and couples counseling. *Family Journal: Counseling and Therapy for Couples and Families, 8*(2), 165–171.

Haley, J. (1971). Approaches to family therapy. In J. Haley (Ed.), *Changing families: A family therapy reader* (pp. 227–236). New York: Grune & Straton.

Haley, J. (1976). *Problem-solving therapy*. San Francisco: Jossey-Bass.

Halford, K., Nicholson, J., & Sanders, M. (2007). Couple communication in stepfamilies. *Family Process, 46*(4), 471–483.

Hanson, S. (1986). Healthy single-parent families. *Family Relations, 35*, 125–132.

Harper, K., & Lantz, J. (1996). *Cross-cultural practice in social work with diverse populations*. Chicago: Lyceum.

Harris, S., & Dersch, C. (2001). "I'm just not like that": Investigating the intergenerational cycle of violence. *Family Journal: Counseling and*

Therapy for Couples and Families, 9(3), 250–258.

Hartman, A., & Laird, J. (1983). *Family-centered social work practice.* New York: Free Press.

Haug, I. (1998). Spirituality as a dimension of family therapists' clinical training. *Contemporary Family Therapy, 20*(4), 471–483.

Helton, L., & Jackson, M. (1997). *Social work practice with families: A diversity model.* Boston: Allyn & Bacon.

Henry, R., & Miller, R. (2004). Marital problems occurring in midlife: Implications for couples therapists. *The American Journal of Family Therapy, 32,* 405–417.

Hepworth, D., & Larsen, J. (1993). *Direct social work practice.* Chicago: Dorsey Press.

Hernandez, M., & McGoldrick, M. (1999). Migration and the life cycle. In B. Carter & M. McGoldrick (Eds.), *The expanded family life cycle: Individual, family, and social perspectives* (3rd ed.) (pp. 169–184). Needham Heights, MA: Allyn & Bacon.

Hernandez, M. (2005). Central American families. In M. McGoldrick, J. Giordano, & N. Garcia-Petro (Eds.), *Ethnicity and family therapy* (3rd ed.) (pp. 178–191). New York: Guilford Press.

Hernandez, M., & McGoldrick, M. (2005). Migration and the family life cycle. In B. Carter & M. McGoldrick (Eds.), *The expanded family life cycle: Individual, family, and social perspectives* (3rd ed.) (pp. 169–184). Boston, MA: Allyn & Bacon.

Hernandez, P. (2002). Resilience in families and communities: Latin American contributions from the psychology of liberation. *Family Journal: Counseling and Therapy for Couples and Families, 10*(3), 334–343.

Herndon, M., & Moore, J. (2003). African American factors for student success: Implications for families and counselors. *Family Journal: Counseling and Therapy for Couples and Families, 10*(3), 322–327.

Hetherington, E., Cox, M., & Cox, R. (1978). Play and social interaction in children following divorce. *Journal of Social Issues, 35,* 26–49.

Hill, J., Fonagy, P., Safier, E., & Sargent, J. (2003). The ecology of attachment in the family. *Family Process, 42*(2), 205–221.

Hines, P., Preto, N., McGoldrick, M., et al. (1999). Culture and the family life cycle. In B. Carter & M. McGoldrick (Eds.), *The expanded family life cycle: Individual, family, and social perspectives* (3rd ed.) (pp. 69–87). Needham Heights, MA: Allyn & Bacon.

Hinton, M. (2003). *A qualitative study of resiliency in women with a history of childhood sexual abuse.* (Unpublished master's thesis). University of Calgary, Calgary, Alberta, Canada.

Ho, M. K. (1987). *Family therapy with ethnic minorities.* Newbury Park, CA: Sage Publications.

Holman, A. (1983). *Family assessment: Tools for understanding and intervention.* Newbury Park, CA: Sage.

Hovestadt, A. J., Anderson, W. T., Piercy, F. P., Cochran, A. W., & Fine, M. (1985). A family of origin scale. *Journal of Marital and Family Therapy, 11,* 287–297.

Horejsi, C., Heavy Runner Craig, B., & Pablo, J. (1992). Reactions by Native American parents to child protection agencies: Cultural and community factors. *Child Welfare, LXXX*(4), 329–342.

Hudak, J., Krestan, J., & Bepko, C. (1999). Alcohol problems and the family life cycle. In B. Carter and M. McGoldrick (Eds.), *The expanded family life cycle: Individual, family, and social perspectives* (3rd ed.) (pp. 455–469). Needham Heights, MA: Allyn & Bacon.

Hudson, W. (1982). *The clinical measurement package: A field manual.* Homewood, IL: Dorsey Press.

Hudson, W. (1985). Indexes and scales. In R. Grinnell (Ed.), *Social work research and evaluation* (pp. 185–205). Itasca, IL: F. E. Peacock.

Hughes, J., & Stone, W. (2003). Family and community life. *Family Matters, 65,* 40–47.

Hunter College Women's Studies Collective. (1995). *Women's realities, women's choices: An introduction to women's studies* (2nd ed.). New York: Oxford University Press.

International Association of Psychosocial Rehabilitation Services. (IAPRS). (1997). PSR standards and indicators for multicultural psychiatric rehabilitation services. *PSR Connection, 4,* 7.

Isaacs, C. (1982). Treatment of child abuse: A review of the behavioral interventions. *Journal of Applied Behavior Analysis, 15,* 273–294.

Ivanoff, A., Blythe, B., & Tripodi, T. (1994). *Involuntary clients in social work practice.* New York: Aldine de Gruyter.

Jackson, D. (1972). Family rules: Marital quid pro quo. In G. Erickson & T. Hogan (Eds.), *Family therapy: An introduction to theory and technique* (pp. 76–85). Monterey, CA: Brooks/Cole.

Janson, G., & Steigerwald, F. (2002). Family counseling and ethical challenges with gay, lesbian, bisexual, and transgendered (GLBT) clients: More questions than answers. *Family Journal: Counseling and Therapy for Couples and Families, 10*(4), 415–418.

Janzen, C., Harris, O., Jordan, C., & Franklin, C. (2006). *Family treatment: Evidence-based practice with populations at risk.* Belmont, CA: Brooks/Cole.

Jaques, J. (2000). Surviving suicide: The impact on the family. *Family Journal: Counseling and Therapy for Couples and Families, 8*(4), 376–379.

Jencius, M., & Duba, J. (2002). Creating a multicultural family practice. *Family Journal:*

Counseling and Therapy for Couples and Families, 10(4), 410–414.

Jencius, M., & Duba, J. (2003a). Searching for the ideal parents: An interview with Al Pesso and Diane Boyden. *Family Journal: Counseling and Therapy for Couples and Families, 11*(1), 89–97.

Jencius, M., & Duba, J. (2003b). The marriage of research and practice: An interview with John Gottman. *The Family Journal: Counseling and Therapy for Couples and Families, 11*(2), 216–223.

Joe, J., & Malach, R. (1998). Families with Native American roots. In E. W. Lynch and M. J. Hanson (Eds.), *Developing cross-cultural competence: A guide for working with children and families* (2nd ed.). Baltimore: Paul H. Brookes.

Johnson, D., & Johnson, F. (2006). *Joining together* (9th ed.). Boston: Allyn & Bacon.

Johnson, H. (1986). Emerging concerns in family therapy. *Social Work, 31*(4), 299–306.

Johnson, J. (1990-91). Preventive interventions for children at risk: Introduction. *The International Journal of the Addictions, 25*(4A), 429–434.

Johnson, L., Ketring, S., Rohacs, J., & Brewer, A. (2006). Attachment and the therapeutic alliance in family therapy. *The American Journal of Family Therapy, 34*, 205–218.

Johnson, T., & Colucci, P. (1999). Lesbians, gay men, and the family life cycle. In B. Carter and M. McGoldrick (Eds.). *The expanded family life cycle: Individual, family, and social perspectives* (3rd ed.) (pp. 346–361). Needham Heights, MA: Allyn & Bacon.

Jones, A. (2003). Reconstructing the stepfamily: Old myths, new stories. *Social Work, 48*(2), 228–236.

Jongsma, A., & Datilio, F. (2000). *The family therapy treatment planner*. New York: Wiley.

Jordan, C. (2008). Assessment. In *Encyclopedia of Social Work* (20th ed.). (Vol. *1*, pp. 1232). Washington, DC: NASW Press.

Jordan, C., & Cobb, N. (2001). Competency-based treatment for persons with marital discord. In K. Corcoran (Ed.), *Structuring change* (2nd ed.). Chicago: Lyceum Books.

Jordan, C., & Cory, D. (2010). Boomers, boomerangs, and bedpans. *National Social Science Journal, 34*(1), 79–84.

Jordan, C., & Franklin, C. (1995). *Clinical assessment for social workers: Quantitative and qualitative methods*. Chicago: Lyceum.

Jordan, C., & Franklin, C. (2002). Treatment planning with families: An evidence-based approach. In A. Roberts & G. Greene (Eds.), *The Social Workers' Desk Reference*. New York: Oxford.

Jordan, C., & Franklin, C. (2003). *Clinical assessment for social workers: Quantitative and qualitative methods* (2nd ed.). Chicago: Lyceum.

Jordan, C., & Franklin, C. (2009). Treatment planning with families: An evidence-based approach. In A. Roberts & G. Greene (Eds.), The Social Workers' Desk Reference. 2nd edition. New York: Oxford. pages 429–432.

Jordan, C., & Franklin, C. (2011). *Clinical assessment for social workers: Quantitative and qualitative methods,* 3rd edition. Lyceum Books.

Jordan, C., Franklin, C., & Corcoran, K. (2005). Measuring instruments. In R. Grinnel & Y. Unrau (Eds.), *Social work research and evaluation: Quantitative and qualitative approaches* (7th ed.) (pp. 114–131). New York: Oxford.

Jordan, C., Franklin, C., & Corcoran, K. (2010). Standardized measuring instruments. In Grinnell, R. and Unrau, Y. (Eds.), *Social work research and evaluation. 9th Edition* (pp. 196–218). New York: Oxford University Press.

Jordan, C., Lewellen, A., & Vandiver, V. (1994). A social work perspective of psychosocial rehabilitation: Psychoeducational models for minority families. *International Journal of Mental Health, 23*(4), 27–43.

Jordan, C., Russe, F., & Cory, D. (2011, June). *Keeping seniors connected with their baby boomer children and others*. Paper presented at the International Conferences on Caregiving, Disability, Aging and Technology–FICC-DAT, 2011, June 5–8.

Juhnke, G., & Shoffner, M. (1999). The family debriefing model: An adapted critical incident stress debriefing for parents and older sibling suicide survivors. *Family Journal: Counseling and Therapy for Couples and Families, 7*(4), 342–348.

Kadushin, A. (1992). *The social work interview*. New York: Columbia University Press.

Kadushin, A. & Kadushin, G. (1997). The social work interview, 4th ed. New York: Columbia University Press.

Kadzin, A. (2004). Psychotherapy for children and adolescents. In M. Lambert (Ed.), *Handbook of psychotherapy and behavior change* (pp. 543–589). New York: John Wiley & Sons.

Kamya, H. (2005). African immigrant families. In M. McGoldrick, J. Giordano, & N. Garcia-Petro (Eds.), *Ethnicity and family therapy* (3rd ed.) (pp. 101–116). New York: Guilford Press.

Kaplan, D., & VanDuser, M. (1999). Evolution and stepfamilies: An interview with Dr. Stephen Emlen. *Family Journal: Counseling and Therapy for Couples and Families, 7*(4), 408–413.

Kaplan, L. (1986). *Working with the multiproblem family*. Lexington, MA: Lexington Books.

Kaplan, L. & Girard, J. (1994). Strengthening High-Risk Families: A Handbook for Practitioners. New York: Lexington Books.

Kaslow, N., & Celano, M. (1995). The family therapies. In A. Gurman & S. Messer (Eds.),

Essential psychotherapies: Theory and practice (pp. 343–402). New York: Guilford Press.

Keefe, S. E. & Casas, M. J. (1980). Mexican Americans and mental health: A selected review and recommendations for mental health service delivery. *American Journal of Community Psychology, 303,* 319–320.

Kerlinger, F. (1979). *Behavioral research.* Toronto: Holt, Rinehart & Winston.

Killian, K. (2002). Dominant and marginalized discourses in interracial couples' narratives: Implications for family therapists. *Family Process, 41*(4), 603–618.

Killian, K., & Agathangelou, A. (2005). Greek families. In M. McGoldrick, J. Giordano, & N. Garcia-Petro (Eds.), *Ethnicity and family therapy* (3rd ed.) (pp. 573–585). New York: Guilford Press.

Kliman, J., & Madsen, W. (1999). Social class and the family life cycle. In B. Carter & M. McGoldrick (Eds.), *The expanded family life cycle: Individual, family, and social perspectives* (3rd ed.) (pp. 88–105). Needham Heights, MA: Allyn & Bacon.

Kliman, J., & Madsen, W. (2005). Social class and the family life cycle. In B. Carter & M. McGoldrick (Eds.), *The expanded family life cycle: Individual, family, and social perspectives* (3rd ed.) (pp. 88–105). Boston, MA: Allyn & Bacon.

Kilpatrick, A., & Holland, T. (1995). *Working with families: An integrative model by level of functioning.* Boston: Allyn & Bacon.

Kilpatrick, A., & Holland, T. (1999). *Working with families: An integrative model by level of functioning.* Boston: Allyn & Bacon.

Kim, J. (2003). Structural family therapy and its implications for the Asian American family. *The Family Journal: Counseling and Therapy for Couples and Families, 11*(4), 388–392.

Kim, B-L., & Ryu, E. (2005). Korean families. In M. McGoldrick, J. Giordano, & N. Garcia-Petro (Eds.), *Ethnicity and family therapy* (3rd ed.) (pp. 349–362). New York: Guilford Press.

Kinney, J., Haapala, D., & Booth, C. (1991). *Keeping families together: The Homebuilders Model.* Hawthorne, NY: Aldine de Gruyter.

Kindsvatter, A., Duba, J., & Dean, E. (2008). Structural techniques for engaging reluctant parents in counseling. *The Family Journal, 16,* 204–211.

Klein, N., Alexander, J., & Parsons, B. (1977). Impact of family systems intervention on recidivism and sibling delinquency: A model of primary prevention and program evaluation. *Journal of Consulting and Clinical Psychology, 45*(3), 469–474.

Kleist, D. (1999). Single-parent families: A difference that makes a difference? *The Family Journal: Counseling and Therapy for Couples and Families, 7*(4), 236–244.

Klever, P. (2004). The multigenerational transmission of nuclear family processes and symptoms. *The American Journal of Family Therapy, 32,* 337–351.

Kohlert, N., & Pecora, P. (1991). Therapist perceptions of organizational support and job satisfaction. In M. Fraser, P. Pecora, & D. Haapala (Eds.), *Families in crisis* (pp. 109–129). New York: Aldine de Gruyter.

Koivunen, J., Rothaupt, J. & Wolfgram, S. (2009). Gender Dynamics and Role Adjustment During the Transition to Parenthood: Current Perspectives. *The Family Journal October 2009, 17*(4), 323–328.

Kozlowska, K., & Hanney, L. (2002). The network perspective: An integration of attachment and family systems theories. *Family Process, 41*(2), 285–312.

Kramer, L., & Radley, C. (1997). Improving sibling relationships among young children: A social skills training model. *Family Relations, 46*(3), 237–246.

Kretchmar, M., & Jacobvitz, D. (2002). Observing mother-child relationships across generations: Boundary patterns, attachment, and the transmission of caregiving. *Family Process, 41*(3), 351–374.

Kusnir, D. (2005). Salvadoran families. In M. McGoldrick, J. Giordano, & N. Garcia-Petro (Eds.), *Ethnicity and family therapy* (3rd ed.) (pp. 256–268). New York: Guilford Press.

L'Abate, L. (2009). The drama triangle: An attempt to resurrect a neglected pathogenic model in family therapy theory and practice. *The American Journal of Family Therapy, 37,* 1–11.

Lambert, M. (Ed.). (2004). *Bergin and Garfield's handbook of psychotherapy and behavior change* (5th ed.). New York: Wiley.

Lambert, M., & Bergin, A. (1994). The effectiveness of psychotherapy. In A. Bergin & S. Garfield (Eds.), *Handbook of psychotherapy and behavior change* (4th ed.) (pp. 143–189). Toronto: Wiley.

Lambert, M., & Ogles, B. (2004). The efficacy and effectiveness of psychotherapy. In M. Lambert (Ed.), *Handbook of psychotherapy and behavior change* (pp. 139–193). New York: John Wiley & Sons.

Lambert, S. (2005). Gay and lesbian families: What we know and where to go from here. *Family Journal: Counseling and Therapy for Couples and Families, 13*(1), 43–51.

Langelier, R., & Langelier, P. (2005). French Canadian families. In M. McGoldrick, J. Giordano, & N. Garcia-Petro (Eds.), *Ethnicity and family therapy* (3rd ed.) (pp. 545–554). New York: Guilford Press.

Langsley, D., Pittman, F., Machotka, P., & Flomenhaft, K. (1968). Family crisis therapy: Results and implications. *Family Process, 7*(2), 145–158.

Laszloffy, T. (2002). Rethinking family development theory: Teaching with the systemic family development (SFD) model. *Family Relations, 51*(3), 206–214.

Laszloffy, T., & Hardy, K. (2000). Uncommon strategies for a common problem: Addressing racism in family therapy. *Family Process, 39*(1), 35–50.

Lawson, D., & Brossart, D. (2004). The developmental course of personal authority in the family system. *Family Process, 43*(3), 391–409.

Lawson, G., & Foster, V. (2005). Developmental characteristics of home-based counselors: A key to serving at-risk families. *Family Journal: Counseling and Therapy for Couples and Families, 13*(2), 153–161.

Ledbetter Hancock, B., & Pelton, L. (1989). Home visits: History and functions. *Social Casework, 70*(1), 21.

Lee, E., & Mock, M. (2005a). Asian families: An overview. In M. McGoldrick, J. Giordano, & N. Garcia-Petro (Eds.), *Ethnicity and family therapy* (3rd ed.) (pp. 269–289). New York: Guilford Press.

Lee, E., & Mock, M. (2005b). Chinese families. In M. McGoldrick, J. Giordano, & N. Garcia-Petro (Eds.), *Ethnicity and family therapy* (3rd ed.) (pp. 302–318). New York: Guilford Press.

LeMasters, E. (1957). Parenthood as crisis. *Marriage and Family Living, 19*, 325–355.

Lero, D., Ashbourne, L., & Whitehead, D. (2006). *Father involvement research alliance.* Guelph, ON: University of Guelph.

Lewandowski, C., & Pierce, L. (2004). Does family-centered out-of-home care work? Comparison of a family-centered approach and traditional care. *Social Work Research, 28*(3), 143–151.

Lewellen, A., & Jordon, C. (1994). *Family empowerment and service satisfaction: An exploratory study of families who care for a mentally ill member.* (Unpublished manuscript). The University of Texas, Arlington.

Lewin, K. (2007). In M. Nichols & R. Schwartz (Eds.), *Family therapy: Concepts and methods.* Boston: Allyn & Bacon.

Lewis, J. (1988). The transition to parenthood: 1. The rating of prenatal marital competence. *Family Process, 27*(2), 149–166.

Lewis, R. (1991). What are the characteristics of Intensive Family Preservation Services? In M. Fraser, P. Pecora, & D. Haapala (Eds.), *Families in crisis* (pp. 93–108). Hawthorne, NY: Aldine de Gruyter.

Littell, J., & Girvin, H. (2004). Ready or not: Uses of Change Model in child welfare. *Child Welfare, 83*(4), 341–366.

Lum, D. (1996). *Social work practice and people of color: A process-stage approach.* Pacific Grove, CA: Brooks/Cole.

Mackie, M. (1991). *Gender relations in Canada.* Toronto: Harcourt.

Magnuson, S. (2000). The professional genogram: Enhancing professional identity and clarity. *Family Journal: Counseling and Therapy for Couples and Families, 8*(4), 399–401.

Magnuson, S., & Shaw, H. (2003). Adaptations of the multifaceted genogram in counseling, training, and supervision. *Family Journal: Counseling and Therapy for Couples and Families, 11*(1), 45–54.

Magura, S., & Moses, B. (1986). *Outcome measures for child welfare services: Theory and applications.* Washington, DC: Child Welfare League of America.

Main, F., Boughner, S., Mims, G., & Logan Schieffer, J. (2001). Rolling the dice: An experiential exercise for enhancing intervention questioning skill. *Family Journal: Counseling and Therapy for Couples and Families, 9*(4), 450–454.

Maisto, S., Galizio, M., & Connors, G. (1995). *Drug use and abuse.* Toronto: Harcourt.

Maluccio, A., & Marlow, W. (1975). The case for the contract. In B. Compton and B. Galaway (Eds.), *Social work processes.* Homewood, IL: Dorsey.

Mannes, M. (1993). Seeking the balance between child protection and family preservation in Indian child welfare. *Child Welfare, 72*, 141–152.

Mannis, V. (1999). Single mothers by choice. *Family Relations, 48*(2), 121–128.

Marks, L. (2004). Sacred practices in highly religious families: Christian, Jewish, Mormon, and Muslim perspectives. *Family Process, 43*(2), 217–231.

Marsh, D. (1999). Serious mental illness: Opportunities for family practitioners. *Family Journal: Counseling and Therapy for Couples and Families, 7*(4), 358–366.

Marsh, J. (2003). Arguments for family strengths research. *Social Work, 48*, 147–149.

Marshall, T., & Solomon, P. (2004). Provider contact with families of adults with severe mental illness: Taking a closer look. *Family Process, 43*(2), 209–216.

Maslow, A. (1968). *Toward a psychology of being.* New York: Van Nostrand Reinhold.

Mason, M. (2005). Theoretical considerations of "resistant families." *Family Journal: Counseling and Therapy for Couples and Families, 13*(1), 59–62.

Masse, J., & McNeil, C., & Masse, J. (2008). In-home parent-child interaction therapy: Clinical considerations. *Child and Family Behavior Therapy, 30*(2), 127–135.

Masson, J. (1994). *Against therapy.* Munroe, ME: Common Courage Press.

May, K. (2001). Theory: Does it matter? *Family Journal: Counseling and Therapy for Couples and Families, 9*(1), 37–38.

May, K. (2003). Family therapy theory: What is important in the training of today's family counselors? *Family Journal: Counseling* and Therapy for Couples and Families, 11(1), 42–44.

May, K. (2004). How do we teach family therapy theory? Family Journal: Counseling and Therapy for Couples and Families, 12(3), 275–277.

May, K., & Church, N. (1999). Families and communities: Building bridges. Family Journal: Counseling and Therapy for Couples and Families, 7(1), 51–53.

McAdams-Mahmoud, V. (2005). African-American Muslim families. In M. McGoldrick, J. Giordano, & N. Garcia-Petro (Eds.), Ethnicity and family therapy (3rd ed.) (pp. 138–152). New York: Guilford Press.

McClurg, L. (2004). Biracial youth and their parents: Counseling considerations for family therapists. Family Journal: Counseling and Therapy for Couples and Families, 12(2), 170–173.

McConnell Heywood, E. (1999). Custodial grandparents and their grandchildren. Family Journal: Counseling and Therapy for Couples and Families, 7(4), 367–372.

McCormick, R. (1996). Culturally appropriate means and ends of counselling as described by the First Nations people of British Columbia. International Journal for the Advancement of Counselling, 18(3), 163–172.

McCubbin, H., & McCubbin, M. (1988). Typologies of resilient families: Emerging roles of social class and ethnicity. Family Relations, 37, 247–254.

McGill, D., & Pearce, J. (2005). American families with English Ancestors from the Colonial Era: Anglo Americans. In M. McGoldrick, J. Giordano, & N. Garcia-Petro (Eds.), Ethnicity and family therapy (3rd ed.) (pp. 520–534). New York: Guilford Press.

McGoldrick, M. (1999a). History, genograms, and the family life cycle. In B. Carter & M. McGoldrick (Eds.), The expanded family life cycle: Individual, family, and social perspectives (3rd ed.) (pp. 141–152). Needham Heights, MA: Allyn & Bacon.

McGoldrick, M. (1999b). Women throughout the family life cycle. In B. Carter & M. McGoldrick (Eds.), The expanded family life cycle: Individual, family, and social perspectives (3rd ed.) (pp. 106–123). Needham Heights, MA: Allyn & Bacon.

McGoldrick, M. (1999c). Becoming a couple. In B. Carter & M. McGoldrick (Eds.), The expanded family life cycle: Individual, family, and social perspectives (3rd ed.) (pp. 231–248). Needham Heights, MA: Allyn & Bacon.

McGoldrick, M. (2002). Re-visioning family therapy: Race, culture, and gender in clinical practice. New York: Guilford.

McGoldrick, M. (2005a). Becoming a couple. In B. Carter & M. McGoldrick (Eds.), The expanded family life cycle: Individual, family, and social perspectives (3rd ed.) (pp. 231–248). Boston, MA: Allyn & Bacon.

McGoldrick, M. (2005b). History, genograms, and the family life cycle: Freud in context. In B. Carter & M. McGoldrick (Eds.), The expanded family life cycle: Individual, family, and social perspectives (3rd ed.), (pp. 47–68). Boston, MA: Allyn & Bacon.

McGoldrick, M. (2005c). Irish families. In M. McGoldrick, J. Giordano, & N. Garcia-Petro (Eds.), Ethnicity and family therapy (3rd ed.) (pp. 595–615). New York: Guilford Press.

McGoldrick, M. (2005d). Women through the family life cycle. In B. Carter & M. McGoldrick (Eds.), The expanded family life cycle: Individual, family, and social perspectives (3rd ed.) pp. 106–123. Boston, MA: Allyn & Bacon.

McGoldrick, M., & Carter, B. (1999). Remarried families. In B. Carter and M. McGoldrick (Eds.), The expanded family life cycle: Individual, family, and social perspectives (3rd ed.) (pp. 417–435). Needham Heights, MA: Allyn & Bacon.

McGoldrick, M., & Carter, B. (2005a). Re-married families. In B. Carter & M. McGoldrick (Eds.), The expanded family life cycle: Individual, family, and social perspectives (3rd ed.) (pp. 417–435). Boston, MA: Allyn & Bacon.

McGoldrick, M., & Carter, B. (2005b). Self in context. In B. Carter & M. McGoldrick (Eds.), The expanded family life cycle: Individual, family, and social perspectives (3rd ed.) (pp. 417–435). Boston, MA: Allyn & Bacon.

McGoldrick, M., & Gerson, R. (1985). Genograms in family assessment. New York: W.W. Norton & Company.

McGoldrick, M., Gerson, R., & Petry, S. (2008). Genograms: Assessment and intervention. New York: W. W. Norton & Company.

McGoldrick, M., & Giordano, J. (1996). Overview: Ethnicity and family therapy. In M. McGoldrick, J. Giordano, & J. Pearce (Eds.), Ethnicity and family therapy (pp. 1–30). New York: Guilford Press.

McGoldrick, M., Giordano, J., & Garcia-Preto, N. (Eds.). (2005). Overview: Ethnicity and family therapy. In M. McGoldrick, J. Giordano, & N. Garcia-Petro (Eds.), Ethnicity and family therapy (3rd ed.) (pp. 1–40). New York: Guilford Press.

McGoldrick, M., Giordano, J., & Pearce, J. (Eds.). (1996). Ethnicity and family therapy. New York: Guilford Press.

McGoldrick, M., Giordano, J., & Garcia-Preto, N. (Eds.). (2005). Ethnicity and family therapy (3rd ed.). New York: Guilford Press.

McGoldrick, M., & Walsh, F. (1999). Death and the family life cycle. In B. Carter & M. McGoldrick (Eds.), The expanded family life cycle: Individual, family, and social perspectives (3rd ed.) (pp. 346–361). Needham Heights, MA: Allyn & Bacon.

McGoldrick, M., & Walsh, F. (2005). Death and the family life cycle. In B. Carter & M. McGoldrick (Eds.), *The expanded family life cycle: Individual, family, and social perspectives* (3rd ed.) (pp. 185–201). Boston, MA: Allyn & Bacon.

McGoldrick, M., Watson, M., & Benton, W. (1999). Siblings through the life cycle. In B. Carter & M. McGoldrick (Eds.), *The expanded family life cycle: Individual, family, and social perspectives* (3rd ed.) (pp. 141–152). Needham Heights, MA: Allyn & Bacon.

McGoldrick, M., Watson, M., & Benton, W. (2005). Siblings through the life cycle. In B. Carter & M. McGoldrick (Eds.), *The expanded family life cycle: Individual, family, and social perspectives* (3rd ed.) (pp. 153–168). Boston, MA: Allyn & Bacon.

McIver, J., & Carmines, E. (1981). *Unidimensional scaling.* Sage Paper Series on Quantitative Applications in the Social Sciences, 07-024. Beverly Hills: Sage.

McKenzie-Pollock, L. (2005). Cambodian families. In M. McGoldrick, J. Giordano, & N. Garcia-Petro (Eds.), *Ethnicity and family therapy* (3rd ed.) (pp. 290–301). New York: Guilford Press.

McNeese, C. A., & Thyer, B. A. (2004). Evidence-based practice and social work. *Journal of Evidence-Based Social Work, 1*(1), 7–25.

McWey, L. (2008). In-home family therapy as a prevention of foster care placement: Clients' opinions about therapeutic services. *The American Journal of Family Therapy, 36,* 48–59.

Menos, J. (2005). Haitian families. In M. McGoldrick, J. Giordano, & N. Garcia-Petro (Eds.), *Ethnicity and family therapy* (3rd ed.) (pp. 127–137). New York: Guilford Press.

Milewski Hertlein, K., & Killmer, J. M. (2004). Toward differentiated decision-making: Family systems theory with homeless clinical populations *The American Journal of Family Therapy, 32,* 255–270.

Miller, B., & Pylpa, J. (1995). The dilemma of mental health paraprofessionals at home. *American Indian and Alaska Native Mental Health Research, 6*(2), 13–33.

Miller, L., & McLeod, E. (2001). Children as participants in family therapy: Practice, research, and theoretical concerns. *Family Journal: Counseling and Therapy for Couples and Families, 9*(4), 375–383.

Miller, R. (2001). Do children make a marriage unhappy? *Journal of Marriage and the Family, 49.* Retrieved from http://marriageandfamilies.byu.edu/issues/2001/April.children.htm.

Miller, S., Hubble, S., & Duncan, B. (1995). No more bells and whistles. *Networker,* 53–63.

Miller, T., Veltkamp, L., Lane, T., Bilyeu, J., & Elzie, N. (2002). Care pathway guidelines for assessment and counseling for domestic violence. *Family Journal: Counseling and Therapy for Couples and Families, 10*(1), 41–48.

Milner, J., & Wimberly, R. (1979). An inventory for the identification of child abusers. *Journal of Clinical Psychology, 35*(1), 95–110.

Mindel, C. (1985). Instrument design. In R. Grinnell (Ed.), *Social work research and evaluation* (pp. 206–230). Itasca, IL: F. E. Peacock.

Minuchin, P., Colapinto, J., & Minuchin, S. (1998). *Working with families of the poor.* New York: Guilford Press.

Minuchin, S. (1974). *Families and family therapy.* Cambridge, MA: Harvard University Press.

Minuchin, S. (1981). Family therapy techniques. Cambridge, MA: Harvard University Press.

Minuchin, S. (1992). Family healing: Tales of hope and renewal from family therapy. The Free Press.

Minuchin, S., & Montalvo, B. (1971). Techniques for working with disorganized low socioeconomic families. In J. Haley (Ed.), *Changing families: A family therapy reader* (pp. 202–211). New York: Grune & Straton.

Miranda, A., Estrada, D., & Firpo-Jimenez, M. (2000). Differences in family cohesion, adaptability, and environment among Latino families in dissimilar stages of acculturation. *Family Journal: Counseling and Therapy for Couples and Families, 8*(4), 341–350.

Mistler, B., & Sheward, P. (2009). Ecosystemic perspective: An interview with Peter A. D. Sheward. *The Family Journal, 17*(1), 77–88.

Molina, B., Estrada, D., & Burnett, J. (2004). Cultural communities: Challenges and opportunities in the creation of "Happily Ever After" stories of intercultural couplehood. *Family Journal: Counseling and Therapy for Couples and Families, 12*(2), 139–147.

Moore Hines, P., & Boyd-Franklin, N. (2005). African American families. In M. McGoldrick, J. Giordano, & N. Garcia-Petro (Eds.), *Ethnicity and family therapy* (3rd ed.) (pp. 87–101). New York: Guilford Press.

Moore Hines, P., Garcia Preto, N., McGoldrick, M., Almeida, R., & Weltman, S. (1999). Culture and the family life cycle. In B. Carter & M. McGoldrick (Eds.), *The expanded family life cycle: Individual, family, and social perspectives* (3rd ed.) (pp. 69–87). Needham Heights, MA: Allyn & Bacon.

Moore Hines, P., Garcia Preto, N., McGoldrick, M., Almeida, R., & Weltman, S. (2005). Culture and the family life cycle. In B. Carter & M. McGoldrick (Eds.), *The expanded family life cycle: Individual, family, and social perspectives* (3rd ed.) (pp. 69–87). Boston, MA: Allyn & Bacon.

Mooradian, J. K., Cross, S. L., & Stutzky, G. R. (2006). Across generations: Culture, history, and policy in the social ecology of American Indian grandparents parenting their grandchildren. *Journal of Family Social Work, 10*(4), 81–101.

Morgan, A., 2000. *What is Narrative Therapy?* Adelaide, Dulwich. www.dulwichcentre.com.au

Morrissette, V., McKenzie, B., & Morrissette, L. (1993). Towards an Aboriginal model of social work practice. *Canadian Social Work Review, 10*(1), 91–107.

Munns, A. (2004). Helping families at home. *Australian Nursing Journal, 12,* (2–37).

Munson, C. (1993). *Clinical social work supervision.* New York: Haworth Press.

Murray, C. (2006). Controversy, constraints, and context: Understanding family violence through family systems theory. *The Family Journal, 14*(3), 234–239.

Murray, K. (2002). Religion and divorce: Implications and strategies for counseling. *Family Journal: Counseling and Therapy for Couples and Families, 10*(2), 190–194.

Myers-Avis, J. (1992). Where are all the family therapists? Abuse and violence within families and family therapy's response. *Journal of Marital and Family Therapy, 18,* 225–232.

Myers, J. (2003). Coping with caregiving stress: A wellness-oriented, strengths-based approach for family counselors. *Family Journal: Counseling and Therapy for Couples and Families, 11*(2), 153–161.

National Indian Child Welfare Association. (n.d.). *Model Curriculum.* Retrieved from http://www.nicwa.org/resources/.

National Network for Family Resiliency (1995). Family resiliency: Building strengths to meet life's challenges. Retrieved from http://www. extension.iastate.edu/Publications/EDC53.pdf Retrieved from the NASW Website and the NASW Center for Workforce Studies (2011). http://careers.socialworkers.org/explore/workforce.asp#trends

Neckoway, R., Brownlee, K., Jourdain, L., & Miller, L. (2003). Rethinking the role of attachment theory in child welfare practice with Aboriginal people. *Canadian Social Work Review, 20*(1), 105–119.

Nelson, S. (1987). *Incest: Act and myth.* London, England: Redwood Burn.

Ng, K. (2005). The development of family therapy around the world. *Family Journal: Counseling and Therapy for Couples and Families, 13*(1), 35–42.

Nichols, M. (2010). The essentials of family therapy: Concepts and methods, 5th ed. Allyn & Bacon.

Nichols, M., & Schwartz, R. (2004). *Family therapy: Concepts and methods.* Boston: Allyn & Bacon.

Nichols, M., & Schwartz, R. (2004). *Family therapy: Concepts and methods* (6th ed.). Toronto: Pearson.

Nichols, M., & Schwartz, R. (2007). *Family therapy: Concepts and methods* (8th ed.). Boston: Allyn & Bacon.

Northwest Indian Child Welfare Institute. (1984). *Cross-cultural skills in Indian child welfare.* Portland, OR: Northwest Indian Child Welfare Institute.

Norusis, M. (1990). *SPSS/PC Statistics 4.0.* Chicago: SPSS Inc.

Nunnally, J. (1978). *Psychometric theory.* Toronto: McGraw-Hill.

Obana, N. (2005). Hawaiian families. In M. McGoldrick, J. Giordano, & N. Garcia-Petro (Eds.), *Ethnicity and family therapy* (3rd ed.) (pp. 64–76). New York: Guilford Press.

O'Connor, L., Morgenstern, J., Gibson, F., & Nakashian, M. (2005). "Nothing about me without me": Leading the way to collaborative relationships with families. *Child Welfare, LXXXIV*(2), 153–170.

Okun, B. (1996). *Understanding diverse families.* New York: Guilford Press.

Olson, D. (1983). *Families: What makes them work.* Beverly Hills, CA: Sage.

Olson, D. (1986). Circumplex model VII: Validation studies and FACES III. *Family Process, 26,* 337–351.

Olson, D. (1991). Family types, family stress and family satisfaction: A family development perspective. In C. Falicov (Ed.), *Family transitions, continuity and change over the life cycle.* New York: Guilford Press.

Olson, D., & Lavee, Y. (1989). Family system and family stress: A family life cycle perspective. In K. Kreppner and R. Lerner (Eds.), *Family systems and life-span development* (pp. 165–193). Hillsdale, NJ: Lawrence Erlbaum Associates.

Olson, D., Russell, C., & Sprenkle, D. (1989). *Circumplex model: Systematic assessment and treatment of families.* New York: Haworth.

Osterlind, S. (1983). Test item bias. Sage University Paper Series on Quantitative Applications in the Social Sciences, 07-030, Beverly Hills, CA: Sage.

Patterson, C. (1995). Lesbian mothers, gay fathers, and their children. In A. D'Augelli & C. Patterson (Eds.), *Lesbian, gay and bisexual identities over the lifespan* (pp. 262–290). New York: Oxford.

Patterson, G. (1974). Interventions for boys with conduct problems: Multiple settings, treatments and criteria. *Journal of Consulting and Clinical Psychology, 42*(4), 471–481.

Patterson, G. (1982). *Coercive family process: A social learning approach.* Eugene, OR: Castalina.

Patterson, G., Capaldi, D., & Bank, L. (1991). An early starter model for predicting delinquency. In D. Pepler & K. Rubin (Eds.), *The development and treatment of childhood aggression.* (pp. 139–168). Hillsdale, NJ: Lawrence Erlbaum Associates.

Patterson, G., DeBaryshe, B., & Ramsey, E. (1989). A developmental perspective on antisocial behavior. *American Psychologist, 44,* 329–335.

Patterson, G., & Fleischman, M. (1979). Mainte-nance of treatment effects: Some considera-tions concerning family systems and follow–up data. *Behavior Therapy, 10,* 168–185.

Patterson, J. (2002). Integrating family resilience and family stress theory. *Journal of Marriage and Family, 64,* 349–360.

Payne, M. (2005). Modern social work theory (3rd ed.). Chicago: Lyceum Books.

Pedhazur, E., & Pedhazur, L. (1991). *Measure-ment, design and analysis.* Hillsdale, NJ: Lawrence Erlbaum Associates.

Peleg, O. (2008). The relationship between differ-entiation of self and marital satisfaction: What can be learned from married people over the course of life. *The American Journal of Family Therapy, 36,* 388–401.

Peluso, P. (2002). Counseling families affected by suicide. *Family Journal: Counseling and Therapy for Couples and Families, 10*(3), 351–357.

Peluso, P. (2003). The ethical genogram: A tool for helping therapists understand their ethical decision-making styles. *Family Journal: Counseling and Therapy for Couples and Families, 11*(3), 286–291.

Peterson, A., & Jenni, C. (2003). Men's experience of making the decision to have their first child: A phenomenological analysis. *Family Journal: Counseling and Therapy for Couples and Families, 11*(4), 353–363.

Peterson, L. (1989). Latchkey children's prepara-tion for self-care: Overestimated, underre-hearsed, and unsafe. *Journal of Clinical Child Psychology, 18,* 2–7.

Petro, N. (1999). Transformation of the family system during adolescence. In B. Carter & M. McGoldrick (Eds.), *The expanded family life cycle: Individual, family, and social perspec-tives* (3rd ed.) (pp. 274–286). Needham Heights, MA: Allyn & Bacon.

Petro, N., & Travis, N. (1985). The adolescent phase of the family life cycle. In M. Mirkin & S. Koman (Eds.), *Handbook of adolescent and family therapy.* New York: Gardner Press.

Pett, M. (1982). Predictors of satisfactory social adjustment of divorced parents. *Journal of Divorce, 5*(4), 25–39.

Piercy, F., & Sprenkle, D. (1986). *Family therapy sourcebook.* New York: Guilford Press.

Piercy, F., & Sprenkle, D. (1996). *Family therapy sourcebook* (2nd ed.). New York: Guilford Press.

Piercy, F., Soekandar, A., Limansubroto, C., & Davis, S. (2005). Indonesian families. In M. McGoldrick, J. Giordano, & N. Garcia-Petro (Eds.), *Ethnicity and family therapy* (3rd ed.) (pp. 332–338). New York: Guilford Press.

Pillari, V. (2005). Indian Hindu families. In M. McGoldrick, J. Giordano, & N. Garcia-Preto (Eds.), *Ethnicity and Family Therapy* (pp. 395–406). New York: The Guilford Press.

Pimento, B. (1985). *Native families in jeopardy—The child welfare system in Canada.* Toronto: Centre for Women's Studies in Education, Occasional Papers, No. 11.

Pinderhughes, H. (2002). African American marriage in the 20th century. *Family Process, 41*(2), 269–282.

Pinkerton, J. (2007). Family support, social capi-tal, resilience and adolescent coping. *Child and Family Social Work, 12*(3), 219–228.

Pinsof, W. (2002). The death of "Till death do us part": The transformation of pair-bonding in the 20th century. *Family Process, 41*(2), 135–157.

Pleck, E. (1987). *Domestic tyranny: The making of social policy against family violence from colonial times to the present.* New York: Oxford University Press.

Pogrebin, L. (1980). *Growing up free.* NY: McGraw-Hill.

Pollack, W. (2000). *Real boys' voices.* New York: Random House.

Polster, R., & Collins, D. (2011). Structured obser-vation. In R. Grinnell & Y. Unrau (Eds.) Social Work Research and Evaluation, 9th Edition. pp. 287–300. New York: Oxford University Press.

Powers, G. (1990). Design and procedures for evaluating crisis. In A. Roberts (Ed.), *Crisis intervention handbook: Assessment, treat-ment, and research* (pp. 303–325). Belmont, CA: Wadsworth.

Prochaska, J., & DiClemente, C. (2002). Trans-theoretical therapy. In J. Lebow (Ed.), *Com-prehensive handbook of psychotherapy: Integrative-eclectic.* (Vol. 4, pp. 165–184). New York: Wiley.

Prochaska, J., & Norcross, J. (2003). Systems of psy-chotherapy. Toronto: Nelson Thomson Learning.

Proctor, E. (2001). Editorial: Social work and vul-nerable families: Economic hardship and service success. *Social Work Research, 25*(3), 131–132.

Proctor, E. (2004). Editorial: Social work's important work: Keeping families safe. *Social Work Research, 28*(3), 131–132.

Pulleyblank Coffey, E. (2004). The heart of the matter 2: Integration of ecosystemic family therapy practices with systems of care mental health services for children and families. *Family Process, 43*(2), 161–173.

Ramage, F., & Barnard, C. (2005). Custody eva-luations: Critical contextual and ethical con-siderations. *The American Journal of Family Therapy, 33,* 339–351.

Rampage, C. (2002). Marriage in the 20th century: A feminist perspective. *Family Process, 41*(2), 261–268.

Rappaport, R. (1971). Ritual sanctity and cybernetics. *American Anthropologist, 73*(1), 59–76.

Razack, N., & Jeffery, D. (2002). Critical race discourse and tenets for social work practice. *Canadian Social Work Review, 19*(2), 257–271.

Red Horse, J. (1980). American Indian elders: Unifiers of Indian families. *Social Casework,* 490–493.

Red Horse, J., Lewis, R., Feit, M., & Decker, J. (1978). Family behavior of urban American Indians. *Social Casework, 59*(2), 67–72.

Reid, W., Davis Kenaley, B., & Colvin, J. (2004). Do some interventions work better than others? A review of comparative social work experiments. *Social Work Research, 28*(2), 71–81.

Ribner, D., & Knei-Paz, C. (2002). Client's view of a successful helping relationship. *Social Work, 47*(4), 379–387.

Richardson, C. (1996). *Family life: Patterns and perspectives.* New York: McGraw Hill Ryerson Limited.

Richman, M. (1917, reprinted 1964). *Social diagnosis.* Philadelphia: Russell Sage Foundation.

Richman, J., & Cook, P. (2004). A framework for teaching family development for the changing family. *Journal of Teaching in Social Work, 24*(1/2), 1–18.

Riley, D., Greif, G., Caplan, D., & MacAuley, H. (2004). Common themes and treatment approaches in working with families of runaway youths. *The American Journal of Family Therapy, 32,* 139–153.

Roberts, J. (2005). Transparency and self-disclosure in family therapy: Dangers and possibilities. *Family Process, 44*(1), 45–63.

Rojano, R. (2004). The practice of community family therapy. *Family Process, 43*(1), 59–78.

Rojano, R., & Duncan-Rojano, J. (2005). Colombian families. In M. McGoldrick, J. Giordano, & N. Garcia-Petro (Eds.), *Ethnicity and family therapy* (3rd ed.) (pp. 192–201). New York: Guilford Press.

Rokeach, M. (1973). *The nature of human values.* New York: Free Press.

Roof, W. (1999). Spiritual marketplace: Baby boomers and the remaking of American religion. Princeton, NJ: Princeton University Press.

Rosen, E. (2005). Men in transition: The "new" man. In B. Carter & M. McGoldrick (Eds.), *The expanded family life cycle: Individual, family, and social perspectives* (3rd ed.) (pp. 124–140). Boston, MA: Allyn & Bacon.

Rosen, E., & Weltman, S. (2005). Jewish families: An overview. In M. McGoldrick, J. Giordano, & N. Garcia-Petro (Eds.), *Ethnicity and family therapy* (3rd ed.) (pp. 667–679). New York: Guilford Press.

Rostosky, S., Korfhage, B., Duhigg, J., Stern, A., Bennett, L., & Riggle, E. (2004). Same-sex couple perceptions of family support: A consensual qualitative study. *Family Process, 43*(1), 43–58.

Rothbaum, F., Rosen, K., Ujiie, T., & Uchida, N. (2002). Family systems theory, attachment, and culture. *Family Process, 41*(3), 328–350.

Rothery, M. (1993). The ecological perspective and work with vulnerable families. In M. Rodway & B. Trute (Eds.), *Ecological family practice: One family, many resources* (pp. 21–50). Queenston, Ontario: Edwin Mellen.

Rotter, J. (2000). Family grief and mourning. *Family Journal: Counseling and Therapy for Couples and Families, 8*(3), 275–277.

Rovers, M., DesRoches, L., Hunter, P., & Taylor, B. (2000). A family of origin workshop: Process and evaluation. *Family Journal: Counseling and Therapy for Couples and Families, 8*(4), 368–375.

Safonte-Strumolo, N., & Balaguer Dunn, A. (2000). Consideration of cultural and relational issues in bereavement: The case of an Italian American family. *Family Journal: Counseling and Therapy for Couples and Families, 8*(4), 334–340.

Saleebey, D. (1992). *The strengths perspective in social work practice.* White Plains, New York: Longman.

Saleebey, D. (1996). The strengths perspective in social work practice: Extensions and cautions. *Social Work, 41*(3), 296–305.

Saleebey, D. (2000). *The strengths perspective in social work practice* (4th ed.). Boston: Allyn & Bacon.

Sanders, G., & Kroll, I. (2000). Generating stories of resilience: Helping gay and lesbian youth and their families. *Journal of Marital and Family Therapy, 26,* 433–442.

Sanders, J., & James, J. (1983). The modification of parent behavior: A review of generalization and maintenance. *Behavior Modification, 7*(1), 3–27.

Sanderson, J., Kosutic, I., Garcia, M., Melendez, T., Donoghue, J., Perumbilly, S., Franzen, C., & Anderson, S. (2009). The measurement of outcome variables in couple and family research. *The American Journal of Family Therapy, 37,* 239–257.

Sandler, J., VanDercar, C., & Milhoan, M. (1978). Training child abusers in the use of positive reinforcement practices. *Behavior Research and Therapy, 16,* 169–175.

Sandler, I., Miller, P. Short, J. & Wolchik, S. (1989). Social support as a protective factor for children in stress. *Children's social networks and social supports.* D. Bell (ed.) (pp. 277–307). New York: John Wiley.

Satir, V. (1967). *Conjoint family therapy.* Palo Alto, CA: Science and Behavior Books.

Satir, V. (1971). The family as a treatment unit. In J. Haley (Ed.), *Changing families: A family therapy reader* (pp. 127–132). New York: Grune & Straton.

Satir, V. (1972). *Peoplemaking.* Palo Alto, CA: Science and Behavior Books.

Satir, V., & Baldwin, M. (1983). *Satir step by step: A guide to creating change in families*. Palo Alto, CA: Science and Behavior Books.

Schact, A., Tafoya, N., & Mirabala, K. (1989). Home-based therapy with American Indian families. *American Indian and Alaska Native Mental Health Research*, 3(2), 27–42.

Sheafor, B., Horejsi, C., & Horejsi, G. (1997). *Techniques and guidelines for social work practice* (4th ed.). Toronto: Allyn & Bacon.

Sheidow, A., & Woodford, M. (2003). Multisystemic therapy: An empirically supported, home-based family therapy approach. *Family Journal: Counseling and Therapy for Couples and Families*, 11(3), 257–263.

Sheperis, C., & Sheperis, S. (2002). The matrix as a bridge to systems thinking. *Family Journal: Counseling and Therapy for Couples and Families*, 10(3), 308–314.

Shibusawa, T. (2005). Japanese families. In M. McGoldrick, J. Giordano, & N. Garcia-Petro (Eds.), *Ethnicity and family therapy* (3rd ed.) (pp. 339–348). New York: Guilford Press.

Shulman, L. (1992). *The skills of helping individuals, families, and groups* (3rd ed.). Itasca, IL: F. E. Peacock.

Shulman, L. (2008). *The skills of helping individuals, families, and groups* (6th ed.). Boston MA: Cengage.

Sims, M. (2002). *Designing family support programs*. Australia: Common Ground Publishing.

Sluzki, C., & Againi, F. (2003). Small steps and big leaps in an era of cultural transition: A crisis in a traditional Kosovar Albanian family. *Family Process*, 42(4), 479–484.

Smith, S. (1984). Significant research findings in the etiology of child abuse. *Social Casework*, 65(6), 337–345.

Snyder, W., & McCollum, E. (1999). Their home is their castle: Learning to do in-home family therapy. *Family Process*, 38(2), 229–244.

Softas-Nall, B., Baldo, T., & Tiedman, T. (1999). A gender-based, solution-focused genogram case: He and she across the generations. *Family Journal: Counseling and Therapy for Couples and Families*, 7(2), 177–180.

Spanier, G., Lewis, R., & Cole, E. (1975). Marital adjustment over the family life cycle: The issue of curvilinearity. *Journal of Marriage and the Family*, 37, 263–275.

Stanley, S., Markman, H., & Whitton, S. (2002). Communication, conflict, and commitment: Insights on the foundations of relationship success from a national survey. *Family Process*, 41(4), 659–675.

Staveteig, S., & Wigton, A. (2000). Racial and ethnic disparities: Key findings from the National Survey of America's Families. *New Federalism: National Survey of America's Families*, The Urban Institute, Series B, No. B-5, 1–6.

Steffen, J., & Karoly, P. (1980). Toward a psychology of therapeutic persistence. In P. Karoly & J. Steffen (Eds.), *Improving the long-term effects of psychotherapy: Models of durable outcome* (pp. 3–24). New York: Gardner Press.

Steinhauer, P. (1991). Assessing for parenting capacity. In J. Veevers (Ed.), *Continuity and change in marriage and family* (pp. 283–294). Toronto: Holt, Rinehart & Winston.

Stern, S. (1999). Commentary: Challenges to family engagement: What can multisystemic therapy teach family therapists. Family Process, 38, 281–286.

Stewart, T., & Mezzich, A. (2006). The effects of spirituality and religiosity on child neglect in substance use disorder families. *Journal of Family Social Work*, 10(2), 35–57.

Stokes, T., & Baer, D. (1977). An implicit technology of generalization. *Journal of Applied Behavior Analysis*, 10(2), 349–367.

Straus, M. (1993). Physical assault by wives. In R. Gelles & D. Loseke (Eds.), *Current controversies on family violence* (pp. 67–87). Newbury Park, CA: Sage Publications.

Straus, M., & Gelles, M. (1988). How violent are American families? Estimates from the National Family Violence Resurvey and other studies. In G. Hotaling, D. Finkelhor, J. Kirkpatrick, & M. Strauss (Eds.), *Family abuse and its consequences* (pp. 14–37). Newbury Park, CA: Sage Publications.

Straus, M., Gelles, R., & Steinmetz, S. (1980). *Behind closed doors: Violence in the American family*. Garden City, NY: Anchor Press.

Suarez-Orozco, C., Todorova, I., & Louie, J. (2002). Making up for lost time: The experience of separation and reunification among immigrant families. *Family Process*, 41(4), 625–643.

Sue, D., & Sue, D. (1990). *Counseling the culturally different: Theory and practice*. New York: Wiley.

Sue, S., & Zane, N. (1987). The role of cultural techniques in psychotherapy. *American Psychologist*, 42(1), 37–45.

Suissa, A. (2004). Social practitioners and families: A systemic perspective. *Journal of Family Social Work*, 8(4), 1–28.

Suissa, A. (2005). Social practitioners and families: A systemic perspective. *Journal of Family Social Work*, 8(4), 1–28.

Sutton, C., & Broken Nose, M. A. (1996). American Indian families: An overview. In M. McGoldrick, J. Giordano, & J. Pearce (Eds.), *Ethnicity and family therapy* (pp. 31–44). New York: Guilford Press.

Sutton, C., & Broken Nose, M. A. (2005). American Indian families: An overview. In M. McGoldrick, J. Giordano, & N. Garcia-Petro (Eds.), *Ethnicity and family therapy* (3rd ed.) (pp. 43–54). New York: Guilford Press.

Sutton, J., Smith, P., & Swettenham, J. (1999). Bullying and "theory of mind": A critique of the "social skills deficit" view of anti-social behavior. *Social Development, 8*(1), 117–127.

Sweeney, T. & Witmer, J. (1991). Beyond social interest: Striving toward optimum health and wellness. Individual Psychology: Journal of Adlerian Theory, Research & Practice, 47(4), Dec 1991, 527–540.

Taanila, A., Laitinen, E., Moilanen, I., & Jarvelin, M. (2002). Effects of family interaction on the child's behavior in single-parent or reconstructed families. *Family Process, 41*(4), 693–708.

Tafoya, T. (1989). Circles and cedar: Native Americans and family therapy. *Journal of Psychotherapy, 6*(1/2), 71–98.

Tafoya, N., & Del Vecchio, A. (2005). Back to the future: An examination of the Native American Holocaust experience. In M. McGoldrick, J. Giordano, & N. Garcia-Petro (Eds.), *Ethnicity and family therapy* (3rd ed.) (pp. 55–63). New York: Guilford Press.

Tambling, R., & Johnson, L. (2008). Relationship between stages of change and outcome in couple therapy. *The American Journal of Family Therapy, 36*, 229–241.

Thayne, T. R. (1998). Opening space for clients' religious and spiritual values in therapy: A social constructionist perspective. In D. Becvar (Ed.), *Family, spirituality and social work* (pp. 13–25). Bingingham, NY: Haworth.

Thomason, T. (1991). Counseling Native Americans: An introduction for non-native American counselors. *Journal of Counseling and Development, 69*, 321–327.

Thomlison, R., & Foote, C. (1987). Child welfare in Canada. *Child and Adolescent Social Work, 4*(2), 123–142.

Thompson, C., & Rudolph, L. (1992). *Counseling Children* (3rd ed.). Pacific Grove, CA: Brooks/Cole.

Thompson, C., Rudolph, L., & Henderson, D. (2003). *Counseling children* (6th ed.). Pacific Grove, CA: Wadsworth.

Thompson, D., & Henderson, C. (2011). *Counseling children*. 8th ed. Belmont, CA: Cengage.

Tomm, K. (1987a). Interventive interviewing: Part I: Strategizing as a fourth guideline for the therapist. *Family Process, 26*, 3–13.

Tomm, K. (1987b). Interventive interviewing: Part II. Reflexive questioning as a means to enable self-healing. *Family Process, 26*, 167–183.

Tomm, K. (1988). Interventive interviewing: Part III. Intending to ask lineal, circular, strategic, or reflexive questions? *Family Process, 27*, 1–15.

Tomm, K. (1991). Beginning of a HIPs and PIPs approach to psychiatric assessment. *The Calgary Participator, 1*(2), 21–24.

Tomm, K., & Wright, L. (1979). Skill training in family therapy: Perceptual, conceptual, and executive skills. *Family Process, 18*, 250–277.

Tomm, K., & Wright, L. (1984). Training in family therapy: Perceptual, conceptual, and executive skills. *Family Process, 18*, 250–277.

Tomm, K., & Collins, D. (2010). Karl Tomm: His changing views on family therapy over 35 years. *The Family Journal, 7*(2), 106–117.

Toseland, R., & Rivas, R. (1984). *An introduction to group work practice*. New York: Macmillan Publishing.

Trepper, T., & Barrett, M. (Eds.). (1986). *Treating incest: A multiple systems perspective*. New York: Haworth Press.

Truax, C., & Carkhoff, R. (1967). *Toward effective counseling and psychotherapy: Training and practice*. New York: Haworth Press.

Tubbs, C., Roy, K., & Burton, L. (2005). Family ties: Constructing family time in low-income families. *Family Process, 44*(1), 77–91.

Tuzlak, A., & Hillock, D. (1991). Single mothers and their children after divorce: A study of those "who make it." In J. Veevers (Ed.), *Continuity and change in marriage and the family* (pp. 303–313). Toronto: Holt Rinehart & Winston of Canada.

Ungar, M. (2002). Alliances and power: Understanding social worker–community relationships. *Canadian Social Work Review, 19*(2), 227–243.

Ungar, M. (2003). The professional social ecologist. *Canadian Social Work Review, 20*(1), 5–23.

Ungar, M. (2004). The importance of parents and other caregivers to the resilience of high-risk adolescents. *Family Process, 43*(1), 23–40.

Unrau, Y. (1995a). *Predicting child abuse and service outcomes in an intensive family preservation services program*. (Unpublished doctoral dissertation). University of Utah, Salt Lake City.

Unrau, Y. (1995b). Defining the black box of family preservation services: A conceptual framework for service delivery. *Community Alternatives, 7*(2), 49–60.

Vazquez, C. (2005). Dominican families. In M. McGoldrick, J. Giordano, & N. Garcia-Petro (Eds.), *Ethnicity and family therapy* (3rd ed.) (pp. 216–228). New York: Guilford Press.

Viere, G. (2001). Examining family rituals. *Family Journal: Counseling and Therapy for Couples and Families, 9*(3), 285–288.

Visher, W., & Visher, J. (1982). Stepfamilies in the 1980s. In J. Hansen & L. Messinger (Eds.), *Therapy with remarriage families* (pp. 105–119). Rockville, MD: Aspen Systems Corporation.

Wahler, R. (1980). The insular mother: Her problems in parent-child treatment. *Journal of Applied Behavior Analysis, 13*, 207–219.

Walker, L. (1984). *The battered woman syndrome*. New York: Springer.

Walker, S. (2003). Family support and family therapy—same difference? *International Journal of Social Welfare, 12*, 307–313.

Wallerstein, J. (1983). Children of divorce: The psychological tasks of the child. *American Journal of Orthopsychiatry, 53*, 230–243.

Wallerstein, J. (1985). Children of divorce: Preliminary report of a ten-year follow-up of older children and adolescents. *Journal of the American Academy of Child Psychiatry, 24*(5), 545–553.

Wallerstein, J., & Kelly, J. (1980). *Surviving the breakup: How children and parents cope with divorce.* New York: Basic Books.

Walsh, F. (1998). *Strengthening family resilience.* New York: Guilford Press.

Walsh, F. (Ed.). (1999). *Spiritual resources in family therapy.* New York: Guilford Press.

Walsh, F. (2002). A family resilience framework: Innovative practice applications. *Family Relations, 51*(2), 130–138.

Walsh, F. (2003). Family resilience: A framework for clinical practice. *Family Process, 42*(1), 1–18.

Walsh, F. (2006). Strengthening family resilience. New York: Guilford Publications.

Wampler, R., Downs, A., & Fischer, J. (2009). Development of a brief version of Children's Roles Inventory (CRI-20). *The American Journal of Family Therapy, 37*, 287–298.

Wares, D., Wedel, K., Rosenthal, J., & Dobrec, A. (1994). Indian Child Welfare: A multicultural challenge. *Journal of Multicultural Social Work, 3*(3), 1–15.

Watts-Jones, D. (2002). Healing internalized racism: The role of a within-group sanctuary among people of African descent. *Family Process, 41*(4), 591–601.

Watts-Jones, D. (2004). The evidence of things seen and not seen: The legacy of race and racism. *Family Process, 43*(4), 503–508.

Watzlawick, P., Beavin, J., & Jackson, D. (1967). *Pragmatics of human communication.* New York: W. W. Norton & Company.

Watzlawick, P., Weakland, J., & Fisch, R. (1974). *Change: Principles of problem formation and problem resolution.* New York: W. W. Norton & Company.

Weakland, J., & Fry, W. (1974). Letters of mothers of schizophrenics. In D. Jackson (Ed.), *Communication, family, and marriage* (pp. 122–150). Palo Alto, CA: Science and Behavior Books.

Weaver, H. (1996). Social work with American Indian youth using the orthogonal model of cultural identification. *Families in Society, 77*(2), 98–107.

Weaver, H. (1997a). The challenges of research in Native American communities: Incorporating principles of cultural competence. *Journal of Social Service Research, 23*(2), 1–15.

Weaver, H. (1997b). Training culturally competent social workers: What students should know about Native people. *Journal of Teaching in Social Work, 15*(1/2), 97–111.

Weaver, H. (1999). Indigenous people and the social work profession: Defining culturally competent services. *Social Work, 44*(3), 217–225.

Weaver, H., & White, B. (1997). The Native American family circle: Roots of resiliency. *Journal of Family Social Work, 2*(1), 67–79.

Weaver, H., & Wodarski, J. (1995). Cultural issues in crisis intervention: Guidelines for culturally competent practice. *Family Therapy, 22*(3), 215–223.

Weaver, H., & Yellow Horse Brave Heart, M. (1999). Examining two facets of American Indian identity: Exposure to other cultures and the influence of historical trauma. *Journal of Human Behavior in the Social Environment, 2*(1/2), 19–33.

Weber, M. (1996). Family preservation can be an appropriate strategy if realistic expectations are maintained. *NRCCSA News.* Retrieved from http://www.casaforchildren.org/site/c.mtJSJ7MPIsE/b.5525205/k.C6AA/Family_Preservation_Strategy.htm (2011,December 20). New York: Norton & Company.

Webster-Stratton, C., & Hammond, M. (1990). Predictors of outcome in parent training for families with conduct problem children. *Behavior Therapy, 21*, 319–337.

Webster-Stratton, C., & Reid, M. J. (2003). Treating conduct problems and strengthening social and emotional competence in young children. *Journal of Emotional and Behavioral Disorders, 11*(3), 130–143.

Wegscheider, S. (1981). *Another chance: Hope and health for the alcoholic family.* Palo Alto, CA: Science and Behavior Books.

Weine, S., Muzurovic, N., Kulauzovic, Y., et al. (2004). Family consequences of refugee trauma. *Family Process, 43*(2), 147–160.

Wells, K., & Whittington, D. (1993). Child and family functioning after intensive family preservation services. *Social Service Review, 9*(6), 505–523.

Wendel, R. (2003). Lived religion and family therapy: What does spirituality have to do with it? *Family Process, 42*(1), 165–179.

Whiffen, V., Kerr, M., & Kallos-Lilly, V. (2005). Maternal depression, adult attachment, and children's emotional distress. *Family Process, 44*(1), 93–103.

White, M. (1986). Negative explanation, restraint and double description: A template for family therapy. *Family Process, 25*(2), 169–183.

White, M. (1989). *The externalizing of the problem and the reauthoring of the lives and relationships.* Adelaide, Australia: Dulwich Centre Publishers.

White, M., & Epston, D. (1990). *Narrative means to therapeutic ends.* New York: W. W. Norton & Company.

Wiggins Frame, M. (2000). Spiritual and religious issues in counseling: Ethical considerations. *Family Journal: Counseling and Therapy for Couples and Families, 8*(1), 72–74.

Wiggins Frame, M. (2001). The spiritual genogram in training and supervision. *Family Journal: Counseling and Therapy for Couples and Families, 9*(2), 109–115.

Wilcoxon, A. (1991). Grandparents and grandchildren: An often-neglected relationship between significant others. In J. Veevers (Ed.), *Continuity and change in marriage and the family* (pp. 342–345). Toronto: Holt, Rinehart & Winston of Canada.

Williams, E., & Ellison, F. (1996). Culturally sensitive social work practice with American Indian Clients: Guidelines for non-Indian social workers. *Social Work, 41*(2), 147–151.

Williams, M., Grinnell, R., & Unrau, Y. (2005). Case-level designs. In R. Grinnell & Y. Unrau (Eds.), *Social work research and evaluation: Quantitative and qualitative approaches* (7th ed.) (pp. 171–184). New York: Oxford.

Williams, L., & Winter, H. (2009). Guidelines for effective transfer of cases: The needs of the transfer triad. *The American Journal of Family Therapy, 37*, 146–158.

Williamson, J., Softas-Nall, B., & Miller, J. (2003). Grandmothers raising grandchildren: An exploration of their experiences and emotions. *Family Journal: Counseling and Therapy for Couples and Families, 11*(1), 23–32.

Winawer, H., & Wetzel, N. (2005). German families. In M. McGoldrick, J. Giordano, & N. Garcia-Petro (Eds.), *Ethnicity and family therapy* (3rd ed.) (pp. 555–572). New York: Guilford Press.

Wilson, P., & Bailey, D. (1990). Early intervention training related to family interviewing. *TECSE, 10*(1), 50–62.

Wolfe, D., Jaffe, P., Wilson, S., & Zak, L. (1988). A multivariate investigation of children's adjustment to family violence. In G. Hotaling, D. Finkelhor, J. Kirkpatrick, & M. Straus (Eds.), *Family abuse and its consequences* (pp. 228–243). Newbury Park, CA: Sage Publications.

Wolfe, D., Sandler, J., & Kaufman, K. (1981). A competency-based parent-training program for child abusers. *Journal of Consulting and Clinical Psychology, 49*(5), 633–640.

Wolfe, L. (2001). *Children, depression, and divorce.* (Unpublished doctoral dissertation). University of Calgary, Calgary, Alberta, Canada.

Wolin, S. (1993). *The resilient self: How survivors of troubled families rise above adversity.* New York: Villard Books.

Wolin, S. J. , & Bennett, L. A. (1984). Family rituals. *Family Process, 23*, 401–420.

Wong, Y., Cheng, S., Choi, S., Ky, K., LeBa, S., Tsang, K., & Yoo, L. (2003). Deconstructing culture in cultural competence. *Canadian Social Work Review, 20*(2), 149–167.

Wood, K., & Geismar, L. (1986). *Families at risk: Treating the multiproblem family.* New York: Human Sciences Press.

Woodford, M. (1999). Home-based family therapy: Theory and process from "friendly visitors" to multisystemic therapy. *Family Journal: Counseling and Therapy for Couples and Families, 7*(3), 265–269.

Worden, M. (1994). *Family therapy basics.* Pacific Grove, CA: Brooks/Cole.

Worden, M. (2002). *Family therapy basics* (3rd ed.). Pacific Grove, CA: Brooks/Cole.

Wright, L., & Leahey, M. (1994). *Nurses and families: A guide to family assessment and intervention.* Philadelphia, PA: F. A. Davis.

Wycoff, S., Bacod-Gebhardt, M., Cameron, S., Brandt, M., & Armes, B. (2002). Have families fared well from welfare reform? Educating clinicians about policy, paradox, and change. *Family Journal: Counseling and Therapy for Couples and Families, 10*(3), 269–280.

Yalof, J., & Abraham, P. (2007). Personality Assessment in Schools. In S.R. Smith & L. Handler (Eds.), *The Clinical Assessment of Children and Adolescents: A Practitioner's Handbook.* Mahwah, NJ: Erlbaum. In Jordan, C. & Franklin, C. (2011), *Clinical Assessment for Social Workers: Quantitative and Qualitative Methods.* 3rd edition. Chicago: Lyceum Books. p. 181.

Young, M. (2004). Healthy relationships: Where's the research? *Family Journal: Counseling and Therapy for Couples and Families, 12*(2), 159–162.

Yuan, Y., & Rivest, M. (Eds.). (1990). *Preserving families.* Newbury Park, CA: Sage.

Ziomrk-Daigle, J. (2010). Schools, families, and communities affecting the dropout rate: Implications and strategies for family counselors. *The Family Journal, 18*, 377–385.

Zurvain, S., & Grief, G. (1989). Normative and child-maltreating AFDC mothers. *Social Casework, 7*(2), 76–84.

Name Index

Subject Index